FEUDAL GERMANY

THE UNIVERSITY OF CHICAGO PRESS
CHICAGO, ILLINOIS

—

THE BAKER & TAYLOR COMPANY
NEW YORK

THE MACMILLAN COMPANY OF CANADA, LIMITED
TORONTO

THE CAMBRIDGE UNIVERSITY PRESS
LONDON

THE MARUZEN-KABUSHIKI-KAISHA
TOKYO, OSAKA, KYOTO, FUKUOKA, SENDAI

THE COMMERCIAL PRESS, LIMITED
SHANGHAI

Feudal Germany

By

JAMES WESTFALL THOMPSON

*Professor of Medieval History in the University of Chicago;
Fellow, The Medieval Academy of America; Fellow, The
Royal Historical Society; Corresponding Member,
The Königsberger Gelehrte Gesellschaft*

Nicht darauf kommt es bei Beurteilung einer Epoche an,
wieviel sie noch vom Alten beibehalten, sondern wieviel sie
neue Resultate gewonnen und gesichert hat.—DEHIO and
BEZOLD, *Die kirchliche Baukunst des Abendlandes*, I, 149.

THE UNIVERSITY OF CHICAGO PRESS
CHICAGO ⋅ ILLINOIS

Composed and Printed By
The University of Chicago Press
Chicago, Illinois, U.S.A.

TO MY WIFE
IN MEMORY OF GOLDEN DAYS
IN GERMANY

PREFACE

IN ONE of those matchless prefaces which Ranke knew so well how to write he has said:

Great peoples and states have a double character—one national, the other pertaining to the destinies of the world. Their history, in a similar manner, presents a double aspect. In so far as it forms an essential ingredient in the development of humanity generally, or records a prevailing influence impressed upon that development, it awakens an intelligent interest which extends far beyond the limits of nationality; it attracts the attention and becomes a subject of study even to those who are not natives of the land whose history is narrated.

Much has been written by German historians upon the history of this epoch, yet it seems to me that an American scholar may still add something to the interpretation of it.

The history of medieval Germany is not merely profitable to study for itself; it is profitable for the light it casts upon the history of other European countries. Yet valuable as the subject is, it has been singularly neglected by French, English, and American historians. The late Viscount Bryce's *Holy Roman Empire*, admirable as it is, is but the history of a great political idea, and it were difficult for one to visualize the real history of feudal Germany from a reading of its chapters. The only book in the English language which does justice to the history of medieval Germany is Mr. Herbert Fisher's *The Mediaeval Empire*, to whose virtue I am glad to pay homage. But the reader who will examine its pages and then turn to those which follow, I think, will discover that both in matter and in method the two volumes are very different. Mr. Fisher's viewpoint is the empire, not Germany; and he has been far less interested in the subject of economic and social history than I have been.

I have not endeavored, even had I the ability, to write a complete history of Germany during the feudal period. Such a work would require a lifetime devoted to uninterrupted study of the subject. My object has been to select certain subjects in the history of feudal Germany whose significance has been of major historical importance. The heart of the feudal age was the epoch lying between the ninth and the twelfth centuries inclusive. But I have sometimes, as the exigency of the subject required, ranged forward of the former century and beyond the term of the latter. By closer construction the book may be said to deal with that period of the history of medieval Germany lying between the accession of Henry the Fowler in 919 and the fall of Henry the Lion in 1181 and the transference of the Hohenstaufen seat of power to Southern Italy and Sicily in 1190. The epoch is almost exactly broken in twain by the reign of Henry IV, the conflict with the papacy under Gregory VII and his successors, and the great rebellion of Saxony—separate yet inseparable subjects which are pivotal both for time and importance in the history of medieval Germany.

The history of medieval Germany is more complex than the history of any other country in the Middle Ages, and almost inexhaustible, less because of its extent than because of its depth. This condition, plus the fact that there is so little in English upon the subject, has been the reason why the notes which I have appended to almost every page are sometimes long and voluminous. They are not put there with any vain desire to make a parade of erudition, but to help the reader search farther and to investigate more deeply if he so wish. In a work covering so large a field as is embraced in this book I have necessarily had to abridge much and to suppress more. I trust, however, that the notes may make partial amends for this abridgment. I have relegated to them consideration of numerous subjects which are germane to the theme of the chapter, yet of subordinate importance.

In the search for material I have taken heavy toll of many libraries, but I am most indebted to the authorities of Harvard University for large use of the magnificent Hohenzollern Collection of German history there, one of the greatest in the world upon the subject, which contains an almost complete set of the local historical periodicals of Germany. When the exigencies of teaching prevented me from remaining in Cambridge, the liberality of Harvard has permitted me to borrow volume after volume from this collection. Without such generosity the completion of this book would have been almost impossible. Needless to say, there is a long list of modern German scholars to whom my homage is due, foremost among whom are Waitz, Nitzsch, Gerdes, Holder-Egger, and Lamprecht. One living scholar has earned my special gratitude—Professor Bernhard Schmeidler, whose masterly editions of Adam of Bremen and Helmold have been of immense service to me. Several of the chapters herein have appeared in part or in whole in the *American Historical Review*, the *Proceedings of the American Historical Association*, the *American Journal of Theology*, the *American Journal of Sociology*, the *Journal of Political Economy*, the *History Teachers' Magazine*, the *Slavonic Review*, and the *Revue Belge de philosophie et d'histoire*.

Among many in the University of Chicago Press who have come in contact with this book in various stages of its preparation, I wish to thank Mr. Gordon J. Laing and Miss Anabel Ireland of the editorial department, Mr. A. C. McFarland of the manufacturing department and Miss Mary D. Alexander of the proofroom. My former student, Mr. R. Clinton Platt, has proved his friendship and his scholarship by compiling the Index. Finally, I am indebted beyond measure to my wife, Martha Landers Thompson, for many patient hours spent in reading the manuscript, the galley proofs, and the page proofs with me.

The device on the cover is reproduced from a thirteenth-century illustration to be found in *Monumenta Germaniae Historica*, *Scriptores*, XVIII, 5.

JAMES WESTFALL THOMPSON

August 15, 1927

INTRODUCTION

ANCIENT GERMANY, the Germany of the time of
Caesar and Tacitus and of the Roman Empire, was a
square bounded on the north by the North Sea and
the Baltic, on the east by the Oder and the mountains of
Bohemia, on the south by the Danube, and on the west by
the Rhine. In the fourth and fifth centuries, under the tremendous pressure of the migrations (*Völkerwanderung*), the
German race surged southward over the Danube and westward across the Rhine, the vanguard tribes penetrating far
into and settling within the Roman Empire, where the first
barbarian kingdoms were established in Italy, in Gaul, in
Spain, and even in Africa. Germany, like an overturned ves-
sel, saw her nations seeping away out of the motherland and
ever flowing toward the west and the south. There was real
danger in the fifth century of the German race being lost to
history through absorption and assimilation by the deeply
Romanized and more highly civilized populations of Italy,
Gaul, and Spain. By the end of the sixth century both nations of the Goths, the Vandals, the Burgundians, the Lombards, and half of the Frankish nation had abandoned the
ancient *Heimland* forever. Only five important tribes yet remained there. The East Franks were in the valleys of the
lower Rhine and Meuse; the Saxons in North Germany with
the small Thuringian tribe wedged in between them and the
Franks; the ancient Suevi, now called Swabians, were spread
over the angle made by the upper waters of the Danube and
the Rhine and were settled even upon the flanks of the Alps
and the Jura; the Bavarians lay along the middle Danube between the Lech and the Inn rivers and bridged the great
stream.

But as the Germans had enlarged their borders toward
the south and west there had been a corresponding shrinkage
along the east and northeast. For when the Goths and Vandals and Lombards had moved out of their ancient seat be-

tween the Oder and the Elbe rivers, the evacuated territory
was slowly filled in from the east by Slavonic incomers, so
that by 600 the Elbe had become the frontier between the
German and the Wendish world. Even the upper reaches of
the Elbe had been crossed by the Wends, and in Central
Germany the Saale was the dividing-line between the races.
The future was to see the recovery and recolonization of these
lost lands. But it is important to observe that a vital distinction must be made in the history of medieval Germany between this "Old Germany," the Germany of the great
"stems" or tribes (East Frank, Saxon, Thuringian, Swabian,
Bavarian), and the "New Germany" beyond the Elbe and the
Saale rivers.

Physiography and natural resources have ever profoundly
conditioned peoples, and a study of the physical map of
Germany is important for an understanding of German his-
tory. North Germany, or Lower Germany, is a broad, flat
plain across which the Ems, the Weser, the Elbe, and the
Oder flow to either the North Sea or the Baltic. South, or
Upper Germany, is composed of mountain and upland and
valleys. The core of Germany and the heart of the German
race are in Thuringia and Hesse, the territory between the
Thuringian Forest and the Rothaar Mountains, the Harz, the
Vögelsberg, the Rhön, and the Teutoburger Forest. Neither
Roman nor Frenchman nor Slav has ever made any impression upon this region, which has "always held the balance
and controlled the natural routes between north and south
Germany." If one will lay his right hand upon a map of Germany he may be interested to discover how remarkably the
human hand reflects the physiography of the land. The area
under his outspread fingers will answer to the plain of North
Germany, his thumb will be the Rhine, his index finger the
Weser, his longest finger will coincide with the Elbe (the
longest river of Germany), the fourth finger will be the Oder,
and the little finger the Vistula. His knuckles will represent
the mountainous ridges extending across Central Germany,
the massif of Thuringia corresponding to the largest knuckle.
Across the back of his hand the Main will flow westward and
the Eger eastward, forming a natural horizontal trough al-

most on the line of the fiftieth parallel, and stretching
straight across Germany from Mainz to Prague. Across his
wrist the Danube will make a blue line from west to east.
Under the palm will lie Upper Germany as under the fingers
will spread the plain of Lower Germany with its rivers wind-
ing northward to the sea. And just as the thumb and the
great knuckle clinch the hand, so does the Rhine clinch and
Thuringia-Hesse articulate together Northern and Southern
Germany.

The tribal ingredients which formed the German race were
as varied as the physical features of the land which it inhabited. As the occupants of the former Roman province of
Lower Germany, and the first of the Germans remaining in
the fatherland to become Romanized—at least partially so—
and Christianized, the Franks of the middle and lower Rhinelands became the first important historical factor in the
formation of medieval Germany. The conquest of the Swabians by the Franks in 496 and that of the Bavarians in 552
incorporated these other Germanic tribes into the Frankish
state of the Merovingians. But the complete union of the
five great German tribes, Franks, Swabians, Bavarians,
Thuringians, and Saxons, was the work of the Carolingian
dynasty, especially of Charlemagne. With this union the
particular history of feudal Germany begins.

But it was tribal union, never tribal consolidation. The
particularism which has characterized German history finds
its root in the important fact that no ruling house in Germany
has ever succeeded in overcoming this original and primordial
heterogeneity of the German race. A common blood, a common speech, and a common body of institutions have never
canceled this sense of separate tribal identity among the
German peoples. And these differences have been accentuated by differences of material and moral culture and were
given added fixity by difference of religion in the sixteenth
century. Every dynasty that has ruled Germany has had to
compromise with or surrender to this inflexible and determined particularism inherent in the German peoples. In the
Middle Ages the Saxon kings, the Salian kings, and the
Hohenstaufen kings had each their own policy of rule and

plan of solution, and each one differed from that of the other. None wholly succeeded, and finally the Habsburgs in the thirteenth century flatly surrendered to conditions beyond their control.

Otto the Great and the Saxon rulers generally sought to use the institutions and the authority of the church as a binding force to unite the state and overcome the incorrigible particularism of the duchies. As in a Gothic cathedral the buttresses are designed to neutralize the thrust and to sustain the weight of the roof, so in the government of Saxon Germany the episcopate was utilized to check the centrifugal thrust of the duchies and to sustain the weight and authority of the crown. But with the rise of the new papacy in the eleventh century with its ambitious plan to subordinate secular authority to that of the church, the Saxon policy, effective as it was in some degree, manifestly carried with it a danger which an independent state could not brook. The Salian emperors abandoned the perilous policy of their predecessors and Henry III and Henry IV labored to establish an absolute monarchy in Germany by drastic coercion and even extinguishment of the duchies, the end of which would have been a centralized Germany in which the ancient duchies would have been reduced to mere administrative divisions. This design—so identical with that which the French kings achieved—was frustrated by the great rebellion of the Saxons against Salian absolutism and the struggle between Gregory VII and Henry IV. This double and simultaneous movement ruined the Salian dream. Feudal and tribal particularism again escaped control by the crown.

The Hohenstaufen in the twelfth century, blood heirs and political heirs alike of the Salian house, again struggled to realize the aspiration of Henry III and Henry IV. But with Frederick I and Henry VI the pernicious effect of the union of Germany and Italy together to form the Holy Roman Empire terminated in disaster both to the Hohenstaufen house and to Germany. Neither Saxon nor Salian had ever permitted the interest of the German kingdom to be sacrificed to imperial prestige and aggrandizement. But Frederick Barbarossa, imbued with the revived ideas of Roman law, with

his head full of vague and grandiose conceptions of imperialism which were partly of Roman and partly of ecclesiastical
origin, endeavored to out-Caesar Caesar, and to establish an
empire of a politico-ecclesiastical nature piered upon Germany and Italy as its foundation, but bending like a mighty
arch over the whole of Christendom.

The majestic ridge of Barbarossa's ambition was the summit over which he fell. In striving to grasp both Germany
and Italy in the grip of absolutism he failed to clutch either
completely, and both Germany and Italy partially slipped
through his fingers. Forces beyond his comprehension to
understand or to measure baffled and frustrated him. These
forces were very different in nature and spirit, but operated
simultaneously and sometimes directly worked together
against him.

In Germany by the twelfth century the former incoherent
and heterogeneous elements embodied in feudal particularism
and the duchies, under Saxon leadership, had been brought
into alignment and given a constructive intention and interpretation. The genius of Lothar of Saxony and Henry the
Proud at last discovered that there was a principle below all
the *Sturm und Drang* of feudal and ducal resistance, and
formulated that principle into a policy. This principle was
that of local sovereignty and state rights to be reserved for
and preserved by the various duchies whose union—loose or
strong—formed the German kingdom. In a word, the Guelf
house worked for the creation of feudal monarchy resting on
a federation of the German duchies; for a form of government that would strike a just balance between the rights of
the crown and the rights of the several ducal states under the
crown. This form of government, if it had ever been realized,
would have given simultaneous and due expression to both
union and severalty, and would have been a form of government intermediate between the intense particularism of the
tenth century and the strongly centralized Germany which
the Salian and the Hohenstaufen strove to create.

The conflict between the Hohenstaufen and the Guelf
culminated finally in the destruction of the great feudal
duchies and the exhaustion of the crown at the same time,

with the result that the real victors in the bitter struggle were the lesser feudatories and the feudalized bishops. The partition of Saxony in 1181 marks the passing of the last great German duchy and tolled the knell of the Guelf design of a federated German kingdom. But as when Samson bowed himself between the columns of the temple of the Philistines in Gaza and pulled down the whole structure upon their heads, so when Henry the Lion fell, the fall of Saxony dragged down the German kingdom with it into wreck. The dissolution of the once splendid duchy of Swabia, the shredding of Franconia, the severance of Brandenburg from Saxony and of Austria from Bavaria, the rise of newly formed and sovereign states within the body of the old duchies immediately preceded or followed the collapse of Saxony. The tragic result was the conversion of the once strong and magnificent German kingdom into a rope of sand, a confused and jarring chaos of small and warring states ruled by petty dynasts neither materially able to accomplish great things nor morally capable of understanding that high things are to know, that deep things are to feel.

In brief, this is the sum of the history of feudal Germany between the tenth and the twelfth centuries. In the intricate evolution and transformation every important element of medieval German life was involved—state and church, ducal territories and crown lands, bishop and abbot, baron and burgher and peasant. The moral factors never absent from the history of any great society, institutions of a national or local nature and those more intimate customs and mores of the people which have to do with daily family life and association, material development like commerce and trade and the sturdy labor of millions of industrious peasants in field and forest, schools and education, the cultivation of literature and the arts (especially in quiet cloisters)—all these separate and mingled strands form the complex warp and woof of the history of feudal Germany. It is a noble history, splendid in idealism and achievement and gravely beautiful even in those portions of it which suffered ruination.

No other field of medieval history presents so rich and varied a history as that of Germany in the Middle Ages, nor is any other more profitable to study. Germany was the first state to establish ordered and settled government after the collapse of Central and Western Europe in the ninth century. When England was sinking into the lees under the spineless rule of the last representatives of the house of Alfred the Great and Edward the Elder, from which the iron hand of William the Conqueror rescued her, when France was in the throes of feudal anarchy and the Capetian kings in Paris could see from its walls the towers of robber barons too strong to be broken silhouetted against the sky, when Italy was "a mere geographical expression," torn by dissension and basely and brutally governed when governed anywhere at all, when the temporal power of the papacy was a byword and a hissing, when in Spain the only government worthy of the name was not Christian but Mohammedan, Germany was a great country ruled by a dynasty of strength and ideas. Violent as the history of Germany in the feudal age sometimes was, the violence was usually a struggle for rights which redeems it from the vice inherent in the violence of France in the tenth and eleventh centuries.

In the invention and application of administrative institutions, while in the eleventh century there are certain provinces, Normandy, Anjou, Norman Italy, in which efficient administration prevailed, nowhere else in Continental Europe except Germany may one find effective administration upon a broad, national scale. In the realm of political theory the Salian monarchs anticipated France in formulation and application of the principles of absolute monarchy, and the Guelfs in like manner anticipated England in the formulation of the principles of constitutional monarchy and attempted to give them realization a generation before the time of Henry Plantagenet. Political principles are never to be wholly approved because they are successful, or condemned because they fail. Both Salian and Guelf failed to achieve their purpose owing to a combination of forces beyond their control and stronger, but no better—indeed, not so good as theirs. It was left to France to win through to efficient absolute monarchical government, and for England to win through to successful constitutional government. But feudal

Germany was a pioneer in both these political ideas. What defeated both issues in Germany was the untoward, even disastrous fact that the destiny of the German nation by an ill freak of fortune was tied up with the history of Italy and the Empire. This made Germany's problem an infinitely complex one, whereas that of France and England was a relatively simple one. The German kings as emperors, especially the Hohenstaufen, wasted untold blood and treasure of the German people beyond the Alps under the malign tyranny of the idea of medieval imperialism. The end spelled the ruin of feudal Germany. But for this medieval Germany would have won through, too, to a great and strong national monarchy. Yet even if failure overcame her, the ideal and the sacrifice were magnificent.

Finally, it is to be noted that in one conspicuous endeavor medieval Germany was splendidly successful. "The great deed of the German people in the Middle Ages," Lamprecht has justly written, "was the recovery of three-fifths of modern Germany from the Slavs." The wars in Italy and along the French border, or even the Crusades never diverted the eyes of the German people away from the great territory beyond the Elbe and the Inn which their forebears had once dwelt in and ruled over. The deep determination in the hearts of the German people to recover these lands from the Slavs, the resolute, though often ruthless way in which the event was achieved, is one of the most stirring stories in the annals of history. The grandeur of the design was matched by the completeness of the conquest. The only thing comparable to this achievement in modern annals is the history of the expansion of the American people westward from the Atlantic seaboard over the Alleghanies, down the rivers and across the great plains. In both instances the work was the work of the common people and independent of governmental initiative, the work of the pioneer and the settler subjugating the forest with the ax, the fields with the plow, and driving Slav or redman, as the case may be, before him by his prowess in arms. What the New West meant to young America that the New East meant to medieval Germany. Each region beckoned the pioneer, the young and lusty of every generation, who sought for cheap lands and new freedom in the wilderness. What Jackson and Clay, Ohio, Indiana, and Illinois meant to the history of the United States between 1815 and 1850, that Albrecht the Bear and Leopold of Babenberg, Brandenburg and Austria, meant to Germany in the twelfth century. When old, west, feudal Germany was falling into dissolution a new frontier, colonial Germany, arose in the east to counterbalance the loss. Without the adventure of knight errantry, without the romanticism of the Crusades, this history of the expansion of a great people has a simplicity and a dignity all its own. But for this splendid achievement Germany today would be a narrow strip of territory wedged in between the Rhine and the Elbe, and the German nation and Germanic culture would exist in the reduced dimension of a minor European state and people.

TABLE OF CONTENTS

APPENDIX

INDEX

LIST OF MAPS

PART I
OLD WEST FEUDAL GERMANY

CHAPTER I

THE CHURCH IN THE CAROLINGIAN AND SAXON GOVERNMENTS

IN THE Middle Ages the church was much more than a religious institution. It was a political, civil, social, economic institution of portentous power and of vast dimension. Its proprietary nature involved it in the network of the feudal régime to a degree which requires some effort of historical imagination to realize. Bishops and abbots were feudal lords, and the machinery of the church was intricately interwoven with the machinery of feudal government. Bishoprics and abbeys were lordships like lay seigneuries and subject to almost identical laws and practices.

By the eighth century the conditions and obligations governing landed proprietorship, whether lay or clerical, had become conventionalized, and, with the transformation of land ownership into benefices in the time of Karl Martel, the church, like secular society, passed completely into the feudal régime. Such a state of things for the church was perfectly adapted both to the ideas and to the practices of a feudal age. There was nothing incongruous or unseemly in the arrangement, however strange it may seem to us today, when fighting abbots and the blazon of episcopacy have vanished. Like every other institution the system was capable of great abuse, and it gave rise to grievous conditions within the church. But we must free our minds from preconceived notions and avoid judging the medieval church by modern conditions. The church was a historical institution, a part of the organic, human life of the medieval epoch. As it functioned in that society it must be studied and judged. Because in its best moments the church taught a quality of life and cherished an ideal above the world, that did not separate it from the world. To have been less human than it was, the medieval church would have had to func-

3

tion in a vacuum or lived in a world of the fourth dimension.

The legislation of Pepin and Charlemagne was particularly instrumental in combining the church with the state. Pepin introduced the bishops into the national Frankish assembly (Marchfeld, Champ de Mars) not only as proprietors but as prelates, in order to counterbalance the power of the lay feudality. Henceforth the councils inclined to supersede the former national assemblies, and civil and ecclesiastical legislation tended to fuse together.[1] It was even within the prerogative of the king to fix dogma (both Childebert and Charlemagne did so), and from Pepin's time forward the state required the *credo* and the *pater noster* as law, and legislated in its capitularies upon the things of the church as well as upon secular matters. The Frankish church was ruled by and for temporal interests.[2] Charlemagne treated the bishops and abbots of his empire exactly as he treated secular dignitaries, and was as cautious in dispensing favors to them as he was to the great lay nobles.

He would never give more than one county to any of his counts unless they happened to live on the borders or marches of the barbarians; nor would he ever give a bishop any abbey or church that was in the royal gift unless there were very special reasons for so doing. When his counsellors or friends asked him the reason for doing this, he would answer: "With

---

[1] Nitzsch, *Gesch. d. deutschen Volkes*, I, 249; Viollet, *Inst. polit. de la France*, I, 356–771; Lesne, *La propriété ecclés, en France*, pp. 424–38. In 755 the Marchfeld was changed to May in order that there might be more pasturage for the horses of those attending (Schröder, *Rechtsgesch.*, p. 155; cf. Einhard, *Ann.*, 820: ". . . . ut primum herba pabulum jumentis praebere potuit"). The councils of the church ceased to be purely eccleciastical bodies, but performed a large amount of civil legislation. See Harzheim, *Concilia Germaniae*, III, 187. Fisher, *Medieval Empire*, II, 92, gives some interesting examples of this fusion of secular and ecclesiastical affairs. "Every bishop and abbot governs his territory by the aid of a little parliament of nobles and ministeriales." From the time of Otto I German bishops had the rank of princes (Hauck, *Kirchengesch.*, III, 28).

[2] The Carolingian policy with reference to church offices may be defined as a sort of right of control and of veto, without, in theory, opposing the free choice of the bishop by the people and the clergy. Louis the Pious went farther and claimed the right to authorize episcopal elections, and under Charles the Bald this practice became so general as to have the force of law, in spite of the influence of the Pseudo-Isidorean decretals and the contentions of Nicholas I (Georg Weise, *Königtum und Bischofswahl im fränkischen und deutschen Reich vor dem Investiturstreit*, Berlin, 1912).

that revenue or that estate, with that abbey or that church I can secure the fidelity of some vassal, as good a man as any bishop or count, and perhaps better."[1]

After Charlemagne everything melted away. The political system established by him was impotent before the power of the revolutionary forces of the time. In the tumultuous laboratory of the ninth century the old order of things was broken up and a new civilization came out of the crucible. Feudalism emerged as a complete political, economic, and social polity, and the feudal states of France, Germany, and Italy came into being.[2] In the anarchy of the times the lands of bishops and abbots were given by the rulers to dukes and counts as the price of their military service, or were seized by the latter and more or less assimilated with their own feudal holdings.[3]

With the break-up of the Carolingian empire in the ninth century, the relations of state and church began to be reversed. Hitherto the state had controlled the church. Now the church began to control the state. The amalgamation of church and state became more complete than before,[4] and the church saw to it that it was well repaid for its services to the government. By the end of the ninth century the dilapida-

---

[1] Monachus S. Galli, *De vita Caroli*, Book I, chap. xiii; cf. Carlyle, *Med. Polit. Theory*, I, 262–79. Guilhiermoz, *L'origine de la noblesse en France au moyen-âge*, p. 126, n. 5, has amassed the evidence to illustrate the Carolingian handling of church offices for political purposes. All abbeys were in the gift of the crown. "Abbatibus quoque et laicis specialiter jubemus ut in monasteriis quae *ex nostra largitate* habeat,"etc. (Cap. Lud. Pii, 823, c. 8).

[2] On the nature and significance of the dissolution of the Carolingian empire see Bourgeois, *Le capitulaire de Kiersey*, esp. pp. 271–83; Prou, *De ordine palatii*, Introd.; Ellendorf, *Die Karolinger und die Hierarchie*; Lavisse, *Histoire de France*, II, Part I, Book 3, and bibliographies there given.

[3] Lesne, *La propriété ecclés. en France*, I, 439–52; Waitz, IV, 165–73; Parisot, *Royaume de Lorraine sous les Carolingiens*, p. 31, n. 5; p. 81 nn.; pp. 185, 331, 687; Poupardin, *Royaume de Provence sous les Carolingiens*, p. 337, n. 6; pp. 373–76, 384; Kurth, *Notger de Liège*, p. 28; Pirenne, *Hist. de Belgique*, I, 39–41. Pope Nicholas I approved the diversion of abbey revenues for the support of Queen Teutberge of Lorraine, Parisot (*op. cit.*, p. 308). Charles the Bald sold the abbey of St. Bertin for thirty gold pieces (*op. cit.*, p. 358).

[4] On this process see Lea, *Studies in Church History*, pp. 326–42; Viollet, I, 370–71; Prou, *De ordine palatii*, Introd.; Ellendorf, *Die Karolinger und die Hierarchie*, Vol. II, chap. iv; Bourgeois, *Capitulaire de Kiersey*, pp. 271–83.

tion of the royal domain, owing to lavish, gratuitous, or forced donations to the church, seriously impoverished the monarchy. It is true that few of them were outright grants. Most of them were in the form of benefices which, at least theoretically, reserved for the crown the right to exact feudal services of the holders thereof. But a crown so weak that it was unable to refuse the demands of the church for more land was too weak to enforce the actual terms of the grant.

The church, however, was not long in discovering that a peril was attached to this rapid acquisition of landed wealth, which, like the shirt of Nessus, was destined to poison the wearer. For its increasing proprietorship entangled the church more and more in the coil of feudalism. The rivalry between the high clergy and the great lay feudality for possession of the crown lands was intense, and the church, in order to sate the land hunger of the feudal nobles, was often compelled to effect an accommodation with them by enfiefing its lands to them. In an age of blood and iron such an arrangement was frequently of mutual advantage. The bishop or abbot did not give or the baron get something for nothing. The baron might have bullied the bishop into making the enfiefment, but he was subject to the feudal contract which always required the rendering of military service by the vassal to the suzerain. Thus originated that class of *milites ecclesiae* which played so great a part in the period of the Crusades; thus the church entered more deeply than ever into the feudal polity. The art of war was not long in becoming an important episcopal accomplishment. The fighting bishop, helmed and hauberked, was a development of the late ninth century.

But it was impossible for any government with a remnant of self-respect to let the church wholly escape from secular control without a struggle, and the kings of the ninth century, weak as they were, had recourse to an expedient which in part recouped their waning material fortune and partially compensated them for the compulsory alienation of their domains to the church. This was the institution of the "advocate" (Fr. *avoué*; Ger. *Vogt*), an outgrowth of the highly feudalized organization of society. The office, in its narrower functions, was almost as old as the church's landed proprietorship. It grew up in the early Middle Ages as a product of the violence of the times. Canon law followed the precept of Paul: "Nemo militans Deo implicat se negotiis secularibus." The bishops and abbots found it desirable, even necessary, to have some secular person to represent them in political, military, and judicial matters as the authority of the state waned and the power of feudalism increased. Before the time of Charlemagne the institution of *advocatus* was an irregular one. But this ruler by law required the permanent presence of such an official in every ecclesiastical establishment, both bishopric and abbey. The spread of immunities gave an enormous extension to the office. For the advocate was first of all a judge in the name of the ecclesiastic whom he represented, and only later, with the dissolution of the Carolingian empire, a defender and protector. But in the disorder of the times the advocate soon became more powerful than his lord. He became a minor pillar in the social edifice of the feudal system, a noble enfiefing the lands of the church which he was once engaged to defend, without any reminiscence of the ecclesiastical title vaguely attached to them. Fiefs *d'avouerie* became insensibly hereditary like other fiefs. The *advocati* became like other feudal nobles, given to war and pillage as they, and blackmailing and bulldozing bishops and abbots like lay barons, so that the restraints of the peace of God became as applicable to them as to others. The office became a menace to the church worse than the evils which it was originally designed to remedy, and the legislation of the synods and the councils of the feudal age involve *advocati* in common condemnation with all other robber barons.

Once become a hereditary fief, the *avouerie* was a terrible weapon in the hands of an ambitious baron, who could mercilessly appropriate the property of the church under guise of "protecting" it. In France the abuse of churches they were supposed to protect drove the episcopate to support the monarchy as a means of relief and to substitute the protection (*gardiennat*) of the crown for the abusive practices of this class of the feudality. The advocate represented his ecclesiastical superior in the administration of the purely secular affairs which fell to the bishop or the abbot to perform in pursuance of his double rôle of an ecclesiastic and a landed proprietor. He pleaded the causes of the bishop or abbot in the courts of the count or suzerain; he administered justice in their name among the church's vassals; he represented his principal in the judicial duel, participation in which was forbidden to ecclesiastics; he presided over cases of trial by battle between the bishop's or abbot's vassals, and, most important of all, he commanded the *milites ecclesiae* when the church was called upon to do military service.

In the anarchy of the ninth century, when the monasteries began to wall their houses,[1] the office of advocate acquired great extension. Protection was the crying need of the time. Often, though, the bishop or abbot had no choice in selecting the incumbent. The post was eagerly coveted by the lay feudality, since it gave the holder control of certain ecclesiastical revenues and the use of certain church vassals for military purposes. As a consequence, in practice the bishop or abbot had frequently to appease the greed of a neighboring noble by purchasing his protection, for otherwise his lands were likely to be pillaged by the noble. Under this form of blackmail the remedy became worse than the disease.[2] The

[1] "Tunc quoque domus ecclesiarum per Gallias universas, preter quas municipia civitatum vel castrorum servarunt" (Rod. Glaber [ed. Prou], Book I, chap. v, sec. 9). For the effect of the Norse invasions in the ninth century and the anarchy of the tenth upon the walling of monasteries, villages, towns, granges, and the erection of castles, first of wood (block houses), later of stone, see Favre, *Eudes, roi de France*, pp. 220–21; Lavisse, *Hist. de France*, II, Part II, 14–16 (bib.); Flach, *Les Origines de l'ancienne France*, II, 312–27, 329–42; Waitz, IV, 629; Parisot, p. 55, n. 2; p. 458, n. 4; pp. 461, 499; Poupardin, p. 337, n. 6; Fagniez, *Documents rélatifs à l'histoire du commerce ... de la France*, Vol. I, Introd., p. xli; Lefranc, *Hist. de Noyon*, pp. 12–14; Mortet, *Recueil de Textes rélatifs à l'histoire de l'Architecture*, Introd., pp. xlii–lii. Cf. also the Index under the words *donjons, mottes de donjons, tours, maisons fortes, fermes, palissades*. In Germany, Henry the Fowler was the first to require monasteries and nunneries to be inclosed (Sommerlad, *Die wirtschaftliche Tätigkeit der Kirche in Deutschland*, II, 234–35; Nitzsch, I, 288). Gorze, Hersfeld, St. Gall, etc., were walled *ca.* 900 as protection against the Hungarians (Hauck, *Kirchengeschichte*, III, 227).

[2] On the institution of the advocate see Waitz, IV, 409 f.; Brunner, *Rechtsgesch.*, II, 320 f.; Bethmann-Hollweg, *Civilprozess*, III, 161 f.; Pischek, *Die Vogtei in den geistlichen Stiftern des fränkischen Reiches* (1886); Hauck, *op. cit.*, II, 598 f.; Sackur, *Die Cluniacenser*, I, 29 f.; Below, *Der deutsche Staat des Mittelalters*, p. 149; Flach,

Capetian kings of France made themselves "lay" abbots of half a dozen of the richest abbeys in France. The counts of Flanders so built up their power. In Germany the practice was carried to an extreme by Frederick Barbarossa, whose Italian campaigns were largely fought with church vassals.

Under these conditions the hierarchy tended more and more to become a military caste like the feudality. Bishops and abbots became dukes and counts. Miter and mace, crosier and coat-of-mail, became interchangeable insignia of the high clergy, who increasingly were recruited from among the powerful families of the feudal noblesse, which put cadets of the house in church preferments, so that bishoprics and abbeys often became dependencies of the feudality.[1] Bishops and abbots became centers of feudo-territorial groups, exercising a temporal sovereignty analogous to the powers they had long practiced within their ancient immunities. In the name of churches and monasteries they granted fiefs, ruled vassals, distributed tenures, and governed serfs. Side by side with the secular feudatories grew up an ecclesiastical nobility composed of archbishops and bishops, who were at the same time dukes or counts, and cathedral chapters and abbeys which as corporations controlled immense territorial possessions. From all sides the weak had recourse to the church's stronger protection, offering it their persons and their prop-

---

Les origines de l'anc. France, I, 437–44; Viollet, *Inst. pol. de la France*, pp. 372–74; Senn, *L'institution des avoueries eccles. en France* (1903); *L'institution des vidames en France* (1907); Heilmann, *Die Klostervogtei im rechtsrheinischen Teil der Diözese Konstanz bis nur Mitte des 13. Jahrhunderts* (1908); Otto Lerche, *Die Privilegierung der deutschen Kirche durch Papsturkunden bis auf Gregor VII* (Göttingen, 1910), pp. 29–32; Blumenstock, *Der päpstliche Schutz im Mittelalter* (1890); Hüfner, "Das Rechtsinstitut der klösterlichen Exemption in der abendländischen Kirche," *Archiv für Kirchenrecht*, LXXXVI (1906), 302 f.; Walter Kraaz, *Die päpstliche Politik in Verfassungs- und Vermögensfragen deutscher Kloster* (Leipzig diss., 1902); Gerdes, *Gesch. des deutschen Volkes*, I, 539–40. Much other literature in Holtzmann, *Französische Verfassungsgesch.*, p. 138, and Luchaire, *Manuel des institutions françaises*, secs. 153–55. For a desperate instance, Richeri, *Gesta eccles. Senon*, I, 17 (*MGH*, SS. XXV). Fisher, I, 319, has a vivid account of the practical working of the advocate's office.

[1] See Schulte, *Der Adel und die deutsche Kirche* (1910). The classic document in the militarization of the bishops is Ep. 112 of the *Letters of Fulbert of Chartres*.

erty. Its tribunals were often preferred to the secular courts of the lay lords, and the church's sway was not only exercised over all ecclesiastical matters, but extended jurisdiction over a host of civil and criminal affairs which primarily were of secular origin and incidence. Gradually the practice of infeudation penetrated the whole body of ecclesiastical offices and functions. The church's lands, offices, altars, prebends, tithes, became feudalized.[1]

Aloys Schulte[2] has shown with a wealth of evidence that before the twelfth century the monasteries were almost wholly groups of freeborn inmates (*freiständische Stifter und Klöster*). From the time of Charlemagne onward the unwritten rule of the kings was that the bishop's office was to be filled by men of free or noble birth, and the German episcopate was emphatically *hocharistokratisch*, even though one sometimes comes upon instances like Benno II of Osnabrück, who was of servile birth. The breakdown of aristocratic control of the German houses began in the eleventh century with the rise of the *ministeriales*, who introduced a non-noble and non-free—in other words, servile—element for the first time into the monasteries, notably at Hirsau. The social decay is still more manifest in the twelfth century, and with it went also the decadence of learning and literary culture in the monasteries. The very catalogues of the monastic libraries, many of whose manuscripts went back to the ninth and tenth centuries, illustrate this intellectual decline, for eleventh-century manuscripts are rare. The subjoined figures from Schulte (pp. 237–39) show it. They are taken from two representative monasteries.

[1] Koeniger, *Burchard I von Worms*, pp. 48–52. For France see Viollet, I, 416–17, and Lesne, pp. 131–42. Walafrid Strabo's ninth-century treatise, *De ecclesiasticarum rerum exordiis et incrementis*, chap. xxxi, has a real value for the historian, for it institutes a striking comparison between ecclesiastical and secular dignities. Thegan, of noble Frank ancestry and biographer of Louis the Pious (*Vita Ludovici imperatoris*, chap. xx), inveighs against the entrance of men of base birth into the church: "De incongrua ignobilium ad ecclesiasticas dignitates promotione et vitiis." Elsewhere we read: "Turpissimam cognationem eorum a jugo *debitae servitutis* nituntur eripere et libertatem imponi." The occasion of this invective was the conduct of Ebbo of Rheims (who was of servile birth) toward Louis the Pious (cf. chap. xli).

[2] *Der Adel und die deutsche Kirche im Mittelalter* (Stuttgart, 1910).

	Reichenau	St. Gall
Eighth century	44	21
Ninth century	100	237
Tenth century	29	86
Eleventh century	7	49
Twelfth century	4	54
Thirteenth century	11	50

The breakdown was further increased by the rapid extinction of the older, noble families in the eleventh and twelfth centuries, which gave room for the entrance of men of base blood and parvenu position. The long civil war into which Germany was plunged in the reign of Henry IV hastened this rapid decay of the older houses. Celibacy also had its influence. It was always detrimental, and sometimes fatal to the survival of a feudal house when one of its members entered the church. When Henry II's brother became bishop of Augsburg it doomed the Saxon dynasty to extinction, for Henry II was childless. From calculations necessarily imperfect, yet significant, Schulte has concluded that in the space of three hundred years 12 per cent of the high feudal families of Germany, 36 per cent of the counts, and 80 per cent of lesser noble families failed to perpetuate themselves owing to so many members of the families having entered holy orders. This was birth control to the point of extinction of many of them, and resulted in actual "race suicide" of some of the greatest feudal families. In 1050 the nobility still had the preponderance in the German church, but not a monopoly. The invasion of the lower classes already was in full swing. Benno II of Osnabrück was the son of a *ministerialis*, and so far as I know, the first German bishop of that status. After 1122 the elevation of men of common origin to episcopal and abbatial dignity becomes frequent. Before that date most of the German bishops were of noble birth. After that date low-born bishops and abbots are often met with.[1]

But neither in Germany nor in France did the king's ecclesiastical sovereignty, conveyed in the term *regale*, become so mutilated and dispersed as his political authority. Some remnants of the complete supremacy over the church,

[1] See Schulte's table, *op. cit.*, pp. 67–68.

formerly enjoyed by the Carolingian monarchy, still remained in the great fiefs, which otherwise had escaped the crown's control. In these areas the vassals and revenues of the church were regarded as part of the military and fiscal resources of the crown and used by the king at his discretion. The bishop or abbot (if the abbey were "royal") was as much the choice of the king as a local priest was the creature of his lord, and the conduct of the hierarchy was assimilated to the condition, if not the status, of the secular feudatories. Bishops and abbots were held to the performance of *auxilia* in the same way and to as great—or even greater—a degree as dukes and counts.

The domain of a bishop or abbot in the Middle Ages was rarely, if ever, a compact, contiguous area. On the contrary, it was composed of a vast ensemble or complex of scattered parcels which had been acquired by gift or purchase during years of time, and was therefore widely located.[1] The unity of the whole was not a physical but a moral one. The bishop or abbot was the proprietor thereof, whose legal position was guaranteed by the immunity which exempted him from any lay jurisdiction or authority save that of the king. Unless feudal usurpation had canceled the theory of the law, no duke nor count could enter within this circumscription, which, in spite of the agglomerated nature of the lands, nevertheless formed a closed circle. Within and on his own lands a bishop or abbot was a royal official. The abbey of Lobbes in Flanders is a good illustration of the feudal com-

---

[1] For example, Corvey had lands in Lorraine, the archbishopric of Magdeburg owned lands in Deventer (Gerdes, I, 536). Outside of Metz proper the bishop had estates in Epinal, Moyen, Marsal, Vic, Habondage, Rambervillers, Conflans, Varnesberg, Radonville, St. Trond, etc. (Klipfel, *Metz, cité épiscopale et impériale* [1866], p. 26). The archbishop of Rheims, though a French subject, owned lands in Lorraine (Parisot, *Le royaume de Lorraine sous les Carolingiens*, p. 37, n. 4; p. 176, n. 3). A Roman papyrus discovered by Kehr in the archives of Marburg (pub. in *K. Gesellschaft d. Wiss. zu Göttingen* [N.F.], I, No. 1 [1896]) shows that Hersfeld owned landed property in Rome. For an extended and particular study see Friedrich Hülsen, *Die Besitzungen des Klosters Lorsch in der Karolinger Zeit* (Berlin diss., 1911). Fulda, Corvey, and Werden owned manors in Frisia (Bunte, *Jahrb. d. Gesellschaft . . . . zu Emden*, X, No. 1 [1892]). The bishopric of Bamberg had holdings as far as the Danube and the Alps, while the cloister of St. Trudo in Liège had possessions along the middle Mosel at Utrecht and even along the coasts of Holland and Frisia. Prüm had holdings in one hundred and eighteen localities, some of them comprising only a few *mansi*.

plications into which a great monastery might fall. Juridically it was situated in the diocese of Cambrai, but feudally the bishop of Liège was its suzerain. The abbot enjoyed high rank among the feudality. His extensive though scattered possessions, being early safeguarded by royal and papal privileges, were settled with a dense population whose labor enriched the abbey.[1]

Both in law and in practice these ecclesiastical lands were regarded as a particular kind of barony or fief which the incumbents held immediately of the king as overlord. This was the view of the church as well as of the state, and neither party looked upon the relation as either incongruous or unusual. Vacant sees and vacant abbeys were treated as knight's fees. After the analogy of lay fiefs the king attached the incomes of ecclesiastical office in the interval between two occupations; the new appointee paid what answered to a "relief" in the secular world in order to qualify for the office; the lands and offices of the church were let to farm, enfiefed, or sold exactly as in the case of secular property.

It is important to appreciate how closely state and church were united in the Middle Ages. The church, not content with regulating faith and morals, actively mingled in politics, inspiring the kings to perform most of the legislative work which they did, and securing the kings' support and defense of their spiritual and temporal interests. As a consequence, however, of this intimate relation the church paid by loss of liberty for the influence and riches which it enjoyed.

In the principle the clergy and people preserved the right of electing the bishop. But it was necessary to have the authorization of the crown in order to exercise the right, and the king might refuse to permit it or might appoint the incumbent himself. Sometimes he outwardly respected the forms, permitting election, but taking care in advance to designate the candidate of his choice. When election had taken place secular confirmation still remained, and only after this formality had been complied with could the metropolitan instal the new bishop.

[1] Koeniger, pp. 52-53; Kurth, p. 16; Pirenne, I, 127-30; Warichez, *L'abbaye de Lobbes depuis les origines jusqu'en 1200* (Tournai, 1909).

No bishop could qualify without the consent of the king. Formal approval was absolutely necessary unless the throne were vacant at the time of election of the bishop. Often the election was a mere formality. Usually the local church authorities and the people placidly accepted the king's choice, for it was desirable that the bishop stand well at court.

In the episcopate heredity could not obtain as in civil functions. But the influence of the feudal tendency toward hereditability of offices was shown in the church also, where nepotism was a common evil. The passage of a vacated see from uncle to nephew was common. Thus, while on the one hand the sovereigns endeavored to keep the bishoprics and the bishops under their control, on the other the prelates themselves were disposed, like all the feudality, to make themselves as independent as possible of any exterior authority. This tendency was all the more pronounced because many of the bishops were of noble families. It is a fair statement that the feudality everywhere in Europe predominantly filled the offices of the hierarchy.

Abbeys no less than bishoprics were dependencies of the crown or of the feudality. Certain of them which had been founded by one of the Merovingian or Carolingian princes, and in general all those monasteries which had been taken under the king's protection, were denominated "royal" abbeys.[1] These belonged completely to the king, who disposed of their revenues as he pleased. Theoretically the abbot was chosen by the monks, as the bishop was chosen by clergy and people. But few abbeys preserved the right of local self-government. If the king were complacent he might approve the selection of the monks. Frequently he brusquely filled the office, even riding down former privileges and immunities. Many abbeys, deprived of liberty by the kings, were united

---

[1] H. Feierabend, *Die polit. Stellung d. deutschen Reichsabteien während d. Investiturstreites* (Breslau, 1913). Upon these "royal" abbeys see Waitz, IV, 153 f.; VII, 189 f.; Lamprecht, *Deutsches Wirtschaftsleben*, I, 682; Parisot, *Histoire du royaume de Lorraine sous les Carolingiens*, pp. 708–9; Fisher, *Mediaeval Empire*, I, 256–57. For Italy, see Karl Vogt, *Eigenklöster im Langobardenreich* (Gotha, 1909). The earliest were patrimonial abbeys of the Lombard kings. Generally these monasteries had been founded by kings and queens, but some by lesser personages, e.g., Farfa, first a private, then ducal, then royal monastery (pp. 50–51).

to a bishopric or another monastery; or, more unfortunate
still, fell into the hands of the feudal aristocracy, who usually
handled them without any reminiscence of their religious
character.

Just as the laity early discovered that it was often a
lucrative thing to found monasteries, so did the bishops.
Many abbeys were "episcopal" abbeys, having been originally founded by a bishop who controlled them and disposed
of their revenues (which arose from the enrichment of the
monastery by pious benefactions) as he pleased, exactly as
the king did in the case of "royal" abbeys. This condition
was particularly common in Lorraine and Swabia, where
ecclesiastical feudalism had progressed farther than elsewhere
in Germany. Here Cornelimünster and Werden belonged to
Cologne; Prüm to Trier; Remiremont to Toul; Saint Stephen,
Andlau, Erstein, Honau, and Hohenburg to Strasburg;
Münster and Murbach to Basel. A monastery might depend
upon a bishopric whether it was within or without the diocese
to which it was attached; it might depend upon another
monastery; it might depend upon the king or some other lord,
even a foreign sovereign or noble; and finally it might depend
immediately upon the pope. Abbeys created by laymen were
the hereditary property of the founders' descendants, and
their revenues formed part of his estate.[1]

Archbishops, bishops, abbots, constituted a body of government officials like the counts, for they were servants of
the state as well as of the church.[2] In virtue of immunities
which may have been granted them, many bishops and
abbots had the powers of a count within the domains of their
church. They were constrained to some sort of personal service to the king, as to attend assemblies, to go on missions, to
act as ambassadors to Rome or to a foreign court. Under the

---

[1] The historical poem of Hroswitha, the Saxon poetess, *De primordiis coenobii
Gandersheimensis*, SS. IV, 306 f., throws interesting light upon how a monastery
was founded and grew during this age. For an abstract of the poem see Ebert,
Gesch. d. mittelalterlichen Litteratur, III, 313–14.

[2] In 871 Charles the Bald denied the competence of the Roman curia over
French bishops in these words: "Reges Francorum .... non episcorum vice-
domini, sed terrae domini hactenus fuimus computati" (*H. F.*, VII, 542–45 [letter
of Hincmar]).

form of "gifts" they were required to make certain contributions to the king's needs, apart from the revenues proper of the bishopric or monastery.

We know more about the political and military obligations of bishops and abbots than about their financial relations to the secular government. As great landed proprietors, in a time when military service was everywhere in Europe dependent upon landed possession, the clergy naturally, as the greatest of such proprietors, were called upon for service of themselves and their vassals, i.e., those who held church lands in fief.[1]

Bishops and abbots had also to aid the king with their counsel like ordinary vassals. Sometimes they sat in general assemblies with the nobles, sometimes in particular ecclesiastical assemblies, as synods and councils. Here too the authority of the king over the church is manifest. For until the Gregorian reform synods could not convene without royal consent.

We have seen that the high clergy was largely recruited from the nobility. Nevertheless, in spite of identical origin, rivalry and even bitter hostility existed between the nobility and the clergy, the former usually being extremely jealous of the landed wealth and exemptions which the clergy enjoyed. In consequence private war accompanied by spoliation of lands and destruction of crops, the driving away of the peasantry, etc., were common features of everyday life; even the kings sometimes despoiled rich ecclesiastics. Yet generally royalty and the hierarchy got along fairly well together. The nobles menaced both the church and the crown, and common interest forced crown and clergy to coöperate.

Ideally the relation of church and state in the Middle Ages, at least before the Gregorian formulation of the dictum of church supremacy obtained, was one of mutual accom-

---

[1] The two documents which have most to do with this subject in Germany are the *Notitia de servitio monasteriorum*, which dates from Louis the Pious, and the *Numeri loricatorum a principibus partim mittendorum, partim ducendorum* (Jaffé, V, 471–72) of the reign of Otto II.

modation. But the relation was capable of great abuse by either party. Neither party was wholly innocent or wholly guilty, and no complete determination of relative responsibility can be made. But one fact is clear: the root of the whole medieval controversy between church and state, the fundamental source of friction, the real bone of contention, was the church's land. If the church had been less secular and more spiritual, if it had been willing to resign, or at least largely to abridge, its temporalities and material possessions, if it had been less devoted to the "royalty of Peter" and the Petrine supremacy and more devoted to the teaching of Jesus that his Kingdom was not of this world, the issue between church and state would probably never have got beyond the limits of doctrinaire discussion.

The land hunger of the church—the most pronounced form of avarice in a day when land was almost the sole source of the production of wealth, the only form of capital, the strongest basis of material power—is a fact calculated to appal and dismay one accustomed to interpret religion in spiritual terms.[1]

Even in the eighth century the enormous monopoly of land enjoined by the church had become a menace to the government and a prejudice to society.[2] Charlemagne complained that gifts to the church were so frequent that freemen were reduced to poverty and compelled to take to a life of crime.[3] "In 817 Louis the Pious was obliged to legislate to prevent clerks from taking gifts which might disinherit the children or near relations of the giver, and the enactment was re-enacted by Lewis II in 875."[4]

As early as 816 the standardization of ecclesiastical

[1] For the church's "working" of the pious for gifts of land and endowments see Lamprecht, *DWL*, I, 2, 670–73

[2] Boretius, *MGH, Leges*, I, 163.

[3] For estimates of the extent of clerical wealth in the Carolingian epoch see Waitz, VII, 186; Inama-Sternegg, *DWG*, I, 291, and his *Grossgrundherrschaft*, p. 32; Lamprecht, *DWL*, I, 703; Sommerlad, *Die wirtschaftliche Tätigkeit der Kirche in Deutschland*, I, 301–16, Werminghoff, *Verfassungsgesch. der deutschen Kirche im Mittelalter*, sec. 8 and bibliography given there.

[4] Boretius, I, 163, 277. The quotation is from Fisher, II, 64.

foundations was attempted.[1] The Council of Aachen divided
the clergy into three strata according to wealth. Those possessed of from 3,000 to 8,000 manors were classified as rich;
those possessed of from 1,000 to 2,000 manors were classified
as medium; those with only 200 to 300 manors were denominated poor. There were a few very wealthy bishoprics whose
riches soared into five figures, and it is obvious that there
must have been a considerable intermediate class between the
first and the second group, and between the second and the
third.

Even the terrible anarchy of the ninth century, owing to
civil wars within and the invasions of the Norsemen from

[1] Mansi, *Concilia*, Vol. XIV, cols. 232–33; ordo canon. 818, c. 122. Cf.
Kötzschke, *Deutsche Wirtschaftsgesch.*, p. 60; Abel-Simson, *Jahrb. Ludwigs d. Fr.*, I,
93; *Cart. de N-D. de Paris*, I, Introd., sec. 14. The genesis of these wonderful surveys
of church property made in the ninth century and later certainly goes back as far as
the time of Pepin the Short, who instituted such an inventory as a part of the partial
restoration of the church's property which Karl Martel had seized for military use
after 732. Susta, *K. Akad. d. Wiss. zu Wien.* CXXXVIII, No. 4, has a valuable
article upon the origin and historical importance of these polyptichs; he finds their
probable origin in the *cadastres* of Rome and Byzantium. There is an interesting
mention of such a survey ordered by Emperor Lothar I of the manors of Lobbes:
"Quarto decimo igitur regni sui [Lothar I] anno redditus villarum nostrarum de-
scribere jussit quod polipticum vocant" (*De gestis abbatum Laub.*; Migne,
CXXXVII, col. 557). Polyptichs of lay nobles for private lands may be inferred but
no example has been preserved (Dopsch, I, 299–300). The best-known example is
the famous *Polyptique* of the abbot Irminon, first edited by Guérard and later by
Longnon (cf. Viollet, I, 366–67, 374–75). Other French examples are Piot, *Cartulaire
de l'abbaye de St. Trond* (2 vols., 1870–75); Pirenne, *Polyptique et comptes de l'abbaye
de St. Trond* (1896); Hansay, *Etude sur la formation et l'organisation économique du
domain de l'abbaye de St. Trond* (1899). The archbishop of Cambrai made a survey
of the abbey of Lobbes in 868–69 (Parisot, p. 283, n. 1). The chief examples in Germany are the *Traditiones* of Corvey; Jaffe, *Monumenta Corb* (1886); Wigand,
Gesch. von Corvey (Höxter, 1819); the *Traditiones Wizentsurgenses* (Wolf, *Erwerts
und Verwaltung des Klostervermögens in der Trad. Wiz.* [Berlin diss., 1883]); and the
Register of the Lands of Prüm, which may have been modeled upon a similar survey
of Ferrières-Lamprecht, *DWL*, II, 84, n. 1. There is a bibliography of German
cartulaires by Oesterly, *Wegweiser durch die Literatur der Urkundensammlungen*
(2 vols.). On these polyptichs in general see *Polyptique d'Irminon* (ed. Longnon),
II, 363 f.; *Polyptique de Saint Remy de Reims* (ed. Guérard), pp. 93 f.; Coulanges,
L'alleu et le domain rural, chaps. i–iii; and Nitzsch, II, 255, 271, who makes an instructive comparison between the culture east and west of the Rhine. Cf. Melchior,
Beiträge zur Kulturgesch. der Rheinlande im 8. und 9. Jahrhundert (Darmstadt,
1904). For the importance of these inventories of the wealth of the church in the
treaties of partition in the ninth century see Meyer von Knonau, *Ueber Nithards
vier Buecher Geschichten. Der Bruderkrieg der Söhne Ludwigs d. Fr. und sein Geschichtschreiber* (Leipzig, 1886), pp. 41, 106, n. 235; Richter. *Annalen*, I, 419–22;
Mühlbacher, *Deutsche Gesch.*, I, 51.

without, was turned to advantage by the church. What I have elsewhere written may be quoted here:

It is undeniable that the distress of the monasteries was frequently deliberately misrepresented in order to prevail upon the crown to enlarge their possessions. Hardship and misery the monks doubtless often endured, but it was a misery wholly relative. They suffered less than ordinary people and were amply compensated for their discomfort. Bourgeois has pointedly said that "the clergy with aid of false charters in general got more than they lost."[1]

The complete separation of the eastern and western kingdoms, i.e., Germany and France, was reached in 870 at the partition of Meersen, and we may take this date as the point of departure for a study now of the proprietary interests of the German church, having cleared the ground for an understanding thereof in the preceding pages, in which the endeavor has been made to explain how the church and feudalism became so closely identified.

The German monasteries, like the Gallican, enjoyed to a high degree the liberality of popular piety. Not infrequently they were enormously endowed at the time of foundation. The nunnery of Gandersheim, the favorite foundation of the Liudolfinger, in the bishopric of Hildesheim was started in 856 with an indowment of 11,000 manors;[2] Hersfeld in the space of thirty years accumulated 2,000 large and small estates scattered in 195 different localities;[3] Tegernsee, in Bavaria, just prior to the secularization of Duke Arnulf (907–37) owned 11,866 manors; Benediktbeuren, which suffered the same fate, possessed 6,700.[4] We have no record of the landed wealth of twenty-five other Bavarian monasteries whose enrichment dates from the Carolingian period. But at the termination of that epoch Fulda possessed 15,000 manors; Lorsch, 2,000; St. Gall, 4,000.[5]

[1] See my article on "The Commerce of France in the Ninth Century," *Journal of Political Economy* (November, 1915), pp. 873–74; but cf. Parisot, *op. cit.*, p. 31, n. 5.

[2] Inama-Sternegg, I, 406.   [3] Hauck, III, 195.   [4] Sommerlad, II, 38 f.

[5] The Swiss monasteries were notoriously rich. The rapid growth of the landed wealth of the monasteries is well illustrated by St. Gall. The *Traditiones* show that before 700 it had not more than 50 *Hüfen;* in the eighth century the number rose to 110, in the ninth to 550; by the year 1000 it had about 4,000 manors. Other figures

Statistics of the extent of episcopal lands have not been preserved so fully as those pertaining to the monasteries. But there is ground to believe that the bishoprics were not as rich as the monasteries. The secular clergy did not appeal as interestingly to the imagination of men as the monks; perhaps the fact that church discipline was administered through the secular clergy, who also mingled more with the outside world, deprived the hierarchy of that bloom of romantic piety which the monks possessed in the eyes of the faithful.

The total number of recorded grants to bishoprics made by the Carolingian rulers in Germany between 814 and 911 amounts to 149, viz., 24 by Louis the Pious, 49 by Ludwig the German, 15 by Charles the Fat, 37 by Arnulf (significant for so short a reign), and 12 by Louis the Child, the last of the house.[1] Of the eight bishoprics in Bavaria, Augsburg and Salzburg were the richest, the former having possessed 1,507 manors in 812, the latter 1,600 manors in the time of Duke Tassilo, who was deposed by Charlemagne in 788.[2] Freising

---

are: Pruem (893), 2,000 *hubae*, 2,402 *Morgenland*; Mettlach, 305 *mansus*; St. Maximin, of Trier, 1284 *Morgenland*, 739 *hubae*; Werden an der Duhr (880), 22 "dominical" estates, 200 *hubae*, and 400 other pieces of land; Weissenberg, properties scattered in 300 localities. The abbey of Lobbes in the diocese of Liège, according to a survey made in 868–69, owned 174 villages and a castle (Vos, *Lobbes, son abbaye et son chapitre*, I, 418; Kurth, *Notger de Liège*, I, 52 and n. 1). For other data see Lamprecht, *DWL*, I, 2, 700; Waitz, VII, 186. Nitzsch (I, 280) well says "Die Zeit der ostfränkischen Karolinger ist die Zeit des Wachstums der kirchlichen Besitzungen. Der Güterbestand besonders der Klöster mehrte sich durch Schenkungen und Zinsübertragungen von Jahr zu Jahr." On the subject further see Waitz, V, 186; Sommerlad, Vol. II, chap. v; Lamprecht, *Deutsche Gesch.*, III, 59; Gerdes, I, 532–40; Roscher, *Ackerbau* (11th ed., 1885, of Stieda), sec. 105. Of course it is not possible to determine absolutely what area of land any monastery possessed, for the unit of measurement, the *mansus* or *Hufe*, was not a uniform area, like an American "section" (Guérard, *Polyptique d'Irminon*, p. 605; H. See, *Classes rurales*, pp. 35–46). The great difficulty in accurately evaluating medieval statistics is illustrated in the case of Guérard, who, careful scholar though he was, made grave errors in his computations with reference to the number of hectares possessed by St. Germain des Prés according to the *Polyptique d'Irminon*. Levasseur, *Acad. d. inscript. et belles-lettres* (July-Aug., Nov.-Dec., 1890), has shown that, according to the calculations of M. Hulin of Ghent, instead of owning 221,019 hectares, the abbey possessed not over 40,000, and probably not more than 37,000. The forest area, instead of representing nine-tenths, Guérard estimated, was not over two-fifths.

[1] Hauck, III, 57.

[2] Rietzler, *Gesch. Bayerns*, I, 327; Inama-Sternegg, *Grossgrundherrschaften*, p. 32.

was credited with estates scattered in 320 localities in the year 835.[1] The archbishopric of Trier, in Lorraine, received ten square miles of land from Charlemagne shortly before his death.[2]

Naturally the enormous landed wealth possessed by the church excited the envy and cupidity of the great lay feudality, especially the powerful "stem" dukes, whose policy, with the dissolution of the Frankish empire in the middle of the ninth century, was to bring the bishoprics and monasteries within their duchies under their sway.[3] With the increasing relaxation of royal authority in Germany after the death of Ludwig the German in 870, the dukes tended more and more to repudiate the Carolingian theory of ducal subordination to kingly authority which Charlemagne had so drastically exemplified in the humiliation of Tassilo of Bavaria, and to assert that they, quite as much as the king, ruled "by the grace of God."[4]

This rise of the great "stem" duchies in Germany in the ninth century is an important and interesting phenomenon. Violent as the measures often were which the dukes practiced toward the clergy in forcibly depriving them of their lands, nevertheless it would be an error to regard their course as merely one of wanton spoliation. Popular feeling in Germany in the ninth and tenth centuries was tribal, not national. The undeveloped and unapprehended popular self-consciousness functioned through the ancient German tribal organisms, of whose complex "personality," so to speak, the feudalized tribal dukes were the most visible and concrete embodiment.

The ducal policy toward the church within the separate duchies was, on a smaller scale, that of Charlemagne before them, namely, the attempt to affiliate or assimilate

---

[1] Sommerlad, II, 27.

[2] Inama-Sternegg, *DWG*, I, 284. Albert Lennarz, *Annalen des hist. Ver. f. den Niedersachsen* (1900), Nos. 69–70, has a very valuable study of the territorial power of the archbishops of Trier about 1220, based on the "Liber annalium jurium archiepiscopi et ecclesiae Trevirensis," which shows both the vast extent of the bishop's lands and the hugeness of his incomes.

[3] Waitz, VII, 45.   [4] Hauck, III, 8.

the administration and resources of the church with secular government. The feudality was not interested in questions of dogma and discipline, but was very much interested in the functioning of the church in government and society within its dukedoms. While the bishops were usually treated a little more leniently than were the abbots of the great monasteries, in general it was of slight moment to the duke whether the lands which they wished to appropriate were owned by a secular or a monastic corporation, so long as the upbuilding of a strong ducal government within their fiefs was to be furthered. As a consequence a double policy of forcible secularization of church lands and the enforcement of the right of advowson by the dukes upon the church within their duchies was general in Saxony, Bavaria, and Swabia.[1] In addition to these measures the dukes drastically thrust their "protection" upon terrorized bishops and abbots. Everywhere the dukes laid a heavy hand upon the church and attempted to impose their feudal authority on the bishops and abbots.[2]

The deposition of Charles the Fat and the accession of Arnulf of Bavaria to the German throne in 887 may be taken as the crucial point in this epoch. For that event, though it did not unseat the Carolingian dynasty, was nevertheless a political revolution. The German church, maddened by the tyranny and the exploitation of its lands by a baronage which had riotously pillaged it under the weak rule of Charles, in self-protection engineered the deposition of Charles the Fat and the enthronement of Arnulf.[3] We get some measure of the

[1] Lamprecht, *DWL*, I, 2, 710, n. 2; Sommerlad, II, 226 f.; Dahn, IX, 518 f.; Hauck, III, 279; Stutz, *Beneficialwesen*, chaps. xx–xxi; Dümmler, *Gesch. des ostfränk. Reiches*, I, 279; II, 107, 285, 290; III, 152.

[2] Waitz, IV, 156 f.; 163, n. 2; Hauck, III, 8–9.

[3] The dethronement of Charles the Fat was chiefly the work of Liutward, archchancellor of the empire, who had been driven from court in June, 887 (the deposition took place in November) by a combination of the great dukes against him, and fled to Arnulf, who already in 884–85 had unmasked his claims as a pretender. The contemporary chroniclers are singularly silent as to causes and motives, which, considering that all were clerics, of itself may be taken as evidence that clerical intrigue, whereof the writers are discreetly silent, was at the bottom of the movement. The conclusion expressed in the text is arrived at by a process of inverse reasoning from the evidence afforded by Arnulf's policy as king and the course of

church's apprehension in the action of the synod of Metz in the following May (888), which expressed fear of general secularization of the lands of the church within the several duchies and implored Arnulf for protection.[1]

By virtue of the circumstances under which he became king, Arnulf was pledged to a pro-clerical policy. In return for the moral support and material backing of the church, whose vassals aided his arms, whose resources repleted the diminished revenues of the Carolingian house, Arnulf showered exemptions and immunities upon the bishops and abbots.[2] At the diet of Tribur in 895 the clergy were given precedence over the feudality.[3] With Arnulf's reign began that intimate alliance between the German church and the German crown which reached a climax of partnership under Otto the Great and his successors.

When the last Carolingian king expired in 911 in the person of Louis the Child, Arnulf's son, the German church lost not a minute in establishing a new dynasty. The ener-

---

the church toward him. Waitz contends that technically it was not a deposition but an abdication by Charles in favor of his rival, and strives to minimize the revolutionary nature of the event (*DVG*, V, 26, n. 2), yet on p. 30 he admits the ascendancy of clerical influence in Arnulf's reign. It seems to me that, looking backward into the policy of the church in the time of Louis the Pious and Charles the Bald, and forward into its policy under Conrad I, especially as expressed at the synod of Hohenaltheim, we are justified in concluding that the church was the controlling factor in the change of ruler. For further literature see Gfrörer, *Gesch. der Ost- und Westfränkischen Karolinger*, II, 293; Dümmler, *Gesch. des Ostfränkischen Reiches*, III, 302 f.; Wenck, *Erhebung Arnulfs*, p. 22; Maurenbrecher, *Gesch. der deutschen Königswahlen*, pp. 25 f.; Harttung, *Die Thronfolge im deutschen Reiche, in Forschungen zur deutschen Gesch.*, XVIII (1874), 134 f.; Phillips, "Beiträge zur Geschichte Deutschlands vom Jahre 887 bis 956," *Abhandlungen der III Classe der Akad. der Wissenschaften* (Vienna), Band III, Abt. 2. For Charles the Bald's recognition of the church's claim to deposition of a king see Flach, *Origines de l'anc. France*, III, 249.

[1] Nitzsch, I, 286. He well says: "Ein neues System nationaler Königtümer war im Entstehen, dessen anerkannten politischen Mittelpunkt der ostfränkische Hof bildete" (p. 287).

[2] Dopsch, *Wirtschaftsgesch. der Karolingerzeit*, II, 328 f. Arnulf denominated himself "ecclesiae catholicae filius et defensor" after 892. There are no less than forty charters in favor of the German church in 888, and thirty-one for 889 (Boehmer-Mühlbacher, *Regesta*, Nos. 1721–92; see remarks of Wattenbach, *Deutschlands Geschichtsquellen*, I, 211–16).

[3] Nitzsch, I, 292. The clergy again expressed fear of spoliation (Regino, *Chron.*, 895).

getic Hatto, archbishop of Mainz, promptly put up Conrad
of Franconia as king, with the backing of the church,
perilous as the course was of choosing one duke in preference
to another.[1]

The formidable nature of this clerical control of the government may be better appreciated when one realizes who
this Conrad I was. The Conradiner were one of the most
powerful feudal families of Franconia. They possessed vast
and rich lands in old Austrasia, along the Rhine, in Hesse
and in Franconia. At the end of the ninth century the family
was represented by four brothers—Conrad, Rudolph, Eberhard, and Gebhard. They were allies of Hatto of Mainz, and
Conrad had married a daughter of the emperor Arnulf. In
892 when the latter deposed Poppo, count of the Sorben or
Thuringian March, he gave the position to Conrad; Rudolph
received the bishopric of Würzburg. This immense advancement of the Conradiner stirred the jealousy of the Babenberger, another ruling family in Franconia, whose seat was
Bamberg. Besides Poppo of Babenberg, just mentioned,
there was another brother named Henry who was killed in
886 during the siege of Paris by the Norsemen. The latter
left three sons—Adalbert, Adalhard, and Henry. The feud
between the clans broke out soon after Arnulf died (901).
A bloody engagement was fought near Bamberg in which two
of the Babenbergers and Eberhard of Franconia were killed.
The third and surviving member of the Babenberger, Adalbert, continued the feud until his capture and decapitation in
906. The ruin of the Babenberger, largely consummated by
the efforts of the Archbishop of Mainz, made the fortune of
the Conradiner, and also assured the church's ascendancy in
Germany during the reign of Conrad I.[2]

But the danger of the church from feudal spoliation was
not over.[3] Henry, duke of Saxony, deprived Mainz of the

---

[1] Nitzsch, I, 296; Hauck, III, 6-10; Lamprecht, *DG*, II, 115; Waitz, V, 61-63.

[2] See Schmitz, *Die Dynastie der Babenberg* (Munich, 1880).

[3] "Freche Menschen schonten selbst der Kirchen und des Kirchenguts nicht.
Wie gross die allgemeine Unsicherheit gewesen sein muss, geht aus der häufigen
Erwähnung von Räubereien und Plünderungen hervor" (Sass, *Die Kultur- und
Sittengesch. der sächsischen Kaiserzeit* [Berlin, 1892], p. 52, n. 10; Koeniger, *Burchard
von Worms*, p. 227).

lands situated within his duchy,[1] while in Swabia, Bishop
Salomon of Constance waged a long and bitter conflict with
Duke Burchard,[2] and when the latter died continued the duel
against his successor Erchanger.[3] In Bavaria the whole
episcopate, headed by Pilgrim of Salzburg, Tuto of Regensburg, and Drachalf of Freising, rallied around Conrad, when
in July, 916, he invaded Bavaria against Duke Arnulf.[4]

The conflict between the church and the crown, on the
one hand, and the feudal dukes, on the other, was furiously
waged. In every duchy the bone of contention was the lands
of the church which the dukes struggled to seize.[5] In Saxony
alone, where the duke was too rich and the church too poor
to tempt feudal covetousness, the local clergy was friendly
with the reigning feudal authority. At the synod of Hohenaltheim in 916, which was strongly imbued with pseudo-
Isidorean ideas of clerical supremacy, and over which a papal
legate presided, the bishops of all Germany, with the exception of those of Saxony who were restrained by Henry the
Fowler from attending, boldly proclaimed their alliance with
the crown.[6] Erchanger of Swabia and Arnulf of Bavaria, who
had revolted against Conrad, were condemned.[7] The synod
tripled the penalty of excommunication, declared the exemption of the clergy from secular courts, asserted the appellate
supremacy of the papal curia, and demanded the restoration
of the property of the church, which the dukes had seized
and secularized, and the enforcement of the tithe.

It was not the fault of the bishops that Conrad's reign
was not successful.[8] Erchanger, it is true, suffered death, but
Arnulf of Bavaria was too strong in his position, and the

[1] Widukind, I, 21; Waitz, *Jahrbuch Heinr. I*, 20; Dümmler III, 585.

[2] *Annal. Allem.*, 911, SS. I, 55; Zeller, *Bischof Salomo III. von Konstanz, Abt von St. Gallen* (Tübingen diss., 1910).

[3] *Annal. Atah.*, 913–16; *Contin. Reg.*, 914–17; Hauck, III, 12.

[4] Dipl. I, 27, No. 30; Nitzsch, I, 303.   [5] Waitz, V, 62 f.

[6] Hauck, III, 13; Nitzsch, I, 303. The Bavarian bishops braved the wrath of Duke Arnulf to come.

[7] Hauck, III, 21.

[8] Even Conrad I abused his popularity with the church in order to increase the family holdings (Hauck, III, 20; Waitz, VII, 134).

Saxon clergy could not be lured away from Henry. Suddenly
the whole program of the church collapsed with the death of
Conrad on December 28, 918. The failure of Conrad's policy
proved two things: first, that the feudal organization of Germany around the great dukes was too deeply rooted to be
overthrown; the day had gone by when the crown could
coerce the dukes as Charlemagne had broken Tassilo of
Bavaria;[1] second, that the time was not yet ripe for the
German church to exercise a dominant sway in political
affairs.[2]

Upon his deathbed Conrad seems to have had some
intimation of this truth, in which the clergy, however reluctantly, appear also to have acquiesced. We cannot explain
otherwise the dying King's action in sending the royal
insignia to Henry of Saxony, and that of the Archbishop of
Mainz in inviting Henry, at Fritzlar, in May, 919, to become
the defender of the church.[3] But Henry I was too wary to
mortgage his freedom of action to the clergy, and with
feigned humility, to the bitter chagrin of the bishops, refused
to be consecrated.[4]

With the accession of the Liudolfinger dukes of Saxony
to the German kingship in 919 Saxony was brought into the
orbit of general German history, and its simplicity, political, social, and economic, began to be modified by the
penetration of more highly developed feudal institutions into
the country. The change particularly affected the church
lands and the people thereon, owing to Otto I's close identi-

---

[1] Popular feeling was tribal, not national (Thietmar, *Chron.*, II, 28). When Con-
rad I executed Adalbert of Babenberg much popular indignation was aroused
(Regino, *anno* 906). The caliph Abd-er-Rahman told the envoys of Otto I that their
sovereign made a mistake in permitting the German dukes so much liberty (*Vita
Johan. Gorz*, chap. cxxxvi, *MGH*, SS. IV, 376). We see the same phenomenon in
feudal France, where the Duke of Gascony denominated his duchy as "regnum"
(Pfister, *Robert le Pieux*, p. 228), and the Duke of Aquitaine was styled "king"
(Bouquet, XII, 451). Thietmar, VI, 30, described the Duke of Burgundy as "miles
est regis in nomine, et dominus in re."

[2] Stein, *König Konrad*, 206 f.; Mühlbacher, *Reg. Kar.*, pp. 743–58; Dümmler,
Gesch. d. ostfränk. Reiches, III, 574–620.

[3] Waitz, *Jahrbuch Heinr.* I, 40.

[4] *Ibid.*, p. 75; Hauck, III, 20–21; Thietmar, *Chron.* I, chap. v.

fication of the German clergy with secular government. Lordship, homage, vassalage, the benefice system, became the order of the day among the Saxon bishops and abbots, as the result of the enfiefing of the enormous grants of land made to the bishops by the Saxon kings. Even church prebends were militarized.[1]

Henry I's feudal policy was to give simultaneous and due expression both to the general and the particularistic interests in Germany. The dukes were permitted to exercise their authority with almost sovereign independence within their duchies, administering justice, coining their own money, and in the case of the Bavarian duke even the right of nomination to bishoprics was abandoned to him.[2] Almost as much latitude was given to Burchard of Swabia and Gilbert of Lorraine.[3] Henry I's policy, in a word, was one of regulation, not suppression of feudalism. But he was no less a king for that. By inner inclination as well as by the compulsion of external events the Liudolfinger were monarchical in sentiment and aspiration.

Only in the last years of his reign did Henry I relax his suspicion of the church. He was not liberal in grants to it.[4] After 933, when his reforms were well established and his power secure, and perhaps not a little influenced by the piety of his wife Matilda,[5] his ecclesiastical policy became more af-

[1] Waitz, VI, 105–7; Guilhiermoz, pp. 126, 182, 243, 264.
"Episcopus eum ad militem suscipiens xxx aratra in praedicto pago in beneficium dedit ea ratione ut in expeditionem iv scuta transmitteret" (Vita Meinwerki, chap. lxx). Henry II permitted Poppo of Trier to do likewise (Thietmar, VI, 51; Koeniger, Burchard von Worms, p. 49). The Franconian kings continued the policy, even Henry III, e.g., ". . . . complacuit quoque ei ut pro eodem beneficio singulis annis sicut et alii milites serviret abbati et in expeditionibus cum sex scutis militaret" (Dronke, Codex dip. Fuld. No. 749 [1048]). The same practice obtained in England and France (Guilhiermoz, p. 124 n.).

[2] Thietmar, I, 10; Rietzler, I, 329; Lamprecht, DG, II, 127; Hauck, III, 16–19; Waitz, Jahrb., p. 52.

[3] Lamprecht, op. cit., II, 127.

[4] Sommerlad, II, 232 f.; Nitzsch, I, 330–32.

[5] The portrait of Matilda in the Vita Mahthildis reginae, SS. X, 573 f., is largely imitated from Fortunatus' Life of S. Radegonde. Yet there are traces of independent treatment, e.g., chap. xvi, where it is interestingly said that the queen in spite of her life in a cloister continued to wear royal purple garments. German cloister life

fable; he even began to abridge the control of the great dukes over the church within their fiefs.[1] But as a whole church politics were at a standstill during Henry I's reign. Yet beyond any doubt Henry I in the last years of his life saw clearly that what had been a policy of wisdom at first could not be wisely adhered to permanently.[2] In feudal Germany the permanent estrangement of church and state was as impolitic as it was impracticable.

This Otto I perceived and symbolically enunciated both his ecclesiastical and feudal (or rather anti-feudal) program in the solemn coronation in Aachen cathedral.[3] Otto cared little for the religious significance of the episcopate, but he was in earnest about its political importance.[4] It was clear in his mind that the German church would have to comply with his will. The German church was on the horns of a dilemma,

---

may have been pious, but it was not addicted to exaggerated asceticism; cf. the comments of Ebert, *op. cit.*, II, 314. On this earliest movement of German pietism see Sybel, *Hist. Zeitschrift*, XLV, 25; Lamprecht, "Das deutsche Geistesleben unter den Ottonen," *Zeitschrift fur Geschichtswissenschaft*, VIII, Part I, 1; Heineken, *Die Anfänge der sächsischen Frauenkloster* (Göttingen diss., 1909); Harnack, *History of Dogma*, VI, 3 n.; Ludwig, Zoepf, *Das Heiligen-Leben im 10. Jahrhundert* (Berlin, 1908); and Walther's article on Matilda, first abbess of Quedlinburg, in *Ztschft. d. Harzvereins f. Gesch..*, XXVII, Heft 2 (1904). She was a daughter of Otto I by his English wife, Edgith.

[1] Lamprecht, *DG*, II, 132–33; Nitzsch, I, 324–25.

[2] Hauck, III, 68; Nitzsch, I, 329–32: "Heinrich I erkannte am Ende seiner Regierung die Bedeutung an, welche die kirchliche Organisation noch immer für das deutsche Leben hatte."

[3] Bryce's exposition of the significance of this ceremony is classic. See *Holy Roman Empire* (2d ed.), chap. viii. The church and the imperialistic ideal of Otto were more easily reconciled than the *imperium* and the ideas of feudal sovereignty of the stem-dukes. The issue between crown sovereignty and feudal state-rights was irreconcilable, as the great struggle of Frederick Barbarossa and Henry the Lion showed in the twelfth century. The absence of the principle of heredity in church offices afforded the crown a powerful means of control of the church which was not applicable to the duchies. Otto finally brought the dukes to acknowledge his authority, but they were always actuated by local and tribal traditions from which the clergy were much more free.

[4] Cf. Hauck, III, 1–19, and notes. In the struggle between two rival candidates at Liège, Otto compelled the Archbishop of Cologne to consecrate the candidate whom he preferred. Bishop Hugo of Verdun was driven from his see for opposing the king, and Benim put in his stead. Political "availability" was the determining factor in the choice of a German bishop.

and Otto perceived it—either to continue to be buffeted and abused by the violence of the dukes and to suffer continual spoliation of its lands,[1] or to purchase peace and protection from the Saxon house at the price of surrendering its independence and renouncing those vague ideas of supremacy which it had cherished since the ninth century. Save for a few irreconcilables like Frederick of Mainz,[2] the German bishops as a whole espoused the king and threw their moral influence and their material resources into the scale with the crown against the feudal dukes. The bishops and abbots not only put at Otto's service their authority and their administrative experience, but their wealth and their church vassals also.

This alliance between the German crown and the German church broke the power of the great German dukes. Otto I disposed of church offices more with an eye to the political bearing of the appointment than with any sentiment for its religious character. He deposed the recalcitrant Archbishop of Mainz and gave the see to his natural brother William; he made his brother Bruno at one and the same time archbishop of Cologne and duke of Lorraine; he made his cousin

[1] Yet, strong as Otto I was, the enormous wealth of the German church still tempted some of the great dukes in his reign to brave the might of the king. Henry of Bavaria blinded and banished the Bishop of Salzburg and castrated the patriarch of Aquileia and divided the episcopal estates among his vassals (Jaffé, III, 358; Waitz, VII, 204). Liudolf of Swabia seized the lands of the Bishop of Augsburg (*Vita Oudal.*, chap. xxx; *MGH*, SS. IV, 399). The Lorrainer dukes Gilbert and Conrad often plundered the estates of the Archbishop of Trier. The frequency with which such acts are mentioned implies the wide prevalence of the practice. The bishops of Bremen, Metz, Liège, Hildesheim, Münster, Paderborn, and Cologne complain time and time again of the greed of their feudal neighbors for their lands (Waitz, VII, 206, and notes; cf. VI, 79 f.). The bishops were much more likely to be involved in this strife with the feudality than the abbots, chiefly because of their greater political ambition and intriguing, and practiced the same violence of which they accused their enemies. They maintained armed bands of bravos for defense or offense as the case might be. Many were the bishops who *praedia multa ecclesiastica pro auxilio distribuit decennium* (quoted in Waitz, VII, 206, n. 1). The anathemas of the church were ineffectual in a land where the high clergy were grossly guilty of the very practices which they reprobated (for examples of anathemas see *Forsch. z. deutsch. Gesch.*, XIII, 497; Lesne, pp. 413–23). The sources abound; see citations in Gerdes, I, 536 nn.

[2] For the opposition of the German clergy to Otto I's measures, see Hauck, III, 33–34.

Henry archbishop of Trier.[1] The German church, so far as the king was concerned, was an instrument of government. There are no examples of German synods in Saxon and Franconian times discussing the general welfare of the church.[2] There are no Saxon capitularies like those emanating from Charlemagne, Louis the Pious, or even Charles the Bald.[3]

Otto I introduced no new principle when he so elevated the church to such a high place in his government, but he enormously magnified the practice of his predecessors. Theoretically the canonical right of episcopal election still continued. But irregularities of the nature of royal designation were so frequent that the rule was far more honored in the breach than in the observance.[4] The chief principle which prevailed with the king was the politico-economic importance of the office to be filled, and the "availability" of the candidate. Expediency was superior to canonicity. The interests of the crown were the decisive factor. Thietmar of Merseburg, the chief historian of the Saxon epoch, depicts the bishops as royal and loyal officials.[5] The feudal ideal was complete. Otto was head of state and (secular) head of the church too. Dogma and discipline were left to the church, but not government, even of itself.

The life of Udalrich, bishop of Augsburg in the time of Henry I and his son Otto the Great, is a typical example of the activities of a German bishop in the depth of the feudal age. Udalrich was descended from an illustrious Allemanic family, his father having been a count of Dillingen, his mother a daughter of Burkhard, the margrave of Raetia. He

---

[1] Hauck, III, 31; Lamprecht, *op. cit.*, II, 153.

[2] Hauck, III, 67; Lamprecht, *op. cit.*, II, 155–56.

[3] Hauck, III, 67 and 230; cf. Fisher, Vol. I, chap. iv.

[4] For a list of episcopal appointments by the German crown see Hinschius, *Kirchenrecht*, II, 530, n. 9.

[5] *Chron.*, I, 15; Lambert of Hersefeld, *Annales* (1071, ed. Holder-Egger), pp. 132–33, has a famous tirade against these "political" churchmen of the Franconian period. The Saxon episcopate has been studied in Hinschius, II, 530–37; Hauck, III, 395–403; Gerdes, I, 566–72; Koeniger, Part II, chap. ii; H. Gerdes, *Die Bischofswahlen in Deutschland unter Otto dem Grossen in den Jahren 953–73* (Göttingen, 1878).

was educated at the monastery of St. Gall, but preferred the life of a secular cleric to that of the cowl, and entered the service of Adalberon, bishop of Augsburg, by whom he was made supervisor of the episcopal revenues as well as grand butler of the episcopal court (*praecoquus*). In 924, through the influence of Burkhard, duke of Swabia, and favored by King Henry, Udalric was made bishop of Augsburg.

Both the city and the see had suffered heavily from the inroads of the Magyars, and Udalric at once set to work to repair and to strengthen the town walls. When he visited the churches in his diocese he traveled in an oxcart, accompanied by a retinue of clerks and vassals. He was himself abstemious, but loved to set a liberal table and was generous in charity. He supported Otto I during the revolt of Liudolph, the king's own rebellious son whom he had unwisely made duke of Swabia, and it was his military contingents, together with those of the bishop of Chur, which so overawed Liudolf in 954 as to prevent a battle on the Iller. In the next year (955) Udalric was the heart and soul of the brave resistance of Augsburg, when the Magyars stormed up the Danube Valley, and won great renown for his prowess in the battle of the Lechfeld. Udalric died in 973 and was succeeded by Henry, a protégé and relative, like himself, of the powerful Duke of Swabia. Less fortunate than his predecessor, Bishop Henry perished in the disastrous battle in Calabria in 982, when Otto II vainly endeavored to extend the German power over the Byzantine provinces of Southern Italy.[1]

Since the defeudalization of the church in Europe, owing to the influence of the French Revolution and especially in Germany through the sweeping changes wrought by Napoleon, it requires an effort of the historical imagination and a large and intimate knowledge of the nature and operation of the feudal régime in the Middle Ages in order to under-

[1] The *Vitae* of the German bishops form a valuable source of culture history, to which may be added the fifth book of Rather of Verona's *Praeloquia*, which is a vivid tableau of the manners and customs of the feudalized high ecclesiastical society of the tenth century, so rich, indeed, in anecdote and color that one suspects it to be a satire, and hence exaggerated. Cf. also Rather's *Qualitatis conjectura cujusdam* (this *quidam* is Rather himself), esp. sec. 3.

stand how and why the church could become so identified
with secular government, and how Otto I was able to make
so large use of it.

The key to the matter is to be found in the proprietary
nature of the medieval church, i.e., the temporal power of
bishops and abbots. For at the same time these ecclesiastics
were churchmen and feudal chieftains. They pertained both
to the spiritual and to the feudal hierarchy. The problem
was to reconcile the dual functions and obligations of bishops
and abbots, and to give simultaneous and due expression to
both their spiritual and their temporal duties. In practice it
was impossible "to split even." Instead of the fief being regarded as the accessory of the bishopric or abbey, the
bishopric or abbey became the accessory of the fief. The state
applied to church lands exactly the same rules and regulations which it enforced in the case of lay lands. Clerical election, when it obtained at all, was a mere formality; in many
cases ecclesiastical election wholly disappeared.[1]

The king lived, in no inconsiderable degree, upon the
revenues of the church[2] and fought his wars in large part with
church vassals. To limit the power of the crown over church
lands was both to diminish the royal authority and to sequester important and necessary revenues. Otto I's theory
of control of the German church was that of Charlemagne
before him. The difference was one of degree only. The
crown's ecclesiastical authority conveyed in the term *regale*,
as said before, was not so reduced as its secular authority.
Considerable remnants of former Carolingian prerogative
still survived in the great duchies, being least in Bavaria,[3] and
thus gave the crown a *point d'appui* in the very heart of the
duchies. This authority was more complete in the case of the
monasteries than in the case of the bishoprics.

Monasteries, from the inception of the movement, were
private foundations, and of all founders of monasteries the

[1] See Erich Laehns, *Die Bischofswahlen in Deutschland von 936–1056* (Greifswald, 1909).

[2] "Alles Reichskirchengut stand im Eigentum des Reiches" (Richter, *Annalen*,
III, Part II, 768).

[3] Giesebrecht, *Kaiserzeit*, I, 227. For details see Waitz, VII, 138 f.

Merovingian kings and the Austrasian mayors had been the greatest. These the Carolingian kings inherited and increased, so that an imposing array of cloisters was within the control of the Frankish crown. Free election disappeared in the abbeys under Charlemagne, who ecclesiastically supervised them through the bishops[1] and assimilated the administration of the monastery lands to that of the fisc in virtue of the "protection" vouchsafed by the crown to them;[2] *Krongut*, *Hausgut* and *Klostergut* were all one in the Carolingian system.[3]

In consequence, despite the fact that during the ninth century the feudality usurped control of many foundations and plundered the crown of its revenues thereby,[4] nevertheless the Saxon house was possessed of many monasteries throughout Germany, although Otto I complained of the spoliation of them under his predecessors and of their reduced number.[5]

With these "royal" abbeys must also be included the new bishoprics like Magdeburg, Brandenburg, Zeitz, Meissen, etc., established during the Saxon epoch in the colonial lands east of the Elbe and Saale rivers, as the Wendish territory was conquered and settled by the German people.[6] By the end of the Saxon period the complete sway of the royal prerogative over all bishoprics and abbeys, save a few of the latter which still remained in private hands by virtue of ancient tradition, was accomplished.

This rapid extension of crown authority over the German church was materially facilitated by the peculiarly concrete conceptions of law which prevailed. It took the medieval, and especially the Teutonic, mind a long time to grasp the highly complex notion of a corporation. The modern legal conception of a juridical personality or of a corporation did

[1] Waitz, III, 433.   [2] *Ibid.*, pp. 155, 158–60.

[3] *Ibid.*, p. 140; IV, 154–60. For the wealth of the monasteries under Otto I see Sommerlad, II, 39.

[4] Waitz, IV, 156, 160, n. 2.

[5] *Ibid.*, VII, 209, n. 4; Koeniger, 101, n. 3.

[6] Waitz, IV, 157, 168, n. 4

not exist. Feudalism was an extremely personal régime. Law had to possess concrete, physical embodiment. Abstract legal conceptions did not prevail and would not have been understood. Accordingly it was universally held that every bishopric and every monastery had to have a physical overlord.[1] In the case of small churches the patron was the local landed proprietor who had founded it, or whose father had founded it, and who controlled it. In the case of monasteries the overlord was the founder. But most of the great German monasteries had been founded by royal initiative and royal endowment, and the same was true, as has been said, of the new bishoprics in the conquered lands. As the king lived in considerable part upon the resources derived from the church lands, especially the abbey lands, to limit the exercise of royal authority over these lands, or to permit them to be enfiefed without royal consent, would not only have diminished the political power of the crown, but also have deprived him of important revenues.[2]

When German history passes from the Carolingians to the Saxons, we find Otto I (936–73) too heavily involved with the church to resist its demands. His father, Henry I, had dangerously estranged the German clergy. It was Otto's policy to mollify them. At the inception of his reign the chief peril to the crown lay in the great power of the feudal dukes. The bishops and abbots, threatened by their usurpations, inclined toward the crown, while the King, for his part, found one of the strongest features of his anti-feudal policy in elevating the clergy as a counterpoise to the high feudality. The lavish generosity of the Saxon kings toward the German church far surpassed that of the Carolingians. Of the 435

[1] "Der Begriff der Kirche als einer juristischen Person war den Germanen fremd. Die kirchlichen Gebäude gehörten dem Herrn des Bodens, auf dem sie standen und wurden von diesem den Geistlichen zur Benutzung eingeräumt" (Richter, *Annalen*, III, Part II, 768; cf. Ficker, 12 [64]; Hinschius, II, 622; Gierke, *Deutsche Genossenschaft*; and Pollock and Maitland, *History of English Law*, I, 469–95).

[2] Henry II, as was his way, sensibly and pithily expressed the crown's position in this matter of secular control of church property: "Oportet ut in aecclesiis multae sint facultates .... quia cui plus committitur, plus ab eo exigitur. Multa enim debet (Fulda) dare servitia et Romanae et regali curiae propter quod scriptum est: Reddite quae sunt Caesaris Caesari et quae sunt Dei Deo." The way in which Abelard made the point is classic (see Bouquet, XIV, 290).

charters which have been preserved of the reign of Otto the Great, 122 are donations to the church.[1] Henry I had made but 5 donations to the clergy during his whole reign. It has been well said that

Otto I perceived that under his father the church of Germany was fast becoming the prey of the nobility. The Bavarian duke had obtained from the Fowler the right to nominate to the Bavarian sees. If the example spread, the church in Germany would split into a number of tribal organizations which would intensify national differences, and possibly destroy the free circulation of talent through the kingdom. Otto was not choosing between a spiritual church on the one hand and a political church on the other. The alternative was between a church dominated and bullied by dukes and counts, and a church controlled and utilized for the service of the nation by the king.[2]

In this policy Otto I had the precedent of Charlemagne, who made large use of the church as an instrument of government. But the Saxon rulers went farther:

These four pious emperors pile donation upon donation. Whereas we have 42 charters of donation proceeding from Louis the German and 37 from Arnulf, we have 122 from Otto the Great. Again, the grants of market rights and toll rights made during this one reign to ecclesiastical foundations exceeded all the grants taken together made by Otto's predecessors. The munificence of the Saxon emperors builds up the territories of the great Rhenish sees, creates the archiepiscopal see of Magdeburg, invests the bishop of Würzburg with ducal powers, creates the new see of Bamberg, endows and founds numerous Saxon abbeys and nunneries, and heaps political and judicial powers upon ecclesiastical foundations.[3]

Otto I was the first medieval ruler who attempted clearly and thoroughly to make the church an ally of the government. The problem and the policy have been admirably formulated by Sohm:

The royal power, upon which, nevertheless, the imperial authority rested, fell far short of the position formerly assumed by the Frankish kings. The feudal system had arisen in the meanwhile, and had changed the constitution of the state. The count was no longer, as before, the official organ of the royal will, but a vassal, whose county belonged to him as a fief

[1] Hauck, III, 58, n. 5.

[2] Fisher, *Mediaeval Empire*, II, 78–79; cf. Waitz, VII, 184.

[3] Fisher, II, 65. For detailed information on the Ottonian church policy see Hauck, III, 58 f.; Eggers, *Der königliche Grundbesitz im X. und XI. Jahrhundert* (Weimar, 1909).

in his own right. Moreover, above the count, the great duchies had arisen, the Swabian, the Bavarian, the Frankish, the Lotharingian, and the Saxon, which possessed a power altogether equal to that of the king. The royal power was in danger of being turned from a real supremacy into a mere feudal overlordship. Otho the Great saved it from this danger by two measures. First he attached the duchies as much as possible to his own family, and thus turned the resources of the duchy into resources of the kingdom. This measure was only partially successful since his own brother, the Duke of Bavaria, and his own son, the Duke of Swabia, were far more inclined to rebel against the royal powers than to be obedient to it.

The decisive measure which Otho the Great employed was to build the new kingdom on the power of the church. Under him it became an express principle of the royal policy to raise the power of the church, especially of the bishops, by enriching them with gifts, bestowing on them public privileges, and even making them counts. And wherefore? In order that the power of the spiritual princes might counterbalance that of the arrogant temporal princes. The king was surer of the spiritual lords than he was of the temporal. The king himself nominated the bishop and abbot of the imperial monasteries by means of the investiture with ring and crosier. He was more free to nominate the bishop and abbot than the count and duke, because spiritual offices were not hereditary, neither could be hereditary. The spiritual dignities in every case fell again into the king's hands at his disposal, and could always be filled by the persons most agreeable to the king.

Even property belonging to the spiritual foundations passed as in some measure the property of the empire. What the spiritual foundation gained was not therefore lost to the empire. On the contrary, it became rather the more certain possession of the empire, by being withdrawn from the hands of the great temporal vassals. The king received subsidies, under the name of gifts, from the church lands, and from church lands the greater part of his troops was supplied in case of war. So over church lands the king set up the bishop or abbot most agreeable to him. Thus the German kingdom and the German empire of the Middle Ages became possible. Its supremacy found a material substratum in the power of the church; and the royal investiture represented the means by which the church was bound to the king.[1]

Otto I, even more than Charlemagne, made the church a political and economic ingredient of the government.[2] He found the German church in a condition of terror and material collapse owing to the violence of the feudality; the

[1] *Outlines of Church History* (Eng. trans.; London, 1895), pp. 97-99. Cf. Paul Merkert, *Kirche und Staat im Zeitalter der Ottonen* (Breslau diss., 1905); Sommerlad, II, 238 f.; Hauck, III, 58 f.

[2] Willigis of Mainz broke two coalitions of the dukes in the time of Otto III and Henry II (Lamprecht, *Deutsche Gesch.* 170, II).

office of advocate of church property converted into a huge device by the baronage for the purpose of levying blackmail upon the monasteries; church endowments almost everywhere except in Saxony, where the church was too poor and his own ducal power too strong to permit practices which elsewhere obtained, divided among families and private persons.[1] To all this spoliation and local "secularization"—to give the practice a euphemistic term—Otto I put an end. In 951 all "royal" abbeys were declared exempt from all and any secular authority save that of the crown, and forbidden to enfief their lands without the consent of the king.[2]

From Otto the Great's time onward until the spoliations of the war of investiture the bishoprics and so-called royal abbeys were a rich source of revenue to the kings. Under Conrad II their lands were assimilated with the fisc and administered as it was.[3] The right to appoint bishops and abbots to church vacancies was a lucrative means of income for the crown. In Italy this prerogative was exercised even more extensively than in Germany, and was more zealously guarded because the Italian sees were richer.[4]

[1] The tendency toward aggrandizement of the temporal power of the clergy, even down to simple priests, appears in *Vita Oudalrici*, chap. vii: "Horum autem, qui in suo episcopatu proprietates habebant, quisquis religiosorum propter amorem Christi ecclesiam componere cupiebat, et cum concessa licentia ab eodem sancto episcopo eam aedificaverat consecrationemque habili tempore ab eo fieri flagitavit, aptissima uniuscujusque petitioni praebuit assensum, si confestim ille consecratae ecclesiae legitimam dotem in terris et mancipiis in manum ejus celsitudinis dare non differet . . . . ea etiam ratione, ut aliis circumjacentibus ecclesiis jura earum in nullis rebus propter illam novam minuerentur."

[2] Gebhardt, *Handbuch der deutschen Gesch.* (1st ed.), I, 258; Nitzsch, I, 348–49; Waitz, VII, 93, n. 3; p. 209, n. 2; Feierabend, p. 1. At the end of the rule of the Saxon house there were 85 royal abbeys in Germany (Matthäi, pp. 96–101; Koeniger, p. 105, n. 1). For discussion of the condition described in the text see Waitz, VII, 209–11; Sommerlad, II, 239 f.; Hauck, III, 30 f.; Lamprecht, II, 154 f.; Nitzsch, I, 340 f.; Dümmler, *Otto der Gr.*, pp. 514 f.

[3] On the distinction of the property of the royal abbeys for monastery and for crown purposes see Waitz, VII, 189–91; VIII, 244; Bresslau, *Konrad II*, II, 364 f.

[4] Bresslau, *ibid.*, pp. 365–67. The Italian cities began to prosper long before the Crusades from the increase of trade through the Alpine passes. "Wenn sich damals in Deutschland selbst in den rheinischen Bischofssitzen noch immer Bauernhof an Bauernhof reihte, so verfügte dieser lombardische Prälat bereits über die Mittel einer wirklich grosstätischen Bevölkerung und einen Komplex fester Adelshäuser in den Ringmauern seiner Hauptstadt" (Nitzsch, II, 31).

The economic advantage derived by the crown from this close articulation between state and church was no less important than the political. Ecclesiastical economy was much ahead of feudal, and even the royal domains, in spite of the precedent of Charlemagne's capitulary *de villis*, could not rival those of the church in intelligent and efficient administration, especially in the Rhinelands.[1]

Until the accession of Otto I in 936 no attempt had been made by the German crown to mobilize the resources of the church in the interests of the government, nor had the kings been distinguished for special generosity to the church. Conrad I, that *Schützling* of the church, gave proof of his piety by a gift of fifteen estates to the church, located in Franconia, Bavaria, and Swabia. The less devout Henry I had made only five donations, chiefly of lands in Saxony. But Otto I, perceiving that the church possessed the most efficient economic régime of the time, gave the church a large share in the administration of the crown lands, and definitely mobilized the church's resources for the benefit of the state.[2] The Ottonian period was the golden age of the "royal" monasteries, whose abbots everywhere, in imitation of the ancient Frankish practice, were used as mayors of the fisc (*villici*).[3]

An examination of Otto I's land policy is evidence of this. The lavish favor of this great Saxon king toward the church far exceeded that of his Carolingian predecessors. Of the 435 charters which have been preserved pertaining to the reign of Otto I, 122 are records of donations of land to the church— almost three times as many as all the gifts combined made

---

[1] *Vita Johan. Gorz.*, chap. lxxxix, SS. IV, 362. On the richness of the Saxon church, Waitz, VII, 183–84; Nitzsch, I, 374–79, and a notable description of the prosperity of Worms in the episcopate of Burchard II (1000–1025), at pp. 388–89.

[2] "Er schützte die Kirche gegen die Habgier der Laien, er schlug alle Säkularisationsfurcht nieder; aber er machte die kirchlichen Erträge zum Hauptposten seines Haushalts, er bildete seine Heere in erster Linie aus den Vassallenschaften der Kirche" (Nitzsch, I, 357–58.)

[3] Inama-Sternegg, II, 129; *Vita Oudalrici*, chap. iii, *MGH*, SS. IV, 389; Lamprecht, *DWL*, I, Part I, 826. For proof of the golden age of the royal abbeys see Jaffé V, 471—a document of Otto II; for use of abbots as *villici*, Waitz, VII, 194, n. 2; p. 198, nn. 1–2; Lambert of Hersfeld, *Annales* (anno 1063). Even Lothar, in spite of his leniency toward the church, so used them (Waitz, VII, 198, n. 3).

to the church by the Carolingian kings from Louis the Pious
to Ludwig the Child. In other words, Otto I in the space of
thirty-seven years gave as much to the church as his predecessors had done in ninety-seven years. Of these grants, 42
were made to Otto's favorite see of Magdeburg, which he
created; 13 to Hamburg-Bremen; the rest are scattered
among various bishoprics and monasteries. In a much briefer
reign Otto II disposed of 50 large and 21 small estates, many
of them to the bishopric of Prague.[1]

Under Otto I the military service of the German bishops,
whose prowess had been severely tested in the strife with the
great dukes and the Hungarians during the reigns of Arnulf
and his son,[2] was systematized, and the long line of fighting
bishops in the Saxon epoch shows how manfully they responded to the call. Late in Otto I's reign the monasteries
were similarly mobilized, though not quite so fully. For example, Fulda was exempt from military service until 972.
The church had known fighting bishops and fighting abbots
in former times, as witness the case of Leodegar of Autun in
Merovingian times, and that of Abbot Fulrad under Charlemagne. But in the tenth century the art of war became an
important episcopal accomplishment.[3] Three-quarters of the
contingents enumerated in the muster-roll of 981 (1,482 out
of a total of 1,990) were drawn from church lands. The
church furnished 74 per cent of the forces for that Italian

[1] "Immer mehr wachsenden Besitzungen der Bischöfe" (Koeniger, p. 74).
Cf., *Libell. I in honor. Willig.*, chap. iii. SS. XV, 745, l. 25; Hauck, III, 58; Eggers,
Der konigl. Grundbesitz im 10. und 11. Jahr. (Weimar, 1909), pp. 58 f.

[2] Between the years 886 and 908 ten German bishops fell in battle. For this
"Kriegshandwerk" of the bishops see Hauck, II, 709; Sommerlad, II, 249–50;
Wattenbach, *Deutschlands Geschichtsquellen* (5th ed.), II, 27. The abbey of Fulda
alone possessed fiefs bound to furnish 6,000 fighting men in the eleventh century.
For statistics of episcopal military service in the time of Otto I see Lamprecht,
DWL, I, 2, 1295.

[3] Gerard, *Viti Udalrici Aug.*, chap. iii: "Concessum est S Udalrico episcopo
ut Adelbero in ejus via itinera hostilia cum militia episcopali in voluntatem imperatoris perageret"; Thancmar, *Vita Bernwardi*, chap. xxviii: "Imperator [Otto
III] et pontifex jubent universos theodiscos episcopos ad illorum praesentiam
destinare cum omni suo vassalatico ita instructos ut ad bellum quocumque imperator praecipiat possent procedere." Cf. Thietmar, *Chronicon*, IV, 20; V, 23.

campaign of Otto II.[1] The German kings gave lands to the church in order to increase its military effectiveness, and the grants were made subject to this stipulation. This is the reason why the kings so resolutely held fast to the right of ecclesiastical appointments, for it was the surest way of controlling the church's resources, both of men and of money. Prior to the middle of the eleventh century, when the

[1] Hauck, *Fulda and Hersfeld*, p. 8. Service *à cheval* was especially imposed upon church vassals (Waitz, V, 325–27; Guilhiermoz, p. 174, n. 10; pp. 182, 187).

An analysis of the roster, in Jaffé, V, 471–72, follows:

BISHOPRICS

Mainz, Cologne, Strasburg, Augsburg, each 100	400
Trier, Salzburg, Regensburg, each 70	210
Verdun, Liège, Würzburg, each 60	180
Seben [Waitz, VIII, 134, erroneously gives 20]	50
Constance, Chur, Worms, Freising, each 40	160
Speyer, Eichstädt, Toul, each 20	60
Cambrai	12

ABBEYS

Fulda, Reichenau, each 60	120
Lorsch, Weissenburg, each 50	100
Prüm, Hersfeld, Ellwangen, each 40	120
Kempten	30
St. Gall, Murbach, each 20	40
Total	1,482
All lay vassals	508
Grand total	1,990

See the detailed analysis of this roster in Sommerlad, II, 250, and literature there given, to which may be added Lehmann, *Forschungen*, IX, 437, and Richter, III, 2, pp. 760–61, who, however, is wrong in his figures. On the infeudation practiced by bishops and abbots see Waitz, VI, 105–7. Examples may be seen in *Vita Meinwerki*, chap. lxx, and Dronke, *Codex diplom. Fuld.*, No. 749. In estimating the number of those summoned it must be remembered that such vassals were *vollehen*, i.e., they held *fiefs du haubert*, which implied the service of at least 12 vassals by each, i.e., 1,990 must be multiplied by at least 12, which would give an army of *at least* 6,096 lay and 17,784 church vassals. This fact does not directly appear, but constructively may be argued from two passages in the *Chronicle of Lorsch*, of the years 1066 and 1107, SS. XXI, 415, 434–35, and other evidence. Cf. Guilhiermoz, pp. 174 and 182. The Italian expeditions of the German sovereigns increased the number and importance of the contingents of the church. For these distant campaigns the emperors needed more reliable troops than the lay vassals usually furnished, and troops more contractually liable than the *Heerban*, which survived until the end of the eleventh century in Saxony, and the intimate relation between the crown and the church made this usage easy and safe. For a case of an abbot complaining of the burden of military service see that of Meginward of Reichenau in Lambert of Hersfeld, *Annales* (ed. Holder-Egger), p. 127 (*anno* 1071). When Henry III went to Italy in 1046 he was accompanied by 3 archbishops, 10 bishops, and 2 royal abbots, with their vassals. The alleged charter of Otto III exempting abbots from military service except expeditions to Rome and the *Constitutio*

Gregorian reform began its attack upon the German monarchy, few contested the right of the crown so to do.[1]

The enormous growth of the church's landed proprietorship, however, and the military use made of it by the German kings were not the only ways in which bishops and abbots reflected the influences of feudalism, mirroring in their historical conditions the dominant political and social ideas of a feudal age. Otto I distributed new immunities, especially to the bishops, with a lavish hand,[2] and confirmed many which had formerly been conferred. After 973 the privilege of immunity was so generally assumed that mention of it was frequently omitted in the charters.[3] Otto III, in a blanket decree, conferred the right of full justice upon all bishops within their domains.[4] The sole judicial officer henceforth within ecclesiastical territories was the *Vogt*, to whom the king yielded his ban.[5] Thus the power of the counts was diminished.[6] The prerogatives of the count and his proprietorship were largely combined in the hands of the hierarchy. Out of this condition sprang the great German "prince-bishops" of the high feudal age.

Yet immunities, despite the advantages derived from their possession, were negative rather than positive in their application. A more substantial means adopted by the Saxon

---

de expeditione romana attributed to Lothar II are forgeries (Schulte, *Der Adel*, p. 213). The statement in the letter of Anacletus II (1133) to Lothar II that German dukes were legally compelled to perform military service in Italy if the emperor was summoned to the relief or protection of the pope is not authentic (Doeberl, *Mon. Ger. Selecta*, IV, 14 n.).

[1] Hauck, III, 397, 402, 404. Ficker, *Abhandl. d. Kais. Akad. zu Wien, phil.-hist. Classe*, LXXII, 90, contends that the crown had legally as full control over bishops as over abbots. Waitz, VII, 199, contests the point, but admits that it has not been sufficiently studied. Cf. also Waitz's article in *Göttinger Anzeiger* (1873), pp. 821 f.

[2] Nitzsch, I, 339; Sommerlad, II, 242–43. Until late Merovingian time the *mundium* was more common than the immunity, which developed with the growth of feudalism in the seventh and eighth centuries (Waitz, VII, 219 f.). In general, episcopal immunities were broader than those of the monasteries (*ibid.*, VII, 228). Otto I was cautious in disposing of the latter (Hauck, III, 60; Seliger, p. 118).

[3] Hauck, III, 60. For an example see case of Hamburg, in *Diplom.*, II, No. 61.

[4] *Diplom.*, II, No. 48, p. 449; Lacomblet, *Urkundenbuch*, I, No. 228.

[5] *Diplom.*, II, No. 16, p. 71.   [6] Waitz, VII, 230.

kings in order to strengthen the church and make it a grateful and willing instrument of the crown was the practice of
directly investing bishops and abbots with the powers of
counts. This policy was not entirely novel with the Ottos, for
as far back as 887 Charles the Fat had given the rights of the
local count to the bishop of Langres,[1] and in 927 Henry I did
the same at Toul.[2]

But until the time of the Saxon kings the bishops were
not the equal of the counts in public authority. To be sure,
within the circumscription of their immunities, as we have
seen, they were independent of the local counts, and exercised
powers analogous to those of the count within the *Gau*, having high and low justice over the population dwelling upon
the church lands. There was a certain inconvenience, however, in this arrangement, for the lands of the bishops were
usually widely scattered, while the jurisdiction of the count
was coextensive with a compact, contiguous territory, and
over all the population living therein. Now the bishops had
whole counties bestowed upon them, with all the rights and
powers of the former counts reigning there.[3] At a stroke they
became the heads of politico-ecclesiastical principalities.
Instead of a lordship over dispersed holdings with no binding
tie save their episcopal authority, the bishops now became
spiritual and temporal lords of vast and compact dominions,
all the more enduring because the power thus newly constituted had that perpetuity and indivisibility peculiar to the
patrimonies of the church. In a word, the Ottos were the
creators of the great ecclesiastical princes of medieval
Germany.[4]

[1] Bouquet, VIII, 643.

[2] Sickel, *Diplom.*, I, No. 16, p. 52.

[3] There is a large-scale map by Otto Curs, "Deutschlands Gaue um das Jahr
1000," in *Deutsche Erde*, VIII, 67, together with a register of places.

[4] Grants of the powers of the count, either in whole or in part to bishops, made
by Otto I are as follows: archbishops of Mainz, Cologne, Magdeburg; bishoprics of
Speyer, Chur, Worms, and Minden (Hauck, III, 62). Otto II gave the county of
Cadore to the bishop of Freising—Reizler, *Gesch. Bayerns*, I, 390. Otto III gave
the counties of Waldsazin and Rangau to the bishop of Würzburg; those of Padergo,
Aga, Treveresga, Auga, Sorethfeld, to the bishop of Paderborn; the county of Huy
to the bishop of Liège. Under Henry II the counties of the old duchy of Franconia

The future danger arising for the German monarchy owing to this arrangement will be seen later on,[1] but there is no denying the immediate benefit of the practice in increased law and order throughout Germany, which is especially manifested in the growth of town life and the development of trade. By Henry II's time (1002–24) the wooden palisades of the Fowler's time were giving way to stone walls around the towns, as at Magdeburg, Verden, Paderborn, and Worms.[2] The ecclesiastical capitals became centers of a rapidly expanding commerce, owing to greater security on the roads and the multiplication of market rights in the hands of the bishops and abbots. For the Ottos were lavish in distributing favors of this nature, together with the right to coin money, among the faithful episcopate.[3]

---

were partitioned between Würzburg and the king's new bishopric of Bamberg, and the bishoprics of Cambrai, Paderborn, Utrecht, Worms, and Hildesheim were further enriched by grant to them of the rights and privileges of the regional counts. For further details and references to sources see Waitz, VII, 208–18, 255–64; Hegel, *Die Enstehung des deutschen Städtewesens*, pp. 73–74; Kurth, *Notger de Liège*, pp. 113–17; Oppermann, *Westdeutsch. Zeitschrift*, XIX (1900), 202 ff.; Schulte, *Rechtsgesch*, sec. 68, n. 4; Ficker, *Forschungen*, II, 12 f.; Berchtold, *Entwickelung der Landeshoheit*, I, 65 f.

[1] For the deep significance both for the present and the future history of Germany of this identification of the church's administrative system with the secular government see Hauck, *Kirchengesch.*, III, 3, and IV, 674–75, and Below, *Der deutsche Staat des Mittelalters*, pp. 190–96; Ranke, *Deutsche Gesch. im Zeitalter der Reformation* (5th ed.), I, 24.

[2] Hauck, III, 410 n.; Sommerlad, II, 234–35, 265–67; Wattenbach (5th ed.), II, 34.

[3] Hauck, III, 61; Waitz, VII, 5–6, 24–33. For the increase of trade and commerce in Saxon Germany see Giesebrecht, II, 11 f.; Gerdes, I, 388–99.

The German episcopate seems to have been more negligent in keeping registers and statistics of its resources than the monastic clergy, and we are consequently driven to the use of indirect evidence and inverse reasoning to ascertain its wealth. While in the nature of things the conclusions are only approximate, it is nevertheless clear that by the year 1000 the German church was exceedingly wealthy. The growing luxury and material self-indulgence of the high clergy and the great abbots shocked the rigid moralists of the age (Richer, *Hist.*, III, 39). Bishops and abbots maintained imposing retinues of servants. This appears even in the time of Arnulf. Salomon of Constance showed some visitors a vase of gold set with precious stones (Ekkehard, *Casus S. Galli*, Book I, chap. xxii). Even Bruno of Cologne dressed his household servants in purple (Ruotger, *Vita Brunonis*, chap. xxx). Purple silk and beaver and marten fur were the usual attire of the bishops on grand occasions (Thietmar, *Chron.*, Book VII, chap. xxxv; Gerbert, *Epp.*, Nos. 33 and 188). Baldric of Liège staggered even Rather of Verona, who was used to the luxury of Italy, with his

The doctrinaire and the religious purist may be tempted to mock at this politico-ecclesiastical system perfected by the Ottos as one of selfish purpose and subversive of the purposes of religion.[1] But both the German crown and the German church faced a condition, not a theory, in the tenth century. Whatever may have been the ultimate results arising from this close affiliation between the church and the state, extending almost to the point of assimilation of the former by the latter, there is no denying the practical efficacy of the arrangement and the immediate benefit to Germany.

Modern historians[2] indorse the opinion of Sigebert of Gembloux[3] in the eleventh century, that Germany's greatness in the Saxon epoch was due to the intelligence of her kings and the public spirit of her bishops.

The German bishops, loyal, efficient, were the pillars of the throne. A roll call of the eminent bishops of the Saxon period would make a brilliant pleiad. Among them were Bruno of Cologne, William and Willigis of Mainz; Henry and Egbert of Trier; Ansfrid of Utrecht; Theoderich of Metz, Wicfrid of Verdun, Gerard of Toul, Ulric of Augsburg, Wolfgang of Regensburg, Pilgrim of Passau, Reginald of Eichstaet, Bernward and Godehard of Hildesheim, Notger of Liège and Meinwerk of Paderborn. Every one of these

---

splendor. Arnold of Halberstadt wrote to his friend Henry of Würzburg: "Praedecessores nostri totam operam suam animabus lucrandis insumebant, nos, quomodo corpora foveamus praecipue satagimus; illi pro coelo, nos pro terra disceptamus" (Jaffé, *Mon. Bamb.*, p. 477). For modern literature on the luxury of the Saxon period see Specht, *Gastmäler und Trinkgelage bei den Deutschen*, p. 8; Gerdes, I, 428 f.; Sass, *Deutsches Leben zur Zeit der sächs. Kaiser.*, pp. 7 f.; Hauck, III, 410–11; Koeniger, pp. 76–77; Vogel, *Ratherius von Verona*, I, 44.

[1] The point was not unseen in the tenth century, and met by the practical argument. See Ruotgerus, *Vita Brunonis*, chap. xxiii; Widukind, *Rerum Gestarum Saxonicarum Libri IV*, I, chap. xxxi, who cites the case of Samuel.

[2] Giesebrecht, *Kaiserzeit*, III, 7; Ratzinger, *Gesch. d. Kirchl. Armenflege*, p. 252; Kraus, *Gesch. der christlichen Kunst*, II, 33; Kurth, *Notger de Liège et la civilisation au Xe siècle*, pp. 1–4.

[3] Jure felicia dixerim Ottonis tempora, cum claris praesulibus et sapientibus viris respublica sit reformata, pax ecclesiarum reformata, honestas religionis redintegrata. Erat videre et reipsa probare, verum esse illud philosophi: fortunatum esse rempublicam, si vel reges saperent vel regnarent sapientes. Praeerant enim populo regni non mercennarii sed pastores clarissimi (Sigebert, *Vita Deoder. Mettensis*, chap. vii).

bishops had more than a local reputation—they were national figures.

The bishops profited more largely than the abbots from this course of the Saxon kings. The reasons are not hard to find. The secular branch of the clergy had an organic unity which the monastic half did not possess. The monasteries were individual, separate houses, not a closely knit organization like the episcopate, and except for the "royal" abbeys[1] almost outside the pale of the crown's control. Most of them were of private foundation and identified with local and feudal interests. Then, too, the abbots had nothing approaching the spiritual and disciplinary authority of the bishops.[2] Finally, the wealth of the monasteries already was so great by the close of Otto III's reign (1002) that it would have been inexpedient, not to say dangerous, as the policy of Henry II showed, to have increased their power.[3]

But there is no gain without some loss. While the German church was an enormous gainer from the royal protection and the royal bounty, on the other hand its close political relation with the government resulted in a certain decline of local and personal interest in it on the part of the feudality, which resented the Ottos' appropriation of revenues to which they believed themselves rightfully entitled, and the political and military use of the church made by the Saxon kings in order to coerce them. To the great German dukes and the half-feudal counts and the big proprietors in general the church was an object of envy and hate on account of its growing

[1] See M. Brennich, *Die Besetzung der Reichsabteien in den Jahren 1138–1209* (1908).

[2] Julius Harttung, *Diplomatisch-historische Forschungen* (1879), has shown that down to the beginning of the twelfth century the liberty of the monasteries from episcopal visitation was very limited and exceptional, the liberty granted the abbeys by Gregory V was curtailed by Sylvester II.

[3] Giesebrecht, II, 86; Gerdes, I, 576. Henry II was the first German king who gave countships to abbots, and this in only two instances, Fulda and Gandersheim (*Diplom.*, Nos. 444 and 509). His actual policy toward the monasteries was one of great restraint, even of suppression. See *infra*. It may be pointed out that this partial assimilation of an abbey's lands with the fisc obviated the necessity of the abbey having an *avoué* or *Vogt* to protect it. For the *vogtis depredationes* were often so great that the monasteries resorted to making forged charters to protect themselves. See Dopsch, *Mitth. d. Inst. f. oesterr. Gesch.*, XIX, No. 4.

wealth and vast political power. Accordingly, the bishops and older monasteries got few benefactions from a sullen feudality. These experienced a distinct and alarming falling off of gifts.[1] Instead, as will be shown shortly, the benefactions of the German nobles went to enrich the newer foundations of French or quasi-French origin, like those of Cluny and Hirsau, with the result that a new and formidable problem for the German monarchy was created thereby.

Naturally the church endeavored to adjust itself to this new condition,[2] and sought to compensate for the decline in private endowments by reorganizing its properties. In addition to introducing greater efficiency in the management of its lands, the church also strove to consolidate its scattered buildings into large complexes, and thus to gain by more scientific management and reduced cost of administration what it lost from the failure of private munificence.[3] The last half of the tenth century and the early part of the eleventh witnessed many sales or exchanges of scattered or remote parcels of land owned by the church for other holdings lying nearer to the bishopric or monastery. Judging from the data preserved, the success of the experiment was considerable.[4]

Endless are the cases of land transfer to cloister and abbey. With the land generally also went the people who lived on it. The service they had owed to their old master, the relationship to him, held good under the new. In making a transfer of lands to the Abbot of Paderborn in 1021 Henry II expressly includes the menservants and maidservants,

---

[1] Hauck, III, 57; Waitz, VII, 184–85; Lamprecht, *DWL*, I, 2, 675, 688, 694, 704.

[2] The *Traditiones Sangallenses* show that between 900–920 St. Gall received 60 benefactions, between 920–1000 only 40, and in the whole of the eleventh century only 5. Before 900 the total grants to Fulda aggregated 646, for the tenth century they were only 80, and for the eleventh 40. Lorsch shows similar depreciation (Waitz, VII, 184 n.; Inama-Sternegg, II, 129).

[3] For details see Sommerlad, II, 27 f.; Hauck, III, 57–59. Yet even as late as the end of the eleventh century the German monasteries did not equal the French in intelligent and effective management (Lambert of Hersfeld, *Annales* [ed. Holder-Egger], p. 84). Expert monastery management came in especially with the Cistercians.

[4] Inama-Sternegg, II, 27 f.; Lamprecht, *DWL*, I, 2, 687; Hauck, IV, 732.

they being amenable to such service and tax to the abbey as they formerly owed the king.[1] But land also changed hands between the nobles and king. Henry III received in 1043 one hundred tilled *mansi* into his possession from Count Esicho of Ballenstaedt, "together with the 'Eigenleute' and 'Lassen,' who live upon the mansi, men, women, and all servants of both sexes . . . . , with the exception of the men servants and maid servants belonging to the manor, who always served the count at the manor."[2]

Episcopal pride and the customary tradition of the church required that a bishop leave his diocese richer than when he found it.[3] The *Miracula S. Balderici* say that it was an exceptional bishop who did not spend his days in annexing lands and increasing the number of his vassals.[4] At his death he left an inventory of the acquisitions made during his incumbency.[5] The *Lives* of Meinwerk of Paderborn, of Bernward of Hildesheim, of Udalric of Augsburg, of Adalbero of Metz, of Burchard of Worms, and the *Chronicon* of Thietmar of Merseburg abound with interesting details as to the administrative duties and manner of life of these active German bishops of Saxon times.[6]

The double political edifice erected by the Ottos, half state and half church, reached its most complete point of development with Henry II (1002–24), the last of the Saxon house.

[1] *Vita Meinwerki*, chap. clxvi.   [2] *Codex Anhalt.*, I, No. 115, 90.

[3] Thietmar, *Chron.*, Book VI, chap. xxvi; Book VII, chap. xxii, where it is related that Bernhard (994–1014), bishop of Verden, in the space of twenty years increased the episcopal domain by 380 manors. A book containing names of donors was regularly kept in every church (Gerdes, I, 535, and notes). Lambert of Hersfeld, *Annales* (1075), p. 243, eulogizes Anno of Cologne for his material enrichment of the see during his incumbency. A medieval German proverb on the impossibility of recovering land from the church was "Kirchengut hat eiserne Zähne."

[4] *Miracula S. Balderici*, chap. ii. Cf. Thietmar, III, 1; IV, 24, 31; *Vita Meinwerki*, chaps. xcvi, xcviii, xcix, cl, clii, clxvi, ccxvii, etc.,; Waitz, VII, 206.

[5] Thietmar, *Chron.*, Book VI, chap. xxvi; and Wattenbach, *Deutschlands Geschichtsq.* (5th ed.), II, 33–34.

[6] For the "day" of a medieval bishop see *Vita Oudalr.*, chap. iii, SS. IV, 390; chap. xxviii; *ibid.*, p. 418; *Vita Adalber.*, chap. x, SS. IV, 485; *Libell. I, in honor. Willig.*, chap. ii, SS. XV, 744. Cf. Gerdes, I, 549–54; Rieger, *Forsch. z. d. Gesch.*, 1877 (on Meinwerk of Paderborn); Dietrich, *Neues Archiv.* XXV, No. 2 (on *Vita Bernwardi*).

There is no king of medieval Germany whose political course is more interesting to analyze for the light which it casts upon problems of feudal government and the relations of church and state in the Middle Ages.

Henry II converted the traditional policy of the Saxon house into a systematic practice, every element of which was carefully planned. He established at court what might be called a "school" for the education of clerics, who were imbued with his ideas and trained in efficiency, and from whom he selected the bishops whom he appointed;[1] he personally invested forty-nine of the fifty episcopal appointees of his reign.[2] In order to magnify the dignity and authority of the episcopal office the emperor surrounded the ceremony of investiture with a pomp and majesty which it had not possessed before.[3] The "ring" ceremony became almost a ritual.[4] It was as Rupert of Dietz wrote: "Convenerunt canonici ad imperatorem . . . . adhuc enim non electione, sed dono regis episcopus fiebat."[5] In vain might the chapters of the cathedrals, which had acquired a larger liberty of election under the weak rule of Otto III, complain that their rights were infringed.[6]

It is one of the eccentricities of history that Henry II should have become known as the "pious," for his ecclesiastical policy had absolutely nothing of the cringing quality of subservience to the church which won the appelation "pious" for Louis Debonair and Robert of France. Henry II was calculating, far sighted, determined, just, but without an ounce of emotionalism in his composition. He looked at things with level eyes, in a practical, not a theoretical, way; he was neither a mystic nor a doctrinaire.[7]

<hr/>

[1] Hauck, III, 405. [2] Ibid., p. 400. [3] Ibid., p. 397; Lamprecht, II, 292.

[4] Thietmar, Chron., Book IV, chap. xxvii; Book VII, chaps. vi–vii; Vita Meinwerki, chap. clxxxii; Waitz, VII, 268 f.

[5] SS. VIII, 267; Hauck, III, 404. [6] Hauck, III, 397 f.

[7] "So kirchlich Heinrich II gesinnt war, so wenig war er der Mann, irgend einer kirchlichen Theorie zu liebe seine Stellung als König zu schädigen [e.g., in the strife at Gandersheim, by the restoration of Merseburg, by the founding of Bamberg]. Das Recht der Bischofsernennung hielt er aufs zäheste fest, über ungetreue Bischöfe sass er zu Gericht, über Abteien verfügte er wie über Reichsgüter, in die Organisation der Kirche griff er direkt ein, er berief viele Synoden und welche Sprache er auf

The functioning of the church in government and society was of more importance to him than its spiritual authority. Religion, *qua* religion, Henry II believed to be the peculiar province of monks. They might be in the world, but their life was not to be of the world. The bishops, on the other hand, were chiefly governmental and military officers. There is no doubt of the sincerity of Henry II's convictions in so thinking. Monks were meant for prayer and worship and religious contemplation, and theirs was a cloistered life; but the duty of the secular clergy was to regulate morals, to govern the land, and to perform the military service exacted of them.[1] What Sir William Ramsay has said of the church in the Roman Empire is just as true of the medieval church:

> The administrative forms in which the church gradually came to be organized were determined by the state of society and the spirit of the age. . . . . These forms were, in a sense, forced on it; [but] . . . . they were accepted actively, not passively. The church gradually became conscious of the real character of the task which it had undertaken. It came gradually to realize that it was a world-wide institution, and must organize a world-wide system of administration. It grew as a vigorous and healthy organism, which worked out its own purposes, and maintained itself against the disintegrating influence of surrounding forces; but the line of its growth was determined by its environment.

One may not dogmatize when considering the part played by the church in the feudal age. Institutions, social structure, ideals, were very different then from what they are today. Feudalism was the rock whence the church was hewn, the pit whence was digged the clay out of which the outward material church was built. It is not always easy to distinguish the line of division between the use and the abuse of the

---

denselben führte, lassen uns überkommene Nachrichten deutlich erkennen" (Koeniger, p. 16). Schulte, *Adel*, p. 68: "[Heinrich II] betrachte die Bischöfe als Beamte des Reiches." The theory of Tomek, *Studien zur Reform der deutschen Kloster im 11. Jahrhundert*, that Henry II was actuated most often by religious consideration in episcopal appointments is not justified by what facts we know of his reign (cf. Hauck, III, 397). In 1014 when Megingaud of Eichstädt died, Henry II appointed one Gunzo, a priest of Bamberg and of servile birth, to the vacancy. A feud soon developed betweeen him and the monks of Herrieden, in which the emperor sustained the latter. His admonition of the bishop shows clearly his conception of the royal prerogative over the episcopate (cf. Schulte, *op. cit.*, pp. 69–70; *MGH*, SS. VII, 260).

[1] Hauck, III, 395; Waitz, VIII, 417.

church's institutions in the history of medieval Germany—
or elsewhere in medieval Europe, for that matter—but it is
an unjust assumption to assert broadly that the German
kings wilfully abused the German church patronage. The
church was a historical institution, the product of long historical development, and the kings used it as such.[1]

A few instances may be cited here from the history of
Henry II's reign which serve to make this point clear. The
empress Kunigunde had a brother named Adalberon, who
was a typical robber baron, a headstrong, quarrelsome Lorrainer. His depredations in the archdiocese of Trier were so
great that he nearly reduced the country to a desert[2] and
drove the Archbishop to seek refuge in Coblenz. The situation required a man of war, not a man of peace. "I will send a
man," wrote the Emperor, "who will put a stop to your wild
deeds." He was as good as his word. For he chose as the new
incumbent of the see not a pious churchman, but a hard-
headed, hard-fisted young Franconian baron by the name
of Poppo of Bamberg, whom he rushed through the various
grades of the hierarchy until he emerged as archbishop of
Trier. Poppo distributed sixty prebends of the see to as many
knights, and with this miniature standing army besieged
Adalberon's castles and finally brought peace and order into
the land again.[3]

Henry II's practical handling of the problem of the
eastern frontier is of a piece with this. The weakest point of
the Slavonic border was in eastern Franconia, where the apex
of Bohemia projected like a salient between the Sorben
Reichsland and the Bavarian Nordgau. The Emperor
bridged the gap here between Magdeburg and the Danube
by re-establishing the bishopric of Merseburg and founding
the new see of Bamberg. Here he built that exquisite Roman-

[1] Fisher, II, 78–84 has some good words on this head.

[2] Following is an account of the depredations of Adalberon: "Urbes certe depopulatae, vici et villae incensae omnes, viri omnes et feminae et totum promiscuum
vulgus ferro, fame, igne pestilentiaque consumptum. Multi etiam nobiles in paupertatem et magnam miseriam devoluti. Multi gladio perumpti" (MGH, SS. IV, 668).
For modern accounts see Giesebrecht, II, 112–16; Pfister, Robert le Pieux, p. 364.

[3] Cf. Thietmar, Chron.VI, 51; Koeniger, Burchard von Worms, p. 49.

esque cathedral which still stands in perpetuation of his memory, and here was his favorite seat of residence.[1]

The superstructure of the Saxon government was built upon and around the hierarchy, as a modern skyscraper is hung upon the steel skeleton within it. The monasteries and the duchies were merely lesser pillars and traverses in the huge edifice of government. Probably if Henry II could have had his way elsewhere in Germany as he had it in Franconia he would have eliminated the duchies from the map. For he gave half of the ducal lands in Franconia to the bishopric of Würzburg and half to that of Bamberg, leaving the duchy little more than a geographical expression with the titular ducal title attached to it.

The obligation of military service, that of appearing at the king's court, the performance of various commissions required by the king, weighed more heavily upon the persons and lands of the church than upon the lay feudality. The "royal" monasteries were practically a portion of the crown lands. The king alienated or enfiefed these domains as he pleased; he employed their revenues when and as much as he pleased for secular uses. The very abbots of the royal monasteries were frequently denominated as *villici*.[2]

Ficker[3] has gone even farther than Waitz and has contended that the lands of the German bishops were assimilated to the status of the royal domain quite as much as abbatial lands. Waitz strongly inveighs against this argument, contending that it is going too far, and demonstrates that the sources do not designate the imperial bishoprics in the same way that the royal abbeys are described, and that there is no

[1] On the founding of Bamberg see Hauck, III, 418–25; Lamprecht, *DG*, II, 293; *DWL*, I, 2, 700; Waitz, VII, 187; Hirsch, *Heinrich II*, II, 42–43. The Emperor enriched the new bishopric with much of the wealth of his own house, to the anger of his brother Bruno, who was bishop of Augsburg, the last survivor of the Saxon line, who coveted the inheritance for his own bishopric. It received 143 separate parcels of land and 6 monasteries (see *Mon. Boica*, XXVIII, 335–407). For the scandalous circumstances under which Merseburg had formerly been abolished for the aggrandizement of Magdeburg and Halberstadt, see Schmidt's Halle diss., *Giselher, Bischof von Merseburg, Erzbischof von Magdeburg* (1886), chap. iii.

[2] Waitz, VI, 189–94.

[3] *Abhandl. d. kais. Akad. zu Wien, phil. hist. Classe*, LXXII, 55 f.; Waitz, VII, 194–265.

example of a bishopric being transferred to a layman.[1] Nevertheless, it is certain that the dioceses of the church were subject to heavy requirements, notably that of military service, and that the material taxes imposed upon episcopal lands by the crown were heavy also. If not so completely assimilated to the condition of the abbey lands, the episcopal lands were yet very largely engrossed by the king.

Henry II made the whole organization and functioning of the church subject to his control. He convoked synods and presided over their debates; he regulated discipline, ritual, and teaching; but he sensibly distinguished between the spiritual and the political functions of the church[2] and was not disposed to abuse his authority. At the same time he was firmly determined not to permit the church to shirk its duties to civil society and the state. The spiritual duties of the high prelates were largely intrusted to coadjutors. The place of the bishops was at court, where they sat in the council of the king, labored in his chancellery, traveled on circuit through their dioceses, much like English sheriffs,[3] and led their vassals to the field of arms, if recourse were had to war upon the border or within the realm in order to crush feudal revolt. The military burden on the church was an exacting one,[4] owing partly to the suspicion attending the service of the lay feudality, partly to the steady decline in the free warrior class, even in Saxony, due to the extension of feudal conditions. The church also had to bear out of its revenues the largest share of the burden of supporting the court,[5] which, owing to the primitive economic régime obtaining, necessarily had to be a wandering one with no fixed

[1] *Ibid.*, p. 199.

[2] According to Thietmar, *Chron.*, Book VI, chap. viii, the emperor was "vicar of God"; according to Wipo, *Vita Chuonradi*, Book II, chap. iii, he was "vicar of Christ." An abbot called Henry III "caput ecclesiae" (Giesebrecht, II, 599).

[3] Waitz, V, 82–83; Gebhardt, I, 258; Hauck, III, 553 and n. 2; Koeniger, *Quellen zur Gesch. der Sendgerichte in Deutschland* (Munich, 1910).

[4] Hirsch, I, 211; Waitz, VIII, 130–31, has nearly two pages filled with references on this subject.

[5] "Nobis pertinent," said Henry VI of the church lands (*Dip.*, III, No. 65. Cf. Hauck, III, 57, n. 1).

capital.[1] Episcopal responsibility, in both ecclesiastical and civil capacity, was a watchword with Henry II. He well rewarded the bishops for their services; but when he intrusted the administration of the crown lands in Saxony to the archbishop of Mainz he expected service.[2]

It was Henry II, too, who devised a way to tap the resources of the reluctant feudal families who had closed their purses to the church under his predecessors by appointing members of these rich families to Saxon sees. Thus Thietmar was made bishop of Merseburg,[3] Meinwerk bishop of Paderborn,[4] Unwan archbishop of Bremen,[5] all of whom were sons of rich and noble Saxon families who gave out of their substance to their bishoprics.

In respect to the monasteries Henry II pursued the most drastic course of any medieval sovereign. Their vows and manner of life alienated the monks from secular activities. The abbots could not be used as freely as the bishops in secular administration or in military affairs owing to the greater isolation and less compact form of government which prevailed in monastic organization. The monks had neither the moral nor the political influence of the hierarchic clergy in Germany. But the material wealth of the monasteries was even greater than that of the secular clergy. In Otto III's reign the monasteries were not only relatively, but absolutely, richer than the bishoprics. For, in the first place, they owned a greater proportion of land; and, second, they had withdrawn a greater amount of it from the taxing power of the state through privileges and immunities.[6] Neither the military nor the financial burden upon the monasteries was so heavy as upon the episcopate.

Under these conditions the monasteries were of little

[1] Nitzsch, I, 325, 358-59.

[2] Nitzsch, I, 388. Cf. Bresslau, II, 354-56; Waitz, VII, 187.

[3] Thietmar, Chron., Book VI.

[4] Vita Meinwerki, SS. XI, 111-12.

[5] Adam of Bremen, Book II, chaps. xlv-xlviii, lviii. Bernward of Hildesheim gave Michaeliskloster 466 manors and 13 churches (Waitz, VII, 186).

[6] Sackur, II, Die Cluniacenser, 156-57; Matthäi, p. 84; Nitzsch, I, 390-91.

practical benefit to either the state or society. Their wealth
was out of all proportion to their material needs, such as the
daily support of the inmates, the maintenance of schools and
hospitals, and poor relief. The "dead hand" kept much of
their surplus wealth from free circulation in society for the
advantage of society, and it was not forced out into the open,
as was the case with the church's wealth, through government use of the church.

Henry II saw the incongruities obtaining in monasticism
and made a heroic attempt to rectify them. The cloistered
life supposedly was a life of poverty and prayer and spiritual
ministry. It had become a life of material ease and irresponsi-
bility so far as public interest was concerned. As individuals
the monks might be "unsocial" (their fundamental ideals
were such), but as an institution monasticism could not be
suffered to continue its antisocial exclusiveness without
detriment to society and corruption of itself.[1]

Contrary to what is usually thought, at this early stage in
the history of medieval monastic reform, Cluny was not yet
at all interested in the reformation of the secular part of the
church. Her aims and interests were still wholly confined to
the reform of monasticism, and when Henry II spilled the
wind out of the sails of the monks who accused him of
flagrantly practicing "simony" by promoting the Gorzean reform movement with dismaying thoroughness, Cluny approved of the emperor's action. "For following the tradition
of monasticism she looked upon the monk as alone fulfilling
literally the words of the gospel, and thus following a higher
ideal than that of the secular clergy."[2]

The monasteries throughout all Europe had appallingly
degenerated during the dark days of the ninth century, and
in Germany had not recovered in the same degree as the
episcopate, which the energy of the Saxon kings had so re-

[1] In *Vita Meinwerki*, chap. clxxxii, Henry II complains: "Qui me bonis con-
cessis cum detrimento regni spoliare non cessas." Cf. also chaps. clxxxiv and clxxxvi.

[2] L. M. Smith, "Cluny and Gregory VII," *Eng. Hist. Review*, XXVI, 21. "Die
cluniacensische Reform hat im 10. Jahrhundert keine hierarchischen Tendenzen"
(Schultze, *Forschungen zur Gesch. der Klosterreform im 10. Jahrhundert* [Halle diss.,
1883], p. 81).

habilitated. Ruined by the invasions of the Northmen in Gaul and the lower Rhinelands, by the inroads of the Hungarians in Germany and North Italy,[1] by those of the Saracens along the whole Mediterranean coast and far up into the Alpine passes,[2] by the trespass of the feudality upon their lands and the seizure of the property and even usurpation of the abbot's title; demoralized by everything which they had themselves originated through abuse of the ideals of Benedictinism, or become the victims of violence from without, the monasteries everywhere in Europe had sunk into debauchery, worldliness, and ignorance,[3]

Many of their inmates had fled the cloister and resorted to a life of pillage like that of the baronage.[4] The serfs upon the monastery lands had run away or perished in the anarchy, and those that were left were often numerically so reduced that the monks themselves were compelled to till the glebe farms.[5] In the tenth century complaints are common against

[1] So many bishops and abbots—to say nothing of lesser clergy—were rendered homeless by the Hungarian invasions in North Italy that it was hard to provide for them (*Ann. Fuld.*, 886).

[2] Poupardin, *Le royaume de Provence sous les Carolingiens*, pp. 248–73; Renaud, *Les invasions des Sarrazins en France* (1836); Devic et Vaisette, *Histoire du Languedoc*, II, 549 f.; Pfister, pp. 351–52; Dümmler, I, 191–94. See the curious story of the capture of Abbot Majolus of Cluny by the Saracens in Rod. Glaber (ed. Prou), Book I, chap. iv, sec. 9.

[3] Ruinés par les invasions des Normands, Hongrois et Sarrazins, par l'installation forcée des vassaux seigneuriaux dans ses domaines, l'usurpation du titre et des biens de l'abbé par les favoris du roi ou les dynastes provinciaux, dégradés par l'intrusion à la place des moines de clercs séculiers ignorants, paresseux et débauchés, les monastères étaient tombés au XIe siècle dans la plus profonde abjection morale et matérielle" (Lot, *Hugues Capet*, p. 34). For the effect of the Norse invasions upon the monasteries in Lorraine see Parisot, *Le royaume de Lorraine sous les Carolingiens*, pp. 498–99, 546–61, 722–24.

[4] Richeri, *Gesta eccles. Senon.*, Book I, chap. xvii, SS. XXV, 264. In the tenth century the miserable *abbatiole* of Ste Celine in the diocese of Meaux, and that of St. Sixtus near Rheims, had only one monk (Lot, *op. cit.*, p. 226 n.). In the life of Odo of Cluny it is related how his friend Adhegrinus sought in vain for a decent monastery, and in despair started on a pilgrimage to Rome, when he hit upon Berno, future first abbot of Cluny, in the little monastery of Baume (*Vita Odonis*, Book I, chap. xxii).

[5] Richeri, *op. cit.*, Book II, chap. xviii. For evidence as to the monasteries of Lorraine see Parisot, p. 723, n. 4.

the monks, who are accused of licentiousness,[1] of neglecting their vows,[2] of eating meat on fast days,[3] of drunkenness,[4] and of refusing hospitality.[5]

The plight of the monasteries was so bad that they seemed incapable of reforming themselves.[6] The initiative came from the piety of the nobility, many of whose members, for the repose of their souls, founded new monasteries, the life of whose inmates was intended to be a reproach to those of older foundation.[7] For it seemed impossible to put new wine into old bottles. Yet, as was the case in the early history of the church when the rural proprietors discovered that it "paid" to establish rural churches, so now there was a considerable measure of self-interest in the movement for restoration of the monasteries, which was not done away with until 996, when the Cluny reform, under the captaincy of the great abbot Odilon, began to be effective. Frequently when a great noble or a bishop, before this term, refounded or reformed a monastery, it was because he controlled the foundation and profited from its revenues, much of which he appropriated for himself.[8]

The movement for monastic reform appeared in France early in the ninth century and gathered force during the two

---

[1] Richeri, *op. cit.*, Book II, chap. xvii; *Mirac. S. Ghisl.*, chap. x, SS. XV, 583; *Vita Gerardi*, SS. XV, 665. As early as 836 the Council of Aachen, chap. xii, declared, "Quae [monasteria] in quibusdam locis lupinaria potius videntur esse quam monasteria" (Mansi, Book XIV, col. 682).

[2] *Mirac. S. Maxim.*, chap. xxiii; *Mirac. S. Basoli*, chap. xi; *Mirac. S. Burcharii*, chap. viii; *Concil. Trosl.* (909); Mansi, Book XIV, col. 682.

[3] Mabillon, *Annal. Benedict.*, III, 305.

[4] Richeri, *Hist.*, Book III, chaps. xxxvii, xxxix, xli.

[5] *Synod. Vern.*, MGH, *Leges*, I, 383–88.

[6] *Vita Joh. abbat Gorz.*, chaps. xxii–xxiii.

[7] Ord. Vitalis, *Hist. Eccles.*, Book VII, chap. xv. This practice was a familiar one in the high Middle Age. William the Conqueror, on his deathbed, took greatest gratification in the large number of monasteries which he had founded, and which he had encouraged his vassals to establish (*op. cit.* [ed. Le Prevost], III, 241).

[8] "Quand un grand laique ou un évêque restaure ou réforme un établissement, c'est qu'il possède cet établissement et qu'il profite de ses revenus qu'il a confisqués" (Lot, *op. cit.*, p. 225, n. 8).

following centuries.[1] The inspiration came not from either Monte Cassino or the imperial court, but from a remote corner of Gaul, Gothia. It was the movement generated by Benedict of Aniane. From Gothia the reform spread into Provence and over Aquitaine; and when the Emperor called Benedict to the abbey of Cornelimünster, the Rhinelands, too, were sowed with the seed of reform. In its complete form it was really the fusion of three separate and independent movements and radiated from three particular foci— Burgundy, Aquitaine, and Brabant. The first two movements soon became identical and culminated in the Cluny reform. The history of the monastic reform movement which began in Brabant, whence it soon spread to the famous Lorraine monasteries of Gorze and Stavelot, must, however, first be traced at this point, because of its immediate influence upon the *Klosterpolitik* of Henry II and Conrad II.[3]

The founder of Brogne (diocese of Liège, duchy of Brabant) was a nobleman of Wallonia, named Gerard, who in 914 established a chapter of canons in one of his allods at

[1] In 845 Raymond of Limoges founded Ruffec; in 860 Count Badilon founded St. Martin d'Autun; Gerard of Roussillon founded the monasteries of Poutières and Vézelay; in 910 William of Aquitaine founded Cluny, Gerald that of Aurillain 914. The Cluniac movement was materially aided by Letald of Macon, Gaufrey of Nevers, and his successor, Adhemar, and Adelaide of Burgundy. Tulle was reformed by Adhemar of Turenne, Sarlat by the counts of Angoulême, Lezat by the viscount of Béziers, Jumièges by William of Normandy, Chanteuge by the counts of Auvergne, St. Pons by Raymond Pons of Toulouse, Fleury-sur-Loire by Count Elisierne. The aristocratic origin of this agitation for reform of the monasteries is to be noticed. The ablest abbots of Cluny, as Odo, Maieul, Odilon, and Hugh the Great, were of noble family. William of Dijon belonged to an illustrious family of Piedmont; Poppo of Stavelot was a Walloon noble. La Chaise-Dieu was established by Robert of Aurillac in 1047 in the forest of Velay near Puy, and spread until it had 297 priories in France and Spain (*Vita Roberti, AASS., Ord. Bened., IX*). La Grande Sauve was founded by Gerard, a Picard noble, in 1079, in Guyenne; it had 70 priories in France, England, and Spain (*ibid.*, p. 857). On all this subject see Sackur, *Die Cluniacenser*, I, 34 ff., and a special article in *Ztschft. f. Soz. u. Wirtschaftsgesch.*, I, Heft 1 (1893); Lamprecht, *Monatschrift f. d. Gesch. Westdeutschlands*, VII (1881), 91 f., 217 f.

[2] Dom Albers, O. S. B. *Consuetudines monasticae, tome III, Antiquiora monumenta maxime Consuetudines Casinenses inde ab anno 716–817* (Monte Cassino, 1907), traces the obscure development of monastic reform from the initiative taken by Pertinax to the reforming synod of Aachen in the third year of Louis the Pious.

[3] Schultze, *Forschungen zur Gesch. der Klosterreform im 10. Jahrhundert* (Halle diss., 1883).

Brogne.[1] Wholly inspired by French monastic ideals, in the next year he was sent to Paris by his suzerain, Count Berenger of Namur, in order to visit the celebrated abbey at St. Denis. There he spent some time in study.[2] In 919 he returned to Brogne and transformed the chapter into a Benedictine monastery.[3] Five years later Gerard was made abbot of Brogne by the Bishop of Liège, and in 927 was ordained a priest at Paris—for Brogne was always regarded as a dependency of St. Denis. It so happened at this time that Count Arnulf of Flanders was in good relation with the church of Rheims, and in 937, through the recommendation of the Bishop of Noyon, Gerard undertook the reformation of the great abbeys of St. Bavon and St. Blandin, in Ghent, and St. Bertin, St. Amand, St. Omer, and St. Vaast, in Flanders. From these points the Brabantine reform movement ran down the channel coast into Normandy, and down the valley of the Oise into the Ile-de-France, where it soon became fused with the Cluny reform.[4]

At the same time the movement also flowed over the Flemish frontier into Lorraine, where St. Ghiselain was reformed in 931.[5] In 933 it took possession of Gorze, near Metz, whence it rapidly spread to the cloisters of St. Maximin in Trier; Senones, near Metz; St. Die, Stavelot, St. Viton, near Verdun; St. Evre in Toul, etc.[6] In the "fifties" of the ninth century the Gorzean reform—for so it may henceforth be called—made headway slowly up the valley of the Moselle. In 951 Metlach joined it; by 973 most of the monasteries in the diocese of Trier, as Echternach, St. Martin, Ste Marie,

[1] *Vita Gerardi*, chap. 1, SS. XV, 2. Of course the institution of collegiate canons was not so radical a reform as the establishment of regular monasticism would have been. L. von Heinemann, *Neues Archiv*, XV, No. 2 (592–96), in an examination of the early diplomas pertaining to Brogne, has determined that the *Vita Gerardi* was written shortly after December, 1038; cf. *Forschungen*, XXV, 223–31.

[2] *Vita Gerardi*, chap. iv.

[3] *Ibid.*, chap. xiii.

[4] Bouquet, IX, 615.

[5] Sackur, I, 126 f.; Lamprecht, II, 210.

[6] Sackur, I, 146 f., 156 f., 163 f., 174 f.; Schultze, pp. 33–58. For the violent opposition of the monks of St. Maximin see *Contin. Regino (anno* 934).

Ste Eucharia, had embraced it. St. Maximin founded two new houses under Gorzean rule at Taben and Appola. From the valley of the Moselle the movement penetrated into the Rhinelands.

Otto I's brother Bruno, archbishop of Cologne, who had been educated at Utrecht, and who therefore must have had immediate knowledge of the reform, introduced the Gorzean reform in Wissemburg, in Lorsch, and probably elsewhere, and founded Soest in Westphalia and St. Pantaleon in Cologne, all of which were put under the new rule.[1] Gradually the movement extended along the middle and upper Rhine. In Alsace two clerks of Strasburg, the canon Benno and a prior named Eberhard, between 929 and 934 founded the monastery of Ste Marioe-Einsiedeln, which soon reached a high degree of prosperity.[2] In Swabia, Udalric of Augsburg became a supporter of Gorze; Gebhard of Constance founded Petershausen.[3] In Bavaria its propagation was rapid. By the year 1000 the monasteries of St. Emmeran, St. Peter, Tegernsee, Altaich, Ebersberg, and the nunneries of St. Paul and Upper and Lower Moutier had been reorganized and three new Gorzean foundations, Michaelsbeuren, Seeon, and Pruel, had been established.[4]

The chief person in propagating the Gorzean reform was John of Gorze, who in his time had a reputation wider than the Christian world, for it was he whom Otto sent on a mission to Mohammedan Spain to the caliph Abd-er Rahman.

[1] *Contin. Regino* (anno 957); *Diplom.*, I, No. 121, 203; Ruotger, *Vita Brunonis*, chap. x; Thietmar, IV, 15; *Chron. reg. Colon.* (anno 964). Bruno's successor, Gero, founded München (*Chron. Gladb.*, *MGH*, SS. IV, 75) and Thankmarsfeld in Saxony. Later still another archbishop of Cologne, Everger, reformed St. Martin (*MGH*, SS. IV, 77, and V, 555). Willigis of Mainz reformed Disibodenburg (Hauck, III, 414 f.); Adalberon of Metz, Epinal (*Vita*, Book II, chap. xiv, SS. IV, 662).

[2] Hauck, III, 376; *Annal. Hersf.* (anno 925) *Annal. Meginr.* (anno 934) *Othl. Vita Wolfgangi*, chap. x. See O. Ringholz, *Geschichte des fürstlichen Benediktiner-stiftes von Einsiedeln* (1905), a monograph of a high order of research. The site was at the beginning a wilderness (*Vita Joh. abbat. Gorz.*, chap. xl).

[3] *Vita Gebeh.*, chaps. x–xiii, SS. X. 586 f.; *Cas. Mon. Petrih*, Book I, chap. ix, *MGH*, SS. XX, 630 f.

[4] Hauck, III, 378–79; *Annal. S. Emmeran.* (anno 975), *MGH*, SS. I, 94 f.; *Vita Wolfg.*, p. 17; *Botae Tegerns*, *MGH*, SS. XV, 1067; *Chron. Ebersp.*, *MGH*, SS. XVII, 363; XX, 11 f.; XXV, 868 f.

His *Life*[1] is one of the most interesting and valuable sources of the epoch. And yet, in spite of his close attachment to Otto I, the Gorzean reform met languid support from the Saxon kings, and of course was violently resisted by the monks themselves.[2] Bruno of Cologne is the only member of the Saxon house who markedly encouraged it. Queen Adelheid, who was a Burgundian princess, seems to have been personally interested in reforming Wissemburg. But as for Otto I, he seems chiefly to have been interested in observing how this new religious emotionalism might increase the wealth of the German church through new gifts and endowments. Otto I's piety was ever practical. Neither Otto II nor Otto III seems to have taken cognizance of the reform.[3] Thus, indifferently regarded by the Saxon kings[4] and bitterly opposed by the monks themselves, the Gorzean reform in course of time lost its force,[5] until it was energetically revived by Henry II and Conrad II, by which time it had begun to be obscured by the far greater reform out of Cluny.

⤳ During the reign of Robert the Pious of France, William

[1] SS. IV, 343 f. esp. chaps. xxii, xxiii, xxvi, xxvii, xxviii.

[2] Mathieu, *De Johannis abbatis Gorziensis vita* (Nancy, 1878). For evidence of resistance see Ekkehard, *Casus S. Galli*, Prolog. and Book IX, chaps. lxxv–lxxx, civ, cv, cxii; Thietmar, *Chron.*, II, 37–38; VI, chap. v; Gerhardi, *Vita Oudalr.*, chap. vi; Widukind, II, chap. xxxvii; *Annal. Qued.* (1013). Cf. Hauck, III, 343–44; Gerdes, I, 599–607; Wattenbach, *Deutsch. Geschichtsquellen*, I, 186; Vogel, *Rather von Verona*, pp. 218–24.

[3] Koeniger, *Burchard von Worms*, p. 108. This fact comes out in the letter of Arnulf of Halberstadt to Henry of Würzberg. Burchard of Worms, in his famous compilation of canon law, does not even allude to the reform (Jaffé, *Ep. Bamb.*, II, 474–76; Migne, *Patrol. Lat.*, CXL, 707, 712, 804, 899, 902, 907, Hauck, III, 440 f.; and *Sitzungsber. der. sächs. Ges. d. Wiss.* [1894], p. 65.

[4] The indifference of the Saxon kings is readily explained by the fact that, like the Cluny reform later, the Gorzean reform soon became a political movement which was a danger to the crown. The great German feudatories like Gilbert of Lorraine, Eberhard of Swabia, and Henry the Wrangler of Bavaria were not slow to perceive the political possibilities implicit in it, and advocated the reform in order to break the grip of the Saxon kings on the church (Sigeh., *Mirac. S. Maxim.*, chap. xii, SS. IV, 232; *Chron. Bened.*, chap. ix, SS. IX, 218; Hauck, III, 364). For the same reason Frederick of Mainz, the leader of the ecclesiastical opposition to Otto I, ardently supported it (Hauck, III, 375 f.; Widukind, III, 37; *Episc. Mogunt.*, p. 14).

[5] Adalberon of Rheims introduced the Lotharingian rule into Rheims, which later gave origin to Austin canons (Freeman, *Norman Conquest*, II, 86 n.; IV, 363, 500; V, 500 f.

of St. Benigne, and perhaps Odilo, who had already labored long and earnestly in France in favor of monastic reform, carried the ideas of Cluny across the boundary into Lorraine, where he stirred up the ashes of the earlier Gorzean reform into newness of life.[1] In the monastery of Stavelot in Lorraine, William came in contact with Richard of St. Vannes and Poppo of Stavelot, destined to be shortly Henry II's and Conrad II's ecclesiastical statesman.[2]

Like Gerard of Brogne, the founder of the Gorzean reform, Poppo was born in the Walloon lands of the German kingdom, and was of noble birth. It was undoubtedly through his persuasion that late in his life Conrad II and his wife were induced to establish the monastery of Limburg in Poppo's native county.[3] When a young man he had made a pilgrimage to Palestine, and later had been to Rome with Count Theodoric of Holland. Although betrothed, he abandoned marriage for the cowl, having been converted, it is said, by a dream.[4] He first entered the monastery of St. Thierry, whence he passed to that of St. Vannes. Then he became abbot of St. Vaast and Beaulieu successively. It was in the last post that Henry II discovered him and took him into his service in spite of the united protest of the abbots of Flanders.[5] In 1020 he was made abbot of Stavelot and Malmedy. Two years afterward he made, under Henry II's direction, that famous reformation of St. Maximin of Trier, the details of which we shall shortly see.

The Lorrainer monasteries, which had formerly yielded to the Gorzean reform, were now in a condition of relapse, and much as they had been before.[6] The Benedictine monas-

---

[1] On William of St. Benigne see Pfister, *Robert le Pieux*, p. 312.

[2] On Poppo, see Hirsch and Bresslau, *Jahrbücher Heinrich II*, III, 235 f.; Bresslau, *Conrad II*, II, 405 f.; Ladewig, *Poppo von Stablo und die Klosterreform unter den ersten Saliern* (Berlin diss., 1883).

[3] *Vita Popponis*, chap. xix.

[4] Hauck, III, 499; Sackur, II, 177, 264.

[5] Hugo Flav., *Chron.* II, 15, p. 391; Adhemar, *Hist.*, III, 37, p. 133; Jotsald, *Vita Odil.*, I, 7; Migne, *Patrol. Lat.*, CXLII, 902; Rodulf. Glaber, *Hist.*, I, 5.

[6] For vestiges of the Gorzean reform at Bamberg as late as 1071 see Lambert of Hersfeld, *Annales* (ed. Holder-Egger), p. 128; *Ann. S. Mich. Bab.*, SS. V, 9.

teries, on the other hand, had scarcely yet been touched. As
they had resisted the earlier reform, so now they even more
violently resisted its revived application, in particular Hersfeld and St. Gall, where Norbert of Stavelot, Poppo's agent,
failed dismally, as Immo of Gorze also failed at Reichenau.
Almost everywhere the monks ridiculed the reform and held
to their old self-indulgent, loose way of living.[1]

But unlike the other kings of the Saxon house Henry II
took a keen interest in the cause of monastic reform, as the
monks soon learned to their sorrow. It may be that the in-
tractability of the monks had its influence in hardening
Henry II's heart toward them. But his *Klosterpolitik* was
undertaken neither in whim nor in spleen; it was an act of
real statesmanship.

Henry II was undoubtedly sincere in his cloister policy,[2]
though it was perhaps not without some cynical satisfaction
that he proceeded to a wholesale reorganization of the German monasteries, in many cases completely disendowing
them. He stripped them of the right of free election[3] and of
most of their property.[4] He held (and here Cluny agreed
with him) that monks were par excellence meant for a life of
poverty and religious contemplation.[5] He forbade plurality
of abbots and insisted upon episcopal visitation of the monasteries.[6] In the case of all the abbeys which survived the

---

[1] "Postquam luxus ac superfluitas accessit, morum insolentia subintravit,
oboedientia torpuit, repulsa est episcoporum reverentia" (*Vita Bernwardi*, chap.
xiv). Cf. *Vita Hathumodae*, chaps. v–vi, SS. IV, 168; Hermann Contract, *Chron.*,
1006; *Chron. Suev.*, 1006; *Catalog. abbat. Aug.*, SS. XIII, 333. Of modern writers,
Sackur, II, 252 f.; Gerdes, I, 599 f.; Hattemer, *Denkmale des Mittelalters*, II, 221,
nn. 4–5.

[2] Koeniger, *Burchard I. von Worms*, p. 108. Cf. Sackur, II, 156–58: Hauck, III,
445, 459; Nitzsch, I, 390–91, 395.

[3] Feierabend, p. 3.

[4] *Ibid.*, p. 4.

[5] Hauck, III, 450. The Register of the lands of Prüm was made at Henry's command, and he must have made many others which have perished (Waitz, VIII, 229,
n. 1).

[6] Matthäi, p. 84; Hauck, III, 450–57; Koeniger, p. 108. Julius Harttung
(*Diplomatisch-historische Forschungen* [Gotha: Perthes, 1879]) has made a minute
study of the question of exemption of the monasteries, and has demonstrated that

reorganization he strengthened the control of the bishops over them, in some instances giving the monastery outright to the bishop.[1] But the last Saxon emperor was not a fanatic. He did not reduce the monasteries to utter poverty,[2] and sometimes he made grants to them in the interest of compacting their estates. In one particular he made a distinct departure from the course of his predecessors, for he conferred the local countship upon the abbots of Fulda and Gandersheim,[3] whereas the Ottos had never given such powers to any churchmen except bishops.

In this great "leveling" process some foundations were leveled up, more were leveled down. The oldest and richest abbeys naturally suffered most. Fulda, Hersfeld, Corvey, Reichenau, Murbach, St. Gall, Benediktbeuren, Tegernsee, Altaich, Gandersheim, had huge blocks of their domains taken away from them.[4] St. Maximin in Trier lost 6,656

at the beginning of the eleventh century the exemption of the monasteries from episcopal surveillance was very limited, and that the liberty granted the regular clergy by Gregory V (996) was sharply curtailed by Silvester II. The forgery of papal privileges by the monasteries in order to secure exemption from episcopal authority became a scandal during the minority of Henry IV.

[1] According to Henry II episcopal inspection of monasteries was divinely ordained in virtue of the bishop's authority: "Canonum statuta non ore hominum, sed spiritu Dei condita praecipiunt" (Diplom., III, No. 371). In order to understand the legal authority which Henry II possessed to institute this reorganization it must be remembered that the control of the crown over monasteries was much more complete than over bishoprics. The king could legally dispose of monastic property much as he wished, employing their revenues, alienating estates or giving them in fief as he might parcels of the royal domain. See Ficker, *Eigenthum*, pp. 72–73, 88 f.; Waitz, VII, 189–227; VIII, 244 f.; Fisher, I, 256 f.

[2] St. Maximin of Trier, after the sharp excision in 1023, was left 209 manors scattered in 40 separate localities, and by the year 1030 had increased its possessions again to 1,000 or more manors. St. Emmeran, in Bavaria, in 1031 still owned 850 manors, and Benediktbeuren possessed 60 *villae* of the total area of 1,350 *Hufen* (Stumpf, Nos. 1815, 1817; Inama-Sternegg, II, 136; *MGH*, SS. IX, 223). By the twelfth century Fulda had so far picked up again that it had 3,000 manors in Saxony, 3,000 in Thuringia, 3,000 in the Rhinelands around Worms, and 3,000 in Bavaria and Swabia (*Gesta Marcuardi, Fuld. Fontes*, III, 171 f.).

[3] *DD*, III, Nos. 444, 509. The grant to the monastery of Niedenburg of a tract of land nine miles long and three to five miles wide, however, was not as generous as it seems, for the abbey belonged to the bishop of Passau.

[4] For a particularly interesting account of Corbie see *Ann. Qued* (*annis* 1014–15), SS. III, 82–83.

manors in 1023, equal to nine square German miles.[1] Some
of the confiscated lands were given to smaller and more struggling monasteries like Lorsch, which, in spite of its ancient
foundation, was poor. For this once favorite abbey of Charlemagne seems to have missed the popular interest of later
generations, and fell away when the Carolingian house
expired.[2]

Naturally the German bishops, who profited much from
this policy, eagerly seconded Henry II's course. For there
was intense rivalry between the two bodies of the clergy.[3]
The feud was an ancient one. Hatto of Mainz, as far back
as the time of Louis the Child, had collected the revenues
of four abbeys;[4] Tagino of Magdeburg reformed Kloster
Bergen; Gebhard of Regensburg that of St. Emmeran; Meinwerk of Paderborn made a 50 per cent reduction in the monasteries in his diocese.[5] In the issue only the older and more
important abbeys were left, and all with a reduced number of
inmates.[6] All were reduced to a mean average of possession;

[1] *Migne*, CXL, 368; Koeniger, p. 108, n. 6; Waitz, VIII, 129, n. 1; Lamprecht,
DWL, I, 2, 710, n. 2. Joerres questions the accuracy of these figures in *Westdeutsche
Ztschft.*, VIII, No. 3 (1889). St. Maximum sought to recuperate in the twelfth century by forging new charters (Dopsch, *Mitteil. d. Inst. oester. Gesch.*, XVII, No. 1
[1896]).

[2] The important sources for this policy of Henry II toward the monasteries are
Vita Godeh., I, 7, 14; II, 7; *Chron. mon. Tegerns.*, p. 3; *Herim. Aug.* (anno 1106);
Annal. Quedlinb. (anni 1014–16); Thietmar, VIII, 13; *Annal. Corb.* (anno 1014);
Vita Popponis, esp. chaps. xviii–xix.

[3] For examples see *Vita Bernwardi*, chap. xv, SS. IV, 765; *Vita Adalb.*, chap. ix,
SS. IV, 584.

[4] Waitz, VII, 212; Ficker, *op. cit.*, p. 87; Nitzsch, I, 292. Henry II gave the
monastery of Seligenstadt to the bishop of Würzburg, St. Stephen and Schwarzach
to Strasburg, Helmswardshausen and Schildesche to Paderborn (Hauck, III, 449–
50). It was rare that a prelate founded a monastery out of his own revenues. Bernward of Hildesheim and Meinwerk of Paderborn did so, but it "paid" them (Lamprecht, *DWL*, I, 2, 826). There was bitter rivalry and even feud between the bishops
for control of monasteries. For cases see Nitzsch, I, 384. Koeniger, p. 69, says:
"Sie Kämpften aber nicht um blosse Rechte ohne reale Grundlage, sondern um
Land und Besitz; im Hintergrunde eines solchen Kampfes stand nichts anderes als
ihre fürstbischöfliche Macht und Stellung."

[5] *Vita Meinwerki*, chap. xvii; Gerdes, I, 576.

[6] The average number of monks varied from 100 to 200; that in the nunneries
was much less, perhaps from 30 to 50. When Henry II reformed Hersfeld he
eliminated over 50 monks, leaving only old men and boys (Hirsch, I, 364).

fourteen were legislated out of existence.[1] What monastery lands did not go to the enrichment of the bishops were reannexed to the fisc, whence many of them had originally come, which sorely needed repletion, owing to the lavish grants of the Ottos.

The monastic writers of Henry II's reign naturally inveigh bitterly against the Emperor, while episcopal authors like Thietmar of Merseburg and the biographer of Meinwerk of Paderborn exult in the ascendancy of the secular over the regular clergy.[2] But Henry II's ecclesiastical policy was neither one of bigotry toward the monks nor one of favoritism toward the bishops. Each group was made to function in the best possible way according to the medieval ideal of the relation of the church to state and society. Monks were intended for prayer and spiritual contemplation apart. Bishops were meant for service in the outside world. The Emperor would have heartily indorsed the Pauline differentiation of functions and duties in the ministry.[3] But the monks were human, and violently resisted the Henrician reform. Some of them were so intractable that Henry put them in irons. Their spiritual professions, which they shrilly advertised, were belied by the desperate way in which they tried to cling to their material possessions. They denounced the bishops, not without some justification, for avarice; but they themselves were quite as avaricious. In high dudgeon many of them forsook their houses. At Hersfeld all the inmates abandoned the monastery; at Corvey only nine remained.

To sum up as to Henry II's ecclesiastical policy: He was a stern, honest ruler, on fundamental issues of the relation of church and state standing with his precedessors and not disposed to abate an inch of royal supremacy over the church. Yet he was more progressive than the Ottos and more in harmony with the new spirit of the age, as when he instructed the synods of Pavia and Goslar to forbid the marriage of

[1] Matthäi, p. 81; Feierabend, pp. 4–5.

[2] Thietmar, *Chron.*, Book VI, chap. v; *Vita Meinwerki*, chap. xvii.

[3] Rom. 12:6–8.

priests, and even ruled that the children of priests should be classed as unfree.[1]

The feud between the German bishops and the German monks, when Henry II died in 1024, was the principal issue in the election of Conrad II, the founder of the Salian house. The two rival candidates were cousins and of the same name. Conrad the Old was supported by the episcopal party, which stood for diminishing the prerogatives of Rome and had triumphed two years before at the Council of Seligenstadt. Conrad the Young, on the other hand, was backed by the monastic party, by a few of the bishops who were already imbued with the ideas of the radical wing of the Cluny movement, and by the dukes of Upper and Lower Lorraine, whose zeal for the "reform" was strongly tinctured with feudal particularism.[2] The former was elected on September 8, 1024, and was crowned by the Archbishop of Mainz. His rival gamely accepted the situation. But his partisans at first obstinately refused to recognize the new king. Headed by Gozelo, duke of Lower Lorraine, a league of opposition was formed in which were Theodoric and Frederick of Upper Lorraine, Renier, Count of Hainaut, the Archbishop of Cologne, and the bishops of Trier, Verdun, and Nimwegen. The feudal and centrifugal implications of the Cluny reform were already clearly manifest.[3]

But the opposition to the German crown, although shortly to become formidable, was as yet unorganized. Pilgrim of

[1] Nitzsch, I, 388; "Henry II had had genuine ideas of reform, albeit they were often mingled with political interest, as when, at the end of his reign, he instructed the synods of Goslar and Pavia to forbid the marriage of priests and declared that their children should be classed as unfree. The affair of Hammerstein, where the court, if not the emperor, energetically sustained Aribo of Mainz, the champion of episcopal rights against the papacy, and friend of Ekkehard of St. Gall, the bitter opponent of reform, shows that on a fundamental issue Henry II stood with his predecessors and would not abate one inch of royal supremacy over the German church" (Gregorovius, *Rome in the Middle Ages*, IV, Part I, 31). Cf. Hauck, III, 528 f.; Sackur, II, 258; Mansi, XIX, 323.

[2] Bresslau, I, 12–13.

[3] *Gesta episcoparum Cameracensium*, III, 50; Pabst, *Forschungen zur deutsch. Gesch.*, V, 339 f.—an extension of his dissertation, *De Ariberto II Mediolanensi primisque medii aevi motibus popularibus* (Berlin, 1864), Pfister, *op. cit.*, pp. 373–74.

Cologne's participation was due to pique and the ancient jealousy existing between Mainz and Cologne.[1] Conrad II adroitly secured his defection by permitting him to have the honor of crowning Queen Gisela.[2] At the same time he turned to Odilo of Cluny, who was known to disapprove of the political programme of the radical Cluniacs, and who believed in still confining the reformation movement begun by Cluny to the reform of monasticism and in keeping it out of politics.[3]

[1] Nitzsch, II, 17.

[2] Wipo, *Vita Chuonradi* (ed. Bresslau), chap. ii, p. 15.

[3] Bresslau, *Konrad II*, I, 34.

CHAPTER II

THE GERMAN CHURCH AND THE SALIAN MONARCHY; SPREAD OF THE CLUNY REFORM IN ITALY AND GERMANY

CONRAD II (1024–39) made no change in the fundamental policy of the German crown toward the church. But he was less considerate in the use of church patronage than Henry II had been. He was friendly with Poppo of Stavelot, the leader of the reform party, and did not actively oppose the movement, but he never let it compromise the political obligations of the church to the government. In the Conradiner theory of church government the bishops were equally vassals and bishops, to be handled precisely as were dukes and counts.[1] The chief office of the church had developed into a feudal institution bearing all the characteristics of a dukedom except hereditability.[2] The bishops ruled the land in place of the former counts; they performed traditional feudal services at court; they led their vassals to the host. They were as much a part of the feudal hierarchy as they were of the clergy, being required to give the oath of fealty and do homage like ordinary vassals. A century was yet to elapse before these princely bishops, territorialized within their dioceses like dukes within their duchies, were formally to assume the rôle of prince-bishops, and haughtily to call their ecclesiastical domains[3] *terra*

---

[1] For Conrad II's ecclesiastical policy see Hauck, III, 544 f.; Nitzsch, II, 18; Fliche, *La reforme grégorienne*, pp. 101 f.; Lamprecht, II, 301; Bresslau, *Jahrb. Konrad II*, II, 389 f.; Feierabend, pp. 5 f.; Voigt, pp. 3 f.; Waitz, VIII, 420–21; Pfenninger, *Die kirchliche Politik Kaiser Konrads II* (Halle diss., 1880); Harttung, *Monatschrift f. d. Gesch. Westdeutschlands* (1878) (on Conrad II's relation with Aribo of Mainz). Conrad dragged the intriguing Italian bishops of Vercelli, Piacenza, and Cremona over the Alps and put the Archbishop of Lyons in chains (Wipo, *Vita Chuonradi*, chap. xxviii; *Herimann of Reichenau*, 1037).

[2] See Waitz, VII, 195. The notes are illuminating on the point.

[3] The earliest instance of this practice is the Bishop of Münster in 1134 (Wermthof, p. 78; Hauck, *Entstehung der geistlichen Territorien*, p. 28). Most of the Ger-

nostra, but they acted on that theory by early Salian times.

Conrad II used church offices with complete indifference to their religious nature, and wholly for political ends. The "school of the palace," established by Henry II for the training of bishops, was abandoned, and bishops and abbots were no longer prevailingly drawn from those of the clergy who were well educated and technically proficient in ecclesiastical duties. They were appointed and ordered about like ordinary feudal officials.[1] While meaning to be "practical" in his handling of church offices, Conrad's almost cynical method offended even those who thoroughly believed in the Saxon ecclesiastical policy, and enraged the ardent reform party. The watchword of this group, "simony," did not necessarily imply corrupt practice with reference to church offices, although the radical advocates of the cause so used the term, and if Conrad II had had more imagination and tact he perhaps might have neutralized their opposition in some degree.[2]

Henry II had frowned upon the frank sale of church benefices,[3] but Conrad II trafficked in them like a *Realpolitiker,* as Feierabend aptly says,[4] invariably exacting a fee from a newly installed bishop.[5] He did not have the vision to see the inadvisability and inexpediency of such practices in view of the growing sensitiveness of the church to secular

---

man bishops were of noble blood and profoundly imbued with feudal ideas (Werminghoff, p. 72). The statement in the text does not mean to say that every possession of a bishopric was regarded as a fief, for a considerable part of the episcopal domains were allods. This is especially true of older holdings. But the donations of the Saxon and Salian emperors were almost invariably fiefs. Ficker (*Vom Heerschilde,* pp. 62 f.) thinks that the title of "prince-bishop" may not properly be applied before the reign of Frederick Barbarossa. Cf. Waitz, *Gött. Gel. Anzeig.* (1862), 170. Conrad's ordinance of 1037 (*Leges,* II, 38) shows that the performance of military service by clerical vassals was subject to the same conditions that governed the service of lay vassals. A bishop who failed to so do was likely to lose his office just as a lay vassal forfeited his lands for the same offense.

[1] Nitzsch, II, 20; Waitz, VII, 210–11.

[2] Hauck, III, 552.   [3] *Ibid.,* p. 544.

[4] Feierabend, p. 5. Cf. Waitz, VIII, 408; Bresslau, II, 366 f.; Sommerlad, II, 228–29; Hauck, III, 544.

[5] Theodoric, bishop of Basel, paid *immensa pecunia* for the see (Wipo, *Vita Chuonradi,* chap. viii).

control over it. The protest of the Cluny reform as yet was little larger than a man's hand in Germany, but Conrad II could not read the sign in the sky. He inadvertently furthered the Cluny reform by failing to distinguish between the _use_ and the _abuse_ of his prerogative.[1]

Yet it is easy to misunderstand Conrad II's policy toward the church. While it may have been more drastic than that of Henry II and more recklessly applied, it was of a piece with that of his predecessor, and as statesman-like. It must be remembered that by Conrad's time the radicals in Cluny had come out into the open and violently inveighed against _all_ secular control of the church as simony, and that, though still a minority, the time was not far off when this radical element was to gain ascendancy over the curia and to claim from Rome domination for a world-church over all the Christian nations of Europe.

A sharp reduction in the number of donations to the church is noticeable in Conrad II's reign. Suspicious of both the great clergy and the high feudality, Conrad II purposely favored the lower feudality, playing them against the higher. In the duchies the principle of hereditary succession had practically become established; but the dukes were reluctant to see the extension of that principle among their vassals, and frequently punished them by deprivation, especially when they showed an inclination to side with the kingly instead of the ducal interests. The degree in which Conrad II strengthened the crown against the feudal princes is manifested by the revolt of Ernest of Swabia, who was easily broken because the lesser vassals would not support him.[2] Internal disorder was less under Conrad II than under his predecessors;[3] yet he accomplished this result without re-

---

[1] Hefele, _Conciliengeschichte_, IV, 703; Giesebrecht, _Kaiserzeit_, II, 292. Conrad II continued the Saxon practice of conferring countships upon bishops, making six such grants, the most important of which were to Trier, Mainz, Utrecht, Brixen, and Paderborn (Bresslau, II, 506), so that the degree of power which the German bishops came to exercise was unparalleled (Gerdes, I, 354 f.).

[2] Wipo, chap. xxv.

[3] For extended discussion of Conrad's feudal policy see Bresslau, _Konrad II_, II, 356, 374; Nitzsch, II, 21–22; Waitz, VI, 261 f.; VIII, 244; Gebhard, _Handbuch_ (1st ed.), I, 288; Sommerlad, II, 227, 233; Gerdes, II, 50–57; Fisher, I, 239–40.

course to the formation of unions for peace in the land (*Landfriedenbund*).

Conrad II's treatment of the monasteries was more rigorous than that of Henry II had been. He personally founded only one new abbey, Limburg.[1] In 1026 he gave the monastery of Kempten outright to the Duke of Swabia in order to purchase his allegiance,[2] and when this intention failed of effect, in 1030 he gave some of the lands of Reichenau to Count Mangold in order to strengthen him in his conflict with the stubborn Swabian duke.[3] Lorsch, which Henry II had spared, was so reduced, owing to the diminution of its estates, that the monks had barely enough *naturalia* for their livelihood. In Tegernsee the monks dwelt in constant terror of losing the small remainder of their property. Lands of Corvey, Hersfeld, St. Maximin, and Echternach were largely distributed among vassals of the crown and even given to *ministeriales*.[4] Schwarzach was given in whole to the bishop of Speyer.[5] But Conrad II did not utterly disestablish any monastery as Henry II had done.[6]

Conrad II had a thrifty German *Haushalter's* dislike of extravagance and inefficiency, and the waste attending the administration of so many monasteries annoyed him. In this sentiment he had the sympathy of Poppo of Stavelot, who clung tenaciously to the austere monastic ideals of poverty and asceticism. Accordingly, Conrad II simplified and reduced the cost of administration of the monasteries by combining no less than ten of the most famous abbeys in Germany, among them Hersfeld, St. Gall, and St. Maximin, in Poppo's hand. It is said that the king contemplated putting all the royal abbeys in his hand. What this change accomplished for economy alone, to say nothing of increased efficiency in monastic administration, must be evident. The mere elimination of ten separate abbots' courts and abbots'

---

[1] *Vita Popponis*, chap. xvi.

[2] Hauck, III, 547; Nitzsch, II, 23.

[3] Bresslau, II, 366.

[4] Hauck, III, 548.

[5] Voigt, *Klosterpolitik*, p. 7.   [6] Feierabend, p. 6.

retinues was a great measure of economy.[1] Conrad II was niggardly in making grants to either branch of the clergy.[2]

In addition to his rigorous insistence upon economy and retrenchment in the monasteries, and strict accountability for intelligent exploitation of their property by the abbots, Conrad II was also keenly appreciative of the growing trade of Germany, which the internal peace and order established by the Saxon kings had promoted, and which was stimulated by the political connection with Italy. He was generous in distributing market grants and coinage rights among the monasteries.[3] The crown was a large contributor to the prosperity of the German church in this way under the Saxon and first Salian kings, in order that the church might be of material assistance to both government and society. We have few secure data to determine what the incomes of the church were from these sources, independently of its wealth in lands, but the aggregate was large.[4]

The gain to both state and church from this arrangement was mutual. The feudal structure and organization of the German church made it an inseparable ingredient of the state. It was impossible to think of a church independent of the state unless the church were willing to resign temporalities which represented nearly half the state, and which the

---

[1] Hauck, III, 483–89, 544; Nitzsch, II, 23–24.

[2] According to the records which have survived twelve monasteries received grants of land from Conrad II, the two most liberally treated having been Eichstädt, 30 manors, and Einsiedeln, 12 manors (Bresslau, II, 506). Limburg, which he and the Empress founded, received but one grant after the initial endowment (DD, IV, No. 216). Fulda and Quedlinburg were the only large monasteries which received grants, for usually Conrad confined his gifts to small monasteries. The same indifference—or economy?—characterized Conrad's attitude toward the bishops. Of 25 grants made to them, 18 were among 5 bishops, the remainder among 7 (Bresslau, II, 506). The gifts made to Meinwerk of Paderborn and Nithard of Freising were not "grants," but rewards for distinguished military service. The bishoprics of Meissen and Speyer were most generously treated (8 and 12 estates, respectively) (Stumpf, Nos. 2193, 2295–98; ibid., Nos. 2216, 2305–6). The Bishop of Naumburg received his reward in the chancellorship of Italy; beyond this he only received one grant of a hundred manors (ibid., Nos. 2249, 2242). Magdeburg got 40 manors in a single grant; Hildesheim, Eichstädt, Brixen, Salzburg, and Passau each one grant (ibid., Nos. 2444, 2416, 2493, 2465, 2330).

[3] Bresslau, II, 381, 389–90; Nitzsch, II, 24, 29.

[4] Lamprecht, DWL, I, Part I, 685 f.

church itself had accepted in times past with a clear understanding of the secular obligations which possession of them entailed. But what if the church became eager not only to be independent of the state, but to subordinate the state to the church? The bishops of Germany—abbots less so[1]—were lords of territorial principalities which equaled the duchies in size and power. They were ecclesiastical princes, often from the same class as the lay feudality, actuated by much the same spirit and subject to similar obligations. The emperor could not renounce control of the great preferments of the church; he could not forego the almost immemorial right of advowson without abdicating his power, if not his office.

The Cluny reform was unveiling its world-wide pretensions.[2] Four years after the death of Conrad II in 1039, Siegfried of Gorze declared that the only law recognizable by the church was that of the canons, and that whoever violated them defied God.[3] William of Benigne wrote to the same effect to the pope.[4] Gerard of Cambrai asserted the supremacy of the canons also.[5] Wazo, bishop of Liège, a former protégé of Poppo of Stavelot, broke away from his master's teaching of the dependence of the church upon the state and repeated the assertion.[6] In Italy, Peter Damieni published his famous tract entitled *Gomorrah*.[7] The guns of Cluny could by this time be heard in the distance. It was merely a question of time now, and that not long, before the attack of the Cluny reform upon the citadel of the German monarchy would begin. What the Cluniacs were accomplishing in France might also be done in Germany. "Away with any one who thinks God is local," exclaims Udalric in the preface to

[1] Yet Damieni, *De contemptu seculi*, Opusc. 21, complained of the insatiable land hunger of the abbots—*terram insatiabiliter concupiscunt* (cf. Anselm, *Ep.*, I, 71).

[2] Gerdes, II, 102.

[3] Giesebrecht, II, 82.

[4] Migne, *Patrol. Lat.*, CXLI, 82.

[5] *Gesta pontif. Camer.*, III, 51.

[6] On Wazo see Cauchie, *La Querelle des investitures dans les diocèses de Liège et de Cambrai.*

[7] Migne, *Patrol. Lat.*, CXLIV, 159 f.

his *Consuetudines Cluniacenses;* "who believes that what He has done in France cannot be done in the region of Speyer."[1] All the earlier local or sporadic movements for monastic reform, like that of Gerard of Brogne and of Gorze, all the accumulated resentment of the monks everywhere in Germany who had writhed under Henry II's and Conrad II's reorganization of the monasteries; all the feudal particularism abroad in Germany, especially in the Lorraines, and in Italy, which perverted a genuine moral force to spurious intent; the ambition of many of the German bishops for greater power, which tempted them to turn against the hand which had so long fed them; and, finally, the enormous ambition of a new and rehabilitated papacy, by the middle of the eleventh century were organized and compacted together into one formidable whole under the name of the "Cluny reform." Some account, therefore, of the origin of this famous abbey and the movement which it generated becomes necessary at this point.

The history of Gerard of Brogne (who died in 959) and the Gorzean movement throughout Flanders, Picardy, and the two Lorraines showed that the church, even in its darkest hours, yet retained some portion of spiritual leaven. But its success had been limited. In striving to revive Benedictine monasticism it had made the mistake of endeavoring to put new wine into old bottles. The Gorzean reform had been too conservative to succeed, and in the course of a century, after the passing of its early leaders, it fell under the yoke of local feudal powers. What was needed was a new and radical monasticism, and this the Cluny reform was.

The birth of Cluny coincided with the most disorganized period of the feudal age. In the midst of the tumultuous disarray which followed upon the collapse of the Carolingian empire, the inroads of the Northmen, the weakness of kings, and the brutality of a riotous baronage, amid the profound oppression of the peasantry and the unparalleled corruption of the church, the establishment of the Order of Cluny was a notable movement of protest and reconstruction. Out of a

[1] "Absit autem ut quisquis credat Deum esse localem, ut quod facit in Francia non etiam possit in territorio Spirensi" (Migne, CXLIX, 638).

soil saturated with blood, out of an iron society, sprang the flower of an ideal.

Cluny introduced into the world a new form of religious life. It was the first successful effort to give homogeneity and compactness to a monastic system which itself had succumbed, like secular things, to the corruption of the ninth and tenth centuries.[1] The rule of St. Benedict had proved ineffective for times which were out of joint. The autonomy and the independence of each monastery had left them a prey to the feudality. Cluny came to prove the truth of the old motto that "in union there is strength."

For a century before Cluny arose the necessity of monastic reform had been perceived, as the labors of Benedict of Aniane[2] show.

The abbey of Cluny, from whose ascetic precincts the movement was destined to come forth to overturn the world, had a humble beginning. In 910 William, count of Auvergne and duke of Aquitaine, for the safety of his soul deeded to Berno,[3] abbot of Beaume and Gigny, a small tract located on the borders of the little river Grosne in the county of Macon, in the midst of the hills which marked the watershed between the Loire and the Saône, whence in clear weather one might descry the blue ridge of the Jura. No spot was more central to Christian Europe, for it was accessible to the Alpine passes into Italy over which ran the pilgrimage roads to Rome, and on the edge between Germany and France in proximity to the future broad commercial highway which was soon to develop through mid-Europe via the Saône and the Meuse rivers. The territory was neither French nor imperial, but part of the "middle kingdom" of Burgundy.

At the time of its foundation Cluny was in a secluded and forested spot. The original group of Cluniacs was made up of six monks from Beaume and six from Gigny.[4] After seven-

[1] See Hauck, IV, 316 f., for the corruption of Benedictinism.

[2] Nicolai, *Der Heilige Benedict, Gründer von Aniane und Cornelimünster, Reformator des Benedictinerordens* (Cologne, 1865).

[3] On Berno's life before he came to Cluny see Poupardin, *Le royaume de Provence sous les Carolingiens*, p. 153.

[4] Sackur, I, 40.

teen years of rule Berno gave way to Odo, a young noble, a
native of the county of Maine, who had for some years been
in the service of William of Aquitaine and had then abruptly
renounced the world and come to Cluny.[1] With him the energetic and expansive history of Cluny really begins. He was
the first of a long list of abbots—all of noble blood—remarkable for their moral force and administrative ability.

While nominally adhering to the ancient Benedictine
rule, actually Cluny created a new type of monasticism, even
though its influence was exerted more to reorganize cloisters
already established than to found new ones. Practically most
of the *de novo* Cluniac monasteries were those belonging to
the Congregation of Hirsau in Southern Germany.[2] Cluny
emphasized manual labor less and study more than did
Benedictinism. It laid more emphasis on moral character
than on sentimental piety. It frowned upon bizarre and extravagant forms of asceticism. It aimed to establish and
maintain a balanced life, physical, intellectual, and moral.[3]
The Cluniac monks wore a comfortable, attractive, even ele-
gant costume; their diet was generous and wholesome, and
included wine and beer.[4] They bathed often, for with them
slovenliness was a vice and filth a sin. The ascetics and fa-
natics in the order were usually foreigners, as Hildebrand.[5]

[1] *Ibid.*, p. 41; *Vita Odonis*, Book I, chap. i.

[2] "Der Einfluss von Cluny im zehnten und in der ersten Hälfte des elften Jahrhunderts macht sich mehr in der Reform des Klosterlebens als in neuen Stiftungen
geltend; dagegen giebt in der zweiten Hälfte Hirsau auch der Klostergründung
einen neuen Impuls" (Waitz, VII, 185). The earliest purely Cluniac foundation in
Germany was the priory of Rüggisberg (1072); see F. Waeger, *Freiburger Geschichtsblätter*, Vol. XXII (1915).

[3] For the library of Cluny see Delisle, *Le Cabinet des manuscrits*, I, 518; II,
Part III, 459; *RQH*, XXXVI, 193–94.

[4] *Vita Majoli*, Book II, chap. viii.

[5] For interesting evidence of female opposition to Cluniac celibacy see Lea, *Sacerdotal Celibacy*, p. 154 and n. 1. The tradition that the Rule of Cluny was not codi-
fied until the time of Hugh the Great is now exploded. The genesis of the Rule of
Cluny has recently been cleared up by Dom Bruno Albers, O.S.B., in perhaps the
most notable research of its kind since the seventeenth-century age of erudition—
scholarly evidence that the genius of Luc d'Achery and his fellow-students in St.
Maur still survives in modern Benedictinism. These volumes are: *Consuetudines
monasticae*, Edidit Bruno Albers, O.S.B. Vol. I, *Consuetudines Farfenses* (Stuttgart:
Roth, 1900). Vol. II, *Consuetudines Cluniacenses Antiquiores* (Typis Montis Casini,

From its foundation Cluny was under the immediate authority of the Holy See and free from the control of any bishop.[1] Its material possessions enjoyed a similar immunity, for early in its history King Raoul of France (923–36) granted Cluny absolute and independent proprietorship of its lands, which made it completely exempt from feudal control—an evil which tortured so many monasteries in the ninth and tenth centuries.[2]

1905). Vol. III, *Antiquiora monumenta maxime consuetudines Casinenses inde ab anno 716–817 illustrantia continens* (Typis Montis Casini, 1907). Before the appearance of these works the oldest written Customs of Cluny were supposed to be the *Ordo Cluniacensis* of Bernard of Cluny, printed in Herrgot's *Vetus disciplina monastica* (1726), and the *Antiquiores consuetudines Cluniacensis monasterii*, compiled by Ulric of Zell and printed in D'Achery's *Spicelegium*, both drawn up in the eleventh century, though the relation of each to the other had not yet been determined. Dom Albers has revolutionized this belief by the discovery of far more ancient compilations among the MSS of the library of Monte Cassino and in the Barberini Library at Rome. The result of his researches shows that Cluny had compiled its rules before 930, that Abbot Majolus (954?–94) revised them, and that a further extension and revision was made between 996 and 1030. The Customs of Farfa are edited from a Vatican MS which materially differs from the version published by Herrgot. Dom Albers has traced back some of the elements of these customs to the Customs of Benedict of Aniane, who in turn was indebted to the *Concordia regularis* of Ethelwold of Winchester, who again goes back to the *Capitula* of 817 and the *Ordo qualiter*, which last was probably composed by an unknown Benedictine monk of Italy or Provence. Ulrich of Zell, author of the celebrated *Constitutiones Cluniacenses*, was born at Regensburg in 1029 and educated at St. Emmeran. In 1044 he became attached to the court of Henry III as his chaplain. His father and his uncle having become involved in a feudal rebellion against the Emperor, Ulrich lost the imperial favor and retired to Freising where his uncle Nitker was bishop. In 1046 he was in Italy, whence he made a journey to Palestine. In 1061 he was received into the Order of Cluny, became chaplain and secretary to Abbot Hugh and later prior of Marcigny. Late in life he returned to Germany at the time when Hirsau was at its height and built the monastery of Zell in Breisgau. He died in 1093, having been blind during his last years (see E. Hauviller, *Ulrich von Cluny*, Münster, 1896). The reader interested in this history may consult further: Dom Albers' summary of his editorial researches in *Untersuchungen zu den ältesten Mönchgewohnheiten* (Munich, 1905) and his article in the *Révue Bénédictine*, XX, 690; Miss Bateson's article on "Rules for Monks and Canons," *English Historical Review*, IX, 690; and Miss Rose Graham's review of Dom Albers' works in the same, XXIV, 121–24.

[1] J. Vendeuvre, *L'exemption de visite monastique* (Paris, 1907). No mention of such exemption of monasteries from episcopal visitation is made in the *Liber Diurnus*. But in the eighth century, and especially in the ninth century, the tendency of monasteries to resent episcopal visitation is manifest. Freedom came rapidly with the Cluny reform.

[2] The text of the bull of John XI is to be found in the *Bullarium S. Ord. Clun.*, p. 1. It is a matter of regret that Sir G. F. Duckett has omitted it in his two admi-

But the most notable feature of Cluny was its form of government. All the monasteries founded by or reformed by Cluny were directly dependent upon it. The mother-monastery alone was a monastery. There was but one abbot of Cluny. The reigning abbot chose his successor before his own powers began to fail through age.[1] The affiliated houses were all priories, though a very few which were so affiliated, out of courtesy, still were permitted to retain the old title of "abbey," as Vezelay, St. Germain d'Auxerre, and St. Bertin. In this wise the famous Congregation of Cluny was formed. The priors were required to convene periodically in the chapter-general under the presidency of the abbot, and the latter made frequent visitations among the priories. How centralized this form of government was, in contrast with the complete separateness of every Benedictine monastery from every other, is manifest. It was the feudal system minus the looseness and particularism of that system. The abbot general was a grand suzerain. It was the adaptation of feudal practices and methods to monastic organization, the conveyance of feudal ideals of lordship, homage, service, fidelity, into the cloister.

This combination of feudal institutions and ideals with monasticism in large part accounts for the rapid spread of the order. Cluny was thoroughly in harmony with the spirit of the age.[3] It also accounts for the attraction Cluny had for men of noble blood and the large part they played in its history.

---

rable volumes, *Charters and Records of Cluny* (privately printed, 1888). Cluny is not the first instance of this immediate dependence of a monastery upon the pope, as Gfrörer, *Kirchengesch.*, I, 42, thinks, but it is the earliest notable one (Blumenstock, *Der päpst. Schutz im MA* [Innsbruck, 1890], p. 33). Robert the Pious forbade the construction of castles in the vicinity of Cluny in order to protect it from the violence of the feudality (Pfister, *Robert le Pieux*, p. 306). For other examples of zones of protection see Mortet, *Recueil de textes relatifs à l'histoire de l'architecture en France au moyen-âge*, p. 114, No. xxxii.

[1] *Electio S. Maioli*; Migne, CXXXVII, 707; *S. Maioli elogium historicum*, *ibid.*, col. 719, chap. xvii; col. 737; chap. l, "Electio Odolonis," *ibid.*, col. 778.

[2] For list of the abbots of Cluny see Duckett, I, 24 f.

[3] On the history of this expansion see Sackur, *in toto*. A brief account may be found in Pfister, pp. 282 ff. Lot, *Les derniers Carolingiens*, pp. 116–17, has interesting data on the religious enthusiasm of the tenth century.

Like all great historical institutions the Order of Cluny gradually developed through processes of change and experiment. The characteristic feature of Cluny—the organization which placed all the religious houses of the order under the control of the central monastery—was an evolution of the eleventh not of the tenth century. When founded, Cluny lay within the bounds of Benedictinism. This intense centralization, the salient feature of the developed system, was not projected in the original organization. Nor was it, when realized, a complete novelty except in so far as it became permanent. For Benedict of Aniane, in the time of Louis the Pious, seems to have vaguely had such an idea of consolidation in his mind as a part of his ideas of monastic reform.

It is interesting to notice the different ways in which the "congregational" system of Cluny grew up. First of all there were "cells," or filial members of the abbey. The parent house would plant them, commonly under a prior, on different parts of its outlying possessions. The prior was a member of the capitular body of the great abbey, and he was able to make himself useful in connection with the management of its property as well as in keeping up the supply of monks. . . . . A second method of extension was by means of influence and the prestige of the ascendant abbey. Monks of Cluny would be elected abbots in other monasteries. . . . . Often the recommendation of the abbot of Cluny would be tantamount to a nomination, so deep was the conviction that what men like St. Odilo advised must be in the best interests of the religious life. It was only a step further to place new or recently founded abbeys under the direct control of Cluny, and from this to the establishment of a definitely organized "congregation" the transition was easy.[1]

Like the earlier reform movement, Cluny's propaganda encountered bitter opposition from the monks. At Fleury the monks barricaded themselves in and hurled stones, shard, and other improvised projectiles at Odo.[2] At La Réole they

[1] From a review of Sackur, *Athenaeum* (Sept. 7, 1895).

[2] *Vita Odonis*, Book III, chap. viii; Sackur, I, 80. "It had long been ravaged by the Normans, and for some years the monks lived . . . . without any regular abbot at all; for there seems to have been a lay abbot, one count Elisiern, who had been granted the monastery in fee, and who after a while repented him of his ways and begged Odo of Cluny to take the monastery in hand. Odo soon made his appearance, accompanied by several counts and bishops. The monks, seemingly not knowing who he was, prepared for a siege and armed themselves with shields and missiles. They sent an ambassador furnished with charters from popes and kings declaring the immunity of the convent from the authority of any other house. They proposed to appeal to the king, some to murder their assailant. But when

killed Abbon, the abbot's representative.[1] But the efficiency of its organization and the immense appeal which Cluny made to the imagination of the time ultimately secured its success over all opposition. Under the administration of Odo it spread over Aquitaine, Upper Lorraine, the valley of the Loire, and North Italy as far as Rome.[2] Every new acquisition in turn became a new center of propaganda.[3] Under the famous Majolus (954?–94), Champagne, Burgundy (the kingdom), German Switzerland, and Provence were brought within its sphere.[4] The great abbeys of Lérins, Marmoutiers, St. Germain d'Auxerre, and St. Maur-des-Fossés then became Cluniac. With Odilo (994–1049) and Hugh the Great (1044–1109)[5] Cluny spread over Germany, Hungary, Poland, Spain, South Italy, and England. The influence of Cluny was strongly manifested in Western Switzerland in the tenth and eleventh centuries. Not only the great abbots of the order, like Majolus, Odilo, Hugh, were in intimate relation with the last kings of Burgundy, Conrad and Rodolph III, and

---

Odo approached, riding on an ass, he was suddenly recognized as the Great Abbot of Cluny. All resistance was forgotten, and Odo entered into possession of Fleury. Henceforward he ruled it as abbot, and under him and his successor Archembald the connection with Cluny continued, Fleury becoming the centre from which the monastic reform was diffused in the province of Rheims and in Upper Lorraine" (*Athen., loc. cit.*).

[1] *Vita Abbonis*, 16–20; Imbart de la Tour, *Les coûtumes de La Réole*; Pfister, pp. 288–89; Pardiac (abbé), *Histoire de St. Abbon ... martyr à La Réole en 1004* (Paris, 1872).

[2] Sackur, I, 71–114.

[3] *Ibid.*, pp. 186–204; II, 133–54. For Normandy, Pfister, pp. 309–10.

[4] Sackur, II, 232–52.

[5] Ringholz, *Der heilige Abt Odilo von Cluny in seinem Leben und Werke* (in *Studien und Mittheilungen aus dem Benedictiner- und dem Cistercienser-Orden*, Vols. V–VI (Würzburg, 1884–85); P. Jardet, *St. Odilon, abbé de Cluny, sa vie, son temps, ses œuvres* (962–1049) (Lyons, 1898); Neumann, *Hugo I der Heilige, Abt von Cluny* (Frankfurt am M., 1879). Odo of Cluny came of a remarkable ancestry. His father Abbo was well versed in the law, who read for pleasure the novels of Justinian and the histories of Livy and Tacitus. As a manorial proprietor he was singularly just and intelligent. He was a trusted counselor of Duke William of Aquitaine and often sat in his court. As abbot of Cluny he was theologian, orator (witness his sermon on the burning of the basilica at Tours), biographer of St. Géraud, count of Aurillac, hymn-writer, musician, for he is the author of a dialogue on music, and with all these capacities, politician, diplomat, man of practical affairs.

with their successors, the German kings Conrad II and
Henry III, but the abbots personally displayed, especially
Odilo, great initiative in the development of foundations
which fell to Cluny owing to the lapse of older monasticism,
or new foundations which Cluny itself promoted. Romain-
motier, Peterlinger, St. Victor of Geneva, Rougemont,
Münchenwyler, Hettiswyl, Petersinzel, Leuzinger, were the
principal of these.[1] At the climax of the order in the twelfth
century Cluny ruled 2,000 priories.[2]

But before this summit was reached the great abbey had also invaded the field of the secular clergy. Without ceasing its
agitation for reform of the monasteries it began to demand
in imperative tones the reformation of the episcopate also.
The French bishops were more deeply involved in the coils of
feudalism than were the monks, and, moreover, many of
them were imbued with the ancient Gallicanism of Hincmar
of Rheims.[3] Indeed, Rheims, Chartres, Tours, and Cambrai
together constituted a school of opposition. Instead of adopting a compromising spirit the Cluniacs aggravated the irritation of the bishops. They refused to acknowledge any rights
claimed by the bishops over them, declared canceled all the
ancient obligations of former monasteries which had become
Cluniac, closed their houses when the bishops on their visitations asked for lodging, refused homage and the payment of
those manorial dues which the bishops had long collected
from the lands of the monasteries, imposed the tithe on their
own account, diverted into the coffers of Cluny gifts which
the bishops used to receive, ignored all diocesan or metropolitan authority, and dealt directly with Rome.[4]

It requires some effort of the imagination to appreciate

[1] B. Egger, *Gesch. der Cluniacenser-Klöster in der Westschweiz* (Fribourg, 1907).
For the history of the Cluniac priories in England see Dom Léon Guillbreau, *Revue
Mabillon* (1912). They were not numerous and mostly founded between 1077 and
1122.

[2] Helyot, *Hist. des Ordres monast.*, Vol. V, chap. xviii

[3] Gerbert of Rheims, later Pope Sylvester II, opposed the Cluniac doctrine of
the supremacy of the papacy (*Lettres* [ed. Havet], Nos. 192, 193, 217).

[4] See Pfister, *Robert le Pieux*, pp. 313 f. The letters of Abbon of Fleury, Migne,
Pat. Lat., CXXXIX, cols. 441 f., abound with information on this matter.

the depth of jealousy, not to say hatred, which divided the
two branches of the medieval clergy. The feud was due to
rival authority, both spiritual and temporal. The bishops
pretended to a kind of ecclesiastical suzerainty over the
monasteries in addition to their episcopal authority and right
of examination, often exacting an oath of homage when
ordaining an abbot.[1] Many monasteries, too, were required
to pay a portion of their revenues into the bishop's coffers.
Then the bishops roundly abused the right of hospitality
which they had the authority to exact upon their visitations,
often quartering a large entourage upon the monastery.
Title to church lands and the right to assess the tithe were
also subjects of feud between the bishops and the abbots.
The former opposed the claim of the monks to collect tithes,
citing the capitularies of Charlemagne and the findings of
councils to the effect that *decimae sint in manu episcopi*. The
monasteries, however, interpreted this regulation in another
way.[2]

The issue between the regulars and the seculars was
fought bitterly at various synods in the last decade of the
tenth century[3] and the first part of the eleventh, when the
kings of France, notably Robert the Pious, threw the weight
of the crown in favor of Cluny.[4] Hugh, archbishop of Tours,
made a special trip to Rome to protest to John XVIII against
the arrogance of Cluny.[5] But the papacy saw on which side
its bread was to be buttered, and that it could diminish the
powers of the bishops by supporting the monks and so enlarge the authority of the pope.[6] But papal intervention or

---

[1] Fulbert of Chartres, *Epistulae*, Bouquet, X, 448 C.

[2] The point is elucidated in a long note in Lot, *Hugues Capet*, p. 184 n.

[3] Pfister, pp. 315–16.

[4] "Les évêques, cette aristocratie de l'église, étaient pour lui [Robert] aussi
redoubtables que l'aristocratie laïque; ils voulaient se rendre maîtres dans les diocèses
comme les seigneurs dans les comtés. Les uns et les autres avaient mêmes intérêts et
représentaient le morcellement féodal" (Pfister, p. 305).

[5] Rod. Glaber, Book II, chap. iv; Sackur, II, 87.

[6] Pfister, pp. 319–20; Lot, *op. cit.*, p. 36. This feeling accounts in part for the
Catilinarian invective of Bishop Arnulf of Orleans at the synod of Rheims in 991
against papal corruption: "O lugenda Roma, quae nostris majoribus clara patrum

even papal anathema never wholly abated the feud. For years there was strife between Fleury-sur-Loire, the Cluniac bastion in Central France, and the bishops of Orleans, which finally came to open fight on the floor of a council and culminated in the offending bishops being summoned to Rome.[1] A similar incident took place in 1025, when the bishop of Soissons and the monks of St. Médard resorted to physical conflict.[2] In the same year the French and Burgundian bishops united at Anse near Lyons declared null and void the papal bull exempting Cluny from the jurisdiction of the bishop of Mâcon.[3] In 1026 Count Landri of Nevers dispossessed the inmates of a monastery belonging to him and replaced them with monks from Cluny, whereupon the Bishop of Autun threw his lands under interdict and so aroused the lay population against him.[4] At Tours there was prolonged quarrel between Archbishop Archambaud and the monks of St. Martin.[5]

Quite as acrimonious as these quarrels dividing the bishops and the monks was the protracted feud between the monks and the feudal nobles, who resented Cluny's attacks upon their immemorial feudal right to appoint to church livings and control church revenues. The history of the first Capetian kings of France, of the dukes of Normandy and

---

limina protulisti, nostris temporibus monstruosas tenebras futuro saeculo famosas effudisti. Olim accepimus claros Leones, magnos Gregorios; quid sub haec tempora vidimus?" (Mansi, *Concilia,* XIX, 131). Cf. Certain's article on Arnoul of Laon in *Bib. de l'école d. Chartes,* XIV, 455.

[1] *Vita Gauzlini,* Book I, chaps. xiv, xv, xvi; Sackur, I, 273 f.

[2] Bouquet, X, 474.

[3] Pfister, pp. 307, 317–18; Lot, pp. 156–57; Hessel, *Zeitschrift für Kirchengesch.,* Vol. XXII (1901). The extension of rural parishes owing to the movements of the peasantry in France has been studied by A. de Charmasse, "L'origine des paroisses rurales dans le département de Sâone-et-Loire," *Mem. de la Soc. Eduenne* (Nouv. sér, 1909), Vol. XXXVII. While such churches were proprietary foundations, there was fierce competition between the local bishop and Cluny for oversight of them—a conflict which generally terminated in favor of the abbey because of the hostility of the nobles toward the bishops.

[4] Petit, *Hist. des ducs de Bourgogne,* Vol. I, éclairissements xvii–xviii, xxvii.

[5] *Lettres de Gerbert* (ed. Havet), pp. 190–91.

Burgundy, and of the counts of Anjou and Champagne is filled with this struggle.[1]

The Cluny reform in its original purpose and policy and in its ultimate application constituted two very different movements, so different that the two were actually separate and distinct propaganda. The original Cluniac movement was a real movement for moral reform and was exerted in the monasteries only. It was a renaissance of the old ideals of poverty and chastity and aimed to emancipate the monasteries from the worldly and feudal practices which had been intruded into them. Owing to the peculiar conditions of its foundation Cluny was free from the prevailing confusion which obtained in other cloisters, for it was independently governed under its own abbot. Thus Cluny tasted of the sweets of independence and was free from political control, as other foundations were not. Moreover, there was undeniably a deeper spiritual life at Cluny.

If the reform had continued to be solely a reformation movement seeking to purify the morals of the clergy and to eliminate the grosser features of feudal abuse, its propaganda would have been both reasonable and salutary. But when the Cluny reform began to preach church independence as well as moral reform it invaded the field of politics and at once took issue with the secular authority, whose supremacy it challenged. This second stage was reached when the Cluny reform became identified with the papacy, in whose hand it became the weapon for the establishment of a universal dominion, and may then be fittingly termed the "Gregorian reform." For its purposes then were less religious than political, less moral than monarchical. This is the Roman stage of the Cluny reform.

Yet the movement was Italian before it became Roman.[2] But even thus early it was anti-German in its direction. Lombard and Tuscan Italy by the middle of the eleventh century had begun to chafe under German domination, and

[1] See Sackur, II, 24 f.; Pfister, pp. 180 f.; Luchaire, *Inst. mon. de la France*, II, 72 f.; Imbart de la Tour, *Les élections épiscopales*, pp. 177 f.; Viollet, *Inst. polit.*, I, 416 f.; Lavisse, *Hist. de France*, II, Part II, Book 1, chaps. iv and v; Book 2, chap. i.

[2] Dresdner, *Kultur und Sittengesch. der Italien Geistlichkeit*, pp. 20 f.

that a domination chiefly maintained by the imposition of German bishops in Italian sees. For the emperors, both Saxon and Salian, distrusting the native ecclesiastics, systematically appointed German bishops to Italian sees. Between 950 and 1000 the presence of 47 German bishops in the bishoprics of Italy is attested, and undoubtedly there were more of such of whom we have no record. Ever since the restoration of the empire in 962 the German kings had followed the practice of setting a certain number of German bishops over Italian sees who would be more devoted to their interests than native clergy were likely to be. The proportion of these foreigners varied according to the time. It was greater under Henry II (about one-quarter) than under the Ottos, when it was about one-sixth. The proportion also varied according to regions. German bishops were thickest in the suffragan sees of Aquileia, in the March of Verona, and in Ravenna. In Lombardy, on the other hand, there were many bishops of Lombard origin, a situation due to the vitality of the tradition of the ancient Lombard church.[1] The precaution was warranted, for by the time of Henry II all the prominent noble familes of North Italy were allied against German domination south of the Alps. Within twenty-four days after the death of Otto III in 1002, on February 15, in the church of St. Michael at Pavia, Arduin, margrave of Ivrea, already famous for his hostility to the Germans in Italy, assumed the iron crown of Lombardy.[2] Two years later the Pavians destroyed the German castle which was the key to the imperial hold upon the city.[3]

But the Pretender had undertaken an impossible task. Henry II crossed the Alps in the spring of 1004 and gave Pavia over to the flames, though Arduin escaped and con-

---

[1] The subject of German bishops in Italian sees in these times has been attentively studied in three dissertations: Groner, *Die Diözesen Italiens von der Mitte des zehnten bis zum Ende des zwölften Jahrhunderts* (Tübingen, 1904); Pahncke, *Geschichte der Bischöfe Italiens deutscher Nation von 951–1004* (Halle diss., 1912); Schwartz, *Die Besetzung der Bistümer Reichsitaliens unter den sächsischen und salischen Kaisern* (Freiburg i. Br. diss., 1913); cf. *Hist. Ztschft.*, CXIV, No. 1 (1915); Dresdner, *op. cit.*, pp. 28–29, 83–87.

[2] Pfister, p. 362, n. 1.

[3] Giesebrecht, II, 231 f.; Lamprecht, II, 278–79.

tinued to call himself "king of Italy" until his death in 1015.[1]
Henry II's humiliation of the Archbishop of Milan and devastation of Parma[2] foiled a plot for the massacre of all the
Germans in Lombardy.[3] The news of the Emperor's death
at Grona, on Saxon soil, in 1024 was received with shouts of
rejoicing in Lombardy, where the populace of Pavia utterly
destroyed the new citadel which Henry II had built.[4]
Conrad II again riveted German domination upon the turbulent country and colonized it with German bishops and German soldiery.

Italy was sullen and sore under the German heel. But
though revolt after revolt failed, nevertheless Arduin of Ivrea
and later conspirators managed to sow dragons' teeth in the
path of the Germans. In 1004 Arduin had vainly made overtures to Robert of France, true to the traditional Italian
policy of seeking some powerful intervention from without,
when he perceived that his cause was failing.[5] The suggestion was not lost. When Arduin died the Italian anti-German
party offered to yield the March of Ivrea to Rodolph, king
of the Two Burgundies, as the price of his intervention,[6] and

---

[1] Thietmar, V, 25–26; Migne, CXL, 96–98; Adelholdi, *Frag. de reb. gestis
Henrici*, chaps. xxiii–xxviii. Pfister, p. 362; Sackur, II, 14; Provena, *Studi critici
sopra la storia d'Italia a' tempi del re Ardoino* (Turin, 1844); Carutti, *Archivio
Storico Italiano*, Vol. X (1882), has traced the history of Arduin's house to the
old kingdom of Burgundy, when it was established in the Val de Mauritaine. One
of the best accounts of the history of Italy in the early Middle Ages is G. Romano,
Le dominazioni barbariche in Italia (395–1024) (Milan, 1909). The work termi-
nates with the failure of the efforts of Arduin to establish an independent kingdom
of Italy at the moment when the German rule was fixed on the north and the Normans were beginning to found their powerful kingdom in the south.

[2] Pabst, *De Ariberto II, Mediolanensi primisque medii aevi motibus popularibus*
(Berlin diss, 1864); cf. the array of sources and authorities in Richter, *Annalen*, III,
Part II, 312–20.

[3] Nitzsch, II, 32. For the Romans' hatred of the Germans in 962 see *Benedicti
chronicon*, Book I, chap. xxxix, SS. III, 719. For general evidence: Liutprand,
Antapod., I, 23; *Gesta Bereng.*, Book III, vss. 80 f.; Regino, *Chron.*, annis 894, 896;
Annal. Fuld., anno 886; Folcuin, *Gesta abbat. Leob.*, chap. xxviii, SS. IV, 69; *Annal. Qued.*, 1014; Sackur, I, 321 ff.

[4] Wipo, *Vita Chonradi*, chap. vii.

[5] The Lombard nobles were too fickle and tricky to be wholly relied upon.
"Principes regni fraudulenter incedentes Arduino palam militabant, Heinrico la-
tenter favebant, avaritiae lucra sectantes" (Arnulf, *Mediol. Hist.*, I, 15).

[6] Pfister, pp. 367–70.

when Henry II died in 1024 they offered the Italian crown
successively to a son of Robert the Pious, to William of
Aquitaine, and finally to Odo, count of Champagne, who in
1037 invaded Lorraine, took Commercy, failed before Toul,
and laid siege to Bar-le-Duc, where he was slain (November
15).[1] Once more retribution was visited by Conrad II upon
the rebellious cities of Italy, especially Pavia and Parma.[2]
However much Italy might be divided against itself with
warring feudal houses and rival bishops, its hatred of German domination and of the Germans has almost the dignity
of a national feeling. The chronicles for every century, even
from before the permanent establishment of German rule by
Otto the Great in 962, bristle with the evidences of it.

Ever since the intervention in Italy in 901 of King Louis
of Burgundy, whom Pope Benedict IV had crowned emperor
after Arnulf's death, Italy had been a field of exploitation for
adventurous and greedy transalpine Burgundians and Provençaux.[3] The overtures of the rebellious Italians in the
reigns of Henry II and Conrad II to Robert the Pious,
William of Aquitaine, Rodolph of Burgundy, and Odo of
Champagne increased this French influx. It was the Italian
national party which saw the political advantage latent in
the Cluny reform, abandoned open revolt for more insidious
conspiracy, and began to agitate against lay investiture as a
means of emancipating Italy from German rule. Then and
there the Cluny reform became a formidable political movement against the German monarchy, all the more formidable
because under the guise of religion it could pursue its purposes. "Reform" became a means to an end, and that end the
liberation of Italy. In soil so fertile with an anti-German

[1] Giesebrecht, II, 231 f.; Lamprecht, II, 278–79; Richter, III, Part II, 273–74
(*annis* 1025–27).

[2] Richter, III, Part II, 311, 319 (*anno* 1037). "The impression that he [Conrad
II] made in west Lombardy was prodigious; only the devil, it was there thought,
could be responsible for so much success" (Previte-Orton, *History of the House of
Savoy*, p. 178); cf. Bresslau, I, 133–34, 188; Rod Glaber, IV, 2.

[3] Poupardin, pp. 65–66, 223, and esp. pp. 377–99; Gregorovius, *Rome in the
Middle Ages*, Vol. III Book 6, chaps. i–ii; Lapôtre, *L'Europe et la St. Siège à l'époque
Carolingien*, pp. 330–34. For Italian feeling toward these adventurers from beyond
the Alps see Liutprand, *Antapod*, Book II, chap. lx; Book III, chap. xliv; Book
V, chap. vi.

spirit the Cluny reform found a congenial field. Many of the rebellious Italian nobles were ardent devotees of Cluny. Arduin of Ivrea, who had rebelled at the death of Otto III and had had himself crowned king of the Lombards at Pavia in 1102, and whom Henry II crushed, terminated his stormy career in Fructuaria, one of the earliest Cluniac foundations.[1]

But if the independence of Italy could be so secured, why not also that of the church in the same way? And if the independence of the church, why not the supremacy of the church? It was this enormous possibility in the application of the Cluny reform which Hildebrand saw, as did no other man, while he was yet little more than a simple monk. He saw the tremendous implications in the issue: that by identifying the papacy with a war to abolish lay investiture the papacy might not only emancipate the church from secular control, but subordinate, even demolish, the state. "Abolition of simony" was to become the slogan of papal victory. The Cluny reform might be made an Archimedean lever with which to overthrow the world. The time was not yet ripe to unveil a program of such colossal magnitude, but it was implicit in the enterprise of the Italian nationalist party.[2] Arduin of Ivrea's rebellion had exhibited marked antiepiscopal tendencies.[3] It is obvious that the original nature of the Cluny reform and this Italian nationalist expression of it were two very different movements.

Italy had early become a seed plot of the real reform, for its clergy in the tenth century was perhaps even more degraded and corrupt than that north of the Alps. Even corrupt and mutilated forms of ancient paganism had resurgence. The Benedictine rule was a reminiscence in such famous monasteries as Monte Cassino, San Vincenzo, Farfa,

---

[1] Fructuaria was founded by William of St. Bénigne in 1003 (Pfister, p. 266); Abbé Chevalier, *Le vénérable Guillaume, abbé de St. Bénigne*, p. 86.

[2] Giesebrecht, II, 30 f.; Lamprecht, II, 278 f.; Sackur, II, 1–14. Contemporary Italian literature at this time shows marked French influence and is prevailingly hostile to the Germans (Zimmer, *Roman. Forsch.*, Vol. XXIX [1911]).

[3] Giesebrecht, II, 240; Lamprecht, II, 284.

[4] Dresdner, *Kultur- und Sittengesch. der italien. Geistlichkeit im X. und XI. Jahrh.* (1890), pp. 51 f., 174 f., 263 f., 307 f., 362 f.; Schulz, *Atto von Vercelli*, pp. 40 f.; Vogel, *Rather von Verona*, I, 43 f.; Sackur, I, 93 f.; Nitzsch, I, 338–39.

Peschiera, and Subiaco.[1] Marozia and Theodora paid their soldiery with money and plate taken from Roman convents.[2]
— The Cluny reform was introduced into Italy by Odo, the second abbot, whom Alberigo, founder of a short-lived Roman republic (932–54), is alleged to have made abbot general over all the monasteries in Rome and its environs. In any case the famous monastery of Sancta Maria, where Hildebrand was educated, was established at this time on the Aventine in a palace given over to it by Alberigo, and a long series of old foundations reorganized by Odo, as St. Lorenzo, St. Andrew, St. Agnes, St. Sylvester, St. Stephen, Subiaco, Farfa, St. Peter in Pavia, and finally Monte Cassino. When Odo died in 944 the progress of the Cluny reform in Italy was interrupted for two decades, but was resumed under Majolus (954?–94).[3]

In 971 St. Savior in Pavia was reformed, in 972 St. Apollinaris near Ravenna, in 982 St. John in Parma, in 987 Monte Celio in Pavia, where Odo had been successfully resisted by the monks some years before. Pavia, significantly for the seat of the Italian national party, at this time indubitably the richest and most populous city in North Italy, became the chief seat of the order in Italy, where Cluny in 967 had acquired extensive lands both within the city and along the banks of the Po.[4] The reformation of Farfa about the year

---

[1] Gregorovius, Book 6, chap. xii, sec. 3 (Eng. trans., III, 307–10).

[2] For the general subject of monastic corruption in Italy see Dresdner, pp. 16–26. Rather of Verona, *Opera, 503*, asked the caustic question: "quorum vero major pars intrat ecclesiam divitumque an egenorum?" (Dresdner, p. 18, n. 2), Sackur I, 96–97. On Farfa see Gregorovius, III, 314–15 (Eng. trans.).

[3] *The Life of S. Guglielmo*, written by Raoul Glaber (Migne, CXLII, 609 f.), informs us that the saint was born in Lombardy, but left his monastery in the diocese of Novara to go to Cluny, whither he accompanied the abbot S. Majolus, when the latter was returning from Rome. S. Guglielmo became successively abbot of St. Saurin and St. Bénigne at Dijon. He was sent to the latter monastery for the express purpose "ad redintegrandum divini cultus ordinem qui in eodem loco omnino defecerat" (Porter, *Lombard Architecture*, I, 157).

[4] Bruel, *Recueil des Chartes de Cluny*, II, Nos. 1143, 1229, 1295. Karl Voigt, *Die königlichen Eigenklöster im Langobardenreich* (Gotha, 1909), is valuable for the history of certain monasteries founded in North Italy by the kings or their queens, upon the lands of the royal domain. The history of San Pietro in Ciel d'Oro in Pavia and of San Salvatore in Brescia is especially well treated (cf. C. W. Previte-Orton, *House of Savoy*, pp. 149–50, 178–88).

1000 was the work of Majolus' successor, Odilo, who founded La Cava near Naples in 1025. Odilo's greatest conquests
though were made in Piedmont, where Fructuaria was established in 1003 by his able assistant William of St. Benigne,
and Novalese in 1027.[1] The last is a curious example of
monastic migration, for the original monastery had been
founded in Bremen.[2]

But by this time—we are within the eleventh century and
in the reigns of Henry II and Conrad II—the Cluny reform
in Italy had ceased to be so much a reform as an anti-German and nationalist propaganda. The Italian who first saw
the Cluny reform in this new light was Guido of Arezzo. He
voiced the earliest deliberate formulation of medieval Italian
nationalism in a letter to Herbert, archbishop of Milan and a
bitter enemy of German rule in Italy, in 1031.[3] He was clever
enough, though, to conceal his political purpose under the
drapery of religion, and inveighed against the "simoniacal"
practices of the German kings in denunciatory fashion. But
"simony" with Guido meant not the *abuse* by the German
kings of their appointive power to church offices in Italy, but
the very exercise of that appointive power at all. He branded
lay investiture as heresy[4] and declared that countless thousands of Christians had suffered eternal damnation because
of it. In this wise the agitation was artfully made to gain the
support of the ignorant and terror-stricken lower classes in
the Lombard cities. A national and popular Italian and anti-
German party was thereby formed in Lombardy, of protest
against "lay" investiture, "simony," and the marriage of
priests, with a political undercurrent and a religious overcur-
rent of enmity against the German bishops. This was the
Pataria, in which the Italian feudality, the lower priest class,
the bourgeoisie of the rising towns, and the rabble were all
commingled.

Milan now, and not Pavia as formerly, was the center of

[1] According to Porter, *op. cit.*, I, 161, the Cluniac churches in Italy were far
from being the magnificent and sumptuous edifices which they were in France.

[2] Bresslau, *Jahrbuch*, II, 164, n. 4; *Vita Odilonis*, II, 12.

[3] Mirbt, *Libelli de lite*, I, 1-4; Bresslau, III, 271-73; Waitz, VIII, 425.

[4] Kayser, *Placidus von Nonantula*, p. 15.

this agitation for Italian independence, but most of the cities of the Lombard Plain were more or less partisans of the movement. Two Milanese clerks named Ariald and Landolph traveled from town to town, preaching in the churches, haranguing the populace in the public squares, and everywhere inveighing against the German bishops, the marriage of priests, simony, etc., in passionate and popular speech, seeking to fan the flame into open revolt and even going so far as to advocate the assassination of all German priests.[1]

The upper clergy in Lombardy, frightened by the violence of the agitation, implored the Archbishop of Milan to suppress it. Ariald and Landolph were condemned in a synod which the Archbishop convoked, and promptly appealed to Rome against the verdict. In 1056 Alexander II canceled the Archbishop's excommunication. The Pataria was formally recognized by the papacy.[2] In the next year Hildebrand, already the power behind the papal throne, and Anselm of Lucca, who had studied at Bec in Normandy under Lanfranc,[3] appeared in Milan as legates of the Holy See and concluded a papal-Patarian alliance, the league being under the captaincy of Landolph's brother Erlenbald, to whom Alexander II sent a special standard which he had blessed.[4] Thus officially recognized by Rome, the Pataria became bolder. The Archbishop of Milan and the German hierarchy in North Italy generally, frightened by the popular fury and the thunders of the Lateran, bowed before the storm. In 1059 they advocated, outwardly at least, the Patarian program at the synod of Rome.[5] The seeds of that revolt against the imperial authority in Lombardy were already sown which came to fruition in the reign of Frederick Barbarossa in the formation of the league between the Lombard cities and the

[1] Arnulf, *Gesta epp. Mediol.*, III, 11, SS. VIII, 19.

[2] *Ibid.*, III, 13, p. 20; Andreas, *Vita Arialdi* (Migne, *Pat. Lat.*, CLXIII, 1439, 1447).

[3] *Vita Alex.*, chap. ii; Labbé, *Concil.*, XII, 69.

[4] Arnulf, III, 14, p. 20; 16, p. 21; Bonizo, VI, 592; Andreas, 33; Migne, *Pat. Lat.*, CLXIII, 1455; Bernold, *Annal.* (1077), p. 305.

[5] Petr. Dam., *Epp.* I, xlii; Arnulf, III, 14-15, p. 21; Bonizo, VI, 593; Meyer von Knonau, *Jahrbuch*, I, 131.

papacy in 1167, when the independence of Lombardy was won on the battlefield of Legnano (1178) and at the peace of Constance (1183). The papacy had scattered dragons' teeth in the imperial path in Italy.

The eleventh century is one of the most fascinating of epochs to the psychological historian, for a religious renaissance, so to speak, then actuated Europe which took many and intense forms of expression. The Cluny reform and the Crusades were the two greatest of these. But the variety of the stirrings of the new consciousness was almost infinite. Almost a craze for the building of new and more magnificent churches developed, from which was born the first positive example of medieval ecclesiastical architecture, the Romanesque.[1] New heresies appeared, symptomatic of fervent religious thought.[2] Relic worship became a mania.[3] The Truce of God attempted to suppress the worst features of private war and made strong appeal to the popular mind.[4] Pilgrim-

[1] Rodolph Glaber's beautiful figure descriptive of this enthusiasm for church building is famous: "contigit in universo pene terrarum orbe, precipue tamen in Italia et in Galliis, innovari ecclesiarum basilicas. . . . . Erat enim instar ac si mundus ipse, excutiendo semet, rejecta vetustate, passim candidam ecclesiarum vestem indueret" (Book III, chap. iv, sec. 13 [ed. Prou]); cf. Mortet, *Textes relatifs à l'hist. de l'architecture*, Nos. XXXI and XLI. For a vivid account of the building of a monastery see Ord. Vit., *Hist. eccles.*, Book VIII, chap. xxvii; Guibert de Nogent, *De vita sua* (ed. Bourgin, 1907), pp. 85, 110, 193–94, testifies to the same enthusiasm. For literature see Viollet le Duc, *Dict. d'architecture*, I, 107–30, 241–42; Merimée, *Études sur les arts au moyen âge*, chap. i; Reinach, *Story of Art*, p. 98; Moore, *Gothic Architecture*, chap. i; Kurth, *Notger de Liège*, Vol. I, chap. xv; Rosières, *La chaire française*, Vol. II, chap. vi; Mortet, *op. cit.*, Introd., pp. xxxi–xlviii; Enlart, *Manuel de l'archéologie franc*, Vol. I, chap. iv, esp. pp. 202, 206, 208–9.

[2] Rod. Glaber, Book II, chap. xi; Book III, chap. viii; Book IV, chap. ii. For literature see Pfister, pp. 325 f.; Lea, *Hist. of Inquisition*, I, 108 f.; Rosières, *La chaire française*, Vol. I, chap. ii; Sackur, II, 30–32; Rénan, *Averroes et averroisme*, pp. 284 f.; Havet, *Bib. de l'école des chartes*, XLI, 570 f.; Lea, *Sacerdotal Celibacy*, chap. xiii; Hahn, *Gesch. der Ketzer im Mittelalter, besonders im 11, 12, und 13. Jahrhundert* (Stuttgart, 1845).

[3] Rod. Glaber, Book III, chap. vi; Petrus Venerabilis, *De miraculis*, Book II; Guibert de Nogent, *De pignoribus sanctorum* (Migne, CLVI, 607–79); Lefranc, *Le traité des réliques de Guibert de Nogent* (in *Études Monod*); Duchesne, *Les origines du culte chrêtien*, pp. 265–90; Reuter, *Gesch. der relig. Aufklärung im Mittelalter*, I, 147 f.; Harnack, *Hist. of Dogma*, V, 267, 302–8; VII, 54 f.; Wattenbach, *Deutschlands Geschichtsquellen*, II, 247 f., has good bibliography for Germany.

[4] On the Truce of God see Luchaire, *Manuel*, pp. 231–33 (bib.); Holtzmann, *Franz. Verfassungsgesch.*, pp. 127, 129, 164 f., 153 (bib.); Lavisse, *Histoire de France*, II, 2, 133–38 (bib.).

ages to the Holy Land enormously increased.[1] The first intimations of chivalry, that curious commingling of the ideals
of a military society and of the faith of the Middle Ages,
began to be manifest.[2]

In such an atmosphere the Cluny reform had operated
until it became identified with Italian nationalist sentiment
in Lombardy, with feudal resistance to the monarchy in
Germany, and finally with the papacy, which saw in it, not
merely an instrument for securing the independence of the
church from secular control, but a means wherewith to overthrow the state. stupid

This stage was reached between 1046 and 1056 with the
ascendancy of Hildebrand in the curia in 1046 and the accession of Henry IV to the German throne in 1056. The first
period of the Cluny reform was a genuine and legitimate
movement for reformation of the medieval clergy, especially
the monks. The second, or Hildebrandine, period was a huge
political propaganda for the establishment of papal supremacy over the national churches and over the nations, masked
under the guise of religion and morality.

When the Cluny reform had first entered Germany out of
France the attitude of the German kings had not been one of
hostility to it.[3] Henry II had encouraged the movement and
can hardly be accused of merely playing politics because he
used the reform in order to secularize much of the lands of the
monasteries whose misuse of their wealth had become a
scandal, and which needed to be bled for their own health's
sake.[4] Conrad II had been a *Realpolitiker*. But though he

[1] See Pfister, pp. 344 f.; Bréhier, *L'Eglise et l'Orient au moyen âge*, pp. 42–54;
Lalanne, "Des pélerinages en Terre Sainte avant les croisades," *Bib. de l'école des
chartes* (1845), p. 1; Riant, "Les établissements latins de Jérusalem au Xe siècle,"
Mem. de l'acad. d. inscrip., XXI, Part II, 151 f.; Lavisse, II, Part II, 81.

[2] Wattenbach, in *Deutschlands Geschichtsq.* (5th ed.), II, 217–23, has some
admirable pages characterizing and summarizing the processes indicated in this
paragraph. See also Flach, *Les origines de l'anc. France*, II, 431–579; Lavisse, II,
Part II, 139–43 (bib.); Luchaire, *Manuel* (index); Guilhiermoz, *L'origine de la
noblesse en France au moyen âge*; Garreau, *L'état social de la France au temps des
croisades*, pp. 165–90. The close affiliation between Cluny and chivalry still is to be
worked out.

[3] Lamprecht, II, 327.

[4] Hauck, III, 448 ff.

seems to have been without the religious sentiment of Henry II, in the main his ecclesiastical policy was sane and just.[1]

Henry III, however, was distinctly a man of the high eleventh century, one deeply and sincerely religious. The argument of expediency was without force with him; his actions had to have a moral sanction as well. This religious earnestness pervaded the whole working of his government.[2] Henry III's marriage with Agnes of Poitiers, daughter of William V of Aquitaine,[3] undoubtedly accented his attachment for things French and inclined him more than ever to be favorable to the Cluny reform, for Cluny had been founded by a duke of Aquitaine, and the house had ever taken interest in its history.

No medieval German ruler assumed the crown under more favorable conditions or exercised his authority with greater power than did Henry III. Of the six German duchies two only, Saxony and Lorraine, had independent dukes. The four others, Franconia, Swabia, Bavaria, and Carinthia were in the king's hands. From the Rhine to Moravia, from the Harz to the Brenta, Henry III was both duke and king. But unfortunately Henry III was less practical than his predecessors and of a more refined education, and fell under the charm of the priest class. The future was already determined when the emperor, without reservation, espoused the Cluny reform. He was betrayed from the beginning of his reign by those in whom he reposed confidence.[4] His endeavor to put a stop to simony was more laudable than successful, for it chiefly diverted the revenues from appointment to church benefices from the treasury of the king into the pockets of his officials.[5]

[1] Voigt, pp. 3–8; Feierabend, p. 5.

[2] For estimates of the character of Henry III see Hauck, III, 572 f.; Nitzsch, II, 38–40; Gerdes, II, 119–21.

[3] Henry III's French marriage irritated the German clergy (Hauck, III, 571; and letter of Siegfried of Gorze to Poppo of Stavelot in Giesebrecht, II, 702 [4th ed.]).

[4] Bresslau, III, 271 f.; Waitz, VIII, 425; Francisz, *Der deutsche Episkopat in s. Verhaeltniss zu Kaiser und Reich unter Heinrich III* (Regensburg, 1878).

[5] Henry III's sacrifice of the royal patronage financially embarrassed his government. He gave generously to the church, which already was perilously rich; the

In the synod of Constance, at the close of a successful campaign against the Hungarians, in gratitude for the victory, and perhaps sentimentally affected by the recent death of his mother, the emperor publicly pardoned all his enemies.[1] He petitioned Siegfried of Gorze, an austere reformer, to pray for him.[2] He wanted to make Richard of St. Vannes in Verdun, the Cluniac leader in Germany, a bishop. While the reform principles of Cluny appealed to his conscience, the Italian Camaldoli appealed to his religious emotion.[3] He abandoned his father's unfinished and sensible plan for consolidated management of the royal abbeys.

Yet Henry III was not clay in the hands of the Cluniacs. His conception of his prerogative was perhaps even more theocratic than that of Charlemagne had been. He treated the papacy as he would a bishopric. Matters of faith were one field, politics was another.[4] He was not afraid of collision with the Cluniacs and those bishops (and there were not a few at this time in Germany) who were tinctured with "reform," but he did not have the discernment to sense the danger in their opposition.

Meanwhile, the immense significance of the Cluniac movement in Italy had been perceived north of the Alps. In 1044 Henry promised the bishopric of Ravenna to a canon of Cologne named Widger, over the protest of a synod at Pavia. The new bishop was so rash as to celebrate mass without yet having received formal investiture from the emperor. For this breach he was summoned to the synod of Aachen, over which Henry III presided. But when Widger was brought forward for trial Wazo, archbishop of Liège, declared that the emperor had no authority to summon an Italian priest before

---

church at Goslar, for example, was given one-ninth of the income from the local crown lands. At one time Henry III was so cramped for funds that he was compelled to pawn the crown jewels (Waitz, VIII, 292).

[1] Hauck, III, 572.

[2] Giesebrecht, II, 718.

[3] Pfister, p. 312; Hauck, III, 572. See W. Franke, *Romuald von Camaldoli und seine Reformtätigkeit zur Zeit Ottos III.*

[4] Hauck, III, 577; Gebhard, I, 280.

a German ecclesiastical body, and that furthermore only the pope had the right to appoint bishops.[1] Italy, Lorraine, and the Flemish lands had struck hands and were all linked together in organized protest by the Cluny reform, now a regular political machine under papal direction. The emperor stood by his guns and deposed Widger, but it was a frontal attack upon the German monarchy. Two years later, when Henry offered the archbishopric of Lyons to Halinard, abbot of St. Benigne, the haughty abbot denied to the king's face his right of investiture and refused to do homage to him at the diet of Speyer in August, 1046.[2] This bold action was applauded by Richard of St. Vannes and the bishop of Toul, the future Leo IX.

But events far more significant than these soon happened in Italy. In 1045 there were three rival popes in Rome. To put an end to this scandal Henry III called a synod at Pavia. Peter Damieni, an enthusiastic admirer of the Holy Roman Empire, who had sustained Henry in the recent controversy over Widger,[3] was inclined to favor Gregory VI, although he was alleged to have bought the papal office, because, as pope, he had openly pronounced against simony.[4] The Emperor hesitated and called another synod at Sutri, where all three popes were deposed.[5] When Adalbert of Bremen declined the

---

[1] Hauck, III, 578–79; Sackur, II, 284; Hegel, *Städteverfassung von Italien*, II, 230; Nitzsch, II, 42; Bresslau, I, 309.

[2] Sackur, II, 274–75.

[3] *Ep.*, VII, 2.

[4] Jaffé-Wattenbach, 4126, 4130.

[5] A mystery still hangs over what happened at the synod of Sutri. Did Henry III depose Gregory VI, as he did the others, or did Gregory VI abdicate? According to Kroymer, *Hist. Vierteljahrschrift*, X, No. 2 (1907), Henry III intervened of his own initiative and called a synod at Pavia; Gregory VI came to find him at Piacenza; Henry then called a second synod where both Sylvester III and Gregory VI were deposed; a third synod at Rome deposed Benedict IX. There is ground to suspect that under Hildebrand's urgency the pope abdicated rather than to have the papacy humiliated by an overt act of deposition performed by the emperor. The act, in other words, was done to save the theory of pontifical authority. This action of self-sacrifice on the part of Gregory VI may have been the reason why Hildebrand, when made pope himself, took the name of Gregory, too, as a tribute to his friend. If true, it shows that Hildebrand was a master of intrigue or an ardent zealot of the "new" Clunyism. See the interesting article by Sir Frederick Pollock,

honor,[1] Henry III chose the Bishop of Bamberg, who took the name of Clement II and crowned Henry emperor. The Cluniacs sullenly acquiesced, comforting themselves with the reflection that Clement II had also pronounced against simony. But when the new pope soon died and Henry appointed the Bishop of Brixen as Damasus II, and a few months later, on his decease, Bruno of Toul became Leo IX, the triple exhibition of imperial control of the Holy See was too much for the Cluniacs. The Bishop of Liège bluntly told the Emperor that he had no right to appoint the pope,[2] and in France an anonymous pamphlet was circulated against Henry.[3]

But the reform party quickly went from despair to elation. Henry III with his passionate idealism, his religious emotionalism, could not read men. Already he had naïvely appointed bishops imbued with Hildebrandine ideas to Italian sees.[4] Now he little realized, when he gave the papal scepter to his uncle Bruno of Toul, that he was undermining his own

"The Pope Who Deposed Himself," *English Historical Review*, X, 123–24, and cf. Sackur, *Neues Archiv*, XXIV, 734 f. R. L. Poole has published a study entitled "Benedict IX and Gregory VI" (*Proceedings of the British Academy*, Vol. VIII). I have not seen the original article, but a review of it in the *English Historical Review* (April, 1918), pp. 278–79, states that "Mr. Poole shows that the usual version that there were three popes co-existing at the same time, whom the emperor Henry III had deposed in 1046, is a mere popular tale given out, he considers, by the imperial entourage, for Benedict IX had abdicated and the anti-pope Sylvester III (John bishop of the Sabina) had abandoned his claims. In fact, at Sutri the reigning pope Gregory VI was deposed for simony, and at Rome the ex-pope Benedict IX was also deposed, presumably because the validity of his abdication was considered doubtful. It would be a natural source of the tale of the three rival popes. . . . . Mr. Poole further makes it probable that the Tusculan popes, though no model ecclesiastics, have been painted in over-dark colors; and gives an explanation of the descent of Gregory VI and his connection with Gregory VII which satisfactorily combines the available evidence."

The question whether a pope may designate his successor has been mooted by some modern historians. Hollweck, *Archiv. f. kath. Kirchenrecht*, LXXIV, Heft 3 (1895), 329, contends that Pius IV, Felix IV, and Boniface III did so, but admits that such instances are very exceptional. In the next volume (1896), Heft 3, Holder severely criticizes this position, and denies that the pope ever has had the right to designate his successor.

[1] *Adam of Bremen*, III, 7. [2] *Gesta epp. Leod.*, II, 65.

[3] *De ordine pontif.*; Hauck, III, 599; Sackur, II, 305, n. 2.

[4] Hauck, III, 609.

throne, for Leo IX proved to be a devoted Cluniac.[1] From his pontificate (1049-54) dates the immense influence of Hildebrand,[2] with whom worked Halinard of Lyons, a notorious ultramontanist,[3] Humbert, soon to be the author of a famous Cluniac tract, and a swarm of Lorrainer and Burgundian prelates.[4]

The Cluny reform betrayed the trust reposed in it by Henry III. Would it have been applied so vigorously without imperial support? In the synod of Sutri in 1046 the Emperor was more radical than the monks, than even Peter Damieni, who were willing to recognize the simoniacal Gregory VI. In the election of the popes the Emperor observed the ancient formalities of election by the clergy and people of Rome; he labored constantly not to offend public opinion and to please the orthodox party. He renounced the dignity of "patrician" at the instance of Victor II, and the gold ring which the Roman government regularly presented to each new emperor; he waived the imperial right to preside over the conference which elected the pope, together with the right of investiture of the pope. At the synod of Aachen (1046) Henry III interdicted simony and never practiced it himself. He encouraged Leo IX; gave him full liberty of action. He did not remove Archbishop Halinard of Lyons, although the Archbishop haughtily refused to take the oath of fidelity to the Emperor. No ruler since Charlemagne had exercised such great sway over the church as Henry III. But he was sincerely convinced that the church must be moral to render effective service.

Hitherto the popes had been accustomed to assign the presidency of synods to legates. But Leo IX traveled from country to country and personally inquired, examined, authorized.[5] The keynote of the future was sounded at the

---

[1] *Ibid.*, III, 600; see Lamprecht's characterization, II, 308, and Drehmann, *Pabst Leo IX und die Simonie* (Berlin, 1908). Bernheim, *Hist. Ztschft.*, CII, No. 2, contests some of his points.

[2] *Ibid.*, III, p. 597, n. 1.

[3] Steindorff, *Jahrbuch*, II, 54 n.

[4] Sackur, II, 314-15.　　　　　[5] Hauck, III, 601 and note.

synod of Rheims in October, 1049.[1] Three canons of that assembly were of great importance. The very first one read: "Ne quis sine electione cleri et populi ad regimen ecclesiasticum proberetur."[2] The second forbade the purchase and sale of altars, church offices, or churches. The third made it obligatory upon all bishops to enforce the canons of election and installation. Bishop after bishop came forward and made obeisance to the pope.[3] From Rheims, Leo IX went to Mainz where he received like homage.[4] The pope preached to the people in their own tongue, presided over the synod, and everywhere proclaimed the teachings of the Cluny reform. The changed relation between pope and emperor is significant. The pope was gradually and artfully edging the emperor out of his legal and traditional headship of state and church.[5]

The policy of Leo IX was new, yet not novel. It was a reassertion of the pretensions of Pope Nicholas I in the ninth century. The new Pope showed the nature of his ideas from the first, for even when still Bruno of Toul, he refused to assume the papal office until he had received confirmation of the Emperor's choice from the clergy and people of Rome. Yet Leo IX was not so uncompromising a reformer as to let principle always rule above policy. In the year after his election (1050) he did not hesitate to violate the principle of free election of bishops by the clergy in the case of the see of Nantes where he thrust in Airard, abbot of St. Paul's in Rome, without any regard for the local clergy. In the Council of Rheims, Leo IX emphatically asserted his position as

[1] Sackur, II, 322–23.

[2] Mansi, *Concilia*, Vol. XIX, cols. 796 f.; Bonizo rightly said of this legislation, "Haec gladium in viscera mersit inimici."

[3] Hauck, III, 613. The pope and the emperor seem to have presided as co-equals at the synod of Mainz. It is significant that Ekkehard, *Chron.*, 1052, SS. III, 70, writes: "Magna sinodus congregata est in Mogontia, cui Leo papa et Heinricus imperator praesidebant." Henry III at this time effected an exchange with the pope of a "complex" of crown lands in Lower Italy for some domains pertaining to the papacy in Germany (Steindorff, II, 216).

[4] *Ibid.*, III, p. 615.

[5] For extended demonstration of this statement see Hauck, III, 600–615, and Lübbersledt, *Die Stellung des deutschen Klerus auf päpstlichen Generalkonzilen von Leo IX bis Gregor VII (1049–1085)* (Greifswald diss., 1911).

head of the church, the universal spiritual sovereign, not only by proclaiming the apostolic supremacy of Rome, but also by summoning divers bishops, and even laymen, before the bar of the Council. The weakness of the French kings made Leo IX's ecclesiastical policy possible in France. The application of the same policy in Germany precipitated, with Gregory VII, a conflict that shook Christendom.[1]

The immense moral prestige which the papacy acquired during the pontificate of Leo IX was not lost; the cumulative force of ideas and things carried the papacy forward and upward. The brief pontificate of Stephen IX saw some of the fruits of his predecessor's reign ripen. Through the clever manoeuvering of Hildebrand and Anselm of Lucca the new Pope qualified without the usual formality of securing imperial approval. This success was followed by the bold stroke of Nicholas II in establishing the College of Cardinals (1059) and thereby emancipating the papacy completely from any legal control by the imperial authority.[2] The minority of Henry IV, the weakness of the empress-mother Agnes, the feud between Anno of Cologne and Adalbert of Bremen, at this time compromised Germany to such a degree that the papacy could do such revolutionary things almost without protest.[3] The provenience of these mid-century popes is instructive in this particular: Leo IX was an Alsatian, Stephen IX a native of Lorraine, Nicholas II a Burgundiun, Alexander II a Lombard. In these regions the Cluniac reform already had secured firm root.

---

[1] W. Bröcking, *Die französische Politik Papst Leos IX* (1891; 2d ed., 1899); cf. Hauck, III, 665 f.

[2] On the establishment of the College of Cardinals see Meyer von Knonau, *Jahrbuch*, I, 134 f.; Hefele, IV, 824 f.; Giesebrecht, *Münchner Jahrb.* (1866); Gustav Schober, *Das Wahldekret vom Jahre 1059* (Breslau diss., 1914). Heinemann, *HZ*, XXIX, No. 1, has shown that it was not the decree of 1059 which brought about the conflict between empire and papacy, for in January, 1059, the convention at Sutri had recognized the emperor's right as patrician of Rome and the decree of May, 1059, required imperial approval before papal enthronement. It was the decree of the Easter council in 1060 which permitted a pope elected outside of Rome to use the property of the church without having been enthroned that provoked the condemnation of Nicholas II and the protests of the imperialists. After the election of the antipope Clement IV the decree of Nicholas II was doctored by his partisans.

[3] Hauck, III, 664.

The monasteries in the reign of Henry III had enjoyed a new lease of prosperity to which they had been strangers since Henry II's time. In addition to recovering the right to elect their abbots,[1] they were liberally endowed again, even acquiring once more considerable parcels of the lands of which Henry II and Conrad II had deprived them.[2] They were protected from the greed of the bishops.[3] The monastic chroniclers are unanimous in testifying to the prosperity of the abbeys under Henry III.[4]

But the monks ill repaid the crown for its generous treatment of them. Henry III's work was ruined in advance, his deeply religious nature abused, the very monarchy betrayed. The Cluny reform which he so favored was at bottom insidiously destructive of secular government.[5] The pro-Cluniac monks who surrounded Henry III were secretly hostile to the German theory of government of a strong church within a strong state and were determined to reverse the relation. What they artfully called the "confusion" of temporal and spiritual authorities was not so in point of fact, for law and order was the ideal of and permeated the whole dual system. But it was this very law and order which maddened the Cluniacs. The mere existence of any sovereignty except that of the papacy was their ground of feud.

The German kings claimed the right of control of the German church because the German church had freely accepted the conditions under which its prosperity had developed. The state contended that if the church wished to possess temporalities it should abide by the responsibilities those temporalities imposed. "You cannot exercise the sovereignty attached to proprietorship without recognizing as all possessors of the soil do, a suzerain above you, to whom you owe homage, fidelity and service; without receiving from him your lands and the rights which inhere in possession of

[1] Nitzsch, II, 54

[2] Bresslau, II, 138, n. 5; Feierabend, p. 6.

[3] For example, the case of intervention in the feud between Herbert, bishop of Eichstädt, and the Abbot of Neuberg (Voigt, p. 15).

[4] Voigt, p. 19.   [5] Gerdes, II, 102.

them."[1] But a party had gradually grown up within the church which was eager to establish, not only ecclesiastical independence, but even ecclesiastical supremacy; which denied that the grants of the emperors had been made conditionally, or that the church had ever willingly entered into such a relation with the state. This party stigmatized all secular control of church offices as "simony," and found the readiest means to attain its end in a denial of the legality of lay investiture. This was the new teaching of the Cluny reform.[2] The war of investiture was at bottom a contest for control of church patronage, and the root of the whole matter was the temporalities of the church. The contest was fundamentally motivated by economic interest. Gregory VII and his successors strove to repudiate those feudal duties and obligations to both government and society which the church's possession of vast landed property naturally and legally entailed, and at the same time to keep the church's lands.[3] This important fact is what Arnold of Brescia and Abelard, the two keenest thinkers of the age, perceived and bluntly said. At the same time they pointed out the remedy.[4]

[1] Reply of imperial partisans reported by Placidus of Nonantula, Pez, *Thesaurus anecdotorum*, II, Part II, 75; Gerhoh, *De statu ecclesial*, cap. 24. On the other hand, the episcopate would rather die than sacrifice their temporalities (Gerhoh, *ibid.*, caps. 22, 24; *Chron. Casinense*, cap. 37; *Muratori*, IV, 516). The church could not possess land without recognizing and staying in the feudal hierarchy. This is what the Concordat of Worms recognized. It was a deviation from the ideas of Gregory VII, a compromise. The opposition of the princes forced the pope's hand. See letter of Albert of Mainz to Calixtus II in Martène and Durand, *Amplissima Collectio*, I, 671). "Sed quia tam imperium quam imperator tamquam haereditario quodam jure baculum et annulum possidere volebant, *pro quibus universa laicorum multitudo imperii nos destructores inclamabat.*"

[2] Hirsch, against the overwhelming evidence amassed by Mirbt, Hinschius, Dresdner, *et al.*, contends that this view was as old as the fourth century (*Archiv. f. Kathol. Kirchenrecht.*, LXXXVI, No. 1 [1906]).

[3] Placidus of Nonantula (1070). "Quod semel ecclesiae datum est, in perpetuum Christi est nec aliquo modo alienari a possessione ecclesiae potest, in tantum ut etaim idem ipse fabricator ecclesiae, postquam eam Deo voverit et consecrari fecerit, in ea deinceps nullum jus habere possit" (*Lib. de hon. eccles.*, chap. vii; Hinschius, II, 628).

[4] "[Arnaldus] dicebat enim, nec clericos proprietatem nec episcopos regalia nec monachos possessiones habentes aliqua ratione salvari posse. Cuncta haec principis

Arnold of Brescia was neither understood by church nor feudality. What his enemies called "political heresy" in him was nothing but the modern doctrine of national sovereignty.

Whatever the weight given to the influence in Gregory's mind of Augustinian ideas of a *Civitas Dei* on earth, whatever the arguments of papal legists and proponents, I am convinced that the papacy never would have attempted to translate these vague, abstract aspirations into actuality if the economic development of the church in Germany had not stimulated the papal ambition and created the opportunity. Naturally the popes kept this materialistic ambition in the background and forced the issue on other grounds. It used phrases like the "Rock of St. Peter" and the "Living Church" as clever watchwords in order to conceal its real purpose and to cover its conduct with the draperies of sanctity. But the real striving of the popes was for wealth and power, in the chief form in which wealth and power were embodied in the feudal age, namely, land.

It is a mistake, however, to think that as yet Hildebrand had complete control of the Cluniac party. There was a radical and a conservative wing in it, a left and a right.[1] Hildebrand, Cardinal Humbert, and the famous curialist Placidus of Nonantula, represented the extreme faction. Its position was that investiture was wholly an ecclesiastical act, and that the grace which was administered through the bishop's office must not be sullied by any form or degree of lay control. It contended that the feudal authority and the temporal functions of the bishop were merged within his episcopal nature, and that no differentiation could be made between them—a contention which was tantamount to depriving the state of all the enormous resources and political

---

esse, ab ejusque beneficentia in usum tantum laicorum cedere oportere. Preter haec de sacramento altaris, baptismo parvulorum non sane dicitur sensisse. . . . . Nichil in dispositione Urbis ad Romanum pontificem spectare, sufficere sibi aecclesiasticum judicium debere" (Otto of Freising, *Gesta Friderici*, II, chap. xxviii).

[1] All the advocates of the two-sword theory came from France or Italy, not Germany, e.g., Bernard of Clairvaux, John of Salisbury, Godfrey of Vendome, Nicholas II, Gregory VII.

authority vested in the bishops by the emperors from Charlemagne down.[1]

On the other hand, Cardinal Damieni was not so radical. He was a sincere admirer of the Holy Roman Empire and appreciated the debt which the church owed to the state. He distinguished between the purely ecclesiastical and the feudo-temporal nature of the bishop's office, and advocated a double coronation ceremony for the bishops, which would give simultaneous and just expression to the claims of both church and state. This is the germ of the idea which finally triumphed in the settlement at Worms in 1122.[2]

By the time of Hildebrand's ascendancy over the papacy, when the church began to pass from prelacy to papacy, the division of Cluny into two parties, an old and a new—or what I have just called a "right" and a "left"—amounted almost to a schism. The real Cluniac party was out of sympathy with the political designs of this radical minority.[3] We are specifically told that Odilo[4] sympathized with the work of Henry II and Conrad II in the reformation of the German

[1] Humbert was the author of the tract *Adversus simoniacos* (1059), which may be with right regarded as the opening gun of the Gregorian party. It is printed in the *Libelli de lite*, I, 95 f., and see comments of Meyer von Knonau, *Jahrb.*, I, 104 f.; Hauck, III, 674 f.; Lamprecht, II, 317 f. There is a large literature on Cardinal Humbert, e.g., Halfmann, *Kardinal Humbert, sein Leben und seine Werke* (1882); Giesebrecht, *Kaiserzeit*, III, 19 f.; Meltzer, *Gregor VII u. d. Bischofswahl*, pp. 37 f.; A. Fliche, "Le cardinal Humbert de Moyenmoutier," *Revue Hist.*, CXIX, 41–76. On Placidus see Kayser, *Placidus von Nonantula: De honore ecclesiae, ein Beitrag zum Investiturstreit* (Kiel, 1888). His tract is in Migne, *Patrol. Lat.*, CLXIII, 613 f.

[2] Damieni argued that the act of royal investiture was only for the church lands and not for the office (*Ep.*, 13, cited by Bernheim, *Zur Geschichte d. Worms. Konkordates*, p. 4). See also Ficker in *Wiener Akad.*, 1872, p. 100, and Kayser, p. 11. Waitz, *DVG*, VIII, 433–51, has summarized the arguments and contentions of both parties. But any secular investiture opened the door to simony, for in investing with the temporalities the crown seemed also to control the spiritual authority attached to the office. How could the two be separated? Cf. *Gesta Trevorum Cont.*, sec. 11: "Artificiosi colore commenti simoniacae haereseos sibi machina menta configunt, asserentes se non spiritualia, sed terrena terrenis acquirere." Pertz, VIII, 184.

[3] Hauck, III, 864.

[4] Odilo ordered the memory of Henry II to be regularly celebrated at Cluny (Migne, *Pat. Lat.*, CXLII, 1038; *Eng. Hist. Rev.*, XXVI, 33, nn. 7, 8).

monasteries; that Henry III "loved him [Odilo] beyond measure and humbly adhered to his counsels."[1] Cluny had

regarded with sympathetic interest every intervention of the emperors for
the reform of the church from the days of Otto I to Henry III. She had
rejoiced at the purification of the papacy, at its gradual ascendancy over
the noble families at Rome, and at the attempt of the reformed papacy to
tighten the reigns of discipline over the bishop. . . . . But further than
this she was not prepared to go, and when the movement under Stephen
IX turned from the reform of the church to its freedom the Cluniac held
back. The anti-imperial bias of the new reform movement estranged his
sympathies, and Cluny had perhaps stood too near to the emperors to get
the proper perspective. When, therefore, the movement for the freedom
of the church took new impetus under Gregory VII, and when the latter
worked to set the church above all worldly and temporal powers, the reformed monasteries took neither a decided nor a unanimous stand for the
papacy. . . . . Against simony in the church and the marriage of priests
Cluny cannot be shown to have been a pioneer. . . . . For any organized
campaign against either simony or the marriage of priests evidence is
wanting. Silence reigns on both points in the *Lives*. . . . . Dangerous as
it may be to argue from silence, it is perhaps still more dangerous to maintain a theory which, with no other proofs, is built up in defiance of that
silence. On this point we believe Kerker's judgment to be sound,[2] while
Hauck cites William of Dijon's zeal against simony as in striking contrast
with the attitude of the other Cluniacs.[3]

The original Cluny reform was designed to purge the
monasteries and to establish a new life within them. It was
indifferent to the condition of the secular clergy and held
aloof from them, frowning upon those members of the order
who were persuaded to accept episcopal appointments.[4]
Otherwise than this Cluny was chiefly interested in promoting the Truce of God, pilgrimages, and church-building.[5]

[1] "Qui supra modum eum diligebat, illiusque consiliis humiliter adherebat"
(*Vita*, II, 12).

[2] *William der Selige* (1863), p. 109.

[3] The quotation is from L. M. Smith, "Cluny and Gregory VII," *Eng. Hist.
Rev.*, XXVI, 25–26.

[4] Miss Mary Bateson says (*Eng. Hist. Rev.*, X, 140) that Odilo "had a strong
desire to be himself a leader or general of an army of monks."

[5] Mansi, XIX, 593; Pfister, pp. 164–73, 266. The influence of chivalry upon
Cluny is very interesting. This fact is the pith of the satire of Adalberon, bishop of
Laon (in Bouquet, X, 65), who attacked the military conception of monasticism in a

Even when the radical Hildebrandines captured the reform and twisted it to the ends of papal supremacy, Hugh of Cluny, although impotent to check the new tide, remained a conservative. Gregory VII reproached him for his indifference in the war of investiture.[1] Hugh was godfather to Henry IV and finally, according to Berthold the annalist, was excommunicated for his loyalty to the Emperor,[2] and when Henry IV was put under the papal ban the monks of Cluny prayed for him.[3] At the conference at Tribur and Oppenheim, Hugh was with the Emperor and did his best to mitigate the verdict.

The real originator of the "new" Clunyism, i.e., the movement to abolish lay investiture in order to elevate the papacy over the state, was Wazo of Liège. But with political Clunyism the conservatives of the order had no sympathy. Peter Damieni was an admirer of the Holy Roman Empire; the *Lives* of Majolus and of Odilo emphasize respect for secular authority and secular dignitaries.[4] To Abbo of Fleury "ascendancy of the crown over both worldly and spiritual

---

fable which Miss Bateson has paraphrased, telling "how a doubt having arisen in a monastery as to the interpretation of contradictory precepts, the bishop considered the matter and sent one of the monks to Odilo for advice. He returned in the evening mounted on a foaming steed. The bishop could scarcely recognize him. He wore a bearskin on his head, his gown was cut short and divided behind and before to make riding easier. In his embroidered military belt he carried bow and quiver, hammer and tongs, a sword, a flint and steel, and an oaken club. He wore wide breeches, and as his spurs were very long he had to walk on tiptoe. The bishop asked: 'Are you my monk whom I sent out?' He answered: 'Sometime monk, but now a knight. I here offer military service at the command of my sovereign who is King Odilo of Cluny' " (*Eng. Hist. Rev.*, X, 140). See further: Hückel, "Les poèmes satiriques d'Aldeberon," *Bib. de la faculté des lettres de Paris*, fasc. xiii (1901). For the influence of Cluny on pilgrimages see Pfister, pp. 344 f.

[1] Jaffé, II, 81; *Reg.*, I, 62, p. 81; VI, 17, p. 351; VIII, 2 and 3, p. 429. Cited by Smith in *Eng. Hist. Rev.*, XXVI, 29. Hugh of Cluny (1024–1109) was a French feudal noble, cf. A. L'Huillier, *Vie de St. Hugues, abbé de Cluny* (Paris, 1888).

[2] Berthold, *Annal.*, p. 289; for Hugh's activity in favor of Henry IV, Lambert of Hersfeld, *Annales* (ed. Holder Egger), pp. 290, 294.

[3] D'Achery, *Spicelegium* (ed. 1723), III, 426. "Neque tamen debita poenitentia errorem cognitum emendavit" (letter of Halinard of Lyons to Countess Matilda).

[4] *Vita Majoli*, I, 7; *Vita Odilonis*, I, 7.

dignities was the foundation of all public laws."[1] Majolus' refusal of the papacy when it was proffered him by Otto II
"showed no consciousness that such power of choice did not
lie with the emperor."[2] Imperialistic Clunyism was born in
Rome, not in France. The unapprehended thought of Wazo
and Cardinal Humbert was seized by the mind of Hildebrand, who, as Pope Gregory VII, converted it into a
thunderbolt: "Man darf geradezu sagen dass eine Parteibil-
dung überhaupt nur von Rom ausgehen konnte."[3] It has
been well said that "the century which is called the century
of Gregory VII, with much better reason might be called the
age of Cluny. For it was only because he was the greatest of
the Cluniacs that Gregory became the greatest of the popes."[4]

For six successive pontificates, from that of Leo IX to
his own ascension of the throne of the Fisherman in 1073,
Hildebrand was the power behind the papal chair. During
that period the Cluny reform had become an organized and
formidable propaganda directed by the Holy See; the creation
of the College of Cardinals had emancipated the papacy from
secular interference; papal power in Europe had been consolidated, especially through the creation of the papal legates;[5] the financial resources of the popes had materially in-

[1] Smith, "Cluny and Gregory VII," *Eng. Hist. Rev.*, XXVI, 23; cf. Sackur, II,
305. Duke William of Aquitaine broke up the synod of Poitiers in 1078, though a
papal legate was present (Mansi, XX, 495). Mr. Smith rightly says that "the
Cluniacs do not seem to have preached any special doctrine as to the papal power."

[2] *Ibid.*

[3] Hauck, III, 515; cf. Grützmacher, *Realencyclopädie für protestantliche Theo-
logie*, XIII, 183. Wazo enjoyed high repute in Flanders and the Rhinelands as a
canonist, and it is to be remembered that Hildebrand had once studied at Cologne.

[4] Dehio and Bezold, *Gesch. der christl. Baukunst im Mittelalter*, I, 387.

[5] Engelmann, *Die päpstlichen Legaten in Deutschland bis zur Mitte des 11. Jahr-
hunderts* (Marburg, 1913). For other literature on the institution of the papal legates
see Werminghoff, p. 205. Gregory VII's legates were nearly all radical Cluniacs, as
Hugh the Venerable, with whom Gregory continually consulted (*Vita St. Gregor.*,
AASS, Bolland., May, VI, 115; *Reg. Greg. VII*, 6; Labbé, *Concil.*, VI, 17); Odo and
Gérault, priors of Cluny (*Reg. Greg.*, I, chap. lxii); Hugh, the prior of St. Marcel de
Châlons, who suspended the archbishops of Rheims, Tours, Bourges, and Besançon
and convoked no less than ten synods or councils (Hug Flav, *Chron.*, p. 194; Bert-
hold, *Annal.*, anno 1078); Simon of Valois, abbot-prior of La Chaise–Dieu and later
of St. Benigne, who was Gregory's ambassador to Robert Guiscard (Hug Flav,

creased, both through extension and through improved methods of collection; the States of the Church were solidly buttressed on either hand by the establishment of papal suzerainty over the kingdom of Norman Italy, and the close alliance
effected between the papacy and Countess Matilda of Tuscany, a strong papal partisan and ruler of the most extensive
and compact territory north of the Norman kingdom.

In Hildebrand's brain were blended a huge ideal and a
practical, vivid political program.[1] There was nothing vague
or indefinite about either. Using the current feudal conceptions of the time he held that God was supreme suzerain of
the world, that the pope was God's vicar and vassal, that
every secular authority, every state, was to be held within
the overlordship of the pope, that national governments were
not rightfully independent sovereignties, but *imperia in
imperio*, that the church was both a political and an ecclesiastical empire as wide as Christendom and as high as
heaven. He claimed all Italy, with Corsica and Sardinia, as
the "States of the Church" in virtue of the alleged donation
of Constantine; that "Spain belonged of old to St. Peter,"
and that this right had never been lost, although the land

Chron., p. 229); Bernard of St. Victor in Marseilles, legate in Spain and Germany,
where he presided over the diet of Forchheim which deposed Henry IV, and was
papal agent among the revolted Saxons (Berthold, *Annal. annis* 1078-79; *Epp.
Greg.*, VII, 15); Richard, a brother of Bernard of St. Victor, who also served in
Spain. "His [Gregory VII's] chief means were synods held by the pope [this was
begun by Leo IX] and new ecclesiastical law books. The nephew of pope Alexander
II, Anselm of Lucca, became the founder of the new Gregorian church law, this
being effected by him partly by making apt use of that Pseudo-Isidore, and partly
by a new set of fictions, e.g., episcopacy everywhere originated from Peter, and
forgeries. He was followed by Deusdedit, Bonizo, and cardinal Gregorius. Deusdedit formulated the new principle that contradictions in the traditional church law
must always be harmonized by letting, not the older but the *greater* authority, that is,
the dictum of the pope, cancel the opposite view. . . . . . A sentence of his [Augus-
tine's] was so manipulated that it came to mean that the papal letters stood on a
level with canonical scripture," Harnack, *Hist. of Dogma*, VI, 18 n.

[1] Hermann Sielaff, *Studien über Gregors VII Gesinnung und Verhalten gegen
König Heinrich IV in den Jahren 1073-80* (Greifswald, 1910).
The question of the genuineness of the *Dictatus Papae* attributed to Gregory
VII has given rise to a large amount of critical literature. As far back as the eighteenth century Fleury declared it apocryphal; Voigt thought it the composition of a
papal partisan; Giesebrecht, who examined the original manuscript in the Vatican
archives, discovered no trace of interpolation, found the spirit of the document in

had been occupied by the infidel;[1] that Hungary belonged to the Roman church by gift of King Stephen; that Charlemagne had given Saxony to the Holy See; that "the empire is a fief of Rome."[2]

With less pretension and more concreteness Gregory VII tried to convert the conferring of the bishop's pallium and his episcopal oath into an act of homage and oath of vassalage to the pope as the bishop's immediate overlord. Except the requirement of celibacy, no demand of Gregory so stirred the opposition of the bishops, for it outraged their national sentiments as well as impugned their long-established political attachment to the emperor.

The most practical and the most successful of Gregory VII's reforms were in the fields of church finance and

---

harmony with Gregory's ideas and practices, and declared it to be of Gregory VII's own authorship; Rocquain, *Bib. de l'école d. chartes* (1872), pp. 378–85, from resemblance between passages in the *Dictatus* and in *Pseudo-Isidor*, thinks it a collection designed to reflect Gregory VII's ideas and known to him. Did Gregory believe the Pseudo-Isidor to be genuine?

[1] The popular spirit with regard to encroachments of Rome in Spain is well illustrated in the *Romancero del Cid* when that doughty warrior urges his sovereign to defy the pope who had just decided that Spain was subject to the Holy Roman Empire.

> "Enviad vueso mensage
> Al Papa, y a su valia,
> Ya todas desafiad
> De vuesa parte y la mia"
>   (cf. Lea, *Studies in Church History*, p. 406).

[2] Jaffé, *Reg. Greg.*, IV, 2, p. 241; *Monumenta Gregoriana*, II, 457, 461 f. For Gregory VII's demand of homage from William the Conqueror see Brook, *Eng. Hist. Rev.* (April, 1911). Weiland, *Ztschft. f. Kirchenrecht* (N.F., 1882), III, Heft 3, prints the letter of Gregory to O'Brien, the Irish chieftain. The question of the genuineness of the registers of Gregory VII has been the subject of new historical examination in recent years. Peitz, *Mitteil. d. Inst. f. oesterr. Gesch.*, XXXIII, Heft 1 (1912), declares that the Vatican example is the original register and was the work of Rainerus, the papal notary. He has attempted to apply the same method of demonstration with less success to the registers of Innocent III and Honorius III (cf. Casper, *Neues Archiv*, XXXVIII, No. 1 [1913]). Pflugk-Harttung, *Neues Archiv*, VIII, 2, finds proof that there was another copy of the register besides that preserved in a collection of canons of Deusdedit in Vatican MS 3833, written in the twelfth century. For imperialists like Wenrich of Treves, Hugh de Fleury, and Sigebert of Gembloux, the state was of divine origin. For the papalists it was of the devil (Mirbt, *Die Publizistik*, pp. 545–46). Gregory VII compared the papacy to the sun, imperial authority to the moon. The glossators calculated mathematically the papacy was

codification of the canon law. Gregory VII's achievements in
the field of finance testify to his administrative capacity and
the essentially material nature of his aims and projects.[1]
Ever since the ninth century, owing to the violence and insecurity of the feudal régime, it had been the practice of
weaker proprietors to commend themselves to the stronger;
sometimes the latter were bishops or abbots. But many
churches and monasteries, in order to protect themselves
from feudal spoliation, gradually fell into the way of putting
themselves under the patronage of the papacy. Through this
practice the pope often became the eminent proprietor of
lands of churches and monasteries widely scattered in Europe.
These foundations, thus liberated from any other human
control, lay or clerical, and protected against spoliation by
apostolic anathema, recognized this protection by paying an
annual sum (*cens*) into the papal treasury.[2] Under various
forms the papal patronage was spread over hundreds of
churches and monasteries in Germany, France, and Italy.
Gregory VII saw in the practice both a means to extend his
authority and a means to reduce the power of the bishops,
and a lucrative source of papal revenue as well, and so widely
extended the system. Not only ecclesiastical establishments,
but private nobles and even towns appeared upon the revenue
rolls of the papacy as "wards" paying for papal protection.
The pope thus became, as has been justly said, "a veritable
suzerain, to whom both homage and money service was due."
If we add to these resources the sums derived from the Peter's
Pence, from administrative fees of many sorts, and from the
Patrimonium Petri, it is evident that not for nothing had

---

47 times greater than the empire. One Laurentius rectified the "error" and found
that the papacy was 1,744 times greater than the empire (Gieseler, *Kirchengesch.*,
II, 2, sec. 54, n. D). In the sixteenth century Bodin ridiculed this calculation and
by pretended use of Arabic and Ptolemaic formulas declared that the papacy was
$6,645\frac{7}{8}$ times greater than the empire (*De la république*, Book I, chap. ix).

[1] W. Schneider, *Papst Gregor VII und das Kirchengut* (Greifswald diss.,
1919).

[2] P. Sander, *Der Kampf Heinrichs IV und Gregors VII von der zweiten Exkom-
munikation des Königs bis zu seiner Kaiserkrönung* (Berlin, 1883), pp. 113–14,
shows the bad condition of the papal finances under Gregory VII and his desperate

Hildebrand been *oeconomicus* of the Roman church before his elevation to the pontificate.[1]

It is difficult for a modern scholar accurately to evaluate the motives and practices of the Cluny reform and to do justice simultaneously to both state and church. On the one hand, one must guard against judging the history of the eleventh century by the standards and practices of the twentieth; on the other hand, it requires an effort of the historical imagination to appreciate the theories and to visualize the conditions which then prevailed.

Only an ignorant or a prejudiced man will pronounce a harsh or bitter judgment either way in this momentous controversy. There is much to be said—and much to be forgiven—on each side. We must discount the raucous, propagandistic, polemical literature which each party circulated. Each side had its rights and its wrongs, its wise men and its stupid, its strong and its weak, its good and its evil men. What Sir Gilbert Murray, quoting Geffcken, has written of the conflict between paganism and Christianity in the fourth century may be said of the struggle between pope and emperor in the eleventh and twelfth centuries: "Dieselbe Seelenstimmung, derselbe Spiritualismus."

It may be premised, however, that the absolute and complete separation of church and state was an impossibility in the feudal age. Granting this, there were two alternative courses open: (1) to define the sphere of authority of each in such a way as to give simultaneous and due expression to the sovereignty of each without jeopardy to the other by the

---

need of money. Schulte, *Der Adel, etc.*, pp. 212–20, shows the zeal of the "reform" monasteries for papal protection in the large number of forged charters which they fabricated. *Per contra*, the anti-reform abbeys forged charters to prove that their lands pertained to the imperial fisc. "Reichenau war eine Schmiede, in der nicht allein für das eigene Kloster, sondern auch für andere geeignete Urkunden fabriziert wurden" (p. 212).

[1] See on this subject Waitz, VII, 218–20; Schreiber, I, 9 f.; II, 463 f.; Werminghoff, p. 70, n. 4, pp. 184–85; Blumenstock, *Der päpstliche Schutz im Mittelalter* (Innsbruck, 1890); Hauck, III, 865 f.; Scheffer-Boichorst, *Mitteil.*, XIV, No. 4. Hinschius' criticism of Blumenstock called forth a reply in *Ztschft. f. Kirchengesch.* (Ser. 3, 1893), III, Heft 2. The fullest account in French of the origin and nature of the papal protection is Daux, *La protection apostolique au moyen âge.* See a review in *RQH*, LXXII, 5–60.

determination of the reserved or particular rights of each, and
at the same time to provide for enough articulation between
the two in order to enable them to function together by
specific delegation and concurrent jurisdiction; (2) failing the
establishment of the coequality of each in separate spheres,
the other alternative was either the supremacy of state over
church or that of church over state.[1]

It may be objected that the first solution was incom-
patible with the Germanic form of government created by
the Saxon and continued by the Salian emperors. This
is probably true. But there are clear indications that such a
solution was possible. The reigns of Henry II and Henry III
had shown that the political functioning of the church did
not necessarily exclude its spiritual working. The church, i.e.,
the radical wing of the Cluny reform which dominated it after
1049, was really the uncompromising party. For it was resolutely bent upon achieving the supremacy of the papacy
over both church and state.

The just and reasonable remedy, if the church chafed
under its relation to the state, would have been for the church
to renounce its feudal possessions and its feudal rights and
privileges—feudal lands, countships, coinage, and market
grants, octrois, regalian perquisites in general—and to be content with its allodial lands, which were of vast extent in themselves. Radical as this solution would have been in the
feudal age, it was thought of and suggested. The imperial
government was willing to make the performance, but the
church was too rich to make the sacrifice. It was determined
to keep its lands and privileges, but to repudiate the obligations to the state which it had assumed with their possession
—a policy little less than robbery under the guise of religion.
Firmly resolved upon this course from the time of Hildebrand's ascendancy at Rome, there was only one way for the
church to attain its ends, namely, to establish its sover-

---

[1] The papalists argued that investiture was a mark of dependence. Pascal II,
Ep. 3 *ad Anselm*, Mansi XX, 982: "Si virgam pastoralitatis signum, si annulum
fidei signaculum tradit laica manus, quid in ecclesia pontifices agunt?" and if
maintained, the church would become a fief and a fief more dependent than a secular
one, for the latter had the guaranty of hereditability while celibacy opened the

eignty over the state.[1] When the state resisted, the church
went to the length of seeking to destroy the state, to dissolve
the historical and legal bonds which centuries had developed,
by organizing rebellion and creating anarchy. In a word, the
policy of the Gregorian church was a rule or ruin one. It was
a policy of no compromise, not even shrinking from the
annihilation of civil society.[2]

The struggle between the medieval empire and the
papacy, some of the history of which has been anticipated in
the preceding paragraphs in order to show the nature of it,
began openly at the death of Henry III in 1056. The Hildebrandine party, already in league with the Pataria[3] and the
Lombard nobility, had also effected an alliance with the

---

door to free disposal of church offices when vacant by the nobles. The only remedy
was prohibition altogether of lay investiture in spite of the fact that it was a
revolution, although Gregory VII denied the utter novelty of it (*Ep.*, V, 5).

[1] Sigebert of Gembloux, the most distinguished man of letters who advocated
the cause of Henry IV, strongly inveighed against the Gregorian theory of temporal
supremacy and said it was heresy (Pertz, VI, 366). He also (p. 362) affirmed that
compulsory celibacy of the clergy was heresy.

[2] "The piety of the Carolings and the Saxons brought a nemesis in the end, for
one of the main agents in the downfall of the mediaeval empire was the territorial
ambition of the princes of the church" (Fisher, I, 81). Helmold, *Chron. Slavorum*, I,
4, says the German bishops were "princes of earth instead of heaven." Cf. Nitzsch,
I, 390; Waitz, VII, 202–3. There is enormous significance in the words of Theoderich, *De reb. Norv.*, chap. v (Langebek, *Scriptores rerum Danicarum*, V, 316), speaking of the policy of Otto II: "Iste est . . . . qui ecclesiam omnemque clerum plus
honorabat et pene plus ditabat quam expediret, subdendo ei pheodatos duces et
comites. Nam ex opulentia nata postea insolentia, ut usque hodieque est cernere.
Unde et illi, ut in Romana historia reperitur, ab angelo est dictum: 'Venenum ad-
didisti ecclesie.' " Cf. also Gerhoh, *De aedif. Dei*, chap. ix, on whom see Fisher,
Mediaeval Empire, II, 117–19. The *Dictatus Papae*, sec. 27, had theoretically formulated the principle that the pope could dissolve the secular organization of society:
"That he [the pope] may absolve subjects from their oath of fidelity to wicked
rulers." Gregory VII gave it practical application in the first deposition and ban-
ning of Henry IV in 1076, which threw Germany into the throes of a long civil
war. How revolutionary the decretalists thought Gregory VII's policy to be is
shown by the fact that Ivo and Gratian lay down the doctrine that obedience to the
secular authority is commanded by God, even when that authority is in the hands of
an unbeliever" (Carlyle, *Political Theory of the Middle Ages*, II, 146–47). Ivo of
Chartres, *Decretum*, V, 7: "Julianus exstitit infidelis imperator, nonne exstitit apos-
tata, iniquis idolatra?"

[3] On the Pataria see Previte-Orton, *House of Savoy*, pp. 223, 227, 230–31, 255;
Mirbt, *Die Publizistik*, pp. 447 f.; Wattendorf, *Papst Stephen*, IX (1883).

feudality of Western and Southern Germany. "Reform" was
the vehicle for expression of the enmity of the German dukes
toward the crown. Feudalism and the papacy were leagued
together. There is deep significance in the fact that the Lotharingian Humbert had been a teacher of Hildebrand.[1]

The chief seat of the movement was Lorraine, the most
refractory of all the feudal principalities in Germany. In the
time of Otto I the duke Gilbert had coquetted with France
and the archbishop Frederick of Mainz who had so resisted
Otto's church policy. Under Otto II, Otto III, Henry II, and
Conrad II, there had been new plots for French intervention
vaguely identified with the French reform movement. But
with Henry III the compact between the feudal elements in
Lorraine and the Hildebrandine "reform" became close. The
whole rule of the German kings over the lands in the valleys
of the Rhine, the Meuse, and the Moselle was challenged.
Most of the religious houses in this vast region were peopled
with offspring of the local feudal families, and Henry III had
been unwise enough to permit the bishoprics of Lorraine to
be filled with representatives of this local aristocracy, thus
letting the strongest instrument of his government of Lorraine, the episcopate, slip out of his hand. Hermann II of
Cologne was made arch-chancellor of the apostolic see; Bruno
of Toul became Pope Leo IX.[2] The feudal aristocracy of Lorraine, and the bishops, most of whom were of noble birth,
combined their political aspirations with the Cluny reform
and worked together against the monarchy. The identification of the Cluny reform in Germany with the elements and
forces of feudal particularism and revolt is plain. The abbey
of St. Vannes in Verdun quadrupled its landed wealth in certain years owing to the generosity of the nobles of Lorraine.

This double feudal and "reform" tendency was incarnated in the person of Duke Godfrey of Upper Lorraine, a

---

[1] Cf. K. Hampe, *Wissenschaftliche Forschungsberichte* (Gotha, 1922), p. 64.

[2] Hauck, III, 482 f.; Sackur, II, 152 f.; Gerdes, II, 519 f. Lambert of Hersfeld
(*anno* 1071, ed. Holder-Egger), p. 133, clearly shows the intimate relation subsisting
between the high German feudality and the Cluny reform, ". . . . principes regni ad
instituendam in Galliis divini servicii scolam Transalpinos monachos evocabant,
nostrates autem, quicumque in illorum instituta ultro concedere noluissent, de
monasteriis cum ignominia eiciebant."

redoubtable warrior and a born adventurer, who was descended from the ancient counts of Verdun.[1] Expelled from his
duchy by Henry III,[2] who awoke too late to the danger of
the situation in Lorraine, Godfrey, in 1051, wandered over
the Alps to Italy, where he captivated Beatrice, the widowed
Marchioness of Tuscany, whose daughter was the great
Countess Matilda, and married her.[2] Thus the string of border states along the French edge of the Empire clear to Rome
was bound together in a papal-feudal association between
1046–55 against the German monarchy.[4] Yet Henry III's
eyes were so sealed to the real import of things that on his
deathbed he commended Empress Agnes and the little Henry
IV to Godfrey's care.[5] The ramifications of the Hildebrand-
ine-Lorraine intrigue even penetrated into Bavaria in Henry
III's reign. In 1042 Henry, son of Count Frederick of Luxemburg (who was also vogt of St. Maximin in Trier), was made
duke of Bavaria by Henry III, who gave it out thus instead
of holding it in the hands of the crown as he should have
done. Thus the feudo-papal program became identified with
Bavarian sentiments of ducal autonomy also.[6]

Meanwhile, in Lombardy, the Pataria, to which allusion
has been made, had also become a formidable movement of
opposition, and it is necessary briefly to relate the origin and
purposes of this party. The organized sale of church offices in
Milan was of long standing. The higher clergy were married
into the chief families, the rest according to their position in
the social scale. The government of the church in Lombardy
formed a hierarchic and social oligarchy. It was manifest to
those who were discontented with this condition of things
that the imposition of celibacy would go far to break this
combination.

[1] Petr. Dam., *Epp.*, VII, 10, SS. XI, p. 450; *Triumph. Remacli*, I, 11, *Ibid.*,
p. 443; Leo Ostiens, *Chron. Cass.*, xi, 97.

[2] For the emperor's drastic discipline of Godfrey see Lambert of Hersfeld,
Annales, 1046. Freeman, *Norman Conquest* (2d. ed.), Vol. II, Appendix O, has a
vivid account.

[3] Dupréel, *Hist. crit. de Godfrey le Barbu*, pp. 59 f.

[4] Nitzsch, II, 47–48.

[5] Lamprecht, II, 266.　　　　　　[6] Gerdes, II, 68.

The agitation was started by a former collegiate priest
of the see of Milan named Anselm da Baggio, whom Henry
III had made bishop of Lucca, and who speedily developed
into a passionate reformer. He found able coadjutors in the
person of Ariald, a deacon of the church of Milan and a clerk
in orders named Landulf. The three agitators soon formed a
party among the discontented lower clergy, many of whom
were hedge-priests without fixed livings. But the movement
soon became more formidable. While Landulf harangued the
rabble in the towns, Ariald journeyed through the country
districts rousing the rustic population against the rural
clergy. In the countryside the Pataria became an agrarian
revolution. The most violent invective was indulged in, and
from verbal abuse matters soon passed to rioting and mob
violence against all married clergy. Religious fanaticism, social prejudice, and economic envy of those who were well-to-
do or rich were united in a seething leaven of discontent. The
most radical among the Patarines went so far as to deny the
right of private ownership of property.

Thus both north and south of the Alps manifold forces of
opposition to the existing order of things were in a condition
of violent unrest, and drifting into co-operation or combination together.

The death of Henry III in 1056 was the signal for open
attack of the papal opposition upon the German monarchy.
The accession of Stephen IX, a brother of Godfrey of Lorraine
and formerly a monk in Verdun, to the papal throne in 1057
was contrived by Hildebrand, the cardinal-abbot of Monte
Cassino, and Godfrey himself. Its effect was definitely to
sever the Holy See from imperial control. The imperial au-
thority was not even consulted.[1] Nonesense a delegation headed by Hildebrand immediately

This action was followed by the creation of the College of approach the Regent
Cardinals in 1059 by Nicholas II, which permanently ex-
cluded German influence in papal elections. In spite of the
guarded phraseology of this decree, it was a declaration of
war upon the imperial authority.[2] In the same year Cardinal

---

[1] Hauck, III, 680; Lamprecht, II, 319.

[2] "Salvo debito honore et reverentia dilecti filii nostri Henrici, qui in praesentia
rex habetur et futurus imperator, Deo concedente, speratur" (Labbé, Concil.,

Humbert issued the famous tract *Contra simoniacos*.[1] At once a storm of indignation arose in Germany. Anselm of Lucca, Hildebrand's agent with him in effecting the papal alliance with the Pataria, was refused a hearing at a German synod in December, 1059, where Hildebrand and Nicholas II were both excommunicated by the irate German bishops.[2] In the next spring the Lorrainer cardinal Stephen was refused audience by the imperial court, and after waiting five days returned to Rome.[3] In 1061 the German bishops condemned the Lateran decree, erased the name of Nicholas II from the list of popes, and declared his decisions null and void.[4]

From such tension to open rupture between the German church and Rome was a matter of a short time. The Lombard bishops, who both detested and feared the growing influence

XII, 50; Hauck, III, 683 f.). Nicholas II was archbishop of Florence, but French-Burgundian by birth. It is to be remembered that Florence was in the center of the Tuscan territory of Godfrey of Lorraine. Panzer, *Ztschft. f. Kirchenrecht*, XXII, Heft 3–4 (1889), has a critical article upon the decree of Nicholas II in 1059, and his encyclical *Vigilantia universalis*. According to him, 125 bishops were in the conclave which debated the question of the creation of the College of Cardinals. The decree promulgated by Nicholas II in 1059 is not identical with the provisions made in the encyclical of 1060. The latter is silent as to the right of the emperor to exert any control over the election of the pope, but the imperial right is not formally denied. The silence was deliberately planned in order to make neglect of the imperial right "convenient" when desirable. Pflugk-Harttung, *Mitt. d. Inst.*, XXVII, 1 (1906), thinks neither version reliable and both "redacted."

L. von Heinemann, *Hist. Ztschft.*, XXIX, Heft 1, argues that the decree of 1059 did not force the issue between empire and papacy, since in January, 1059, the synod of Sutri had recognized the emperor's prerogative as "patrician" and the May decree provided for imperial confirmation before the pope was enthroned. It was the decree of the Easter council in 1060, Heinemann contends, which permitted a pope, though named outside of Rome and before enthronement, to use the property of the church, that provoked the condemnation of Nicholas II, and called for the imperial protest. After the election of the anti-pope Clement IV the decree of Nicholas II was falsified by the Hildebrandines. For additional bibliography relating to the history of the origin of the College of Cardinals see Delarc, "Le pontificat de Nicolas II," *RQH*, XL, 361 n.

[1] Halfmann, *Cardinal Humbert, sein Leben und seine Werke* (Göttingen, 1883).

[2] Hefele, VI, 404.

[3] Petr. Dam., *Disc. synod*, p. 88; Scheffer-Boichorst, *Mitteil. des Institut.*, XIII, 125.

[4] Deusdedit, *Contra Invasor.*, cap. ii; Mirbt, *Libelli de lite*, II, 309; Meyer von Knonau, *Jahrb.*, I, 285.

of the Pataria, especially since its union with Rome, vainly urged the Empress to appoint Cadalus, bishop of Parma, a well-known opponent of the "new Clunyism," to the papal office.[1] Hildebrand countered with his friend Anselm of Lucca, who was elected by the cardinals as Alexander II,[2] and in order to thwart the possibility of imperial intervention summoned the Norman chief Richard of Aversa to Rome, with whom he had had an interview some years before at Melfi, under the shadow of whose soldiery Alexander II was elected.[3]

The German party was more alarmed than ever. In October, 1061, the German and Lombard bishops (most of whom, it should be remembered, were either German or German sympathizers) met at Basel, proclaimed young Henry IV "patrician" of the Romans, and, in order to rebuke the Hildebrandine party, elected Cadalus of Parma, a bitter enemy of Hildebrand, to be pope under the name of Honorius II.[4] For the next ten years a war of the partisans racked Northern Italy. The empire was powerless to interfere, and most of the German bishops were too busy grinding their own axes at home to give attention to things beyond the Alps.[5] Hildebrand was not yet quite ready to carry the war overtly into the German kingdom, but was soon to do so.

In the meantime, Germany was sown and watered with the "new Clunyism." No attentive student of the history of the war of investiture can fail to be impressed with the conjuncture of circumstances in the middle of the eleventh century. The years between 1056, when Henry III died and the minority succession of Henry IV ensued, and 1075, when Hildebrand, as Pope Gregory VII, opened the great struggle, saw the development of conditions which profoundly affected the history of both empire and papacy.

[1] Petr. Dam., *Epp.*, I, 20, p. 242; Leo Ostiens, *Chron. Cass.*, III, 19; Benzo, VII, 2.

[2] Meyer von Knonau, *Jahrb.*, I, 669 f.

[3] Hauck, III, 704; Leo Ostiens, *Chron. Cass.*, III, 19; Benzo, *ibid.*

[4] Hauck, III, 705–6.

[5] For the unimportant details of this schismatic conflict see Hauck, III, 717 f.; Giesebrecht, III, 80 f.

The rapid growth of the order of Cluny in Germany during the minority of Henry IV is not merely interesting; it was ominous for the future.[1] In this process the regent-mother Agnes was an unwitting tool in the hands of Anno, the crafty archbishop of Cologne. Already a patroness of the Italian Cluniac foundation at Fructuaria, in 1060 she colonized a group of Italian Cluniacs from Fontello in the old monastery of St. Blasien in the Schwarzwald.[2] In 1066 Anno colonized Sigeberg and St. Pantaleon near Cologne with Piedmontese monks, and in 1071 expelled the Benedictines from Saalfeld and Grafschaft and filled their places with Lorrainer and Burgundian monks.[3] By 1075 the influx of French and Italian monks into Germany seemed like an invasion. Lambert of Hersfeld gives a glowing account of this migration of "transalpinos monachos" from Cluny, from Gorze, from Fructuaria, and rejoices in the discomfiture and exile of the Benedictines, who fled the cloisters, often taking the treasure and vessels of the monasteries as spoil with them.[4]

The shining product of this revolution—for it amounted to that—was the monastery of Hirsau in the Black Forest. Founded in the ninth century by Louis the Pious, it had long

[1] Upon this significant sympathy of the German feudality for the Cluny reform see Hauck, III, 490 f.; Gerdes, II, 369–70 and notes, 519 f.; *Chron. Hirsaug.* (1099); Lambert of Hersfeld (*anno* 1071); *Chron. Bern. S. Blas.* (1091), SS. V, 452.

[2] Meyer von Knonau, *Jahrb.*, I, 280.

[3] *Vita Annonis*, chaps. xvi–xvii, xxiii; Lambert of Hersfeld (*anno* 1071), p. 132; (*anno* 1075), pp. 244–45.

[4] Lambert (*anno* 1071), p. 133; cf. (*anno* 1075), pp. 244–45. A monk of Gorze found St. Michael's in Bamberg empty when he arrived (Berthold, *Annal.* [1071], *MGH*, SS. V, 184). The old-line Benedictine abbeys, especially those which were "royal," violently resisted the incomers, satirizing their "unascetic" costume (*MGH*, SS. XXI, 432, vss. 84 ff.; *Casus S. Galli contin*, XXXI, 82; *Chron. Lauresham*, SS. XXI, 421; Hauck, III, 869), inveighing against their hypocrisy and stigmatizing them as tares and thorns among wheat (*Vita Oudalr.*, p. 24; *MGH*, SS. XII, 259). "Haec pestis de Francia transfusa in Lothrangiam quam sit detestabilis, nostro tempore Petrus Damianus Alexandro papae hujusmodi invectione deplanxit," is another description of the monastic reform movement out of France (*Chron. Huberti Andagin*, chap. lxxviii; Migne, CLIV, 1426), Meyer von Knonau, *Mitt. zur vaterländischen Geschichte*, Vols. XV–XVI (1877), on the sources of the history of S. Gall, analyzes the *Casus S. Galli* of Ekkehard IV line by line, and shows how the monks lauded the good old times in opposition to the Cluny reform.

fallen into decay. About the year 1066 it was colonized by a band of monks from Einsiedeln, one of the earliest offshoots of Gorze.[1] The Black Forest soon became a veritable drill-ground of Clunyism. Around Hirsau were St. Blasien, Grüningen, Ruggisberg, Peterlingen, etc.[2] A new codification of the Rule of Cluny was drawn up by Udalric,[3] the prior of Hirsau.

Within an amazingly brief time branch houses of Hirsau multiplied in Germany, especially in the south. By 1080 St. Blasien and Schaffhausen were united with Hirsau. In Franconia it absorbed Hasungen, Komburg, Schönrein. In Swabia it acquired St. Savior in Schaffhausen, St. George, St. Gregory, Zwifalten, Petershausen, Weilheim, Blaubeuren, and Sindelfingen. In Bavaria, Kremsmünster, St. Paul, Admont, St. Margaret in Zell. In Thuringia, Reinhardsbrunn and St. Peter in Erfurt. In addition to all these Hirsau either founded or absorbed more outlying or detached monasteries, as Altdorf, Kloster Bergen near Magdeburg, Hugshofen, St. Michael's in Bamberg, Paulinzelle, Prüfening, Breitenau, Bosau, Langenau, Elchingen, Amorbach, Mettlach, Schwarzach on the Rhine and another of the same name on the Main, Theres, Wessobrun, Meherau in

---

[1] Migne, *Pat. Lat.*, CL, 927.

[2] Hauck, III, 865–76; Lamprecht, II, 368–70. The Black Forest region of Germany was very strongly pro-papal in the war of investiture (*Bernold S. Blas.*, SS. V, 439 [1083]; 452–53 [1091]). "Die Richtung und Entwicklung der Kirche, welche mit Gregor VII zur Herrschaft kam, ging vornehmlich von Cluny aus, und einer ihrer stärksten Vorposten, in engster Verbindung mit Cluny, waren die Klöster des Schwarzwaldes. Hier verkehrten die Legaten und Gegenkönige, hier feierten sie ihre Feste, hier suchten sie und ihre Anhänger Zuflucht in Zeiten der Noth. Die Mönche von Ebersheimmünster im Elsass haben Rudolf von Reinfelden sogar seine Krone geschmiedet. Es war nicht wie bei den Sachsen eine zufällige Uebereinstimmung in der Opposition gegen das Reich, welche diese Mönche mit Gregor zusammenführte, sondern der reine dogmatische Eifer" (Wattenbach, *Deutschlands Geschichtsq.* [5th ed.], II, 44).

[3] Lambert (*anno* 1071), p. 133; *Vita Oudalr.*, Book II, chap. xxxiv; Berthold, *Annal.* (1077). It was Bernhard, abbot of St. Victor in Marseilles and the legate of Gregory VII, who suggested to William of Hirsau the adoption of the Cluniac rule (Wattenbach, II, 45). For the text see Migne, CXLIX, 635f.; and for the history thereof, CL, 929. For the discipline of these Consuetudines Cluniacenses see *Const. Hirs.*, II, 21, col. 1067; II, 9, col. 1048.

Bregenz, Lorsch, Bleidenstadt, Hornbach, Deggingen, Beinwil, Odenheim, Mölk, Scheuern, St. Emmeran, Prühl, Biburg, Mallersdorf, Reichenbach, Michelfeld, Ennsdorf, Weinhenstefan, Weltenburg, Münchenmünster, Kastel, Benediktbeuren, Seeon, Corvey, Pegau, St. Jacob in Regensburg, etc.[1] At the same time Cluny proper founded or reformed Ilsenburg, Hillersleben, Harsefeld, Huysburg in North Germany, while St. Blasien in the south did the same with Muri, Kempten, St. Ulrich, Wiblingen, Ochsenhausen, Alpirsbach.[2]

The great German nobles were little less active. Welf of Bavaria, since 1070 duke there, and a bitter anti-imperialist, founded Weingarten; Berthold of Zähringen founded St.

---

[1] Hauck, III, 870; Mayr, "Die Hirsauer Congregation," *Mitteil. des Inst.*, I (1880), 126 f.; Helmersdörfer, *Forsch. z. Gesch. des Abtes Wilhelm der Heilige*, p. 118. According to *Annal. Hirs.*, Prolog and pp. 225–27, 266–68, 294, the total number of Hirsauer foundations was 97. The bibliography of the Hirsauer movement is extensive. Süssmann, *Forschungen zur Gesch. des Klosters Hirsau, 1065 bis 1105* (Halle diss., 1903); Messing, *Papst Gregors VII Verhältniss zu den Klöstern* (Greifswald diss., 1907); Ernest Hauviller, *Ulrich von Cluny* ("Kirchengesch. Studien," Band III, Heft 3), (Münster, 1896); Haffner, *Regesten zur Gesch. des schwäbischen Klosters Hirsau* ("Studien und Mitteil. aus dem Benediktiner- und Cisterzienserorden," Band XIII); Cless, *Versuch einer kirchl.-polit. Landes- und Kulturgesch. von Würtemberg*, II, Teil I, Abt., pp. 237 f. (Gmünd, 1807); Kerker, *Wilhelm der Selige* (Tübingen, 1863); Richter, *Annalen*, III, 2, pp. 86–87, 269–72, 347, 411–12; Godeke, *Die Hirsauer während des Investiturstreites* (1883); Egger, *Gesch. der Cluniazenser-Klöster in Frankreich und in der West-Schweiz bis zum Auftreten der Cisterzienser* ("Freiburger Hist. Studien," Heft III, Freibourg [Switzerland], 1907); Karl Schott, *Kloster Reichenbach im Murgtal in seinen Beziehungen zu Hirsau und den Markgrafen von Baden* (Freiburg i. B., 1912); Schreiber, *Kurie und Kloster im 12. Jahrhundert* (2 vols.) (Stuttgart, 1910); Gieseke, *Die Ausbreitung d. Hirsauer Reform*; C. H. Baer, *Die Hirsauer Bauschule* (1895); Max Fischer, *Studien zur Entstehung der Hirsauer Konstitution* (1910). Odilo Ringholz, *Des Benediktinerstiftes Einsiedeln Tätigkeit fur die Reform deutscher Klöster vor dem Abte Wilhelm von Hirsau* ("Studien und Mitteilungen aus dem Benediktiner und Cistercienserorden," VII [1886], 1); Bruno Albers, *Hirsau und seine Gründungen vom Jahre 1073 an* ("Festschrift des deutschen Campo Santo," pp. 115–29). Weber, "Hirsau-Paulinzella-Thalbürge," *Ztschrft. d. Ver. f. Thüring. Gesch.* (N.F., XII); Hafner, *The Treaty of Confraternity between the Benedictine Monasteries of Hirsau, St. Blasien and Muri* ("Studien und Mitth. aus dem Bened. und dem Cisterc.-Orden," Band XVI, Heft 4 [1895]). Text with commentary on monastic confraternities in the Middle Ages. Thudichum, *Wuertemb. Vierteljahrshefte f. Landesgesch.*, Band II, Heft 3 (1893), has shown how in envy of and imitation of Hirsau other monasteries in Germany forged privileges of the nature of those of Hirsau. Thus in the twelfth century Ellwangen did so in order to reduce the rights of the *vogtei* and limit the authority of the bishop of Augsburg.

[2] Hauck, III, 869–71.

Peter in the Schwarzwald.[1] Two Swabian counts united in founding Wiblingen on the Iller. Count Udalric of Bregenz founded Ochsenhausen. The bishops Adalberon of Würzburg, Gerard of Salzburg, Altmann of Passau, severally founded one or the other of the following: Lambach, Admont, Reichersberg, Göttweih, St. George, St. Polten, St. Florian, St. Paul, St. Lambert. In Saxony, Burckhard of Halberstadt, Herrand, abbot of Ilsenburg, Gilbert, abbot of Rheinhardsbrunn, sowed the north and east with Hirsauer or Cluniac houses, as Ilsenburg, Hillersleben, Harsefeld, Huysburg, Pegau, Kloster Bergen, Hammersleben, Reinsdorf, Paulinzelle, Oldisleben, Hadmersleben, Vizenburg, Drübeck, Notterlingsburg, Kalterbrunn.[2] Whole villages got the contagion of the new monasticism, which was fired by fanatic, wandering preachers, and resolved "to have all things in common" like the apostles.[3] Wealth and numbers poured in upon the monasteries so fast that the Cluniac rule against lay brothers was broken down.[4] Gregory VII saw in this popular growth of Hirsau the possibility of establishing a German Pataria.[5] The monasteries in these years grew like Jonah's gourd vine. When Otto I died in 1073 there were 108 monasteries in Germany; when the war of investiture began there were over 700.[6]

[1] Bernoldi, *Chron.* (1093), SS. V, 456-57.

[2] Hauck, III, 871-72.

[3] Bernold, *Chron.* (1091); *De unitate ecclesiae conservanda*, II, 38; Gerdes, II, 272, 528 f.; Kerker, pp. 156 f.; Richter, III, 2, pp. 412-13 nn.

[4] Bernold, *Chron.* (1093); Hauck, III, 875, n. 3; Gerdes, II, 530; Helmsdörfer, pp. 90 f.; Kerker, pp. 135 f. They are first mentioned by Lambert of Hersfeld in 1076 (ed. Holder-Egger), p. 277. The lay brothers were used in gardening and working on the grange (*grangiae*) farms and were called *conversi laici*, or more familiarly, *fratres barbati* or *Bärtlinger*, i.e., "bearded." For the economic activity of these "lay" brothers see Wattenbach, *Deutschlands Geschichtsquellen*, II, 88. Although not unlike Cluny, the Hirsauer monasteries were not so compactly associated together as the Cluniac (*Chron. Zwifalt.*, 16, SS. X, 82). Many of the older monasteries, as a popular move, during the war of investitute, in imitation of Hirsau, enrolled lay brothers in their midst (Wattenbach [5th ed.], II, 88). "Die Mönche der älteren Art kamen durch diese neuen Regeln, welche rasch verbreiteten, mehr und mehr in Missachtung *beim Volke* und bei den Grossen und sahen sich dadurch manchen Gefahren ausgesetzt" (*ibid.*, p. 89).

[5] Berthold, *Contin.* (1079), p. 317; Richter, II, 2, p. 293; Feierabend, p. 25 n.

[6] Hauck, IV, 49, n. 10; Koeniger, p. 101, n. 3.

By the time the struggle between Henry IV and Gregory VII opened, all West and Southwest Germany and large areas in the center and north had been colonized by Cluny or Hirsau, the German form of the Cluniac movement. More ominous still for the monarchy was the intimate alliance between Cluny-Hirsau and the powerful lay feudality. Its support is not to be attributed to disinterested or religious motives. Just as earlier the great dukes had espoused the Gorzean reform in the hope of finding in it a means to injure the crown's power over them by using the German church against them, so in the eleventh century the German feudality advocated reform for self-advantage. Lorraine, Bavaria, and Swabia were notorious storm centers of opposition to the Saxon kings.[1]

By the third quarter of the eleventh century the controlling influences in the church, namely, the Cluniac party and Gregory VII (1073–85), were more interested in church supremacy than in church reform; more interested in enlarging the political power and material wealth of the church than in furthering its spiritual ministry. Of course the real remedy for church corruption and the solution of the friction between the state and the church was for the latter to have renounced its vast material wealth and temporal powers, much of which was not necessary to it as a religious institution. But this the church was unwilling to do. Its love of wealth and its love of power were too great. The church's policy, with the accession of Hildebrand to the papacy, was one of uncompromising supremacy of church over state. It laid the ax at the root of the emperor's power by attacking the state's right of proprietary control over the church through the prohibition of lay investiture.

Before 1050 the Catholic Church, however universal in theory, had hardly been universal in fact. The period of the Frankish, the Saxon, and the early Salian emperors had been a period of what German writers called the *Landeskirche*. The power of the bishop of Rome had not yet been fully established, and the great churches of Rheims and Mainz and Milan were practically independent centres. Independent of the papacy, they were not independent of the lay rulers within whose dominions they lay. On the contrary, their members were deeply engaged in lay activities; they

[1] Lamprecht, II, 135 f., 151 f., 163 f., 249 f.

were landlords, feudatories, and officials in their various countries. In the face of these facts the Gregorian movement of the eleventh century pursues two closely interconnected objects. It aims at asserting the universal primacy of the papacy; it aims at vindicating the freedom of the clergy from all secular power. The one aim is a means to the other: the pope cannot be universal primate unless the clergy he controls are free from secular control, unless the universal primacy of the papacy effects their liberation.

Gregorianism .... establishes the theory, and in a very large part the practice, of ecclesiastical unity..... The days of the church universal under the universal primacy of Rome are begun. But when the universality of the church has once been established in point of extension, it begins to be also asserted in point of intensity. Once ubiquitous, the papacy seeks to be omnicompetent. Depositary of the truth, and only depositary of the truth, by divine revelation, the church under the guidance of the papacy seeks to realize the truth in every reach of life, and to control in the light of Christian principle every play of human activity. Learning and education, trade and commerce, war and peace, are all to be drawn into her orbit. By the application of Christian principle a great synthesis of human life is to be achieved and the *lex Christi* is to be made a *lex animata in terris*. This was the greatest ambition that has ever been cherished.[1]

"Reform" was a means to an end, not an end in itself. It was a convenient watchword, like so many political shibboleths, embodying self-interest in an outward guise of virtue and ethicality which fooled the emotionally religious and the unthinking masses of mankind, but which never deceived the initiated and those who had the penetration to see that though the hand might be the hand of Esau, the voice was the voice of Jacob. The English historian, William of Malmesbury, who lived in the reigns of Henry IV and Henry V, clearly perceived the justice of the emperor's position. He writes:

This was the period in which Germany for fifty years bewailed the pitiable and almost fatal government of Henry [IV]. .... He was neither unlearned nor indolent; but so singled out by fate for every person to attack, that whoever took up arms against him pretended, to himself, to be acting for the good of religion. .... There were many things praiseworthy in the emperor: he was eloquent, of great abilities, well-read, actively charitable; he had many good qualities both of mind and of person.[2]

[1] Barker in Marvin, *The Unity of Western Civilization* (Oxford, 1915), pp. 99–100.

[2] Cf. *De unitate eccl. conserv.*, especially chap. vii, and *Vita Heinrici IV, passim.*

ARCHBISHOPRICS AND BISHOPRICS IN MEDIEVAL GERMANY

CHAPTER III

THE WAR OF INVESTITURE; THE CONFLICT BETWEEN HENRY IV AND GREGORY VII

HISTORY affords few more striking examples of revolutionary change than the contrast between the relations of the German crown, the German church, and the papacy in Saxon (919–1024) and Salian (1024–1125) times. Under the Saxon emperors the church was the friend and ally of the dynasty. This good relation became somewhat strained under Conrad II and Henry III, the first Salians, and under the last two Salian rulers, Henry IV, and Henry V, the German church in large part, and the papacy wholly, were the implacable foe of the emperors and strove with might and main to compass the destruction of the German crown.

The conflict between Henry IV and Gregory VII has usually been portrayed with the dramatic grandeur of a Greek tragedy. Dramatic qualities and dramatic personalities that struggle certainly possessed. But in general its history has been pitched upon too high a plane. The character of Hildebrand is one of the most complex and difficult to understand in all history. He was at once a superlative idealist imbued with the Augustinian dream of a world-church supreme over a world-state, and a shrewd politician. Such a man is rarely always consistent in his conduct. Depending upon mood or circumstance he sometimes responds to one motive or stimulus, sometimes to another.[1] It is the endeavor of this chapter to show that the root of the struggle between Gregory VII and Henry IV was an economic one; that the immediate and fundamental, though carefully con-

---

[1] The life and time of Gregory VII are too packed with great men and great events for a single writer or a single volume adequately to present the complex issues. No epoch of medieval history is more dependent upon the co-operative labor and researches of a large number of historical students. See the suggestive paragraph by Giry, "Grégoire VII et les évêques de Térouanne," *Revue Hist.*, I, 387.

cealed, purpose of the papacy was to acquire complete proprietary control of the German church (indeed the church
throughout all Europe); and that the Cluny reform was
sedulously propagated as a means to that end. Karl Wilhelm
Nitzsch (1818–80) in his *Geschichte des deutschen Volkes* was
the first who discerned this factor in the war of investiture.[1]
Since his death other scholars, in many monographs, have
widened the field which he first tilled, and the enormous influence of the proprietary interests of the German church upon
the history of the medieval empire has been abundantly
demonstrated.[2]

One of the most certain achievements of modern historical
research is the proof which precludes denial of the interrela-
tion of all the facts and forces of an epoch. The war of investiture cannot be rightly understood except in the light of
the economic and social history of Germany in the tenth and

---

[1] Cf. Nitzsch, *Deutsche Gesch.*, II, 15, and Döllinger, *Akad. Vorträge*, Vol. II, Lecture 1; Inama-Sternegg, *DWG*, II, 135.

[2] Harnack, *History of Dogma*, V, 7, has suggestively said, "The task of administering property was more important to the German church than the political
and dogmatic debates of the neighboring French hierarchy." So again, *ibid.*, VI, 16,
he says, "It was about the property of the bishops and . . . . who was the true
ruler of the divine state that the great battle was really waged between the empire
and the reformed papacy."

Ficker first clearly formulated the idea that the war of investiture was primarily
one for control of the church's proprietary power (*ein Eigenthumsrecht*)—"Ueber das
Eigenthum des Reiches am Reichskirchengute," *Sitzungsberichte der philosoph.-
histor. Klasse der kaiserl. Akad. d. Wissenschaften*, LXXII (1872), 55–146, 381–450.
To this article Waitz replied the next year in the same journal (1873), p. 825, admitting the presence of proprietary elements in the struggle between emperor and pope,
but contending that Ficker exaggerated its importance. Cf. Waitz, *Deutsch Verfassungsgesch.*, VII, 199, n. 1. Since these epoch-making articles a large amount of
supplementary work has been done by more recent scholars, which, it seems to me,
bears out Ficker's contention, as Matthäi, *Die Klosterpolitik Kaiser Heinrichs II*
(Göttingen diss., 1877); Stutz, *Die Eigenkirche als Element des mittelalterlich-
german. Kirchenrechts* (Berlin, 1895); and his *Gesch. des kirchlichen Beneficialwesens*
(1895) and article entitled "Lehen und Pfründe" in *Zeitschrift der Savignystiftung
für Rechtsgesch.*, XXXIII (N.F., 1899), 20, 213–47; Hauck, *Kirchengesch. Deutschlands*, III (1905), 441 ff.; Werminghoff, *Gesch. der Kirchenverfassung Deutschlands im Mittelalter* (Leipzig, 1905), pp. 179 ff.; Feierabend, *Die politische Stellung der deutschen Reichsabteien während des Investiturstreites* (Breslau diss., 1913);
Voigt, *Die Klosterpolitik der Salischen Kaiser und Könige mit besonderer Beruck
sichtigung Heinrich IV biz zum Jahre 1077* (Leipzig diss., 1888); Koeniger, *Burcha
I von Worms* (1905), chap. iv. Waitz's great work, Vol. VII, chap. ii, *Die hoh
Geistlichkeit*, is invaluable for the wealth of references to sources. For the "royal"
abbeys see *ibid.*, III, 434–35; IV, 153–57.

eleventh centuries.[1] The root of the problem between church and state in the Middle Ages, and the chief root of the evil in the church, was its immense landed wealth. Between the alternative of renouncing her feudal revenues, her temporalities, her privileges, her political power, and so seeking deliverance from secular control, and the alternative of keeping her temporalities and yet securing freedom from the authority of the state by crushing the state, the church did not hesitate. She chose the latter course, and the identification of the Cluny reform with the papal power by Hildebrand went far toward making the aspiration a reality.

Henry IV, when he reached his majority, was not hostile to the reform. If the issue between him and Gregory VII had been one merely of traffic in church dignities and the celibacy of the priest class, the rupture between emperor and pope would probably never have come to pass. There is no reason to doubt Henry IV's sincerity when in 1082 at Milan he took an oath not to practice simony, and when, in 1083, his anti-pope Clement II urged the clergy to live in chastity—and that at the very moment when Gregory VII had begun to waver upon the question of celibacy owing to the adverse situation in which he found himself. All these issues were minor ones between emperor and pope. Much smoke was raised over them at times, but there was really little fire in them.

The real issue was otherwise: the aspiration of Gregory VII for universal rule over both church and state, his passion for wealth and power, his pretentions to the right to set up and dethrone kings—these were the marrow of the conflict. In giving a new and formidable connotation to the word "simony," in dissolving the tie of fidelity and investiture which bound the German clergy to the king, Gregory VII attempted to cut the very nerves of the Salian monarchy. It is true that much of the property of bishoprics and abbeys was considered as royal property; but the church derived enormous benefit from the possession of it nevertheless, in

[1] In his recent work, *Belgian Democracy* (Eng. trans.), p. 30 n., Professor Henri Pirenne has written, "There is here, i.e., in economic history, a whole group of phenomena in general too little heeded by the students of this great conflict."

spite of heavy political, financial, and military burdens imposed upon its clergy. The benefits resulting from the arrangement were worth the price exacted, as most of the German bishops perceived, and accordingly advocated the king's cause instead of that of the pope.

The war of investiture was a maze of cross- and countercurrents. While the struggles between emperor and pope and between the German crown and the rebellious Saxons were the two main streams, the strife between the bishops and the abbots was no unimportant chapter.[1] The feud between the "regulars" and the "seculars," as we have seen, was an old one. The monasteries for centuries had chafed under the superior jurisdiction of the bishops, and the papacy had developed a lucrative trade in selling them exemptions from episcopal authority. The German kings, too, had always sustained the bishops against the monks. Naturally most of the monasteries, except conservative ones like St. Gall and Lorsch, supported the Cluny reform as a means of emancipation from both the episcopate and the crown.[2]

While Henry III had lived he had attempted to hold the balance even between the rival groups of clergy. But when his strong hand was removed the weak regency of the empress-mother was unable to cope with the situation. The bishops as well as the lay feudality at once began a wholesale policy of spoliation of the monastery lands. When Agnes was removed from the regency and the rivalry of Anno of Cologne and Adalbert of Bremen ensued for control of the boy king Henry IV, the condition of things grew more aggravated than ever. For both were fierce and ambitious bishops who hesitated at nothing to attain their ends, whether by fraud or violence.[3]

The years of the minority of Henry IV were favorable days for the bishops. Between 1057 and 1065 we have the record of 20 grants of land made to them, and only 5 for the ensuing seven years (1066–73), when the king had attained

---

[1] Cf. Messing, *Papst Gregors VII Verhältnisse zu den Klöstern* (1910).

[2] Hersfeld, Fulda, Corvey, and Ottobeuren were notorious seceders (Feierabend, p. 27). On the whole see Sackur, II, 270–99.

[3] Hauck, III, 728 f.; Voigt, p. 40 f.

his majority. For immediately upon the decease of Henry III the bishops waxed bold in their demands of the crown. The Bishop of Brixen bullied the empress-mother into giving him the monastery of Dissentis and seized Kloster Polling; the Bishop of Speier got Conrad II's foundation of Limburg, St. Lambert's, and the abbey of Schwarzach; the Bishop of Freising obtained Benediktbeuren; the Bishop of Halberstadt received the monastery of Drusbeck in the Harz as settlement for claims against the royal estates in his diocese; the Bishop of Constance seized Reichenau; the Bishop of Bamberg, Kloster Kitzingen. A typical case is the spoliation of the lands of St. Michael's in Bamberg by Ulrich, a *ministerialis* of the Archbishop of Mainz. The years 1062–65 were even worse for the monasteries. The Archbishop of Salzburg seized Chiemsee in 1062; the Archbishop of Mainz acquired Selingenstadt in 1063; Adalbert of Bremen tried to seize Malmedy and Cornelimünster.[1]

During the time of Henry IV's minority it seemed as if the suppression of the monasteries by the bishops and the German princes would be accomplished. By 1065 fourteen of the greatest and richest abbeys had been appropriated by the bishops and the Fürsten.[2] Otto of Nordheim, the new duke of Bavaria, devoured Nieder Altaich; Rudolf of Swabia laid his hand on Kloster Kempten. As Gerdes says, "Fast jeder grosse und kleine Fürst geistlichen und weltlichen Standes erhielt ein Stück aus der Beute."[3]

Sometimes, however, the rivalry between two jealous bishops for possession of the same foundation resulted in a deadlock. The distribution of the prizes might be made on paper but was impossible in practice.[4] For example, Anno of Cologne and Adalbert of Bremen were both contestants for possession of Corvey and Lorsch, and neither got them.[5] Anno was thwarted in his contemplated seizure of Stablo

[1] Adam of Bremen, III, 45.

[2] *De unitate eccles. conserv.*, chap. xxxiii; *Libelli de lite*, II, 258 f.; Waitz, VII, 211–13; Voigt, pp. 38–43.

[3] Gerdes, II, 158.

[4] Voigt, p. 40.

[5] Hauck, III, 729; Voigt, p. 55; Adam of Bremen, III, 45.

by the Abbot of Malmedy, aided by his vassals.[1] The monastic chroniclers of these early years of Henry IV, especially Lambert of Hersfeld, give a vivid picture of the spoliation of the monasteries at the hands both of the German episcopate and the lay feudality.[2]

The feud between the bishops and the great nobles to enlarge their lands was quite as bitter as that between the bishops and the monasteries. The history of the archbishopric of Bremen is perhaps the best example of this struggle. This see, in early Saxon days, was very poor.[3] Its enrichment began with the accession of Archbishop Unwin (1013–30), of the wealthy Immedinger family, who gave a substantial portion of his family inheritance to Bremen.[4] Under the careful administration of the archbishops Liawizo (1030–32) and Hermann (1032–35) the riches of Bremen increased.[5] But the greatness of Bremen really began with the famous Archbishop Adalbert (1043–71).[6]

Adalbert was the son of a Saxon noble, Count Frederick of Goseck. If he had been permitted to grow up as a feudal lord instead of a bishop the history of Saxony might have been very different from what it was. While yet provost in Halberstadt, Adalbert's ability, striking personality, and no less striking physical bearing made him a marked man. Henry III made him archbishop of Bremen. The ambition of the Billunger dukes of Saxony was at this time giving serious anxiety to the Emperor, and Henry wanted a strong man to hold it in check. In 1046 Adalbert accompanied the Emperor to Italy, and when Gregory VI died he was offered the papacy but waived the honor in favor of his old colleague of Halberstadt days, Bishop Suidger of Bamberg, who became Pope Clement II.

[1] Voigt, p. 46; Lambert of Hersfeld, (anno 1071).

[2] Lambert of Hersfeld (annis 1060, 1064, 1066, 1070, 1071, 1072, 1074, 1075, etc.).

[3] The large powers of the archbishop of Bremen date from the charter of Otto I (967), DO, II, 16; cf. Adam of Bremen, III, 5, Henry IV's confirmation of this grant.

[4] Adam of Bremen, II, 40, and schol. 46.

[5] Ibid, II, 44, 65; Thietmar, Chron., VI, 53.

[6] For a character sketch see Meyer von Knonan, Jahrb., II, 124–45.

Bremen historically was the ecclesiastical center from which the conversion of the North had radiated. Its episcopal overlordship extended over Denmark, Scandinavia, the Northern Islands, Iceland, and the newly conquered Slavonic lands; Adalbert dreamed of erecting his see into a huge patriarchate of Northern Europe; almost, one might say, to make himself pope of all Baltic and North Atlantic Christendom. The resistance of the Danish kings, of Harold Hardraade of Norway, and of Hildebrand, then the power behind the papal throne, who naturally could not tolerate such a separatist ecclesiastical project, ruined Adalbert's scheme.

Adalbert's early years in Bremen were his happiest and best. He admirably organized the diocesan administration and began work on the great cathedral. His court became one of the most brilliant in Europe, a refulgence possibly influenced by the commercial importance of the city. Italians, Greeks, Mohammedans, Spaniards, French, English, Norse; musicians, actors, literati, physicians, artists, were hospitably received within its gates.[1]

But the most substantial opposition came from the dukes of Saxony. The upgrowth of such a powerful episcopate within their immediate lands, and one intimately identified with Salian power, was most unwelcome to them. The Billunger feared, with good reason, that Henry III had planned to abolish the dukedom and vest its authority in Adalbert.[2]

---

[1] The names of some of these persons have been preserved, as John of Ireland; Gualdo Gallicus (*Hamb. Urkundenb.*, No. 101); Transmundus the artist-monk (Bruno, *De Bello Saxonico*, I, 4); Guido, a musician (Adam of Bremen, II, 66). Schumacher, *Brem. Jahrb.*, Vol. 5 conjectures he may have been Guido of Arezzo which is denied by Schmeidler, p. 129, n. 1; the most recent editor of Adam of Bremen, Aristo, probably a Byzantine Greek; Adamatus, from the medical school in Salerno; Bovo, a famous traveler who had been three times to Jerusalem and even to Cairo. For larger information see Adam of Bremen, III, 35–38, 44; for Adalbert's revenues see Adam of Bremen, II, 45; Dehio, *Gesch. des Erzbistums Hamburg-Bremen*, I, 175–277; Giesebrecht, *Kaiserzeit*, III, 95–138, 153–66; Beazeley, *Dawn of Modern Geography*, II, 516–21; K. Maurer, "Islands und Norwegens Verkehr mit dem Süden im IX. bis XIII. Jahrhundert," *Zeitschrift für deutsche Philologie*, II, 446; Riant, *Pèlerinages des Scandinaves en Terre Sainte*, p. 58. The Golden Psalter now in the Hofsbibliothek at Vienna is believed to be the one mentioned by Adam of Bremen, III, 45, as once belonging to Adalbert of Bremen. See Schmeidler's edition, p. 187, n. 5. Adam of Bremen, III, 58, mentions a colony of merchants in Bremen in 1072.

[2] Blumenthal, *Adalbert of Bremen*, p. 18.

The assignment of the county of Frisia to him, when Duke Gottfried of Lorraine died, readily made the Duke of Saxony so believe. Be this as it may, the enrichment of Bremen was a rapid one.[1] Adalbert tried to purchase the Duke's good-will by alienation of numerous estates of the church of Bremen. The old duke Bernward seems to have been not unwilling to compound with Adalbert, but nothing could pacify his sons, Bernhard, Ordulf, and Hermann.[2] The episcopal estates in Frisia were lost to Adalbert owing to a raid which the Duke and his two sons made in 1059, and seven hundred pounds of silver were collected by them.[3] Henry III had too many irons in the fire to be able to help the Archbishop to any great degree, and all that Adalbert seems to have acquired during his reign were the forest lands in Loragau and Stiergau, with the donation of two royal *villae*, Bolga and Fivelgoe.

I should think so, he was dead by 1056.

What could not be accomplished in the lifetime of Henry III was done in the earlier years of the reign of his son, when the weakness of the crown gave opportunities for seizures. Thus soon after the death of Henry III the Frisian counties on the left bank of the river Ems[4] were given to Adalbert, and in 1063 the promised estate Lesum[5] of approximately seven hundred *hubae*, with the rights of coinage and toll, and much land about the city of Bremen, were ceded. In the same year the countships Emsgau and Stade came into his possession, not as gifts, however, for the King demanded one hundred pounds of silver as the purchase price for Emsgau.[6] A short time afterward three more estates were transferred to his posses-

---

[1] Adam of Bremen, III, 8, p. 41.

[2] *Ibid.*, III, 9; Steindorff, II, 41.

[3] Adam of Bremen, III, 41–43. The abbey of Luellberg was also destroyed about the same time (*ibid.*, III, 35). Ordulf blinded some of the serfs on the episcopal lands. Henry III sent money to aid in rebuilding.

[4] Stumpf, No. 2540; cf. Adam of Bremen, III, 8, 45.

[5] Stumpf, No. 2622; cf. Steindorff, II, 16; Adam of Bremen, III, 8. Lesum was an old North German county which had once belonged to the Billunger, and had been "revindicated" by Conrad II. Hermann Billung at this time hoped to have it restored to him. Naturally the Billunger were incensed to see a territory to which they believed they had rightful claim pass into the hands of their worst enemy.

[6] Stumpf, Nos. 2630, 2632; Adam of Bremen, III, 35; Meyer von Knonau, I, 357.

sion, as well as the privilege of hunting in four royal forests.[1]
In 1065 the King awarded to Adalbert the countships of the
counts Bernhard and Werl, and the margraviate of Udo, with
the fiefs, immunities, market, and toll privileges pertaining
thereto. But as the King was in need of money at this time,
the Archbishop paid a thousand pounds of silver for the
acquisitions.[2] The abbeys of Lorsch and Corvey, however,
never came into Adalbert's possession, although transferred
to him by the King.[3]

During the absence of Adalbert at the King's court the
Billunger played havoc with the lands and serf population of
the Bremen diocese. In the end he was forced to buy off his
enemies by alienating a thousand mannors to Magnus Billung and nearly as much more in fief to Magnus' friend,
Count Udo of the Nordmark, before he dared return to
Bremen from his ancestral estates near Goslar, whither he
had fled. He died in 1071, four years before the death of his
implacable rival, Anno of Cologne.[4]

The rapacity of the German church, besides being manifested in the bitter feud between "regulars" and "seculars,"
in the strife between clergy and feudality, and in the exhaustion of the conquered border peoples by clerical taxation, is also reflected in the famous "Tithe War" of the early
years of Henry IV. Since its institution by Charlemagne[5] the
tithe had always been a lucrative source of income to the
church. Under the Saxon kings the church had labored hard
to subject all land, lay and clerical alike, to its imposition.[6]
While such a blanket right was not acquired, nevertheless the
church got a substantial reward. Otto I gave the Bishop of

[1] Stumpf, Nos. 2633, 2634, 2638.

[2] Adam of Bremen, III, 45. For a remarkable story told of Udo see Freeman,
Norman Conquest (2d ed.), IV, 245–46.

[3] Adam of Bremen, III, 27 and 44.

[4] Meyer von Knonau, I, 513–22; Gerdes, II, 162–63. The moral difference between Adalbert and Anno is to be observed. Anno of Cologne strove for personal
aggrandizement; Adalbert of Bremen for the aggrandizement of the church of
Bremen (Wattenbach, II, 71).

[5] Capit. Herist., anno 779; Leges, I, 50.

[6] Stein, Konrad I, p. 184; Dümmler, Otto I, Vol. I, p. 47; Koeniger, pp. 55–56.

Osnabrück permission to levy the tithe on all lands within his diocese.[1] Otto II permitted Corvey to collect it in Ammergau.[2] These rulers were complacent in allowing the tithe to be imposed upon the royal domain. Naturally there was contention between bishops and abbots for the right, all the more so because the bishops tried, in turn, to impose the tithe upon the monastery lands.

The Tithe War was a feud between the Archbishop of Mainz and the abbots of Fulda and Hersfeld, in which Thuringia was the bone of contention. Ecclesiastically the country was subject to Mainz, but part of the region paid tithe to the monasteries. The rest was exempt. The origin of this partial exemption is not known. Shortly before the death of Henry III, Liutpold of Mainz attempted for the first time to levy the tithe upon all Thuringia. The Thuringians resisted, pleading ancient customary law, no writ of exemption being in evidence. Liutpold claimed that Henry III had recognized the legality of his demand and included even the royal estates in Thuringia under the imposition. It was a barefaced piece of effrontery. The weak empress-mother Agnes compounded with the Archbishop and alienated one hundred and twenty manors of the fisc as the price of quittance.[3] But Fulda and Hersfeld repudiated the Archbishop's claim. While the struggle still endured Liutpold endeavored to extend the tithe over the lands of the Thuringian nobles too. The triangular conflict dragged along for years without settlement and finally became one of the eddies in the war of investiture.[4]

[1] Waitz, VIII, 347, n. 2. Pages 347–72 contain a long account of the history of the tithe in Salian Germany. In the reign of Henry IV, Benno of Osnabrück forged new documents for the extension of the tithe over Corvey and Herford (Wattenbach, II, 28–29), which precipitated another Tithe War in Saxony; cf. Loeffler, *Hist. Jahrb.*, XXIV (1903), 2; Philippi, *Osnabrücks Urkb.*, pp. ix f.; Brandi, *Westdeutsche Ztschft.*, XIX, 142 f. For its history in the twelfth century see Schreiber, *Kurie und Kloster im 12. Jahrhundert* (2 vols.; Stuttgart, 1910), Part III, pp. 2.6–94.

[2] Waitz, VIII, 355. The same privilege was given to Memleben.

[3] Waitz, VIII, 347; Stumpf, No. 2569; Lambert of Hersfeld (*annis* 1062, 1067, 1069, 1073, 1074, etc.). The synod of Quedlinburg (1085) forbade lay collection of the tithe except in cases where the right had been "legally" granted.

[4] For the history of this Tithe War see Giesebrecht, III, 1116 f.; Hauck, III, 730 f.; Voigt, pp. 56 f.; Wolf, *Eichsfeldische Kirchengesch.* (1816), pp. 60 f.; Ausfeld,

Meantime, in 1070 Henry IV had got the reins of government into his own hands. The change, so far as the German church is concerned, is reflected in two ways: first, in the diminution of grants of land to the bishops; second, in recovery of the "lost" royal abbeys by the crown.[1] Henry IV clearly perceived the importance of the monastery lands to the fisc and attempted to regain possession of those which had been seized by the episcopal cabal during his minority.[2] By strong pressure all but four of these were recovered, not, however, without their having suffered considerable reduction, owing to the rapacity of the bishops during their short possession of them,[3] and naturally while in the hands of such "politicals" the monasteries had received few benefactions.[4]

Such, as we have described it, is the complex background,

Lambert von Hersfeld und der Zehntstreit zwischen Mainz, Hersfeld und Thüringen (1880); Dronke, *Codex diplom. Fuld.*, pp. 370 f. Koeniger (pp. 55–56) has a good brief account of the tithe in the Saxon epoch. There is no proof that Henry IV promised the Archbishop of Mainz the collection of the Thuringian tithe if he would divorce him from the queen Bertha (Giesebrecht, III, 1116). The pretensions of Mainz emboldened the Archbishop of Salzburg to attempt the same measure in Bavaria, and he proceeded with such energy that most of the monasteries and nobles either paid or compounded. The sources abound with examples of feud between bishops and abbots, between bishops and bishops, between abbots and abbots, over the tithe, e.g., *Vita Bernwardi*, chaps. xiii–xv; *Vita Deoderici*, chap. xvi; *Vita Adalb.*, chap. ix. In 1123 Adalbert of Mainz at last succeeded in imposing a tithe upon crops and fruits in Thuringia (*Ann. Pegav.*, SS. XVI, 254).

[1] Lambert (1063) points out the dependence of the abbeys on the fisc: "Nihil minus regem juris ac potestatis in abbates habere quam in villicos suos vel in alios quoslibet regalis fisci dispensatores." *Ibid.* (1071): "Abbatiae publice venales prostituuntur in palatio, nec quisquam tanti venales proponere queat, quin protinus emptorem inveniat."

[2] *De unitate eccles. conserv.*, chap. xxxiii; *Libelli de lite*, II, 258 f.; Voigt, pp. 38–43.

[3] "Bald ein Theil der Einkünfte verschenkt, bald der Besitz selbst in fremde Hände gegeben" (Gerdes, II, 178); cf. Voigt, p. 51. During Henry IV's minority the bishops had annexed eleven countships. In all by 1073 the German episcopate is estimated to have held possession and collected the revenues from 53 countships.

[4] Even Adalbert of Bremen, whom Henry IV trusted much, could not persuade the King to be generous with him. Henry saw the necessity of hanging on to all the resources of the crown. When Magnus Billung surrendered after the revolt of Saxony, Henry, however, restored to Bremen the lands which the Duke had seized. Adam of Bremen asserts that the estates of Plisna, Duspure, Gronningen, and Sigoriem were restored, but no record has survived by which we may control this statement.

of the war of investiture upon the verge of which we now are. It was a series of wheels within wheels, of struggle within struggle, at the bottom of every one of which, in last analysis, the church's lands and the church's resources were the subject of feud. One other factor yet remains to be mentioned, the great revolt of the Saxons under Henry IV,[1] although this is not the place to enter into consideration of its causes. It was inspired by a blend of tribal jealousy, political and economic grievance, and social unrest. It was in no sense due to any religious or ecclesiastical issue, even remotely. But so decisive was the influence of the Saxon rebellion that it has been said with good reason that a compromise between state and church might have been possible "in an atmosphere undisturbed by the Saxon war," but that this "was from the first rendered abortive by the obstinate determination of the Saxon race."[2] Rebellious Saxony and the papacy had a common enemy in Henry IV, and Gregory VII was acute enough to perceive the value of Saxon support. The coincidence between the rebellion of the Saxons and the prohibition by Gregory VII of lay investiture was not accidental. The Pope's action was deliberately timed.[3]

The rebellious Saxon nobles favored the Gregorian cause solely out of self-interest, and in spite of his detestation of the Germans the Pope welcomed their alliance.[4] No thinking person of the time was duped by the Saxon professions of religious devotion.[5] Their special and local motives were clearly perceived.[6] Real Gregorianism probably had less actual sway in Saxony than anywhere else in Germany. The Saxon hierarchy was notoriously political and secular in spirit and practice, and the lower clergy were almost totally

---

[1] See chapter **v**.   [3] Gerdes, II, 176–77.

[2] Fisher, I, 133.   [4] Meyer von Knonau, I, 140.

[5] It is to be noticed that most of the northern bishops backed Henry IV in spite of their metropolitans of Mainz, Cologne, and Magdeburg (Loeffler, *Die Westfälischen Bischöfe im Investiturstreit*). In Osnabrück, Benno II (1088) was an imperialist; Markwald, former abbot of Corvey, a Gregorian—deposed in 1093; Wido (1093–1101) an imperialist; cf. Klem, *Mitteil. d. Ver. f. d. Gesch. von Osnabrück*, Band XXVII (1902).

[6] Guill. Malmesb., *Gesta regum Anglorum*, III, 288; Bruno, *De bello Saxonico*, chaps. 108, 116; *De unitate eccles conserv.*, II, 16.

illiterate.[1] The cleverness with which Henry IV and his partisans maneuvered at Tribur,[2] and the wavering course of
Gregory VII are in striking contrast. Gregory VII at first had
no idea of dethroning the King, and after Canossa recognized
him as such, although in 1080 he denied that he had restored
Henry.[3] The Pope's dealings with Rudolph of Swabia were
ambiguous. On the other hand, there is nothing to prove that
Henry IV falsified his promise of October, 1076.[4] When the
war began, Rudolf of Swabia, whom the feudal party put
up as king on March 15, 1077, was compelled to purchase a
following by promises of land, not only from the royal fisc,
but out of the domains of the church.[5] The first thing striven
for by all parties, and the last thing surrendered, was the
lands, whether belonging to one or another of the partisans,
or to the fisc, or to the church.

The princes of Germany, who were already intriguing with Gregory
for support in their perennial revolts against their sovereign, were delighted to seize the opportunity of at once obliging the pope, creating
disturbance at home, and profiting by the church property which they
could manage to get into their hands by ejecting the unfortunate married
priests. . . . . Add to this the attraction which persecution always pos-
sesses for the persecutor, and the license of plunder so dear to a turbulent
and barbarous age, and it is not difficult to comprehend the motive power
of the storm. . . . . A contemporary writer whose name has been lost, but
who is supposed by Dom Martène to have been a priest of Treves, gives
us a very lively picture of the horrors which ensued, and as he shows himself friendly in principle to the reform attempted his account may be
received as trustworthy. He describes what amounted almost to a dissolution of society.[6]

As early as 1078 Gregory VII was compelled to order that no
more church property was to be enfiefed, and threatened to
put everyone who sought to enrich himself by seizure of

---

[1] *Vita Bennonis*, chap. v, Gregory VII, *Ep.*, IX, 3, admitted even most of Italy
favored Henry IV: "Cui ferme omnes Italici favent."

[2] Cf. Brackmann, *Hist. Vierteljahrschrift* (1912), No. 2.

[3] See Martens, *Ztschft. f. Kirchenrecht*, N.F., 1882 Band II.

[4] Cf. Schaefer, *Hist. Ztschft.*, Band LX, Heft 3.

[5] Bertholdi, *Annal.* (1077); Bruno, *De bello Saxonico*, chaps. xcix, cviii; Hauck,
III, 810; Gerdes, II, 268–70.

[6] Lea, *Sacerdotal Celibacy* (3d ed.), I, 278–79; Martène and Durand, *Thesaurus*,
I, 230–31.

church land under the papal ban.[1] Six months later the synod of Rome ordered every noble, every bishop, and every abbot who had seized any church land to restore it whence it came.[2] In 1085 the legate Leo of Ostia, at the synod of Quedlinburg, issued a blanket ban against all despoilers of church lands.[3] Nevertheless, for years the lands of the church were subjected to almost perpetual pillage. The sources abound with such references.[4] As a result of the anarchy there was a great exodus of monks from Germany into France.[5]

The masterly stroke of Henry IV at Canossa in defeating Gregory's designs with reference to Germany,[6] and the utter

---

[1] Hefele, V, 109.   [2] *Ibid.*, p. 114.   [3] *Ibid.*, p. 333.

[4] *Gesta Trevorum*, chaps. iv, xvi, xxii; *Gesta Alberonis*, chaps. xii, xiv; *Gesta episcop. Mettens. cont.*, I, chap. i; *Laurentii gesta episcop. Virdun*, chaps. ix, x, xxii, xxv; *Vita Churnadi archiep.*, chap. vii; *Ann. Augsb.* (annis 1077, 1084, 1088, 1090); *Ann. Sax* (anno 1077): Bruno, chap. cxii; *Vita Norberti*, chap. xviii; *Chron. episc. Merseburg*, chap. xiii; *Chron. Gozecens*, II, chaps. xxii–xxiv, xxix; Ekkehard, *Casus S. Galli, passim; Gesta abbat. S. Trudon*, X, chap. xii, *Ruperti chron. S. Laurent. Leod.*, chaps. xlv–xlvi, l; *Chron. S. Huberti-Andag.*, chap. lxxxix. For Corvey's losses, Martiny, *Grundbesitz Corveys*, p. 305; for Fulda's, Dronke, *Trad. Fuld.*, p. 153; Bunte, *Güterbesitz des Kloster Fulda* ("Jahrbuch für Emden"), Band X, Heft 1; Ekkehard, *Chron.* (annis 1098, 1125); Ortlieb, *Chron. Zwifaltens.*, chap. v; Cosmas of Prague, III, chap. xx; *Chron. S. Petri Efford* (anno 1105); Jaffé, V, 232, 517.

[5] Gerdes, II, 272. Pro-Gregorian monks wore beards, pro-Henrician ones shaved the face clean (*Gesta Trev.*, chap. x, SS. VIII, 183).

[6] Every historical scholar today who is worthy of the name knows that Canossa was a victory for Henry IV, and not for Gregory VII. The prevalent popular and erroneous belief, which has been carefully cultivated and fostered by the Church of Rome and has even deceived most Protestant historians, as Milman and Michelet, for example, is based upon the account of the incident as described by Lambert of Hersfeld, supplemented by later legendary materials. Von Ranke was the first scholar who challenged the integrity of Lambert ("Zur Kritik fränkisch-deutscher Reichsannalisten," *Abhand. d. Akad. d. Wiss. zu Berlin* [Phil.-hist. Cl., 1855]. This was followed in 1873 by Delbrück's crushing critical study, "Ueber die Glaubwürdigkeit Lamberts von ████████feld," and later by Döllinger, *Kirchengesch.*, II, 1, pp. 131 f.; Hefele, *Conciliengesch.*, V, 89 f.; and D. Schaefer, *Deutsche Gesch.*, I, 226, since which it has been impossible to attach any credence to Lambert. Although he seems to have had copies of Gregory's letters before him when he wrote, Lambert, by transposing the Pope's words, garbled the meaning (cf. ed. Holder-Egger, p. 291 nn.). Henry was *not* kept outside the courtyard of the chateau of Canossa, and merely "intra secundum murorum ambitum receptus," as Lambert says, while "foris derelicto omni comita u suo." Both statements are false, for Henry and his company were admitted to the place before the gate of the inner castle, according to Gregory's own account (*Reg.*, IV, 12) which is confirmed by Berthold; Berthold, *Annal.*, p. 289; cf. Haller, *Neues Jahrb.*, IX (1906), 2. The "castellum triplici muro septum" is a description of Lambert's own fancy borrowed from

failure of effect which his second ban had, gradually gave Henry IV the upper hand.[1] By 1093 Germany and Italy were under imperial control once more.[2] With the death of William of Hirsau in 1091 the Cluniac movement in Germany collapsed.[3]

By 1085 Henry IV had succeeded in winning control of almost every bishopric in the kingdom. Only Gebhard of Salzburg, Altmann of Passau, Adalbert of Worms, Hermann of Metz, and Adalbert of Würzburg resisted to the last. In the Council of Mainz in April of that year these, too, were deposed. But in the next year, following upon a new rising of the Saxons and the King's defeat at Pleichfeld (August 11), Adalbert of Würzburg recovered his see for a season. Actually, however, the Gregorian episcopal party collapsed with the death of Burckhardt of Halberstadt.[4]

Vergil vi. 549. Moreover, Henry did *not* stand *en chemise*, as Michelet says, *nor*, "while the fierce winds of the Apennines were sweeping the sleet upon him in their passage from Monte Pellegro to the plain, [he] knelt barefoot, clothed in sackcloth, fasting from dawn till eve, for three whole days," as Symonds (*Sketches in Italy*) has written, *nor* "clad only in the thin white linen dress of the penitent," as Milman has said. Henry naturally, since he was appearing as a penitent, put off his royal insignia and assumed the garb of a penitent. But all that Gregory (*Reg.*, IV, 12) says is that "deposito omne regio cultu, miserabiliter utpote discalciatus et laneis indutus," which shows that he was comfortably clad beneath his white dress. Again, Henry did *not* "a mane usque ad vesperam perstabat," i.e., stand "three days" outside the castle door. Gregory himself, Berthold, and Donizo all say only that "on the third day" Henry was admitted to the papal presence (Lambert of Hersfeld [ed. Holder-Egger], p. 292 nn.). The famous "hostia-scene," in which Gregory is alleged to have prayed that he might be stricken dead if guilty, when swallowing the holy wafer, and challenging Henry to the same ordeal, is a dramatization imitated by Lambert from Regino of Prüm's account (*anno* 869) of the interview between Pope Hadrian II and King Lothar II of Lorraine. The incidents and the language are nearly identical. Neither Gregory nor Bruno has any such account of the incident, and Berthold's and Donizo's versions are much less sensational (see Holder-Egger, p. 297 nn.). Finally, it must be remembered that an act like that of Henry IV at Canossa, dramatic as it seems to us, was not fraught with novelty for men in the Middle Ages. It was no new thing in

[Footnote continued on page 140]

[1] "Er [Gregory VII] weiss, mit der Absolution, ist Heinrich auch wieder König," (Dehnicke, *Massnahmen Gregors VII gegen Heinrich IV*, Halle diss., 1889).

[2] Lamprecht, II, 36.

[3] Feierabend, p. 28. For the completeness of Henry IV's ecclesiastical control see Herbordus, *Dialogus*, III, 35; *Vita Otton. ep. Babenb.*, I, 7; Jaffé, V, 595, 828.

[4] Hauck, III, 839–50; Stein, *Gesch. Frankens*, I, 178 f.

Gregory VII died May 25, 1085 in self-exile in Salerno, whither he had sought refuge with the Norman king, Robert Guiscard, his spirit indomitable to the last. If the words reputed to him lack positive authenticity—"I have loved justice and hated iniquity. Therefore I die in exile"—they are true in fact if not perhaps in form.

The cardinals gathered at his bedside besought him to designate his successor, who might safely steer the ark of the church through the troubled waters. The dying pontiff is said to have recommended to the suffrage of the College of Cardinals Desiderius, the abbot of Monte Cassino; Archbishop Hugh of Lyons; Otto, bishop of Ostia; and Anselm, bishop of Lucca. Meanwhile, Henry IV's anti-pope had been driven from Rome by the mob. At first the Abbot of Monte Cassino seemed the most likely person to secure the tiara, but he hesitated to accept the honor so nearly thrust upon him, and finally quit the city and returned to his monastery. His election would have been a good omen for Henry IV to whom he was favorable, and he was supported by the Nor-

---

medieval Europe, either before or after the time of Henry IV, for a king to do public penance and even to be flogged. Otto I, Otto III, Henry II, Henry III, all did such penance without forfeiting the loyalty of their subjects. The imposition of penance was a discipline of the church and was universal. It was not even a humiliation. Gregory had to absolve Henry, for the moral sentiment of Europe would have regarded it as a monstrous abuse of the authority of the church if he had refused to do so. Henry professed penitence; he had to be forgiven. By the absolution Gregory was balked from going into Germany to try the King at Augsburg, and although the Pope later claimed that the absolution did not restore Henry to the kingdom, it is a quibble to say the ban deprived him of the right to rule, but that the raising of it did not restore him to the kingship. The utter failure of the second ban shows the futility of the Pope's efforts, for it helped Henry's cause instead of hurting it. The real victor at Canossa was Henry IV, not Gregory VII. He foiled all the plans of his enemies. As Nitzsch, II, 100, has said: "Dieser Akt einer furchtbaren, rücksichtslosen Energie gab den Vermittlern die Oberhand über das Misstrauen des Päpstes." Whether Henry himself devised this astonishing way out of the situation in which he found himself at the diet of Tribur ("inito tam occulto quam astuto consilio" [*Vita Heinrici*, chap. iii, p. 13]), or whether it was suggested to him by someone else, is a matter of conjecture. Personally I am inclined to think that the suggestion came from Hugh of Cluny, always one of Henry's staunch supporters, who was with him when he was suspended from the kingship at Tribur. Lambert of Hersfeld ended his history at this point (1077), giving up in despair any hope of resolving the complex mass of material which he had collected, and using almost the identical valedictory words of Lampridius, in his *Vita Sept. Severi*. After the exhibition of partisanship, falsification, and mendacity which he perpetrated under the guise of "history" it is small wonder that he did so.

man influence. Fortunately for the papacy his timidity frustrated his election.

A long deadlock ensued. The intervening months had seen a new broadcasting of that polemical literature to which the war of investiture gave rise. Guido of Ferrara endeavored in a pamphlet to demonstrate that Gregory VII had been a schismatic, and implored the factions to recognize the anti-pope. The imperialist blast was all the more disconcerting to papalists for the reason that their own camp was divided. Hugh of Lyons and the Gregorian intransigeants formed a radical group of "die-hards," who would accept no compromise. Things seemed to be coming Henry IV's way of themselves. Rudolf of Swabia, the first anti-king, had been slain in battle (1080). The second anti-king was a hopeless nonentity. The rebellious Saxons were cowed, if not completely crushed. The papal partisans in Germany were silent and submissive. With great astuteness the Emperor had expressed his wish to have peace, his regret for the misfortunes of Gregory VII, and declared himself willing to submit to the second excommunication provided its legality were established. To this end he convoked the Saxon bishops at Gerstungen. The papal legate in Germany, Otto of Ostia (the future Pope Urban II), who had been sent thither to draw together again the threads of papal interest, made a tactical blunder in consenting to this conference and designated Gebhard, archbishop of Salzburg, as the Gregorian advocate.

But the cards were stacked against him in advance. Wezil of Mainz, a Henrician partisan, boldly produced a false decretal which seemed to favor the Emperor's contention, and the Archbishop was not a clever enough scholar to discern the forgery. The result was that the bishops refused to sustain the alleged papal act. Udo of Hildesheim, his brother Conrad, Count Theodoric of Katlenburg, and others made their peace with the King. After Easter, 1085, Henry IV convened a synod at Mainz whose members triumphantly sustained the King's cause. The composition of this synod is worth noting. Besides the three Rhenish bishops—Wezil of Mainz, Egilbert of Trier, Sigwin of Cologne—sixteen other bishops had responded to Henry's summons, among them

Theodoric of Verdun, Conrad of Utrecht, Robert of Bamberg, Otto of Constance, and Udo of Hildesheim. Hermann of Metz was the sole prelate west of the Rhine not an avowed Henrician partisan. He had appealed to Gregory VII for counsel and had been the recipient of that famous papal epistle in which the Pope had fully set forth his theocratic ideas. Hermann henceforth was an eager papal partisan, so that Henry IV now deposed him and established the Abbot of St. Arnulf in his stead.

Certain now that the German episcopate was well in hand, Henry IV turned to Saxony to achieve its final pacification. Here, where Udo of Hildesheim and Hartwig of Hersfeld had labored earnestly in the King's behalf, affirming that the crown would not displant the old Saxon privileges, most of the Saxon nobles made their submission. The counterking, and the few supporters which he still had, fled across the Elbe. The Abbot of Hersfeld was installed in the archbishopric of Magdeburg; Merseburg, Meissen, and Minden were filled with Henrician bishops. The same sort of displacement of Gregorian bishops by loyal supporters of the imperial cause took place in Bavaria. All feudal and ecclesiastical opposition to Henry IV was dead in Germany. From the Elbe to the Rhine, from the Alps to the sea, the cause of anti-king and pope seemed at an end. In Italy the Countess Matilda of Tuscany was shut up in the castle of Canossa, practically a prisoner.

Meantime, what of the papacy? In the College of Cardinals at this juncture the Norman influence was in control. The policy of Robert Guiscard was both anti-imperial and anti-Gregorian. He feared both the German power in Italy and the growth of the theocratic power of the papacy. Guiscard's candidate for the throne of St. Peter was the pliable Abbot of Monte Cassino, and in the issue he was elected pope, taking the name Victor III. The choice antagonized the Bishop of Ostia and Hugh of Lyons, each of whom had been strong candidates, and a rupture of the College of Cardinals ensued. The new Pope's early demise, however, soon liberated the papal office from immediate Norman control. The factions were united again, and finally, nearly three years after Gregory VII's death, his ideas may be said to have returned to their august seat when Otto of Ostia was finally elected to be pope, taking the name of Urban II, a name destined to win everlasting renown in history. For Urban II was the organizer of the First Crusade (1095).[1] The zeal of the cleric and the avarice of the feudality had consumed the land. When there was nothing else for the Pope to offer the nobles as an inducement for further support he proffered the enslavement of the wives of married priests as a bribe.[2]

The influence of the First Crusade upon the peace of Germany was manifested in a drawing off toward the east of the most boisterous fighting element. In 1101 a German army under Welf of Bavaria and the archbishops of Salzburg and Passau went on an expedition to the Orient. Welf died on the return homeward.

The authority of Henry IV was everywhere acknowledged in Germany.[3] But the overture which the Emperor made to Rome in 1101 was repulsed, and the excommunication[4] of him renewed in sharper form. At the diet of Mainz in 1102 a general peace for the whole Empire was decreed to last for four years. The peasantry, and especially the burgher class in the towns, profited much from the order which prevailed in the realm. Cologne became notoriously prosperous.

[1] The intricate history of papal politics in the years immediately following the death of Gregory VII has been best studied by F. Chalandon, *La domination normande en Italie et en Sicilie*, Vol. I, chap. xii; and more recently by A. Fliche, "La crise religeuse depuis la mort de Grégoire VII jusqu'à l'avènement d'Urban II," *Revue des cours et des conférences*, Vol. XXIV, Nos. 1–2.

[2] *Synod. Melfi.* (1089), canon 12, cited by Lea, *Sacerdotal Celibacy* (3d ed.), I, 289.

[3] Even Henry IV's enemies, when not blinded by prejudice and indulging in vituperation, admitted his ability and force of character. Ekkehard, *Chron.* (1106); Pertz, VI, 239: "Pluribus autem testibus comprobare poterimus, quod nemo nostris temporibus, natu, ingenio, fortitudine et audacia, statura etiam totaque corporis elegantia videatur fascibus imperialibus ipso aptior, si tamen in conflictu vitiorum homo non degeneraret vel succumberet interior."

[4] Urban II declared it was not murder to kill those who were excommunicated (*Ep. ad Godfred episcopum Lucan*, citing Gratian, *Decret.*, cap. xlvii, Qu. 5: "Non enim eos homicidas arbitramur quos adversus excommunicatos zelo catholicae matris ardentes, aliquos eorum trucidare contigerit." A council in 1105 ordered the disinterment of bodies of excommunicates (*Annal. Hild.* [Pertz, III, 108]).

But there were tares in the wheat. Many of the German nobles who had battened on the civil war for years were loath to obey the peace. Others who had once supported Henry IV's monarchical designs now took alarm at the growth of the royal power and drifted over to the side of the Pope and his feudal partisans in Germany. The *ministeriales*, of whom by now there were thousands, who had been fed on the meat of power too much, in imitation of the feudality built their castles on the hilltops and assumed the life of a riotous baronage, to the anger and dismay of the peasantry.

The insurrection of the Emperor's son Henry was based upon these elements, and by 1103 the kingdom again began to be racked by civil war.[1] The reason given by the latter, that he was not bound to obey an excommunicated ruler, was a mere pretext. His main motive was that he was fearful of losing the succession, and the instigation of the papal partisans and the discontented feudality urged him forward. The insurrection, as was natural, rapidly spread over Thuringia and Saxony, the ancient battle-ground of opposition to the Salians. To make matters worse for the emperor, the bishops who had hitherto largely supported him now deserted the imperial cause on account of Henry IV's friendly attitude toward the burghers in the towns, between whom and the bishops there was an enduring feud. The secession of the bishops, too, was accelerated, owing to the fact that Henry IV, on account of the dilapidation of the fisc, had increased the taxes upon the church.

[1] "Patria ab utraque parte nimio incendio vastatur."—*Ann. Rosenv.* (1103). Herman of Tournai explicitly says that Urban II provoked the rebellion of Henry V: "Interea callidus papa Henricum adolescentem filium Henrici imperatoris litteris adversus patrem concitat et ut ecclesiae Dei auxilietur, admonet; ille, regni cupidus .... (Achery, II, 914). Even Gerhoh, *De statu ecclesiae*, chap. xviii, a papal partisan, says that Henry V was crowned "Urbani papae hortatu accedente." The *Annales* of Hildesheim declare that the idea of inciting Henry IV's son against him was of divine inspiration: "Apostolicus autem ut audivit inter patrem et filium discidium, sperans haec a Deo evenisse." Herman of Tournai, who saw the letter Henry IV wrote to Philip of France in regard to Prince Henry's rebellion, wrote: "Quam si quis legerit et non fleverit, videtur mihi duri esse cordis," Achery, II, 914. The *Chron. Breve Leodiense* (Martène and Durand, *Anecd.*, IV, 1407) flays Prince Henry: "contra jus naturae et fas legum." Alberic of Trois-Fontaines said: "Sub specie religionis eo quod pater ejus a romanis pontificibus excommunicatus .... videres .... quod contra legem naturae, filius in patrem assurgeret."

After two years of desultory conflict Henry IV was compelled to resign the crown; he had even to recite the form of confession of his sins—the *Confiteor*—as a crowning humiliation. Henry IV fled from Ingelheim and threw himself upon the protection of the Rhenish burghers. Flanders, Lorraine, and the Rhinelands joined with Saxony and Thuringia. In the midst of the struggle the Emperor died, on August 7, 1106, his last act having been to send his signet ring and sword to his rebellious son.

It now remained for Henry V to settle the long controversy. He had played with his father's enemies as a means to an end. His professions had been mere pretenses, for he was a true Salian in the conception of his prerogative. But his path was smoother than that of his father. For the struggle had dragged on so long[1] and the exhaustion of both combatants was so great that room had been made for a compromise party to get a hearing. A generation of rack and ruin began to bring surcease of combat through very exhaustion. The strife had given birth to an enormous amount of polemical literature.[2]

Out of the bewildering maze of passions and conflicting ideas a mediate thought gradually crystallized. An unknown monk of Hersfeld, who was the author of the tract entitled *De unitate ecclesiae conservanda*, and Wido of Ferrara, author of the *De scismate Hildebrandi*, were the chief imperialist pamphleteers, and urged a double and simultaneous investiture by both church and state: the one for the bishop's office, the other for his lands. Already before the close of the eleventh century Yves de Chartres and Hildebert of Lavardin, bishop of Tours, had begun diligently to labor in search of a general principle which would reconcile the

---

[1] For the anarchy in Germany see Hauck, IV, 105.

[2] For this literature see Mirbt, *Libelli de Lite*, and his *Die Publizistik im Zeitalter Gregors VII* (1894); Bernheim, *Zur Gesch. des Wormser Konkordats* (1878); Willing, *Zur Gesch. des Investiturstreites* (1896); Heinzelmann, *Die Farfenser Streitschriften, etc.* (1904); Imbart de la Tour, "La polémique religieuse et les publicistes à l'époque de Grégoire VII, *Revue des Questions Historiques* (1907), pp. 226 f.; Fliche, *Études sur la polémique religieuse à l'époque de Gregoire VII: polémique durant la querelle du Investiture* (1916)."

issue yet preserve the principle for which the church contended.[1]

In his perturbation Pascal II turned toward France for support, and in rapid succession sent four separate legates thither: John of Gubbio, cardinal of Ste Anastasia; Benedict, cardinal of Ste Eudoxia; Richard of Albano, deacon of St. Stephen's in Metz; and Bruno, bishop of Segni. On December 2, 1104, the Pope raised the ban of excommunication under which King Philip I had been living for years, closed his eyes to the latter's misconduct with Countess Bertrada of Anjou, and followed this action by liberal concessions concerning episcopal elections in France, yielding papal preferment to royal choice.

There is ground for the probability that some sort of compromise was arrived at not unsimilar to the Concordat of 1107 made between Henry I of England and Anselm, which certainly was the prototype of the Concordat of Worms in 1122. In that instrument the English king renounced the right to invest the bishop with ring and crozier, but retained the prerogative to exact homage of the bishop.

Some such entente seems to have been arranged between Philip I and Pascal II, owing, so far as we can judge, to the conciliatory influence of Yves of Chartres.[2]

How far along the road of compromise the papacy had traveled within twenty-two years may be appreciated when we compare these terms with the uncompromising ones of Gregory VII. In his eyes the church had the whole and exclusive right to dispose both of the bishop's office and the lands pertaining to the see. But now, in Pascal II's time the lands of the church are conceded to be fiefs of the king (*regalia*) which the kings had donated to the church subject to the exaction of feudal rights and including royal investiture.

If we cut the issue of lay investiture down to the marrow

[1] Barth, *Hildebert von Lavardin (1056–1135)* (Stuttgart, 1906), chap. ii. For French indifference to the significance of the war of investiture in its early stages see Flach, *Origines de l'anc. France*, III, 279.

[2] B. Monod, *Essai sur les rapports de Pascal II avec Phillippe Ier (1090–1108)* (Paris, 1907), pp. 90–91.

by putting the question of simony to one side for a moment, an analysis of the evidence, as Scharnagel has made it, shows that there were three interpretations of what was meant by the term "investiture."[1] According to the first, lay investiture concerned not only the property of the church, but the church itself, its independence, its dignity, its authority. The Gregorians gave the word this sweeping application in order to make the contention of Henry IV appear to be as monstrous as possible. According to the second theory, investiture could only be given to those bishops canonically elected, and had to be given to them; but the bishop was bound to swear homage and fidelity to the secular power. Until his open espousal (after long hesitation) of the cause of Rudolph of Swabia, whom the German rebels put up as counter-king to Henry IV, Gregory VII seems to have been inclined to tolerate this form of investiture, but the Emperor refused to concede any abatement of his prerogative. But as the conflict became more bitter the papacy hardened, and Urban II in 1095 forbade the bishops to perform homage. The third interpretation took a middle stand between these two extremes, acknowledged the legitimacy of both contestants, and aimed to effect a compromise by providing for simultaneous and due recognition of the rights both of the church and of the secular power.

The pacific current of French ecclesiastical thought at this time was peculiarly effective, for in France the strife over lay investiture never reached the colossal dimensions it had within the Empire, although the Gregorian claims had produced acute relations between the papacy and Philip I, the dukes of Normandy (who were at the same time, be it remembered, also kings of England), the counts of Anjou, and others of the great French feudality.

In this atmosphere, less surcharged with enmity, a moderate and liberal group of the French clergy was formed, imbued with the ideas of Cardinal Damieni, who in the early days of the Cluny movement had attempted to distinguish between the purely ecclesiastical and the feudo-temporal

[1] Scharnagel, *Der Begriff der Investitur in den Quellen und der Literatur des Investiturstreites* (Stuttgart, 1908).

nature of the bishop's office, and had advocated a compromise settlement of the issue.[1] Progressive without being radical, resolute without being violent, this third party of moderates gradually grew in influence until, with the exhaustion of both combatants, it at last began to find a hearing.[2]

This compromise form of settlement slowly increased the number of its adherents and formally triumphed in England in 1107 with the concordat made between Henry I and Anselm, by which election of bishops and abbots was to be in the hands of the chapters, but held at the king's court, the consecration to be in the hands of the bishops, but the temporal estates of the church to be conferred by the king. This English form of settlement had a powerful influence upon France and French politico-ecclesiastical thought.[3]

[1] Hinschius, *Kirchenrecht*, II, 552 ff.; Kayser, *Placidus von Nonantula:* Gierke-Maitland, *Political Theories of the Middle Ages*, nn. 34, 38, 46; J. de Ghellinck, "Polémique durant la querelle des investitures," *Révue des Quest. Hist.* (N.S.), XCIII, 71–89. The last article contains much additional bibliography. It is significant of the depth to which Rome had intellectually degenerated that during the whole eleventh century the Hildebrandine propaganda had no Roman representative. All the thinking was done by Lombard and Franco-Burgundian publicists (Wattenbach, II, 195). Donizo of Sutri is an exceedingly untrustworthy source. Originally a zealous partisan of the papacy and author of a tract against simony, when removed from the see of Piacenza by Urban II for misconduct, he became a violent detractor of the Pope and the countess Matilda. See Fournier, *Bib. de l'école d. ch.* (May-Oct. 1915); Martens, *Theol. Quartalschrift*, Vol. LXV (1883).

[2] Consult Esmein, *La question des investitures dans les lettres d'Ive de Chartres* (1889); Fournier, "Yves de Chartres et le droit canonique," *Compte rendu du quatrième congrès scientifique internat. des catholiques* (Fribourg en Suisse, 1898); Lavisse, *Histoire de France*, II, 2, pp. 218–20; Gierke-Maitland, *op. cit.*, n. 38. Fournier, *Bib. de l'école d. chartes*, LVII, 645–98; LVIII, 26–77, has an exhaustive study of *Les Collections canoniques attribuées à Yves de Chartres*. These are the *Panormia*, the *Decretum*, from which the *Panormia* was abridged, and the *Tripartita*. He concludes that Yves was the author of the first two and of two-thirds of the last, and that the Bishop's purpose was ecclesiastical reform in anticipation of the councils called by Urban II. Yves of Chartres' ideas may be summarized as follows: ecclesiastical election, popular acclamation, papal approval, lay investiture of temporalities. Barth, *Hildebert von Lavardin*, chap. ii, deals largely with the conciliatory ideas of Yves of Chartres. Schum, *Die Politik Papst Paschals II gegen Kaiser Heinrich V im Jahr 1112*, gives interesting details about Ives de Chartres, Geoffrey de Vendome, etc.

[3] The best presentation of the Anglo-French angle of the conflict over investiture will be found in Boehmer, *Kirche und Staat in England und in der Normandie im XI. und XII. Jahrhundert* (Leipzig, 1899), Part II, in which he surveys all the literature pertaining to the issue in France and England before 1107, i.e., the writings of Yves of Chartres and Hugh of Fleury, of Lanfranc and Anselm, of Gilbert Crispin

This compromise solution was ultimately applied to Germany and Italy in the Concordat of Worms in 1122, with the difference that in the former kingdom homage preceded consecration, while in Italy and Burgundy consecration was made to precede homage.

But there were still rocks and shoals ahead, and years were to elapse before a settlement finally could be made. The idea of compromise was distasteful to both Emperor and Pope, and even when each began so to incline from sheer exhaustion, neither dared take the initiative for fear of letting his cards slip out of his hand.

Henry V began his reign aided by the papal party.[1] His election was at Mainz on December 25, 1105, while his father was yet alive. Henry IV was deserted by almost all in Germany except the burghers of the Rhine cities.[2] The new emperor—or rather counter-Emperor—immediately sent an embassy to Rome,[3] the chief members of which were Bruno, archbishop of Trier; Henry, archbishop of Magdeburg; Otto, bishop of Bamberg; Eberhard, bishop of Eichstädt; and Gebhard, bishop of Constance, the last an intimate friend of Pascal II. It is important also to notice that the historian, Ekkehard of Aura, was in the embassy, a circumstance which gives his narrative unusual weight.[4]

But the embassy sent by Henry V failed to reach Rome. It was intercepted by a young count named Adalbert, acting for Henry IV, according to Ekkehard, and all the members of it were captured except Gebhard of Constance, who finally got to Rome.[5] Presumably Gebhard performed the mission of the entire embassy, for at the Council of Guastalla no evidence of friction between Henry V and the papacy was evidenced. This Council convened in the last week of October,

---

and Hervert of Norwich (Thetford). The hundred pages (pp. 177–269) are masterly in which the chronology of these writings is examined and the ideas of the authors analyzed with reference to ordination of priests' sons, celibacy, relations of church and state, etc.

[1] Ekkehard, *Chronicon Universale*; Migne, CLIV, 999.   [2] *Ibid.*

[3] Gregorovius, *Rome in the Middle Ages*, IV, 2, p. 324.

[4] Ekkehard in Migne, CLIV, 1005.   [5] *Ibid.*, col. 1003.

1106. Ekkehard was present and records that Pascal II promised to come to Mainz at the next Christmas.[1] A serious endeavor seems to have been made at Guastalla to adjust the grounds of feud between pope and emperor. A decree was issued ecclesiastically legitimizing those bishops and lesser clergy who had been ordained during the war of investiture.[2] No mention was made of that formidable word "investiture."

If the papal party had cherished the hope that the new ruler would be inclined to their interests it was soon disillusioned. A Guelf emperor was as impossible as a Ghibelline pope. Before the year 1106 was far along it was evident that the Salian leopard had not changed his spots. Henry V invested the bishops in Germany with both ring and staff,[3] against which the Council of Troyes in the next year protested. It is not surprising, therefore, to find that the Pope did not come to Germany as he had promised.[4] Instead, he went to France and spent the whole winter (1106–7) either at Cluny or at St. Denis.[5] At Châlons-sur-Marne in May, 1107, Henry V's ambassadors made uncompromising demand for a

[1] *Ibid.*, cols. 1013, 1015.

[2] *Chronica regia Coloniensis* (folio ed.), p. 45.

[3] William of Malmesbury, the English historian, was not far wrong at this time when he wrote (*Gesta*, sec. 420): "The emperor had in his favor all the bishops and abbots of the kingdom . . . . because Charlemagne . . . . had conferred almost all the country on the churches, most wisely considering that the clergy would not so soon cast off their fidelity to their lord as the laity; and besides, if the laity were to rebel, they might be restrained by the authority of episcopal excommunication and weight of power" (cf. Waitz, VII, 203, n. 2).

For a modern characterization, which shows that William of Malmesbury knew what he was writing about: "Seit Otto dem Grossen nahmen die deutschen Bischöfe eine kirchlich-weltliche Doppelstellung ein, sie waren zugleich hohe Würdenträger der Kirche und des Reiches. Als Diener der Kirche waren sie ihrem Oberhaupte, dem Nachfolger Petri, Gehorsam schuldig. Als Inhaber von Reichsgütern waren sie dem Könige verpflichtet; ihm hatten sie auch meist die Erhebung auf ihre Stühle zu danken. Und endlich haben sich nicht wenige Bischöfe auch an den Bestrebungen der weltlichen Fürsten beteiligt" (Löffler, *Die Westfälischen Bischöfe im Investiturstreit* [Halle, 1903]).

[4] Ekkehard, *op. cit.*, col. 1015.

[5] For his activities in France at this season see Suger, *Vita Lud. Crassi* (ed. Molinier, 1887), chap. ix, and Luchaire, *Cat. des actes de Louis VI*, Introd., pp. cxxxiii–iv; *Inst. mon. de la France*, I, 140; Mühlbacher, *Papstwahl*, p. 42; D'Arbois de Jubainville, *Hist. des comtes de Champagne*, II, 96–97.

settlement of the war of investiture.[1] Deserted by the Countess Matilda, abandoned by the Normans in Italy, even indifferently regarded by Cluny, save the "irreconcilables," with the Gregorian party everywhere in Germany and Italy broken and reduced,[2] the Pope was powerless. A synod at Troyes protested against the Emperor's demands,[3] a cry of indignation went up from the Italian clergy.[4] But their wrath was impotent, for no one moved a hand. For four years Pascal II hesitated and temporized, while a torrent of invective and reproach was poured out in Europe.

Meanwhile, in 1110, after the diet at Regensburg was over, Henry V had entered Italy with his army.[5] Reluctantly the Pope, early in 1111; when the Emperor was at Sutri, made an overture, proposing a convention by the terms of which the state was to resign the right of investiture in return for renunciation to the crown by the church of the fiefs and political rights acquired by the church since the reign of Charlemagne.[6]

[1] They were Bruno, archbishop of Trier; Reginard, bishop of Halberstadt; and Burchard of Münster. Suger, who characterizes Bruno as "vir elegans et jocundus, eloquentie et sapientie copiosus," gives a vivid account of the meeting. Cf. B. Monod, "Étude sur les rélations entre le St. Siège et le royaume de France de 1099 à 1108," *Bib. de l'école d. Chartes* (1904), pp. 99 f.

[2] *Annal. Hild.* (1104, 1105); Hauck, III, 885.

[3] Suger, p. 28. The acts of the Council are lost, but the evidence for its deliberations may be found in Mansi, *Concilia*, XX, cols. 1217-20. Cf. Hauck, III, 894 f. The *Annal. Hild.*, p. 60, says that even Gebhard of Constance was censured.

[4] *Chronica regia Coloniensis* (ed. Waitz), p. 48.

[5] Suger, *Vita Ludovici Crassi*, chap. ix, says that Henry V had 30,000 men with him. Ekkehard, *op. cit.* (1019), gives an account of the diet of Regensburg.

[6] *Paschalis II Privilegium primae conventionis* (February 12, 1111), in Doeberl, *Monumenta Selecta*, III, No. XX A; also in *MGH, LL.* II, 68 f. The preamble, after reciting the evils which have penetrated the church by reason of its participation in feudal affairs concludes: "Tibi itaque fili karissime rex Heinrice, et nunc per officium nostrum Dei gratia Romanorum imperator, et regno regalia dimettenda precipimus, que ad regnum manifeste pertinebant, tempore Karoli, Lodoicy, et ceterorum predecessorum tuorum. [This spared the temporal power of the pope.] Interdicimus et sub anathematis districtionem, ne quis episcoporum seu abbatum, presentium vel futurorum, eadem regalia invadant. Id est, cyvitates, ducatus, marchias, comitatus, monetas, teloneum, mercatum, advocatias regni, jura centurionum, et curtes que manifeste regni erant, cum pertinentiis suis, militia et castra regni. . . . . Porro, ecclesias cum oblationibus [i.e., pious gifts in the form of produce or money], et

Henry V accepted the terms on condition that they were
ratified by the bishops and nobles of Germany. It is difficult
to believe that either the Emperor or the Pope conceived for a
moment that such a radical solution would be possible.
Henry V must have been "bluffing"; as for Pascal II, perhaps he hoped that latent sympathy might be stirred in his
behalf if he thus exposed the papacy's extremity.. He could
hardly have indulged the illusion that the German bishops
would passively renounce their great worldly power. He
knew them too well for that.[1] Had not Urban II at the Council of Milan in 1096 said that even parish priests conducted
themselves like petty kings? The German clergy had too
long been fed upon flesh by the Saxon and Salian kings to renounce it now. Temporally, feudally, they were unwilling to
yield and too strong to be coerced by either emperor or pope.

The supreme test of the church's sincerity was made in
1111, when Pascal II offered to buy the church's freedom
from lay investiture at the price of renunciation of the
church's temporalities and secular power. At once a storm of

---

hereditariis possessionibus [i.e., gifts of land owned in fee simple, and not feudally],
que ad regnum manifeste non pertinebant, liberas manere decernimus."

Not every landed possession of the church was a fief; for if it had been an allod
at the time of donation, it so remained. Most of the donations made since the beginning of Saxon times were fiefs, however, so that the effect of the decree, if executed,
would have been to reduce the church to the proportion of land which it had possessed in the time of Louis the Pious. This would have been far from cutting the
church to the quick, for even so early the church's landed wealth was enormous.
Placidus of Nonantula, an ardent curialist, argued that the church needed its great
wealth for support of the poor, and that tithes, etc., were not enough (see Kayser,
Placidus von Nonantula, p. 17). There is little doubt of the wisdom of requiring the
church to evacuate its purely feudal lands. But it may have been going too far, in an
age of *Naturalwirtschaft*, to expect the church to renounce, too, its endowments in the
form of tolls, market rights, etc. These were the very sources of income which tended
to emancipate it from the *Naturalwirtschaft* of the earlier medieval period, and which
would enable the church to keep abreast of the economic changes of the time. The
question was not a doctrinaire one, but one of enormous practical interest. I owe
this important suggestion to my friend, Professor Charles H. Haskins of Harvard
University. The latest work on Pascal II is by Korbe, *Die Stellung Papst Urbans II
und Pascals II zu den Klöstern* (Greifswald, 1910).

[1] "In your kingdom," Pascal II had written Henry V the year before, "bishops
and abbots are so occupied in secular affairs that they are compelled to frequent the
county courts and to do soldiering. The ministers of the altar have become ministers
of the court" (*Gesta Trev.*, I, 222). The Pope refused to go to Germany, alleging the
"barbarous" manners of the people there (Ekkehard, *Chron.* [1107]).

protest arose. Like the rich young man who came to Jesus (Matt. 19:16–22), the church had too great possessions to make the sacrifice. Its idealization of poverty was belied by its avarice. A few rare spirits like Arnold of Brescia[1] daringly advocated the true remedy and expiated at the stake the zeal of the reformer born out of due season. The greatest spirits of the Middle Ages, like St. Francis, Dante, Nicholas de Clamanges, for example, deplored the church's choice. But few churchmen, and never any pope save Pascal II, had the courage to advocate the true solution of the church's corruption. The argument and the protest of the church of Liège, at the height of the strife over lay investiture, fell upon deaf ears.[2]

Pascal II was compelled to cancel the agreement, but proffered no other form of settlement.[3] Henry V brusquely demanded imperial control of episcopal elections and unconditional right of investiture. The Pope, after enduring two months of imprisonment, yielded.[4] If the first concession had angered the German bishops, the second enraged the Gregorians.[5] A council at Vienne condemned the papal action,

[1] In spite of the enmity between St. Bernard and Arnold of Brescia they were at one over the evils flowing from the temporal position of the church (see Bernard, *Epp.*, No. 238, to Eugene III, and his *De consideratione, passim.* Gerhoh of Reichersberg shared Arnold's views (Gregorovius, *Rome in Middle Ages*, IV, 2, 547, n. 2).

[2] In justifying itself against the threats of Pascal II the church of Liège quoted St. Ambrose with telling force: "Si Christus non habuit imaginem Caesaris, cur dedit censum? Non de suo dedit: sed reddidit mundo quae erant mundi. Et tu, si non vis esse obnoxius Caesari, noli habere quae mundi sunt. Sed si habes divitias, obnoxius es Caesari. Si vis nihil debere regi terreno, dimitte omnia et sequere Christum" (Udalr. Babenb., *Cod. Lib.*, II, chap. ccxxxiv).

[3] Pascal II seems honestly to have regretted the church's temporalities (*Ep. 22 ad Henricum V*; Mansi, *Concilia*, XX, 1007; cf. *Vita Paschalis*, Muratori, SS. III, 360; *Annales Romaldi* (1111), (Pertz, V, 473). Schum (*Jenaer Literatur-Zeitung*, 1877, No. 8) demonstrates that Pascal II really sought liberty of the church by separation of the temporal power.

[4] Doeberl, *op. cit.*, No. 20 B. On these two privileges see Gerson Peiser, *Der deutsche Investiturstreit unter König Heinrich V bis zum päpstlichen Privileg vom April 13, 1111*, and Hauck, III, 894–903.

[5] Pascal II's letter of October 29, 1111, to the Emperor shows the sentiment of revolt abroad in the church: "Ex quo vobiscum illam quam nostis pactionem fecimus, non solum longius positi, sed ipsi etiam qui circa nos sunt, cervicem adversus nos erexerunt, et intestinis bellis viscera nostra collacerant et multo faciem nostram rubore perfundant" (Jaffé, V, 283; Migne, *Pat. Lat.*, CLXIII, 291); *Chron. Cass.*, IV, chap. xxxi; Suger, *Vita Lud. Crass.*, chap. ix; cf. Hauck, III, 904–5.

reaffirmed in energetic words that lay investiture was heresy, and held Henry V up to the obloquy of Christendom.[1]

The radical Gregorians in Italy raised a furious outcry. Bruno of Segni even attacked Pascal II himself, for which insult he was deprived of the abbotship of Monte Cassino. The unfortunate Pope cast about for some means of renouncing the agreement which he had made, and a council was convened at the Lateran on March 28, 1112. The representatives were all Italians except two transalpine bishops. This fact is interesting, for it indicates that the old pro-imperial and German clergy in Italy had become wholly displaced during the long conflict.

The spokesman of the Gregorians was Bishop Gerard of Angoulême, who argued that the agreement made by Pascal II did not expressly forbid a revocation of it. The resolution of the council is a masterpiece of ecclesiastical casuistry, though it must be said that the method of revocation was no worse than the means by which the agreement had first been obtained.[2]

Neither the findings of the Council of Vienne nor those of the Lateran had any appreciable effect on Henry's position in Germany.[3] The ban served as a pretext for a feudal noble here and there to rebel against the king. But the crown was too strong to fear a repetition of what had happened in Germany in 1076, until the Emperor's defeat at the battle of Welfesholz on February 11, 1115, gave new courage to the Gregorians and filled Henry V with misgiving.[4] Then Kuno of Praeneste was bold enough to carry the excommunication of the Council of Vienne into Germany. But Pascal II was too timid to heap the papal excommunication upon the ban of the Council.

The reason for the pope's prudence is to be found in the fact that Henry V had again come into Italy, where the great Countess Matilda had just died (1115), in order to prevent the execution of her will, in which she had made the papacy the beneficiary of her vast possessions in Tuscany. In spite

---

[1] Labbé, *Concil.*, XII, 1183. For extracts from sources, Richter, III, 2, pp. 575-77.

[2] Labbé, XII, 1163-82. [3] Giesebrecht, III, 862. [4] *Chron. Ursperg.* (1116).

of the Emperor's efforts to secure a conference with Pascal II, he was unable to bring it about. The pope was too wary again to be caught in the imperial clutches and replied that all matters touching the relation of pope and emperor must be deferred until another council, which he would summon in due time. But the Pope's call was never issued, for Pascal II died on January 21, 1118. After the death of Pascal II the influence of the conciliatory party rapidly increased. The control of things almost wholly passed out of the hands of the Pope, less out of the hands of the Emperor, into those of the penetrating canonists who finally resolved the issue.[1]

His successor was John of Gaeta, the late Pope's chancellor, who took the name of Gelasius II. Henry V, by this time grown impatient of the way in which Pascal II had dodged him, tried unsuccessfully to take the pontiff prisoner by a *coup de main*. Failing this attempt, the Emperor had recourse to the old practice of creating a counter-pope and put up Archbishop Burdinus of Braga, who took the name of Gregory VIII.[2] He was a mere tool whom Henry V soon discarded and imprisoned when the door opened to another solution to the controversy.

Meantime, Gelasius II had fled to France, summoned a synod at Vienne, of whose deliberations nothing is known,[3] and excommunicated Henry V and his papal puppet.[4] At the same time, in Germany, Kuno of Praeneste and Adalbert of Mainz called an opposition synod at Cologne in May, 1118, and at Fritzlar on Saxon soil in July.[5]

The whole situation abruptly changed when Gelasius II died on January 18, 1119, and was succeeded by Gui of

[1] For a masterly exposition of the whole complex issue—the opinions and contentions of the two contending parties, the obscurities which enveloped the theories of secular and ecclesiastical supremacy, the extent of the domains of the Church and of the Empire, always a bone of contention between the principals, the exhaustion of both parties, the passionate desire for peace with honor, the pressure of the German nobility upon Henry V, the pitiable turning and twisting of Pascal II, the rapid development of the influence of the canonists, etc.—see Bernheim, *Zur Geschichte des Wormser Koncordates* (Göttingen, 1878).

[2] *Chron. Cassinense* (Migne, CLXXIII, 885); *Annales Romani*, SS. V, 478–79.

[3] Labbé, XII, 1249.   [4] *Chronica regia Col.*, p. 57.

[5] Ekkehard, *ibid., col.* 1039.

Burgundy, the archbishop of Vienne, who, on February 2, 1119, became Pope Calixtus II.[1] During this decade the conciliatory ideas of Yves of Chartes and Hugh of Fleury gained ground, which the English settlement of 1106 reinforced.

It seemed a favorable opportunity to terminate the bitter strife. Calixtus II had been a violent opponent of Henry V, but seems to have been sobered by the serious position of his office. On the other hand, the Emperor, too, was in a more conciliatory mood than he had been in the early part of his reign. He sorely wanted peace, for the situation in Germany gave him great anxiety.

Henry V summoned the diet at Tribur, the date of which we do not know, where he proffered the olive branch to ambassadors of Calixtus II. The incongruity of the Pope dealing with an excommunicated ruler does not seem to have occurred to anyone. After these preliminaries the Pope began to negotiate more directly with the Emperor and sent the Bishop of Châlons and the Abbot of Cluny to Strasburg. We have a detailed account of these negotiations in the *Relatio de concilio Remensi*, written by one Hesso, "scholasticus."

The argument which seems to have had greatest weight with Henry V was that the English King had surrendered the right of investiture without losing the regalia. Calixtus II was at Paris when word was brought to him of the Emperor's inclination to make peace with the church after the compromise form. But he still mistrusted. "Utinam jam factum esset: si sine fraude fieri posset," he exclaimed. The Pope now sent Cardinal Gregory and the Bishop of Ostia to confer with Henry V, who met them between Verdun and Metz. Here the formal documents were prepared which the Emperor agreed to exchange with Calixtus II in person at Mouzon on October 23.

On October 19, 1119, the council opened at Rheims, where hopes for peace ran high. Four days later the Pope went to Mouzon. His suspicions were made more certain when he discovered that Henry V had come with an army at his back.

---

[1] Ulysse Robert, *Histoire du pape Calixte II* (1891); Hauck, III, 907; Lamprecht, II, 383–87; Ender, *Die Stellung des Papstes Calixt II zu den Klöstern* (Greifswald, 1913).

He had no mind to fall into the trap which had caught Pascal II, and returned to Rheims. Henry V was re-excommunicated and the council was dismissed. But the door was even then left ajar for the possibility of peace, for a canon was adopted which specifically declared that the prohibition of lay investiture applied *only to the office* of bishops and abbots as such, and not to their regalia.

In Germany everyone wanted peace. In a short time a commission of twelve princes was established, the members of which were divided equally between the two factions, who should draft an agreement to be submitted to a diet which was to be held at Würzburg.

The diet convened on September 29, 1121. The Emperor was now as politic as he had been impolitic at Mouzon, and left everything, at least outwardly, to the princes. The separation of investiture from regalia was agreed upon, and Bishop Otto of Bamberg, Duke Henry of Bavaria, and Count Berenger were sent to Rome to secure the cancellation of the ban of excommunication. Later the Bishop of Speyer and the Abbot of Fulda were also sent to Rome and returned to Germany in company with two cardinals and the Bishop of Ostia.

Exactly a year had elapsed since the diet of Würzburg had met. On September 8, 1122, a council met at Worms. The Concordat of Worms in 1122 distinguished between the spiritual and the temporal functions of bishops and abbots and instituted a double investiture, the Emperor investing the new incumbent with the fiefs and secular authority of the office, the Pope or his legate with the spiritual title and authority.[1] The loaf was divided, apparently into equal portions. But the pope had the difference between a half loaf and no bread.

Yet the Concordat of Worms really settled nothing permanently, for the papacy soon claimed that the terms of the Concordat were only applicable to the rule of Henry V and that the church was not so bound to his successors. Neither Pope nor Emperor, as the future was to show, nor the German bishops, were satisfied with the halfway nature of the

[1] Ulysse Robert, *Calixte II*, chap. x.

arrangement. At most it was only an armistice. It glossed
the question; it did not determine it. The most that it proved
was the temporary exhaustion of both combatants. It was
too irrepressible a conflict to be settled by any half-measures.
The real winner was the German episcopate, who in the preliminaries in 1121 had declared that they would make the
right of imperial investiture their own. They kept their word
only too well. For they made the claim for secular investiture not only the emperor's, but their own. The real
Prinz-Bischof of Germany dates from this time. The episcopal lands became less church domains than fiefs. It is not long
before we find the bishops boldly alluding to their episcopal
lands as *terra nostra*.[1]

The Concordat of Worms did not terminate the struggle
between the Empire and the Holy See; it did not mark the
ruination of the Holy Roman Empire; it did not destroy the
Ottonian-Salian monarchy. Its terms were made neither by
the German King nor the Pope, but by the German feudal
princes. The German feudality were the arbitrators between
Henry V and Calixtus II. The German clergy still remained
dependent upon the Emperor.. The crown still retained the
right of eminent domain over church property, the right of
proprietorship remained, and the bond which bound the
clerical feudality to the crown as supreme proprietor was
guaranteed in the article of the pact; the bishops were compelled to swear fidelity and to do homage; the heavy financial
exactions long laid upon their lands were continued; the resources of the Staufer kings in the twelfth century were
chiefly derived from the property of the church.

The famous clause requiring the *presentia regis* for valid
election and that requiring investiture before consecration,
saved not only the honor, but the authority of the king. He
could block the candidacy of a bishop who was displeasing to
him. The great purposes for which Gregory VII had struggled were unfulfilled at Worms. Calixtus II renounced the
pretensions of his predecessor.[2]

[1] Cf. Hauck, *Die Entstehung der geistlichen Territorien.*

[2] It is interesting to observe the marked influence of the revived study of Roman
law and the legists of Italy upon the policy both of imperialists and papalists. The

What loss of power the German king suffered in 1122 redounded, not to the profit of the papacy, but to that of the German princes, whose influence henceforth was vital in episcopal elections. Hadrian IV recognized that the Concordat of Worms was merely a suspension of hostilities, not a victory for the Holy See, when he renewed the conflict under Frederick Barbarossa. The complaints of Gerhoh of Reipersberg regarding the dependence of the German clergy upon the feudal princes are very instructive. If other proof be asked to demonstrate the real discomfiture of the papacy at Worms, the opposition of the Lateran Council in 1123 which refused to ratify the settlement, and the positive repudiation of the Concordat by the Lateran Council in 1139, are sufficient evidence. The Roman church's programme of "revindication" is recorded at length in the *Narratio de electione Lotharii.* The contention of the papacy was that the concession *de presentia regia* was a simple personal concession to Henry V and had no force in church law with his successors![1]

two seats of this study were Ravenna and Bologna, the former being imperial in sympathy, the latter pro-Italian and papalist. Petrus Crassus, who was the author of the remonstrance of the German bishops against Gregory VII in the Council of Brixen (1080), was a teacher of law at Ravenna (Ficker, *Forschungen zur Reichs-und Rechtsgesch. Ital.,* IV, 106 f.; Rashdall, *Rise of the Universities,* I, 107–9). Bologna, "a link between the papal states and Lombardy" (Rashdall, I, 117), owed its importance to the patronage of Countess Matilda and "the need the countess Matilda experienced of learnéd defenders for the cause of the church and of testamentary freedom" (*ibid.,* p. 133). It was not until the time of Frederick I that the school at Bologna deserted the papal cause for the imperial, and even then not entirely. Roland Bandinelli, afterward Alexander III, as Lambert of Fagnano, later Honorius II before him, were both teachers of law at Bologna.

[1] Dietrich Schaefer, *Zur Beteilung des Wormser Konkordates* (Berlin, 1905), contends that the imperial promise of September 23, 1122, was valid for the church in general; that it constituted a permanent agreement which bound the Emperor and his successors to Peter and Paul and to the Holy Catholic Church; but that, on the other hand, Calixtus II's concessions were personal to Henry V alone, and not binding upon the Pope's successors—a condition which gave room for future conflict between Empire and Papacy. Schaefer attempts to prove his contention by an examination of subsequent episcopal elections from the beginning of Lothar's reign down to the death of Frederick I (1125–90). His conclusion is that the terms of the Concordat of Worms played no part in episcopal appointments during this period, and that political considerations alone were decisive. In other words, politically the settlements at Worms really concluded nothing.

This view has been attacked by a number of scholars, notably by Hauck,

The application of the Concordat of Worms varied in time
and place according to the interest of politics and the obstacles or the support which it met. Lothar II was conciliatory; Frederick I, the opposite. The consequence was that
conflicts over the election of bishops tended to throw a large
amount of control into the hands of the canons, who often
succeeded in eliminating outside influences in the choice, both
imperial and papal. The Council of the Lateran in 1139 encouraged this practice as a means to extrude the secular factor
in episcopal elections and the Lateran Council in 1215 made
it general, saving always the confirmation of choice by the
papacy.[1]

The oft-repeated statement that Lothar weakly surrendered to papal pressure and sacrificed the "saving clause"
of the Concordat is a legend, or rather a misrepresentation of
the Roman party in order to gloss over the defeat of the
Pope and afford pretext for a future renewal of the papal
claims. It is beyond doubt that Lothar resolutely insisted
upon the rights of the state in all nominations to vacant
bishoprics and abbeys during his reign.[2] He never showed
himself either indifferent or negligent on such occasions, but

---

Kirchengesch. Deutschlands (3d and 4th ed., Leipzig, 1906), III, 1047-49; by Bernheim, *Das Wormser Konkordat und seine Vorurkunden hinsichtlich Entstehung,
Formulierung, Rechtsgültigkeit* (Weimar, 1906), who bases his argumentation upon
the preliminary documents of 1111 and 1119, and endeavors to show that these do
not justify Schaefer's conclusions. Bernheim argues for the substantial permanence
of the terms in spite of exceptional instances. This is also the conclusion of H.
Rudorff, *Zur Erklärung des Wormser Konkordates* (Weimar, 1906); of Meyer von
Knonau, *Jahrb. . . . . unter Heinrich V*, VII, Exkursus I; and is the one made
traditional by Giesebrecht. Paul Kopfermann, *Das Wormser Konkordat im deutschen Staatsrecht* (Berlin, 1908), shows that in the fourteenth and fifteenth centuries
the legal writers attached no importance to the Concordat. It was the Reformation
which elevated it to a false eminence—an eminence which became almost consecrated in the view of Protestant historians owing to the influence of Planck. May I
add that Werminghoff has made an important suggestion which it is hoped may bear
fruit. He points out that the whole conflict had turned upon the higher *Reichskirchengut*—bishoprics and abbeys; but that after 1122 an obscurer but very important struggle was carried on over control of parish temporalities. A study upon this
neglected phase of the war of investiture is much needed.

[1] Roland, *Les chanoines et les élections épiscopales du XIe au XIVe siècle (1080-
1350)* (Aurillac, 1909).

[2] A. Friedberg, *Forschungen zur deutschen Gesch.*, Band VIII.

made it an absolute rule not to grant regalian rights to bishop or abbot until the candidate had taken oath of fidelity, and that before his consecration. The sole concession made by Lothar seems to have been the waiver of homage from those ecclesiastics already in office, a renunciation which did not later prevent him from enforcing the right of investiture in all its fulness during the schism occasioned by the double election of Innocent II and Anacletus. The most that may be said in reproach of Lothar is that his conciliatory policy toward the papacy opened the door to a new series of papal usurpations which culminated in the breach between Frederick Barbarossa and Hadrian IV in 1157.[1]

Unfortunately, the evidence is not so plentiful for the history of Conrad III, but it is quite as certain that the first of the Staufer was not disposed to relax the vigilance of the crown in so important an issue. The most that can be conceded is that Conrad III, since he owed his election not a little to the ecclesiastical princes and the legate (a fact which in itself is indicative of papal discontent with the policy of Lothar II), admitted appeal to Rome in the case of a double election, a contingency not provided for in the Concordat of Worms.[2]

Under Frederick I the German church was the right arm

[1] Bernheim, *Lothar III und das Wormser Konkordat* (Strasburg, 1874), has shown that Lothar made it an absolute rule not to accord regalian rights to the bishop until the oath of fidelity had been taken, and before consecration. The only concession made by him seems to have been postponement of ecclesiastical homage immediately after his election—a circumstance which did not prevent him later, in the schism produced by the double election of Innocent II and Anacletus, of enforcing the right of investiture with full force. Nevertheless, it must be admitted that Lothar by abandoning the old practice opened the door to papal usurpations— usurpations which he could not prevent owing to the fact that at his coronation as emperor he failed to demand the recognition of the former law. It is this laxity which perhaps accounts for Conrad III's weak ecclesiastical policy. Moreover, Conrad III owed his election chiefly to the support of the bishops.

Hampe defends Lothar against Hauck, who accuses him of having constantly sacrificed the interests of the crown to the claims of the church (*HZ*, LVII, Heft 3). Henry V evaded the limitation imposed upon the crown in 1122 by recourse to a garbled form of the text now preserved in the *Codex Udalrici*. Lothar and Conrad III adhered to the Concordat but Frederick I and Henry VI followed the example of Henry V.

[2] H. Witte, *Forsch. zur Gesch. des Wormser Konkordates: Die Bischofswahlen unter Konrad III* (Göttingen, 1877).

of his power, the most effective instrument of his policy. The bishops were finally and permanently englobed in the German feudal system. Frederick I, when the bishops of Oldenburg and Halberstadt refused to do military service for him in Italy (1155), promptly seized their manors and annexed them to the fisc.[1] The evidence of it is the hot protest of the German clergy after the episode at Besançon against the pretensions of Hadrian IV (1157). At Würzburg in 1165 all the bishops except two adhered to Frederick's anti-pope. In the last conflict of Frederick I with the curia in 1186 every bishop present protested against Urban III's interference with German politics, and affirmed their feudal obligations to the Emperor. From his right of proprietorship over the property of "royal" churches Frederick I drew consequences of far-reaching power, appropriating as regalia all rights, authorities, and revenues of vacant sees. As to nominations to ecclesiastical dignities, while an appearance of election was pretended, actually Frederick I claimed the right to designate incumbents to vacant church offices; his control of ecclesiastical offices was complete and decisive.

He used the high clergy of the German kingdom as commanders of his armies, as diplomats, as governors. Rainald of Dassel, archbishop of Cologne, was a trusted military leader; Christian of Mainz was practically his viceroy in Italy. And what shall be said of Wibald of Stavelot, Philip of Cologne, Arnold of Mainz, Wichmann of Magdeburg, Eberhard of Bamberg, Hartmann of Brixen, Otto of Freising? There is not a single bishop in Germany during the reign of Frederick Barbarossa who can be mentioned for his spiritual desert; there is hardly one who was not a politician or a warrior.

As the result of his defeat by the Lombard communes at Legnano in 1176 Frederick I was compelled to renounce his grandiose purpose of establishing a powerful monarchy in North Italy at the Peace of Venice. But his power in Germany still remained undiminished. The fall of Henry the Lion in 1181 (whose alleged "treason" at Legnano is impossible of occurrence since the lay princes of Germany were not

[1] Otto of Freising, *Gesta Frid.*, II, 12; Helmold, *Chron.*, I, 83.

obliged to participate in Italian expeditions) and the brilliant diet of Mainz in 1184 are striking evidences of the abiding power of Frederick I. Pope Alexander III, in spite of the magnitude of his pretensions, recognized the "schismatic" bishops whom Frederick I had appointed to German sees, and declared to the chapter of Bremen in 1177 that the *favor principis* was essential to episcopal election. So far as Germany is concerned, the settlement at Venice no more compromised the prerogative of the King with reference to control of church offices than the Concordat of Worms had done.[1]

The doctrine of the Two Swords, clearly enunciated in the eleventh century, crystallized in the next century and at last triumphed in 1198.[2]

But the final victory of the Holy See over the Empire in the time of Innocent III was more owing to the civil conflict then raging in Germany than to the natural power of the papacy. With the fall of Henry the Lion in 1181 and the passing of the old duchies of the high feudal age, the ancient sectionalism which had often made the dukes protagonists of regional aspirations and sentiments passed away also. In its stead grew up the rank weed of feudal particularism, something ignoble and vicious, and unpossessed of those virtues of local pride and patriotism which, with all its faults, had been attached to the motives and the policy of the ancient duchies, now mutilated or destroyed. The ambitious and selfish feudal princes of Germany, lay and clerical, ruined the autonomy of the once glorious kingdom, and in so doing wrecked the Empire too.[3] But the victory was not unto the Pope. The

---

[1] Hauck, IV, 196, 304.

[2] Cf. Ivon. Carnot., *Ep.* 106; John of Salisbury, *Policrat.*, V, 2, 13, 26; VI, 9; Gierke, *Genossenschaft*, III, 112, 526, 547. "Nun ist der Papst nicht mehr primär Priester, sondern vor allem Weltherr" (Hauck, IV, 685).

[3] One of the papal partisans in the time of Frederick I admitted that the purpose of the Pope was a broken and divided Germany incapable of threatening the popes in future. Gerhoh, *In Psalmum*, p. 64: "Haec nimirum spectacula nunc regibus partim ablatis, partim diminuto eorum regno humilitas, et exaltato sacerdotio, delectant spectatorem benevolum, torquent invidum quo ut amplius crucietur ...., succedet in seculari dignitate minoris nominatis potestas diminutis regnis magnis in tetrarchias aut minores etiam particulas, ne premere valeant ecclesias et ecclesiasticas personas."

Fürsten demanded the right of investiture in their own territories.[1] As princes the German bishops were as free of papal
control in the thirteenth century as their predecessors had
been in the eleventh and twelfth. The mastery of the emperors over the German church was destroyed, but the mastery
of the papacy was not established in its room.

Certainly not the state nor yet the church was the ultimate winner in the great controversy. The real winners were
the feudalized bishops and abbots and the German feudality.
The prince, bishops and warlike abbots of Germany, with
their worldly ways, their hard faces, their political interests,
lords of church lands which were actually huge ecclesiastical
fiefs,[2] and the German feudality were the real victors in the
war. The sources upon this subject are rich, varied, and
unanimous. In the bitter warfare of the partisans both sides
had pillaged wantonly. Probably there was not a bishopric
or monastery in all Germany which was not despoiled at
least once. When Adalberon became archbishop of Trier in
1131, the revenues of the see would hardly support him for a
day. The condition of Metz and Verdun was similar. Augsburg was captured and pillaged twice. Salzburg fared no better. The losses of Mainz were huge. Of the abbeys, all were
more or less plundered, and numbers of them completely de-

---

[1] Hauck, IV, 196–97.

[2] "Episcopi non essent pastores ecclesiarum, sed ductores bellorum" (De
unitate eccles. conserv., chap. xviii). "Lo, what lusty and warlike archbishops there
are in Germany," wrote Richard to Prince Edward of England during the War of
the Barons. "It would not be a very bad thing for you if you could create such archbishops in England" (Annals of Burton, MGH, SS. XXVII, 489). For discussion
of this feudalization of the episcopate see Below, Der deutsche Staat des Mittelalters,
pp. 336–37, and Stutz, Ztschft. der Savigny-Stiftung, XX, 217 and 242–44. To
Louis VII of France, according to Walter Map, an archdeacon of Oxford, who has
reported an interesting conversation he once had with the French king, the chief
difference between Germany and France was in the greater material wealth and comfort in France, and the great political and military power of the bishops in Germany
(De nugis curialium [ed. Wright, Camden Soc.], p. 215). Caesar of Heisterbach relates that a clerk at Paris sustained the thesis that no German bishop was capable
of being saved "because almost all the bishops of Germany have both the spiritual
and the temporal sword; because they judge cases of blood and practice war; because they are more solicitous for military power than for the cure of souls" (Distinctio, II, chap. xxvii).

stroyed, as Goseck, St. Gall, Schaffhausen, Prüm, Stablo, Lüttich, St. Trudo, St. Hubert, and Corvey.

Neither Germany nor the church was the same ever again. While nominally the former form of government seemed still to remain, actually the government of the Hohenstaufen was very different from that of their predecessors.

From the national ruination of the war of investiture the German church rapidly recovered under the Staufer. But the moral recuperation is not so manifest. As new evidences of the institutional development of the church in Germany in the twelfth century the most striking phenomena are internal rather than external. It is true that the eastward expansion of the German people still had the effect of creating new episcopal sees; but most of these had been founded in the tenth or eleventh centuries, and had passed their infancy in the twelfth. The internal growth of the church, though, during the Staufer period is an interesting and important matter. Examples of this process are many: multiplication of rural deaneries, increase in the number of almost every cathedral staff, new urban parishes, the increasing importance of the lay element in ecclesiastical affairs, which is especially manifest in the schools and in eelymosinary administration. More intangible phenomena, and difficult to trace, are the real and genuine religious manifestations like pietism.[1] But often poverty, not will, compelled people to enter the church.

The immediate effect of the papal mothering of the monasteries naturally was to bind them close to Rome and to make the monks zealous propagandists of pontifical supremacy. The monks became a standing army of the popes in Europe and the monasteries papal garrison points. The ultimate effect, however, was to work their deterioration. By donations and privileges of indulgence the curia augmented the fortune of the monasteries with the result that they became richer and more self-indulgent than ever, until by the end of the twelfth century the manners and morals of the regular clergy in Europe had again become notorious for their cor-

[1] Hauck, IV, 1-9.

ruption,[1] a condition which gave rise to the two great reforming orders of the thirteenth century, the Franciscans and Dominicans. "The condition of the church," wrote Caesar of Heisterbach at the beginning of the thirteenth century, "has become such that it is not worthy to be governed save by reprobate bishops."[2]

[1] *MGH*, SS. XVII, 232, l. 31, *ca.* 1200: "Canonici cum militibus, moniales nobiles cognoscebant."

[2] *Distinctio*, II, chap. xxviii.

CHAPTER IV

OLD SAXONY

THE HISTORY, institutions, and culture of the Germans of the fifth century have for three generations been a hunting-ground for the student of social origins. Almost nothing new may be found there. It is threshing old straw to study them.

But there was a great German tribe living in late Roman times where their descendants live to this day, namely, the Saxons of Lower Germany, who did not come in contact with Roman civilization or Christianity, as the other Germans had done, in the fifth century, and knew nothing of the Romano-Christian-German culture of early medieval Europe until the end of the eighth century. Accordingly, a study of early Saxon history when this people, still in a state of barbarism, first came in contact with medieval civilization has a freshness that is denied to the earlier period. For, compared with the study of the social origins and practices of the early Germans, that of the Saxons has been neglected.

In superficial area Saxony was the greatest of the German tribal duchies. It included the entire territory between the lower Elbe and Saale rivers almost to the Rhine. Between the mouths of the Elbe and the Weser it bordered upon the North Sea. The only parts of the territory which lay across the Elbe were the little counties of Holstein and Ditmarsch. Adam of Bremen, writing in the eleventh century, compared the shape of Saxony (including Thuringia) to a triangle, and estimated that from angle to angle the distance was eight days' journey. Roughly speaking, Old Saxony was an equilateral triangle measuring approximately two hundred miles on each side.

For the most part, the land was a broad plain, save on the south where it rose into hills and the low mountainous country of the Harz and Hesse, where are the sources of the Weser,

the Ems, the Lippe, and the Ruhr rivers. This low divide
was all that separated the country of the Saxons from their
ancient enemies and ultimate conquerors, the Franks. The
lack of clear physical definition along this border, from time
immemorial, had been the cause of incessant tribal conflict
between the Saxon and the Frank.[1]

Along the Frisian border and in the bottom lands of the
Ems and the Weser the soil was very marshy until drained by
Dutch and Flemish colonists in the twelfth and thirteenth
centuries. But, as a whole, Saxony was a rich alluvial plain
of alternating prairie and forest, the fertility of which was
highly praised in the eleventh and twelfth centuries by Adam
of Bremen and Helmold, the ablest North German chroniclers
of the feudal period.[2]

As a people the Saxons were divided into four kindred
groups: the Angrians, along the right bank of the Weser; the
Westphalians, along the Ems and the Lippe; the Eastphalians, on the left bank of the Weser; and the Nordalbingians,
in modern Schleswig-Holstein.[3] But not even with these four
tribal groups was the term of tribal division reached. For the
Saxon, "nation" was really a loose congeries of clans of
kindred stock.[4] For example, the Nordalbingians alone were
subdivided into lesser groups—Holsteiners, Sturmarii, Bardi,
and the men of Ditmarsch.[5] The primitive bond of kindred

---

[1] History can add little to or take little from Einhard's brief statement in *Vita Karoli*, chap. vii: ". . . . Termini videlicet nostri et illorum paene ubique in plano contigui praeter pauca loca, in quibus vel silvae majores vel montium juga inter-jecta utrorumque agros certo limite disterminant, in quibus caedes et rapinae et in-cendia vicissim fieri non cessabant."

[2] Adam of Bremen, *Gesta Hammaburgensis ecclesiae pontificum*, I, 1, 2; Hel-mold, *Chronicon Slavorum*, I, 12, 88.

[3] The *Chauci* and the *Chauci minores* of Tacitus may be the earliest recorded division between the Eastphalians and the Westphalians.

[4] "Sed variis divisa modis plebs omnis habebat. Quot pagos tot pene duces" (*Poetae Latini*, *MGH*, SS. IV, 8).

[5] Einhard's *Annales* for the years 775, 776, 783, 797, 810; Widukind, *Rerum gestarum Sax.*, I, 14; Helmold, *passim*. Schmidt, *Hist. Vierteljahrschrift*, XIV (1911), 1, has studied all the earliest textual references to the Saxons. For the origin of the name Holstein see Adam of Bremen, II, 17. They were *Holcetae, dicti a silvis, quas accolunt*—"those who dwelt in the woods" (*Holz*). "The inhabitants of Ditmarschen are supposed to be Saxon, with a leaven of Frisian blood. Wagrien, the eastern part

and clan was particularly strong among the Saxons, and in spite of these many divisions the Saxons were an unusually homogeneous nation living as late as the eighth century as the early Germans had lived.

The long warfare with the Franks largely reduced, though it did not wholly obliterate, the identity of these ancient tribal groups, and the ducal leadership of the house of Widukind, the first important person mentioned in Saxon history, was confirmed by the heroic resistance of the people under him for thirty years (772–802) against Charlemagne. *"Gens dura Saxonum"* was a Frank byword as early as Einhard's time.[1]

The Saxons were composed of an aristocracy of nobles, not a landed proprietary class, but a free warrior class of distinction and renown, simple freemen, and many unfree.[2] Social differences were jealously guarded by social prescription. The death penalty was imposed upon any man who married a woman above his rank; the marriage of a man below his station was severely condemned; bastardy was not tolerated; intermarriage between Saxons and other Germans was

---

of Holstein, left desolate by migration, or so it is said, was given over to the Wends by Karl the Great, and won back in the twelfth century. Lauenburg seemed to have originally been Slavic, but the Slavs were gradually ousted by Saxon colonists in the twelfth century. That there was a large subject population of Wends in most Saxon districts is revealed by the thirteenth century Sachsenspiegel. . . . . The history of Ditmarschen is . . . . sharply divided from that of Holstein . . . . though from an ethnological point of view it is very similar, the population being of Saxon origin, though perhaps with a Frisian admixture. . . . . The solidarity of the kindred has left its mark on every sphere of Ditmarschen life. It was the kindreds, or *Schlachte* ["agnatic clans"], which in the tenth and eleventh centuries built the great dykes to prevent the sea flooding the marsh lands" (B. S. Philpotts, *Kindred and Clan*, pp. 103, 125).

[1] "Saxones, gens dura, bellis aspera, tam praeceps ad arma quam audax, vendicans sibi praerogativam laudis ex incepto furoris" (*Vita Heinrici IV*, chap. iii). Cf. *Poeta Saxo*, V (772), 13; *Poetae Latini*, IV, 1, 7: "Saxonum . . . . pectora dura"; Alcuin, *Versus ad sanctos Eboracensis ecclesiae, ibid.*, V, 47; Jaffé, *Bibl.*, VI, 83: "Gens . . . . duririam propter dicti cognomine Saxi" (as if "Saxon" were derived from the Latin word *saxum*, a "rock"!).

[2] Nithard, *Historia*, IV, chap. ii; Rodolph. Fuld. *Translatio S. Alexandri*, chap. i; Widukind, *Rerum gestarum Sax.*, I, 14. Cf. Moeser, *Osnabrückische Gesch.*, Part I, sec. 44. The *lazzi* of Nithard means *Leute* (Moeser, Vol. I, Part III, sec. 32, n. E).

frowned upon; and strangers were hated.[1] So tenaciously
did the Saxons cling to their ancient customary law that
clear traces of these social survivals persisted in Saxony
down through the Middle Ages.[2]

The nobles, as a class, seem to have been of late origina-
tion and to have developed greatly during the long wars with
the Franks, for the earliest designation of them is found in a
capitulary of the year 797, *cc.* 3 and 5 (*nobiliores*), and Bede's
well-known characterization of the Saxons of the eighth century makes no mention of any noble class, but only of war-
chieftains.[3] But once arrived, the Saxon nobility displayed a
tenacity and a durability not found elsewhere in North Germany. In the tenth century, Saxony was the only country of
North Germany still retaining its own historic and old-line
noblesse.

The various stages in the Frankish conquest of Saxony
may be discerned from careful analysis of the chronicles, and
the variety of methods employed by Charlemagne to maintain the subjugation of the country is worth observing. In
775 Charlemagne established two Frankish garrisons: one at
Eresburg, the other at Syburg. These fortified points marked
an advance line of protection, a "mark," at some distance
from the imperiled Hessian frontier. Soon afterward the fortress of Karlsburg was established on the Lippe. Thus a triangle of fortified posts and a segment of occupied territory
was marked out in the heart of the Saxon land. At the same
time a civil and ecclesiastical administrative organization began to be installed through the medium of counts, bishops,
and abbots who were introduced into Saxony.[4] The method
of reduction of the country was exactly similar to that employed by Pepin earlier in Frisia in the time of Willibrord and

[1] *Translatio S. Alex.*, *MGH*, SS. II, 674–76; Widukind, I, 9; Adam of Bremen, I,
6, and III, 55; Bruno, *De bello Saxonico*, chap. xxiii; *Sachsenspiegel*, III, art. 64,
sec. 3.

[2] Widukind, *op. cit.* (ed. Waitz), p. 15, n. 3.

[3] Bede, *Historia ecclesiastica*, V, 10. On the nobility and freemen among the
Saxons see Waitz, *Deutsche Verfassungsgesch.*, III, 148–50.

[4] Waitz, III, 129; Abel and Simson, *Jahrb. Karl d. Gr.*, I, 417; Hauck, *Kirchengesch.*, II, 382; Kenzler, *Forschungen zur deutschen Gesch.*, XII, 350; Schroeder,
Ztschft. der Savigny-Stiftung f. Rechtsgesch.: German. Abt., XXIV, 350.

Boniface. Although the Franks were driven out time and again, they always returned and ultimately wore down the Saxon resistance into submission both to Frankish rule and to Christianity. The most intractable region was the low, marshy country between the lower course of the Elbe and that of the Weser, called Wihmode or Wigmodia, and in Nordalbingia.[1] The whole Frankish policy is registered in the ferocious capitulary *De partibus Saxoniae* (785?). But continual and desperate risings of the Saxons, united with the humane protest of Alcuin, gradually induced Charlemagne to moderate the drastic nature of the government in Saxony.

The Saxons were too inflexible (*gens dura*) to be utterly reduced, and had to be compromised with in certain ways. The change is measured by comparing and contrasting the capitulary just mentioned with a new law proclaimed in 797, which evidently was the result of long deliberation between the king, the clergy, the nobles, the counts, and the Saxon leaders themselves. It is most significant that the Saxons in 797 were permitted the right of public assembly and to retain their own ancestral laws and customs. The country lost its independence and was incorporated within the great Frankish Empire. But the Saxons still preserved many of their native manners and customs, which they were too indomitable to surrender.[2] The chief change in Saxony effected by the con-

[1] The old practice of blood revenge and even paganism was to be found in these localities until the twelfth century.

[2] A remarkable example of the inflexible nature of the Saxons and their strenuous adherence to their ancient laws and customs, even in the face of the authority of the church, is afforded by the case of Gottschalk, a Saxon monk in the ninth century. He protested against the oblation of young boys, i.e.. against the monastic practice of persuading the parents of young children to commit them, while still infants, to the monastic life. When still a little boy, Gottschalk, who was of noble Saxon lineage, had been dedicated by his parents to cloister life in the monastery of Fulda. He bravely asserted that this was a deprivation of liberty in violation of Saxon law which declared that no freeman could be deprived of liberty without the judgment of competent persons of his own class and nation. We have in Gottschalk's case the example of a Saxon appealing to his law, but also of the deep antagonism between Frank and Saxon. For Rabanus Maurus, archbishop of Mainz, published a reply to Gottschalk in which he poured contempt and scorn upon the Saxons as being half-pagan barbarians yet. See Migne, *Pat. Lat.*, CVII, 432; Ebert, *Gesch. d. Lat. Lit. d. Mittelalters*, II, 138–39; H. O. Taylor, *Mediaeval Mind*, I, 224.

Wala is another example somewhat similar to Gottschalk. He was also of noble

quest was in the matter of religion. Yet, as we shall see later, the ancient Germanic paganism persisted and was strong in Saxony for many years.[1]

Charlemagne, with that unerring judgment which distinguished him, when the subjugation of the Saxons was completed, treated the Saxon nobles with great consideration, and we find many of them at his court in the latter years of his reign.[2] But the freeman class, which was not so large as once was believed, was only very slowly worked into the Frankish military system.[3] When the Frankish conquest ended

the dependent peasant was already the rule. When peasant holdings are given to a monastery, the donor is not the cultivating peasant, but his small landlord, who gives the land and the peasant on it. What happened in the Carolingian epoch was not the birth of landlordship, but a new allot-

---

Saxon birth, and abbot of Corvey until exiled by Louis the Pious in 822. Though a monk, he never forgot that he was a Saxon. His biographer relates that he often said he wished he might still wear the Saxon national clothing instead of the Benedictine frock, and to the end of his life he insisted upon wearing Saxon shoes (*Vita Walae*, chaps. xii, xvi).

How unfamiliar Saxony was in the ninth century with the popular Christianity of the Frank land is illustrated by the *Translatio S. Viti* (*Mon. Corb.* ed. Jaffé, pp. 319–22). Relic worship was still a novelty in Saxony, as the account vividly shows. Cf. Ebert, *Gesch. d. Lat. Lit. d. Mittelalters*, III, 205–6; Dümmler, *Otto I*, pp. 331, 343, 347, 354, 357.

[1] The *Translatio S. Liborii* written by a Saxon clerk, probably of Paderborn, toward the close of the ninth century, is highly interesting for the evidence it furnishes upon the deep religious change in Saxony made by the conquest. Cf. Ebert, II, 204–6. Of equal value is the *Translatio S. Viti* (836), in Jaffé, *Mon. Corb.*, I, 319 f.; and see Ebert, II, 336–37. A glimpse of pagan Saxony before the Frankish conquest is found in Hucbald, *Vita S. Lebuini*, chap. ix; cf. Abel, *Karl der Grosse*, I, 96; Ebert, II, 190–91.

[2] For this policy of Charlemagne, see Nitzsch, *Deutsche Gesch.*, I, 222–29, 234–35, 320–21.

[3] In 855, when Louis the Young invaded the West Frank kingdom of his uncle, Charles the Bald, his army was composed of Franks, Thuringians, Swabians, and Bavarians, i.e., of South Germans (*Miracula S. Martialis*, Bouquet, VII, 370); some Saxons were with the East Frankish host in the battle of Andernach in 876 (*Ann. S. Bert.*; *Ann. Fuld.*; *Regino, Chronicon*), but it is evident that they were not many, since the *Ann. Fuld.* tell us that on account of the large number of horses the army had to be widely scattered for forage, and we know that the Saxons were almost wholly foot-forces. Arnulf's army in the battle of the Dyle against the Norsemen in 891 was chiefly drawn from Bavaria and Swabia, though there were some Saxons in it (*Cont. Ratisb.* [891]).

ment of the permanently dependent peasants, leading to the formation of a relatively small number of great lordships instead of a larger number of little ones.[1]

Thirty years of bitter and wasting wars between the Franks and the Saxons, while it created an aristocracy of warrior nobles among the Saxons, also left in its wake thousands of broken freemen, serfs, and slaves. This is evident from the account of Nithard, the Frankish chronicler of the middle of the ninth century, who relates that during the civil war between the sons of Louis the Pious, after the defeat of Lothar at Fontenay in June, 841, he sought assistance from the Saxons. His relation is very interesting for the light which it throws upon the texture of lower Saxon society and the profound social and religious effect which the Frankish conquest had had. He writes:

As all Europe knows . . . . the great emperor Charles . . . . turned the Saxons from the vain worship of idols to the true and Christian belief in God. . . . . All this nation is divided into three classes. First there are those who in their speech are called *aedhillingi*, the second are the *frilingi*, finally there are those known as *lazzi*, that is to say in Latin, nobles, freemen and serfs.[2] In the strife between Lothar and his brothers the nobles were divided into two factions, one of which espoused Lothar, the other Ludwig. This being the case, Lothar perceiving that after the victory of his brothers the people who had been with him wished to desert him, compelled by various exigencies, sought assistance wherever and however he could.

---

[1] W. J. Ashley, *Economic Journal*, IX, 255, a review of Knapp's *Grundherrschaft und Rittergut*.

[2] These three classes are indicated in Hucbald, *Vita Lebuini:* "Statuto quoque tempore anni, semel ex singulis pagis atque eisdem ordinibus tripartitis singillatim viri duodecem electi et in unum collecti in mediae Saxonia"; and again late in the tenth century, Widukind, I, 14, writing of social stratification among the Saxons, says: "usque hodie gens Saxonica triformi genere ac lege preter conditionem servilem dividitur." It is evident from an examination of the texts that serfdom was a new social condition in Saxony in the ninth century. Meitzen, *Siedelung und Agrarwesen*, I, 297, citing Nithard, says that in the *lazzi* we are to see conquered Saxon freemen who had been permitted to remain upon their formerly free ancestral acres, but who were subjected to manorial impositions, and with a "diminished" freedom. But how far diminished? Was manorial proprietorship introduced into Saxony by Charlemagne? Or did it exist before in some degree? If so, then the Frankish conquest merely aggravated an already existing process toward lordship and serfdom in Saxony. Wittich, *Die Grundherrschaften in Nordwest Deutschland*, and Knapp, *Grundherrschaft und Rittergut*, have contended that a dependent peasantry was the rule in Saxony even before 800. See further Ashley, *Surveys, Economic and Historical*, pp 129–30, 134–35.

He distributed the crown lands for his own advantage, he gave liberty to some and promised that he would give it to others when he had won. He even sent messengers into Saxony and promised both freemen and serfs, whose number was immense, if they would support him, that he would restore to them the law which their forefathers had possessed when they were worshippers of idols. Won over by this means these classes formed a league, adopted a new name for themselves, that is *Stellinga,* and having almost driven their masters out of the country, began to live the law which each pleased after ancient Saxon custom. . . . . But Ludwig . . . . suppressed the rebels in Saxony both by legal process [i.e., by confiscations and forfeitures] and by executions.

What was the *Stellinga?*[1] Is it an example of the ancient German gild surviving in Saxony, but which Charlemagne and the church had stamped out among the other Germans? It seems to bear resemblance to those *conjurationes servorum* which existed in the salt marshes of Flanders and Frisia, and which the legislation of Louis the Pious condemned in 821.[2] If so, then it was a rebellion of broken freemen and serfs. There can be no doubt that the *Stellinga* was an insurrectionary movement in Saxony which intended to secure the restoration of those old Saxon rights and liberties which the conquest had suppressed or destroyed.[3] We know

[1] Nithard, IV, chaps. ii, iv, and vi. The *Annal. Fuld.* (842) mention *liberti,* i.e., *liti;* the *Annal. Xanten* (841) speak of *servi.* The *Annal. Ruod. Fuld.* refer to this movement in Saxony as a "validissimam conspirationem libertorum legitimos dominos opprimere conantium, auctoribus factionis capitali sententia dampnatis, fortiter compescuit." Prudentius, *Annal. S. Bert.,* says that 140 conspirators were beheaded, 14 hanged, and "innumerable" others suffered mutilation. For commentary on these sources see Derichsweiler, "Der Stellingabund," *Progr. des Fr.-Wilh. Gymn. zu Köln* (1868); Meyer von Knonau, *Über Nithards vier Bücher Geschichten. Der Bruderkrieg der Söhne Ludwigs d. Fr. und sein Geschichtsschreiber.* (1866), pp. 77 f.; Dümmler, *Gesch. d. Ostfränkischen Reiches,* I, 178; Waitz, III, 148–50, and IV, 689; Gfrörer, *Gesch. d. Ost- und Westfränk. Carolinger,* I, 27–30. As to the derivation of the word *Stellinga,* modern philology favors its derivation from German *stellen,* or *sich herstellen.* Graff, *Althochdeutscher Sprachschatz oder Wörterbuch,* VI, 674, associates the word with *stallo* and *Notgistallo,* which points to the ancient German gild associations which Charlemagne and the church endeavored to suppress as *conjurationes.*

[2] That the *Stellinga* was very similar to the *conjurationes servorum* which had been formed earlier in the seaboard regions of Flanders and Frisia, and which the legislation of Louis the Pious condemned in 817, admits of no doubt. For this statute see Baluze, *Capitularia regum Francorum,* I, 875; (ed. Boretius), I, 301; cf. p. 437.

[3] See Wachsmuth, "Aufstände und Kriege der Bauern im Mittelalter," *Historisches Taschenbuch,* V, 294–96.

from the biographer of Louis the Pious[1] that the Emperor restored many of those Saxons who had suffered under his
father to their rights and liberties, and this restoration of the
Saxon nobles may have infuriated the peasantry, who were
not partakers of the imperial clemency and who endured
the exactions of church and feudality, to rebellion.[2] The
tyranny of the tithe was a potent source of their dissatisfac-
tion.

But the *Stellinga* was also a pagan reaction. The *Annals of
St. Bertin*, indeed, emphasize this nature of the rebellion.[3]
After fifty years of professed Christianity, actually it was but
a gloss in Saxony. Deep below all outward profession of the
conquering faith, in the hearts of the Saxon people were the
memories of old worship, old strivings and victories which
the imposed religion could not efface. Even Saxon Christianity was tinctured with these ancient aspirations. We find
it in the *Heliand:*

> To the old Saxon poet Christ is a king over his people, a warrior, a
> mighty ruler. . . . . The Christ in the *Heliand* is a hero of the old Germanic
> type, an ideal of courage and loyalty, and his disciples are noble vassals
> from whom He demands unflinching loyalty in return. . . . . The back-
> ground of the events in the *Heliand* is the flat Saxon land with the fresh
> North Sea. . . . . "Nazarethburg," "Bethlehemburg," "Rumuburg"
> [Rome] called up more vivid, if more homely pictures than any description
> of Palestine or Rome; the marriage at Cana and Herod's birthday-feast be-
> come drinking bouts in the hall of a German prince.[4]

But traces of this pagan persistence may be found much later
than the ninth century in Saxony. In 1013, when Bishop Unwin came to Hamburg, he found pagan rites still celebrated

---

[1] Theganus, *Vita Ludovici imperatoris*, chap. xxiv.

[2] It was a tantalizing suggestion of Potgessier (a writer of the eighteenth century), *De statu servorum*, Vol. I, chap. ii, sec. 84, p. 94 n. C, that in the Stedinger
movement of the twelfth century in Lower Saxony we have the survival or at least
the outcropping of the ancient *Stellinga* once more.

[3] *Ann. S. Bert.* (841), "Ut Saxonibus qui Stellinga appellantur, quorum multi-
pliciter numerus in eorum gente habetur, optionem cujusque legis vel antiquorum
Saxonum consuetudinis, utrum earum vellent, concesserit; qui . . . . magis ritum
paganorum imitari quam christianae fidei sacramenta tenere delegerunt." Under
anno 842, it is added: "Qui et christianam fidem pene relinquerant."

[4] J. G. Robertson, *History of German Literature*, p. 20.

in some parts of the diocese, the fasts of the church ignored, and even, we are told, bloody sacrifices.[1]

It is significant that in 852 there is record of a third revolt of the *Stellinga*.[2] The seat of the discontent was Angraria and the *pagi* in Eastphalia of Hardego, Suabengo, and Hohsingo, localities in which to this day old Saxon characteristics and ancient Saxon customs still persist with remarkable fidelity.[3]

The conquest of Saxony by Charlemagne, it is manifest, was the point of departure of enormous political, economic, social, and religious changes. But the innate and rock-ribbed conservatism of the Saxons was more proof against the thrusts and pressures imposed by the growing feudalization of things than any other part of Germany. According to Meitzen, there are villages today in this portion of Germany in which nine-tenths of the *Höfe* may be traced back as far as changes which took place during the tenth and eleventh centuries.[4] A modern French historian (and the only one who is

---

[1] Adam of Bremen, II, 48 and 62. Even in the second half of the eleventh century Saxon prejudice against new-fangled church ritual was strong (*ibid.*, III, 26). For traces of Germanic paganism in the popular beliefs around Braunschweig see Voges, *Ztschft. d. Harz Ver. f. Gesch.*, Vol. XXI, No. 2 (1889). See also the valuable work of Pfannenschmidt, *Germanische Erntefeste im heidnischen und christlichen Cultus mit Beziehung auf Niedersachsen* (Hannover, 1878), and his earlier book, *Das Weihwasser im heidnischen und christlichen Cultus* (Hannover, 1869).

[2] *Annal. Fuld.* (852): [Hludovicus] "profectus est in Saxoniam ob eorum vel maxime causas judicandas, qui a pravis et subdolis judicibus neglecti et multimodis, ut dicunt legio suae dilationibus decepti graves atque diuturnas patiabantur injurias. Suberant etiam et aliae causae ad se ipsum specialiter aspicientes, possessiones videlicet ab avita vel paterna proprietate jure hereditario sibi derelictae, quas oportuit ab iniquis pervasoribus justa repetitione legitimo domino restitui. . . . . Habito generali conventu tam causas populi ad se perlatas justo absolvit examine quam ad se pertinentes possessiones juridicorum gentis decreto recepit. . . . . Apud Erpfestfurt habito conventu decrevit inter alia ut nullus praefectus in sua praefectura aut quaestionarius infra quaesturam suam alicujus causam advocati nomine susciperet agendam, in alienis vero praecausis agendi haberent facultatem" (cf. Waitz, IV, 410, n. 2).

[3] Cf. the notes of Pertz to the *Annals of Fulda* (852). Of all the Saxons bishoprics founded in the time of Charlemagne, Hildesheim most preserved its ancient character and original condition through the Middle Ages. See Otto Heinemann, *Beiträge zur Diplomatik der älteren Bischöfe von Hildesheim (1130–1246)* (Marburg, 1895).

[4] *Siedelung und Agrarwesen*, I, 562. Wittich, *Die Grundherrschaften in Nordwestdeutschland* (Leipzig, 1896), admits the same thing, but with more qualification.

a competent authority upon the history of medieval Germany)
relates how he found a peasant of Drantum near Osnabrück
who in his (the historian's) belief was living still upon the
same farm which his ancestors had worked a thousand years
before.[1] Winckelmann claims that a considerable proportion of the present farming population in what was once Old
Saxony can trace their family history, at least in family tradition, back to the time of Widukind.[2]

The agrarian economy of the Saxons reflected simple and
homely farming conditions.[3] The social texture was the result of the agricultural system. While manorial conditions
and practices prevailed upon the lands of the church and
those of the greater nobles, on the other hand there were
thousands of allodial freeholders in Saxony and great blocks
of freehold land. In a word, freeholds, not tenures, were the
rule. Moreover, the tenacity of family ties and the stubborn
persistence of the spirit of the old clan group gave protection
and support to this condition.[4] What another has written has
pertinence here:

> It is generally agreed that the isolation of the small landowner was his
> undoing, since it rendered him unable to withstand adverse circumstances,
> such as a bad year, a fire, a plague among his beasts, or a piratical raid
> upon his homestead. This is all quite true of the isolated small landowner,
> but we cannot believe it at all true of the small peasant proprietor who was
> surrounded by a kindred. . . . . In regions where the kindred preserved
> its solidarity it would be far less easy for a wealthy landowner, or even for
> ecclesiastical foundations, to exploit the financial and social difficulties of a
> poor neighbor by acquiring his lands, or by extorting rights over him at a
> period of want.[5]

[1] G. Blondel, *Études sur les populations rurales de l'Allemagne*, p. 69.

[2] Winckelmann, *Schriften des Vereines f. Sozialpolitik*, XXIII, 53.

[3] The *Heliand* furnishes interesting evidence that horse-raising was important
in ancient Saxony, for instead of "shepherds watching their flocks by night" on the
eve of the nativity, we find *ehuscalos* watching over their horses in the fields. The
whole poem is redolent of German antiquities. See Vilmar, *Deutsche Alterthümer im
Heliand* (2d ed.; Marburg, 1862).

[4] Inama Sternegg, *Grundherrschaften*, p. 54; Sering, *Erbrecht und Agrarver-
fassung in Schleswig-Holstein*, p. 199; Nitzsch, *Das alte Ditmarschen* (Kiel, 1862).
These authors are cited by Philpotts. See next note.

[5] Philpotts, *op. cit.*, pp. 247–48.

This is precisely what we find in early Saxony, indeed until as late as the end of the twelfth century, whereas in all the rest of Germany this condition had disappeared centuries before.

Remnants of the primitive Germanic *Gemeinde* evidenced in the "plowlands" pertaining to each householder, and the common meadow and duck-pond were everywhere visible in Saxony until late in the Middle Ages.[1] Forms of tillage grown obsolete in older Germany survived in Saxony, as the ancient one-field and two-field systems, found side by side with the three-field system.[2]

Drastic as the conquest of Saxony had been, the native Saxon temper was too sturdy to be wholly altered in genius and character by it. The influence of the church's organization did not wholly extirpate the ancient *Gau*-system, although Adam of Bremen would have us so believe.[3] Nor did the church succeed in utterly stamping out the immemorial pagan religious practices of the Saxons. Fragments of the cult of Woden and Thor survived for centuries in the mutilated form of folk-lore, custom, superstition.[4] The same vitality characterizes the persistence of primitive social institutions. The *comitatus*—the ancient German war-band or "following" of a war-chieftain or Herzog—can be clearly traced in Saxon history long after it was lost in feudalism in the rest of

[1] Long after the Allmend had been appropriated by the greediness of both lay and secular nobles, the currency of certain sayings shows how tenaciously the Saxons clung to the memory of free villages and common lands, e.g.: "Allmend ist nicht Nachbarngut"; "Was der Ochs mit dem Horne nicht biegen kann, das weiset man für Markland"; "Wenn der Müller aus der Mühle tritt, so steht er auf der Allmend."

[2] Meitzen, II, 53–97.

[3] Adam of Bremen, I, 3. Cf. Thietmar, *Chronicon*, II, 20, and the spurious charter (see Sickel, *Acta Karol*, II, 393–94) for Bremen cited by Adam of Bremen in I, 13: "Huic parrochiae decem pagos subjecimus, quos etiam abjectis eorum antiquis vocabulis et divisionibus in duas redigimus provintias, his nominibus appellantes Wigmodiam et Lorgoe." Usually in Saxony the limits of the dioceses were deliberately made different from the lines of the ancient tribal boundaries.

[4] Widukind, I, chap. xii; cf. Grimm, *Myth.* (1st ed.), I, 210 n.; Müllenhoff, *Zeitschrift f. deutsch. Alt.*, XXIII, 3; Halthaus, *Cal. med. aevi*, p. 131, has collected a mass of evidence on this matter. The *Chron. ducum de Brunsw.* chap. ix (*Deutsche Chron.*, II, 581), shows that the festivities of *die Gemeine Woche*—the week beginning with the first Sunday after the feast of St. Michael—preserved ancient pagan German practices as late as the sixteenth century.

Germany.[1] The stubborn nature of Saxon social texture
yielded ever so slowly to the pressure of the feudal social
structure around it.[2] The *Sachsenspiegel* retained a force in
North Germany long after the law of the Swabians (*Schwabenspiegel*) and of the Bavarians had gone the way of feudalism.[3] In the dissolution of the Frankish Empire in the ninth
century the native institutions of the Saxons asserted their
supremacy over the external and exotic Carolingian institutions which Charlemagne had imposed upon them.[4]

The core of the Saxon army for years was the ancient
German Heerban, led to the rally by the counts, and interspersed with the more compact fighting groups of the *comitatus*. The free farming peasantry of Saxony in a trice, if occasion demanded, could be converted into a fighting force, as
the Saxon bishop, Thietmar of Merseburg, gleefully records
in 1002, when Henry II was in Saxony with a rout of Bavarian troopers, who "with that insatiable avarice which
they curb at home, but wantonly indulge abroad, began
to waste the crops of our Saxon farmers," and got soundly
thrashed by the infuriated peasants. The brother of the
King's chancellor, together with several other Bavarians, was
killed in the mêlée. The remainder fled to the royal court,
which was soon surrounded with augmented bands of irate
peasants who were not dispersed until Duke Bernhard of
Saxony appeared upon the scene with a strong force.[5]

The army with which Henry II invaded Poland in 1004

[1] Widukind, I, 21–22 and III, 51; Lambert of Hersfeld, *Annales* 1070, (ed.
Holder-Egger), p. 116. The Saxon army as a popular assembly appears as late as 929
(Widukind, I, 38). Cf. Richter and Kohl, *Annalen d. deutschen Gesch.*, III, Part II,
758–63.

[2] Schröder, *Deutsche Rechtsgesch.*, p. 389; Michael, *Gesch. d. deutschen Volkes*,
I, 298; Schulte, *Deutsche Staats- und Rechtsgesch.*, sec. 62.

[3] For this subject of legal complexities and ancient survivals see Waitz, V,
149 f.

[4] Widukind, I, 36; II, 3, 16, 33; III, 45, 51, 54, 67. Cf. Schröder, p. 166, n. 18.
Some of the Carolingian officials passed into the feudal hierarchy, e.g., Dietrich,
count of Kallenburg, was descended from a *preses Saxonicus* (*Annal. Ratisb. anno*
1085).

[5] Thietmar, *Chronicon*, V, 19; *Acta Henrici (II) imper.*, chap. xvii (Migne,
Pat. Lat., CXL, 97).

contained many Saxon footmen and the same is true of that
which he led into Italy,[1] although mounted service prevailed
everywhere else in Germany, a fact which shows how un-
feudal Saxony was. During the civil war in the reign of Henry
IV (1103), the feudal soldiery of the Emperor, most of whom
came from the Rhinelands and South Germany, were astonished still to find in Saxony freemen cultivating their fields
in time of peace and in war swarming to the fyrd, as their
forefathers had done before them, raw peasant levies fighting
on foot, armed with antiquated equipment,[2] and perhaps
wearing homemade straw hats, as Otto the Great's army did
when it invaded France in 946.[3] "Go back to your fields from
whence you came," cried Henry IV once to a rebel Saxon
army over against him.[4]

As a people, the Saxons as late as the twelfth century were
a simple folk, wholly agricultural in their means of livelihood,
west of the Weser dwelling in isolated farmsteads bounded
by a hedge or ditch, east of the river living in jumbled villages, with the "long fields" of the community lying round
about the hamlet,[5] every man among them proud of his

---

[1] Thietmar, *op. cit.*, VI, chaps. viii, x.

[2] Widukind, I, 21; II, 39, and Liutprand, *Antapod.*, II, 25, would seem to show
that Henry I's forces at the battle of the Unstrut in 933 was wholly composed of the
Heerban. Cf. Waitz, VII, 124; Baltzer, *Zur Gesch. des deutschen Kriegswesens*, p. 31;
Lambert of Herzfeld, *Annales* (anno 1012, 1075; ed. Holder-Egger), pp. 195, 216,
238, 260. *Carmen de bello Sax.*, II, vss. 118 f., and III, vs. 94; Bruno, *De bello Sax.*
(ed. Wattenbach), chap. iii, p. 20.

[3] The curious information in regard to straw hats is found in Widukind, III, 2;
pillea foenina, according to cod. A, 2, 3; *pillei ex culmis contexti*, according to cod. i.
This is confirmed by a passage in Rather of Verona cited in Pertz's edition of Widukind, *Rerum Ger. Scrip. in usum schol.*, p. 60, n. i; *Opera Ratherii* (ed. Ballerini),
p. 310; Vogel, *Ratherius von Verona*, I, 260; Lauer, *Le règne de Louis IV d'outre-mer*,
p. 146, n. 5.

[4] Reddite agris quos ex agro deputastis armis, coequate numerum satellitum
ad mensuram facultatum" (*Vita Heinrici Quarti*, 1103 [ed. Eberhard], p. 21). The
medieval Latin syntax in this sentence is almost as curious as the historical matter
in it.

[5] See Meitzen, *Siedelung und Agrarwesen*, II, 53–97, and Fuchs, *Epochs of
German Agrarian History and Agrarian Policy*, translated in T. N. Carver, *Readings
in Rural Economics*, pp. 224–30, where the theories as to the origin of this dualism
are given. Cf. also Seebohm's review of Meitzen in *Economic Journal*, VII, 71,
and Ashley's in his *Surveys, Historic and Economic*, pp. 116–28, and Wuttke's in
Neue Jahrb. d. klass. Alterthumsgesch. und deutschen Literatur, Vol. I, No. 5 (1898).
Meitzen's work strongly emphasizes the importance of agricultural practices and

"long knife,"[1] the *sachs*, from which they were believed to have derived their tribal name, and hating strangers.[2]

Feudalism in Saxony was almost rudimentary when compared to the system elsewhere in Germany. There was hardly any *ordo militaris* there. Suzerainty and vassalage—overlordship and underlordship—were less formal relations than

---

agrarian economy for the interpretation of history. But the honor of first perceiving this valuable fact and formulating the principle is to be given to Justus Moeser, who wrote in the Preface to his *Osnabrückische Geschichte:* "The history of landed property in Germany is the most important chapter in the history of German civilization." Elsewhere in the same work, Vol. I, p. 2, sec. 1, he returned to this thought in these weighty words: "Die Einrichtung eines Landes hängt gar sehr von der Natur seines Bodens und seiner Lage ab. Viele Bedürfnisse der Menschen werden allein dadurch erweckt und befriediget. Sitten, Gesetze und Religion müssen sich nach diesen Bedürfnissen richten." It is evident that the early Saxons dwelt both in nucleated villages and in tiny hamlets and scattered farmsteads. According to Meitzen (and others have followed him in this interpretation of the origin of these differences), where the population is found dwelling in rambling villages and outlying farms it is evidence that we have an autochthonous population, or at least peaceful occupation, e.g., the territory of the great Saxon plain. On the other hand, where the population is found settled in compact villages, it is the proof of German conquest, or at least of settlement made with more or less force. House construction and house decoration also shed some light on this distinction in the nature of ancient Germanic settlement in Old Saxony, and the elements which went to form the Saxon nation. West of the Weser the popular ornamentation is a horsehead; east of the Weser, on the other hand, pillars or columns reminiscent of the Irminsaeule are to be found. See Hartmann's monograph on house and gable ornamentation in Old Saxony (*Monatschrift f. d. Gesch. Westdeutschlands,* Band VIII [1882]; cf. Brandi, *Mitteil. d. Ver. f. Gesch. von Osnabrück,* Band XVIII [1893]). He determines the line of division as running through Detmold, Bielefeld, Osnabrück, Hanteburg, and Petershagen. The southern limit of the Low German type of peasant-house today does not coincide with the dividing-line between the Low and High German peoples, but runs to the north of that line. Since the eighteenth century the High German type of peasant-house has steadily trespassed on the region of the Low German peasant-house so that the latter seems doomed gradually to disappear and to be known in future only in pictures. See Andree, *Ztschft. f. Ethnologie,* Band XXVII, Heft 1 (1895).

[1] Widukind, I, 6–7; Nennius, *Hist. Britton,* chap. xvliii; Schaten, *Hist. Westphal.* (2d ed.), p. 119, says: "Usus hujus vocis hodiedum in Saterlandia obtinet apud incolas prisci sermonis retinentissimos, apud quos coram audivi loquentes 'sachs' cultrum sonat." For information on the Saterland see Kretschmer, *Hist. Geographie von Mitteleuropa,* sec. 121, where other literature is cited.

The Goths, too, earlier seem to have been partial to this short blade. For in the *Gesta Francorum* by Rorico, a monk of Moissac, we find the Visigoths using it against the Franks in Clovis' time: "Gothi . . . . cultellos permaximos quos vulgariter 'hantsaccos' corrupto vocabulo nominamus, etc." (Migne, CXXXIX, 609.)

[2] For Saxon hatred of outsiders (*advenae*) see Adam of Bremen, III, 55; Helmold, *Chron. Slavorum,* I, 83.

in Swabia and Bavaria. While there were many nobles, there was also a large body of free peasants. Moreover, these nobles were not many of them great landowners. Their distinction was a social one rather than one of political superiority. They lived much like English country gentlemen upon their estates. The early Saxon noble was more a rich proprietor farming his ancestral acres than a great baron. His life was rustic and his activities and interests rural. He was proud of his class but he wore no escutcheon.[1]

The true-born Saxon was opposed to new-fangled feudal laws and feudal methods like rigid definition of the relations of overlord and underlord, relief (i.e., inheritance tax for succession to a fief), new judicial processes, new kinds of taxes, extension of the king's ban over the forests, etc. He was a staunch conservative in this attitude, and in the sentiment the peasantry shared.[2] The Saxons were proud of the *crudelissima lex Saxonum*,[3] opposed to the new invention of the church to regulate and restrain private war, the Truce of God,[4] resented efforts to stamp out the good old blood feud (*faida*),[5] were sticklers for the old legal idea of personality of law,[6] were democratic within their class, but clung tenaciously to social distinctions, and detested outsiders (*advenae*) of any kind, Swabians, Bavarians, Flemings, etc., and hated *ministeriales* both as men of servile origin and as outsiders.[7]

Such is a picture of the culture of Saxony and the Saxon people in the depth of the feudal age—a bit of older Germany surviving and persisting in Central Europe when all the rest of Europe had gone the road of feudalism. Racial instincts, customs and inhibitions, primitive Teutonic religion, primi-

---

[1] Nitzsch, II, 10; Müller, *Sachsen unter Herzog Magnus* (1881), p. 9; Huebner, *Germanic Private Law*, p. 94.

[2] Bruno, *De bello saxonico*, chap. xxv. Cf. what Huebner, pp. 6–7, says about the conservatism of Saxon law. The revolt of Margrave Dedi of the Ostmark, or Thuringian Mark was due to the fact that having married the widow of the former margrave, Henry IV demanded payment of an inheritance tax (relief) for the lands which she brought him (Lambert of Hersfeld, p. 106; Bruno, *op. cit.*, chap. xxvi).

[3] Wipo, *Vita Chuonradi*, chap. vi.   [5] *Ibid.*, pp. 108, 116.

[4] Lambert of Hersfeld, p. 160.   [6] *Ibid.*, pp. 158, 270.

[7] *Ibid.*, pp. 114, 151, 152, 158, 172, 178, 217, 235, 236, 246, 262, 287; Bruno, chaps. xvi, xxiii–xxvi, cxxvii.

tive Teutonic law, a simple Teutonic society, gradually broken down by stronger outside contacts—such is the history of early Saxony.

Longinqua odia et inexpiabiles irae had existed between the Saxons and the Franks from the time of Charlemagne, and may have been aggravated in 1024 when the scepter passed from the Saxon to the Salian (Frankish) house. But in the eleventh century this factor was probably less concrete than the separatist ambition of the Billunger dukes. This purpose, veiled under Conrad II, became clear in the reign of Henry III (1039–56),[1] who took drastic measures for the coercion of Saxony by erecting and garrisoning castles there, so that long in advance of their rebellion the Saxons already were treated much as a conquered people.

In spite of the large part which Saxony played in German history during the rule of the Saxon house (919–1024), the Saxon people always had preserved a certain aloofness toward Germany as a whole, and revolved in an orbit of their own defining. Two reasons were mainly responsible for this: One was the fact that the Slav world not only impinged upon the eastern edge of Saxony, along the Elbe River, but actually imperiled Saxony. Accordingly, the interests and the energies of the Saxons for two hundred years were chiefly directed toward the conquest of the Wendish tribes. The colonization and upbuilding of Mecklenburg, Brandenburg, the Thuringian East Mark, and Pomerania absorbed all the resources of the Saxons. They had neither time nor inclination to participate in the affairs of the rest of Germany.

The other influence which held Saxony aloof from Germany at large was the fatal blunder of Otto I in failing to retain the duchy in his own hands, and instead conferring it upon his friend, Hermann Billung.[2] From the first the Bil-

---

[1] See Hauck, *Kirchengeschichte*, III, 313 and notes.

[2] Hermann Billung in 961 owned twenty counties in Saxony, and in Nordalbingia from Ditmarsch to the Peene River he possessed the tithe (Richter and Kohl, *Annalen*, III, Part I, 139, 143, 147, 185, 194). The tale that the Billunger in the beginning were mere peasant farmers is a legend (Giesebrecht, *Kaiserzeit*, I, 247–48). The family was originally from Nordalbingia and owned several counties in the dioceses of Bremen and Verden (*ibid.*, pp. 237–38; Waitz, *Deutsche Verfassungsgeschichte*, VII, 102, 109, 138; Steindorff, *De ducatus qui Billungorum dicitur in Saxonia progressu*).

lunger dukes played their hand wholly for themselves, and worked tooth and nail to build up a great lordship in the north which would be all but independent of the German crown. Henry II was well advised when he built a royal citadel in Bremen.[1] The result was a wall of partition, as it were, between Saxony and the rest of Germany which accentuated the isolation of Saxony.[2]

Until the decease of Duke Benno in 1011 the Billunger had been loyal, though with diminishing fidelity, to the German crown. With the accession of Duke Bernhard the alienation of Saxony became an estrangement which Conrad II was not the man to brook. His lenient treatment of the Wendish peoples (the hereditary foes of the Saxons) and the revindication of the fisc which he began were intimations not lost upon the Billunger. Thanks to Conrad II's effective measures, by 1039, when Henry III succeeded his father, only two of the six German duchies, Saxony and Lorraine, were independent. From the Rhine to the Morava, from the Harz to the Brenta, Henry III was both a local prince and a sovereign. Even the string of marches along the eastern border of Saxony were under his control. For after the death of Eckhard of Meissen in 1046, who made the king his heir, the crown had retained Eckhard's allodial lands, while the Thuringian March and Lausitz were given to Dedi of Wettin, a jealous rival of the dukes of Saxony.

[1] Adam of Bremen II, 48 (anno 1011).

[2] How far the factor of interracial antagonism between North and South Germany is to be allowed is doubtful, and it may have been rather a result than a cause. It was not greatly apparent before the war of investiture, and then the elements were so complex and kaleidoscopic that it is quite impossible to differentiate and to evaluate them all. Innocent III, though, used the racial argument in 1198 (*Reg. de neg. Rom. Imp.* [Migne, *Patrologia Latina*, CCXVI, 1067]; Toesche, *Heinrich VI*, Beilage X, pp. 587–92). Yet there was no love lost between Saxons, Bavarians, Swabians, and Franks, The Bavarians had a bad reputation for plundering whenever possible (*Adelboldi Fragmentum de rebus gestis Henrici (II) imperatoris*, chap. xviii; [Migne, CXL, 95]).

CHAPTER V

THE REBELLION OF SAXONY[1]

IT WAS with Henry III (1039–56) that the real coercion of Saxony was begun. His instruments of coercion were the archiepiscopal authority of Bremen, the fisc, and royal castles spread like a mesh over the duchy. He wrought to make Adalbert, archbishop of Bremen,[2] the great lord of the north in room of the Billunger dukes, to crush their feudal power under the weight of an enormous politico-ecclesiastical authority backed up by the military and financial resources of the crown, and at the same time to bleed the Saxon nobles and high clergy of the lands which they had obtained from the fisc in huge amounts and by questionable methods in times past.[3]

But Henry III's intentions were bigger than the coercion of a sullen and recalcitrant duchy. Possession in his own hands of each and every one of the German dukedoms was but preliminary to greater things still. What Henry III

[1] The literature pertaining to this subject is so great that it may seem temerity to hope to write anything new upon it. See Meyer von Knonau, *Jahrb. Heinrich IV*, II, 153 f.; Nitzsch, *Hist. Ztschft.* (N.F.), IX, 1, 193 f.; Vogeler, *Otto von Nordheim*, pp. 65–66; Lindner, *Anno der Heilige*, pp. 83 f. Ullmann, *Zum Verständnis der sächsischen Erhebung* (*Aufsätze für Waitz*); Zweck, *Die Gründe des Sachsenkrieges* (Königsberg, 1881); Eckerlin, *Die Ursachen des Sachsenaufstandes* (Burg, 1883); Hahn, *Ueber die Gründe des Sachsenkrieges* (Dramburg, 1885); Tieffenbach, *Die Streitfrage zwischen Heinrich IV und den Sachsen* (Königsberg, 1885); Sieber, *Haltung Sachsens gegen Heinrich IV* (Breslau, 1883); Meyer, *Lambert von Hersfeld* (Königsberg, 1877); Delbrück, *Ueber die Glaubwürdigkeit Lamberts von Hersfeld* (Bonn, 1873); Wagemann, *Die Sachsenkriege K. Heinrichs IV* (Celle, 1882); Floto, *Kaiser Heinrich IV und sein Zeitalter*, I, 351 f.; Giesebrecht, *Kaiserzeit*, III, 155 f.; Gerdes, II, 178 f.; cf. Richter, *Annalen*, III, Part II, 117 n.

[2] Adam of Bremen, III, 34, 35, 36, 56, 57, 65; Lambert of Hersfeld, *Annales* (*anno* 1057); Steindorff, *Heinrich III*, II, 366 and n. 6. Ordulf called Adalbert a spy—*quasi exploratorem* (Adam of Bremen, III, 5). On the other hand, Adam calls Magnus' followers *latrones* (III, 48).

[3] For Adalbert's use of *dispensatores fisci* see Lambert of Hersfeld (ed. Holder-Egger), pp. 89, 91. The Archbishop's fiscal operations and castle-building angered the Saxons (Adam of Bremen, III, 36).

dreamed of was the transformation of the feudalized German kingship into a real monarchy, the defeudalization of it by concentrating all provincial authority in the person and office of the king, the welding of the separate duchies into a compact whole—in a word, to transform the German kingdom from an agglomeration of duchies into a compact, united realm.

As a means to this end Henry III planned to centralize the Salian monarchy in a fixed capital at Goslar, and abandon the age-old practice of a wandering, itinerant government with the capital situated wherever the king happened temporarily to be at any given time.[1] Goslar at this time was nothing but a hunting lodge of the kings, with a little mill hard by it, in the Harz. But the locality had recently acquired great importance because of the discovery of the silver deposits of the Rammelsberg in the reign of Otto I.[2] The increased importance of a money economy is faintly discernible in Europe at least fifty years before the Crusades which created a widespread necessity for it, and Henry III seems to have felt the peculiar value of Goslar as a capital.[3] In spite of its apparent remoteness and isolation Goslar actually was singularly well situated for a capital. The great Heschenwege, or Hessian Way, the most important vertical highway in Germany between the Rhine and the Elbe, terminated at Goslar, so that the town was readily reached from Franconia, the homeland of the Salian kings, and even

[1] This is a moot point among historians of Germany, and many doubt if Henry III's ideas were so concrete. But it seems to me that Nitzsch (*Deutsche Gesch.*, II, 45-47, and Anmerkung, pp. 352-60) has proved the point. Goslar originally pertained to the house lands of the Ludolfinger dukes of Saxony, whence came Henry I and Otto I. The appropriation of Goslar by the Salian kings was one of the many grounds of feud between the Billunger and the crown in the eleventh century. Cf. Begiebing, *Die Jagd im Leben der Salischen Kaiser*, p. 48 (Bonn diss., 1905); Borchers, *Villa und civitas Goslar* (Leipzig, 1919).

[2] Widukind, *Rer. gestar. Sax.*, III, 64; Thietmar, *Chron.*, II, 8. Legend ascribed the discovery to the reign of Henry I (Waitz, *Jahrb. Heinrich I*, Excursus XV; Kretschmer, *Hist. Geographie von Mitteleuropa*, p. 210).

[3] See Gebhardt, *Handbuch d. deutschen Gesch.* (1st ed.), I, 298, n. 10; Justus Möser, *Osnabrückische Gesch.*, Part III, sec. 18, is the first historian who emphasized this fact.

from Swabia and Bavaria.[1] Here the Emperor built a palatium, erected two churches, and established a market which
soon became an important rendezvous of merchants.[2]

The Saxon feudality and their duke regarded the new
policy of Henry III with deep distrust, a sentiment also extended to the King's favorite, Adalbert of Bremen, whom the
royal largess enriched with the reversion of the county of
Frisia, 700 manors in the royal Herrschaft of Lesum (or
Lismona), other estates (*praedia*) in Sinzig, Duisburg, and
Altenburg, navigation rights on the lower Weser and along
the coast, king's ban and hunting rights in Stedingerland and
Vieland, in addition to gold bullion and plate for the cathedral church at Bremen.[3] Even more ominous than this
increase of the power of his favorite in Saxony was Henry
III's castle-building in the Harz, where he erected Regenstein
and Heimburg, fit companions to Goslar. It was evident that
the machinery of the metropolitanate of Bremen and that
of the fisc were to be utilized to coerce Saxony. Duke
Bernhard and the ring of northern bishops around Anno of
Cologne, Adalbert's bitter rival, of whom Burckhard of
Halberstadt, Anno's nephew, and Werner of Magdeburg,
Anno's brother, were the most prominent, regarded Henry
III's measures with secret and sullen anger.[4]

[1] Lambert of Hersfeld frequently mentions this road (pp. 116, 117, 156, 225).
Modern (and medieval) Eschwege in Hesse-Nassau, about eighteen miles southeast
of Cassel, preserves the remembrance of this famous highway. The town consists of
the old town on the left bank of the Werra River and the new town on the right bank,
and Brückenhausen—expressive name—on a small island connected with the old
and new towns by bridges.

[2] Adam of Bremen, III, 27. Goslar, Boppard, Hammerstein, Dortmund,
Engern, Nürnberg, were the chief toll stations of the German *Reich* (Waitz, VIII,
203; Richter and Kohl, III, Part II, 145 n.).

[3] Adam of Bremen, III, 8, 27, 44, gives a detailed account of these donations.
For further information see Kretschmer, p. 238; Dehio, *Gesch. d. Erzbistums Hamburg-Bremen*, I, 233 f.

[4] Adam of Bremen, III, 5, 34; Bruno, chap. xxvi; Vogeler, *Otto von Nordheim*,
pp. 44–45. For a particular account of Burckhard's spoliation of the fisc see Sellin,
Vita Burchardi II . . . . ep. Halberstadensis (Halle, 1866), pp. 13–15; Wackermann,
Burchard von Halberstadt, der Führer der Sachsen in dem Krieg gegen Heinrich IV
(1878). Henry IV imprisoned him in the Harzburg at one time (*Ann. Palad.*, SS.
XVI, 70). Lambert of Hersfeld, *Annales*, abounds with details as to the plundering

The fire was not long in breaking out. Apparently the enrichment of Adalbert was the chief grievance, although the irritation was commingled with fear of loss of some of their own ill-gotten lands.[1] In 1047 matters reached a crisis when Thietmar, the brother of the Saxon Duke, was charged with a plot against the life of Adalbert of Bremen. When summoned to trial before the Emperor, Henry III commanded him to clear himself through trial by battle, and as if in deliberate humiliation of the accused, appointed as his combatant a royal *ministerialis* named Arnold. Thietmar refused to fight under such conditions. The cause was adjourned for a few days, and in the meantime Thietmar was murdered by Arnold. Shortly afterward the dead Count's son waylaid and killed Arnold and then hanged the corpse between two dead dogs, for which the King exiled him.[2] The relation of Saxony to the German crown was year by year becoming more and more tense. Already, since the death of Otto III in 1002, one representative of the ducal house had been besieged, one killed, and the third exiled. It is no wonder that for the next five years Henry III stayed almost uninterruptedly in Saxony and pushed forward the works around Goslar.[3]

The sudden death of the Emperor in the prime of life in 1056 delayed, but did not avert, the struggle between Saxony and the crown. The duchy began to steam with rebellion. As soon as it was known that Henry III was dead the Saxon nobles commenced to take measures to safeguard their interests, although Lambert of Hersfeld's statement[4] that a plot

---

of the "royal" monasteries and the fisc during Henry IV's minority, e.g., pp. 41, 42, 47–56, 58, 67–69, 77–79, 89–91, 192, etc. For the graft and rapacity Anno displayed in order to enrich Cologne see Lambert, p. 143.

[1] "Metropolitanus autem e contra bonis studiis certans et beneficiis" (Adam of Bremen, III, 9; Steindorff, II, 15–16, 366).

[2] Adam of Bremen, III, 8; Lambert of Hersfeld, p. 61. For this gruesome old German method of punishment see Grimm, *Rechtsalterthümer*, p. 685.

[3] Herim. Aug., *Chronicon* (*annis* 1048–52).

[4] "Principes Saxoniae crebris conventiculis agitabant de injuriis quibus sub imperatore affecti fuerant, arbitrabanturque . . . . si filio ejus dum aetas oportuna injuriae esset, regum eriperent. . . . . Accessit . . . . adjumentum Otto frater Wil-

was at once set on foot to dethrone the infant Henry IV, and
even to kill him, is open to doubt. It is impossible to believe
that the conspirators ever seriously contemplated putting up
as king Otto, the half-brother of the heroic William, the margrave of the Nordmark, who had recently died of wounds received in a campaign against the Hungarians, and with whose
prowess Germany rang. For Otto's mother was a Bohemian.
It is preposterous to think a man of half-foreign and base
extraction could have been contemplated for the kingship.
The truth would seem to be that the conspirators planned to
use Otto (whose claim to the vacant margraviate was im-
peached by his low birth as well as against the feudal law of
the time, for the hereditability of the marches was not yet
established as a legal principle) as a stalking-horse behind
whom to further their own designs. But the murder of this
ambitious and unscrupulous adventurer, as he was en route
to Saxony, by two of the King's cousins, Bruno and Ekbert
of Brunswick,[1] certainly nipped a contemplated rebellion of
the Saxon nobles in the bud.

Perhaps nothing but the strength of Adalbert of Bremen
saved the crown of the infant Henry IV from being at once
stripped of all power in the north. But in the end the great
Archbishop was overwhelmed by his foes. First Henry IV,
who had nominally attained his majority in 1065, was compelled to dismiss Adalbert from his service (1066); then the
Billunger fell upon Bremen and terribly wasted the diocese.
In vain Adalbert, who had fled to Goslar, sought to compound with his enemies by proffering a thousand of his manors. "He shall not rest," said Ordulf, Duke Bernhard's son,
"while I and my house last." In the issue, the archdiocese of

---

lehelmi marchionis sed matrimonio impari, matre scilicet Sclavica. . . . . Is. . . .
comperta morte fratris, magna spe obtinendae hereditatis regressus in Saxoniam,
a cunctis illic principibus benigne excipitur, magnisque omnium adhortationibus
instigatur non modo marcham, quae sibi jure hereditario competeret, sed ipsum
quoque regnum affectare. . . . . Fidem omnes dicunt, suas quisque manus, suam
operam pollicentur, regemque, ubicumque fortuna oportunum fecisset, interficere
constituunt" (Lambert of Hersfeld, *Annales* [1057], p. 71).

[1] Their grandmother was Gisela, formerly wife of Bruno, count of Brunswick,
who after his death married the emperor Conrad II.

Bremen was stripped of two-thirds of its lands, half the spoil
going to the Duke, the rest to his partisans.

In the welter which followed the fall of Adalbert it must
sometimes have seemed as if the German kingship would be
dragged down, too, and the King become a lean and solemn
phantom like the kings of France at this very time, with scant
domains and little save the theory of royal authority to sustain the fabric of government. For with the general lapse of
the crown's power in Saxony, Bavaria, Swabia, and Lorraine
also exhibited ominous centrifugal tendencies. Fortunately
for the crown at this critical juncture, the German episcopate
as a whole, even in Saxony, remained loyal to the monarchy.
Why should it not? For a century and a half the kings had fed
and favored the bishops, and protected them against the
violence of the feudality.

Henry IV was made of sterner stuff than either his father
or Conrad II. The greatest of the Salians, as able as Frederick
Barbarossa and far wiser (indeed, if I may hazard my own
judgment, the ablest German ruler between Charlemagne and
Charles V), Henry IV was not the man to cry quits. With a
courage, a cunning, and an energy that is amazing to observe,
when Henry IV became a free agent at the termination of his
disastrous minority, he patiently set himself to repair the
shattered fabric of German kingship which Conrad II and
Henry III had built up.

During the King's infancy the disloyal bishops and the
Fürsten in Saxony had boldly seized huge blocks of the lands
of the fisc by means of forged charters or by force, and then
erected castles in defiance of the law with which to hold the
land.[1] Dedi, margrave of the Thuringian March, built Beich-

---

[1] A portion of the fisc was the remnant which remained from the largesses
which had been made by the Ottos. The residue was represented by the revindica-
tions of Conrad II and Henry III. The penury of the royal fisc in Saxony is manifest
from the admissions even of the king's enemies (Lambert of Hersfeld [1065; ed.
Holder-Egger], p. 100; *ibid*. [1073], p. 173; Bruno, *De bello Sax.*, chap. xliii—letter of
Werner of Magdeburg to Siegfried of Mainz; *Carmen de bello Sax.*, I, 26, 45). Much
of the property of the crown had been seized by means of forged charters, especially
in the case of the bishops. For further information see Vogeler, *Otto von Nordheim*,
pp. 41–43; Waitz, *Abhand. d. k. Gesellschaft d. Wiss. Göttingen*, Band XV; Schaumann, *Gesch. des niedersächsischen Volkes*, pp. 190–91. The best study of Henry IV's
attempt to "revindicate" the fisc in Saxony and Thuringia is M. Stimming, *Das*

lingen and Burgscheidungen; Otto of Nordheim constructed Hanstein, Burghasengun, and Desenburg; Magnus Billung fortified Lüneburg.[1]

But the Saxon nobles soon discovered that two could play at the game of castle-building. Henry III had pointed out the way to coerce the duchy by erecting Goslar, Regenstein, and Heimburg. His son proposed to cover the country, especially the region of the Harz, with a network of castles, garrisoned by loyal Swabians, Bavarians, and Franconians, most of them *ministeriales* of the king.[2] The plan was not unsimilar to Otto the Great's method in the tenth century, when he gridironed the newly conquered Thuringian March, just wrenched from the Sorben, with timbered blockhouses like those which his father Henry I had built in Saxony to protect it against the Magyar raids. But Henry IV's erections were more substantial than these earlier structures, for the art of castle-building had much advanced in the eleventh century.[3]

The precaution had first been pointed out to the King by Adalbert of Bremen in 1066, and he had begun speedily to act upon the advice.[4] The first and strongest of these castles was the Harzburg,[5] which was another Goslar in magnificence

---

deutsche Königsgut, pp. 86 f., who shows that much the richest block of the crown lands was in Eastern Saxony and Thuringia.

[1] Lambert of Hersfeld (1069), p. 108; *ibid.* (1071), p. 119. Anno of Cologne was the original sinner in this violation of the law (Delbrück, *Ueber die Glaubwürdigkeit Lamberts v. Hersfeld* [Bonn dis., 1873], p. 30), having built them during the feud with the abbots of Fulda and Hersfeld—a fact which Lambert carefully conceals, but which is revealed by the *Annal. Corb.* (*anno* 1067), SS. III, 6. Cf. Bruno, *De bello Saxonico,* chap. xvi; Ekkehard, *Chronicon* (*anno* 1068); Berthold, SS. V, 275; *Annal. Altah.* (anno 1073).

[2] "Rex . . . . privata praesidia nimirum potentibus regni non satis fidens instituere . . . . coepit" (Ekkehard, *Chron.* [1068]).

[3] "Castella non tam pulchra quam forta esse laborabat" (Bruno, *loc. cit.*).

[4] ". . . . ipsius [Adalbert] suasionibus coepit in desertis locis altos et natura munitos montes quarere, et in his hujusmodi castella fabricare, quae si in locis competentibus starent, ingens regno firmamentum simul et ornamentum forent" (*ibid.*). Stimming (*Das deutsche Königsgut,* pp. 98 f.) significantly shows the contiguity of the lands of the leaders of the Saxon revolt, bishops as well as nobles, to the royal domains in Saxony and Thuringia.

[5] Bruno, *loc. cit.;* Lambert of Hersfeld (*anno* 1071); Meyer von Knonau, II, 231, n. 76; *ibid.,* p. 871, n. 5.

and strength. At first the Saxon Fürsten smiled derisively, and said that Henry IV was merely playing at castle-building.[1] But when the hills of Thuringia and the Harz country fast began to bristle with frowning fortresses they looked graver.[2] Among them were Wigantestein, Moseburg, Sachsenstein, Spatenburg, Hasenburg, and Volkerode.[3] Without counting the castles which his father had erected, Henry IV soon had five other castles in the Harz, and two in Thuringia.

The royal architect in the erection of these structures was Benno II, bishop of Osnabrück, the earliest military engineer of medieval Germany.[4] If Bernward of Hildesheim (died 1022) be Germany's first great architect,[5] Benno was certainly the second and Otto of Bamberg the third.[6] Swabian born, and of servile birth, Benno was educated at Reichenau, whence he went as master to the cathedral school at Hildesheim, of which church he became provost. Henry III took a fancy to him and made him mayor of his palatium at Goslar and superintendent of the fisc. Finally, having tested Benno's talents, the Emperor appointed him bishop of Osnabrück in 1054. He died in 1088, the most able and loyal supporter Henry IV ever possessed. Besides building the King's castles Benno drew the plans and laid the foundations of Henry IV's Romanesque cathedral at Speyer, where the prob-

[1] ". . . . puerilis ludus videbatur" (Bruno, *loc. cit.*).

[2] "Montes omnes colliculosque Saxoniae et Turingiae castellis munitissimis . . . . (Lambert of Hersfeld [1073], p. 141); ". . . . totam Saxoniam castellis novis et firmis coepit munire" (*Vita Bennonis*, chap. xi); to the same effect: *Annal. Corb.* (1067), SS. III, 6; *Annal. Sax.* (1067), *ibid.*, VI, 695; *Compil. Sanblas.*, *ibid.*, V, 275; Bernold, *ibid.*, p. 429; *Annal. Altah.* (1073).

[3] Lambert of Hersfeld (1073), p. 179. For location and details about these structures see Holder-Egger, *Neues Archiv*, XIX, 190 f., 425 f.; Meyer von Knonau, *op. cit.*, II, 871 f.; Richter and Kohl, III, Part II, 130–31. Helmold, *Chron. Slavorum* (written a century later), I, 27, in order to make an effective quotation from Deut. 32:10, exaggerates the wildness and isolation of the site of the Harzburg. Lambert of Hersfeld's description (pp. 155–56) is probably fairly accurate. There were no roads in the region, only hunters' trails. The Harzburg, like the Star Chamber in England, became a synonym for royal tyranny. Arnold of Lübeck in the thirteenth century refers to it as the "jugum totius Saxoniae" (*Chronicon Slavorum*, II, 18).

[4] See the long and interesting accounts in *Vita Bennonis*, chaps. xi, xxi, xxvii.

[5] On Bernward see Thangmar, *Vita Bernwardi*, SS. IV, 758 f.

[6] See Herbordus, *Vita Ottonis ep. Babenb.*

lem of protecting the foundations from being undermined by the floods of the Rhine was a difficult one. In addition to these abilities Benno was a notable manager of the lands and resources of his diocese.[1]

Henry IV's drastic course in the building of these châteaux stirred up bitter resentment in the countryside roundabout, for he impressed into service the whole laboring population, employing not only serfs from the crown lands in the region, but those on the manors of the Saxon nobles too, and even, it is said, Saxon freemen.[2] When completed the castles were garrisoned with Bavarian and Swabian troops, who instead of living upon the produce of the royal manors in the vicinity, made levies upon the Thuringian monasteries and raided the countryside for forced contributions.[3]

And yet there is reason to believe that the chroniclers hostile to Henry IV, like Bruno and Lambert of Hersfeld, exaggerate these grievances. As has been before observed, by the middle of the eleventh century Europe was beginning to manifest signs of an economic awakening, trade was commencing to have an international relation, and a money economy was slowly supplanting the old practice of barter and exchange. With the silver mines of the Rammelsberg so close at hand Henry IV seems to have attempted to force forward these economic changes too rapidly for the backward population of Thuringia to understand them. For Lambert inadvertently admits in two places that those supplies which the fisc or the royal abbeys (which were actually part of the fisc) failed to furnish were purchased—an inadvertence as damaging to the annalist as it is creditable to Henry IV. It probably not infrequently happened on such occasions that

---

[1] Norbert's *Vita Bennonis* ranks as one of the most valuable episcopal biographies of the Middle Ages. For modern appreciations of him see Von Thyen, *Benno von Osnabrück* (Göttingen diss., 1869); Stenzel, *Gesch. Deutschlands unter den fränkischen Kaisern*, II, 93 f.; Bresslau, *Neues Archiv*, Band XXVIII; Löffler, *Die Westphälischen Bischöfe*, pp. 39–44.

[2] Bruno, *loc. cit.* For a similar instance in Lorraine see *Frag. de gestis Henrici imp.* (Migne, *Pat. Lat.*, CXL, 98).

[3] Bruno, chaps. xvi, xxv; Lambert of Hersfeld, pp. 118, 141; *Annal. Altah. (anno* 1073); Waitz, VIII, 429. For an instance of one of the royal *ministeriales* being killed by a woman at Ingelheim while making a forced levy see Lambert of Hersfeld, p. 101.

the simple peasantry, unused to money and not knowing what to do with it, refused to take it when proffered in payment for supplies taken, whereupon the King's officers seized the goods wanted.[1]

That Henry IV should have been misunderstood and violently opposed, not only by those who had selfish interests to guard, but by others who were quite genuine and sincere in their hostility to him, was natural. Bruno's charge is true: ". . . . ut solus omnium dominus esset, nullum in regno suo dominium vivere vellet,"[2] provided "dominus" be understood as an absolute king and not a tyrant, and "dominium" to mean intelligent and efficient rule and not mere brute force on the part of a prince. Goslar, both because of its strategic position in Saxony, the storm center of opposition to the Salian purpose to establish a strong monarchy in Germany, and perhaps more because of its proximity to the Rammelsberg silver mines, was Henry IV's intended capital.[3] Here was the seat of Henry IV's court until the great rebellion of 1075 drove him out. It was the *königlicher Hof*. Here foregathered, when not afield, Henry IV's most trusted counselors and friends like Benno II of Osnabrück, Ebbo of Naumburg, Liemar of Bremen, Adalbert's successor, lesser nobles of the feudal hierarchy like Werner of Hesse, William of Utrecht, Liupold of Merseburg, Giso, count of Gudensberg-Hollenden, Udalric of Cosheim, a count Adalbert, whose fief (if he were not a favored *ministerialis*) seems to have been too insignificant to record the name of, with his four sons, and two counts of Nellenberg—one from Zurichgau, the other from the upper Rhinelands.[4]

[1] Lambert of Hersfeld, pp. 100, 173. Lambert seems to be confirmed by Bruno (chap. iv), who clearly fails to understand this kind of transaction.

[2] Bruno, chap. lx. The same charge is made by the *Annal. Sax.* (1076), which quotes the harangue of a Saxon leader: "Nolite servitutis jugum recipere, nolite hereditariam vestram tributariam facere."

[3] Nitzsch, *Deutsche Studien*, p. 133 (also printed in *Hist. Ztschft.* [N.S.], IX, 1 f., 193 f.); Thyen, p. 34 and n. 5. Vogeler (*Otto von Nordheim*, p. 39), however, thinks Henry IV had no greater purpose than to make Goslar his chief military base. But, as developed in the text, Henry IV's public economy was toward getting away from the old *Naturalwirtschaft* and basing his system of government upon the new *Geldwirtschaft*.

[4] Adam of Bremen (ed. Schmeidler), p. 192, n. 3.

The fisc, as already intimated, was an important instrument of Henry IV's administration, and he used it like a screw to bring pressure upon Saxony. For he enormously increased the burden upon the crown lands there both for days of service and in amount of produce to be contributed. The heaviness of Henry IV's hand in these two requirements was so great that one is led to think that there was a political intention in the policy as well as an economic purpose; that, anticipating protest, and even rebellion, he planned to break the backbone of opposition in advance by sheer weight of the burdens imposed.

Be this conjecture as it may, the fact is certain that the inventory of services required in the year 1064–65 shows that the exactions laid upon the fisc in Saxony were from four to five times as great as elsewhere in Germany. According to this highly important document,[1] the crown then possessed twenty-one manors in Franconia, twelve in Bavaria, and twenty in Saxony. Nothing is said of the number of the crown lands in Lorraine or Swabia or Carinthia, and we know that there was no fisc in the new colonial lands across the Elbe.

An analysis of these important *Tafelgüter* reveals that while the fiscal manors in Bavaria were charged with only thirty-six days' service and those in Franconia with eighty-five days' service, the Saxon manors had a total of four hun-

---

[1] The full title is *Indiculus curiarum ad mensam regis Romanorum pertinentium* (text in *MGH Const.*, I, No. 440, 646; better edition in *Neues Archiv*, XLI, 572–74). Haller, "Das Verzeichnis der Tafelgüter des römischen Königs," *Neues Archiv*, XLV, 48–81) argues against the generally accepted date (*ca.* 1065) and holds that it pertains to a century later (1185). But I cannot see the force of his argumentation. It seems impossible to me that the document can be of the time of Frederick I, though it is plausible to indulge the thought that it was made by Frederick I after the fall of Henry the Lion in 1181. See B. Heusinger, "Servitium regis," *Archiv f. Urkundenforschung*, VIII, 26–159, for further critical study. While by far the most important, this famous *Indiculus* is not the sole source of information which we have upon the royal exactions in Thuringia.

In Boehmer, *Fontes*, III, 397, or *MGH LL*, IV, 1, 647–49 (also in *Reg. Thur.*, No. 853), is found a similar document showing the undue burden imposed upon the manors there. It reads: "Iste curie tamen de Saxonia dant regi tot servitia, quot sunt dies in anno et XL plus. Item notificamus tamen vobis, quod sit regale servitium in Saxonia: Sunt XXX magni porci, III vacce, V porcelli, L galline, L ova, LXXX casei, X anseres, V carrate cervisie, V libre piperis, X libre cerae, vinum de cellario suo ubique Saxonie." Cf. also *ibid.*, Nos. 837 and 940.

dred and five days' service imposed upon them each year.
This means that the average long working day of the Saxon
peasant was prolonged far beyond customary exaction elsewhere. The same enormous discrepancy is apparent also
when we compare the exactions in produce (as distinguished
from services). It may be presented in the subjoined table.

	Cows	Hogs	Chick-ens	Geese	Eggs	Chees-es	Beer	Honey	Wine	Pepper
Saxony	60	600	1000	200	10,000	1,800	100	200	.....	100
Franconia	20	160	200	40	2,000	360	.....	40	16	20
Bavaria	15	120	150	30	1,500	270	.....	30	12	15

If Henry IV had gone no farther than the reorganization
of the fiscal system upon the crown lands in Saxony[1] he
would have dealt only with an unfree peasantry. But he
touched the whole body of Saxon freemen, of whom there
were thousands, on the quick when he revived the almost
obsolete royal impositions (*census*; Ger. *Zins, steora*), formerly exacted of freemen in Carolingian times. These were collected on farm produce.[2] The menace of manorial serfdom
threatened the largest and freest body of free peasantry in
Germany. It is small wonder that the Saxon peasantry grew
disquieted. Always tenacious of their native institutions and
jealous of outside and newfangled innovations of any kind,
whether in state or church, they were apprehensive lest the
new policy of the fisc might extinguish the *Allmend*, inclose
the forests, restrict their hunting rights, and draw the net of
manorialism tighter around their free villages.[3]

[1] For the management instituted upon the manors of the church from which the
crown drew revenues see *Vita Bennonis*, chap. x; Eggers, *Der königliche Grundbesitz*,
pp. 133–34; Inama Sternegg, *DWG*, II, 150.

[2] Waitz, IV, 111 and n. 6; Schröder, *Rechtsgesch.*, p. 187. For an example under
Otto I see *Codex Anhalt.* (965), I, No. 42, p. 32. On the other hand, tribute was only
exacted of the conquered non-German peoples of the east border, e.g., Widukind,
I, 35, 40; *ibid.*, III, 53; Wipo, chap. vi; Lambert (*anno* 1041); Otto Fris., *Gesta
Frid.*, III, 2.

[3] Even in the reign of Henry II, who was of Saxon blood, the Saxons had showed
alarm by compelling the King to take an oath "not in any point to corrupt Saxon
law" (Thietmar, *Chron.*, V, 16–17; Giesebrecht, II, 24, 593).

The Salian forest policy was as alarming as its fiscal policy. The old order of things formulated in Vridank's rhyme,

Dem richen walt es lützel schâdet,
Ob sich ein man mit holze ladet,[1]

was fast becoming obsolete in the eleventh century. One of the most significant evidences of the growth of feudalism is the gradual appropriation of the forests by private proprietors, both lay and clerical. Year by year since Charlemagne's death the area of free forest land in Germany had shrunk, and the rights of the peasantry to the timber, fish, and game therein had been curtailed by the spread of private proprietorship.[2] With the revival of royal authority by the Saxon kings a stop was put to this indiscriminate practice of forest appropriation, and all unappropriated forest land was declared to be *Königswälder* and a part of the fisc, special license being required for use of it.[3] But unfortunately, while the Ottos thus tried to save at the spiggot, they wasted at the bung. The Saxon kings were lavish in gifts of forest land to the bishops and abbots.[4] The drop-off of private donations to the bishops in the eleventh century, owing to the great popularity of the religious orders, especially Cluny, gave a fillip to the land-hunger of the bishops, who found compensa-

[1] Quoted by Lamprecht, *DWL*, I, Part I, 517.

[2] *Ibid.*, p. 110; and his *Deutsche Gesch.*, III, 54–55; Von der Goltz, *Landwirtschaft*, I, 186; Huebner, *Germanic Private Law*, p. 271.

[3] Lamprecht, *Deutsche Gesch.*, III, 53.

[4] Lamprecht, *DWL*, I, Part I, 148. This is especially true of Henry II. In 1002 he enriched the Bishop of Worms, in 1008 the Bishop of Liège, in 1012 the Abbot of Fulda, with huge tracts of forest. See his *Acta* (Migne, CXL, 245, 281, 295).

In 1065 Henry IV gave Adalbert of Bremen the *Bannforst* over the forest between the Ruhr, the Rhine, and the Düssel, through which the great road from Cologne ran, which at that time was dotted with villages of the free peasantry. "Addimus insuper cum banno nostro praedictae ecclesiae forestum unum in triangulo trium fluminum scilicet Rein, Tussale et Rurae positum, ita quoque determinatum per Ruram se sursum extendens usque ad pontem Werdinensem et exinde per stratam Coloniensem usque ad rivum Tussale, et per descensum ejusdem rivi ad Rhenum, et per alveum Rheni usque ad quo Rura influit Rhenum" (Lacomblet, *Urk. B.*, I, 205; cf. Averdunk, *Gesch. der Stadt Duisburg*, I, 44; Begiebing, *op. cit.*, pp. 33–36).

tion by inclosing the forests, a practice which the lay nobles quickly imitated.[1]

By the middle of the Salian period most of the forest land in Western and Southern Germany had become inclosed. But this was not true of Saxony. Here the forest was the poor man's home, in whose depths he might escape the coils of manorialism, farm a little clearing, and pasture his swine upon the nuts and acorns without money and without price. This free condition especially prevailed in the Harzwald and Thüringerwald.[2]

Henry IV, with that passion for efficiency which so characterized him, determined to realize upon all the resources of the crown, and revived the almost forgotten prerogative of king over unappropriated forest tracts and sought to assimilate the forests in Saxony with the fisc.[3] The project stirred the Saxon people, especially the masses of freemen, enormously. If he had alarmed and antagonized the free farming peasantry of the open country by imposing the *Zins*, he now still more alarmed and antagonized those thousands of humbler, lowlier freemen who dwelt in tiny hamlets in clearings in the forests. They believed that the King contemplated nothing less than the reduction of all of them to a state of serfdom. They resented being compelled to pay for pasturage and firewood which from time immemorial had been as free as air, and the curtailment of their ancient right of "squatter sovereignty."[4]

Farther and farther into the remote valleys of the Harz and the depths of the Thüringerwald, had the Saxon free peasantry pressed, only there to be sought out by land-hungry bishops, abbots, and barons, or the agents of the

[1] Lamprecht, *DWL*, I, Part II, 688; Inama Sternegg, *Grundherrschaften*, p. 44.

[2] Thietmar, V, 19; *Vita Bennonis*, chap. x. For the wildness of the Harzwald see Lambert of Hersfeld (1073), p. 156.

[3] Waitz, VIII, 388; Richter and Kohl, III, Part II, 123; Lambert of Hersfeld (1073), p. 146. For other mentions by him of government invasion of the forest see pp. 141, 147, 155, 158, 159, 270; Bruno, chaps. xxx, xlii; *Carmen de bello sax.* I, ll. 42–46. Delbrück (*op. cit.*) has shown the exaggerated nature of this popular apprehension. Cf. Thimme, "Königsgut und Königsrecht," *Archiv. f. Urk.* (1909).

[4] ". . . . qui vulgo dicuntur werlude" (Lacomblet, *Urk. B.* [1026], I, No. 164, cited by Lamprecht, *DWL*, I, Part I, 148).

royal fisc.[1] The Harzwald must have been dotted with
tiny forest villages founded thus,[2] among whose inhabitants
Henry IV's announcement that the king's ban was to be extended over the three great heaths of Saxony spread con-
sternation. For the heaths had been *Ödlandereien* as far back
as the memory of man.[3] The forest around Castle Iburg
seems to have been dotted with these pioneer borderers (*com-
marchiones*), who were driven to fury by the royal appropriation and leveling of the woods to make a cleared space for
another of Henry IV's castles.[4]

The bitter tithe wars waged at the same time in Saxony
between the bishops and the abbots for exclusive right to
exact tithes of the peasantry increased the rage of the peasantry. The bishops claimed that the right was an episcopal
one in which the abbots had no part. In Osnabrück there
was a feud between the Bishop and the Abbot of Corvey,[5]
Burckhardt of Halberstadt waged a long controversy with
Hersfeld.[6] The Archbishop of Mainz and the Abbot of Fulda
were at swords' points in Thuringia. Inevitably the feudality
were drawn into the struggle. Dedi of the Thuringian Ostmark and Albert of Ballenstadt sought to fish in the troubled
waters. Royal intervention became necessary to enforce
peace in Thuringia, but increased the sullen resentment.

Henry IV emerged victorious from the struggle with Margrave Dedi only to discover that he had a new and more
formidable conflict upon his hands in the rebellion of Otto of

---

[1] For a striking instance see "Gesta Marcuardi," *Fuld. Fontes* (*ca.* 1150), III,
166. The upper Moselle was not invaded until the twelfth century (Lamprecht,
DWL, I, Part I, 147).

[2] There is a valuable article by Bruhns, "Geographische Studien über die Wald-
hufensiedelungen in Sachsen," with a map, in *Globus*, XCV, 197–200, 220–25.

[3] For these three heaths see *Sachsenspiegel*, II, 61, and for the *campestris
Heidibae* (Hadeby) south of the Schlei River see Adam of Bremen, II, 79. Cf.
Zeitschft. f. Ethnologie, XXXVI (1904), 688–90. An interesting account of the multi-
plication of these forest villages during the tenth and early eleventh century may be
found in the *Mittelrheinisches Urkundenbuch*, Band II (Einleitung); Inama Sternegg,
I, 207–17; Arnold, *Ansiedelungen und Wanderungen deutscher Stämme*, II, 20–44; Von
der Goltz, I, 140 f.; Rietzler, *Gesch. Bayerns*, I, 135 f.; Lamprecht, *DWL*, I, Part
I, 124–48.

[4] *Vita Bennonis*, chap. xvi.

[5] *Ibid.*, chap. xvi.   [6] Lambert of Hersfeld (1059), p. 75.

Nordheim and Magnus Billung. Few characters in the history of feudal Germany are more enigmatical than Otto of Nordheim. Even the exact reason for his rebellion still eludes complete explanation. Was Otto a deeply wronged man, or was he a shrewd adventurer? Was he knave or hero? Certainly, whatever be the verdict, it is impossible to deny Otto's great influence upon the course of events.

Otto of Nordheim first appears in history in 1061 as a favorite of Agnes, the queen-mother, who gave him the then vacant duchy of Bavaria in that year. He was of Saxon lineage and already marked as a man of capacity.[1] Gossip said that out of pique at not obtaining the duchy of Swabia instead, Otto turned against the Empress. At any rate, he was a party to the abduction of the young King in 1062 and for a time shared the power with Anno of Cologne and Adalbert of Bremen.

When Henry IV took the reins of government into his own hands he may possibly have feared so powerful a counselor. He had no reason to repose confidence in any ministers of the regency except Adalbert, least of all a Saxon. For Otto of Nordheim, through his landed possessions, was one of the greatest of the Saxon nobles and boon companion of Magnus Billung to boot.[2] The crisis came in 1069 when Henry IV was sojourning in Bavaria, having just returned from a victorious campaign against the Ljutizi beyond the Elbe.[3] A violent feud broke out between some of the men of the Duke and a favorite *ministerialis* in Henry IV's train named Conon,[4] whom Otto detested, perhaps for no other reason than that Saxon pride of birth hated all parvenus. The other *ministeriales* in the entourage took a hand in the fray, among them a friend of Conon named Egino.[5] The affair was temporarily appeased. But soon afterward Egino publicly accused Otto of conspiracy to kill the King.

[1] Stenzel, I, 217; Voigt, p. 14.

[2] *Annal. Altah.* (*anno* 1061); Ekkehard, *Chron.* (1071); Lambert of Hersfeld (1061), p. 78; Vogeler, p. 7 n.

[3] *Annal. Weissemb.* (*anno* 1069); Sigeb. Gembl., *Chron.* (1069).

[4] He appears as a recipient of the King's bounty in a charter of October 26, 1064 (Stumpf, *Regesta*, No. 2652).

[5] Vogeler, pp. 12 and 14, n. 3.

The incident so far seems only to have led to some estrangement between the King and the Duke.[1] Now Otto was summoned to appear before the *Hofgericht* at Mainz (June 19, 1070), where he denied the charge and was given a delay of six weeks, at the termination of which he was commanded to appear at Goslar to clear himself, according to custom,[2] by trial by battle with his accuser. The form of solution was needlessly humiliating,[3] for Otto of Nordheim was a high noble and Egino a man of servile origin. The Duke demanded a safe-conduct to court and a trial by his peers. The King granted the security but evaded pronouncing upon the form of the process. Otto feared, perhaps with good reason, to come to Goslar, was tried and condemned in his absence by a court of Saxon nobles,[4] and deprived of his benefices, which were immense.[5] The north country soon flamed with war. The armed *ministeriales* of the King devastated Otto's estates, while he himself sought asylum in the depths of the Thuringian forest, whence he made forays upon the adjacent crown lands. In August, Henry IV himself came with a rout

[1] Otto of Nordheim's name appears very rarely in the *Urkunden* in 1069–70, although frequent before (Vogeler, p. 17).

[2] ". . . . ut mos est" (Ekkehard, *Chron.*, SS. VI, 200).

[3] For an analysis of the psychology of this incident see Meyer von Knonau, II, 9 f.

[4] As Otto was a Saxon and lived Saxon law the process was strictly proper. But was he guilty? Saxon chroniclers, like Bruno and Lambert, believe him innocent; the Bavarian author of the *Chronicle of Niederaltaich* thinks him guilty; Bertold of Swabia brings in the Scotch verdict "not proven." The various sources are analyzed by Giesebrecht, *KZ*, III, 1033 f.; Richter, III, 2, 71, n. B. A puzzling feature is that Saxon nobles themselves condemned Otto. Lambert alleges private envy of him: "principes Saxoniae . . . . propter privatas inimicicias maxime invisum eum haberent" (p. 114), which Riezler, *Gesch. Bayerns*, I, 484, thinks plausible, but which Franklin, *Das Reichshofgericht im Mittelalter*, II, 129, 160, denies; Delbrück, pp. 21–26, thinks Lambert's account one of studied mendacity. Where doctors so disagree, perhaps I may be justified in making my own conjecture. In feudal society at this time honor was, originally a social conception, had come to have a legal valuation. Saxon law, in especial, shows great sensitiveness to this quality (Huebner, *Germanic Private Law*, p. 102 [trans. Philbrick; Boston, 1918]). Even impeachment of a man's honor was sufficient ground for *Ehrlosigkeit*, although actual guilt might not be proved. May not Otto's peers sitting as a jury have regarded the charge itself as sufficient to justify condemnation? Helmold (*Chron. Slavorum*, I, 27), writing a century later, says Otto was condemned *quia Saxo erat*, which is absurd.

[5] "Beneficia quae immensa habuerat, perdidit" (*Annal. Altah. Maj.* [*anno* 1071]; Waitz, VI, 497, n. 5).

at his heels, stormed the castles of Hassenstein on the Werra, and Burg Tesenberg near Paderborn. With less justice he harried the Westphalian lands of Otto's wife, who had been the widow of Count Hermann of Werla. Within a short time Otto of Nordheim had a following of three thousand men who lived partly on booty and plunder of the manors of the fisc, partly upon the resources furnished by his friend Magnus Billung.

The Saxon, especially the Thuringian peasantry, who hated the new and heavy taxes and tithes which had recently been laid upon them,[1] rallied around Otto, as did also many of the Saxon nobles, for reasons of their own, which were far different from those of the peasantry. The war gave vent to all the accumulated grievances of the Saxon and Thuringian people of all classes of society. It was at once a political and military conflict and a social and economic uprising.[2]

Meantime, humiliation and ignominy were heaped upon Otto of Nordheim. He was deprived of his duchy of Bavaria, which was given to Welf, the first of this famous house to hold the dignity.[3] In Saxony the war widened to formidable dimensions, the smoldering wrath of the peasantry undoubtedly being aggravated by the hard times due to failure of the harvest during three consecutive years.[4] Henry IV feverishly

---

[1] *Vita Bennonis*, chap. xiii: "Redditus inde per singulos annos exacti sunt pro quantitate agrorum." The weight of these exactions and the resentment of the peasantry were undoubtedly greatly aggravated by the successive crop failures and famine conditions which existed in Saxony in the six years between 1066 and 1072 (see graphic details in Adam of Bremen, III, 57 and 64). Wolves even penetrated into the streets of Hamburg. The hunger in 1075 noticed by Bruno, chap. liii, was not due to failure of crops but to the destruction wrought by the civil war.

[2] The sources abound with evidence: *Annal. Altah.* (1070); Ekkehard, *Chron.* (1070–72); *Annal. Sax.*, SS. VI, 720; *Ann. Avent.*, V, 12. Convenient extracts are in Richter and Kohl, III, 2, 75. For the Thüringerwald at this time see Kirchoff, *Mitteil. d. Geogr. Gesellschaft zu Jena* (1885), III, 18 f.

[3] Welf had married Judith, a daughter of Count Baldwin IV of Flanders and niece of Matilda, queen of William the Conqueror. Her first husband had been the famous English earl, Tostig, who was exiled by Harold in 1066 and fled to Normandy. Judith brought a fortune with her into Germany. In order to marry this rich lady he put away his first wife Ethelinda, who was a daughter of Otto of Nordheim. Welf's enmity with Otto of Nordheim and his wealth undoubtedly commended him to the favor of Henry IV. He was forced to pay well for the duchy: "praediorum suorum et pecuniarum quantitatem regi donavit."

[4] *Vita Bennonis*, chaps. xiii, xiv, xv.

pushed forward the construction of new fortresses by forced labor, even freemen being compelled to work. Bishop Benno of Osnabrück built Castle Iburgen in the heart of Widukind's ancient country;[1] Otto of Nordheim fortified Burg Hasungen in Hesse, a basalt hill a mile from Cassel as his chief base.[2] Fruitless efforts were made to patch up a peace. Neither antagonist would trust the other. Moreover, it was apparent that Henry IV had the stronger following of the two, for Otto was only supported by local interests, while with the King were the dukes of Bavaria, Swabia, Lower Lorraine, and many bishops.[3] In desperation Otto of Nordheim and Magnus turned to Adalbert of Bremen and offered to restore the manors of which he had been despoiled.[4] Finally, when the court was celebrating the consecration of the new cathedral at Halberstadt, the two rebels came in and made submission. Magnus was promptly thrown into prison in the Harzburg for life. The outlawry against Otto was canceled, his allods restored, but his feudal lands confiscated, and he was imprisoned for a year.[5]

Henry IV seemed everywhere the master. "Tanto rex erat omnibus terrori," wrote Bruno, the Saxon chronicler.[6] Otto of Nordheim appeared to be crushed, the Billunger seemed cowed, the peasantry in despair, and Henry's castles were rising or completed on almost every hill in Thuringia. But the calm was too furtive to endure. It was the lull before a new and greater storm. The various ingredients of enmity in Saxony were too explosive to remain quiescent. In the spring of 1072 Otto of Nordheim was released,[7] but Magnus Billung was still kept in prison. At this juncture Duke Ordulf Billung of Saxony died (twelve days after the death of his implacable

[1] Adam of Bremen, III, 57.

[2] Meyer von Knonau, II, 42; Hauck, *Kirchengesch.*, III, 725; Delbrück, p. 27; Vogeler, p. 38.

[3] See the list of vassals in the King's train at Liège in 1071 (Stumpf, No. 2743); cf. *Annal. Sax.*, SS. VI, 698.

[4] Adam of Bremen, III, 39; *Annal. Altah.* (1071).

[5] Sources collected in Richter and Kohl, III, Part II, 82, n. C, and p. 93, n. E.

[6] Bruno, chap. xviii.

[7] Lambert of Hersfeld, p. 137.

enemy Adalbert of Bremen), and Magnus became the new
duke, although a prisoner in the Harzburg. Henry IV, in the
flush of his success and fulness of pride, refused to recognize
the succession, and seemingly with the resolution to annex
the great duchy of Saxony to the crown by forfeiture, seized
the Billunger stronghold of Lüneburg.[1]

It was a high-handed as well as an inexpedient act. Ordulf
had never been popular with his people, but young Magnus
was popular among them.[2] The King was simply courting
new rebellion, the more so as the Saxons soon found a leader
in Otto of Nordheim. Henry IV's reckless conduct crystallized the widespread resentment into hard and sharp form.
The enmity of the feudality because of the King's political
and administrative methods, especially the revindication of
the fisc and the use of *ministeriales*, the ambition and suspicion of some of the bishops, notably Burckhardt of Halberstadt, the wrongs, real and fancied, suffered by the Saxon
peasantry,[3] both freeborn and servile, the menace of the
King's castles, the feuds with Otto of Nordheim and Magnus
—all these forces and factors coalesced.[4]

The King, if we may believe Bruno, seems to have thought
that holding Magnus as a hostage would avert revolt.[5] But
the surprise and capture of the garrison which had been left
in Lüneburg by Hermann Billung, Magnus's uncle, made the
King change his mind, and in return for the release of these
seventy captives Henry IV was compelled to give Magnus his
liberty, "whence the saying ran through all Saxony that one
Saxon was worth seventy Swabians." Saxony was jubilant,
and for a time it was thought that greater concessions were

---

[1] *Annal. Sax.*, SS. VI, 698; Bruno, chap. xxi.

[2] Bruno, chap. xix.

[3] According to *Vita Benonnis*, chap. xiv, Henry IV's procrastination exasperated the nobles and peasantry to rebellion.

[4] The *Ann. Altah.* (1073) sum up the situation thus: "Igitur per longum tempus
potentes quosque rex ceperat contemnere, inferiores vero divitiis et facultatibus
extollere et eorum consilio, quae agenda erant, amministrabat, optimatum vero
raro quemquam secretis suis admittebat, et quia multa inordinate fiebant, episcopi,
duces aliique regni primores de regalibus se subtrahebant."

[5] Bruno, chap. xxi.

in the air. But when, shortly afterward, a deputation which went to Goslar to ask for redress of grievances which still rankled, was kept waiting a whole day and then dismissed without seeing the King amid the jeers of the royal *ministeriales*, the anger of the Saxons was again stirred to its depths.[1] A rush would have been made at once upon the Harzburg by the desperate crowd if the cooler head of Margrave Dedi had not restrained them.

That night the leaders held a conference in a nearby church and resolved upon a great open-air meeting to be held at Wormsleben near Eisleben. "Illa dies et haec causa bellum primatus incipit." There Otto of Nordheim took the parole and in an impassioned speech set forth all the accumulated grievances of the Saxons. Below the medieval Latin surface of Bruno's account, deep in the fibers of the parchment, one can feel the pulse and throb of a tremendous popular movement, the kind of deep, national passion which makes Bruno's *Liber de bello saxonico* a prose epos. The *Carmen de bello saxonico*, the other contemporary account of Saxon authorship, on the other hand, is tinctured with aristocratic sympathies.[2] The same is true of Lambert of Hersfeld. He has no real sympathy with the Saxon peasantry, but uses their grievances as a means to abuse Henry IV.

It is interesting, in the long list of grievances, to distinguish the particular *gravamina* which each writer emphasizes. The unknown author of the *Carmen* demands the leveling of the castles; the return of confiscated and forfeited estates; the exclusion of *ministeriales* from the royal council; the restoration of Otto of Nordheim to the duchy of Bavaria; amnesty for all, especially for Otto, Magnus, Anno of Cologne, Siegfried of Mainz; the integrity of ancient Saxon law; the abandonment of Goslar as a capital; justice to church and cloister; and the "return to kingly honor." On the other hand, Bruno reflects popular feeling. He demands destruction of the King's castles, relief from fiscal exactions,

[1] Bruno, chaps. xxii–xxiii. The *Annal. Altah.* (1073) are more moderate but to the same effect.

[2] See Roehrig, *De secularibus consiliariis Henrici IV* (Halle diss., 1886), p. 4; "Die höfische Färbung des Carmen," Richter and Kohl, III, Part II, 127 n.

Saxon representation in the King's council when the court is on Saxon soil (an extremely interesting demand from the point of view of medieval law), and general amnesty.[1] This programme, while chiefly having to do with redress of grievances, yet had within it certain constructive recommendations or demands. The germ of a new and important theory of government was embodied in them.

The cleavage between the feudo-ecclesiastical party and the popular or peasant party is clear through all the war which soon followed, in spite of the confusion and apparent identity of issues. Otto of Nordheim's failure to bridge this cleavage, and to effect a more perfect union between the two factions, accounts for his downfall at last, as it also partly accounts for Henry IV's success at Langensalza. Otto was too much of a noble to be wholly trusted by the common freemen and the servile class; on the other hand, the Saxon nobles, lay and clerical, were suspicious of him because of his professions of sympathy with the peasantry—he protested too much—and his popularity with them.

In the alignment against the King were the Saxon bishops Wezel of Magdeburg, Burckhardt of Halberstadt, Hezel of Hildesheim, Werner of Merseburg, Eilbert of Minden, Immet of Paderborn, Frederick of Münster, Benno of Meissen. Among the nobles were Hermann Billung (uncle of Magnus), Dedi (margrave of the Ostmark), Ekbert of the Thuringian March, Frederick (count palatine in Saxony), Diedrich of Cadalenburg, Adalbert of Ballenstadt, and some lesser nobles like the counts Otto, Henry, and Conrad whose fiefs are not known. Lambert of Hersfeld dismisses the rest of the rebels as "a common herd."[2] The German episcopate as a whole adhered to Henry IV, including three Saxon bishops, viz., Benno of Osnabrück, Eppo of Zeitz, and Liemar of Bremen, as did also most of the high feudality throughout the country. The cloisters were not drawn into the struggle until the conflict with the papacy began.

Henry IV was at the Harzburg, a mile from Goslar, upon a steep hill commanding the valley of the Ocker clear to

[1] See Richter and Kohl's analysis, *op. cit.*, p. 149 n.; Vogeler, pp. 65–66.

[2] *Vulgus promiscuum* (Lambert of Hersfeld, p. 150).

Brunswick. For fear of being entrapped there, on the night of August 9–10, 1073, he fled through the forest, narrowly escaping his enemies who lay in wait for him along the roads, through the guidance of a hunter who took him by devious trails to Hessewech.[1] Here the ban was issued for meeting of the King's forces on the Werra at Bredingen on the seventh day after the feast of St. Michael. Meanwhile, at an assembly held at Tritburg, a hill near the Unstrutt River, the Thuringians joined the revolted Saxons and the whole country was soon in flames.[2]

The winter of 1073–74 was a hard one for the Saxon peasant levies, most of whom were on foot. Many of them were suspicious of the leaders, lay and clerical, who had their own axes to grind.[3] The Hasenburg was taken, and the siege of Spatenburg and Volkerode begun, but the Harzburg still held out. It was impossible for the King to humiliate the valiant garrisons of these strongholds by surrendering them. The friction between the Saxon *Landwehr* and the leaders grew apace. The revolted peasants were at sea, knowing not what to do.[4] Their inclination increasingly was to make one more effort to persuade Henry IV to moderate his policy, while at the same time the Saxon leaders thought that they might fish advantageously in the troubled waters. They were indifferent to the grievances of the peasantry if they could force the King to give them what they wanted.

The whole body of insurrectionists, accordingly, sought the King, who was at Gerstungen (February 2, 1074), and presented their demands.[5] Henry IV quickly sensed the division which prevailed among them and played his hand deftly. The hostile forces were double his own, a fact which frightened some of his following until the King pointed out to them that many of them were peasants without horses, and bearing

---

[1] *Ibid.*, p. 156; Adam of Bremen, I, 13; cf. Kretschmer, p. 402.

[2] Bruno, chaps. xxvii–xxviii.

[3] Bruno, chap. xxxii.

[4] ". . . . nulla Saxonibus viderentur satis tuta consilia" (Lambert of Hersfeld, p. 180).

[5] Bruno, chap. xxxi.

homemade arms.[1] Henry IV suavely promised amnesty for all, relaxation of the harshness of the fisc, to choose Saxons for his advisers in Saxon affairs, not to introduce Bavarian, Swabian, or other outsiders into the land in an administrative capacity, and to level the royal castles except that the chapel and convent in the Harzburg were to be preserved, provided that the Saxon nobles also destroyed their castles.[2] According to Lambert of Hersfeld, the King even promised to restore Otto of Nordheim to the duchy of Bavaria within a year; and, according to the *Carmen de bello saxonico*, he gave gold to the Saxon leaders. The terms were astutely made, for Henry IV well knew that the rebellious Saxon nobles would not level their fortresses, so that he could plausibly refuse to fulfil his terms as long as his enemies failed to execute theirs.

The thousands of Saxon freemen soon discovered that they had been euchred by the King and betrayed by their leaders,[3] and their fury was great—all the greater because in that spring the border Slavs had raided their country while it was without defenders, destroyed farms and granaries, and carried off some of their wives and children into captivity.[4]

The popular rage soon passed beyond all restraint by the nobles. The Harzburg was to them the symbol of Salian despotism, an emblem of the reduction to serfdom with which they felt themselves threatened.[5] Three days later a wild rush was made upon the Harzburg by the maddened folk. The royal manors were sacked and burned, the castle destroyed with all its rich furniture by pickax and fire, the treasure of the chapel looted, the altar smashed to fragments, the tomb of Henry IV's little son and his own brother

---

[1] Berthold. Const. (1075) sums up the Saxon demands in a very few words, "Imprimis exoptata vitae securitas, pacis fideique non fictae, foedus inviolabile: justitiarum legumque paternarum suarum, plenaria libertas."

[2] Bruno, *loc. cit.*; Lambert of Hersfeld, p. 180; *Carmen*, II, 215–19.

[3] According to the *Carmen*, II, 190, there were 60,000 men, mostly freemen, in the Saxon army.

[4] Bruno, *loc. cit. ad fin.*

[5] Lambert of Hersfeld, p. 183.

Conrad, who were buried there, torn open and their bones, together with those of a defunct abbot and the skull of St. Anastasius, a sacred relic which the King had given to the church, thrown into a ditch.[1]

The sack of the Harzburg was an act of wild, popular fury for which the Saxon leaders were not responsible. Indeed, the news of it threw them into dismay, for it gave the King a ready pretext to declare that the terms of peace had been violated. The whole cause of the Saxons was compromised by it.[2] Moreover, the sacrilege which had been committed thrilled the people with horror, the more so because the event took place just before Easter. The wantonness shocked religious sentiment and offended the feelings of common humanity.[3] Werner, bishop of Merseburg, wrote a letter of grievance, apology, and alarm to Archbishop Siegfried of Mainz[4] which must have been intended for public circulation. It is even said that a mission was sent to Rome by the King to accuse the rebels.[5]

The Saxon rebellion now took a new departure. The entrance of the burgher class of the Rhine cities into the struggle (1074) upon the King's side is a very important political and social event.[6] With Henry IV against the vested and political interests of the high German feudality, the rebel bishops, the Saxon peasantry—and the papacy was soon to enter the lists—were now aligned the loyal bishops, the lower feudality (including a host of *ministeriales*), the "royal" Benedictine abbeys whose inmates resented the Cluniac re-

---

[1] Lambert of Hersfeld, pp. 184–85; Bruno, chap. xxxiii; *Carmen*, III, 1–23; Ekkehard, *Chron.*, SS. VI, 200, etc. For the tomb see Lambert of Hersfeld, p. 70; for the relics, p. 135.

[2] Lambert of Hersfeld, p. 184.

[3] *Ibid.*, p. 185; Bruno, chap. xlii.

[4] Reproduced in Bruno, *loc. cit.*

[5] Lambert of Hersfeld, p. 185. The statement seems doubtful since there is no evidence in Gregory VII's *Epistulae*. But see Pauli Bernried, *Vita Gregorii VII*, chap. lxiv. The alleged letter of Henry IV inserted in the *Registrum Greg. VII*, Bk. I, between Epp. 29 and 30 is a manifest forgery. It is without number and date.

[6] Lambert of Hersfeld, pp. 169, 170, 186, 187, 192, 193, 280; *Carmen*, III, 199–200; Boos, *Urk. B. der Stadt Worms*, I, 47, n. 56; Richter and Kohl, III, Part II, 141–46; Sudendorf, *Registrum*, I, No. 3 (Cologne); Nitzsch, II, 82–84.

form and the propaganda of the "new" papacy, and finally the burghers of the middle Rhinelands.[1]

In the middle of the winter (1074) Henry IV had come to Worms to celebrate Christmas there. It happened to be the very time when the revolted Saxon princes had sent emissaries to solicit the support of the Rhine princes, especially that of the bishops of Mainz, Worms, and Cologne, and to propose the elevation of Duke Rudolf of Swabia as counterking.[2] The plot stirred the burghers of Worms deeply, and when the *milites* of Bishop Adalbert tried to bar the King's entrance into the city they rose in rebellion, drove the Bishop out, and enthusiastically welcomed Henry IV. The King promptly showed his gratitude by exempting the Wormser merchants in future from all tolls in the seven royal villas (*Zollstätten*) of Frankfort, Goslar, Boppard, Dortmund, Nürnberg, Engern, and Hammerstein. By Easter week the burgher revolt had spread to Cologne, where Henry IV's intriguing foe, Archbishop Anno, also was driven out.[3] The wild rumor was spread through the Rhine country that the angry Archbishop had appealed to William the Conqueror to restore him, and in spite of its absurdity it was sufficient to call the King back hastily from Bavaria, where he was upon the point of making an expedition against the Magyars.[4]

Meantime, the Cluny reform movement, since the identification of Gregory VII with it, was assuming vast proportions. The cardinal legates, Hubert of Palermo and Gerald of Ostia, with the bishops of Chur and Como, were working secretly among the Saxons and intriguing with the German bishops, while Henry IV resumed his interrupted Magyar campaign.[5] The great conflict between Henry IV and Greg-

---

[1] "Heinricus rex . . . . principes despicere, nobiles opprimere, inferiores sustollere . . . . coepit" (Ekkehard, *Chron.* [1068]).

[2] Lambert of Hersfeld, pp. 168–69.

[3] Lambert of Hersfeld, p. 169. *De unitate eccles. conservanda* (chap. xxviii; Lindner, *Anno der Heilige*, p. 85; Meyer von Knonau, II, 391 f., 805 f.).

[4] Lambert of Hersfeld, p. 195; *Vita Annonis*, II, chap. xxii; Meyer von Knonau, II, 390, n. 108; Freeman, *Norman Conquest*, IV, 568.

[5] Lambert of Hersfeld, pp. 193–97. The critical notes of the editor, Holder-Egger, need to be read carefully to control the text. Cf. the critical notes in Richter, III, 2, pp. 167–72, n. A.

ory VII was impending, to add the touch of grandeur to the approaching war and inject the element of religious fanaticism into the already complex issue.[1]

But before the Pope was quite ready to throw down the gauntlet to Henry IV, Saxony flamed anew into rebellion. In the spring of 1075 Otto of Nordheim, Frederick, count palatine in Saxony, and Burckhardt of Halberstadt took the field, the alleged ground of revolt being Henry IV's failure to fulfil the pact of Gerstungen. The initiative was taken by the Saxon Fürsten, but many Saxon and Thuringian freemen joined their standard.[2] Yet many of the peasantry hesitated, and even some of the Saxon nobles held back, especially those who held lands elsewhere in Germany, out of fear of losing them. Families were divided against one another.[3]

The King established his headquarters at Bredingen, in the lands of the abbey of Hersfeld, whence he sent word to the rebels saying that he was willing to confer with the Saxons in regard to their grievances, provided they put away their leaders. This firm stand was enough to cause the desertion of some of the lesser Saxon nobles to the King.[4] Early in June, Henry IV moved his quarters from Bredingen to Langensalza on the Unstrutt River,[5] so as to be closer to the Saxon encampment, declaring that the time for words had passed.[6]

It was a motley army which lay over against the royal host. Mingled with the Saxon nobles and their vassals, who of course were armed after the feudal manner, were thousands of freemen, "a tumultuary levy," fighting on foot, armed with homely weapons, and more used to wielding the pick and spade than a sword. There were even serfs who had been impressed into service by their masters. The King's

[1] Already the rebel bishops had worked upon the fears of the masses in Saxony and Thuringia by utilizing the sacrilege at Harzburg (see Lambert's account, p. 214).

[2] Berthold. Cont. (anno 1075), Bruno, chap. xxxix.

[3] Bruno, chaps. xxxvii, xlvi; Lambert of Hersfeld, p. 221.

[4] Bruno, chap. xlv.

[5] Berthold. Const. (1075) notices Henry IV's careful attention to military detail.

[6] Bruno, chap. xlvi.

strength was in his horse, for his army was wholly of feudal formation.[1]

The charge of Henry IV's Swabian contingents[2] under Duke Rudolf—who was soon to turn his coat and espouse the papal cause—broke the Saxon center immediately, and the rest of the battle of Langensalza (June 9, 1075) was a rout. The very camp-followers (*plebei et rustici*) took a hand in the fray. The rebel leaders saved themselves, thanks to the swiftness of their horses, but the Saxon foot forces were slaughtered like sheep. Several thousand, it is said, perished by drowning in the river.[3] Prodigious spoil fell into the victors' hands.[4]

The fratricidal nature of the battle of Langensalza, the frightful slaughter, shocked Germany. The Saxon nation was so shaken that the Archbishop of Mainz had to threaten to excommunicate the Thuringians, who had refused to pay the tithes, in order to raise new funds for the war chest of the rebels.[5] The harrying of Saxony and Thuringia followed upon the triumph, so that the country was reduced to starvation. Men and women fled to the forests for refuge.[6]

The Archbishop of Magdeburg, after consultation with his fellow-insurgent Burckhardt of Halberstadt, in a letter to the Archbishop of Mainz and the Bishop of Würzburg, undertook to discover what terms the King would accept.[7] Henry IV, after keeping them on tenterhooks for weeks, returned an evasive answer as to the grievances of the Saxon peasantry;

---

[1] *Ibid.*, chap. xxxviii; Lambert of Hersfeld, p. 216; *Carmen*, III, 97–126.

[2] The Swabians, in accordance with ancient German law, had the honor of the van in battle (Berthold. Const. [1075]: "ad primam coitionem ut et se lex habet Allemanica"). Cf. Lambert of Hersfeld, p. 218. The privilege is recorded in the *Schwabenspiegel*, sec. xxxii. Stahlin, *Gesch. Württemb.*, I, 393, has collected a series of passages from historians and poets in evidence of the honor.

[3] See accounts in Bruno, chap. xlvi; Lambert of Hersfeld, pp. 218–21; *Carmen*, III, 127–208; Richter and Kohl, III, Part II, 176 n.

[4] Lambert of Hersfeld, p. 221.

[5] *Ibid.*, p. 222.

[6] Lambert of Hersfeld, p. 221 *ad fin.*, pp. 223–25; Bruno, chaps. xlvii, liv; *Vita Heinrici IV*, chap. iii.

[7] This letter is in Bruno, chaps. xlviii–xlix. Cf. Lambert of Hersfeld, p. 222.

but his terms were clear and hard regarding the rebel Saxon nobles. Yet hard and humiliating as they were, they were accepted. They were sentenced to six months' imprisonment and the confiscation of their fiefs, which were distributed among the King's adherents.[1] Then followed a dramatic event. On the broad plain between Creussen and Kindel-brücken near Speyer, on October 25, 1075, the whole Saxon army, bishops, nobles, and freemen, disarmed and bare-footed walked submissively between the files of the King's army on either hand and laid their act of surrender at Henry IV's feet.[2]

Saxony was so broken and divided against itself that its complete subjugation seemed accomplished. The rebel leaders were crushed and humiliated. The mass of the people, who felt that great numbers of their class had been slain like sheep for the benefit of the feudality, were bitterly angry with the nobles, who returned the hatred.[3] Many a broken noble, many an impoverished freeman, with his family, left the country and trekked to the colonial land beyond the Elbe, while other nobles sought asylum in France.[4]

Apparently Henry IV had won a conclusive victory. But the invincible nature of the Saxons was soon to belie the outward appearance. Actually the Saxons had scarcely begun to fight.[2]

The King's hand had fallen heavily on the duchy. The way seemed open now for him to realize that absolute monarchy which was the aspiration of the Salian kings. But Henry IV was not a mere tyrant, and once the opposition to his purposes was crushed he was in the mood to be just, or at least

[1] Lambert of Hersfeld, p. 232.

[2] Lambert of Hersfeld, pp. 238–39; Bruno, chap. liv, glosses the event. Perhaps it was too humiliating for a Saxon to describe.

[3] Lambert of Hersfeld, p. 237.

[4] Lambert of Hersfeld, pp. 233, 239, 256, 258, 259, 260; Bruno, chap. lxxxiv. For additional material on all this see Richter and Kohl, III, Part II, 186, n. F.

[5] The author of the *Vita Heinrici IV* (chap. iii, p. 12) writing years later, and viewing the past in perspective, appreciated this. He says: "Nam licet eos in pugna congressos vinceret, victos fugaret, fugatos persequeretur; licet bona eorum devastaret, munitiones everteret, et omnia quae victorem libet, faceret, non tamen ad deditionem cogi potuerunt."

politic. He knew that a constructive policy could not be built up upon the eternal hatred of the Saxons.

Accordingly, the chief princes of the realm were summoned to a diet at Goslar at Christmas (1075) in order to confer about the Saxon question, at which the King took the precaution to assure the succession of the Salian dynasty by securing from them (after the French royal practice) the recognition of his infant son Conrad as the heir of the throne.[1] Then Henry IV unfolded his programme for the conciliation of Saxony, Otto of Nordheim was released from imprisonment, given the royal amnesty, and formally admitted to the King's council.[2] Even more significant was the elevation of Otto to the position of king's viceroy in Saxony, with official residences in the Harzburg and the Steinberg.[3]

The sincerity of both Henry IV and Otto of Nordheim in this arrangement has been impugned by numbers of historians, who have accused the King of alienating the ablest leader of the Saxons by bribery, and have condemned Otto for selling himself. It seems to me that this is an unjust verdict in either case. We know, even from Bruno's testimony, that Henry IV had a high opinion of Otto's ability.[4] Why may not Henry IV have calculated that the reconstruction of Saxony might be facilitated by identifying the fallen Saxon leader, who was popular with the masses of the Saxon nation, with the Salian policy? And why may not Otto have figured, now that Saxony was beaten and broken, that he could do more for the cause of his countrymen by working with Henry IV than sulking in his tent? That the policy of either the King or of Otto of Nordheim was a cynical one, it seems to me is an excess of adverse historical criticism.[5]

[1] Lambert of Hersfeld, p. 251; Bernold, SS. V, 43; Jaffé, *Mon. Greg.*, V, 100, n. 46; Waitz, VI, 30–32; Maurenbrecher, *Königswahlen*, p. 110.

[2] Lambert of Hersfeld, p. 261; Bruno, chap. lvii.

[3] Lambert of Hersfeld, p. 261. Vogeler styles him *Statthalter*.

[4] Bruno, *loc. cit.*

[5] Vogeler (chap. v) thinks that this arrangement was made secretly at the time of the humiliation of the Saxon army in the plain of Speyer in the autumn before. I think an evidence of Otto's sincerity is to be found in the fact that he had no secret dealings, in the early months of 1076, when the conflict with Gregory VII had begun,

Lambert of Hersfeld's accusation that Otto was secretly a willing party to the humiliation of the Saxon army in the field of Speyer, and purchased his own safety and promotion by consenting to the King's deportations and other drastic acts, seems so far fetched that it must be taken with great caution.[1]

But it was not Henry IV's intention to restore Saxony to its ancient position among the German duchies. Saxony was regarded as a conquered country, which had forfeited its feudal autonomy and was treated accordingly, much as a faction in the victorious north in the Reconstruction Era declared that the southern states of the United States had forfeited their rights and were to be treated as conquered provinces. The King's intention, beyond a doubt, was to annex Saxony permanently to the crown by abolishing its ducal autonomy, and to make it, with Goslar as the capital, the keystone of the strong monarchy which he had in mind to build up, much in the same way that the French kings used Paris and the Ile-de-France in the upbuilding of the Capetian monarchy. It was the dream of all the Salian kings, it was the purpose of the dynasty, and both Henry III and Henry IV were close students of the course followed by the French kings. In the mind of Henry IV the day of German sectionalism and feudal particularism was a passing one.

Temporarily a hard government in Saxony could be the only effective government, for the country was infested with robbers and brigands, refugees and desperate men of broken fortune who haunted the thick forests, whence they plundered the farming peasantry and even the lands of the clergy.[2] Merely as a police measure, if not as a precaution against another rebellion, the castles in Thuringia and Saxony which had been destroyed, were rebuilt. Simultane-

---

with the Pope. There are numerous letters in Gregory VII's correspondence at this time with Rudolf of Swabia, Welf of Bavaria, Gozelo of Lorraine, Berthold of Carinthia, and Wratislaw of Bohemia, but none with Otto of Nordheim, who had been in Rome in 1068 (*Ann. Altah.* [1068]).

[1] Lambert of Hersfeld, p. 261.

[2] Lambert of Hersfeld, p. 260; cf. Bruno (chaps. liii–lv), who is graphic upon the economic ruination of Saxony.

ously[1] the restoration of the fisc was begun. So energetic
were the King's measures that although the people mur-
mured at being compelled to work upon the castles, nevertheless law and order soon again prevailed in Saxony, and economic recovery and prosperity returned.[2]

So terminated the first rebellion of Saxony. No historian
may pronounce with finality upon what the ultimate success
of Henry IV's policy might have been. Yet to me it seems
probable that Henry IV would have created a great German
state coeval with Norman England and anticipating the
French monarchy of Philip Augustus, if at this critical juncture the conflict between him and Gregory VII had not be-
fallen, which tore open all the old wounds of Germany and
made many new ones, and irrevocably changed the form of
government and the social texture. The Pope chose the moment to open battle with the Emperor with shrewdness.

[1] Lambert of Hersfeld, pp. 246, 259, 261; Bruno, chaps. lvi, lx.

[2] "Tanta siquidem tamque inopinata rerum prosperitas evidens" (Lambert of
Hersfeld, p. 261).

CHAPTER VI

SECTIONALISM AND PARTY STRIFE IN
THE WAR OF INVESTITURE

THE EPOCH of German history between 919, when
the Saxon house of Henry the Fowler and the Ottos
came to the German throne, and 1181, when Frederick Barbarossa rent the duchy of Saxony to shreds after his
victory over Henry the Lion, is a single whole. But the period
is sharply broken into two parts in the reign of Henry IV, and
is intimately connected with the history of the war of investiture in Germany (1075–1122). That conflict is the most important turning-point in the history of medieval Germany between Charlemagne and the Reformation.[1] It was as important for Germany as was the Norman Conquest for England,
or the Crusades for all Europe.

In that protracted triangular struggle which broke out in
1075 between Henry IV and Gregory VII, between Henry IV
and his revolted vassals, and between the King and the
rebellious Saxon peasantry, it is comparatively easy to understand the contention of each party separately. But to understand them in their relation, each to the other, is very difficult. For the organic compound was a very complex one.
And the condition becomes all the more complex when one
discovers that both the feudality and the hierarchy were
divided, some nobles and some bishops adhering to the King
in spite of feudal or clerical preponderance against them; that
the burgher class of the Rhenish towns sympathized with the
King, were hostile to the peasant revolt, and anti-feudal and
anti-clerical to boot; and that the nobility, too, lay and
clerical, was bitterly opposed to the cause of the peasantry.
In this confusion worse confounded, the most invariable and

---

[1] "Seine lange, im ganzen 50 Jahre umfassende Regierung, ist ein Wendepunkt
in der Geschichte der deutschen Verfassung geworden" (Waitz, *Deutsche Verfassungsgesch.*, VIII, 427).

steadfast elements were the Emperor and the Saxon peasantry.

Every ingredient in the war of investiture except that of papal participation had been in insurrection before against Henry IV. The tithe war between the Archbishop of Mainz and the Thuringians, which began in 1062 and drew into its eddies Margrave Dedi of the Ostmark and Adalbert of Ballenstadt, and which was prolonged for more than ten years, finally merging into the war of investiture,[1] the bitter feud between Archbishop Anno of Cologne and Archbishop Adalbert of Bremen, the rebellion of Otto of Nordheim and Duke Magnus of Saxony in 1070–71, the great rebellion of Saxony during 1074–75, culminating in Henry IV's victory over the Saxons at Langensalza in June, 1075—all these were preliminaries of and became factors in the struggle between the Emperor and the Pope.[2] The variety of issues involved in the war of investiture made it a bundle of discords. Aside from the fact that both bishops and nobles were divided into two factions, a natural bond of union between the feudality and the revolted Saxon peasantry, or between the Rhenish burghers and either the feudality or the Saxon peasantry, was unthinkable. Not even Gregory VII was ever able to reconcile them; adroit as the Pope was in choosing that particular time, when Germany was seething with discord, to challenge the imperial prerogative, the issue of the conflict between him and the Emperor proved the wisdom of the old story about Pandora's box. For the greater war gave birth to forces which neither Pope nor Emperor was able to exorcise.

The ashes of the recent Saxon rebellion, not yet grown cold, were fanned into new flame, while every dissident and ambitious noble, every adventurer who sought to mend his fortune by desperate means, every ambitious or disgruntled bishop, was given a plausible pretext to rise against the royal authority. As a result Germany was rent asunder as never

---

[1] This complex subject is analyzed by Dieffenbacher, *DZG*, VI, 2, 305 f.; Meyer von Knonau, *Jahrb. Heinrich IV*, II, 795 f.; Holder-Egger, *Neues Archiv*, XIX, 185 f., 519 f.; Ausfeld, *Lambert von Hersfeld und der Zehnstreit* (1878); Hesse, *Thüringen im Zehnstreit* (1892). Cf. Richter and Kohl, *Annalen*, III, 2, pp. 33, 65, 66, 99, 125.

[2] Richter and Kohl, *op. cit.*, III, Part 2, pp. 71, 79, 81.

before in her history, and never again until the great inter-regnum and the seventeenth century. Even families were divided against one another.[1]

Aside from the inflexible attitude of Henry IV through all this struggle, the only other factor in the movement which was without variableness or shadow cast by turning was the Saxons. Even Gregory VII for a long time wavered and wobbled. With the Saxons it was not the opposition of a class, but the rising of a great people against oppression and for the vindication of their popular rights. In Bruno's *De bello Saxonico* the forthrightness of the Saxon people is apparent on every page. In Lambert of Hersfeld's account, on the other hand, the Saxon cause is often confused with the other issues, and frequently misrepresented, owing to Lambert's incorrigible partisanship and remarkable mendacity.

The sincerity of the Saxons is the brightest spot in the whole bitter controversy. An incident which Bruno relates of the first Saxon rebellion of 1074–75, which Henry IV so crushed at Langensalza, is in point here, for it illustrates this sincerity. It has a ring of genuineness about it, and a pathos, too, which carries the authentic note. He tells how when Udo of Trier was preaching on Easter Sunday in the cathedral at Mainz, a messenger handed to him in the pulpit a letter in the form of a prayer in the name of the whole Saxon people, and begged the Archbishop to read it aloud. Henry IV, who was present and apparently sensed some danger, forbade him to do so, whereupon the bold envoy, in spite of the King's anger, declared the substance of the missive to the congregation.[2]

Otto of Nordheim's speech as reported by Bruno[3] is the

[1] "Multi etiam de majoribus qui bona in utrisque regionibus habebant, ut utraque servarent, sponte sua hic relicto filio sive fratre ad regem transibant, vel ipsi hic remanentes, fratres vel filios ad regem transibant, vel ipsi hic remanentes, fratres vel filios ad regem transmittebant" (Bruno, *De bello Saxonico*, chap. xxxvii; cf. chap. xlvi, and Lambert of Hersfeld, *Annales* [ed. Holder-Egger], p. 221).

[2] Bruno, chap. xliv.

[3] Bruno, chap. xxv. Every word of this speech needs to be read in order to appreciate the measure of its importance; cf. chap. xxx. In Lambert of Hersfeld the Saxon arguments are nowhere so succinctly stated, and the Saxon contentions must be pieced together by fitting many scattered paragraphs together. But the popular

clearest formulation of the Saxon demands which we have, although Otto himself is open to suspicion of the sincerity of his own professions and the charge of double dealing. In brief, the points are: that the Saxons were born free but are now being reduced to serfdom owing to the royal tyranny; that Henry IV's castles are a just ground of grievance; that Henry has violated the principle of kingship by his misrule and injustice, and that therefore the Saxons are released from any bond of allegiance to him; that he has forfeited the right to rule, even though not formally deposed.

Gregory VII acted upon this argument on February 22, 1076, when he deposed Henry IV and absolved his subjects from their oath of allegiance to him. It was the surrender of Germany to violence and anarchy, for lordship and homage, suzerainty and vassalage, were the political bonds which held a medieval state together.[1] Whether magnificent idealist, religious fanatic, or stupendously ambitious man utilizing his formidable authority for the elevation of the monarchical papacy over Europe,[2] the fact remains that the German people were thrown into an appalling civil war by the Pope's initiative.

By the spring of 1076 a widespread conspiracy was under way, engineered by the papal legates in Germany, the disaffected and ambitious feudality, and the Saxons.[3] The

---

note is unmistakable throughout the whole of Lambert's account, even if it is sometimes nearly drowned by the writer's shriller declamations concerning the wrongs suffered by the church and the feudality, with whom Lambert's sympathies lay.

[1] See the text of the first deposition in Doeberl, *Monumenta Selecta*, III, No. 9, or in Jaffé, II, 223. The *Vita Heinrici IV*, chap. iii, strongly inveighs against the monstrousness of the Pope in thus dissolving the feudal bond which held society together.

[2] *Dictatus papae*, sec. 27, in Jaffé, II, 174; Doeberl, III, No. 6. As early as 1073 Sigfried of Mainz wrote to Rome that the German crown should be regarded as "apostolic"—"ut apostolicum non solum imperii Romani diadema, sed etiam regni Germanici coronam appellaret" (*Codex Udalrici* [ed. Jaffé], *ep.* 126). Gregory VII's own disclaimer of worldly ambition is in the first deposition.

[3] "Facta est igitur conspiratio non modica et magis in dies roboratur" (Lambert of Hersfeld, p. 258). Cf. *Vita Heinrici IV*, chap. iii; Berthold. Cont., p. 283; Bruno, chap. lxxiv; *Hugo Flav.*, SS. VIII, 458. The papal legates were intriguing in Germany in the early months of 1076 (Lambert of Hersfeld, p. 251).

bishops Hermann of Metz and Adalberon of Würzburg, and
the Dukes Welf of Bavaria, Rudolph of Swabia, Berthold of
Carinthia, "and many others" held a secret meeting "to
consider what should be done."[1] Some of the Saxon nobles
who had been released on parole after Langensalza were
absolved from their oath by Bishop Hermann.[2] The loyal
burgrave of Meissen was assaulted in his city and barely
escaped owing to the fleetness of his horse.[3] Bishop Burckhardt of Halberstadt haughtily refused to perform the military service required of him against the Hungarians.[4] The
exiled Saxon nobles came trooping back across the frontier
from the Wendish lands whither they had fled when the
first rebellion of the Saxons was crushed, chief among whom
were Dietrich and William, the two sons of Gero, count of
Brelma, who were veritable sons of Zeruiah for valiancy.[5]
A guerilla warfare followed in Saxony. The King's castles
were assailed, the manors of the fisc devastated. The crown
officials fled the country. The fragility of Henry IV's government in Saxony was shown by its swift collapse.[6]

The real leader of the second Saxon rebellion and the
brains of the insurrection was Burckhardt of Halbserstadt.[7]
Unlike the first rebellion, in which there was a large popular
participation, the second Saxon rebellion was primarily a
feudal and ecclesiastical movement. The old catchwords of
"Saxon liberties" and the old grievances were again alleged,
but they had a hollower ring.[8]

[1] Lambert of Hersfeld, p. 257.

[2] *Ibid.*, pp. 258, 260; Bruno, chap. lxxxii.

[3] Bruno, chap. lxxx.

[4] Bruno, chap. lxxxiii.

[5] Lambert of Hersfeld, pp. 260, 269; Bruno, chaps. lxxxiv, lxxxv. For the dramatic escape of two of the King's Saxon hostages see Lambert of Hersfeld, pp. 265–
68.

[6] Lambert of Hersfeld, p. 261, although he exaggerates.

[7] This is admitted by both Lambert of Hersfeld, p. 265, and by Bruno, chap.
lxxxiii. Modern criticism concurs. See Leers, *Burckhardt von Halberstadt* (1894). The
first edition (1892) contained a valuable bibliography omitted in the second.

[8] ". . . . pro patria, pro liberis, pro conjugibus . . . . patriam libertatemque
armis recuperare" (Lambert of Hersfeld, pp. 260, 262; cf. Bruno, chap. lxxxiv).

But Otto of Nordheim, the leader of the former insurrection, held aloof, to the exasperation of the nobles, who needed his support more because of his hold upon the mass of the Saxon people than for his military talents. Accordingly, a deputation visited him in the Steinberg which he had recently completed at great expense, both to advise with him and to warn him. At first Otto hesitated, but either fear or self-interest finally persuaded him to join the rebellion.[1] However, according to Lambert of Hersfeld, before taking the step he had an interview with the King at Saalfeld, in which he tried in vain to induce Henry IV to moderate his policy toward the Saxons, alleging their just grounds of grievance, and only at last, when his plea failed, dramatically washed his hands of the consequences.[2]

Henry IV turned to the Bohemian duke Wratislaw for help to check the Saxons, and offerred him the margraviate of Meissen, since the fealty of young Ekbert of Meissen was dubious.[3] But Ekbert was too quick for him and withheld the city and the castle of the march. At the same time (summer of 1076), Gero's two intrepid sons, with seven thousand men, by a *coup de main* endeavored to capture the King, and probably would have succeeded if a flood in the Mulde had not given Henry IV opportunity to make his escape.[4]

In the autumn (1076) at the diet of Tribur and Oppenheim, where the hostile parties met on opposite sides of the river, Henry IV showed that he still could ride the storm. His enemies cried for his deposition; his friends, among whom was Hugh, abbot of Cluny, parried the demand, which would have been almost fatal to the King if executed, by securing a compromise judgment to the effect that Henry IV was to be suspended from his royal functions until he was released from

[1] Lambert of Hersfeld, pp. 261–62; Bruno, to whom Otto of Nordheim is a hero, suppresses this fact of Otto's hesitation.

[2] Lambert of Hersfeld, pp. 169–72; Delbrück, *Ueber die Glaubwürdigkeit Lamberts von Hersfeld* (Bonn, 1873), pp. 59–61, thinks Lambert's account mere declamation.

[3] Apparently Henry IV also sought aid from the Ljutizi, too, for the *Annal. Yburg*, SS. XVI, 436, record that the Saxons raided their territory at this time.

[4] Lambert of Hersfeld, pp. 272–73.

the papal excommunication.[1] Meantime, while the King was under the ban, following the Pope's instructions, his enemies wasted the crown lands.[2]

The dramatic act of Henry IV at Canossa absolved him from the ban and automatically made him every inch a king again.[3] Gregory VII dared not refuse absolution after such a striking manifestation of repentance, and the possibility of the Pope trying Henry IV at Augsburg before his rebel vassals—which would have been the last word in royal humiliation—was removed.[4]

The chagrin of the Pope and the anger of the rebel bishops and nobles in Germany at the King's adroit stroke were great. But the Pope was cautious; the rebels were not. While Gregory VII tried to steer a middle course and fenced for time, the revolted nobles met at Forchheim in March (1077) and "elected" Duke Rudolf of Swabia to be king.[5]

[1] Text in Doeberl, III, No. 12.

[2] Mirbt, *Libelli de Lite*, I, 372.

[3] The modern conditions of church and state are so different from what they were in the Middle Ages that it requires a conscious effort of reason to perceive the truth of this statement. In the Middle Ages the church was not a state; it was *the* state. This state had "one basis of unity denied to the modern—religion. Baptism was a necessary element in true citizenship in the Middle Ages, and excommunication was its antithesis. No heretic, no schismatic, no excommunicate, has the rights of citizenship. This principle, admitted as it was by Catholic princes and founded on the Code of Justinian, was the ground of the Pope's claim to depose sovereigns" (Figgis, *The theory of the divine right of Kings*, p. 17). Accordingly, when Henry IV recovered his status in the church he *ipso facto* recovered his position as king.

[4] The oath which Henry IV took at Canossa guaranteeing the Pope safe-conduct if or when he wished to come to Germany, and to "do justice according to his judgment or make peace according to his counsel," was qualified by a saving clause —*nisi impedimentum*, etc.—which actually left the King's hands free (see text in Doeberl, III, No. 13 *bis*).

[5] No confidence can be placed in Lambert's assertion (pp. 165–66) that the revolted Saxons participated in the election of Rudolf of Swabia at Forchheim. His statements are contradicted by Bruno, chaps. xvii, xxxi, xxxv, and by the unknown author of the *Carmen de bello Saxonico*, II, ll. 31–44. See, too, Holder-Egger's edition of Lambert, p. 165 n., and O. Grund, *Wahl Rudolfs von Reinfelden*, pp. 32 f. We know that that act was not an act of the German people, but of the feudality. Elsewhere, too, Lambert's statements may be checked and controlled by other contemporary observers. After reciting the grievances of the Saxons and Thuringians he asserts, like Bruno, that an oath of allegiance by a vassal is not binding toward an unjust king, and makes the distinction between a king and a tyrant; that a council of the princes has the right to investigate the charges made against Henry like a

The war now became general,[1] and the cross-graining of
the rival parties is interesting and complex. Nevertheless,
in spite of the confusion, certain lines of cleavage and of
sectional feeling may be discerned. The German bishops,
with individual exceptions, thanks to the long-established
policy of the Saxon and Salian kings of elevating them as a
counterweight to the power of the dukes, as a body were
faithful to Henry IV.[2] The most hostile bishops were those
of Halberstadt, Magdeburg, Merseburg, and Paderborn.[3]
The monasteries of the Benedictine order (except those of
Fulda and Hersfeld), led by St. Gall, being as hostile as the
bishops to the Cluny reform, sided with the King. The most
solid provinces against Henry IV were Saxony, whose participation in the war of investiture was a war within a war, and
Swabia, where the feudality was much influenced by the
Hirsauer or German Cluniac monasteries.[4] The lower feudality as a whole supported the crown, as was natural, for the
Salian kings had always been favorable toward them.

The geographical sectionalism is clearer than the social
cleavage. The most pronounced pro-Salian region was Franconia, the homeland of the Salian house, where all classes

high court, and finally that deposition is a lawful remedy against the abusive government of a bad prince. See the essential passages in Lambert, pp. 151–52: ". . . . ut
principibus Saxoniae, quibus sine legittima discussione . . . . pro fide christiana, pro
libertate etiam sua dimicaturos"; p. 165: "Cumque toto triduo . . . . eligerent";
p. 166: "Et profecto Rudolfum . . . . decerneretur"; pp. 177–78: "Tunc missi sunt.
. . . . Deo manus suas operamque nos negaret." The critical notes of Holder-Egger
need to be carefully studied in connection with these passages. Carlyle, op. cit., III,
113, 130–32, 155–57, has paraphrased them.

[1] "Undique igitur hujusmodi motus per provincias omnes ab utriusque partis
sectatoribus promiscue . . . . per totum annum illum agebantur" (Bernold, p. 434).

[2] Loeffler, "Die Westfälischen Bischöfe im Investiturstreit," Mitth. d. Ver. f.
Osnabrück. Gesch., Vol. XXXVIII (1903). The list of bishops, twenty-six in all,
who signed the letter of protest of January 24, 1076, to Gregory VII, is a good index
of the way the episcopate was divided. See it in Jaffé, V, 103. For other similar lists
see pp. 127, 130, 133, 154.

[3] Bruno, chap. xxxix.

[4] "Mox episcopi, tam illi quos amor quam quos timor in partem regis traxerat,
metuentes ordini suo, ab ejus auxilio plerique se retrahebant; quod et major pars
procerum factibat" (Vita Heinrici IV, chap. iii; cf. chap. viii and Richter and Kohl,
III, 2, 477, n. D).

sided with the King.[1] All classes in Saxony and the upper feudality in Swabia were dead against h:m. Henry IV made sure of the allegiance of Bavaria and Carinthia by clever distribution of confiscated lands and the patronage of the church among the nobles there. Neither Welf of Bavaria nor Berthold of Carinthia could control their duchies.[2] The parish priests in most of Germany, too, sympathized with the King, for most of them were married, and they deeply resented the papal requirement that they put away their wives. In Saxony, however, the rural priests sympathized with the grievances of the peasantry.[3] The most original group in support of the King were the burghers of the Rhine cities. The news of the counter-kingship was the signal for the spontaneous insurrection of the people in Mainz, Worms, and other towns.[4]

Roughly speaking, North Germany and Southwest Germany were the most hostile portions of the kingdom. Middle Germany from the far eastern border to Lorraine, and the

[1] Although written a century after the conflict the statement of Helmold, *Chron. Slav.*, I, 28, is so explicit on this point and so sustained by an abundance of contemporary evidence that it cannot be doubted: "Ceteri principum civitatesquequaesunt circa Renum non receperunt eum [Rudolf], omnesque Francorum populi eo quod jurassent Heinrico et juramenta temerare noluissent."

[2] Bruno, chap. lvi; *Vita Gebehardi*, chap. vii; Waitz, VIII, 232, n. 4. The King gave Carinthia to Liutpold of Eppenstein; the patriarch of Aquileia acquired Friuli, later also Istria and Carniola, by which Henry IV kept his lines open toward Venice and the eastern trade. Control of Bavaria gave him contact over the Brenner Pass with Lombardy, from the commerce of whose cities Henry IV drew his chief supply of gold (Berthold. Cont., chap. xii, p. 299; Nitzsch, *Deutsche Gesch.*, II, 102; cf. Bruno, chap. xv). The western passes were not so much in Henry IV's hands, though Sigeb., *Chron.*, SS. VI, 364, exaggerates when he says Rudolf and Welf controlled all of them. The adherence of the Bishop of Basel was of great advantage in enabling the King to keep an open road over the western Alps. In Swabia, to counteract the influence of Rudolf, Henry gave the duchy to Frederick von Beuren, a simple knight, whose allods were at Staufen, and the hand of his daughter Agnes in marriage—a high reward for his loyal accompaniment of him over the Alps to Canossa. Frederick founded the Hohenstaufen dynasty.

[3] In the *Annal. Altaich.* (anno 1071) is an interesting instance of a simple priest voluntarily giving his substance to Henry IV. It is not an isolated instance. For other examples see Meyer von Knonau, I, 93.

[4] Berthold. Cont., p. 292; Bernold, p. 433; Sigb. *Chron.*, SS. VI, 364; Lambert of Hersfeld, pp. 280–83; Bruno, chap. xcv; Richter, III, 2, 258–60; Hegel, *Neues Archiv*, XVIII, 219 f.

territories in the valley of the Rhine from Basel to Utrecht, adhered to Henry IV. The obvious military practice of the King was to maintain possession of the zone between, and to subdue his enemies separately.[1] This accounts for Rudolf of Swabia's furious siege of Würzburg in 1077 and the double battle on the Neckar and the Streu in 1078. We see the mixed ingredients in the parties and the evidence of sectionalism in the makeup of the opposing armies in this engagement. There was friction between the nobles and the armed *ministeriales* with the King. In the battle on the Neckar the burgher force could not stand against the charge of the Swabian horse, showing that the art of war was a noble's accomplishment. On the other hand, in the simultaneous engagement on the Streu, the burghers fought well when supported by cavalry, and, elated with victory, took frightful toll of the bishops in Rudolf's defeated army, who were the first to run, and shamefully maltreated some of the nobles who fell into their hands.[2] Picturesque to Henry IV's mailed and mounted nobles were the swarms of Saxon peasant freemen, fighting without armor, with antiquated weapons, and on foot.[3] They made good fighters in a mêlée, but showed great reluctance to fight beyond the home borders. To them the war was a Saxon affair. They were not interested in either the cause of the feudality or the papacy. It required all the influence of the papal legates to keep the Saxons in the field, and then they were not always successful.[4]

Gregory VII's policy of "watchful waiting" for three whole years so exasperated the Saxons that passionate ex-

[1] ". . . . a partibus Austri-Franciae et Moinonis fluvii per Nechoram fluvium et Ezzlinga oppidum ad usque Ulmam et Danubium" (*Annal. Augsb.*, SS. III, 129; cf. Gebhardt, *Handbuch d. deutschen Gesch.* [1st ed.], I, 315–16).

[2] The Archbishop of Magdeburg was killed; the Bishop of Paderborn plundered by the Wendish hillmen; the Bishop of Worms and Magnus and Hermann Billung were captured. Certain of Rudolf's men were castrated by the foe in derision of celibacy (Bernold, p. 435; Berthold. Cont., p. 311).

[3] Bruno, chap. cxxii; Guilhiermoz, *L'origine de la noblesse en France au moyen âge*, pp. 457–58.

[4] ". . . . domi unanimiter se continuerant" (Berthold. Cont., p. 320). "Nostra multa festinatione simul et asperitate fatigati, multis in via prae lassitudine derelictis adveniunt et se . . . . ad defensionem suae patriae disponunt" (Bruno, chap. cxxii; cf. chap. cxvii).

postulation was made in Rome.[1] They could not understand the Pope's long hesitation in recognizing Rudolf of Swabia, and in proportion as Gregory VII hesitated, the Saxon complaints grew more shrill.[2] At last the Pope acted, and on March 7, 1080, the second ban was hurled at Henry IV and formal papal recognition of the counter-king given.[3] This was followed, on October 15, by the bad defeat of the King on the Elster, although Rudolf was slain in the battle. "Facile est regnum accipere, difficile tueri," comments the author of the *Vita Heinrici*.[4] Perhaps it was Henry's own bitter reflection.

The luckless counter-king had never been anything but a partisan chief. The Saxons had never loved him, for he came from the southland, and, moreover, he was too much the creature of the great feudality to enlist any popular support.[5] His advocacy of Saxon liberties was always regarded by the Saxons themselves as a pose, and a mere bid for support. In addition, the insatiable appetite of Rudolf's supporters for lands exhausted his resources, and compelled him, though against his will, to lay his hands upon the church lands.[6]

The war of investiture had by this time taken on a tinge of religious animosity and bitterness worse than ever.[7] In the battle on the Elster, Rudolf's troops went into the fray singing the Eighty-second Psalm, as the Huguenots of the six-

---

[1] See the bitter letter in Bruno, chap. cviii, which describes the horrors of the civil war. Henry IV's threat to put up a counter-pope is what forced Gregory VII to act. The papal curia certainly never had an inkling of the psychology of the Saxons in the war. Petrus Crassus, the jurist of Ravenna, in 1086, exhorted the Saxons to adopt the eighth book of Justinian's *Code* as their law! (Fisher, *Mediaeval Empire*, I, 191). For Gregory VII's hatred of Germans see Meyer von Knonau, I, 140.

[2] Bruno, chap. xcv.

[3] Doeberl, III, No. 14. For the Pope's argument for his powers so to do see *Greg. Reg.* V, No. 14; Jaffé, II, 404; Labbe, *Concilia*, XII, 637.

[4] See Erich Topp, *Die Schlacht an der Elster* (Berlin diss., 1904). Henry IV's defeat was largely due to the enterprise of Otto of Nordheim who followed up the initial repulse, and prevented Rudolf's troops from stopping to plunder the King's camp (Bruno, chap. cxxii).

[5] Berthold (*anno* 1077), SS. V, 295; Bruno, chap. xciii.

[6] Berthold, SS. V, 295, 310; *De unitate eccles. conservanda*, II, 25; Waitz, VIII, 166. Only thirteen bishops supported him.

[7] *De unitate eccles. conservanda*, chap. xvi.

teenth century and the Ironsides of Cromwell of the seventeenth were to do.[1]

But although Henry IV had been badly beaten, he was not downhearted. The second papal ban had helped him more than it injured him. For many now became disillusioned as to the sincerity of the feudo-papal party; the Pope's act savored of persecution; his procrastination had made men dubious or suspicious about the sincerity of his professions; it was evident that many nobles had espoused Rudolf in order to enrich themselves by spoliation and pillage; when the lands of Henry IV's supporters and the crown lands failed them these did not hesitate to plunder and to seize the lands of the church; and, finally, the discrepancy between the popular nature of the Saxon revolt and the class interests of the feudality widened into an open breach. The Saxons felt, not without reason, that they were being exploited by the nobles, that their blood was being shed without sufficient reward to themselves, that the aim of the leaders "to carry the war into Saxony" was a selfish ruse in order that they might spare their own territories from carnage and spoliation.

The resentment of the Saxons might have been mollified if Otto of Nordheim had been chosen as counter-king after the death of Rudolf. But Otto was distrusted by all the feudal leaders. He could not live down the suspicion which he had incurred by his long hesitation before taking sides. Moreover, the nobles detested him for his real or pretended sympathy for the common people.[2]

But the designation of a new counter-king lay with the Pope, with whom the question of family riches availed more than any other qualification. For Gregory VII was dismayed at the price the German church was being compelled to pay in the war, since both parties seized church property to defray the costs of the conflict. The Pope wanted to find a rich

[1] Bruno, chap. cxxii. For the religio-social feeling engendered by the war see Meyer von Knonau, I, 114 f., who gives an interesting quotation from Hermann of Reichenau.

[2] A tentative suggestion was made to put up Henry IV's young son Conrad in his father's stead. But Otto of Nordheim blocked it with a jibe, saying: "Ex bove malo malum vitulum vidi generatum, ideoque nec filii nec patris habeo desiderium" (Bruno, chap. cxxv).

noble whose fortune could be made to bear the expense of the
papal cause. The choice lay between Duke Welf of Bavaria
and Count Hermann of Luxemburg.[1] Each was very rich;
but the German nobles were intensely jealous of Welf, so the
Pope's approval fell upon Hermann.[2]

The issue was now more sharply drawn than ever "Nisi
rex deponeretur, aut papa."[3] The real leader of the feudo-
papal party in Germany was not Hermann of Luxemburg but
Burckhardt of Halberstadt. The monks of Hirsau in Swabia
contributed fanaticism,[4] and the big feudal nobles like Welf
and Berthold fished in the tumultuous waters. In these years
the war lost almost every reminiscence of its original character. It became a war for aggrandizement on the part of
the feudality. These were fertile times for the upgrowth of
the *Grundherrschaften*. As for the mass of the common people,
the wish for peace became widespread.[5] The Truce of God
became popular. In 1085 the bishops of Mainz and Bamberg
each issued a decree ordaining the *treuga*.[6] In this year Henry
IV was so far victorious that Hermann of Luxemburg and
Burckhardt of Halberstadt were both compelled to fly to
Denmark for safety. Many of their partisans fled across the
Elbe.[7]

But Henry IV was too confident. The moment he licensed
his troops the refugees returned. For the King in excess of
confidence made the bad blunder of releasing his army before
he had carried his policy in Saxony to completion. The rebel
bishops and rebel nobles determined to make a supreme
effort to save their offices from forfeiture and their lands from

---

[1] See Hugo Müller, *Hermann von Luxemburg, Gegenkönig Heinrichs IV* (Halle
diss., 1888), pp. 5–8.

[2] The election of Hermann estranged Otto of Nordheim from the cause. He died
on January 11, 1083, of a fall from his horse (Bruno, chap. cxxxi; cf. *De unitate eccles.
conserv.*, chaps. xxxviii and xlii).

[3] *Vita Bennonis*, chap. xviii; Bernold (*anno* 1083), p. 439.

[4] Müller, *op. cit.*, shows this abundantly.

[5] Bernold (*anno* 1084); *Ann. Sax.* (1085), SS. VI, 722; *Ann. Disibod.*, SS. XVII, 9.

[6] *MGH, LL*, II, 55; new ed. by Weiland, I, Nos. 424, 425.

[7] *De unitate eccles. conserv.*, chap. xxviii; *Ann. Sax.*, p. 723.

confiscation.[1] Henry was compelled hastily to improvise new support for this unexpected emergency by lavish bestowals to the loyal bishops out of the crown lands,[2] and to promise to restore to Ekbert of Meissen the estates in Flanders of which he had been deprived[3]

Having thus mended his fences in Saxony at heavy cost, Henry IV moved to the relief of Würzburg, which was being besieged by Hermann of Luxemburg and a Swabian force. But his Rhenish burgher militia again was beaten by the knights at Bleichfelt (August 11, 1086). The divided condition of his foes, however, both geographically and politically, enabled Henry IV luckily to get the upper hand. Burckhardt in desperation, since now no one would serve Hermann, offered the crown to Ekbert of Meissen.[4] Events thereafter rapidly thickened. Burckhardt of Halberstadt, who had come into Franconia to brace the anti-Henrician cause, was murdered by the infuriated burghers of Würzburg[5] on April 7, 1088. In September, Hermann of Luxemburg died.[6] Except for Ekbert of Meissen, who had finally screwed his courage to the point of rebellion in August, the opposition was everywhere collapsing. For two years more the war was continued in Saxony in a guerilla manner by Ekbert of Meissen and his partisans,[7] but the peasantry took no hand in it.[8]

---

[1] Sigeb. *Chron.*, SS. VI, 365; Ekkehard, *Chron.*, SS. VI, 206.

[2] *Ann. Aug.* (anno 1086). See the charters in Stumpf, *Regesta*, Nos. 2870–78.

[3] Stumpf, *op. cit.*, Nos. 2880, 2893. The estates were the Ostergau and the Westergau, and had been given to the Bishop of Utrecht in 1077 (Richter and Kohl, III, 2, 268 n.).

[4] For his cupidity see *Vita Heinrici IV*, chap. **v**.

[5] *Ann. Sax.* (anno 1088).

[6] The *Vita Heinrici IV*, chap. iv, stingingly says of Hermann: "Nam cum Saxones de terra sua proturbaret, quicquid illud fuerit, quod eis in illo displicuit, reversus in patriam suam portans inane nomen regis, ad Herimannum Trevirensem episcopum se contulit."

[7] *Ann. Hild.* (1089), SS. III, 106; *Chron. Hild.*, chap. xviii, SS. VII, 854; *De unitate eccles. conserv.*, II, chap. xviii. After the death of Gebhard of Salzburg the papal party had but four bishops in Germany: Adalberon of Würzburg, Altmann of Passau, Adalbert of Worms, and Gebhard of Constance (Gerdes, *op. cit.*, II, 292).

[8] "Saxones a fidelitate S. Petri discedentes, Heinricum quem multotiens abjuraverant receperunt" (Bernold [anno 1088]; cf. *Gesta ep. Halb.*, SS. XXIII, 100;

The land suffered fearfully from privation and devastation.
Abrupt termination was brought to the war by the murder
of Ekbert on July 3, 1090.[1] In the year following, Berthold
of Carinthia and Welf of Bavaria made their submission.
Peace at last had come to Germany to stay, after fifteen
years of civil war. Gregory VII had already been dead for
five years. When Abbot William of Hirsau died in 1091 the
last flame of opposition to Henry IV expired.[2]

Out of the enormous disarray caused by the fusion of
the Saxon rebellion, the revolt of the feudality, and with the
war of investiture, the injection of religious fanaticism into
the already complex body of issues and antagonistic forces—
political, economic, social—which engrossed all authorities
and all classes of society, a new Germany was born. What the
fifth century had done for the Roman Empire, what the ninth
century had accomplished in France, that the reign of Henry
IV saw done in Germany. All the elements and institutions
of Germanic life were melted as in a tumultuous laboratory,
and fused in new proportions into new political and social
forms. The government was altered, the texture of society
changed, unwonted economic and social conditions introduced. The very psychology of the German people took on a
new cast.

Materially Germany was reduced nearly to a state of
ruination. Both sides in the long war had swept the land as
bare as a threshing floor. The manors of the fisc, the lands
of the church and the nobles, the farms of the peasants, had
been devastated again and again. *Raubrittertum* was universal.[3] As early as 1078 Saxony was more like a wilderness
than an abode for men. Immense areas of it had gone over to

Ekkehard, *Chron.*, SS. VI, 206; *Ann. Sax.*, SS. VI, 724; *Ann. Magd.*, SS. XVI, 178).
Many of the Saxons and Thuringians who had enriched themselves by the spoil of
the church had become indifferent (*De unitate eccles. conserv.*, chap. xxii).

[1] *De unitate eccles. conserv*, chap. xxxvi.

[2] "Sed jam aliquantulum diuturna regni discordia inter catholicos et scismaticos
tepescere cepit, ut non jam bellum ad invicem, sed pacem componere sanius judi-
carent" (Bernold, p. 450).

[3] Bruno, chap. cxxii.

bramble and brier, to the forest and the wolf.[1] Bishop Rupert
of Bamberg, between 1093–95, declared that there were large
parts of Saxony without inhabitants.[2] Frederick, count palatine in Saxony (i.e., Henry IV's chief agent of the fisc there),
collected around him a band of freebooters who carried away
with them or destroyed what either friend or foe had spared,
and the last remnants of a plundered manor-house or home-
stead were taken by the desperate and hungry peasantry, itself brutalized by the brutality it had suffered.[3] In the raids
that time and again had swept over Saxony the Swabians
were notorious for their plundering ways.[4] Both parties, as
we have seen, were compelled to buy partisans, and the only
means of purchase was land. The result was the dilapidation
of the domains of both the crown and the church, and the
spoliation of each party's lands by the other.[5]

Hardly was the German kingdom on the fair road to recovery from this condition when the rebellion of Henry IV's
sons in 1103 renewed all the former horrors.[6] Even before the
first rebellion of Saxony a distinct drift of the Saxon population eastward across the Elbe is discernible, which was seeking relief from the rapacity of the baronage and the tithes of
the church.[7] This tide of refugees and men of broken fortune
who hoped to repair their losses in old Germany by finding

[1] At the diet of Regensburg Henry IV "dixit namque Saxones in proximi proelii
conflictu sic esse prostratos, ut nisi de gentibus exteris agrorum cultores advenirent,
Saxonica tellus in solitudinem versa bestiis silvestribus habitanda remaneret"
(Bruno, chap. ciii).

[2] ". . . . in vacuis illius partibus Saxoniae" (Jaffé, *Mon. Greg.*, V, 171).

[3] Bruno, chap. ci. They used to sing for joy while so doing: "cum magno
gaudio cantuque."

[4] Bruno, chap. ciii.

[5] For dissipation of the fisc see Bruno, chaps. xxxviii–xxxix, cviii, cxii; Lambert
of Hersfeld, pp. 201–2; *Ann. Sax.*, SS. VI, 712; *Ann. Aug.*, SS. III, 129. See, further,
Richter, III, 2, p. 372, n. G; Gerdes, II, 377–89. The evidence of spoliation of church
lands is even fuller; see the notes in Gerdes, II, 485–98. The letter of Sigfried of
Mainz to Gregory VII may be cited as an example: "Hostili praeda et pervasione
magna ex parte dispierierunt res et reditus episcopi nostri" (Jaffé, V, 99).

[6] For a vivid description of the dire condition of Germany see *Vita Heinrici IV*,
chap. viii, and Jaffé, *Mon. Greg.*, V, 241–46.

[7] Adam of Bremen, III, 49, *anno* 1066.

homes in the new East Germany became a flood in the latter years of Henry IV's reign.[1]

Thus by breaking down within and emigration abroad the ancient integrity of Saxony disappeared more and more. The tentacles of sectionalism clutched the shattered territory. Already during the civil war Westphalia showed a tendency to separate from Eastphalia, a separation which became final in the next century when Albrecht the Bear inherited one-half of the Billunger lands and acquired Brandenburg as an independent fief in 1134, while the north and west of the once glorious duchy passed into the hands of Henry the Proud and the Welfs.

Alas for the land of the Liudolfinger, of Henry the Fowler, and Otto the Great! The nobles like a pack of wolves fed upon the carcasses of the state and the church, gorging themselves on the property of both. But they could not take or keep all the spoil, though the lion's share fell to them. For a crowd of petty lesser vassals and *ministeriales*, as hungry as their superiors, followed like jackals at the heels of the lions, and picked up what they could of the remnants. The condition of chronic local warfare which prevailed compelled every high noble, lay and clerical, to divide with his following by enfeoffing his lands in order to keep his supporters. Thus the number of the lower feudality was increased tenfold. The long war had sowed dragon's teeth which sprang up as men.[2]

Castles began to bristle on every hilltop. The practice which Henry III had initiated in Saxony, which Henry IV had continued in Thuringia, which the bishops and nobles has imitated, became general. The Wartburg is first mentioned in 1080.[3] Castle Böckelheim appears in 1105.[4] A writer of the twelfth century says that the castles multiplied

---

[1] See chap. xiv.

[2] Waitz, V, 475 f., Giesebrecht, *Kaiserzeit*, III, 2, 960 f., 1004 f.; Gerdes., *Gesch. d. deutsch. Volkes*, II, 410 f.

[3] Bruno, chap. xcvii. The story that the Landgrave of Thuringia, while hunting, discovered the site and said, "Warte, Berg, du sollst mir eine Burg werden," of course is pure legend.

[4] *Chron. S. Hub. Andag.*, SS. VIII, 629. For Trifels see Heintz, *Mittheil. d. hist. Ver. f. d. Pfalz*, VII (1878).

as fast as the churches had done in the eleventh century.[1] Many of these strongholds were dens of robbers.[2]

Henry V's policy in this strait was to play off the South German princes against the Northern—the Staufer and the Welfs against Lothar. This he was able to do the more readily since Frederick of Hohenstaufen, the duke of Swabia, was Henry V's nephew and heir. The party situation in Germany, therefore, was a triangular one, the Saxon and Hohenstaufen parties being the two greater ones, each of which fished for the support of the third, or Welf party. The sectionalism manifest in the distribution of these three parties is interesting and important. The Saxon-Lotharian party was spread over the whole north; the Hohenstaufen field was Swabia; the Welfs were centered in Bavaria. The difference in folk-ingredients, historical tradition and development, economic and social conditions, between these three regions of feudal Germany accentuated these distinctions. The analogy of the history of the United States between 1800 and 1825, when North and South and New West were clearly differentiated, will occur to an American historian. And as both North and South then angled for the support of the West, so in Germany in the twelfth century both the North (Saxony) and the South (Swabia) angled for the support of the other section (Bavaria, the Southeast). The Rhinelands stood aloof. Their interest was in trade and breaking the bishops in the cities.

The political situation in Germany when Henry V died (1125) was a tense one. For in spite of his father's and his own failure to do with Saxony as they pleased, and the inability of the Salian kings to convert the royal prerogative into an absolute one, nevertheless the power of the crown had increased so greatly that both the feudal and the clerical parties were filled with apprehension. The Concordat of Worms in 1122 had given the King the kernel of the controversy and

---

[1] Ekkehard of Aura, *Chron.* (1116–17), SS. VI, 252; Herbordus, *Vita Ottonis ep. Babenb.* I, 26.

[2] Thus the *Ann. Patherb.* (1107) relate of Henry V: "Inde [from Regensburg] per Thuringiam ad Saxoniam vadit, Radinburg [Radelburg] et Bemelburg [Boineburg in Hesse], presidia munitissima in Thuringia, propter latrocinia que inde in finitimos exercebantur, cremari precepit."

left the papacy the shell. The feudal party was in better state than the ecclesiastical, for Henry V had been signally repulsed in Saxony, while in Swabia and Bavaria the Welf and Hohenstaufen party had expanded. Even the power of the lesser Fürsten had been growing greater.

In the election at Mainz after Henry V's death the Saxon-clerical party, whose candidate was Lothar of Supplinburg, was pitted against the Salian party, represented by Frederick of Hohenstaufen. No other candidate was seriously considered. The issue was at once political, ecclesiastical, and sectional.

At the death of the Emperor precedent provided that the Archbishop of Mainz, as the German primate, should call a conference of the highest clerical and secular princes for the purpose of electing a successor.[1] In times past, however, dynastic preponderance had always been so great that the choice was practically assured in advance, and the "election" of the eldest son of the deceased monarch was a certainty. In this wise, while the German kingship was in theory an elective office, in practice its hereditability tended to obtain de facto.

Adalbert of Mainz was determined that in this instance the hereditary principle should be defeated. He was resolved that the freedom of the church and the integrity of the rights of the feudality and the people, both of which issues were sharply sustained in Saxony, should prevail in the coming election.[2]

It is important to analyze the party and sectional forces and currents which eddied around Lothar's elevation, since his election to the kingship was the confirmation of nearly everything for which the anti-Henrician opposition had fought in past years.

In the first place, Lothar was a Saxon, and by birth, tradition, and training represented the things most dear to

[1] See the monograph by Stutz, Der Erzbischof von Mainz und die deutsche Königswahl, and the review of the same in Hist. Ztschft. (3d ser.), XIV, Heft 1.

[2] The pertinent documents have been collected by Mario Kramer, Quellen zur Gesch. der deutschen Königswahl (1911). Naturally the literature upon this turning-point in the history of feudal Germany is large. The thesis of R. Niemann, Die Wahl Lothars von Sachsen (Göttingen, 1871), is suggestive.

the Saxon heart. He was a son of Count Gebhard of Supplinburg, his mother having been Hedwig, a daughter of Ordulf
Billung. In 1106 when the Billung house expired with the
death of Magnus Billung, Lothar had been reluctantly recognized as duke by Henry V, who would have been glad to
escheat the duchy but dared not to do so for fear of offending
the Saxons to the point of new rebellion.[1] Moreover, this influence of Lothar with the Saxon people had been strengthened by his marriage to Richsa, a daughter of Otto of Nordheim, the leader of the great revolt of the Saxons in 1075; and,
finally, Saxon admiration for their new Duke was raised to a
patriotic pitch in 1115, when Henry V, casting discretion to
the winds, invaded the north country with an army in order to
break the great lord of the north, and got badly beaten by
Lothar in the battle of Welfesholz.[2] Lothar also had other
qualities which endeared him to his people. In the winter of
1124-25 he had made a victorious campaign against the
Wends, the hated enemy of all Saxons, and won a victory
the like of which Germany had not seen in years.

With the feudality, too, Lothar was popular, for his own
succession to the duchy of Saxony had been a triumph of
collateral and female succession to imperial fiefs, a principle
which the Salian kings had steadfastly resisted and for which
the great dukes had as strenuously contended.

But the most decisive of all Lothar's qualifications was his
popularity with the German hierarchy. If the dukes grasped
at the opportunity to register their power in electing Lothar,
the bishops did so even more. The extinction of the Salian
house with the childless Henry V in 1125 afforded them, as
well as the feudality, the chance once and for all to declare
the destruction of the hereditary principle with reference to
the German kingship, and to assert a genuine elective principle.[3]

---

[1] *Annal. Sax.*, SS. VI, 744-45.

[2] *Ibid.*, SS. VI, 750-51; Ekkehard, *Chron. (anno* 1115).

[3] Carlyle, *op. cit.*, III, 151. The electoral character of the German crown is asserted frequently in the *Sachsenspiegel*, III, 52, 1; 54, 2; 55, 1; cf. Carlyle, III,
153 nn., and Sugenheim, *Gesch. d. deutschen Volkes*, II, 314. Wattenbach, in the
Preface to his edition of the *Narratio de electione Lotharii*, SS. XII, 509, writes:

The call which the Archbishop sent out to the German bishops and Fürsten at this time is exceedingly interesting to analyze in the light of this purpose. Instead of being a perfectly formal document, after announcing the primary purpose of the conference, seemingly as *obiter dicta*, but really of great significance, he adds: "It is our thought then that the princes should meet and take necessary action in regard to the serious problems which confront us, viz.: the general state of the kingdom, the question of a successor, *and other matters*."[1] This seemingly casual allusion to "the general state of the kingdom" and "other matters" was artfully made.

The reign of Henry IV had established two precedents which the liberal party in Germany was not going to suffer to be lost. One of these principles was the contention that state affairs should be subjected to a general discussion by the princes;[2] the other was that henceforth the King had to give a reason for exacting military service of vassals, whether of lay or ecclesiastical condition, and that he might not levy troops at his pleasure.[3]

The Saxon party had no intention of permitting the coming conference to act, as so often before, in a merely mechanical way, and passively register the wish of the lately deceased ruler by choosing as his successor the person whom he had selected and designated to be his heir. The conference was to be a free and independent deliberative body in which the sovereignty of the German state was vested ad interim, between the decease of the late King and the election of a new ruler. No one denied that Frederick of Hohenstaufen

---

"Lotharii regis electio ea de causa praecipue notabilis est, quia tum primum praevaluit sententia episcoporum, qui hereditariam regum successionem tamquam simoniae cujusdam speciem abominabantur et liberam tam in regno quam in sacerdotiis electionem postulabant."

[1] Doeberl, *Monumenta Germaniae Selecta*, IV, No. 1; Jaffé, *Monumenta Gregoriana* V, 396.

[2] Waitz, *Deutsche Verfassungsgeschichte*, VI, 348. The germ of the later diets is to be found in these sessions of the German nobility (*ibid.*, pp. 321 f.).

[3] Schulte, *Deutsche Verwaltungsgesch.*, sec. 74, 2; Homeyer, *System*, p. 378; Sachsenspiegel, *Lehnrecht*, art. 4, sec. 1.

was the personal heir of his uncle Henry V, and as such entitled to inherit his private estate. But it was meant to have done forever with the idea that the German crown was a dynastic possession and the property of a single house.

The electoral college (if one may anticipate the phrase by which the conference came in later years to be designated) was not to be a mere board of registration like the French *parlement*, but an independent body sovereign in its peculiar sphere and its particular function. A precedent was afforded for this contention in the group of bishops and Fürsten which had formerly elected Rudolf of Swabia and Hermann of Luxemburg. The principle of election was asserted in a positive way, with the corollary of a responsible crown and recognition of fixed and traditional rights pertaining to the feudality and to the people.[1] These rights were historical and legal, and the crown could not lawfully inhibit or destroy them. They were the lawful, vested rights of their possessors.

When the electoral college convened on August 24, 1125, at Mainz, all the great princes of Germany, lay and clerical, were there, each with a train of vassals and *ministeriales*. So high was the political tension and so keen the rivalry between the parties that the two groups occupied opposite banks of the Rhine. After an amount of "logrolling" and "wirepulling" at which we can hardly guess from the evidence, a nominating committee of forty was chosen, to consist of ten members from each of the four great "stems" or Germanic tribes (Saxons, Swabians, Franks, Bavarians), whose choice the entire concourse bound themselves in advance to accept. Only Frederick of Swabia refused to commit himself to this pledge—a tactical blunder on his part.

[1] This is evident from the studied manner in which the author of the *Narratio* follows the language of Berthold of Constance in his description of the assembly which elected Rudolf of Swabia. The *Narratio* reads: ". . . . et facta seorsum principum collectione non modica, utpote qui animum jam in regnum intenderat et quasi spe certa preoccupaverat. . . . ." The language of Berthold is: "Proinde episcopi seorsum et senatorius ordo seorsum pro constituendo rege diu multumque consiliati" (SS. VI, 292). Kalbfuss, *Mitteil. d. Inst. f. oesterr. Gesch.*, Band XXXI, (1911), Heft 4, has traced the genesis of the political ideas enunciated in the *Narratio*. For bibliography on this exceedingly important document see Doeberl, *op. cit.*, IV, 2 n. The *Pactum* of the *Narratio de electione Lotharii* was not an electoral regulation, but a program drawn up after Lothar's election by the bishops and legates to lay down the policy to be pursued by Lothar.

After long deliberation the choice of the forty electors[1] fell upon Lothar of Saxony, and was spontaneously applauded, not only by the greater part of the bishops and nobles, but also by the people who were present. The moral participation of the German people in this election is to be noted. While in former elections this popular approval had sometimes been manifested, it was merely incidental. But in Lothar's election in 1125 it would seem that there was some reversion to the old German method of popular election of a chieftain. For the new King was enthusiastically raised aloft upon the shoulders of his followers when the news was announced.[2]

That the accession of Lothar was a triumph of the principles for which the Saxons had contended during the reign of Henry IV is clear if we compare the diet of Forchheim, which elected Rudolf of Swabia in 1077, with the body that elected Lothar in 1125. The words of Bruno's De bello Saxonico, chapter xci, apply equally well to the event of 1125 as to that of 1077. In both cases the designation rested upon election and not upon inheritance; in both cases the validity of the customary law of the duchies and the rights of the people were asserted; in both cases the principle of limited monarchy was affirmed.

The relief which was felt throughout Germany when the result was known was great. The erudite monk who penned the account records the astonishment and gratification that a board of unlettered laymen who could neither read nor write should have manifested such wisdom.[3] The tension had been very great during the interval, and Germany not im-

---

[1] Weiland, in Forschungen zur Deutsch. Gesch. XX, 303–39, has shown that the privilege of election little by little became an appanage of the great clerical and lay lords. This doctrine was favored by the popes, propagated by the Mirror of Saxony, and finally triumphed in the election of 1257.

[2] Narratio, sec. 4. Popular approval seems to have been really spontaneous in the election of Otto I (Widukind, Rerum gestarum saxonicarum, II, chap. i. For Conrad's II election see Wipo, De vita Chuonradi, chap. ii).

[3] "Hoc itaque magnum decus, et memorabile nec prius auditum, jam nostro tempore Dominus suae concessit ecclesiae, ut laicorum scilicet illiteratorum humilitas sanctissima ostenderit in majoribus non ambiendis, quam perniciose clericorum et literatorum in minoribus, magis tamen spiritalibus, ambicio dampnosa delinqueret" (Narratio, sec. 2 [ad fin.]).

probably would have been thrown again into civil war if Lothar had not been elected.[1] As it fell out, the only disgruntled person was Frederick of Hohenstaufen, who quitted the assembly in a fit of rage and soon afterward came out in open rebellion. Fortunately, however, that revolt was localized and soon crushed.

The determining factor in this happy result had been Duke Henry the Proud of Bavaria, a Welf. The balance between the two rival parties, without him, was so close that the card might have fallen either way. The Welf, or Guelf, influence was decisive in settling the issue—a fact of enormous significance in the future history of Germany. For it meant that the two greatest duchies in the kingdom, Saxony and Bavaria, the one in the north, the other in the southeast, were aligned together, and were united in support of an identical and constructive political program. When in 1127, two years later, the Welf Duke married Lothar's only child, his daughter Gertrude, the political alliance was cemented by a family one as well.[2]

[1] *Ibid.*, sec. 5.   [2] *Monumenta Welforum*, chap. xvi.

CHAPTER VII

POLITICAL THEORIES AND CONSTITUTIONAL PROGRESS DURING THE WAR OF INVESTITURE (1075–1139)[1]

IN THE history of medieval Germany one does not find that continuity of monarchical policy which prevailed in England and in France. The fortunate establishment and persistence through several centuries of a single dynasty enabled the kings of England and of France to maintain a consistent monarchical policy for generation after generation. In Germany, on the other hand, we find three successive dynasties, each with a different policy. But it would be an error to assume that because the Saxon, Salian, and Hohenstaufen dynasties were short-lived when compared with the Plantagenets and Capetians, that, therefore, their political theory and their political practice made no permanent contribution to the fund of medieval political experience and political philosophy.

Long before the French Capetians were able to do more than tentatively to discuss the theory of their authority, before even those two brilliant Norman rulers, Robert Guiscard in Southern Italy and William the Conqueror in England, had laid the foundations of real monarchy by the Tyr-

[1] The literature upon this subject is extensive, but there is little in English except the Carlyles' *A History of Mediaeval Political Theory*, Vol. III. For literature on the subject of the *Libelli* consult: Mirbt, *Die Publizistik im Zeitalter Gregors VII* (1894); Giesebrecht, *Die Gesetzgebung der römischen Kirche zur Zeit Gregors VII* (1866); Bernheim, *Zur Gesch. d. Wormser Konkordats* (1878); Meyer von Knonau, *Jahrbücher unter Heinrich IV und V*; Heinzelmann, *Die Farfanser Streitschriften: Beitraege zur Gesch. d. Investiturstreites* (1904); Imbart de la Tour, *Questions d'histoire religeuse*, pp. 225 f.; Ghellinck, "La littérature polémique durant la querelle des investitures," *Revue d. Quest. Hist.*, XCIII (N.S.), 71 f.; Scharnagel, *Der Begriff der Investitur in den Quellen und der Literatur des Investiturstreites* (1908); A. Fliche, *Études sur la polémique religeuse à l'époque de Grégoire VII. Les prégrégoriens*, esp. chap. v, and his article in *Revue Historique*, CCXXV, 1–67, on "Les théories germaniques de la souveraineté." The only article on the subject in English is by Father Ghellinck, *Irish Theol. Quart.*, VII (1912), 329.

rhene Sea and across the channel, Conrad II and Henry III
in Germany had felt some intimation of what the future had
in store for Europe, and were the first of medieval kings to
sketch the large lines of a really monarchical form of government. Conrad II laid the foundations of the new German
kingship; Henry III began to build the superstructure; his
untimely death not only left the edifice far from completed,
but much of what he accomplished was torn down in the reaction which followed during his son's minority. When Henry
IV took the reins of government into his own hands the
fabric which his father and grandfather had labored to erect
was so badly breached that little was left but a great tradition and an urgent necessity.

The Saxon chronicler Bruno has a wild tale to the effect
that Henry IV in the year 1074 dreamed of appealing for
help to William the Conqueror.[1] The story is preposterous.
Yet Henry IV must have envied the untrammeled way in
which William and Robert Guiscard were able to act in their
dominions. For with them authority rested upon conquest
and might largely made right; Henry IV, on the other hand,
was not only bound by the inherited prerogatives of his office
as king, but also by a mass of traditions, laws, and feudal
practices which were woven into the very texture of German
life, much of them unwritten and customary and difficult to
modify or discard. This was particularly true in Saxony,
where the conservatism of the people was very strong, and
the vested interests of the feudality, both lay and clerical,
very deep.

The outstanding features of Henry IV's administrative
policy are the establishment of a fixed capital, the establishment of the inalienability, indivisibility, and extension of
the royal domain, the subordination of the feudal dukes and
the feudalized clergy to royal authority, and finally the
creation of a bureaucratic form of government, that is, the
administration of public affairs through a specially created
and technically trained official class known as *ministeriales*,
to be as the fingers of the king's hand, touching every part of
the kingdom, and imbuing every activity of the administra-

[1] *De bello Sax.*, chap. xxxvi.

tion—justice, law, taxation—with the king's will. The King's design was nothing less than the creation of an absolute monarchy in Germany; not a reckless despotism, but a supreme royal authority able to put the German baronage, lay and clerical, under its feet by gradually converting suzerainty into sovereignty and hardening the royal prerogatives into an instrument able to coerce, and even to destroy, particularistic feudalism. It was to be a feudal monarchy, for the spirit of the times and the institutions of society were feudal, but every element and line of it was to be vitalized and controlled by the King's authority. This is what the Capetians in France and the Plantagenets achieved, and what Henry IV struggled to establish in Germany. If real morality is "the will to discern life," and a man is to be judged not by what he achieves, but by what he labors to accomplish, then the paradox is true that Henry IV succeeded though he failed.

Henry IV was not the man to be daunted by adverse conditions, nor dismayed by the formidable opposition he knew he must encounter if he would carry out the political designs of his house. Once legally free from the restraints of his minority, and out of the hands of the "robber gang"[1] which for years had exploited the government, Henry IV revived the monarchical policy initiated by Conrad II and Henry III, and set to work to establish the royal authority along larger lines and on a firmer foundation than ever before. Neither the design nor the policy was new with Henry IV. What was new was the energy which the King displayed, the formidable nature of the opposition, and the complications which ensued, which profoundly altered the conditions of the struggle, the most important of which was the entrance of the papacy under Gregory VII into the conflict for reasons which had to do with the tremendous ambitions of the pontificate at this time. For no sooner was the Salian principle of kingship formulated and begun to be applied than it was challenged with forthright boldness, first by the Saxons, then by the feudality of Germany, and finally and most formidably by the new papacy. The Saxons, the great dukes, and the papacy had each a different theory which each translated

[1] Adam of Bremen, III, 46; "in den Händen von Räubern," says Giesebrecht.

into practice. Out of the fusion was generated the first cogent and genuinely original political theory the Middle Ages developed.

Whence came this authority of kings? Was it of God, or was it of men? The church, arguing that all power was from God (*omnis potestas a Deo*), proclaimed the supremacy of the church over the state. With some the church was regarded as a superstate; with others the state was regarded as a man-made institution, and accordingly evil, and the right of the existence of the state was denied. The latter was the attitude of Gregory VII,[1] in his moments of extreme exaltation, or of despotic spirit, from which he sometimes sank to a lower and more practicable plane of endeavor, and admitted the right of the state to exist, though only in dependence upon the church.[2]

The function of authority is to administer justice. As long as the prince fulfils this duty the duty of subjects is to obey. Upon these two points the medieval political theorists agreed. But divergence appeared upon the question whether subjects were bound to obey an unjust or tyrannical prince. Some jurists, the spiritual ancestors of the future apologists of absolute monarchy, contended that the teaching of the Bible and the wisdom of the fathers was that a sovereign must be obeyed under all circumstances save in case of his heresy. During the war of investiture the imperial partisans adopted and propagated this theory.[3]

---

[1] See his letters to Hermann of Metz, *Reg.*, IV, 2; VIII, 21.

[2] Gregory's letters to Harold of Denmark and William the Conqueror, *ibid.*, V, 10; VII, 25.

[3] So Henry IV wrote to Gregory VII: "Me quoque qui licet indignus inter Christos ad regnum sum unctus, tetigisti, quem sanctorum patrum traditio soli Deo judicandum docuit, nec pro aliquo crimine nisi a fide, quod absit, exorbitaverim, deponendum asseruit; cur etiam Julianum apostatam prudentia sanctorum patrum non sibi sed soli Deo judicandum deponendumque commiserit" (*MG. LL.*, II, 47). Otto of Freising says that he vainly searched history for a precedent for the pope to depose an emperor or any king (*Chronicon*, p. 35: "Lego et relego Romanorum regum et imperatorum gesta, et nusquam invenio quemquam eorum ante hunc a romano pontifice excommunicatum vel regno privatum"). With St. Thomas Aquinas the reserved right of insurrection and deposition of a tyrranical king passed definitely into law (Viollet, *Inst. polit. de la France*, II, 4, n. 1). The German nobles had resolved on deposition of Henry IV before Gregory VII became pope (Lambert of Hersfeld, *anno* 1073: "Eum sine magna Christianae religionis jactura non posse ulterius regnare").

The opponents of this school, on the other hand, argued that a prince who failed to do justice ceased to be a prince and became a tyrant, and as a tyrant forfeited the right to rule.[1] But if so, who had the authority to try the prince or to depose him? The church, or the prince's own subjects? It is manifest that this contractual idea contains the germ of the principle of the liability of princes, of constitutional monarchy, of the right of revolution. John of Salisbury in the next century went so far as to justify resort to the murder of a bad prince, to make assassination a principle.

Thus little by little a body of political theory was formed, a new political system, which crystallized at the end of the eleventh century, during the conflict between Henry IV and Gregory VII in the writings of Manegold of Lautenbach.

The rights of the people became the corollary of the coronation oath of the king. What guaranteed the people against abuse of princely power? The refusal of service and the threat of deposition. Neither barons, burghers, nor peasantry possessed yet the right to vote subsidies as in a later age, but the feudality could refuse to do service for the king, and the burghers and peasants could at least rebel against tyranny. The remedial process was therefore a species of feudal "strike," with the principle of revolution involved in it. The feudal tie as embodied in the coronation oath was contractual in its nature and bound ruler and ruled by reciprocal obligations of protection and obedience. "The doctrine of the social contract became the watchword of popular resistance to the growth of arbitrary despotism." It is important to observe that in this feudal society the oath of the prince preceded that of the subjects. The consequence of this anteriority of the prince's oath was that the oath of the

[1] In the diet at Oppenheim the princes practically said: Henry has been cut off from the communion of the church by the Pope's anathema. It would be folly for us now not to seize the opportunity thus afforded to accomplish that which we have been long premeditating.

"Nunc vero, cum ab ecclesiae corpore propter flagicia sua apostolici anathematis mucrone precisus sit, cum ei communicare sine communionis ecclesiasticae damno et fidei jactura non possimus, cum fidem nostram multis apud eum sacramentis implicitam, Romanus pontifex apostolica auctoritate explicuerit: extremae profecto dementiae esset, divinitus oblatam salutis occasionem non obviis, ... et quod diu premeditatum sit, ut *agatur tam oportuno tempore non agere, cum leges humanae et ecclesiasticae sinant.*" Lambert of Hersfeld (*anno* 1076), p. 280.

prince's subjects was a conditional one. If the prince broke
the contract, the oath of his subjects ceased to be obligatory.
This right (*securitas*) was inherent in feudal society as a right
of the feudality, but until the end of the eleventh century,
and more especially until the twelfth century, no precedent
had extended this right downward to the lower classes of the
people. The theory that the power of the ruler emanated
from God, the source of all power, and that, accordingly, the
sovereign was only responsible to God for his acts, could not
resist the evolution of popular right. First the baronage qualified the principle of absolutism, and then the people. We
have thus in the reign of Henry IV the conflict between two
principles of authority, two theories of government—the
idea of the absolute prerogative and the divine right of the
prince, and the idea of monarchical authority tempered by
the right of resistance of the nation, first by the baronage,[1]
next by the burghers, and finally by the body of the people.

The germ of limited monarchy, the doctrine of popular
sovereignty, and the theory of the state as a contractual
social organism were potentially in these new doctrines.[2] It
was a demand for a social organization which should rest less
on force and more on law; for a system of government which
would substitute contract for compulsion; which would recognize definite relations and mutual rights and obligations. If a
lord, even the king, failed to do justice and to perform the
services which society expected of him, what right had he to
rule? If he oppressed, why continue to obey him?

In this new conception of the nature of government, the

---

[1] Nitzsch, II, 101, points out that the election of Rudolph of Swabia was an
enunciation of a new constitutional theory, and the first "lay" election of a German
king. The Fürsten identified popular sovereignty with their purposes and interests,
but their democracy was a class democracy, and "popular" only as contrasted with
Salian absolutism. Henry V, when prince, by uniting with the rebellious feudality against his father in 1105 was compelled to admit this contention. It comes out
in his address of March 25, 1106, to the German nobles: ". . . . injuria mea regni
potius est quam mea; nam unius capitis licet summi dejectio, reparabile regni
dampnum est; principum autem conculcatio, ruina regni est" (*Vita Heinrici IV*, chap.
xiii). For commentary on this important passage see Waitz, VI, 371; Below, *Der
deutsche Staat des Mittelalters*, p. 184; Ranke, *Zeitalter d. Reformation* (5th ed.), I, 24.

[2] See Gierke, *Political Theories of the Middle Ages* (Maitland's trans.), pp. 37–67,
for development of this thesis. Cf. Carlyle, *Mediaeval Polit. Theory*, III, 12–13.

church and the common people struck hands.[1] The church, for all its temporal power, intense feudalization, and plenitude of vested interests, never wholly lost sight of the dignity and authority of justice as a principle among men.[2] The church's greatest leaders in their best moments remembered that justice was the habitation of God's throne, that mercy and truth met together before it. Above the wrack of feudal warfare the clergy held up the doctrine of better laws, the duty of kings and nobles to judge with honor and govern with equity. Time and again, in the writings of the ninth, tenth, and eleventh centuries, we find this principle of social justice reiterated. Century after century the teaching returns, even though it be with an alienated majesty.[3]

One must not be deceived by terminology. Theology was

[1] Gregory's appeal to laic opinion was a thing unheard of—to subject church offices to the mob, said the opposition. Cf. Gregory's reply, *Ep. ad Rudolphum Suaviae et Bertulphum Carentanum duces, Ep.* II, No. 45: "Multo melius nobis videtur justitiam Dei vel *novis* reaedificare *consiliis*, quam animas hominum una cum legibus neglectis." The German bishops reproached the Pope for appeal to popular sentiment. *Conc. Worms*, 1076 (Pertz, *Leges*, II, 45): "Omni rerum ecclesiasticarum administratione *plebeio furore* te attributa." Cf. the letter of Dietrich of Verdun in Martène and Durand, *Thesaurus*, I, 218: "Legum de clericorum incontinentia per laicorum insanias cohibenda, legem ad scandalum in ecclesia mittendum tartaro vomente prolatam."

[2] Apropos of the church's influence in preservation of the idea of justice, and the idea of the state, a French historian has written: "Cette notion était inconnue à l'aristocratie et aux basses classes. Heureusement, la littérature orale se charge à de perpétuer chez les illétrés, nobles ou vilains, le sentiment d'une certaine solidarité entre les div:ses parties dont se composait le royaume. ... Aux époques même les plus sombres du moyen-âge il y a eu une opinion publique dont les souverains féodaux ont dû tenir compte." Lot, *Hugues Capet*, p. 238 and n. 2. Gregory VII wrote to Alphonso of Castille not to hesitate to appoint clergy of foreign blood or low birth if they were capable men. (*Ep.* IV, No. 2; Mansi, XX, 341): "Quod non tam generis aut patriae nobilitatem, quam animi et corporis virtutes perpendendas adjucaverit." Hadrian IV wrote to Frederick I that there were no strangers in Rome, all men were equal in opportunity: Baronius, *Annales* 1159, sec. 3: "Ipsa enim ecclesia Romana, viros et scientia adornantos praeditos honestate et sanguinis nobilitate praeclaros, ad se libenter evocat, et eos aliunde consuevit admittere."

[3] Alcuin, *MGH, Ep.* IV, No. 18; Jonas of Orleans, *De inst. regia*, pp. 3–5, Hincmar, *De ordine palatii; ad episc. de inst. Car.*, p. 7; *de regis persona*, p. 25; Sed. Scotus, *De rect. Christ.*, pp. 2, 3; Agobard of Lyons, *MGH, Ep.* V, No. 6; Hrabanus Maurus, *In Genesim*, II, chap. viii; Rather of Verona, *Praeloquiorum*, III, 1; Wipo, *Vita Chuonradi*, chap. iii. Extracts from all of these are conveniently collected in Carlyle, *op. cit.*, I, 200, 203, 224, 255–56; III, 100, 108, 109. Rather of Verona said that an honest peasant deserved to be called a king (Carlyle, III, 127 n.).

the dominant, almost the only mode of medieval thought. But, it has been well said:

When this characteristic is recognized, it is found to supply not only the explanation of the distance which seems to separate the middle ages from modern times, but also a means of bridging over the interval. Men thought theologically, but when we penetrate this formal expression we discover their speculations, their aims, their hopes, to be at bottom not very different from our own; we discover a variety beneath the monotonous surface of their thoughts, and at the same time an unity, ill defined perhaps, but still an unity, pervading the history.[1]

The claim made by Gregory VII of the right "to absolve subjects from their allegiance to wicked men" was based not merely on Scripture, but upon the implied pact which held feudal society together, and which entailed mutuality and reciprocity, with the reserved right of repudiation by either party for failure to abide by its terms.[2]

Whatever the amount of self-interest which actuated the three elements hostile to Henry IV, the rebellious dukes, the revolted Saxons, and the papacy, it is nevertheless not to be forgotten that there was a principle at stake for which they contended, even admitting that a large number of baser motives were commingled therewith. The scientific historian may not pronounce categorically either one way or the other. There were honest, sincere men on each side who acted according to conviction, even though their comrades were often knaves. It is a wise old saying that "politics makes strange bed-fellows."

[1] Lane Poole, *Illustrations of the History of Mediaeval Thought*, p. 3. To the same effect is Figgis, *op. cit.*, p. 2: "In these lectures we shall be regarding a literature without charm or brilliancy or overmuch eloquence, voluminous, arid, scholastic, for the most part dead it seems beyond any language ever spoken. Dust and ashes seem arguments, illustrations, standpoints, and even personalities. . . . . Yet it was living once and effectual. . . . . These men whose very names are only an inquiry for the curious are bone of our bone, and their thought, like the architecture of the middle ages, is so much our common heritage that its originators remain unknown."

[2] Dietrich of Verdun demanded what right Gregory had to dissolve allegiance. *Ep. ad Greg. VII* (Martène, *Thesaurus Anecdotorum*, I, 219): "Illud vero reminisci pudet, literae vestrae domini regis dispositionem continentes, ad quantum per omnium ora ludibrium circumferuntur, quomodo eis vestrae, ut dicitur, testimonium pertinaciae prolatis, *nostrum et omnium pro parte vestra loqui volentium ora obstruuntur.*" Henry's friends declared the Pope was destroying the social order. Hugonis Flav., *Chronicon* (anno 1184), (Pertz, VIII, 462): "Jam vero si quis esset qui Gregorio communicaret, hic publice conviciis appetebatur, hic hereticus, *destructor regni.*"

In Gregory VII's mind the issue was not wholly one of the supremacy of church or state; it was also the issue of righteous government, as he understood it, against tyranny. With the revolted feudal nobles in Germany likewise, some, at least, were fighting for maintenance of their rights as they understood them, for their *consuetudines feudorum*, which they honestly believed to be imperiled by Henry IV's absolutistic designs. The same was true of some of the German churchmen, even of those who did not sympathize with the Gregorian theory. While they still adhered to the belief that the German crown had a legitimate right to use the church as an instrument of government, they yet believed that the immense use of the church made by the Salian kings was an abuse. They did not believe in a free church in the state, least of all a church superior to the state. But they did think the right and natural functioning of the church was impaired by too gross use of it for secular purposes.

The case of the Saxon peasantry is similar. They believed that their ancestral liberties and immemorial customs were jeopardized by the Salian policy; that they had a right to rebel and seek to depose Henry IV because of his failure to live up to the terms of kingship, namely, to maintain the laws, to protect society, and to do justice among men. The divine authority of kingship was acutely challenged by the Saxons. The right to revolt was inherent in the compact theory of government, and this contractual theory of government not only existed in the mind of the feudality, it had become fused with the theocratic conceptions of the papacy, and at the same time gravitated downward until it filled the collective consciousness of the people too.

The war of investiture was the first issue in medieval history to excite a popular interest. To the masses it was not a doctrinal question, as so many church issues heretofore had been, but a question in which were involved far-reaching considerations and implications of morality and ethics, economic rights and wrongs, social conditions, hopes and purposes. For the first time in medieval history all classes of society from bishops and abbots and barons down to the lower classes of the people, even the servile peasantry, were interested in a common matter. It is this fact which makes the reign of

Henry IV and the pontificate of Gregory VII of such sur-
passing importance. The conflict between pope and emperor,
at least as much as the Crusades, first awakened the common
consciousness of Europe.

From the point of view of the definition and the spread
throughout the consciousness of Europe of the idea of social
justice the conflict between Henry IV and Gregory VII is
very important to the student of social ethics. The princes
and peoples of Europe watched this struggle with far more
interest than we of today imagine. It was the first event in
medieval Europe before the Crusades which attracted the attention of each and every class in society, and it would be an
error to think that this interest was wholly due to the high
position of the two combatants. It is not exaggeration to say
that much of the common people of Europe, wherever the
controversy between Gregory VII and Henry IV was known,
felt that the Pope was battling for their rights in the church.
Henry, bishop of Speyer, wrathfully denounced the Pope for
having deserted the authority of the bishops and subjected
the church to the madness of the laity.[1] Granting that the
personalities of Pope and Emperor were great, the principles
involved in the conflict were greater; it was these which made
Europe at times almost breathless with attention.

The abstractions of political dreamers began to give way
before the practical demands of society for the enforcement
of law, for better protection of life and property, for better
recognition of the rights and clearer definition of the duties
of the multiple authorities which existed in feudal society.
The crux of the whole argument was the nature of justice.

We see this new and more practical, positive ideal reflected in the historiography of the eleventh century.[2] At
this same time the student of medieval law begins to detect elements in it which are neither of Roman nor of ecclesiastical origin, but which may be described as feudal. It is
evident that some new and constructive ideas are beginning

[1] See the observations of H. C. Lea, *Sacerdotal Celibacy* (3d ed.), I, 276.

[2] Wattenbach, *Geschichtsquellen* (6th ed.), II, 6; Marie Schulz, *Die Lehre von
der historischen Methode bei den Geschichtschreibern des Mittelalters* (Berlin, 1909),
p. 97.

to leaven the feudal organism too. The day of anarchy and sheer brute force, of unrestrained violence and brutality such as characterizes so much of the history of the tenth century, is beginning to pass away, and a new epoch to dawn in which the mutuality of rights and duties, of privileges and obligations, will be better understood and more regarded.

Feudalism was a régime founded upon personal devotion or duty—and more still upon the contractual relations—which obtained between man and man. The form of government so constituted was the very antithesis of autocratic or absolute government; rather each noble was a ruler within his sphere or fief. But of whatever degree that power was, it was nevertheless contractual. Theoretically the members of a society established on these bases were liable only for obligations which they had voluntarily accepted. But the theory and the fact were far from coinciding. In practice the feudal régime exacted and required a compulsory relation of man with man, of the greater with the less, of the stronger with the weak, of the upper members of the secular hierarchy with the lower members—in brief, the whole feudal world was held together as in a net by the ties of lordship and homage, of vassal and suzerain.

From the point of view of political philosophy the feudal régime was, perhaps, the nearest approach to philosophical anarchy the world has ever seen, and it not unnaturally often approximated actual anarchy in practice. But too wholesale condemnation either of the theory or the practice of feudal government would be an error. For feudalism, after all, was prevailingly a constructive organism, and manifested the phenomena of social progress more than those of social decadence.

The very sensitiveness (one might almost say supersensitiveness) of the men of the feudal age to the question of justice is proof of this. The idea of justice was never less a theory and never more actual than in the feudal age. But justice implies a sanction, and this sanction must be law. Now law, for the medieval man, was the product of experience and tradition. It was custom, the accretion of generations in the past, and silently accepted by the men of the present. Even the prince could not contravene this customary law. Customary law was the supreme law, and any modification of it had to be accepted by all, or at least, if the community were too large and too widely dispersed to make approval or disapproval possible, then it had to be accepted by the governing class, by the *major* or *sanior pars*. The prince himself was not above the law, for he was of the noble class and contributed to the formation of the law of his kind. He, too, was subject to the customary law of the land. His authority was very far from being that of a despot.

But parallel to this theory of customary law we discover another political theory running: the principle of the national state, in virtue of which a relation of subordination exists between the prince and all the people who form the nation. This new principle asserted itself more and more strongly with the legists of the twelfth and thirteenth centuries. It even penetrated into a purely feudal society like that of the Kingdom of Jerusalem; from the twelfth century, the supremacy of the central or national organism represented by the prince's own person and privileged blood, i.e., by the crown, over the relations between the vassal and his immediate lord begins to be admitted. By the thirteenth century the principle is uncontested, according to the opinions of the feudal jurists, that the king has jurisdiction over all persons within the realm.

These are the principles which neutralized, and finally overcame, the centrifugal forces in feudalism. For centuries the history of the public law of Europe is the history of the struggle between these two tendencies.

All over Europe, in the late eleventh and through the whole of the twelfth century, we see this disposition on the part of the lower classes to assert, peaceably if they may, forcibly if they must, the integrity of their traditional rights (*consuetudines*), to resent abuse or deprivation of them, and to demand justice. A spirit which had lain dormant for centuries—nay, which had never existed before—in the hearts of the common people of Europe began to awake and to stare about, determined to acquire liberty and secure justice for all conditions of men, but ignorant of the ways and means by which to obtain them. Instinctively, more than by a process of reason perhaps, the people contended that the contractual nature of the relations between noble and noble was as valid for them as for their overlords; as applicable in the seigniorial régime as in the feudal world. "These are the true seigniorial rights established by our ancestors in the interest of peace and tranquillity," writes one in the twelfth century, "but which are daily perverted to unjust practices."[1]

The twelfth-century doctrine that an unjust government need not be obeyed, indeed may rightfully be rebelled against, is not so far as it seems from the modern doctrine that government rests upon the consent of the governed. The former asserted the doctrine negatively; the latter expressed it positively. In fundamental principle the two political doctrines are so nearly alike that they amount almost to the same thing.

The double rebellion in Germany of the Saxon peasantry and the high feudality, combined with the struggle of Henry IV with Gregory VII, was one of the most fruitful periods of the Middle Ages in the progress of political theory. When Henry IV labored to establish absolute monarchy in Germany he denied the validity of the nature of feudal government, which was based upon contract. When also Gregory VII deposed Henry IV he *ipso facto* assumed to sit as a supersovereign in Europe. Each in his own way challenged the form of existing government. Few periods in history, therefore, are of greater importance for the definition and the progress of political theory than the last quarter of the eleventh century and the first quarter of the twelfth.

The fact that the chief energy of the German emperors was expended in policies largely external to Germany, namely, against the papacy and the revolted Lombard cities, has diverted attention too much from the development of political thought within the German kingdom in the eleventh and twelfth centuries. The simultaneous revolt of the Saxon

[1] "Porro quia he consuetudines, cum gratia pacis et quietis a majoribus institute sunt, in pravos usus quotidie perverteruntur" (Flach, *Les origines de l'anc. France*, I, 407). So in the *Miracula de St. Privat* (ed. Brunel; Paris, 1912), p. 136, the Bishop of Mende in 1193 is made to swear: "Populum et clerum amicabiliter gubernabo et juste et juxta bonos mores et bonas consuetudines."

peasantry and of the great feudality in Germany during the strife between the Emperor and the Pope raised issues and unfolded political theories of very great significance, and quite distinct from the issue of papal or imperial supremacy. While the Pope intervened in both struggles, the issues themselves were neither imperial nor papal, but peculiar and local to Germany. The very principles and practices of medieval kingship, upon which its past policy rested and its future course was keyed, were challenged in this double conflict, and the contribution made to medieval political theory during this duplex battle is of high importance.

Wenerich, archbishop of Trier, attacked Gregory VII for absolving vassals from their allegiance and fomenting the rebellion of the Saxon peasants, and accused him of throwing a double brand of civil war into Germany;[1] Berthold of Constance said that some of the German clergy asserted that neither the Pope nor any other authority could judge a king, however unjust, except for heresy;[2] Duke Berthold of Carinthia is reported to have admitted the justice of the complaints made against Henry IV by the feudality, but urged that these grievances should be submitted to a meeting of the princes.[3] Even the Pope was not at all times clear in his own mind as to the justice of the issues or the justice of his own course;[4] else why did he hesitate for three whole years after the deposition of Henry IV by the rebellious nobles at Forchheim before he acknowledged the act and recognized the counter-king, Rudolf of Swabia?[5] Why did Gregory VII for three years continue to address Henry IV as "king" (rex) and style Rudolf of Swabia a "pretender" (rex dictus)? If the Pope had been actuated solely by ambition and had

---

[1] *Wenricus scholasticus Treverensis, Epp.* 1, 2, 3, 6; *De unitate ecclesiae conservanda,* II, 1. Cf. Carlyle, *History of Political Theory in the Middle Ages,* III, 118–24, 163. Weneric's letters are also in Mirbt, *Libelli de lite,* I, 284–99.

[2] Berthold of Constance, *Annales* (1076), SS. V, 296; *ibid.* (1077), p. 297; Carlyle, *op. cit.,* III, 119, 132.

[3] Lambert of Hersfeld, *Annales* (1073; ed. Holder-Egger), p. 197. For a consideration of the constitutional issues involved in Rudolf's election see Richter and Kohl, *Annalen d. deutschen Gesch.,* III, Part II, 251–57 nn.

[4] See the references in Carlyle, *op. cit.,* III, 94–99.

[5] Berthold, *op. cit.,* SS. VI, 291.

played the game of practical politics he should at once have sided with the revolted baronage and the rebel Saxons. Instead he came perilously near to alienating the Saxons altogether by his delay,[1] and sorely tried the patience of the feudal party in Germany. Why did Gregory VII hesitate? Was his course one of double-dealing? or watchful waiting? or timidity? or scruple?

It was inevitable, as party lines became tauter and the issues clearer, that the rival contentions and opinions should crystallize into sharp-cut propositions. But of more interest is the rapid popular circulation of these demands. The organized nature of the propaganda of both parties is a matter of astonishment. The Cluny reform had already given birth to a widely disseminated polemical literature, but this volume was enormously increased when the struggle between Henry IV and Gregory VII broke out. By a stroke of genius Gregory VII made an appeal to the sentiment of Christendom, and his imperial antagonist forthwith followed his example. The result was the showering of Germany and Italy—France to a less degree—with a pamphlet literature of very great interest and value to the student of history. Those who were able to read were instructed to read these circulars to those who could not read. The diffusion of them was accomplished through the medium of monks and traveling priests, through pilgrims, and even through the use of itinerant merchants. The machinery of the church was far more effective for this employment than the means available to the emperor, and it is not a matter of surprise, therefore, to find Weneric of Trier, one of Henry IV's most ardent supporters, complaining of the success of the papal propaganda.[2] Yet, on the other hand, we find Gebhard of Constance, a devoted Gregorian, inveighing against the political activity among the people of the German

---

[1] Bruno, *De bello Saxonico*, chap. cxii. It is significant that the shortest chapter in his history of the Saxon rebellion is only six lines long, in which he pours out the gall of bitterness upon the papal legates whom he flatly accuses of double dealing and of taking money from both sides. As late as the summer of 1083 Gregory VII positively denied any papal element in the election of Rudolph of Swabia: "Deo teste Rodulfum qui rex ab ultramontanis ordinatus est, non nostro precepto sive consilio regnum tunc suscepisse" (*Reg.*, VIII, 51; Jaffé, II, 503–4).

[2] *Libelli*, I, 293–94.

bishops in Henry IV's behalf.[1] Mirbt, who has edited these controversial tracts, known to historians as the *Libelli de lite imperatorum et pontificum*, assigns eight of these pamphlets to the years 1073–85; sixty-five to the years between 1085 and 1112. The years 1076, 1080, 1081, 1084–86, 1098, and 1112 are especially prolific in the production of these *Flug-schriften*. Fifty-five of the *Libelli* are of German authorship; forty-eight are of Italian origin; a few are French; and one of them is probably of Spanish authorship.

The popular nature of this controversial literature, and the manner in which it was circulated, is a striking evidence of the value and the power attached to collective opinion.[2] It was intended to be read not only by the clergy, but to be read to and expounded to the laity of the time, to nobles, burghers, and even the common peasantry. The pamphlets were produced in multiplied copies in abbey and cathedral schools and disseminated by priests, journeying monks, pilgrims, wandering merchants, at market places, fairs, and wherever concourses of people were met together. The high tide of the controversial literature came not during the most bitter period of the struggle, but following it; after the man who had thrown the age into a turmoil had disappeared from the scene and when vague political theory was beginning to crystallize into new law. This seems to indicate an attempt to mold public opinion.

Manegold of Lautenbach wrote that the works of an opponent were scattered through the streets and public places in many parts of the kingdom. He also speaks of calumnies about the Pope "echoed in streets and shouted in the market

[1] *Ibid.*, I, 270.

[2] Manegold, Preface and chap. lxviii, in *Libelli*, I, 311, 420; Sigeb. Gembl., *Apologia*, chap. ii, in *ibid.*, II, 438. The wide publicity intended to be given to this propagandistic literature is evident from the language employed: ". . . . libellus . . . . undique circumfertur . . . . per plateas et andronarum recessus propalatur; muliercularum textrina et opificum officinae jam ubique personant . . . . ; libellis . . . . longe lateque disseminatis; consiliis et cartis undique missis . . . . errorem totum spargendo per orbem; quamvis undique plateae personent, muliercularum textrinae commurmurent, ... etc." The appeal made to women in these tracts should not escape the psychologist. It is a very early evidence of the value attached to female public opinion and an appreciation of the influence of the quality of religious emotionalism so strong in women, both medieval and modern.

places, and even gossiped about by women at their spinning."[1] This is undoubtedly an exaggeration. Concerning the activities of the Hirsauer monks it is said that "they moved about through the entire country as though they were doctors craftily teaching the common masses."[2] Again we find the schismatic cardinals in a protest charge that their opponents' "books corrupt the earth with heresy, scattering erroneous beliefs far and wide through their followers."[3] That these pamphlets were widely distributed is also evident from the fact that the polemics continually make references to one another.[4] The technique of the production and spread of this propagandistic literature designed to sway public opinion is highly interesting.[5]

Several of the pamphlets have been found in the handwriting of different monks, showing that they were often recopied in different countries. Manuscripts written by Italian monks were circulated extensively in Germany. Many manuscripts were also lost in transit, while others were destroyed when they fell into hostile hands. It is perhaps for this reason that the Gregorian polemics are in the majority, for the followers of Gregory were in a more favorable position to intercept.

Another means of giving the polemics a wide audience was the medieval system of instruction. Nearly every monastery, convent, and cathedral had schools of various degrees of efficiency. Some of them had instructors whose reputation in special faculties was widely known, and scholars eager in search of knowledge traveled extensively from one institution to another. The prevailing educational system gave rise to the wandering students, who often traveled from country to country. Then, too, the church, in order to hold Christendom together, had countless channels for the rapid

[1] *Libelli*, I, 311.

[2] Mirbt, *Publizistik*, p. 96: "qui quasi doctores discurrent per regiones, simplicum mentes versute discipientes."

[3] *Libelli*, II, 406.

[4] Ghellenick, *Revue d. Quest. hist. XCIII*, p. 82.

[5] Mirbt, *Die Publizistik*, pp. 102–21.

conveyance of papal decisions, and other necessary information. Besides the wandering scholars, there were wandering
monks, and traveling merchants, who served as convenient
carriers of polemics in the interest of both Gregory and
Henry.[1] In this bitter war of words calculated to influence
the opinions of men we may readily believe the papacy was
more successful than the secular power, although the imperial
propaganda was of no mean dimension. The very bitterness
of Lambert of Hersfeld's invective against it shows its efficiency.[2] The imperialists seem even to have employed dramatic farce imported out of Italy in ridicule of Gregory VII.[3]
On the other hand, the papal partisans utilized the assertion
of signs and wonders and the machinery of miracles to further
their ends.[4] While much of the argument in these writings

[1] *Ibid.*, p. 108.

[2] ".... varios sermones per populum serebat [p. 187] .... per occultos
indices .... hostes publicos et insidiatores regni qui sub pretextu legationis men-
dacia sua per populum sererent ad sollicitandos animos [p. 213]."

[3] This fact, although it has escaped the observation of every student of the
medieval drama, so far as I know, seems to be certain. It is recorded by Lambert
of Hersfeld (*anno* 1075), p. 253: "Commode quoque conficiendis tantis rebus inter-
venit quidam ex cardinalibus Romanis, Hugo cognomento Blancus, quem ante
paucos dies propter ineptiam ejus et mores inconditos papa de statione sua amo-
verat, deferens secum de vita et institutione papae *scenicis figmentis consimilem
tragediam.*" There is a similar allusion on p. 195. No editor of Lambert has noticed
these observations, nor can I discover them mentioned in either Mirbt, *op. cit.*, or
Dresdner, *Sittengesch. Italiens* Gregorovius, *Gesch. d. Stadt Rom im Mittelalter,* IV,
185 n., says it was "ein förmaliches Pasquill," whatever he may mean by that
term. Bernried, chap. lxvii, says that Cardinal Hugo came with forged letters.
Hugo was an Alsatian by birth. In the time of Nicholas II he was identified
with the anti-papal party in Rome and allied with the Roman nobility against the
papal power. As Hildebrand's influence in the curia grew he turned his coat, and
Gregory VII sent him as his legate to Spain soon after his accession. But in 1075 he
was expelled from the College of Cardinals for espousing Henry IV's cause. We do
not yet know enough about the culture of Italy in the eleventh and twelfth centuries. Dresdner's *Kultur- und Sittengeschichte der Italienischen Geistlichkeit im
10. und 11. Jahrhundert* (Breslau, 1890) is but a *Vorarbeit.*. The history of literary
relation between Italy and Germany also still remains to be worked out with fulness. Paul Bernried corresponded with Italian clerics (*Neues Archiv,* XII, 340 f.;
XIV, 570 f.). Literary production in Germany was more versatile than is usually
thought. There is evidence in the *Vita Godehardi,* bishop of Hildesheim (1022–38),
of religious drama at the beginning of the eleventh century, and Walther of Speyer
sent his work, *De passione S. Christopheri,* to Salzburg-Wattenbach, *Geschichtsq.,* I,
304. Organized book trade dates from the thirteenth century in Germany, and in
Italy perhaps obtained right through from antiquity (Mirbt, p. 121).

[4] See notes in Lea, *op. cit.,* I, 281.

necessarily dealt with questions of theology and canon law, and so went over the heads of the people, on the other hand there were elements in this literature which were designed to appeal to the imagination of the masses and to convince them, such as alleged signs and wonders, miracles, etc. Moreover, a note of popular appeal was struck in the commingling of a coarse, rustic humor, buffoonery, and lampooning with the language of satire and invective.

The most valuable of all these tracts for a study of the new political theory of the state as a body politic united by contract, with the attendant concomitants of popular sovereignty and right of deposition, is one in the form of an open letter entitled *Liber ad Gebehardum*, addressed to the Archbishop of Salzburg of that name and written by a young monk of Lautenbach named Manegold.[1]

The historical importance of Manegold's monograph is that for the first time the whole mass of inchoate and unsettled questions was acutely analyzed and the conclusions systematically formulated. For this reason the tract constitutes a landmark in the history of medieval political theory. Manegold's conclusion may be summarized.

Briefly it was that the temporal power was of divine origin and the office of the king a sacred one, its primary function being to maintain justice; that the king's power, however, was not immediately from God though founded upon the

[1] *Libelli*, I, 310–430. Manegold's arguments are summarized by Mirbt, *Die Publizistik*, p. 233, and by Meyer von Knonau, III, 511–19. Miss M. T. Stead has an excellent article on Manegold in *Eng. Hist. Rev.*, XXIX (1914), 1–15, but she has missed the dissertation of G. Koch, *Manegold von Lautenbach und die Lehre von der Souveränität unter Heinrich IV* (1902), and "Manegold von Lautenbach. Ein Beitrag zur Philosophiegesch. des 11. J.," *Historisch-Politische Blätter*, CXXVII (1901), 389–401, 486–95; and the same author in *Historisches Jahrbuch*, XXV (1904), 168–76; nor does she mention some important earlier literature: Giesebrecht, "Ueber Magister Manegold von Lautenbach und seine Schrift gegen den Scholasticus Wenrich," *Sitz. ber. d. k. bayr. Akad. d. Wiss.*, II (1868), 297 f.; Spohr, *Ueber die politische und publizistische Wirksamkeit Gebhards von Salzburg* (Halle, 1890); Bezold, "Die Lehre von der Volkssouveränität während des Mittelalters," *Hist. Ztschft.*, Band XXXVI (1876); Endres, "Manegold von Lautenbach, modernorum magister magistrorum," *Hist. Jahrb.*, Band XXV, Heft 2 (1904); Paulus, "Nouvelles études sur Manegold de Lautenbach," *Revue Catholique d'Alsace* (1886). The most recent examination of Manegold's writings is by A. Fliche, "Les théories germaniques de la souveraineté à la fin du XIe siécle," *Revue Hist.*, CXXV, 41. Ewald has studied the chronology of Manegold's tracts in *Forschungen zur deutschen Gesch.*, Band XVI, Heft 2.

authority of God, but was derived mediately from the people whom he ruled; that the oath of allegiance was not an obligation which must be unhesitatingly and undeviatingly obeyed by the subject, but a pact which entailed mutual and reciprocal obligations while also conferring mutual and reciprocal rights and privileges; that, in a word, duties and rights were reciprocal and that government was a two-sided relation; that the state rested upon compact, not upon absolute authority; that there is a distinction between king and tyrant, and the latter, *ipso facto*, forfeits his right to rule because of misgovernment; that either the people or the papacy, together or separately, has the right for cause to declare a king's authority void and to depose him and to put another king in his room.[1] For, in last analysis, royal authority rested on delegation by the people.

This theory of the nature of sovereignty, government, law, society, was far and away the most important result of Henry IV's reign, and the greatest and most enduring constructive emanation out of the gigantic struggle. The seminal influence of these ideas now first enunciated may be traced through the succeeding centuries clear down to the Renaissance and beyond. The greatest publicists of the later Middle Ages reflect them in whole or in part—John of Salisbury, Marsiglio of Padua, Liupold of Bebenberg, William of Ockham, Wyclif, Nicholas of Cusa. Overlaid and obscured, even suppressed, by the great monarchical papal-

---

[1] The salient passages in Manegold are quoted in the notes by Carlyle, *op. cit.*, III, 103, 111–12, 136, 162–66. The first English writer to treat of Manegold was Reginald Lane Poole, *Illustrations of the History of Mediaeval Thought* (London, 1884), pp. 229–32. Modern American and English historians are at fault (e.g., Dunning, *History of Political Theories*, pp. 46 f.) in thinking that the compact theory of government began with John Locke, or at most with Hotoman's *Franco-Gallia* and the *Vindiciae contra Tyrannos* in the sixteenth century. Locke owed more to the political theorists of the Middle Ages than is usually supposed. Lambert of Hersfeld is full of allusions to "natural rights," "natural law," etc. (e.g., *humana lex*, p. 99; *jus gentium*, pp. 90, 149, 159; *mos et jus*, p. 119; *lex gentis*, p. 160).

John of Salisbury in the twelfth century went farther than Manegold in the treatment of tyrannical kings, and advocated, not deposition, but assassination. "Imago deitatis, princeps amandus venerandus est et colendus; tirannus, pravitatis imago, plerumque etiam occidendus" (*Policraticus*, VIII, 17; cf. VII, 17 and VIII, 20). See also Gierke, *Genossenschaft*, III, p. 524, n. 16, 565, n. 130; Lane Poole, *op. cit.*, p. 201. The *Policraticus* has recently been translated into English, with a valuable historical introduction, by John Dickinson, under the title: *The Statesman's Book of John of Salisbury* (New York, 1927).

ists and scholastics of the thirteenth century like St. Thomas Aquinas, nevertheless even they borrowed something from the teaching.[1] In spite of his turgidity and lack of arrangement Manegold of Lautenbach is an important figure in the history of the development of European political theory.

The dream of the Salian house of establishing an absolute monarchy in feudal Germany was ruined morally and materially[2] in the great struggle between Emperor and Pope. Despite the fact that the drift of things from the time of the election of Hermann of Luxemburg as new counter-king was away from the Volksaufstand idea and toward a feudo-aristocratic form of government,[3] yet the essential principles of the revolution triumphed with the extinction of the Salian house and the accession of Lothar II in 1125.

The failure of the Salian house to establish a solid royal domain in Saxony, their inability to compel the Saxon nation to come into their system and accept their theory of government, ruined their aspiration to create a strong, compact monarchy in medieval Germany which, if it had been realized, might have anticipated that of Norman-Plantagenet England and that of Capetian France. Without Saxony no greater Germany was possible. With Saxony almost anything was possible.

Those historians of medieval Germany who see German imperialism as the sole axis around which Germany history revolved in the Middle Ages have been inclined to depreciate the character of Lothar II because he made the Italian interests of the crown subordinate to those of Germany, and was wise and just enough to acknowledge that the church, in spite of the portentous temporal claims of the papacy, yet contended for a principle. Lothar II was a constructive compromiser—not a weakling, but a strong man, as prudent as he was just, one who could look at both sides of an issue, who was willing to give as well as take.

[1] For proof of this proposition see Gierke, *Political Theories of the Middle Ages* (Maitland's trans.; Cambridge, 1900), sec. 6, pp. 37–60, and even more valuable, the notes, Nos. 137 and 211.

[2] Walraum of Naumburg, *De unitate ecclesiae conservanda* (1092), is already conscious of this.

[3] Müller, *Hermann von Luxemburg*, p. 2.

He has been condemned for having renounced the "saving clause"[1] in the Concordat of Worms; for yielding to the contentions of the papacy in the matter of the Tuscan lands of Countess Matilda, who had willed them to the Holy See, but which Henry IV and Henry V had held confiscate on the ground that the Countess had been a revolted vassal of the Empire and therefore had forfeited her lands; for his general indifference to the authority and the dignity of the imperial prerogative.[2]

These writers (and it is significant that they are modern ones like Droysen and Sybel and Treitschke, whose laudation of Hohenzollern pretorianism finds a prototype in the imperialism of Frederick Barbarossa) fail to measure the significance of the change which brought Lothar II to the throne. Like Jefferson's "revoluton of 1800" the change of dynasty in Germany in 1125 was a revolution, the triumph of new theories, new principles, and new policies of government.

To Lothar II, Italian and imperial politics were of secondary importance to those of Germany. Home affairs came first. He felt the futility and the injustice of squandering German blood and German treasure in maintenance of German domination beyond the Alps.[3] Within the German kingdom he regarded the old historic and tribal duchies as separate components of one whole, but yet having reserved rights of local independence and an internal polity and economy which it was not the province of the crown to interfere with. In a word, to use American political parlance, Lothar II was a "state rights" man who believed in the preservation of the

---

[1] The last clause of art. 6 of the *Narratio* guaranteeing the "liberty" of the church, and entailing renunciation of the terms of 1122, is a forgery later appended (Doeberl, *op. cit.*, IV, 5 n., 17 n., 18 n.).

[2] See the document in Doeberl, *op. cit.*, IV, No. 6C. The alleged act of homage made by Lothar to the Pope was commemorated by Hadrian IV, who had a picture set up in the Lateran representing it, with a haughty inscription attached. This is what so irritated Frederick Barbarossa in 1155, when the "stirrup episode" occurred (see Watterich, *Pont. Rom. Vitae*, II, 327 f.; Bryce, *Holy Roman Empire* [ed. 1904], p. 169).

[3] Was Bryce thinking of Lothar II when he wrote: "But the real strength of the Teutonic kingdom was wasted in the pursuit of a glittering toy: once at least in his reign each emperor undertook a long and dangerous expedition and dissipated in a costly and ever to be repeated strife the forces that might have achieved conquest elsewhere, or made him feared and obeyed at home" (*op. cit.*, p. 199)?

local sovereignty of the feudal duchies under the crown, and
that historical tradition and just law alike imposed limitations
upon the right of the crown to regulate the internal affairs
of the feudal dukedoms. If Lothar II had lived in the
United States in 1850 he would have been a statesman of the
Old South and would have stood with Calhoun. If that great
Southron had known the history of feudal Germany he would
have found food for reflection in the political theories of the
Guelfs. For the genesis of the contract theory of government
goes back to the tract of Manegold of Lautenbach, the rebellion of the Saxon peasantry, the revolt of Rudolf of Swabia,
and the contentions of Lothar II and Henry the Proud.

The principles of modern constitutional history go back
to the Guelfs. Medieval Germany shares honor with medieval England, in this distinguished particular. The ruin of
the Guelfs by Frederick Barbarossa ruined the principles for
which they struggled, and thus permitted English history to
snatch the glory of creating the first constitutional monarchy
in recorded history. I do not wish to pit the history of
medieval Germany against that of medieval England in the
matter of value and importance. But in the matter of
priority of constructive political development Germany certainly stands first—the first and earliest effective state that
emerged out of the chaos of the ninth and tenth centuries.[1]

An analysis of Lothar II's administration refutes the
charge of weakness and clerical servility[2] His concession
with regard to the installation of bishops forbade investiture

[1] English writers are fond of attributing the honor of creating the earliest
ordered government in Europe since Charlemagne to the Angevin kings. Thus Professor T. F. Tout, *France and England in the Middle Ages*, p. 20, has recently declared: "It was in the Angevin lands that the first adequately administered and
ordered state was established that bridges the gulf between the Carolingian administrative machinery of the early middle ages and the beginnings of quasi-national administration in the England and France of the thirteenth and later centuries."
Elsewhere (p. 64) he writes that the Angevin state was "the most orderly and
effective state that western Europe had known since the Carolingian." I do not
think this is so. The government of Germany under Henry II, Conrad II, Henry
III, Henry IV (after the abuses of his minority had been rectified and the rebellion
during the investiture strife been crushed), was as sound as that of the Norman
kings. And be it noted that the reigns of all these kings except the last antedated
the reign of William the Conqueror and his sons.

[2] See Karl Lessmann, *Die Persönlichkeit Kaiser Lothars II im Lichte mittel-
alterlicher Geschichtsanschauung* (Greifswald, 1912).

until the king had first been paid the homage due from the
bishop's regalia.[1] His theory and his practice were the antithesis of those of the Salian emperors, but they are not to be
condemned because they were different. Lothar II was not
one to abate his prerogative as German king.[2] He bluntly
told Otto of Bamberg that he would confiscate his episcopal
property unless he returned to his diocese. He is the only
German king who possessed any large ideas with reference to
the destiny of Germany beyond the Elbe River. To every
other German sovereign, both before and after him, these
colonial lands were merely a region into which the German
people were expanding and settling; they had no vision of
the great future of Germany there; they made no effort to
build up the royal fisc there. But Lothar II showed a keen
interest in and an understanding of the problem of the
colonial lands in the East, as his appointment of the Praemonstratensian Norbert to the see of Magdeburg and his
promotion of the colonizing foundations of the monasteries
give evidence.[3]

    Lothar II had some perception of the nature of the state
as an abstract political entity distinguishable from the person
and authority of the ruler, a very great advance from what
had formerly obtained. His treatment of the fisc shows this.
Conrad II a century earlier had partly discerned this distinction. But the absolutistic theories of Henry III and Henry
IV had confused the idea of the state with the man who ruled.
The Salians had regarded the crown lands as private property

---

    [1] "Nos [the Pope] igitur, majestatem imperii nolentes minuere, sed augere, im-
peratorie dignitatis plenitudinem tibi concedimus et debitas et canonicas consuetudines presentis scripti pagina confirmamus. Interdicimus autem, ne quisquam
eorum, quos *in Teutonico regno* ad pontificatus honorem vel abbatiae regimen evo-
cari contigerit, *regalia usurpare vel invadere audeat, nisi eadem prius a tua potestate
deposcat,* quod ex his quae jure debet tibi, tuo magnificentio faciat" (*MGH, LL.,*
Sec. IV, 1, 168; Jaffé, V, 522; for commentary, see Friedberg, *Forschungen zur
deutsch. Gesch.,* VIII, 84; Mühlbacher, *Die streitige Papstwahl,* pp. 183 f.; Bernhardi,
Jahrb. Lothar II, p. 478).

    [2] ". . . . pacem . . . . firmiter observari praecepit" (*Annal. Sax.* [1135]), and
cf. the letter of the Emperor himself in Jaffé, *Mon.,* V, 523. The *Chron. Reg. Col.*
(*anno* 1137) is straight to the point: "Merito a nobis nostrisque posteris pater
patriae appellatur quia erat egregius defensor et fortissimus propugnator nihili
pendens vitam suam contra omnia adversa propter justitiam opponere."

    Vita Norberti, SS. XII; Bernhardi, *op. cit.,* p. 92.

and as pertaining to their house, and tended even to regard the kingdom as a gigantic possession with which they might do much as they pleased. This was not the case with Lothar II. The distinction between *Reichsgut* and *Hausgut*, between public and private property, was first clearly formulated by Lothar II at the diet of Regensburg.[1]

The government of Lothar II and the political theories of the Guelfs were the first attempt in medieval Europe to establish a government which aimed in law to give simultaneous and due expression to the rights of the crown, to the rights of the church, to the rights of the feudality, to the rights of the great duchies, and to the rights of the peasantry. It recognized the rights as well as the duties of these different classes of medieval society. It practiced what it preached and preached what it practiced.

The Germany of Lothar II was neither a tyranny nor a rope of sand; it was not a mere agglomeration of feudal provinces given superficial coherence by the overlordship of the suzerain-king. It was an organic union of organic duchies. It was a feudo-federal monarchy. The operation and the extent of the powers of the several elements which formed this state were not defined in written form (for the "constitution," so to speak, was chiefly derived from custom and tradition), although recent events had produced a few important written instruments,[2] and the long conflict in the Salian epoch had developed certain principles in which the rights of the crown, the rights of the feudality, the rights of the church, and the rights of the people were acknowledged and vaguely defined.

---

[1] "Rege apud Radisponam in conventu principum inquirente praedia judicio proscriptorum a rege, si juste forifactoribus abjudicata fuerint vel pro his quae regno attinent commutata, utrum cedant . . . . vel proprietati regis. Judicatum, potius regiminis subjacere ditioni quam regis proprietati" (*Ann. S. Disibod.* [1125], SS. XVII, 23; cf. *Ann. Sax.* [1127], SS. VI, 765), and see Below, *op. cit.*, 185 f.

[2] It must be kept in mind that the German people in the twelfth century were yet largely a rude peasantry, unused to a highly developed or abstract law, and tenaciously adhering to their traditional rights and customs. With them law was almost wholly customary, and they looked with suspicion upon written instruments. ". . . . nec aliis legibus utuntur, sed nec eidem recte utuntur, tanquam gens agrestis et indomita" (*Chr. Ursperg.* [1187], SS. XXIII, 361). "Denique vetus consuetudo pro lege aput Francos et Suevos inolevit" (Rahewini, *Gesta Frid.*, II, 46).

CHAPTER VIII

GUELF AND GHIBELLINE

ONE of the greatest, most critical, most penetrating historical controversies waged in the nineteenth century was that between the eminent Prussian historian von Sybel and the equally eminent Austrian scholar Ficker.[1] Before its conclusion many of the ablest German medievalists had been drawn into the current, and the controversy gave rise to a large amount of new and stimulating historical literature.[2]

The intellectual genealogy of this famous controversy, now become of classical importance in modern historiography, may be briefly summarized. The battle of Austerliz on December 2, 1805, gave the death-blow to that venerable and desiccated medieval antiquity known as the Holy Roman Empire of the German nation, which Voltaire had already in the eighteenth century wittily described as "neither holy nor Roman nor an empire." Then had come the German war of liberation in 1813 and the fall of Napoleon. The effect of this event upon German historiography was great. As Mr. Herbert Fisher has written: "The Napoleonic wars in the realm of fact, and the romantic movement in the realm of fancy, set men seeking for the history of the Germans."[3] The roots of the history of new Germany began to be sought for in the soil of past centuries. Raumer's brilliant *Geschichte der Hohenstaufen* was the first product of the new historical spirit. Later Giesebrecht, who had come out of Ranke's seminar, began to issue volume after volume of his monumental *Geschichte der deutschen Kaiserzeit*. With vast erudition and

---

[1] For a discussion of this controversy see G. von Below, *Der deutsche Staat des Mittelalters* (1914), pp. 353–57; E. Fueter, *Gesch. der neueren Historiographie*, pp. 539 f.; Gooch, *History and Historians in the XIXth Century*, pp. 122–27.

[2] Below, p. 353, n. 6, cites the important literature upon the subject. But see also Herbert Fisher, *Mediaeval Empire*, Vol. I, Introd.

[3] Fisher, *op. cit.*, I, 3.

an almost magic pen—a qualification rare among German historians—Giesebrecht wrote the history of Germany's most glorious and most potent period.

But his eloquent panegyric of medieval German imperialism was not universally accepted. The nineteenth century pulsated with a spirit which had been dormant before 1789 —the new spirit of nationality. The Poles, the Bohemians, the Danes, the Magyars, protested vigorously against Giesebrecht's assertions that the border nations of Germany owed all their civilization and culture to medieval German teaching and example.[1]

But far more important than this protest of minor nationalities was von Sybel's attack upon Giesebrecht. The latter had argued that the union of the German kingship with the imperial crown had been a beneficent event from which both Germany and Italy had derived benefit. Sybel challenged this interpretation, declaring that the effect had been to work injustice to and was disastrous for both peoples; that the event of 962 had diverted the national history of the German people out of its natural orbit, stimulated a false ambition in the minds of the German kings, and entailed the expenditure of an enormous amount of German blood and treasure beyond the Alps to no profitable use. Owing to this vicious tradition the German kings were drawn into the disastrous strife with the papacy, and the German Fürsten encouraged to rebellion against the crown, with the ultimate result that the Hohenstaufen lost the rule of Germany, nor were able to acquire Italy.

The Austrian scholar Ficker flew to the rescue of Giesebrecht in a lecture delivered at Innsbruck entitled "The German Nation in Its Universal and National Relations," in which he argued that the restoration of the Holy Roman Empire was both a medieval necessity and a great historical benefaction.[2] Not Lombardy, but Sicily, destroyed the Ger-

---

[1] Lepar, *Ueber die Tendenz von Giesebrecht's Geschichte* (Prague, 1868). For literature upon the influence of German feudalism upon Poland, Bohemia, Hungary, etc., see Below, *op. cit.*, p. 335 n.

[2] J. Ficker, *Das deutsche Kaiserreich in seinen universalen und nationalen Beziehungen* (1862). It was this famous controversy which first suggested to the late

manic kingship. It was Henry VI's mad dream for Mediterranean imperialism which ruined Germany and the Empire
together.

Unfortunately this controversy acquired a polemical character owing to the strained relations between Prussia and
Austria at this time. But the fundamental question it raised,
namely, the worth and merit of medieval Germany's *Kaiserpolitik*, still remains a live and unsettled issue. Unfortunately
for the discovery of historical truth, in more recent years and
since the initial controversy, the development of German
Weltpolitik and the influence of the so-called "Prussian school
of historians" represented by Droysen and Treitschke took
the German Clio captive, and Hohenstaufen imperialism was
so construed as to give validity to Hohenzollern pretensions.
The Guelfs were represented as factious partisans and Henry
the Lion as a rebel because of his opposition to the imperialistic ambitions of Frederick Barbarossa.

It is high time now to revaluate this historical verdict of
the nineteenth century. In the dimming of the lights of modern kaiserism the great Duke of Saxony is now beginning to
stand forth in true focus, and seen to have been one of the
very greatest of medieval German statesmen, with the exception of Henry IV probably the greatest German between
Charlemagne and Luther. Superficial opinion too often light-
ly assumes, when the weaker goes to the wall in a great
struggle, that his cause was a bad one and deserved to fail.
But reflection not infrequently proves that the victory of the
strong is sometimes morally a barren triumph, and that the
real virtue inheres in the vanquished.

The Germany which emerged from the civil wars of the
reign of Henry IV, like the United States in 1865, came out of
the conflict with certain new principles of government and of

---

Lord Bryce the idea of writing *The Holy Roman Empire*. See my article on "Bryce's
Holy Roman Empire," *Historical Outlook*, XIII (Philadelphia, 1922), 125 f. For further reading see H. Finke, *Weltimperialismus und nationale Regungen im späteren
Mittelalter* (Freiburg im B., 1916); Below, *op. cit.*, pp. 353 f. and his most recent
work: *Die Italienische Kaiserpolitik des deutschen Mittelalters mit besonderem Hin-
blick auf die Politik Friedrich Barbarossas* (Munich, 1927); J. Harttung, *Die Lehre
von der Weltherrschaft im Mittelalter* (Halle diss., 1909); F. von Kampers, *Kaiserpro-
phetien und Kaisersagen im Mittelalter* (1895).

law, which had before been nascent and inchoate. Even though the "constitution" was an unwritten one, there was a body of recognized principles and postulates which together formed a new politico-social organism, a state which, as Burke said of the American colonies, was "in the gristle, if not yet in the bone." The feudal duchies were conceded to have certain intraducal rights which the crown had hitherto refused to admit; in other words, a "states-rights" theory of feudal government had been dimly evolved,[1] and a "strict construction" of the constitution recognized. The field of operation of the powers, both central and local, was defined as never before, and the principle of limitation of the royal prerogative asserted.[2]

The test of the new government came soon after Lothar II's election. Frederick and Conrad of Hohenstaufen were not long in raising the standard of rebellion.[3] They could not dispute the legality of the election. But they put forward a claim, as the heirs of Henry V, not only to his personal property, but also to those lands which had been acquired by the Empire during the whole Salian period.[4] Already the

[1] Witness this remarkable utterance of Henry II given in *Adelboldi Fragmentum de rebus gestis S. Henrici II imperatoris*, chap. xv (Migne, *Pat. Lat.*, CXL, 94): ". . . . Hezelo, Bertholdi filius, quem tempore ducatus sui ultra omnes comites regni hujus ditaverat, legatos quos in ipso exercitu meliores eligere poterat, ad ipsum transmisit [et] ut Bavariensem ducatum sibi concederet, inconsulte rogavit. Sed inconsultae quaestioni consulta paratur responsio, et festinanti petitioni, ponderata monstratur deliberatio. Patienter enim audita legatione ait: Quos semper praecipimus inter omnes gentes, habui quosque semper toto mentis affectu amavi, hos adepta benedictione regali, in lege sua nec deteriorare volo, nec deteriorari patiar, dum vixero. *Legem habent et ducem eligendi potestatem ex lege tenant:* hanc ne dum ego frangam; quicumque frangere tentaverit me inimicum habebit. . . . . Exspectet ut in Bavariam redeam: ibi, si illum eligerint, eligo et laudo; si renuerint, renuo Nec etiam existimo illum esse tantae insipientiae ut ex meo dedecore honorem suum quaerat amplificare." Cf. Thietmar, *Chron.*, V, 8.

[2] I think that as much as this may be inferred from a reading of Otto of Freising, *Gesta Friderici*, I, 20–21, and his *Chronica*, VII, 17–18. Niemann, *Die Wahl Lothars von Sachsen*, p. 18, says: "Wir müssen des halb den Wert dieser Nachricht sehr hochschätzen, zumal Otto, wenn auch ein Verwandter und Verehrer der Staufer, doch durchaus kein Feind Lothars war, sondern diesem und seiner Regierung die höchste Anerkennung zollt."

[3] It was not until 1127 that Conrad, Frederick's brother, raised himself as counter-king (Richter and Kohl, *op. cit.*, III, 2, 657).

[4] "Utrum cedant ditioni regiminis, vel proprietati regis" (*Ann. S. Disob*, SS. XVII, 23). "Fridericus namque, dux Sueviae, et frater ejus Conradus. . . . .

widowed Empress Matilda, who was a daughter of Henry I of England, had managed to spirit away the imperial crown jewels to England as if they were her own private property.[1]

The formidable nature of this claim of the Hohenstaufen may be appreciated when it is said that, if allowed, it would have given them for their own all the feudal lands of the late Countess Matilda in Tuscany, the city and castle of Nuremberg, besides all other lesser domains which had been escheated to or confiscated by the crown during the one hundred and one years of rule of the Salian house.[2] Such a claim, if made today by a prince, would be sufficient to send him to a madhouse. It would be as if the heirs of President McKinley had claimed Porto Rico and the Philippines in 1898 as their inheritance.

Yet monstrous and fantastic as this claim seems to us today, it was not so absurd in the twelfth century. For the Hohenstaufen claim was simply an assertion of the old traditional right of the grosser feudal age which fused *Hausgut* and *Reichsgut* together.[3] As we have already seen, it was only very slowly that this distinction had been made, and the principle was not clearly asserted until the Hohenstaufen forced decision of the issue at the diet of Regensburg. How hardly the older, feudal conception died is manifest. It was far from being obsolete in 1125, although the claim was an anachronism in the light of the progress which the idea of the state, of government, of law, was making.

The war which ensued was of the nature of that "struggle for rights" which characterizes so much feudal strife.[4] In

---

Heinrico imp. decedente, plurima castella et multa alia regii juris sibi vindicantes temeraria potestate, sub principatus sui conditionem hereditario jure usurpaverunt" (*Ann. Sax.*, VI [1125], 765; Otto of Freising, *Chronica*, VII, chap. xxiv).

[1] Roger of Hoveden, I, 181; *Ordericus Vitalis*, XII, 43; Stubbs, *Introd. to Rolls Series*, p. 190; Otto of Freising, *Gesta Friderici*, I, 16; Freeman, *Norman Conquest* (3d ed.), V, 200.

[2] *Monumenta Welforum*, chaps. xvi, xxiv; Otto of Frising, *Chronica*, VII, chaps. xxiv–xxv; Waitz, *op. cit.*, VIII, 40.

[3] Toesche, *Heinrich VI*, p. 20.

[4] *Monumenta Welforum*, chaps. xvii–xxiv. For a brilliant elucidation of this theory of much warfare in the feudal age being a "struggle for rights" see Stubbs, *Seventeen Lectures on Mediaeval and Modern History*, chap. ix.

order to understand it aright one must remember that in
twelfth-century Europe law was not written, but was customary; and tradition was susceptible of various interpretation. Moreover, the distinction between what is public and
what is private in the feudal age was not clear, and the very
idea of the state a hazy conception.

It requires an effort of historical imagination to appreciate the incredible uncertainty and indefiniteness which prevailed in the feudal period with reference to the nature and
extent of political rights.

Every kind of power took on a personal aspect. It was easy to say that
the empire had acquired a territory; but where was the empire? When the
emperor died, what became of the rights which he had held in his hands?
There was no permanent machinery of administration, such as we think
of as essential to the existence of a state. There were frequently long inter-
vals in which the imperial title lay in abeyance. The very idea of an
imperial possession was obscure. Matilda had become a vassal of the
emperor. Did that mean of the empire? If so, where was the person to
whom her lands should offer their service?[1]

The new monarchy of Lothar II weathered the storm of
the Hohenstaufen reaction. But it could not survive the
event of Lothar II's death in 1139. The Guelf principles of
government had hardly sprouted and begun to bear fruit before they were cut down and destroyed. The growth and
development of those principles depended upon the establishment of hereditary monarchy in the Guelf house. By that
alone could they be guaranteed stability and permanence.
The continuity of the principles, the application of the practices, was contingent upon the continuity of the house which
represented them. As in feudal France the evolution of the
absolute monarchy was achieved through the establishment
of primogeniture, so in feudal Germany the nascent form of
state for which the Guelfs stood depended for its endurance upon the hereditability of the dynasty which incarnated
those ideas. For the elective character of the German crown
gave room for the assertion of personal, particularistic, and
reactionary interests not only capable of compelling each
newly elected king to compound with them, but even to ac-

[1] Emerton, *Mediaeval Europe*, p. 276.

quire possession of the crown and so throw the government
back again upon the old rails.

Lothar II perceived this peril and felt that the security
and success of the Guelf ideas depended upon establishing
hereditary succession of the Guelf house. Therefore, so far as
he was able to do, he designed and designated his son-in-law
Henry the Proud to be his heir to the throne. With Saxony
and Bavaria in Germany, and Tuscany in Italy in the hands
of Henry the Proud as king,[1] the rule of Germany might have
been stabilized and the new principles firmly grounded. Upon
two such anchorages as Saxony and Bavaria the superstructure of a new Germany might have been erected as strong, as
permanent, as the French crown, though a government of
different principle and different form.

But fate determined the history of Germany to be otherwise. The Hohenstaufen succession to the throne in 1139
was a reaction against the Guelf political ideas, a reversion
to the older feudal type of state, "red in tooth and claw"
once more.

The medieval German kingdom was the first constructive
state which appeared above the welter into which Europe was
thrown by the break up of the empire of Charlemagne in the
ninth century. The first dynasty which ruled it, that of the
Ottos in the tenth century, put the kingdom upon its feet.
The second, or Salian house, that of the Henrys, anticipated
the French monarchy in unfolding a program and a policy
working toward the establishment of an absolute monarchy.
But the great rebellion of the Saxons and the revolt of the
high feudality in 1075 (two separate and distinct movements
in origin, but which more or less coalesced), combined with
the gigantic struggle between Henry IV and Pope Gregory
VII, which synchronized in time with those two rebellions
and partially fused with them in project and policy, destroyed the Salian dream of German absolutism. Out of the
Sturm und Drang a new theory of government and a new
polity gradually emerged and took more than inchoate form
in the reign of the Emperor Lothar II (1125–39).

[1] ". . . . Princeps . . . . potentissimus . . . . a mari usque ad mare, id est a
Dania usque in Siciliam" (Otto of Freising, *Chronica*, VII, 23).

This political theory was that the German kingdom was a union of historically different but equal feudal duchies, each of which possessed a body of intraducal or "states-rights" (*consuetudines*); that within each duchy these rights were sovereign rights; that though customary and unwritten, these rights were the law of the land within each duchy, and inviolable by the crown. From these historical conditions it was argued that the German kingdom was not rightfully, nor could be, an absolute monarchy. Instead, the tradition of the past and the drift toward the future pointed toward the formation of a monarchical federation, a federal feudal kingdom[1] under a king not with absolute but with limited prerogatives. In terms of political science it might be defined as a *Staatenbund* with a king as sovereign, united by compact or contract.[2]

I do not mean to say that these political ideas were either as clear or as cogently expressed as I have defined them. But they were more than implicit in the Germanic organism. For under Lothar II the German kingdom actually was organized on the lines of, and governed in harmony with, these political ideas. But in order to make the new form of government permanent, the hereditary succession of the dynasty which represented them had to be assured. For only by hereditability could continuity be secured. Lothar II had no son to follow him, and accordingly endeavored to make his son-in-law Henry the Proud, of the famous Guelf family, his successor.

[1] Waitz, *Abhandlungen zur deutschen Verfassungs- und Rechtsgesch.* (ed. K. Zeumer), p. 315, truly says: "Die Verfassung [des Lehnstaates] erhält mitunter etwas von einem föderativen Charakter." For further reading on the federative elements inherent in feudalism see Schröder, *Rechtsgesch.*, pp. 78 and 869; Hinze, *Ztschft. f. Politik*, VI, 488; Below, *op. cit.*, pp. 279, 323-24.

[2] "In Germanic law there was a simple ideal of keeping the peace, of satisfaction of the social demand for general security put in its lowest terms. . . . . The middle ages . . . . thought of the end of law as maintenance of the social status quo by enforcing *reciprocal* claims and duties involved in relations established by tradition and maintained by authority" (Pound, *Interpretations of Legal History*, pp. 30-31). "In the middle ages natural law protected the nations against the caprice of princes and papal power, defended German from Roman law, and upheld the demands of what was reasonable in the face of what had become historical. . . . . *It was vitalized . . . . with the contractual theory of the state*" (Josef Kohler, *Philosophy of Law*, p. 6).

Unfortunately this purpose failed to carry. In the election which followed Lothar II's death in 1139 reaction triumphed, and the former Salian dynasty, under a new name,[1] that of the Hohenstaufen, got the throne, and Germany was thrown back upon the old course. Before the Guelf principles had had time to develop and harden they were thrown into the discard. Unfortunately, the new dynasty, for all the ability its kings displayed, had neither the imagination to understand nor the ethical sense to appreciate the fact that the twelfth century was the dawn of a new epoch in European history.

Conrad III (1139–52) in order to break the Guelf preponderance in Germany sheared off Brandenburg from Saxony and Austria from Bavaria, thus resorting to the old tooth-and-claw policy of the Saxon kings, and thereby imperiled, if he did not ruin, the power of the Guelfs, the only house in Germany with large and constructive ideas of rule.

Worse still, counting upon the land hunger of the lower baronage to support him if there were prospect of spoil for them, Conrad III maneuvered through the *Reichstag* held at Würzburg an *ex post facto* act[2] prohibiting the possession of more than one duchy by any duke. The law manifestly aimed to cut the power of the Guelf to the bone. Henry the Proud was given his choice of retaining either Saxony or Bavaria; he might not have both. When he refused to do so and appealed to the sword he was broken.

His defeat was more than a personal humiliation. For Henry the Proud was not only the private heir of Lothar II; he was the heir of his political ideas. But the principles did not utterly perish, and were the issue in the tremendous conflict between Henry the Lion, the proud Duke's son and successor, and Frederick I, Barbarossa, the second of the

[1] Otto of Freising, *Chron.*, VIII, 23; *Historia Welforum*, chap. xxiv. The Saxon party made a futile effort in the diet at Bamberg in May, 1138, to save the situation (Cont. Cosmas, SS. IX, 144; Jaffé, *Ep. German Fürsten to Archbishop Conrad of Salzburg*, V, 529). Ranke, *Weltgesch.*, VIII, 140, bluntly says: "Für das Reich bedeutete Konrads Erhebung ein öffentliches Unglück. Wenn es die Absicht gewesen wäre, einen unauslöschlichen neuen Krieg in Deutschland anzuzünden, so konnte man es nicht besser anfangen." See also the trenchant comments of von Below, *op. cit.*, p. 354, and D. Schäfer, *Deutsche Gesch.*, I, 273.

[2] *Hist. Welf.*, chap. xxiv.

Hohenstaufen. And although the weaker again went to the wall in 1181 as in 1139, defeat did not vitiate the principles for which the vanquished fought, nor triumph justify the victor. Then, as so many times in history, might did not make right.

What his uncle impaired Frederick I ruined,[1] for his was a "rule or ruin" policy. Infatuated with the grandiose idea of medieval imperialism, he strove to unite more firmly than ever before Germany and Italy, whose destiny really lay along different lines.[2] The Emperor's attempt so to do revived the ancient feud between pope and emperor, and involved him in the bitter and exhausting struggle with the Lombard cities. His ambition cost the German people untold blood and treasure. Frederick I's failure to read some of the most manifest signs of the time seems like stupidity. But his defect was not that. It was a colossal egotism which so warped his brain that he had not the intelligence to understand, the sympathy to tolerate, the new political philosophy, the new economic conditions, the new social transformations which Europe was undergoing. His obstinate adherence to obsolete prerogatives, both in Germany and Italy, his obdurate determination "to maintain the honor of the empire which from the foundation of Rome has been glorious and undiminished,"[3] in a time when the whole drift of European political development was away from the older medieval idea and toward nationalism—all this conduct makes Frederick I, in spite of his brilliant talents and strict enforcement of justice,[4] a dangerous anachronism; but unfortunately he was

[1] Simonsfeld, in an article on the election of Frederick I, *Bayer. Akad. d. Wiss.* (1894), Heft 2, has shown that the Archbishop of Mainz vainly attempted to secure the election of Conrad's minor son instead of his nephew Frederick, in the hope of perpetuating the principles of Lothar II's reign.

[2] A. Cartellieri, *Neue Heidelberger Jahrbücher*, Band XIII, Heft 1, argues that Frederick I's Italian policy was necessary in order to reduce the pretensions of the papacy, and defensive of the interests of Germany. I cannot so read history.

[3] ". . . . Ne honorem imperii qui a constitutione Urbis et christianae religionis institutione ad vestra usque tempora gloriosus et imminutus extitit . . . . (Manifesto, Oct., 1157, *Doeberl.*, IV, No. 35B).

[4] Cf. Hauck, *Kirchengesch. Deutschlands*, IV, 197. It is little wonder that when the anarchy of the great interregnum prevailed the people idealized the stern justice of Frederick I.

not a lean and solemn phantom as anachronisms usually are, but a power terrible to pervert the present and to maim the future.

He came to his imperial duties without any exact knowledge of the difficulties which awaited him, and without any guiding principles beyond those which were afforded by the code of knightly honour and the romantic legends of the empire. To do justice, to keep troth, to humble the rebellious, to protect the weak, to honour the church were honourable ambitions, but insufficient rules for the guidance of a statesman. . . . . Even in 1154 when powerfully re-enforced by Henry the Lion, Frederick could only muster 1,800 knights for Italy. Funds for hiring mercenaries were not available; without the service of the princes he was helpless; and though he had the legal right to demand service under pain of the imperial ban, we only know of two Saxon prelates, out of all his contumacious vassals, against whom he ventured to launch the ban in 1154, and these happened to be mortal enemies of the Saxon duke, his chief supporter. That he was prepared to purchase troops for the Romfahrt at the cost of extravagant concessions is clear from his treaty with Berthold IV of Zähringen concluded in the first weeks of the reign. Not only did he cede the Burgundies as a fief to the Zähringen, but he even promised to assist in reducing them, provided that Berthold would furnish a substantial contingent for the Italian war. . . . . The military assistance of Berthold was eventually secured at a lower price and Frederick obtained Upper Burgundy for himself by a marriage of convenience. . . . . The grant of the Slavonic bishoprics to Henry the Lion is another instance of the recklessness with which Frederick purchased aid for his Italian expedition . . . . though he found a subsequent opportunity of revoking the compact. . . . . But the most decisive proof of Frederick's preoccupation with Italy is afforded by his settlement of the dispute regarding Bavaria. To perpetuate the union of Bavaria with Saxony was in itself a blunder; bad was made worse by the compensation given to Henry Jasomirgott under the Privilegium Minus which created an exceptionally privileged duchy of Austria and gave a precedent for promiscuous claims of the Landeshoheit on the part of the princes.[1]

Frederick Barbarossa little deserves the consecrated shrine which he has found in the hearts of the German people. From Henry IV to Frederick I the German people, strongest in Saxony, had been slowly and painfully, often blindly and intuitively too, for institutions develop unconsciously, working toward the formation of a government which would give simultaneous and due expression both to the rights of the

[1] H. C. W. Davis, review of Simonsfeld, *Jahrbücher* . . . . *unter Friedrich I* (1152–58), in *English Historical Review*, XXIV, 770.

crown and to local rights, the latter being represented by the historical, traditional customs of the several duchies, which actually were each an organic historic entity, and each older than the kingdom, save Lorraine and Carinthia.

Frederick I's caesaristic madness[1] and his mania for application of the Roman law was destructive of the best political traditions of medieval Germany. It is ineffectual argument for his admirers to claim that he never had any intention of introducing the Roman law into Germany, and to cite the decision of 1181 as evidence thereof.[2] For the same man had earlier, in 1165, repudiated German law in the face of the bitter opposition of Worms on the ground of the decrees of his "predecessors." And whom did he mean by the word? Constantine and Valentinian, whose "sacred laws" he venerated as "oracles."[3]

The crowning wrong perpetrated by Frederick Barbarossa was the destruction of Saxony, the greatest and strongest state in feudal Germany, the real cornerstone on which a new Germany in harmony with the spirit of the age and the conditions of the time might have been founded, and representative through the Guelf duke, Henry the Lion, of the new, constructive ideas of government. By the time of Henry the Lion the nascent principles of his house had acquired clarity and substance; they were no longer inchoate political ideas, but practicable realities. He was against abortive and expensive campaigns in Italy, wars waged for the achievement of purposes which were false and ideals which were meretricious. He believed that the great deeds of the German people should be accomplished in Germany, not beyond the Alps. He believed in a forward-looking government, not one that looked backward to ancient Rome or even to Charlemagne for its sanctions. He believed that the feudal state, like all feudal society, was held together by compact; that a king was not of right an absolute monarch, but

---

[1] See Goette, *Zeitschrift f. Kulturgesch.*, Band II, Heft 5 (1895), for the history of this development.

[2] Schäffner, *Das römische Recht in Deutschland*, p. 56.

[3] Weiland, I, No. 227

that he was bound by the rights and liberties of his subjects; that his prerogative was a limited one, and that misgovernment or tyranny justified rebellion. He believed in states-rights for the historic duchies which composed the German kingdom. Finally, as no king in Germany ever had, Henry the Lion possessed a vision of the great destiny of the German people in the New East (like our own New West in 1830) beyond the Elbe River, and labored for its expansion and settlement.[1]

Henry the Lion was not a political theorist nor a metaphysician, in these contentions, like Calhoun. But his political policies have kinship with those of that famous statesman of the Old South. One may find a concrete illustration in his doctrine (if it may be called by so formal a term in the twelfth century) of the preservation of ducal rights, or what I have denominated "states rights" in this feudal age.

The regalia of the dukes represent an example of these rights. The administration of civil and ecclesiastical matters within the German duchies pertained to the duke alone, save in case of counts palatine and bishops, and control of the so-called "royal abbeys." The vassals in each duchy were responsible, as a military force, to the duke; their obligation lay to him and not to the crown. In the matter of the law-making power, Henry the Lion contended that the local *Landtage* had the right—and should have the power—to make all laws necessary and proper for the immediate internal welfare of the duchy.[2]

A conspicuous instance of the difference between the

---

[1] Otto of Freising, though uncle of Frederick Barbarossa, and in general a supporter of Hohenstaufen policy, was too honest a historian not to recognize that the Guelfs in Germany represented a principle. Wilmans well says in the Preface to his edition of Otto's *Chronicle:* "Videmus Ottonem quamvis Stoffensibus imperatoribus arctissimis familiae vinculis obstrictum, tamen medium ut ita dicam inter illam et Welficam gentem obtinuisse locum, ut jure Aeneas Sylvius dicere posset in ipso neque cognationem veritati neque cognationi offecisse."

[2] We have clear reference to the Saxon *Landtage* for the year 1138, and the Guelf policy of favoring them: "Imperatrix Richenza indixit conventum principum in festo purificatione sancte Mariae Quedilingsburg," *Annal. Patherb.* (1138); cf. *Ann. Sax.* and *Ann. Col. Reg.* for the same year. One of the complaints which the Fürsten made against Henry IV was his opposition to convening public assemblies, and his disposition to administer through a group of officials.

Guelf and the Hohenstaufen view of government is afforded by the question of the *Landfrieden*. Henry the Lion claimed that its enforcement was a matter of ducal and feudal juris- diction; Frederick I claimed that its enforcement was a pre- rogative of the crown alone. Another example of difference: Frederick I tried to make Swabian law (his own ancestral law) the supreme law of the land, and to beat down or nullify the traditional and historic law of the several duchies. Yet Saxon law, Bavarian law, Salian law, Swabian law, were each equally old, had obtained for centuries each in its own sphere and among its own people; and each, one might think, had as valid a right to exist in its own region.

On the pretext that the Guelf house was remotely of Swabian origin, although Henry the Lion was of pure Saxon lineage on his mother's side, and the Guelfs though not originally of Bavarian stock had nevertheless been resident in Bavaria for five generations, Frederick Barbarossa contended that Henry the Lion was under Swabian law—a contention which, aside from the fact that the argument was a violent distortion of all precedent, would have put the Saxon Duke utterly at the mercy of his formidable antagonist. It was the old trick of Henry IV, who had tried to practice the same method on Otto of Nordheim; the old ruse which the Hohen- staufen brothers had tried to play in 1125 when they claimed the lands of the fisc as their own as the heirs of the personal estate of Henry V.

All these claims made by the Guelfs, which were of the very cortex of German legal and institutional history, Fred- erick I either traversed or crushed.

The question of Goslar was an added source of friction between Guelf and Hohenstaufen. It was the key to Saxony. In the hands of Frederick it was a menace to everything for which the Saxon nation had struggled in the time of Henry IV, for everything which Lothar II had saved, for everything for which Henry the Lion contended.[1]

It would be an error, no doubt, to assume that these

[1] The close student of modern German history perhaps may detect the per- sistence of the Guelf traditions in the history of Hanover. He will hardly fail to perceive the parallelism between Staufenism and Hohenzollernism.

theories and rights for which the Guelfs struggled were always clearly and sharply defined. But they were more than
inchoate, flabby principles, and of real force and actuality.
Unfortunately, the Guelf cause had not such skilful publicists
as the Hohenstaufen had, and one has sometimes to determine the nature of it by examining the negative side of Frederick I's positive action, by studying his conduct, by judging
what he did of what he had no right to do, by analyzing the
Guelf protests, occasionally by a resort to inverse reasoning
and calculating the probable yet indistinct from the known.
Henry the Lion may frequently have been as much prompted
by instinct as by the logic of the law or the weight of historical
tradition. But even when admitting so much, it is not saying
that the brief for the defendant is a piece of special pleading
and the evidence *ex parte*.

An examination of Frederick Barbarossa's policy toward
the Lombard cities may help to illuminate German history
at this juncture. For it is in analyzing the Emperor's Italian
course that we get the clearest light upon his conception of
his prerogative, since both the documentary and narrative
material is more abundant for the history of Italy than for
that of Germany. Moreover, the difference between the issue
in Germany and the issue in Lombardy is not so great as to
make a comparative study of them unjust.

At bottom the Lombard cities and Henry the Lion were
fighting for much the same principles. Henry fought for the
local sovereignty and the historical rights of the German
duchies. The wish of the Lombard cities was to be assimilated to the status of grand vassals of the crown as collective
or corporate urban feudatories. South of the Alps, as north of
them, the test of the rival principles of Guelf and Hohenstauf-
en was made. The issue was much the same after all allow-
ance had been made for difference in local traditions and in
milieu. Henry the Lion and the Lombard cities were the advocates and representatives of genetic and progressive political and social principles sprung from the womb of feudalism—a self-developing and constructive adjustment of European society to changed conditions. Frederick I, on the other
hand, insisted upon the public law of Europe as it had been

in the time of Charlemagne, Louis the Pious, and Otto the Great, which was equivalent to a denial of the traditional rights and the new liberties for which both the Guelf and the communes asked recognition.[1]

It is not necessary for our purpose to enter into a consideration of the thorny question of the origin of the Lombard towns. We can see the vague lineaments of them as far back as the beginning of the German domination in Italy in 962. When Otto I appeared in the peninsula the nobles, lay and clerical, there as elsewhere in feudal Europe, had usurped the whole body of regalian rights which had once pertained to the Italian crown in the time of the Carolingians. Before the German intervention the whole kingdom was in a state of ruination, and the petty princelings of Northern and Central Italy were quarreling over the spoil and remnants of it.

Otto I made no effort to restore the Carolingian system in Italy any more than in Germany. He was content with regulating the feudal condition he found there, but he did not fundamentally change the régime. In so doing he rendered immense service to Italy. The public order established by the German kings naturally promoted the welfare of the Lombard towns, already beginning faintly to show the influence of the stimulus of commerce and trade. But the Saxon emperors took no hand in the evolution of the towns. They held aloof almost completely from the communal movement. That was an issue between the feudal nobles, ecclesiastical and secular, and the unfree population of the towns. Unless, as at Pavia in the time of Henry II, the townsmen did violence to the prerogatives or the property of the crown (i.e., the local lands of the fisc), the emperors did not interfere, but left the nobles to fight their own battles out by themselves with their rebellious subjects.[2] The Salian emperors, except

---

[1] "Sed cum ea quae vicissim petebantur, ad imperatoris notitiam referrentur, ipse in cunctis modum nimis excedens, et ab ecclesia in spiritualibus postulavit, quod nulli umquam laico inveniretur concessum, et a Lombardis ultra quod Carolus et Ludovicus atque Otto imperatores contenti fuerunt, exegit" (*Vita Alex. III papae*, Migne, *Pat. Lat.* CC, col. 44).

[2] Frederick I complained bitterly of this policy of his predecessors: "Haec [Longobardia] quia propter longam absentiam imperatorum ad insolentiam declinaverat, et suis confisa viribus aliquantum rebellare coeperat, nos animo indignati,

Conrad II in 1037, had been too busy, especially Henry IV and Henry V, with the question of investiture to intervene in Italy, even if they had been so inclined, so that the Lombard cities continued to develop without royal or imperial restraint.

True to the Saxon-Guelf policy Lothar II had not interfered with this state of things. In a diet held at Roncaglia (1136) he impliedly recognized the legality of the consular institution of the Lombard cities, and referred the case of Landulf of St. Paolo to the College of Consuls (*coetus consulum*) at Milan. In the Emperor's eyes the consular colleges in the Lombard cities formed courts of first instance from which an appeal lay to the imperial tribunal. Conrad III had never appeared in Italy, and during his reign the Lombard cities, from the point of view of the public law of Europe, had acquired a status as legitimate as customary law could give them.

Thus when Frederick Barbarossa came to the imperial throne a complete revolution in the political condition of North Italy had taken place. It would tax the ability of a modern historian better to describe this condition than did Otto of Freising. His account is as sound and fresh and clear today as when it was written:

> Almost the whole country pertains to the cities, each of which forces the inhabitants of her territory to submit to her sway. One can hardly find, within a wide circuit, a man of rank or importance who does not recognize the authority of his city. . . . . . They surpass all other cities of the world in riches and power; and the long-continued absence of their ruler across the Alps has further contributed to their independence. . . . . Although they boast of living under law, they do not obey the law. . . . . Among all these cities Milan has become the leading one. . . . . The bishop of Asti and William, marquis of Montferrat, a noble and great man [are] almost the only princes in Italy who have kept themselves independent of the cities.[1]

A careful analysis of this excerpt will make evident that the Lombard communes were the product of a slow, double

---

etc." (*Proem. Gesta Friderici*). "Deinde [the allusion is to the second diet of Roncaglia] super justitia regni et de regalibus, quae longa tempora seu temeritate pervadentium seu neglectu regum imperio deperierant" (Radevic, II, 5).

[1] *Gesta Friderici*, II, 13–15.

revolution. In a socio-economic sense these townsmen had risen out of serfdom and become freemen, burghers, through increase of wealth accumulated by industry and commerce. In a political sense the Lombard cities had emerged out of the débris of the ancient count administration, assumed the prerogatives and functions of those vanished officials of the Carolingian time, and established and practiced self-government. The key to this change is found in the office of the consuls in each city. This elective office was the keystone of their municipal structure; it was the palladium of their liberties.

The communes energetically asserted the right of self-government in this particular, and Frederick I as energetically denied it. From the point of view of ancient law Frederick I was theoretically right, if one goes back far enough. He stood upon the letter of the law. But the cities stood upon the new spirit, the new condition born out of that spirit, the new tradition which in their eyes had supplanted the older tradition. They based their claim upon custom, alleging what was quite true, that they had enjoyed the right to elect local magistrates since the time of Henry III and Henry IV.[1]

But there was no room in Frederick Barbarossa's political or social philosophy for these city republics of burghers, who claimed the right to be recognized as corporate feudatories of the Empire. Both the principle raised by the new condition and the magnitude of it shocked him. How could descendants of serfs become vassals when the very status of vassalage implied nobility of birth? How could a collective group become a feudatory? Personal vassals Frederick could understand. Group or corporate vassalage was beyond his perception. It is true that already in Germany there were some free burghers, but not free cities, to say nothing of whole provinces, as in Lombardy, composing city republics

---

[1] Muratori, *Ant. Ital.*, IV, 261A (oath of the Lombard League); *MGH*, IV, 169 (*Pacta Placentina, petitio societatis*); *MGH*, *LL*, II, 151 (peace overture of the cities, Art. 2); *ibid.*, IV, 175 (Peace of Constance, Arts. 1 and 22, *consuetudines*). Frederick's total incapacity to understand the real issue in Lombardy is shown in his appeal (1155) to the German princes (*ibid.*, *Leges*, II, 99): ". . . . Quia Mediolansium superbia jamdiu caput contra erexit imperium, ne gloriam nostram plebs improba usurpare vel conculcare valeat."

and a thronging urban population capable of putting a formidable army of town militia into the field.

Noluimus hunc regnare super nos, nec Teutonici amplius dominabuntur nostri ("We will not have him to reign over us, nor the Germans to rule us more"), declared the towns. *Maluimus honestam mortem inter hostes* ("Better a brave death among enemies than that"), declared Frederick.[1] Neither peace nor compromise was possible between two such antipodal points of view.

After years of wasting war, in the Peace of Constance in 1183 the Lombard cities finally won recognition of themselves as grand corporate vassals of the imperial crown. The oath of the Lombard delegates was a feudal oath; the investiture of their consuls a feudal investiture; the communes henceforth had the status of the great feudal duchies, as sovereign states with local, internal sovereignty under the crown. Their form of government differed from that of the duchies, but their legal relation to the Empire was identical with that of the duchies. The principle of states rights had triumphed in them. The Lombard cities won in Italy the principle for which Henry the Lion vainly struggled in Germany, and as the victory of the former spelled progress for Italy, so the defeat of Henry spelled reaction and retard for Germany.

But we have not yet reached the term of consideration of this issue between Guelf and Hohenstaufen. Even if we admit the legitimacy of Frederick Barbarossa's contention respecting the sovereignty of the crown, the degree of that sovereignty and the conditions of its exercise still remained a fair subject of debate in Germany, unless it be admitted out of hand that the crown was a 100 per cent absolute monarchy, which would not be true either in law or in fact and would make Henry the Lion nothing but a mere rebel. Positive law may be legitimate in principle, but the degree of acceptance of that law yet be subject to definition.

In a justly organized state both sovereignty and liberty require definition, guaranties, and sanction. Frederick I offered no guaranties, no sanctions, as security for the justice

---

[1] *Curia Roncaliae* (1159), *MGH*, IV, 116.

of the state against the power of the state. Sovereignty to him was the supremacy of his independent, unhampered will. His clemency was the only security of the subject against his power. Frederick I took his stand on the revived Roman law, which tended toward absolutistic concepts of royal prerogative. Henry the Lion appealed to the traditional, active, living feudal law of his time, which fostered liberty and the recognition of individual rights.

How vital was the principle at stake between these two, between the Guelf and the Hohenstaufen parties, may be seen by a glance at English history at this time. The struggle between English customary, traditional liberties and Norman-Plantagenet tendency in the twelfth century offers a parallel to that which was happening in Germany. Stephen stood for the maintenance of old English liberties; Henry Plantagenet, for Roman absolutism.[1] For Roman civil law, introduced into England by the canonists after 1066, within little more than a generation had become so great a menace to English traditional rights and liberties that Stephen silenced Master Vacarius, the chief teacher of it, and suppressed his books.[2] It was as Liebermann describes:

> The political instinct of the English government, influenced more than ever before or after by the lay baronage, stood up for the Teutonic feudal law of the Anglo-Normans against the decrees of Roman popes and emperors. The foreign foe . . . . opposed systematic jurisprudence to unwritten customs. It was neither the first nor the last time that the barons replied to canonistic pretensions. *Noluimus leges Angliae mutari.*[3]

In essence Henry the Lion was struggling for the same principle for which the barons contended with John at

[1] "The writer of the *Tractatus Eboracensis* under Henry II developed a theory of royal omnipotence by divine right as complete if not as systematic as that which we shall have to consider later" (Figgis, *Political Thought from Gerson to Grotius*, p. 13).

[2] John of Salisbury, *Policraticus*, VIII, 22. For this instance, and the general subject of the introduction of Roman law into England at this time, see Liebermann, "Master Vacarius," *English Historical Review*, XI, 305 f.; Holland, *ibid.*, VI, 244; and his article on Vacarius in *Dict. Nat. Biog.*, LVIII, 80 f.; Pollock and Maitland, *History of English Law*, I, 99; Rashdall, *Universities*, II, 335 f.

[3] Liebermann, *op. cit.*, p. 310. For Lanfranc's instrumentality in promoting these absolutistic influences by means of forged documents see Boehmer, *Die*

Runnymede. A reference to the twelfth and fourteenth articles of Magna Carta will help to make this clear. That instrument is a summary and definition of the political franchises of the English people. The barons admitted the king's right to levy aids and impose scutage, but the charter adds:

No scutage or aid shall be laid on our realm except by the common counsel of our realm. . . . .

And to have a common counsel of our realm on assessing an aid . . . . we will cause to be summoned archbishops, bishops, abbots, earls and greater barons singly by our letters, and we will also cause to be summoned in general by our sheriffs and bailiffs, all those who hold of us *in capite*, at a certain day, to wit, at least forty days after, and a certain place; and in all letters we will express the cause of summons, and when the summons is made the business assigned for the day shall proceed according to the counsel of those who are present, though not all who are summoned come.

These were the guaranties. The barons were faithful to English feudal traditions as Henry the Lion strove to be loyal to German feudal traditions, which Frederick I, deeply imbued with the theories and the practices of the Roman law, aimed to suppress and efface. The English King was compelled to give guaranties for the exercise of his sovereignty. The German King refused to do so. He was obdurate and evasive in the matter of sanction, and without sanction law and liberty are whimsical or arbitrary. But in Magna Carta we find that sanction; Articles 39 and 40 read:

No freeman shall be seized or imprisoned or disseized or outlawed or exiled or injured in any way, nor will we enter on him, or send against him except by the lawful judgment of his equals or by the law of the land. . . . . We will sell to no one or deny to any one or put off right or justice.

If Henry the Lion had been backed by the bishops and princes of Germany in the cause for which he fought as the English baronage and bishops were united in support of English traditional rights and liberties (*consuetudines*), as they had grown up out of feudalism, Germany would have laid

---

Fälschungen Erzbischofs Lanfranks von Canterbury, pp. 82 f. For John of Salisbury's argument for the superiority of intelligent, reasoned law over customary law see *Policraticus*, V, 16.

the foundations of a future constitutional monarchy in 1181 as England did in 1214.[1]

But fate determined otherwise. The German bishops and small nobles had been so long fed on the spolia of the church and the regalia which the Hohenstaufen had bartered away in order to purchase their support, that their hunger for lands knew no limit. When Frederick Barbarossa offered them the spoil of the Guelf lands, the whole of the great duchy of Saxony as the price of their assistance against Henry, the ravenous pack charged upon the Lion and dragged him down. He was a noble quarry, and the depth of his fall is measured by what the ruin of his ideas meant for Germany, by what the partition of Saxony entailed for Ger-

[1] The *Sachsenspiegel* even asserted that the Pope could not issue decretals in prejudice of local laws and institutions (Lea, *History of the Inquisition*, II, 349). It hardly need be said that in instituting this comparison with Magna Carta I am regarding that instrument in the light of its own time and not as the palladium of liberty which the legists of Coke and his school represented it to be, who in their conflict with the Stuart kings attributed to it a constitutional importance which it did not possess. The practical effects of Magna Carta did not extend beyond the fourteenth century. Article 39 insisted not so much upon a particular form of judgment as upon the necessity of protection against the arbitrary acts of King John which violated the customary law of England; it was of interest not only to the barons, but to all *liberi homines* who invoked the common law and demanded strict observance of the *consuetudines* of Englishmen by the crown. The guaranties exacted of the King by the barons in 1215 are precisely of the nature of those for which Henry the Lion struggled and failed to secure. He asserted the right of revolution against royal tyranny exactly as Magna Carta asserted it. Frederick I, like King John, claimed to rule as an absolute sovereign—a claim which both in England and Germany was declared to be contrary to "the law of the land." The difference lies in the fact that in Germany the effort failed, while in England it succeeded. A comparative study of the constitutional development of Germany and England in the twelfth century is very instructive. I borrow the subjoined quotation from a review by Mr. H. C. W. Davis (*Eng. Hist. Rev.*, XXIV, p. 772) of Dr. Simonsfeld's *Jahrbuecher unter Friedrich I*: "The Landfriede ordinance in fact is chiefly valuable as a record of the new legal principles which were shaping themselves in the minds of German statesmen at this period . . . . for example, the idea that the legal rights and duties of the knightly class ought to be distinguished from those of the peasants, but that no such distinction need be drawn between the free and the unfree. Following a hint of Jastrow-Winter, Dr. Simonsfeld suggests that the Landfriede edict may profitably be compared with the English law of the same period. He might with advantage have followed up this train of inquiry. The 6th art. of the Landfriede edict anticipates to some extent the measures of Henry II against criminous clerks just as the imperial constitution of 1157, restraining appeals to Rome, anticipates another clause in the Constitutions of Clarendon. The 7th art., which provides for the extradition of criminals who escape from public justice by fleeing into a seignorial borough, reminds us of the powers given to the sheriff in the Assize of Clarendon,

many. The splendid duchy was torn into a tangled mass of jarring clerical and petty lay principalities. The last chance for achieving the unity of Germany was lost.

Frederick I's "kaiserism" ruined Germany and destroyed the most progressive and constructive political ideas to which feudal Germany gave birth in the Middle Ages. Like all shortsighted politicians, he won the point for which he aimed. But it was not worth fighting for. He staked everything on it, and Germany was all but ruined by his victory.

History has done tardy justice—if so much—to the aims and purposes of Henry the Lion. When the "New Germany" now on the way comes to re-read her past history Henry will come into his own. Instead of the slow realization of a federal feudal monarchy, based upon institutions vivid and helpful, the expressions of the essentially healthy things which were in feudalism, medieval Germany fell into chaos in less than a century.

To one who feels the greatness of the history of medieval Germany and realizes that the destruction of Henry the Lion and the dismemberment of the glorious duchy of the north at the hands of Frederick I entailed the loss of Germany's political unity, the reckless waste of German blood and treasure, the perversion of her rightful destiny to wrong ends, the wrenching of her out of her natural historical orbit into a path strewn with dragon's teeth and incumbered with thorns, the territorial reduction of the kingdom to a thing of shreds and patches, the tyrannical rule of a swarm of petty

---

although the German measure characteristically shows greater respect for the lord's privilege. The 11th art., empowering counts to fix the price of corn at the Nativity in each year, after consultation with seven men of good report, may be compared with the English Assize of Bread. The 12th art., if understood to prohibit the wearing of arms by men of the non-feudal classes, corresponds to the edict of Henry II 'that no man should carry arms on this side of the river Severn.' Dr. Simonsfeld, it is true, thinks that the German law forbade the *possession* no less than the wearing of arms, in which case the difference between the views of the English and the German legislator would be as great as we can imagine. . . . . It is not to be supposed that these coincidences, remarkable though some of them appear, are due to deliberate imitation on the part of English lawyers. But they may serve to remind us that English legal development cannot be understood without the employment of the comparative method. The principles which we associate with the name of Henry II were in the air before he entered upon his career of legislative reform."

feudal barons as narrow and brutal as they were politically
incapable and morally ignoble—when one realizes, I say, that
all these things were poured out like a witches' broth on Germany because of Frederick I's exaggerated egotism, which
brooked no opposition, tolerated no other ideas than his own,
then one is divided between sentiment of wrath for the victor and sympathy for the vanquished.

Frederick I and the late Kaiser Wilhelm were fellows of
the same school, and had much the same psychology. The
latter's speeches ring curiously like those of Frederick I
as found in Otto of Freising and the Lombard chronicles.
Egotism, megalomania, *Weltmacht*,[1] obsessed them both—and
both in the event ruined the Germany which they ruled.

The fall of Henry the Lion in 1181 not only marks the
passing of the last of the great historic duchies of feudal Germany; it marks further the last chance which Germany had
of becoming a strong national monarchy, which might have
spared her the anarchy of the interregnum in the thirteenth
century and the praetorianism of Prussia in the twentieth
century.[2]

Modern German historians, imbued with Hohenzollern
imperialism and fascinated by Hohenzollern praetorianism,
have exalted the merits of Frederick I and depreciated those
of Henry the Lion. The time has come for Germany to revaluate her past history. When she does the Lion of Brunswick will come into his own and tardy reparation will be done
his memory.

The lower nobles of the land, some of them of parvenu
origin, who had been raised to power by the Salian policy,

[1] O. von Heinemann, *Braunschweigisches Magazin*, Vol. I (1895), makes much
of Henry the Lion's opposition to the establishment of universal monarchy as an
element of Frederick I's hatred of Henry the Lion. The rebellion of Saxony in 1193
against Henry VI was rooted in this feeling (Bloch, *Forschungen zur Politik Kaiser
Heinrichs VI in den Jahren 1191–1194* [Berlin, 1892]).

[2] Arnold of Lübeck opens the third book of his *Chronica Slavorum* with the
verse in Judg. 21:25: "In those days there was no king in Israel: every man did
that which was right in his own eyes," and follows it with a picture of anarchy which
anticipates that of the interregnum. If the words put in the mouth of Frederick I
by Arnold of Lübeck [II, 1], were truly said to Henry the Lion, then the brilliant
Hohenstaufen added hypocrisy to his other faults, although it is difficult to believe
that insincerity was one of Frederick I's vices. For Frederick was usually forthright,
and not given to deception. The issue between the two was a clear-cut and definite
one, and neither was disposed to hedge or to compromise.

or had usurped it during the anarchy of Henry IV's reign, saw in Henry the Lion the menace to their own selfish ambitions. The clergy, especially the bishops, who had become princely in station since 1122 and had been fed upon the strong meat of secular power, were hostile to him. Henry the Lion's power and great wealth were his undoing. He had been confronted at different times by coalitions of the nobles and bishops against him, the most formidable of which was that in 1166 headed by Rainald of Dassel (archbishop of Cologne), Archbishop Hartwig of Bremen, Wichmann (archbishop of Magdeburg), and Bishop Hermann of Hildesheim.[1]

The intervention of Frederick I had saved him then, for his support was necessary to the Emperor and Henry had participated in Frederick's Italian campaigns, though his judgment was against them. Whether Henry did or did not withdraw his vassals from the battle on the day of Legnano is of little matter. Henry's doom was sealed the moment the Italian question was settled. After the Peace of Venice in 1177 and Frederick's reconciliation with the Pope, the Emperor had no more use for Henry. He had tolerated and even protected Henry when it was expedient for him to do so. When the hour for his use had passed, Frederick ruined him. Henry the Lion was the victim of an imperial theory imbued with the madness of caesarism, of an almost criminal political ambition, of envy of his great wealth, of personal malice toward him.

No event in the history of medieval Germany is so charged with the elements of tragedy as the fall of the Guelf house. The drama has the imaginative fire and the tremendous scale of *Die Götterdämmerung*. Henry the Lion is the Siegfried of German history, without the loyal vassals which that hero possessed who silently raised the body of the fallen leader and bore it on their shields across the distant hills. The Volsung-motif, the sword-motif, and the Siegfried-motif are all in the drama, if only one reads aright the pages of history and has the spiritual discernment to hear the deep undertone amid the percussion of conflicting ideas and the clangor of arms. Wagner's *Twilight of the Gods* may well be regarded as a funeral oration in music over Henry the Lion.

[1] Helmold, *Chron. Slavorum*, II, 6–7.

But—one may say—was the Guelf solution possible? Could Saxony have extended her sway over the rest of Germany, imposed her will upon reluctant duchies, ruled all Germany, and at last molded the kingdom into a new and national form? Of course no absolute answer can be given to this objection, for the reason that the Guelf experiment was never fairly or fully tried. It was hardly given form before it was ruined.

Feudalism had its weaknesses as well as its virtues It may be that the weaknesses inherent in German feudalism might have militated against the firm establishment of the Guelf form of government. History shows that in spite of its admitted virtues, feudalism was incapable of founding a state upon the bases of fidelity and the sense of justice of the seignior. Justice and law had to have higher authority and a different sanction. The ideals of chivalry and the chansons of the troubadours might laud in vain the feudal state as the perfect state, feudal society as the perfect social structure.[1] Unfortunately, the men of the feudal age were not abstract paragons of virtue, but flesh-and-blood human beings whose virtues (when they had them) were traversed by their vices and their wickedness. It is easier to found a state in which all shall be subject to the will of a single prince than to hold a society together by ties of mutual right and mutual privilege—in a word, to establish a state without a strong central authority, but based on mutual contract. Perhaps this is the reason why the French monarchy succeeded and the German monarchy failed.[2]

The problem of all government is to give simultaneous and due expression to the aspirations, the rights, and the needs of the central and the local interests.

[1] The following passage illustrates the utopian nature of German chivalry: "Cujus mors genti Teutonicorum omnibusque Germanie populus lamentabilis sit in eternum quia aliarum terrarum divitiis eos claros reddidit, terroremque eorum omnibus in circuitu nationibus per virtutem bellicam incussit eosque prestantiores aliis gentibus nimirum ostendit futuros" (SS. XX, 328).

[2] See the exceedingly wise and keen observations of Lot, *Huguus Capet*, p. 236, n. 2, and p. 245, nn. 1, 2, 3; cf. Luchaire, *Manuel*, pp. 219–34. The feud of the Abbot of Fulda and the Archbishop of Cologne at the great diet of Mainz in 1184 shows the emptiness of Frederick I's pretensions to power and authority. See Arnold, *Chron.*, III, 8. The passage is translated in Fisher, *op. cit.*, I, 339–40.

CHAPTER IX

GERMAN FEUDALISM

WHILE the roots of the history of feudal Germany may be traced as far back as the time of Charlemagne, and beyond, it is unnecessary for the purpose of this chapter to go farther back than the dissolution of the Carolingian Empire in the ninth century. In the awful crucible of that age, a period of vast disintegration of political and social institutions within, combined with attack from without by formidable enemies like the Norsemen and the Magyars, Central and Western Europe was transformed. A new polity and a new society emerged out of the vortex.

But the process of change was not simultaneous in France and Germany; it was not accomplished in equal degree everywhere, nor did it result everywhere in establishing identical conditions. While feudalism became universal in medieval Europe, the local variations and differences between French feudalism, English feudalism, German feudalism, and Italian feudalism are often so great that the four forms may usually be studied more profitably by contrast than by analogy.

Roughly speaking, the process which began in France as early as 814 affected Germany but slightly until 887, except in the lower Rhinelands. The deposition of Charles the Fat in 887 and the accession of Arnulf was the real turning-point of German history. From that date forward the old Carolingian régime rapidly dissolved, and a new, more feudal form of government and structure of society took its place. This process of transformation may be said to fill the reigns of Arnulf and his son, Ludwig the Child (d. 911), the last eastern Carolingian; the abortive reign of Conrad I (911-19); and the reign of Henry I (919-36), the first Saxon king, by whose time a new Germany had been formed, a new kind of government, a new social texture, which harmonized with the spirit and the condition of the new age.

The enormous disarray which characterized the history of Western Europe in the ninth century was less ruinous to Germany than to France. The German kings were made of sterner stuff than those across the Rhine. The invasions of the Norsemen had only menaced the lower Rhinelands, and were not nearly so prolonged in Germany as in France. The chief danger was along the eastern border, where Slavonic and Magyar pressure, even before the notable military reforms made by Henry the Fowler, had their influence upon the development of predial serfdom and the growth of feudal practices.[1]

Germany in the ninth century had a solidity which France did not possess. Actual anarchy such as prevailed in France almost continuously from the time of Charles the Bald (840–77) to the time of Louis VI (1108–37) is not found in Germany except during the minority reign of Ludwig the Child.[2] It is true that the reign of Conrad I, his successor, was fraught with violence; yet the power of the church and the strength of the great dukes in some measure compensated for the weakness of the crown.[3]

Germany being less exposed to attack from the outside and possessed of a firmer texture within than France, German feudalism did not become as hard and set a system as was French feudalism. "Old" France crumbled away in the ninth and tenth centuries; "old" Germany, anchored to the ancient duchies which remained intact, retained its integrity. The tribal dukes recognized the office of the king, but they did not admit that they held their duchies of the crown, or that they held their lands of the king, even when such lands had the aspect of fiefs. The German nobility always included a large number of landed nobles who regarded their possessions as huge allods which they might partition as fiefs when it so pleased them; but they rhetorically called their

---

[1] Waitz, *Jahrb. Heinrich I*, p. 63; Hauck, *Kirchengeschichte Deutschlands*, II, 686, n. 6; Sommerlad, *Die wirtschaftliche Tätigkeit der Kirche in Deutschland*, II, 226.

[2] Waitz, *Deutsche Verfassungsgeschichte* (2d ed.), V, 59 ff. Cf. the elegy upon Salomon, bishop of Constance, in *Mittheil. der Antiq. Gesellschaft in Zürich*, XII, 233, vss. 117 f.

[3] Waitz, *DVG*, V, 65–66.

own great fiefs *Sonnenlehen*, or "sun fiefs," in order to express their complete freedom—they held only of the sun.[1] Fiefs of the sun (*Sonnenlehen*) were originally allodial seigniories, and it was because of the penetration of feudalism everywhere that they were thus assimilated with fiefs.

The power of the great German dukes had been formed during the troubled times of Arnulf and his son. The separate German "nations," Franks, Swabians, Bavarians, which had developed into dukedoms under the Merovingians (Saxon ducal development originated in Charlemagne's time), and had been suppressed but not extinguished by Charlemagne, rose again into newness of life. With the break-up of the Empire came a recrudescence of ancient tribal consciousness. The grouping of the various German "nations" was instinctive and pronounced.[2]

The rise of the stem-dukes whom Charlemagne had so coerced was the result of the instinctive and spontaneous rally of the German people, owing to the stress of the time, around their natural and historical tribal representatives.[3] In Saxony especially the ducal movement was strong, for

[1] Later these *Sonnenlehen* came to be called *Fahnlehen*, or "banner-fiefs," because investiture was conferred by a *vexillum*, or "banner." At first only the duchies were of this rank, then margraviates, and finally any princely fiefs. Its gift conferred the right to levy military service of vassals, hence the saying: "*Es erhöhet nichts des Mannes Schild denn Fahnlehen.*"

[2] Arnold of Bavaria assumed the title of "duke by the grace of God"; *Vita Oudalrici*, chap. iii (*MGH*, SS. IV, 389). Under Henry I the dukes coined their own money, convoked assemblies, administered justice, and controlled the church within their territories (Waitz, V, 72; Hauck, *op. cit.*, III, 8–9; Lamprecht, *Deutsche Geschichte* [3d ed.], II, 127). When Conrad I put Adalbert of Babenberg to death in 906 his people were furious (Regino, *Chronicon* [*anno* 906]). The position of the great dukes in the tenth century really represented a reversion to the type of duchy which prevailed in Merovingian times. The dukes had then exercised all the rights of sovereignty as dukes, and not as Frankish officials, although they depended upon the Merovingian crown. Royal confirmation was mingled with popular choice and quasi-hereditary right. In Swabia and Thuringia the dukes had to pay tribute and to follow the king in war. The fall of Tassilo in 788 ended this ancient status, and during the reign of Charlemagne the duchies were practically administrative provinces of the Frankish empire. When the empire went to pieces the duchies emerged and resumed their old condition once more. See Bornhak, *Forschungen zur Deutschen Geschichte*, XXIII, No. 3.

[3] Henry II in 1002 recognized this local feeling in the German duchies when he refused the demand of Henry, count of Schweinfurt and margrave of the Bavarian Nordgau, that he be made duke of Bavaria. The King said: "Nonne scitis . . . . Bawarios ab initio ducem eligendi liberam habere potestatem; non decere tam subito

there the ancient Germanic tradition was less impaired than elsewhere.[1] The stem-dukes were only able to reappear after the collapse of the Carolingian system. The same thing is true of the German nobility, which had disappeared during the sixth and seventh centuries and been supplanted by Frankish officials. When the latter vanished, the old nobility came up.

At this moment when the old German duchies arose once more the territory of Germany was not divided into a swarm of petty sovereignties as in France. The power of the great dukes still rested upon a considerable body of freemen who cultivated the soil in person, upon some vassals without fiefs, upon certain local officials such as counts and *centenarii*. In a word, in Germany until the end of the ninth century much of the Carolingian régime persisted. In France, on the other hand, all the ancient political and social bonds were loosed and new ones had to be formed in order to save the country from utter dissolution.[2]

When the power of the crown was reduced to impotence under Charles the Bald private enterprise or usurpation stepped in and performed the functions of government.[3] When the cry arose for protection against invading Norsemen in the north and foraying Saracens in the south, the land of France began to bristle with feudal castles. By the year 1000 the horizon of every province of France was fretted with looming bastions profiled against the sky.[4]

---

eos abicere neque constitutionis antique jus absque consensu eorum frangere? Si voluisset exspectare usque dum ipse ad has regiones venirem, cum communi consilio principum eorundem ac voluntate sibi libenter in hoc satisfacerem" (Thietmar of Merseburg, *Chron.*, V, 14).

[1] Waitz, *Jahrb.*, p. 9; *DVG*, V, 43.

[2] For details of this history see Guilhiermoz, *L'origine de la noblesse en France au moyen-âge*, p. 143 and notes; Flach, *Les origines de l'ancienne France*, Vol. II, Book III, chaps. vi–viii; and my article on "The Commerce of France in the Ninth Century," *Jour. Pol. Econ.* (November, 1915).

[3] "Damit ist das Staatswesen feudalisiert" (K. von Amira, *Grundriss d. German. Rechts* [3d ed.], p. 156). "Von den letzten Karolingern an datiert die Verfassung die wir als Feudalstaat bezeichen" (Below, *Der deutsche Staat des Mittelalters*, p. 350).

[4] See the striking descriptive paragraph in Ferdinand Lot, *Hugues Capet*, pp. 236–37.

Inchoate feudalism first crystallized in France into a form of government and a structure of society by the union of the benefice or fief with vassalage, and adoption of the principles of recommendation and homage.[1] In Germany the benefice was long unknown.[2] Great lay and ecclesiastical proprietorships were first developed in France, especially in old Neustria.[3] In Germany both forms were chronologically of later origin, and when formed were technically different from the French practices. In France feudalism was rapidly militarized as the result of chronic conditions of warfare. In Germany the old German *Heerban* survived for centuries, and when the art of war at last became feudalized, the conditions were very different from those prevailing in France. The earliest instances of the delegation or seizure of the sovereign power of the state, which is of the very essence of feudalism, by public officials or vassals, occur in France, not Germany.[4] The partibility of fiefs appeared in France long before the practice became manifest in Germany. In France the principle of the heritability of fiefs was old when it was yet new

---

[1] Brunner, *Deutsche Rechtsgeschichte*, II, 262; Guilhiermoz, *op. cit.*, pp. 77, 127.

[2] The *Historia Welforum Weingartensis*, chap. iv, relates an incident of Eticho, one of the founders of the house, which, however legendary it may be, yet illustrates this spirit of allodial pride and indisposition to recognize the drift toward feudalism. Eticho, the father of Empress Judith, was filled with anger when his son Henry accepted a benefice from his brother-in-law, Emperor Louis the Pious; that a man of noble blood would renounce such proud condition and become a vassal was too much for the old conservative—it was demeaning his class.

"Heinricus cum ad militares annos pervenisset et sue voluntatis compos fieret, ignorante patre ad imperatorem se contulit. Cumque illi summa familiaritate sociaretur et totius imperii vires terminos ejus circueundo et pertranseundo cognosceret, tandem consilio principum et maxime ipsius imperatoris instinctu hominium ei et subjectionem fecit, et in beneficio quatuor milia mansuum in superioribus partibus Bajoarie ab eo suscepit."

As late as the second half of the twelfth century, when Frederick I passed through Thun a local magnate, instead of saluting the Emperor after the feudal manner merely raised his hat in courteous greeting. The act piqued Frederick, who upon inquiry found that the Baron of Krenekingen was so old, so free, and so noble that he owed neither homage nor service to any man (Grimm, *Deutsche Rechtsalterthümer*, p. 279).

[3] Brunner, *op. cit.*, II, 226; Guilhiermoz, p. 77.

[4] Brunner, II, 253–55; Waitz, VII, 10; R. Schröder, *Lehrbuch der Deutschen Rechtsgeschichte*, III, 128.

in Germany.[1] The ancient French maxim, *"Nulle terre sans seigneur,"* never became universal or anything like it in medieval Germany, and allodial ownership was far more widespread in feudal Germany than in feudal France.[2] Feudalism transformed aristocracy of race into aristocracy of function. Government pertained to the most capable. But if superiority conferred rights it also imposed duties.

It is a fallacious belief that medieval society was divided into close and hard castes; that all the privileges were with one class and all the obligations with the other. In reality the fief was, if not a servitude, at least a service; it was a noble as distinguished from an ignoble service. Like serfs, vassals too were given away, sold, bequeathed by will by their overlords.[3]

The military reforms made by Henry the Fowler, remarkable as they were, did not make that radical and immediate change in institutions or social texture usually attributed to them. Military feudalism was of relatively late appearance in Germany when compared with France. Indeed, until the twelfth century, anything approaching the régime which prevailed in France was foreign to Germany, except along the French border.

As a whole, both administratively and socially, medieval Germany until the end of the Salian period was predominantly Carolingian. What the ninth century did for France in transforming her into a feudal country was not done in Germany until the civil wars of the reign of Henry IV, and even then the process was less complete and very different in result. Feudalism, at least in the French sense of that term, neither deeply permeated the German military or administrative system, nor saturated the land and society so fully as in France. When feudalism at last became "formed"

---

[1] Heritability of fiefs began to prevail in Italy in the eleventh century, and in Germany in the twelfth (Guilhiermoz, p. 241). The Italian word *capitaneus* ("vassal") penetrated into Swabia, but not elsewhere in Germany (Waitz, V, 464).

[2] Lamprecht, *op. cit.*, II, 87–88, 109–11; Brunner, *Forsch.*, I, 39, and his *Rechtsgeschichte*, II, 246–47, 250, 255 ff., 265 ff., 273 ff.; Maurer, *Einleitung zur Geschichte der Mark-, Hof-, Dorf- und Stadtverfassung*, p. 214.

[3] Guerard, *Polypt.*, I, 422 and n. 5.

in medieval Germany the contrasts between its institutions and those of France are more striking than the analogies. As for feudal identities they hardly may be said to have existed.

The benefice system in Germany, except in the case of church lands, was not widely spread. Vassalage in France was primarily a military relation. In Germany it was chiefly an economic one until the time of the Hohenstaufen.[1] In France, outside of Auvergne, where freemen were still in preponderance as late as the eleventh century, to cultivate the soil in person implied loss of status and often loss of liberty.[2] In Germany, and above all in Saxony, agriculture did not condition status until the twelfth century. By that time the general rebellion of the German feudality in the west and south, combined with the revolt of the peasantry in Saxony, had so nearly ruined the land that freemen everywhere were depressed, great nobles, lay and clerical, had become greater, and a swarm of parvenu nobles had come into being, all of whom rose upon the débris of the Salian system.

In France warriors without fief, living in the château of the lord and doing his service, were yet noble. In Germany castle-guard and similar services were performed by ex-serfs, i.e., *ministeriales*.[3] In France, at least in theory and in principle, every noble had a château and a fief. In Germany the lord rewarded his vassals with gifts, as horses, arms, etc.; suzerainty and vassalage were largely an economic and social relation.[4] In the *Ruodlieb*, one of the earliest of medieval

---

[1] Lamprecht, II, 106; Brunner, II, 248, 262 ff.; Roth von Schreckenstein, *Ritterwürde*, p. 59; Guilhiermoz, pp. 197 (n. 5), 265, 298. Even in the thirteenth century the *Sachsenspiegel* represents the tradition of early practice, i.e., that the fief is the wage of a function or service—"Das Lehn ist der rittere Sold" (Homeyr, *Sachsenspiegel*, II, 314).

[2] Guilhiermoz, p. 115 and notes; Lamprecht, *Études sur l'état économique de la France pendant la première partie du moyen-âge* (trans. Marignan), p. 199; Levasseur, *Histoire des classes ouvrières*, I, 162.

[3] Guilhiermoz, p. 114, n. 28.

[4] *Ibid.*, pp. 143 (n. 20), 165 (n. 77), 242–43. In Ottonian times the real nobility of Germany was composed of counts who were paid out of the public domain (Gerdes, *Geschichte des Deutschen Volkes*, I, 404). Rear-vassalage was stimulated in its development both by the evolution of the *ministeriales*, who came, as they rose, to be looked upon as the vassals of their lord, who was in turn a vassal himself, and by

German poems, being of the eleventh century, there is no mention made of fiefs in the enumeration made to the hero of the advantages which will arise from his entering the king's service.[1] Not until the twelfth century does the reward of a German vassal regularly take the form of a gift of fief.[2] In the eleventh century almost all the instances of benefices conferred upon condition of military service occur in the border lands adjacent to France, as Lorraine and Burgundy.[3]

Even then these German feudatories but slightly resembled their French congeners, for they were checked on every hand by the counts, the bishops, and the counts palatine, who were strictly royal functionaries; they could not indulge the right of war as in France without peril, nor coin money nor administer anything save simple justice. They had few political attributes, and no sovereignty.[4] In brief, German vassalage was simple and curtailed when compared with the institution as it prevailed in France.[5] The strong hand of the German kings prevented the growth both of a tyrannous higher feudality and the nuisance of a petty feudality until the war of investiture and the rebellion of

---

the disintegrating effects of the war of investiture which drove small nobles to larger ones for protection, or who else, owing to the collapse of the royal authority, lost their direct relation with and protection by the crown and were reduced to vassalage by the strong. See Below, *op. cit.*, pp. 239–42, and literature cited in notes (pp. 276–78).

[1] *Ruodlieb*, Frag. I, vss. 97 ff.; Waitz, *DVG*, VI, 44. Edited by F. Seiler, *Der aelteste Roman des Mittelalters* (Halle, 1882), the *Ruodlieb* has been usually regarded as of German origin (near Tegernese) and dated about 1030. But Wilmotte, *Romania*, XLIV, 373 f., assigns it to Northeastern France (valley of the Meuse between Namur and Liège) and to the early twelfth century. However, the fact that the *Ruodlieb* seems not to have had any influence on subsequent German poetry argues for its earlier date as probable.

[2] Ficker, *Vom Heerschilde*, p. 165; Guilhiermoz, p. 163, n. 4. The conservative nature of the benefice in Germany is shown in the *Constitutio* of Lothar II in 1136 (*MGH, Leges* [N.S.], IV, 176); the grant is still Carolingian in character. Cf. Guilhiermoz, p. 114, n. 26 *ad fin.* Even as late as the thirteenth century German law carefully distinguished fiefs formed from allods from the older type of benefice (Guilhiermoz, *ubi supra*, and pp. 265 [n. 30], 298–301).

[3] Thietmar, *Chron.*, VI, chap. xxxvi; *Vita Meinwerki*, chaps. lxxii–lxxvi; *Chron. Laureshamense* (Lorsch) (*anno* 1066) (SS. XXI, 415, 434–35); Dronke, *Codex Diplomaticus Fuldensis*, p. 359, No. 749.

[4] Gerdes, I, 396; Schröder, pp. 536–37.   [5] Brunner, II, 273–74.

Saxony threw all Germany into confusion and anarchy, the effect of which was to relax the power of the crown and profoundly to alter the institutions of feudalism and the texture of society.

Personal vassals, i.e., vassals without fief, are to be found in Germany as late as the *Sachsenspiegel*, although by that time they were an exception to the general condition.[1] This archaic form of vassalage especially survived in Saxony, but even in North Germany much of the old order of things passed away during the reign of Henry IV.[2] Then strong freemen became nobles and were bound to higher lords by ties of vassalage and homage, while weaker freemen went down to serfdom under the stress.[3] The Saxon and Thuringian peasantry rebelled against Henry IV in 1075 just because they were free and determined to preserve their freedom when the peasantry almost everywhere else in Germany had already sunk, or were sinking, to serfdom. As a whole, in Germany the tie of vassalage evidently was not a political and social principle strong enough to maintain the necessary political cohesion of the social body without force to sustain or coerce it. The history of feudal France illustrates this necessity.

As it was with vassalage so also was it with rear-vassalage or subinfeudation. French law never imposed a limit upon the number of successive subinfeudations. In Germany subinfeudation itself was a late practice as feudal origins go, and never reached the meticulous degree that obtained in

---

[1] Homeyer, *Sachsenspiegel*, I, Part II, 159; Guilhiermoz, p. 236, n. 2 *ad fin.*

[2] Thus Adam of Bremen, *Gesta Hammaburg. Eccles. Pontif.* (III, 35), says of Adalbert, the archbishop: "cum omnes qui erant in Saxonia sive in aliis regionibus clari et magnifici viri adoptaret in milites, multis dando quod habuit, ceteris pollicendo quod non habuit. . . . ." Farther on (III, 48) he writes, again of Adalbert: "cum tyranno [Magnus Billung] fedus pepigit ut, qui hostis erat, miles efficeretur, offerens ei de bonis ecclesiae mille mansos in beneficium et amplius." Lambert of Hersfeld abounds with details about Henry IV's Saxon policy and its effects, but see especially *Annales* (ed. Holder-Egger), pp. 238, 260.

[3] Lambert of Hersfeld, pp. 141, 146–48; Bruno, *Liber de Bello Saxonico*, chaps. xvi, xxiii–xxv, cxxvii. The symbolic procedure employed had a relation of significance to the rights or privileges granted. Thus the use of a piece of turf indicated that the vassal received land, the ring and crozier signified the collation of a bishopric, the scepter implied that the vassal secured his regalian rights, etc. The study of feudal ceremony is valuable for the light it casts upon the nature of fiefs.

France. Until the time of the Staufer, Germany had a powerful nobility, but that nobility was not oppressive, while
France as late as the reign of St. Louis exhibits many of the
phenomena of feudal anarchy. In their relations with the
king the German nobles had more liberty than English and
Norman barons under the Angevins, but it was a liberty preserved only through allegiance to the king's law.

In Germany, as compared with France, the proportion of
great nobles was small, and the number of lesser nobles not
nearly so large as in France.[1] On the other hand, there were
many more freemen in Germany than in France—at least
until the late twelfth century. Aside from the bishops and abbots of the "royal" monasteries, of whom military service
was rigidly exacted in virtue of the vast landed possessions
which the largess of the Saxon kings had conferred upon
them, there were relatively few real military vassals in the
strict sense of that term, i.e., nobles who held fiefs subject to
military service, and most of these were to be found along the
French border. In Germany field service and castle-guard
were sharply distinguished until Hohenstaufen times; in
France there is close relation and often confusion between
the practices.[2]

In medieval Germany "the art of war was a necessary
episcopal accomplishment" to a far greater degree than in
either France or England. Feudal France produced few
bishops like Adhemar of Puy and Philip of Beauvais. The
latter accompanied Philip Augustus to the East on the Third
Crusade, faced the furious charge of the Turkish horse at
Arsuf, and shared in the repulse at Acre; his bloodstained
hauberk was sent to the Pope with the message: "This we
have found. Know now whether it be thy son's coat-of-mail
or no." As for English fighting bishops, who does not know
Richard of Cornwall's famous letter to his brother Edward
in 1257 from Cologne? "Lo," wrote Richard, "what mettle-
some and warlike archbishops are in Germany. It would be a

[1] The children of small nobles were often pledged to the service of the larger
ones. For examples see Ruotger, *Vita Brunonis*, chap. xiii; Thietmar, IV, 15, 22,
and VI, 52.

[2] Guilhiermoz, pp. 298 ff.

fine thing for you if you could create such archbishops in England."[1] The barons' war in England in the thirteenth century might have had another issue if the crown had possessed such fighting clergy as feudal Germany possessed.

As far back as the reign of Otto the Great the Saxon policy had engrossed the bishops and "royal" abbots within the German military hierarchy. But the provisions of the Concordat of Worms in 1122 formally made the princes of the German church also princes of the German kingdom, and at this moment the great bishops and abbots officially entered into the military hierarchy with papal consent.[2] This status once established, in proportion as the ecclesiastical princes entered into the feudal life and institutions of Germany, the differences which had formerly distinguished them from the great lay nobles tended to blur together. Their office alone distinguished them from the secular feudality. In blood, in policy, in psychology, they were wholly feudalized. But this observation would not justly fit the high clergy of either France or England in the twelfth and thirteenth centuries. It is this difference of historical process and condition which enabled medieval Germany to produce such fighting bishops as Rainald of Dassel and Christian of Mainz, and not possess such churchmen as Becket, Grosseteste, John of Salisbury, Ivo of Chartres, Maurice de Sully, and Jacques de Vitry.

[1] *Annals of Burton* (SS. XXVII, 480). The author of the tract entitled *De unitate ecclesiae conservanda*, chap. xviii, written during or soon after the war of investiture, says of the bishops of that time: "quales scilicet episcopi non essent pastores ecclesiarum, sed ductores bellorum, non custodes dominicarum ovium, sed ut graves lupi persecutores earum, interfectores animarum pariter et corporum."

[2] See Heinrich Schaefer, *Pfarrkirche und Stift im Deutschen Mittelalter* (1903). A sharp distinction must always be made between church and lay fiefs; the former were always conferred with ring and staff, the latter with the banner and the sword. Yet in one particular the two kinds became one in nature, for a distinction developed between great or princely fiefs and fiefs of lower rank. Both bishoprics and great territories became regalian fiefs and hence of the same degree. In proportion as the bishops became of greater and greater importance in the feudal world the differences which distinguished them from great lay nobles become blurred. By the beginning of the thirteenth century the two classes are much alike. A new insignia appears among the ecclesiastical princes. It is the banner (*die Fahne*), which, at first a symbol of the right of high justice, ends by signifying actual right of sovereignty. The requirement of personal appearance before the Emperor soon disappeared. The princes, whether lay or clerical, contented themselves with sending their ambassadors.

In Germany feudalism became politically sovereign. In France the growth of the royal power gradually deprived the feudality of power and authority, and reduced it to a social caste. In England the opposition of the baronage and liberal bishops became a constitutional opposition and developed one of the most remarkable and beneficent institutional and political processes in history. In Germany bishops, abbots, and barons were bitterly divided against one another after 1197, when the strong hand of the Hohenstaufen was removed, and in the end they wrought the ruin of the German kingdom. In France clergy and nobles alike were made to bend to the king's will. Yet what happened in England might have been achieved in Germany, too, in the twelfth century (a full hundred years before Edward I and Simon de Montfort) if the Guelf programme could have triumphed. The Hohenstaufen emperors were as self-willed and absolutistic as the Capetian kings, but they could not make their will prevail over Germany as the French kings did in France. The dream of the Guelf house was to establish a federal feudal monarchy in Germany composed of a union of the separate duchies, each of which was to preserve its local "states rights"—to establish a form of government which would have given simultaneous and due expression to the rights of the crown and the rights of the duchies. But this great and constructive programme was ruined by the despotic policy of Frederick Barbarossa, and the fall of Henry the Lion in 1181 dragged ducal Germany down with Saxony. Never again in German history did the great old duchies play an important part. Upon the débris of the great duchies a swarm of petty particularistic feudal states arose and Germany, which in the twelfth century hovered upon the verge of creating a wholly new kind of state in Europe, a federated feudal and limited monarchy, drifted in the thirteenth century into the anarchy of the interregnum. By destroying the Guelfs the Staufer ruined the only element in feudal Germany capable of accomplishing something like what the barons accomplished for English liberty at Runnymede. The germ of constitutional limited monarchy was implicit as much in the Guelf programme as in the demands of the English barons in 1215.

If now we turn from things feudal to a consideration of things servile and manorial in medieval Germany, again we find marked variations and differences from similar conditions west of the Rhine or in England.

The distance which separated the lord of the manor from his servile dependents in Germany was wider than the same kind of separation in France. In the latter country the necessity of protection threw nobles and peasantry more closely together than in Germany. In France the villages were often, even usually, in close proximity to the castle, crowded against the cliff on which the château stood, or huddled at the foot of the hill within the shadow of the keep. In Germany, on the other hand, we find few castles until late in the eleventh century. The nobles lived as country gentlemen upon their estates, moving as necessity bade from one to another. The villages of the peasantry were rambling hamlets, often widely scattered. In consequence of these different conditions the German noble lived more aloof from the lower classes than the French noble; he knew less of them and their life; he was less familiar with them. But, on the other hand, owing first to the fact that thousands of freemen survived in Germany until as late as the twelfth century, whereas this class in France had long before this date diminished almost to invisibility; and, second, owing to the further fact that predial serfdom was late in development in Germany and slow in its spread, the German noble did not have that contempt for the lower classes which is found in medieval France, nor did the German peasantry as a class exhibit that servility which characterized the French peasantry in the eleventh and twelfth centuries.

The growth of proprietorship—or, to use the convenient German term, *Grundherrschaft*—and of serfdom was both slower and later in Germany than in France. Moreover, the manorial régime which resulted in Germany never had that systematic character which is attached to French manorialism, nor was it ever so universal. *Systemsucht* has been too much a disposition of recent German historical writers in this particular. On the other hand, the contention of Gerhard

Seeliger[1] that too much economic determinism has been introduced into the interpretation of medieval German serfdom, it seems to me, errs in the other direction.

Until relatively late in medieval Germany, as compared with medieval France, a German baron's[2] daily life was not unlike that of an English squire. He was more a proprietor farming his ancestral acres with the labor of a free peasant population than a feudal chieftain with a rout of men-at-arms and retainers always around him, and all living on the forced toil of a servile peasantry. This was especially true in North Germany. His possessions were likely to be surrounded by the outlying farms of free peasants who were his neighbors. His life was "rustic." In the *Ruodlieb* the chief occupation of the baron is to work his fields.[3] He is more concerned about the state of the weather and the condition of his crops than about politics and war; he has few vassals, or none at all, and they are personal vassals without fiefs; a handful of *ministeriales* is enough for house-guard.[4]

A few castles began to creep into the country in the tenth century, but they were simpler and ruder erections than those of France, and most of them were in the west near the French border.[5] Until the war of investiture and the

[1] *Die soziale und politische Bedeutung der Grundherrschaft im früheren Mittelalter* (Leipzig, 1903).

[2] The word *baro* was rarely used in the eleventh century, and not common even in the twelfth. I have not found it in Lambert of Hersfeld. It occurs six times in Otto of Freising, *Chronica*. Frequently a qualifying adjective is employed with the word, as *liber baro*, the Latin equivalent of *Freiherr*. Cf. Guilhiermoz, p. 158, n. 54.

[3] Frag. IV, vss. 15 ff.; Zoepfl, *Deutsche Rechtsgeschichte*, p. 351.

[4] Seifrid Helbling, I, vss. 826–29; Ottokar, *Reimchronik*, vss. 30727–55. Cf. Haupte, *Zeitschrift für Deutsches Altertum*, IV, 164.

[5] Regino, *Chron.* (anno 892); Lamprecht, *DWL*, I, 2, 1297, 1316, n. 6; Dubrille, *Cambrai*, pp. 2–3. Castle-building was a typical phenomenon of the ninth century, and a concrete evidence of the breakdown of the central authority. Castles were first built as places of protection against the inroads of the Northmen in France. As such they were mere blockhouses erected on some natural escarpment or artificial *agger*, and surrounded by a palisade and a ditch. In Parmentier's *Album Historique*, I, 100, may be seen a picture of the château of Ste Eulalie-d'Ambarès (Gironde), of the late ninth or early tenth century. An earlier and still simpler one is in Grégoire and Gaillard's *Histoire du moyen âge* (Paris, 1895), p. 312. Taine, *Ancient Régime*, p. 7, has a striking description of this age of castle-building. They first appear, as has

rebellion of Saxony, with the ensuing anarchy, all castles in Germany were regarded as "adulterine" save the citadels pertaining to the crown, most of which were in the towns, as Frankfort and Regensburg.[1] But as German life partook more and more of feudal ways of living, as institutions tended to crystallize and the structure of society to harden, individual castrametation gradually developed and the German nobles began to build castles of their own.[2] First they converted a favorite *Pfalz* into a walled or moated grange (*curtis*); from this the transition was made to a more formidable edifice.[3] But until the last quarter of the eleventh century there were comparatively few independent châteaux in Germany. Such structures were "adulterine" in the eyes of the Saxon and Salian kings and were usually destroyed or else forfeited to the crown.[4] Only royal officers might

---

been said, in the north of France. Cf. *Vita S. Romani*, chap. xiii (*AASS Boll.*, V, [May], 158); *Cart. de St. Père*, I, 6; Hincmar, *Annales* (862, 866, 869); *Annal. St. Vaast* (885). In 862 Charles the Bald enjoined the erection of private castles as a means to defend the country, but rescinded—or attempted to rescind—the edict in 864 owing to the fact that these strongholds became rendezvous of robbers (*MGH, Leges* [N.S.], II, 86). Thenceforth castle-building increased rapidly; every castle-owner defied the crown. See Regino, *op. cit.* (879); *De Gestis Abbat. Laub.*, chap. xvi; *Hincmarus ad Carolum Calvum*, in Migne, *Patrol. Lat.*, CXXV, 954; Flach, *Les origines de l'anc. France*, II, 82–86, 301 ff. Richer, *Historiarum Libri IV*, is full of vivid details in regard to early castles, e.g., I, 19, 27; II, 7, 8, 9; III, 20 (the first mention in 964 of the famous château of Coucy), 103 (Verdun); IV, 17 (Laon), 76 (Melun). Until the eleventh century the castles were chiefly, even entirely, made of timber, and part-wooden, part-stone castles are even met with in the twelfth century, as Sugar's *Vita Ludovici Crassi* shows. But Richer, IV, 27, indicates that stone towers and battlements were in use by the middle of the tenth century. Besides the word *castellum*, the words *oppidum, municipium, castrum*, and *arx* were employed in the same sense. The art of castrametation was much more advanced in France than elsewhere, and the ability of the French in building castles astonished both the Germans and the Italians. *Mon. S. Gall.*, II, 17; Richer, II, 10; III, 106; Flodoard, *Annales* (938); *Mirac. S. Bened.* (ed. Soc. de l'Hist. de France), p. 245. The counts of Anjou excelled in this kind of engineering (Halphen, *Le Comte d'Anjou au XI* siècle, Part II, chap. ii).

[1] E.g., *MGH, Dipl.* (N.S.), I, 169, l. 14; 232, l. 8; 242, l. 35; 499, l. 27.

[2] "Nobiles in villis turres parvulas habuerunt quas a suis similibus vix defendere potuerunt," quoted by Schulte (*Hofleben*, I, 124). Waitz, VIII, 203–4, has a striking paragraph on this evolution.

[3] Waitz, VIII, 200; Maurer, *Geschichte der Fronhöfe*, I, 126, 136.

[4] Waitz, VIII, 201.

legally have castles, and then they were emanations of the
king's authority and often citadels garrisoned and muni-
tioned by government.[1] Before the twelfth century most of
the so-called "castles" of the German dukes with whom the
kings were continually struggling were not actual castles but
merely fortified manor-houses.[2]

Even the German kings before Henry IV were without
real castles, except for their citadels, which, as said, were
provincial police headquarters. All the Saxon monarchs and
the first two Salians, Conrad II and Henry III, lived much as
Charlemagne had lived, as described in the *Capitulare de
villis*, that is to say, in a great low-roofed, rambling manor-
house, or *palatium*, leaving what castles they possessed to
garrisons who were usually armed *ministeriales*.[3]

Wood was the universal fabric of castle construction for
years in Germany, until French building technique and
engineering introduced stone construction. Even the Wartburg in 1080 had two wooden towers.[4] The genuine feudal
castle crept gradually into Germany from Lorraine.[5] Already
by the eleventh century in France military engineering had
become a profession and the names of some of these architects
are known.[6] But the first German castles were cruder constructions than those found in France at the same time, al-

[1] For examples see *Annal. Hild.* (971) (SS. III, 62); Thietmar, *Chron.*, V, 9;
VI, 36; *MGH, Dipl.* (N.S.), I, 169, 232, 242, 499. Cf. Otte, *Baukunst*, pp. 134–35;
Nährer, *Kunst und Alterth. in Württemb.*, III, 150.

[2] See Wipo, *Vita Chuonradi*, chap. xxii; *Vita Oudalrici*, chap. x; *Vita Balderici*,
chap. vii; *Vita Deoderici Mett.*, chap. xii.

[3] Waitz, VIII, 205–7; Heyne, *Wohnungswesen*, p. 139; Lamprecht, *Deutsches
Wirtschaftsleben*, I, Part I, 544; Schulte, *Hofleben*, I, 42. For Belgium see Kurth,
Notger de Liège, p. 301, n. 5; Pirenne, *Histoire de Belgique*, I, 128.

[4] Otte, *Baukunst*, p. 269. For description of such a wooden castle see *Gesta
Abbatum Trudonensium* (SS. X, 243).

[5] Kurth, *op. cit.*, pp. 25–27. For instances see Regino (*annis* 903, 906); Flodoard, *Annales* (951, 960, etc.); Herimann of Augsburg, *Chron.* (1044) (castle Böckelheim). Yet even in Henry IV's time the castle of Zabern was still of wood, *arca ex
tabulis ligneis confecta* (SS. XI, 669, l. 25).

[6] Ordericus Vitalis, *Hist. Eccles.*, VIII, 24; X, 5; Bouquet, XII, 528; V. Mortet,
Recueil de textes relatifs à l'hist. de l'architecture, Introd., sec. 22. Lambert of Ardres,
Hist. Comitum . . . . Ardensium, chap. lxvii, has preserved a vivid description of the
erection of a castle early in the twelfth century.

though they were sometimes capable of making a long resistance against siege. Henry III lay for three months before Hammerstein before he was able to take it.

The backwardness of German siegecraft before Frederick I's experiences in Lombard Italy, when improved siege engines began to be introduced into Germany, made even simple fortresses formidable. Fire was commonly the most effective means to reduce a castle, since most of them were really little more than timbered blockhouses. Early German castles were without bastions, portcullis, pontlevis, all of which devices were imported from France. Even the donjon was not a "keep," but the *Gross Turm* in which the lord dwelt.[1]

The real castle age in Germany began during the reign of Henry IV, when castles arose, first in Thuringia and Saxony, but soon were to be found all over the land as if raised by an enchanter's wand.[2] Then appeared the Wartburg, *nomen omen* among such frowning citadels, Trifels, Kyffhausen, Drachenfels, Wolkenburg, the last two having been erected by Frederick of Cologne.[3] Ambitious *ministeriales* soon followed the example set by rebellious barons, and on all sides the châteaux of these upstarts began to rival the towers of the barons. Henry V, in spite of his power, never was able to suppress them.[4] Frederick of Swabia, the Emperor Lothar II's arch-enemy, sowed castles from Basel to Mainz. It was said of him that he dragged a castle at his horse's

---

[1] G. Köhler, *Entwicklung des Kriegswesens*, III, Part I, 351–52; Piper, *Burgenkunde*, pp. 168, 218, 228 ff., 279, 284; Heyne, *op. cit.*, p. 134. According to Köhler (*op. cit.*, p. 402) the donjon first appeared in Swiss Burgundy. There is an interesting article by Leo in *Hist. Taschenbuch*, Vol. VIII.

[2] "Montes omnes colliculosque Saxoniae et Thuringiae castellis munitissimis" (Lambert of Hersfeld, *Annales* [anno 1073; ed. Holder-Egger], pp. 140–41; Giesebrecht, *Kaiserzeit*, III, Part II, 1221 ff.; Henne am Rhyn, *Kulturgeschichte des Deutschen Volkes*, I, 20 ff.). The Wartburg is first mentioned by Bruno, *Liber de Bello Saxonico*, chap. cxvii, in 1080; Trifels is first mentioned in *Annal. Paderb.* (1113).

[3] Stein, *De Fred. Archiep. Colon.*, p. 27.

[4] See the vivid description of the anarchy in Germany in 1116 by Ekkehard of Aura (SS. VI, 252) and cf. *Recens. de Annal. Paderb.* (1107); *Chronica Regia Coloniensis* (1107); *Vita Heinrici IV*, chaps. viii, ix, xiii; Herbordus, *Vita Ottonis ep. Bab.*, I, 25.

tail.[1] In the reign of Frederick I Swabia bristled with castles of the Zähringen.[2] By the next century Germany was as thickly studded with castles as France, and their occupants were far bolder in depredation, for the royal authority in Germany then was rapidly collapsing.[3]

The burgher population in the German towns, especially in the Rhinelands, where town life first appeared and was most developed, because it was numerically strong enough within the towns to overpower the bishops and was protected from the baronage without by the town walls, weathered the storm of the civil war in Henry IV's reign. But the rural population of feudal Germany had no such defenses, nor did they possess that compact organization which the burghers had, to enable them to resist the pressure of the time and the violence of the age.[4] Thus insecurity, tyranny, poverty, famine, reduced the free class, even in Saxony, to serfdom, and thrust those already unfree down to lower social depths.[5]

In social texture feudal Germany before the reign of Henry IV was quite different from France. Except the clergy and some of the official count class, at the beginning of the Saxon epoch there were few who were very rich. Great lay properties were slow to accumulate in Germany. The *Grossgrundherrschaften* surrounded by a nimbus of vassals and retainers were not widely known until the last half of the twelfth century.[6] In Saxony the old blood nobility of the German tribes, like the free peasantry, persisted long after it had disappeared everywhere else.[7]

[1] Otto of Freising, *Gesta Friderici I*, I, 12; Heyne, *Wohnungswesen*, p. 333; Gebhardt, *Handbuch der Deutschen Geschichte* (1st ed.), I, 226.

[2] *Chron. Otto S. Blas.* (1165) (SS. XX, 311). For the Wartburg in Barbarossa's time see *Gesta Frid.*, I, chap. iv.

[3] Raumer, *Geschichte der Hohenstaufen*, I, 208; Piper, *Burgenkunde*, pp. 122 ff.

[4] Gerdes, *op. cit.*, II, 305–6, 577 ff.

[5] For the effect of famine see Curschmann, *Hungersnöte des Mittelalters* (Leipzig, 1900).

[6] Cf. Lamprecht, *DWL*, I, Part II, 713, and n. 6 (*anno* 1198).

[7] Wazo of Liège, *Gesta Episcop. Leod.* (SS. VII, 225), writing to Henry III in 1047, strikingly shows the contrast, for he says: "Rarus apud nos miles et securus agricola." The primitive Germanic solidarity of kindred is another evidence of

The feudal tendency toward heritability of fiefs affords an interesting contrast in the cases of France and Germany. While the old idea is now exploded that the famous capitulary of Kiersy in 877 established the general heritability of fiefs in France, it yet remains true that in practice the inheritance of fiefs obtained in France from the end of the ninth century; that deviation from this tendency was the exception, not the rule.

On the other hand, in Germany this form of transmission long remained an act of grace on the part of the overlord.[1] While the succession of the eldest son was probably customary,[2] it was far from invariable. The ancient Germanic law of equal inheritance of the sons survived in many quarters of Germany for centuries—indeed, it never entirely became obsolete—and along with partibility of fiefs other liberal practices gradually were legalized also, as protection of the rights of widows and the right of female succession or inheritance through the female line.[3] Often, in fact, designation of the heir was made in advance by the possessor.[4] If, however, the possessor was a vassal who had died without having made a will providing for the succession, or the act of infeudation had not so provided, then the suzerain had the right to dispose of the inheritance among the heirs as he chose.

---

the persistence of early social conditions. This was especially persistent in Ditmarsch where in the eleventh and twelfth centuries the dikes were built by the *Schlachte*, or agnatic clans (cf. R. S. Philpotts, *Kindred and Clan*, pp. 103, 125). Hugo of St. Victor's homesickness for Saxony perhaps reflects this simplicity of Saxon life: "Ego a puero exsulavi, et scio quo moerore animus arctum aliquando pauperis tugurii fundum deserat, qua libertate postea marmoreos lares et tecta laqueata dispiciat" (*Didascalicon*, III, 20 [Migne, CLXXVI, 773]).

[1] Thietmar, *Chron.*, I, 7; Lambert of Hersfeld (*anno* 1075; *ed. cit.*), p. 232.

[2] The *Continuator of Regino* (ed. Kurze), p. 164, records it as an unusual fact that Otto I permitted a count to divide his fiefs upon his deathbed among his sons.

[3] Waitz, VI, 88-89; Homeyer, *Sachsenspiegel* (3d ed.), Part I, p. 371, and I, Part II, 143-44. The most notable instance of female succession is in the case of Saxony in 1106 when the Billunger house expired and Lothar of Supplinburg forced the succession in his own favor, his mother having been a daughter of Duke Ordulf Billung (*Annal. Sax.* [SS. VI, 744-45]).

[4] Lambert of Hersfeld (*anno* 1071), p. 121.

It is true that from the moment of their appearance the stem-duchies tended to become hereditary. But numerous examples of revocation and dispossession occur in Saxon and Salian times. Not until the Hohenstaufen epoch did heritability of the duchies become an accomplished fact.[1] The Ottos regarded the ducal office as a function of the crown. Only from Henry IV's time forward does the idea of the ducal prerogative as a strictly dynastic possession of a local family become preponderant. Then the Guelfs in Bavaria, the Hohenstaufen in Swabia, and Lothar of Supplinburg in Saxony strongly manifest this inclination.[2]

Conrad II in 1037 recognized the principle of primogeniture for Lombardy.[3] But this act had no binding force in Germany, where the church long resisted primogeniture in protection of younger sons and collateral heirs.[4] Even at the end of the twelfth century Henry VI was unable to establish primogeniture after the French and Plantagenet practice.[5] The truth is that in medieval Germany no uniform and invariable law of succession ever triumphed to the exclusion of any other form.[6] As to "relief," that feudal institution was unknown in Germany until late in the eleventh century, and uncommon before the twelfth.[7]

In France as early as the ninth century to be a "noble" was to sit a horse and to bear arms; such a person was a *miles*, or "knight," and belonged to the *ordo pugnatorum*.[8]

[1] But already in Henry II's reign the heritability of countships had been admitted (Giesebrecht, II, 70, 284, 594, 625).

[2] H. A. L. Fisher, *The Medieval Empire*, I, 321–25.

[3] *MGH, Const.*, I, 90. For the popularity of the act see Wipo, *Vita Chuonradi*, II, 6.

[4] See *Chron.* of Lorsch for the years 1066 and 1119 (SS. XXI, 415, 534–35) *Codex Udalrici*, Ep. 103, in Jaffé, V, 190; Homeyer, *System des Lehnrechts*, sec. 42.

[5] Gervase of Tilbury, *Otia Imperialia*, II, 19.

[6] Frederick I's decree at Roncaglia in 1158, which probably was meant to apply to Germany as well as Italy, while it declared duchies, counties, etc., indivisible, did not prescribe a rule of inheritance.

[7] Waitz, VI, 35 ff.; Guilhiermoz, pp. 338 ff., nn. 52, 53.

[8] Guilhiermoz, pp. 388–89; cf. Richer, I, 5, 57; II, 3, 5, 28, 39, 54; III, 71, 88, 93; IV, 11, 28.

The right to wear arms and armor distinguished him from the unarmed peasantry.[1] Per contra, personal cultivation of the soil implied a servile condition. In France in the eleventh century—perhaps even in the tenth century—it was necessary to be knighted to be a chevalier, to be a noble. Nobility and knighthood were two sides of the same coin. In Germany neither knights nor knighthood were known before the twelfth century. The term *ordo militaris* (or *equestris*) first appears in France in the pages of Richer; and the context of the various passages shows that already before the year 1000 the French nobility was a closed order and had become a caste.[2] In Widukind, on the other hand, although he uses a similar term, *ordo equestris*, the context shows that it applies only to the great dukes[3] and it seems more like a rhetorical flourish than a historical description, for it is used in connection with Widukind's account of the grand banquet in Charlemagne's palace at Aachen after Otto I's coronation in 936. In France the nobles early became a hard-and-fast privileged group divided into classes by somewhat inflexible lines of partition, while in Germany the nobility remained for two centuries after the beginning of the feudal régime merely the upper stratum of German lay society, not sharply divided from ordinary freemen nor antagonistic toward them, and loosely held together more by family tradition than by pride and prejudice. In France the gulf became wide and fixed between even the lowest noble and the servile class; a mere *châtelain* with nothing but a single castle and a few roods of land was nevertheless a noble.[4] In Germany, on the other hand, the social distinction was less a cleavage than a gradual shading off of the nobility, through the intermediate grade of the *ministeriales*, into the serf class. German feudal society hardly even approximated the condition of French feudal society before the twelfth century. For two hundred years

[1] Guilhiermoz, pp. 379–80.

[2] Lamprecht, *Études sur l'état écon. de la France* (trans. Marignan), p. 199 and notes.

[3] Waitz, VI, 265.

[4] Guilhiermoz, pp. 143–44. Hence the excessive subdivision of fiefs in France. In Flanders, Picardy, Poitou, the Orléannais, and Normandy we find *demi-pairies*, *demi-fiefs*, *demi-fiefs de haubert*, and even fractional *roncins de service*, less than half (Guilhiermoz, pp. 190–92).

the meticulous differences and the social prejudices which had characterized the French noblesse since the ninth century were almost unknown in Germany.

In France, when compared with Germany, chivalry developed early and rapidly. In Germany knighthood and chivalry did not blossom until the middle of the twelfth century. One of the earliest examples, possibly the very first, is the knighting of the Hungarian king by Conrad III in 1146 in imitation of the French practice with which he became familiar while on the Second Crusade.

Freehold or allodial tenure persisted longer and was much more general in Germany than in France, and freemen were much more numerous, particularly in the north.[1] Even as late as the battle of Bouvines (1214) many Saxon freemen fighting on foot were still to be found in the German army of Otto IV, and probably had taken an oath of loyalty to him as in Charlemagne's day.[2] But what was true of Saxony was not true of the rest of Germany then or earlier. For, as has been pointed out, by the time of Henry IV most of Germany had become feudalized, though not after the French form. During the civil war the Lorrainer and Swabian horsemen of Henry IV were astonished to find in Saxony freemen still cultivating their own fields and fighting as their ancestors had fought, on foot.[3] When their free position became difficult to maintain, many of these freemen became *ministeriales*,

[1] Lamprecht, *Deutsche Geschichte*, III, 93–96; Schröder, *op. cit.*, pp. 407, 458–59; Waitz, V, 185, 325, 393 (n. 1), 386, 430; Below, *Entstehung der Deutschen Stadtgemeinde*, p. 13; Walter, *Deutsche Rechtsgeschichte*, sec. 451. These freemen were the *liberi viri*, the *friman*, the *frigebur*, or the *schoppenbarfreye* of the *Sachsenspiegel*, who acted as jurors and made up the *Heerban* when it was called out. This class was especially abundant in the north of Germany (Lamprecht, III, 93). It is significant that in the west, particularly in Lorraine, where French conditions prevailed more, donations to the monasteries were chiefly made by nobles, whereas in Bavaria until late, and in Swabia and Franconia until relatively late in the feudal age they were made by freemen and *ministeriales* (Waitz, V, 431). These freemen had the same *wergeld* and the same *fredum* as the *Ritter* class. The *Sachsenspiegel* (III, sec. 1) puts them on the same plane as the *ministeriales*, who at the time the *Mirror of Saxony* was written had become a petty nobility (Schröder, pp. 458, 591; Walter, *loc. cit.*).

[2] Waitz, VIII, 122–23; Schröder, p. 525; Lamprecht, *DG*, III, 96; cf. Rigord, X, 686.

[3] *Carmen de Bello Saxonico*, II, vss. 118 ff., and III, vss. 94 ff.; Lambert of Hersfeld (*anno* 1075); Bruno, *op. cit.*, chap. xxxi.

and thus escaped the rigors of serfdom.¹ The real noble class
in Germany, in the legal sense, under the Saxon and first
Salian kings, was composed of the counts and dukes. But
their prestige from Henry IV's reign onward was more and
more compromised by the elevation of men of servile origin
to church and lay offices—men who had everything to gain
by the cultivation of parvenu practices and parvenu vir-
tues.²

In France the early Capetians were compelled by the
feudal drift of the times to enfeoff public offices like lands.
In Germany enfeoffment of public offices does not occur until
after 1100, when its appearance is a manifestation of the
rapid growth of feudalism as a result of the upheaval and collapse of things during the war of investiture and the Saxon
rebellion. Thenceforward the swift extension of the practice
of enfeoffment of offices, in the words of Huebner, "made
futile in Germany the hope of such growth of royal power as
resulted in France and in England."³

In France the ownership of land early became an index
of social position. Yet in Carolingian times poverty did not
entail loss of liberty or degradation of class,⁴ and it is not
until late in the eleventh century that we begin to detect in
Germany a sentiment of contempt for the poor who were well
born, who have the misfortune either not to own land or to
have lost the land which they once possessed.⁵

¹ Waitz, VI, 41; Dümmler, *Geschichte des Ostfränkischen Reiches* (2d ed.), III, 635.

² Gerdes, I, 404; Schröder, pp. 441 ff.; Zallinger, *Ministeriales und Milites*
(1878), pp. 58 ff.; Lamprecht, *DG* (4th ed.), III, 103. Ekkehard of St. Gall's comment on the rise of the *ministerialis* class is very illuminating: "Majores locorum de
quibus scriptum est 'quia servi si non timent, tument,' scuta et arma polita gestare
incoeperant; tubas alioquam caeteri villani clanctu inflare didicerant" (*Casus S.
Galli* [SS. II, 103]).

³ Huebner, *Germanic Private Law* (Eng. trans.), p. 340.

⁴ "Quamvis pauper sit, tamen libertatem suam non perdat nec hereditatem
suam" (*Lex Baiuvariorum*, in *MGH, Leges*, III, 298). Cf. *Trans. S. Magni* (*ca.*
850), chap. xv (SS. IV, 426): "quamvis pauperculus tamen ex bonis parentibus
natus."

⁵ "Erant duo cujusdam Geronis comitis filii, satis quidem edito loco nati, sed
propter inopiam rei famularis inter principes Saxoniae nullius nominis vel momenti"
(Lambert of Hersfeld [*anno* 1076; ed. Holder-Egger], p. 260). Cf. *ibid.*, pp. 233,
256; Bruno, chaps. xcix, cxvii. Lamprecht, *DWL*, I, Part II, 1162, cites other
examples.

In France the lapse of royal authority and the upgrowth of a violent baronage resulted in the universal prevalence of private war. In Germany private warfare was unusual and soon crushed. The commonest kind of local violence was the persistence of the old German *faida* among the peasantry.[1] When private war is found in feudal Germany it usually occurs along the French border in Flanders, Lorraine, and Burgundy.[2] Germans looked with mingled horror and contempt upon the "French" anarchy. To maintain the king's peace was the first duty of a German sovereign.[3] In theory a *faidosus* was subject to the death penalty; in practice, however, the offender was commonly banned and his property confiscated and devoted to church endowment.[4] Ludwig the German asserted the best tradition of Carolingian times with reference to enforcing law and order in the realm.[5] The principle lapsed temporarily during the minority of Ludwig the Child and the weak reign of Conrad I. Yet even then Adalbert of Babenberg was cited before the diet of Tribur, and when he failed to come was besieged in his castle, taken, and sent to the scaffold.[6]

In the eleventh century, an age of intense religious emotionalism, the idea of the Truce of God began to spread from France into Lorraine and Burgundy. It mattered little to its enthusiastic advocates that what might be good, even necessary, in France, was unnecessary in Germany. Henry III, too sensitive of the royal prerogative and too proud openly to approve of a movement which in its very nature

[1] For the curious complaint and regulations in the legislation of the Bishop of Worms governing his *familia* in the year 1023 see *MGH, Leges* (N.S.), I, 640, art. 3. Cf. Nitzsch, *Ministerialität und Bürgertum*, I, 366–76. The time-honored judicial duel lingered in Franconia until the sixteenth century (Zimmermann, *Hist. Taschenbuch* [1879]).

[2] See the interesting work by Dubois, *Les assurements au XIIIᵉ siècle dans nos villes du nord; recherches sur le droit de vengeance* (Paris, 1900). Charlemagne's efforts to stamp out the ancient German feud were successfully continued by the German kings (Schröder, pp. 353 ff.; Lamprecht, *Deutsche Zeitschrift fur Geschichtswissenshaft*, VII, 8–9).

[3] Waitz, VI, 522–23.

[4] *Dipl.* (N.S.), I, 303, 434, 447; *Continuator of Regino (anno 958).*

[5] Dümmler, II, 416; Gerdes, I, 525.

[6] Regino, *Chron.* (902, 906).

implied the inability of the crown to maintain law and order, endeavored to compromise by instituting the *Landfrieden* instead, which attempted to effect the purposes of the *treuga* but saved the honor of the crown.[1] For the extension of the Peace of God in Germany was due to psychological and religious contagion, not to necessity as in France.[2]

Legally the *Landfrieden* was a revival of the old Carolingian ban reinforced by ecclesiastical penalties.[3] No more formidable police power can well be imagined than the exercise of this double-shotted authority by a sovereign like Henry III. Almost any infraction of law under its provisions was capable of being construed as a violation of the "peace," and the culprit could be condignly dealt with. As subsequent history was to show, in the hands of the German kings the *Landfrieden* became a means of coercion powerful enough to break the greatest of foes, as Frederick Barbarossa's employment of it against Henry the Lion illustrates. Herimann of Augsburg was not far wrong when he declared the "new peace" a *pacem multis saeculis inauditam.*[4] The chief defect of the law was that its enforcement was so dependent upon the personal presence of the king.[5]

The Archbishop of Cambrai introduced the *Landfrieden* into his dominions in 1032; the Bishop of Worms soon followed.[6] In 1041 Henry III confirmed it in Burgundy in spite of his suspicion of the bishops.[7] But the Peace of God did not acquire a firm foothold in Germany until 1081, when the

---

[1] Cf. Giesebrecht, II, 366 ff.; Stenzel, *Geschichte Deutschlands*, I, 89; Hauck, *Kirchengeschichte Deutschlands*, III, 581; Schröder, I, 669; Nitzsch, II, 39.

[2] See Rosenstock, *Herzogsgewalt und Friedensschutz* (Breslau, 1910).

[3] Richter and Kohl, *Annalen der Deutschen Geschichte im Mittelalter*, III, Part II, 341, n. *a*, and 351, n. *g*, have collected quotations from the sources pertinent to history of the *Landfrieden* at this time. For the spread of the Truce of God in France see C. Pfister, *Études sur le règne de Robert le Pieux*, chap. iv; Luchaire, *Manuel des Institutions Françaises*, pp. 231–33, with bibliography.

[4] Herimannus Aug., *Chron.* (*anno* 1043) (SS. V, 274).

[5] "Nam [rege] recedente justicia terras reliquit, pax abiit," bitterly wrote the unknown author of the *Vita Heinrici IV* (ed. Wattenbach, *in usum scholarum*, 1876), chap. i.

[6] Nitzsch, II, 36–38.

[7] Richter and Kohl, *Annalen*, III, Part I, 337, 351.

anarchy of intestine war promoted it. Henry of Liège was one of its earliest exponents. Sigwin of Cologne soon imitated his example in 1083.[1] But Gerard of Cambrai was violently opposed to the movement.[2] In 1084 the counter-king Hermann ordained the peace in Saxony.[3] In the same year the synod of Bamberg took a similar measure.[4] At the diet of Mainz in 1085 Henry IV extended the provisions of the Peace of God to the whole kingdom. Warfare was forbidden on four days in each week and certain classes of persons, as clerks, merchants, the peasantry, women, and children, declared inviolable at all times.[5] Thenceforth peace legislation is the capital element in German legislation.[6]

This brings us to a brief consideration of the legislation of the German kings in the Middle Ages. The contrast between their legislative energy and the lassitude of the Capetian kings of France before Philip Augustus and Louis IX is very striking. While there are only 12 diplomas of Hugh Capet for the nine years of his reign, we have 425 for that of Otto III. And if we go back into the earlier history of the Saxon house we find the same display of energy. There are 43 diplomas of Henry I, 434 of Otto the Great, 317 of Otto II. Yet much of the energetic legislation of the Saxons got nowhere, for it was all of a special, particular nature. It lacked co-ordination and the organic quality of real law.

With the accession of the Salian emperors this defect began to be remedied. Conrad II's legislation, though not large in volume, is singularly constructive in quality,[7] and Henry III's legislation had a unity and directness which is in harmony with the absolutistic purposes of that monarch.

But all the intelligent designs of the Salian house were

---

[1] Aegidius Aureaevallensis, *Gesta Episcoporum Leodiensium*, III, 13 (SS. XXV, 89); Ekkehard, *Chron.* (SS. VI, 206); *MGH, Const.*, I, 602; Hauck, III, 843; *Forschungen zur Deutschen Geschichte*, XXIII, 134 ff.

[2] *Gesta Pontificum Cameracensium*, III, 27, 52.

[3] *Annales Bernenses* (1084); Hauck, III, 843.

[4] *MGH, Const.*, I, 605.

[5] *Ibid.*; Ekkehard, *Chron.* (SS. VI, 205); *Annal. Bern.* (1085); *Annal. Augustani* (SS. III, 131); text in Doeberl, *Monumenta Germaniae Selecta*, III, No. 17.

[6] Schröder, p. 669.   [7] Nitzsch, *Deutsche Gesch.*, II, 26.

frustrated when the rebellion of Saxony and the war of investiture broke out. Then, with the enormous progress of feudalism, sectionalism gained the upper hand, the courts lost their connection with the crown, the German baronage and the princely bishops and abbots established their power, freemen lost their freedom, and serfdom became the general condition of the lower classes. The one redeeming feature in the transformation of German society is the rise of the burgher class. Except for them the triumph of the *Landeshoheit* was nearly complete.

Nothing is more melancholy and more futile than the legislative activity of Frederick Barbarossa. In spite of the "new legalism" introduced by the revived study of the Roman law during his reign, in spite of Frederick I's own organizing ability and tremendous energy, the evidence of Frederick's futility is spread over all his works. Otto of Freising, fond as he was of his brilliant nephew, was too honest a historian to gloss the truth.[1] By Hohenstaufen times feudalism was in the saddle and the great feudality, lay and clerical, not Frederick, really ruled Germany.

So far as the reign of law is concerned, in Germany the triumph of feudalism prevented the spread of any single, uniform system of law. This is exactly opposite to the tendency in France, where the growth of the crown gradually reduced, and even effaced, the law of the provincial dynasts, and the *établissements* and *ordonnances* of the French kings became more and more the law of the realm.

Not only the ancient Germanic codes but the Carolingian capitularies also became obsolete in Germany by the tenth century. Few traces of them are manifest in legislation or other sources.[2] When we meet with such terminology as *jus* or *lex Francorum, Alamannorum, Bajuwariorum, Saxonum,* the allusion is not to the old codes, but to a body of local,

---

[1] Otto of Freising, *Gesta Frid.*, II, 28, and the remarkable evidence in Weiland, *Constitutiones et Acta Publica*, I, No. 198. For the anarchy in North Germany after Henry the Lion's death see Weiland, II, No. 10.

[2] The most notable mention of the validity of former capitularies is found in *Const. Francofurtana* (951) (*MGH, Leges* II, 26). Cf. *Concilium Triburiense* (895), chap. i, and see Waitz, V, 149; VI, 407; also Schulte, sec. 57.

customary practices.[1] The German kings, whether of Saxon, Salian, or Swabian birth, always "lived" Frankish law.[2] But the tendency of legal development in medieval Germany was toward heterogeneity and away from homogeneity,[3] exactly opposite to the drift of law in France, where the growth of the monarchy made toward unity. This particularistic tendency in feudal Germany finally obliterated all conception of general law. The more feudalism won, the more the law became local, particularistic, sectional. By the thirteenth century the law of Germany had become the will of petty dynasts commingled with the débris of the past. There was greater drift toward uniformity of law under the Saxon and Salian kings than under the Hohenstaufen. The appeal made to and the use made of the petty feudality by the Swabian rulers during the conflict with the Guelfs canceled the progress legal development had made under their predecessors, cheapened their own legislation, and consecrated at last the vicious principle of the supremacy of local lordship law.

While Frederick I and his son Henry VI wasted the blood and substance of Germany in bootless campaigns in Italy, Germany slipped more and more out of their hands into the hands of the feudality. The old bonds of government and so-

---

[1] The *Lex Salica* apparently was still in force in the ninth century (Hincmar, *De Divortio Lotharii et Teutbergae*, interrog. 5). But Otto of Freising's mention of it in 1158 is extremely hazy (*Chronicon*, IV, 32). Cf. Schulte, sec. 23. Henry II took an oath "not in any point to corrupt Saxon law" (Thietmar, V, 16–17; Giesebrecht, II, 24, 593). A vestige of the ancient Allemannic code comes out in 1077, when Welf of Bavaria and Berthold of Carinthia were condemned by the papal partisans for espousing the cause of Henry IV (*Annal. Augustani* [SS. III, 129]; cf. Heyck, *Deutsche Geschichte*, I, 36). Schröder (*Forschungen z. Deutschen Geschichte*, Vol. XIX) has a monograph on the diffusion of the Salian Franks and shows the persistence of Salic law in Hesse. Schultz, *Zeitschrift des Vereins für Thüringische Geschichte und Altertumskunde* (N.S., 1878), Band I, has studied Frankish immigration into Thuringia and the spread of the *jus Francorum*. Karl von Amira, *Die Handgebärden in den Bilderhandschriften des Sachsenspiegels*, has examined the illustrations in manuscripts of the *Mirror of Saxony*, for the attitudes and motions of the principals in a case at trial were of technical importance and are interesting for the light cast upon juridical processes in feudal Germany.

[2] Otto Sanblasianus, *Chron.*, chap. li.

[3] "Secundum legem et ritum gentis . . . . secundum judicium et legem patriae" (Lacomblet, *Urkundenbuch*, Nos. 192, 309).

ciety dissolved, and the new ones which were formed were of
a wholly different nature. They had neither the genius nor
the binding force of those which they supplanted.

The partition of Saxony in 1181 ruined all prospect or
possibility of German political and territorial unity, for
Saxony was the premier duchy and the very cornerstone of
the kingdom. Its ruin, combined with the triumph of the
feudality and the breakdown of the ancient German noble
class, owing partly to the power of the kings,[1] partly to the
rise of the lesser nobility and *ministeriales* to higher place,[2]
and partly to the incurable habit of the great families to commit family suicide by permitting so many members of their
families to enter the church,[3] finally ruined Germany.

It is a defect of German historians that they have too
exclusively studied the Italian policy of the Hohenstaufen;
their attention has been too much fixed upon the conflict
with the pope and the Italian cities. Accordingly, they have
failed to appreciate the enormous significance of the interior
changes in Germany, in ideas and especially in institutions.
The rising of the nobles in 1193 marked a reaction against
the policy of the house of Swabia, and is the more important
because it took place when Henry VI's eyes were fixed on the
conquest of Norman Italy and Sicily, while he believed that
he had established order in Saxony and the Rhinelands. With
Henry VI the center of gravity of the Hohenstaufen house

---

[1] This breakdown of the old nobility was reached in Saxon times: "Multi . . . .
nobiles in paupertatem et magnam miseriam devoluti" (*Vita Adalberonis II Mettensis* [written *ca.* 1000], chap. xxvii; cf. Lamprecht, *DWL*, I, Part II, 1163).

[2] See a striking paragraph in Lamprecht, *op. cit.*, p. 1063, and cf. p. 1029.

[3] Aloys Schulte, *Der Adel und die Deutsche Kirche im Mittelalter* (Stuttgart,
1910), p. 278, has the appended statistical table to illustrate the gradual extinction
of the great families of Germany between 900 and 1500.

	Fürsten.........	69 per cent married, 31 per cent celibate
Men	Grafen..........	64 per cent married, 36 per cent celibate
	Freiherren.......	50 per cent married, 50 per cent celibate
	Fürsten.........	74 per cent married, 26 per cent celibate
Women	Grafen..........	68 per cent married, 32 per cent celibate
	Freiherren.......	65 per cent married, 35 per cent celibate

There is a review of this book in *Eng. Hist. Rev.*, XXVI, 164–65.

was definitively transferred from Germany to Italy, and Germany more and more drifted into the whirlpool of the great interregnum.

The history of Germany from the time of the Hohenstaufen onward proves that feudalism had no ethnic ingredients, but was the product of social and economic conditions played upon by political purposes. Germany in the late twelfth and thirteenth centuries (from 1193 to 1273) repeated the history of France of the ninth and tenth centuries. The German kings and the German feudality, dukes, margraves, counts palatine, and burgraves were the victims of the same psychological phenomenon that had so weakened and reduced the last Carolingians and first Capetians in France, namely, the detachment of the vassal from the overlord, and rear-vassals in their turn from their suzerains. This centrifugal tendency finally was carried so far that Germany, territorially and politically, like France earlier, was reduced to a rope of sand, and the kingship became a lean and solemn phantom.

The history of England is essentially the history of the rights and liberties of the people; that of France is the history of the development of the rights and the power of the kings; that of Germany the history of the triumph of feudal particularism over monarchy and people. In Germany feudalism was less a constitutional system than the dissolution of all public power. From the twelfth century the principalities were regarded much more as patrimonial territories than as fiefs of the Empire, and the triumph of the principle of heredity transformed these lordships into sovereignties. This transformation was essentially the result of a combination of fief with function. It gave birth to a body of diverse rights which gradually reduced the former rights of the crown to mere suzerainty.

I have deferred unto the close of this chapter extended treatment of the *ministeriales*, for the reason that this influential class was a unique group in German feudal society, with slight counterpart in either France or England. On the continent outside of Germany proper, the class is only to be found in the provinces bordering upon France, like Flanders and Lorraine.[1]

In theory medieval society was supposed to be divided into three classes: clergy, nobility, and the common people.[2] *"Nunc orant, alii pugnant, aliique laborant,"* ran the proverb.

But, as so often happens in history, close examination of social evidences has proved that the theory and the fact were far from coinciding. We know that feudal society never was truly tripartite and that the sharp line of division between the classes upon which the legists laid so much emphasis never actually existed. Bishops and abbots were both priests and nobles; they had a dual status. The Knights Templar, the Knights Hospitaller, and the Teutonic Knights were no less chevaliers because they enjoyed benefit of clergy. As the condition of the two privileged orders blurred at the upper edges, so at the lower edge the noble class shaded off into the servile through obscure gradations of *minores, minocres, mediocres,* upon whose status Du Cange and all the rest of the great expounders of medieval institutions have not a word.[3] Similarly, the decline of serfdom and the burgher revolution split the masses into three classes, bourgeois, free

[1] The *colliberti* of French cartularies are the closest French analogue to the German *ministeriales* (Lamprecht, *op. cit.*, Part I, pp. 820 ff., 1128 ff., 1167 ff., and his *Études sur l'état économique de la France* [trans. Marignan], p. 214 and notes). But remnants of a rudimentary *ministerialis* condition are to be found in Normandy and Brittany as late as the twelfth century (Guilhiermoz, p. 114 and n. 28). Chevaliers-serfs, or knights of servile extraction, were not uncommon in Flanders (Kervyn de Lettenhove, *Histoire de Flandre*, I [1846], 215–16, 349–50, 365). The most remarkable illustration is in the Hacket family in the time of Charles the Good (d. 1127). See Galbert de Bruges, *De Multro, Traditione, et Occisione gloriosi Karoli Comitis Flandriarum* (ed. Pirenne), esp. chap. vii, and cf. van Houtte, *Essai sur la civilisation Flamande au commencement du XIIe siècle* (Louvain, 1898), pp. 42–43; Hansay, *Étude sur la formation et l'organisation économique du domaine de l'Abbaye de St. Trond* (Ghent, 1899), pp. 62–63.

[2] For larger treatment of this social attitude see Guilhiermoz, pp. 357–58, 370–74, but to the literature there cited add Rather of Verona (Migne, *Patrol. Lat.*, CXXXVI, 236); *Gesta Episcoporum Camerac.* (SS. VII, 485); Garreau, *L'etat social de la France au temps des Croisades*, pp. 215–16; Luchaire, *Social France at the time of Philip Augustus* (Eng. trans.), p. 391, quoting John of Salisbury; Mary M. Wood, *The Spirit of Protest in Old French Literature* (New York, 1917), chap. i.

[3] Cf. my article in *Amer. Hist. Rev.*, XVIII, 500; Hessels, "Medieval Latin," *Jour. Phil.* (London), XXXI, 474, 480, 486–88, 538, 561–68.

villains, and serfs. Neither legally nor historically are the three groups identical.[1]

These variant conditions and these social and economic changes were common to all Europe in the Middle Ages; but the degree of the transformations differed widely in different countries. France remained always socially the most aristocratic country, with England next, thanks largely to the operation of the law of primogeniture. In Lombard and Tuscan Italy the triumph of city states suppressed the political power of the feudality, and even the blood of the nobility was largely absorbed by the bourgeoisie. The victory of the Guelf party almost everywhere in Northern Italy by the end of the thirteenth century destroyed forever the domination of the nobility. Henceforward it was often true, as Salvemini has written: "Scratch a knight and you find a burgher."[2] In medieval Germany, on the other hand, in spite of the great number of the towns there, the burghers never suppressed the baronage. The two classes never fused together as in Italy, but lived side by side in permanent hostility.

A cardinal social fact in the history of medieval Germany is the degradation of the nobility from below by the penetration of men of servile birth and condition upward into the privileged plane. This phenomenon is the rise of the *ministeriales*. There are isolated and rare instances of the same thing in French and English history, but they occur early in the feudal age, never later when feudal society had become more crystallized. But in medieval Germany the elevation of

---

[1] Chivalry was not a nobility but a function; it could not be a closed class, for its privileges were not hereditable. It was recruited from below as much as from its own social level. Otto I raised a simple warrior to dignity of knighthood (Wid. III, 44). The Hohenstaufen regularly employed its reward as a means of recruiting followers (Otto of Freising, *Gesta Frid. I*, p. 18; Petrus de Vineis, *Epist.*, VI, 17). As warfare, especially the Crusades, thinned the ranks of the aristocracy the void was filled from below. The *Contin. Will. Tyr.* says: "Il n'avait adonc à la cité que deus chaveliers qui estoient eschappés de la bataille. Lors fit Belin d'Helin cinquante fils de borgois chevaliers" (Martène, *Amplissima*, V, 209). In a few generations all memory of origin of these families was lost.

[2] Salvemini, *La Dignità Cavalleresca nel Comune di Firenze* (1896). Cf. *Eng. Hist. Rev.*, XII, 552.

men of servile condition to the rank of a petty nobility took place on so large a scale that the result approximated a social revolution. The formation of the *ministerialis* class is a historical development unique in German history and not found elsewhere.[1]

In its origin and inception the rise of the *ministeriales* is to be found in the economic conditions of the manorial system. Originally the *ministeriales* were a preferred class of serfs employed for service instead of for labor, who were not bound to the glebe except theoretically, but were installed in administrative and military offices of inferior responsibility, and rewarded by stipends derived from manors.[2]

Officials of such lowly origin are to be found in Charlemagne's *Hof* and upon the estates of the Carolingian fisc, where they acted as managers or stewards of the property.[3] But in a day when lands and public offices both tended to become fiefs it was difficult—and in Germany impossible—

[1] Ashley, *Surveys*, p. 245, however, cautiously says: "Such a class of *ministeriales* certainly does not stare us in the face in the English sources, but we should possibly find them if we looked for them, even if they do not play with us quite the leading part ascribed to them in Germany."

[2] Lamprecht, *DWL*, I, Part II, 902; Wittich, *Die Grundherrschaft in Nordwestdeutschland*, p. 75; Guérard, *Polyptique de l'Abbé Irminon* (proleg.), pp. 801–2, 819–20; Fürth, *Die Ministerialen*, p. 34; Hansay, *op. cit.*, p. 63, n. 4. The diversion of servile tenures for support of the *ministeriales* naturally increased the economic burden upon the serfs (von der Goltz, *Geschichte der deutschen Landwirtschaft*, I, 112). The literature pertaining to the origin of the *ministeriales* is voluminous. The chief matter of debate is whether the class first appeared upon ecclesiastical or secular lands, and whether it was primarily used for domestic or military service. The servile origin of the *ministeriales* is almost universally admitted. But Heck, *Beiträge zur Gesch. der Stände im Mittelalter* (2 vols.; Halle, 1905), and "Der Ursprung der sächsichen Dienstmannschaft," *Vierteljahrschrift f. Soz.- und Wirtschaftsgesch.*, Band V (1907), with whom Wittich agrees, in *ibid.*, IV, No. 1 (1906), and Ganzenmueller, in *Westdeutsche Zeitschrift*, XXV, No. 4 (1906), have recently contended that at least in Saxony the *ministeriales* developed out of free and not servile condition. Schulte, *Der Adel*, app. 1, and Bode, *Der Uradel in Ostfalien*, both argue against this theory, which cannot be more than a thesis. Cf. *Hist. Zeitschrift*, CXIV, No. 1. The best and most recent discussion of this intricate subject is Keutgen, in *Vierteljahrschrift für Sozial- und Wirtschaftsgeschichte*, Band VIII, a series of four articles. For Flanders and Lorraine see F. L. Ganshof, *Étude sur les ministeriales en Flandre et en Lotharingie* (Brussels, 1926). The second section surveys all the literature on the general subject.

[3] *Capit.* 789 (ed. Krause), Vol. I, chap. iv, p. 88; *Capitulare de villis*, chaps. x, l; Waitz, II, 174 and notes; Nitzsch, *Deutsche Geschichte*, I, 237; Lamprecht. *DG*, II, 101.

to prevent these stations of humble authority from being assimilated to the condition of fiefs. For both lay and ecclesiastical lords often preferred, rather than enfeoff their lands in order to secure vassals, to recruit men-at-arms from among their dependents.[1] The *ministeriales* thus became armed domestics. The practice was both cheaper and safer. These preferred servitors, who were usually managers of farm properties, became messengers, stood castle-guard, acted as a bodyguard for the lord when he traveled, and on a pinch performed actual military service either afoot or *à cheval*.[2] The last duty was so privileged a one that Charlemagne in 789 ruled that a *ministerialis* performing genuine military service was *ipso facto* made free.[3] The *ministerialis*, while personally remaining a serf, thus came to enjoy the honors and emoluments of a petty noble. He had the privilege of a liegeman without a social status.

The inchoate beginnings of the *ministerialis* class are discernible in the Merovingian period,[4] but the hardening of the occasional practices of that epoch falls within the ninth and tenth centuries. The stages of development are relatively clear and rapid. At first the position and the privilege of this class within a class was an informal one, and varied accord-

---

[1] They are the *milites agrarii* of Widukind (*Rerum Gestarum Saxonicarum*, I, 35), and the *milites gregarii* of Wipo (*Vita Chuonradi II*, chaps. iv, xxxiv). The term first occurs in Alcuin's *Epistola, 174,* (ed. Jaffé), VI, 623: *gregarios, id est ignobiles milites*. See also Waitz, V, 439 (in his dissertation at the end of this volume on the *ministeriales*), and cf. II, 42 (n. 4), 390 (n. 3); IV, 126 (n. 2), 488. It should be added, however, that although the passage in Widukind, I, 35, is usually interpreted as meaning *ministeriales*, since the rise of the "garrison theory" of town origins some recent German historians like Varges, *Zur Entstehung der deutschen Stadtverfassung* in Conrad's *Jahrbücher für Nationalökonomie*, LXI, 175, and Keutgen, *Untersuchungen über den Ursprung der deutschen Stadtverfassung*, do not regard these *milites agrarii* as armed serfs, but as freemen keeping castle-guard. The former calls them *wehrhaftige, heerpflichtige Dorfbewohner*; and the latter, *heerbannpflichtige Bauern*. Buecher, *Die Entstehung der Volkswirtschaft*, p. 45, is to the same effect. For a discussion in English of the garrison theory see F. W. Maitland's famous essay of that title, and W. J. Ashley, *Surveys*, pp. 188–93. Dietrich Schaefer, "Die agrarii milites des Widukind," *S. B. Berliner Akad. d. Wiss.*, XXVII (1905), 577.

[2] Lamprecht, *DWL*, I, Part II, 713 (n. 4), 880, 1313 (n. 4); Schulte, *Rechtsgeschichte*, sec. 83, 4; Guilhiermoz, pp. 108–9, 462.

[3] *MGH, Leges* (ed. Krause), I, 67. This privilege fell into decay after Charlemagne (Guilhiermoz, p. 458).

[4] Zallinger, *Ministeriales und Milites*, pp. 3–20.

ing to the liberality of the lord. Gradually, however, this position and privilege became fixed and a body of *ministerialis* "rights" was formed, not recognized in written charters, but sanctioned by practice and custom. In this evolution the *ministeriales* of the crown first developed as farm managers, bailiffs, or stewards upon the lands of the fisc; they next appear in the same capacity upon the lands of the church;[2] and finally, we find them in the courts of the great nobles.[3] For uncertain of the allegiance of their vassals, the upper feudality, lay and clerical, more and more inclined to rely upon *ministeriales* as soldiers, and rewarded them with lands and honors.[4] The practice was an old one, but it acquired enormous extension during the Salian period.

But the rank of *ministerialis* was not open to serfs of every condition. A distinction obtained, and only those called *dagewardi* or *fiscalini* were eligible to ministerial degree. Omitting the lowest variations of class among the lowly, the upper serfs in medieval Germany may be said to have been divided into two groups, viz.: the *fiscalini* (or *fisgalini*) and the *dagewardi* or *dagewehrten*, the former being the higher in social scale; they had a share in the *wehrgeld* of their kindred, were not compelled to render services except of specified kind,

---

[1] Waitz, V, 337–38, 341–42; Schröder, p. 448; *Bamberger Dienstrecht*, in Jaffé, V, 51.

[2] For the large employment of the *ministeriales* by the church see Nitzsch, *Ministerialität und Bürgertum*, I, 371–74; II, 24. The distinction between *ministeriales* engaged in agricultural economy and those employed in the industrial arts first appears on the manors of the church.

[3] In *Annales Fuldenses* (880) is an account of an invasion of Lower Germany by the Norsemen. In the battle two bishops, twelve counts, and eighteen *satellites regii* (*ministeriales, milites gregarii*) fell. The names are very interesting, for they clearly indicate the base origin of the bearers of them. In *Annales Altahenses Majores* (1042) Adalbert, margrave of the Ostmark, encountered the Hungarians "cum parvissima manu militum et servitorum, quippe nec triginta habentes scutatorum."

[4] Gerdes, II, 386 f.; Waitz, V, 343 f., 386–87. Lambert of Hersfeld describes the method (*anno* 1074), p. 198: "Sed alii temporis angustias, alii rei familiaris inopiam, plerique quod opes suae bello Saxonico nimium attritae fuissent, item alii aliud excusationis genus obtendentes, omnes pariter miliciam detrectabant. Ipse tamen, ne tantum reipublicae commodum casu oblatum sua ignavia corrumperetur, gregario tantum ac privato milite contentus, etc." Bruno, chap. lxxviii, gives the king's *ministeriales*, with justice, an evil reputation for tyranny: "Nam familiares praedicti Henrici qui ab omni regno infamia notantur, etc."

or in certain departments of the lord's household, and could
inherit and devise property. It has been inferred from these
facts that their ancestors had once been freemen and had become bondmen for the sake of protection. This is Wittich's
contention. If true at all, it is truer for North Germany than
for the South and truer of northwest Saxony than of the
northeast. The *fiscalini*, at least those who dwelt on lands of
the bishops, seem to have been divided into two classes—
those who lived in the town, who no doubt were artisans and
craftsmen, and those living in the country, who were peasant
farm laborers.[1] If a *fiscalinus* married a *dagewarda* or a *dage-
wardus* married a *fiscalina* their children belonged to the
status of the parent who was the lower of the pair. Usually,
if not invariably, the *ministeriales* were recruited from the
fiscalinus class of serfs.

The development of the *ministerialis* class has been
illustrated by the appended diagram:

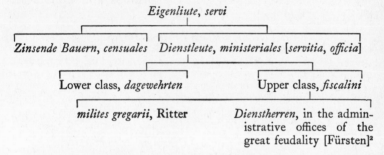

The formation of the *ministerialis* class may be said to
have become completed by the twelfth century, by which
time the performance of military service, the supreme dignity
of a noble, had become theirs, and the status in fact, though
not in law, become a hereditary one.[3] Certain servile tradi-

---

[1] The classic document illustrating the condition of episcopal *ministeriales* is
the law for the *familia* of Burchard of Worms (1023) (*MGH, Leges* [N.S.], I, 640 ff.;
Altmann and Bernheim, *Ausgewählte Urkunden*, No. 62, esp. secs, 9, 13, 16, 22, 29).

[2] From Paul's *Grundriss der Germanischen Philologie*, XI, 122; also in Schauffler,
Quellenbuch zur Kulturgeschichte der Deutschen im Mittelalter (Leipzig, 1894), p. 130.

[3] By the twelfth century a *ministerialis* is often qualified as "noble." Waitz,
V, 500, *Chron. Ebersheimense:* "Familia ministerialis . . . . adeo nobilis et belli-

tions, however, still clung to the position of the *ministerialis* which it was their constant effort to obliterate.[1]

Tempted by the advantage of the position many freemen sought to become *ministeriales*, and, of course, to rise to the level of one was the supreme ambition of many a serf, to whom emancipation by economic change was a desperately slow one and too much for his patience, while emancipation by revolt was impossible.[2]

In this wise the armed domestic and petty bureaucrat became constituent elements in the social fabric of feudal Germany. Kings, dukes, bishops, and abbots were surrounded by a crowd of *Hofdiener*.[3] The clergy in particular were partial to the formation of this class. For although the heaviest landowners they were the least willing to enfeoff their lands, a course in which the crown sustained them, since the Saxon and Salian kings drew vastly more upon ecclesiastical sources for men and money than upon lay sources. Instead of sending real vassals to the army the bishops and abbots sent

---

cosa." The *Vita Bennonis II, Episcopi Osnabrugensis*, chap. i (he died in 1088), illustrates the position to which the *ministerialis* class had risen at the end of the eleventh century. Benno was born of this class, yet he reached the episcopate and became one of Henry IV's greatest ministers: "ejus parentes non nobiles quidem sed tamen plebeam conditionem transgressi." He was the first German bishop of *ministerialis* class (Schulte, *Der Adel und die Deutsche Kirche*, p. 72; Schulte, *Schriften für Geschichte und Naturgeschichte der Baar*, V, 142).

[1] The "rights" of the *ministeriales* were first legally recognized in the ecclesiastical principalities (Steindorff, *Jahrbücher Heinrichs III*, II, 342; Jaffé, V, 51). The earliest effort to formulate them is found in the *Hofrecht* of Burchard of Worms in Henry II's reign (*Urkundenbuch der Stadt Worms*, I, 40), and in the Bamberger *Dienstrecht* of Bishop Gunther (1057–64) (Gerdes, II, 441). In the *Sachsenspiegel*, *Dienstmann* is glossed with *puer* (*MGH, Const.*, I, 88). In the letter of the law the rights of a freeman were denied to a *ministerialis*. He could be bought and sold with the land like a serf (Kluckheim, *Zeitschrift für Deutsches Altertum*, LII, 135 ff.; Waitz, V, 358); marriage with a free woman was forbidden; he could be beaten (*MGH, Leges* [N.S.], IV, 609). But these disqualifications by the twelfth century, and even before that, were really obsolete for many of the *ministeriales*, and their presence in the codes merely illustrates the conservatism of the law which preserved old, time-worn dicta which had long since become anomalous and out of date.

[2] Lamprecht, *DG*, III, 67.

[3] Waitz, V, 323. It is apparent from Wipo, *Vita Chuonradi*, chap. iv, that by the time of Conrad II freemen were a negligible quantity around the court, and that the officials were either clerics, nobles, or *ministeriales*.

bodies of armed domestics.[1] Such men were far more trac-
table than vassals and less dangerous also to intrust with
power.[2] Serfs were meant to obey, and in spite of the parvenu aspirations of the *ministeriales*, the tradition of obedience and servility was still strong among them. When the
expedition was over they returned to their former occupations, contented with their "service fiefs," which did not
entail homage but were servile tenures of magnified dignity.

In the reign of Henry I and the Saxon epoch in general,
the *ministeriales* seem chiefly to have formed small mounted
contingents.[3] But the great cost of the Italian expeditions[4]
of the medieval emperors and the reluctance of many of the
German vassals to do service so far away gradually induced
the emperors to make larger and larger use of *ministeriales*
instead of vassals. It is evident from Wipo's *Life of Conrad
II* (1024–39) that feudal service in Italy had much declined
by the first quarter of the eleventh century.[5] Henry V in
1124 had great difficulty in getting vassals to serve in France
"quia Teutonici non facile gentes impugnant exteras."[6] A

---

[1] The evidence is abundant and some of it very interesting. See *Gesta Abbatum
Trudonensium*, IX, 12; *Vita Godehardi*, chap. xxxi; *Chron. Gosec.*, chaps. i, ii, xxvii.
The sarcasm in Henry IV's speech, as related by the author of the *Vita Heinrici* (ed.
Everhard), chap. viii, p. 29, in announcing the unpopular ordinance of 1103 to the
discontented nobles is manifest when it is remembered that their following was
chiefly made up of armed domestics: "Reddite agris quos ex agro deputastis armis,
coequate numerum satellitum ad mensuram facultatum." Cf. Waitz, V, 325, 328.

[2] For examples of the hazard in using regular knights as bodyguard see Thietmar, VIII, 14, and cf. Guilhiermoz, p. 253, n. 23.

[3] Widukind, I, 38; Thietmar, IV, 28; Cosmas of Prague, II, 9.

[4] See *Constitutio de Expeditione Romana* (cited by Waitz), V, 373. The war of
investiture greatly multiplied the number of *ministeriales*, for each side made much
use of them, rewarding them out of the spoliated lands (Waitz, V, 332; Schröder,
p. 448; Lamprecht, *DG*, III, 68). From some military statistics for the years between 1096 and 1146 it would appear that vassals formed 71 per cent of the army.
But between 1147 and 1191 this proportion drops to 23 per cent; and between 1191
and 1250 the figure declines to 3 per cent. The balance of the troops, i.e., 29, 77, and
97 per cent, were composed of *ministeriales* (Kluckhohn, *Die Ministerialität in
Süd-Deutschland* [Göttingen, 1909]). However, it must be remembered that these
figures pertain to South German contingents only.

[5] *Vita Chuonradi*, chap. xxiv.

[6] Ekkehard of Aura, *Chron.* (SS. VI, 262); Waitz, VIII, 103, n. 5.

large portion of the army of Conrad III on the Second Crusade was made up of *ministeriales*.[1]

It was always difficult for the Salian emperors to make Saxons serve in Italy, and even Henry II, though a Saxon, had trouble.[2] Accordingly, *ministeriales* were increasingly used for military service. Conrad II's legislation in 1028 for the Weissenburger *ministeriales* (if genuine) marks an epoch in the evolution of this class.[3] Henceforward military *ministeriales* took an oath similar to that of the feudality. One of the grievances of the Saxons against Henry III was his large use of *ministeriales* for garrison duty in the citadels of the crown in Saxony. Their swaggering ways and their base origin angered the pride of the Saxons.

There was nothing essentially new in the use of *milites gregarii* or armed domestics by the Salian kings. The Ottos had done the same; they merely extended the employment of *ministeriales* for military service. What the kings of the Salian house are remarkable for is the introduction of this class into the civil offices of the crown. Occasional instances of favorite *ministeriales* near the person of the king may be found in the Saxon period. But Conrad II was the first German sovereign who created the "royal" *ministeriales*, as a class, and organized them into an executive staff of officials. Werner was his chief *ministerialis* and the earliest secular minister in the history of medieval Germany. In his capacity of supervisor of the fisc he was a kind of chief intendant or comptroller general.[4]

Henry IV pushed the Salian policy of employing *ministeriales* in the administration of the fisc so far that almost all

---

[1] Bernhardi, *Konrad III*, Part I, p. 598, nn. 18, 19; for high Hohenstaufen times see Otto of St. Blasius (ed. Hofmeister), pp. 26, 27, 68.

[2] For Henry II's difficulty see Helmold, *Chronica Slavorum*, I, 14.

[3] There is much division of opinion in regard to this document. Giesebrecht (4th ed.), II, 633, thinks it genuine; Riezler, *Geschichte Bayerns*, I, 441, n. 1, wholly rejects it. Waitz, *Forschungen*, XIV, 32, and *DVG*, V, 334; Bresslau, *Konrad II*, I, 252, n. 1; II, 379; Steindorff, *Heinrich III*, I, 415; Zallinger, *Ministeriales und Milites*, p. 4, and other historians think it genuine, but glossed or corrupted by later additions.

[4] Wipo, *Vita Chuonradi*, chap. iv: "Werinharii militis, quem rex longe ante cautum consiliis, audacem bellis, frequenter secum experiebatur."

such officials in his reign seem to have been *ministeriales*,[1] the chief of whom was Eberhard of Nellenburg. These hated tax-gatherers and counselors were the persons for whom the hostile chroniclers reserved such opprobrious epithets as *parasiti, scurrae, facinorum ipsius* (Henry IV), *conscii et fautores*, etc., and whom the Fürsten detested as *obscuri et pene nullis majoribus nati*.[2]

The arrogance and petty tyranny of this parvenu class made the *ministeriales* detested by the peasantry, and feuds between the *ministeriales* of one lord and those of another were frequent, for they readily took up the causes of their patrons.[3] Even the Bambergers complained of Henry IV's *ministeriales*, although Bamberg was the favorite seat of the Salian emperors.[4] Barefaced seizure or compulsory secularization of ecclesiastical lands to the profit of *ministeriales* in the employ of the church was common all through Germany during the strife between Henry IV and the rebel partisans of the Pope and the revolted Saxons.[5]

For during the Saxon rebellion and the war of investiture

[1] See the dissertation of Roehrig, *De Secularibus Consiliariis Heinrici IV* (Halle, 1866). Waitz, VI, 292, is very brief. But see Nitzsch, *Historische Zeitschrift* (N.S.), IX, 200. Lambert of Hersfeld voices the aristocratic protest against them: "Quod, remotis a familiaritate sua principibus, infimos homines et nullis majoribus ortos summis honoribus extulisset, et cum eis noctes perinde ac dies in deliberationibus insumens, ultimum, si possit, nobilitati exterminium machinaretur" (*Annales* p. 277).

[2] For all his large use of *ministeriales*, the sight of them in the ranks of the enemy angered Henry. In 1103, when a new rebellion was on his hands, he cried out sarcastically to the army against him: "Reddite agris quos ex agro deputastis armis, coequate numerum satellitum ad mensuram facultatum recolligite praedia vestra quae stulte sparsistis, ut multos armatos haberetis, et redundabunt omnibus bonis horrea et cellaria vestra" (*Vita Heinrici IV*, chap. viii).

[3] The history of the strife of Bishop Salamon of Constance (d. 871) with the Kammerboten Erchanger and Berchtold has been unraveled by Baumann in *Vierteljahrshefte für Württemb. Geschichte* (1878). It was almost legendary by the time of Ekkehard of St. Gall (see *Casus S. Galli*, chap. i) and gave rise to some of the earliest German ballad literature.

[4] Jaffé, V, 395. The famous ordinance of Bishop Embricho in 1128 for the government of the Bamberger *ministeriales* must have been called out by this abuse. Cf. Fürth, pp. 509–10; Gengler, *Beiträge zur Rechtsgeschichte Bayerns*, IV, 153–54. Fisher (*Medieval Empire*, I, 80) has translated part of the ordinance.

[5] Cf. Martiny's study in *Mittheilungen des Ver. für Geschichte von Osnabrück*, Band XX (1895). By the twelfth century we find *ministeriales* assuming titles from landed possession like nobles (Ficker, *Vom Reichsfürstenstand*, I, 77).

the power of the *ministeriales* enormously increased. Both sides recruited their fighting men from among this class of armed servitors and created new members for the express purpose of warfare, in so much that the boldest of the *ministeriales* succeeded in converting their service tenures into real fiefs, and even demanded benefices as the price of their services.[1] *"Dienstmann ist nicht Eigen"* was their slogan.

Yet it would be an error to assume that military service was the predominant function or activity of the *ministeriales*. It was the most distinguished but the rarest form of service. Most of them were employed in small administrative capacities upon the crown lands, the manors of the clergy and nobles, as stewards, or bailiffs, and in household offices. Writing in 1135 and describing the monastery community of Zwifalten in Swabia, Ortlieb takes pride in the obedience and humility of the *ministeriales* who belonged to the abbey. He writes:

> Among our men some owe service of this kind, namely, when the lord abbot, prior, provost, or others among the brethren would travel anywhither, these men with their horses do accompany them and minister to them. And in order that this service may be rightfully required of them they are granted certain benefices. They assuredly rejoice to be honored by this distinction because they have the right to have under them men whom we call *clientes* or *ministeriales*. Yet in spite of this, no man of ours has ever become so perverse or so haughty that he presumed to ride with us, in military array, or refused to carry the wallet of any of our monks upon his pack-horse. The founders of our monastery did not intend to give us such men, and we have not consented to receive any one who might prove troublesome to us or to our successors.[2]

Farther on in this interesting chronicle of Zwiefalten, Ortlieb quotes the caution given the monks by Count Liutold, one of the monastery's benefactors, lest the monks let the *ministeriales* in the service of the abbey increase too much,

[1] *Annal. Hild.* (1103) (SS. VIII, 202); Walter, *Rechtsgesch.*, sec. 210; Lamprecht, *DWL*, I, Part II, 881. For a remarkable instance of the boldness of a *ministerialis* in the time of Frederick I see *Gesta Frid.*, II, 3. For the misconduct of Conrad III's *ministeriales* in Saxony see SS. XVI, 82, and Bernhardi, *op. cit.*, Vol. I, p. 162. By 1200 we find these parvenu knights as "wandering knights" in Germany; Gislebertus Montensis, *Chronicon Hannoniae* (ed. Pertz, *in usum scholarum*), p. 66; "milites . . . . in imperio Theutonicorum gyrovagantes."

[2] *Ortliebi Zwifaltensis Chronicon* (SS. X, 78).

a warning which shows some of the inconveniences, and even dangers arising from the ambitious pretensions of this parvenu class.

He told us that *ministeriales* were the greatest factor in the decay of monasteries, and the chiefest cause of their penury and poverty. He used to say that monks who had *ministeriales* never had peace and tranquillity and were never without fret, trouble and turmoil. Moreover the *ministeriales* acquired the property of the monastery for themselves and consumed that of others by strife, warfare, fire and sword. How could unarmed and unwarlike monks withstand such pretentious and quarrelsome upstarts whom neither the very nobles nor even tyrants can control?[1]

Only the most ambitious and the most fortunate of the *ministeriales* succeeded in rising into the *Ritter* class and became noble. Such were those who had shown distinguished prowess in war.[2] It was rare in France, if not impossible, for a serf to become a chevalier. But in feudal Germany it was not unusual, even if not common. When this transformation was reached the *ministerialis* acquired the status of a petty noble. He had entered—albeit his foot was on the lowest rung of the ladder—the blue-ribbon membership of the *Heerschild*,[3] assumed a title, was lord of a castle and a mano-

---

[1] "Dixit etenim, milites maximam occasionem destructionis monasteriorum et quietis monachorum perturbationis fore, maximam penuriae et paupertatis causam milites esse. Monachi, inquam, qui milites habent semper pace et quiete carent, numquam sine ira, rixa et disceptatione manent. Insuper res monasterii inter se dividunt, alia rixando, bellando, igne ferroque consumunt; et quomodo inermes monachi et imbelles his possunt resistere, quibus proprii domini vel ipsi etiam tyranni vix et vix possunt imperare?" (*MGH, SS*, X, 100, chap. vi).

[2] The first instance of the knighting of *ministeriales* is of those of the Archbishop of Mainz in 1126 (Boehmer, *Fontes*, III, 278, 328). The practice first obtained in the Rhinelands (Waitz, V, 397).

[3] In its original, primary sense the *Heerschild* was the royal host. The king himself, as a noble, was the first degree (*Sachsenspiegel*, chap. lxxi, sec. 6, ed. of Homeyer, I, 286). The first clear definition of the *Heerschild* is in *Chron. Lauresh*. (SS. XXI, 415, 434–35). Ficker's book, *Vom Heerschilde*, is a classic. Cf. Guilhiermoz, p. 264, n. 27. "The Thuringian family of Reuss, which has maintained its independence to our own day, springs from the imperial *ministeriales* who administered the Voigtland, or district of Weida, Gera, and Plauen. The peculiar interest of its history lies in the fact . . . . that it attained its rank not through any noble connexion or in virtue of the office of *Graf*, but solely through reliance upon the position of imperial *Vogt*. The family was 'unfree,' and was in part subject to the landgraves of Thuringia. By means of their judicial rights, which, as imperial officers, they retained over the small territory which came to them, the various members of this house gradually founded a claim to be immediate vassals of the empire. Assisted in the

rial proprietor, adopted a heraldic device, and aped the court-
ly fashions of the age of chivalry.[1] By the time of the Hohenstaufen a considerable proportion of the German noblesse,
especially the knights, were composed of former *ministeriales*.
But we find counts, dukes, and bishops risen from this class.[2]
The poets and minnesingers of the twelfth and thirteenth
centuries all arose from this class, as did many of the heroes
of whom they sang. Their technical feudal language, when
it is not of French troubadour origin and often used in order
to air their "culture," betrays their parvenu ancestry.

To all these forces which have been enumerated, which
tended to break down the old German feudal aristocracy,
should be added the democratizing (or shall one say the cor-
rupting?) influence of the new monastic orders like the Cistercians and the German Cluniacs or Hirsauer monks, whose
brotherhoods were far less aristocratic than the older orders
were. In addition to hundreds of lay brothers or *conversi*,
these two orders developed *ministeriales* to an unprecedented
degree.[3]

The social practice of feudal Germany in thus elevating
domestic serfs to the rank of small nobles gave a banality to
the late medieval German aristocracy which one does not
find in the English or French nobility. The German nobility
of the thirteenth century lacked the culture, the grace, the
urbanity, and the pride which one so habitually associates

---

thirteenth century by the emperors who were opposed to the house of Wettin, the
family of Reuss finally received a golden bull from Lewis of Bavaria in 1329, and
were legally established in their princely rank" (review of W. Finkenwirth's *Die
Entwicklung der Landeshoheit der Vorfahren des Fürstenhauses Reuss, 1122–1329*
["Jenaer Historische Arbeiten" (Bonn, 1912), Band II], in *Engl. Hist. Rev.*, XXVIII,
603).

[1] Moeser, *Osnabrückische Gesch.*, II, 105, says the rush to become *ministeriales*
was so great that "liberty almost became an indignity."

[2] Roth von Schreckenstein, p. 335; Waitz, V, 385; Köhler, II, Part II, 63;
Gerdes, I, 482–83; Lamprecht, *DWL*, I, Part II, 1173; Kluckhohn, *Zeitschrift für
Deutsches Altertum*, LII (1910), 135 ff.

[3] Aloys Schulte, *Der Adel und die Deutsche Kirche im Mittelalter* (1910), has
shown by abundant evidence that in the early period of the Middle Ages the high
offices of the church in Germany were very largely filled by men of noble family, but
that in the later period men of unfree birth and ministerial condition invaded the
very highest grades of the hierarchy.

with the aristocracy of England and France. Birth and blood always counted in France and across the channel. But in Germany by the twelfth century these qualifications, while not unimportant, had lost the unique quality they preserved elsewhere. The distinction between real knight and *ministerialis* was a blurred social difference, not a sharp cleavage.[1]

By 1134 we find mention of the *ordo equestris major* and the *ordo equestris minor*, the one composed of real nobles, the other formed of *ministeriales*. But by 1152 even this distinction has disappeared and the two orders have fused into one. The law of 1187 shows the hardening of the process; the two groups were welded socially and politically.[2] Even before this development was reached the *ministeriales* of the crown and of the great nobles had forced their way into the diets and courts of the realm,[3] where they sat as proudly as real princes, and in Saxony only does their arrogance seem to have been regarded as effrontery.[4]

When we reach the reign of Frederick Barbarossa we find that the most ambitious of the *ministeriales* have blossomed

[1] Thus the *Chronica Regia Coloniensis* (ed. Waitz, *in usum scholarum*), p. 60, writing of the year 1122: "orta seditio inter armigeros *de re modica*, uti sepe fit, usque ad *milites armatos* pervenit." The former are genuine knights; the latter, *ministeriales* who have become knights. Cf. *ibid.*, pp. 144, 249. Struben, *Nebenstunden*, IV, 424 f.; V, 250 f., says most of German nobility actually were of servile or bourgeois origin by the fourteenth and fifteenth centuries.

[2] Waitz, V, 453; Köhler, III, Part II, 35; Schröder, p. 458; Roth von Schreckenstein, p. 291; Lamprecht, *DG*, III, 182; Schauffler, p. 131. Otto of Freising twice uses the term *ordo militaris* (*Chronica* [ed. Hofmeister], pp. 74, 175), and once the words *militares viri* (p. 88).

[3] *Chronica Regia Coloniensis* (1142), p. 78.

[4] *Annales Palidenses* (1146) (SS. XVI, 82): "Hoc anno res mira et hactenus inaudita in regno exorta est. Nam ministeriales regni et aliarum potestatum, non jussi ad colloquium sepius convenientes, inconsulto tam rege quam ceteris principibus justiciam omnibus interpellantibus se judiciali more fecerunt." Werner of Bolland possessed 17 castles in the time of Frederick Barbarossa and had 1,100 knights in his service (*Chron. Hanoniense* [*ed. cit.*], p. 145). His *Stammtafel* is given by Schulte, *Der Adel und die Deutsche Kirche*, pp. 312–13. For the high position of *ministeriales* around Frederick I see *Gesta Frid. Imp.*, II, 3; Arnold of Lübeck, *Chron. Slav.*, II, 17. For those in Germany during Frederick II's reign see Huillard Bréholles, *Historia diplomatica Friderici Secundi*, Introd., p. clx. In general, see Gudenatz, *Schwäbische und Fränkische Freiherren und Ministerialen am Hofe der deutschen Könige, 1198–1272* (Bonn, 1909).

into full-fledged nobles,[1] and many of them among the *Ritter-schaft*. Externally nothing distinguishes these parvenus from the old aristocracy except their low-born speech and rude manners. They, too, boasted title and assumed escutcheons like the real nobility, and their dynasties were recorded in the medieval *Almanach de Gotha*, the book of the names of those privileged to be included in the *Heerschild*, at the apex of which stood the king-emperor.[2]

And yet it must not be forgotten that these fortunate climbers who thus attained knighthood and nobility were, of course, proportionately few compared with the vast number of the *ministeriales* in all Germany. The great majority of the class, still in the twelfth century, as before, continued to be found in managerial capacities upon the lands of the fisc, of the church, and of the nobles.

The evolution and importance of this new class in medieval German society, a blend of serfdom and knighthood, constitutes one of the most striking differences between German feudalism and French or English feudalism. France, by taking a different and more aristocratic road from that of Germany, eliminated the débris of those Carolingian institutions which were the residuary legacy of the Frank Empire to both, while Germany retained it. Such indifference to social distinctions, such slight stress put upon ancestry, and such lack of class pride as feudal Germany displayed were unthinkable in feudal France in the twelfth century. There the law of primogeniture was a selective process which kept out upstarts and social climbers. Germany did little of the kind, and the result was that the ancient German nobility was undermined by the lower classes, its authority weakened, its prestige debased. The French noble was by ancestry and remained a *gentilhomme*—he was gentle born. The German noble class became filled with parvenus, men of low birth,

---

[1] By the charter granted by the Archbishop of Cologne to his *ministeriales* in 1154, art. 1 required that they take an oath of fidelity like any noble; art. 12 specifically calls the lands they held "fiefs" (text in Altmann-Bernheim, No. 70). On the assimilation of ministerial benefices to fiefs see Walter, *op. cit.*, sec. 210.

[2] Ficker, pp. 51 ff.; Schröder, p. 452; Lamprecht, *DG*, III, 97; Gebhardt, *Handbuch* (1st ed.), I, 465.

without family pride, and actuated by grossly materialistic
motives and ambitions, without the culture and the idealism
of the French noblesse. "As cheap as a German baron" was
an adage as far back as the twelfth century. One has only to
read the puzzled and critical comments of Suger and Gilbert
of Mons to discover this.[1]

[1] Suger, *Hist. Ludovici VII* (ed. Molinier), chap. ii, p. 148; *Chronicon Hanoniense* (SS. XXI, 538); Guilhiermoz, pp. 258–59.

CHAPTER X

THE CROWN LANDS IN FEUDAL GERMANY[1]

IN AN age when *Naturalwirtschaft* was almost universal,
and when even kings had to "live of their own" in large
part, that is to say, from the resources of their house and
crown lands, and when, too, little distinction was made between public revenue and private fortune, a feudal monarch
could have no fixed capital. He was compelled to be forever
on the road traveling from one royal domain to another. This
is true of the medieval kings of England, France, and Germany. Neither London nor Paris became permanent seats of
the English and French governments before the end of the
twelfth century.

In Germany, owing to three changes of dynasty, fixation
of capital was even less possible. The Saxon house manifested
a preference for residence in Saxony when the exigency of the
time permitted; the Salians sojourned in the middle Rhinelands when they could; the Hohenstaufen in Swabia. But the
crown lands of Germany (the fisc) were scattered in patches
and parcels in every duchy. Among the *villae* or *curtes* (*curiae
regales*) there was a certain number which were called *pertinentes ad mensam regis*, which were exploited after practices
laid down by Charlemagne in the *Capitulare de villis*. In
time the custom grew up of fixing a set number and kind of
commodities exacted from these, as beef, animals, pork, beer,

---

[1] Waitz, *Deutsche Verfassungsgesch.*, Vol. VIII, chap. xv, has 200 pages. The
best detailed study of the fisc is Eggers, *Der königliche Grundbesitz im 10. und beginnenden 11. Jahrhundert* (Weimar, 1909) (see important reviews of this work in
Hist. Viertelj. [1910], No. 4; *Goettingische . . . . Anzeiger* [March, 1911]; *Mittheil. d.
Inst. f. oesterr. Gesch.*, Band XXXIII, Heft 1 [1912]); Frey, *Die Schicksale des
königl. Gutes in Deutschland unter den letzten Staufen* (1881); M. Stimming, *Das
deutsche Königsgut im 11. und 12. Jahrhundert* (Ebering, *Historische Studien* [Berlin,
1922], No. 149); B. Heusinger, "Servitium regis in der deutschen Kaiserzeit,"
Archiv. f Urkundenforschung, VIII, 26–159. Niese, *Die Verwaltung des Reichsgutes
im 13. Jahrhundert* (1905), deals with the dissipation and dilapidation of the fisc
in the thirteenth century.

wine. But vegetables, grain, flour, and forage were expected as a matter of course. This condition was a transition stage between direct kingly exploitation and lease.

We have a few sources of uncertain value in regard to the expenses of the court of Otto I (936–73). According to these data, about 30 pounds of silver were required, per diem, for support of the king's *Hof*, or about 10,000 pounds per annum. Most interesting are the daily demands of the court in *naturalia*, which show the predominantly agricultural character of the economy, and the enormous rout of officials, counts, palsgraves, guardsmen, vassals, both lay and clerical in attendance, besides visiting guests of the king, *ministeriales*, etc., by whom the king was perpetually surrounded. According to the *Saxon Annals* (*anno* 968), Otto the Great's entourage daily consumed 1,000 swine and sheep, 10 *Fuder*, or 2,700 gallons of wine, the same amount of beer, 1,000 measures of grain, 8 oxen, chickens, ducks, geese, eggs, vegetables, fish, etc.[1] Of course, not all of these supplies came from the crown lands. The king "lived of his own" when it was convenient for him to do so. But as king and liege lord, he and his suite were entitled to hospitality from vassals in whose territories he was temporarily, or through whose lands he was passing. This right of hospitality often became a serious grievance of the feudality, who looked upon its exaction as a heavy burden.[2]

The revenues of the fisc, which were almost all in kind (*naturalia*), were supplemented by other resources which were fixed by the customary law of the manorial régime, such as tolls, *corvées* and fines and court fees payable to the king as a manorial proprietor. The most important of these impositions was the *Zins* (Fr., *cens*), a tax upon immovable property and nearly approaching in nature the later rent. The amount of the *Zins* varied according to the importance of the locality. In regions where the population was fairly dense and trade of some magnitude, it might be paid in money. In sparsely peopled regions of a backward economy,

[1] See Waitz, VIII, 223–25. For modern money equivalents, p. 223, n. 2.

[2] Waitz, VIII, 226–29.

it was usually paid in produce of the land or the forests. In any case, the revenues were not different from those collected by every feudal lord from his domains.[1]

The very fact that the fisc was formed of a widely scattered complex of domains, whose administration differed in no whit from the management of the surrounding and neighboring manors of the great proprietary class, exposed it to constant depredation by the latter. Moreover, counts and other local officials were prone to abuse the trust reposed in them and expropriate both lands and revenues to their own aggrandizement. Even Charlemagne was compelled at least once to institute a "revindication" of the fisc.[2]

In the ninth century the royal domain both in Germany and France was much reduced owing to the weakness of the kings, who were compelled to purchase from their rebellious vassals by grants from the fisc a support which they were unable to compel, or else the royal domains were boldly seized by the feudality, lay and clerical—barons, bishops, abbots. Louis the Pious seems to have made a weak effort to restrain such spoliation,[3] but the first effective check in Germany was imposed by Ludwig the German, in 852, who instituted the earliest reclamation or "revindication" of the fisc of which we have record.[4] The results, however, must have been unsatisfactory, for eight years later at Coblenz we find the King still complaining of rapine and depredation.[5]

[1] Waitz, IV, 113–20; Richter and Kohl, *Annalen d. deutschen Gesch.*, II, 1, 569–71; Nitzsch, II, 14.

[2] In the *Capitulare de justitiis faciendis*, chap. vii, we read: "Ut non solum beneficia episcoporum, abbatum, abbatissarum atque comitum sive vassalorum nostrorum, sed etiam nostri fisci describantur" (Boretius, *Capitularia regum Francorum*, I, 177). In *Vita Ludovici*, by the Astronomer, chap. vi (*MGH*, SS. II, 610), there is mention of this revindication, which was probably of the year 795. As Bloch says: "Nous sommes en présence d'une de ces vastes révisions des aliénations domainiales comme plus tard la royauté capétienne en fournira tant d'examples" (*Revue Historique*, CXLIII, 49).

[3] Boretius, *Capitularia regum Francorum*, I, 288, sec. 7; 291, sec. 22.

[4] ". . . . possessiones videlicet ab avita vel paterna proprietate jure hereditario sibi derelictas, quas oportuit ab iniquis pervasoribus justa repetitione legitimo domino restitui" (*Annal. Fuld* [anno 852]; cf. Mühlbacher, *Regesta*, No. 1403; Dopsch, *Wirtschaftsentwicklung der Karolingerzeit*, I, 174).

[5] ". . . . rapinas ac depraedationes quas jam quasi pro lege multi tenent per consuetudinem" (*MGH, Leges*, I, 472, art. 6). See also Bourgeois, *Le capitulaire de Kiersey*, p. 257, n. 7.

When Ludwig died, in 870, the spoliation of the crown lands went on apace under his successors.[1]

When the house of Charlemagne expired in Germany in 911, nothing but tattered remnants and scattered fragments of the former great patrimony of the Carolingians remained. At the accession of the Saxon dynasty in 919, it has been calculated that there were left only 83 crown lands in Franconia,[2] 50 in Swabia, 21 in Bavaria, 12 in Thuringia, 5 in Saxony, and 5 in south Friesland[3]—in all, about 375 square miles (Ger.) of farm lands once subject to the intelligent management laid down in the *Capitulare de villis*.[4] Of this heritage, the Franconian estates were the richest and most compact, and represented over 20 square miles (Ger.). The bishops in this rich Rhineland region had very largely succeeded in getting possession of the crown lands in the vicinity of their sees by the end of the Carolingian period. But there were still many old royal *Pfalzen* along the Rhine, of which Tribur, Coblenz, Boppart, Wesel, Oppenheim, and Hagenau were the most important.[5]

When the Saxon dukes became kings of Germany in 919, these scattered crown lands were united with their own ducal domains in Saxony, the whole forming the new fisc. After the extension of German rule to Italy in 962 by Otto I, these royal *Pfalzen* extended from the Harz to the Apennines in a long, ragged line, the denser complexes being in Saxony and

[1] Regino, *Chronicon* (*annis* 885, 887, 906).

[2] A considerable block of these, however, were not of Carolingian origin, but were the lands confiscated from the Babenberger by the government of Ludwig the Child in the time of the regency of Hatto of Mainz. *Regino* (906): "Facultates et possessiones ejus [Adalbert of Babenberg] in fiscum redactae sunt et dono regis inter nobiliores quosque distributae." The church, though, got the lion's share of this spoil. See Dümmler, *Forschungen*, III, 327–30.

[3] Inama Sternegg, *Grundherrschaft*, p. 26; Lamprecht, *Deutsche Wirtschaftsleben*, I, 718, n. 1; Kerrl, *Ueber Reichsgut und Hausgut der deutschen Könige des früheren Mittelalters* (Tübingen, 1912). Some of these domains, however, were remnants only, and mere *Meierhöfe*.

[4] For literature on Charlemagne's management of the crown lands see Gareis, *Die Landgüterordnung Kaiser Karls des Grossen* (Berlin, 1895), being the best text of the *Capitulare de villis*, with notes and commentary. It is evident that registers or rolls of receipts and expenditures were required by Charlemagne (Pirenne, *Mélanges Julien Havet*, p. 745).

[5] Wenck, *Hessische Landesgesch.*, I, 35–36.

Franconia.[1] The Saxon kings also further increased their revenues by taking the richer abbeys, whose landholdings were immense and which accordingly excited the cupidity of the baronage, under their protection,[2] and using a large portion of the revenues arising from them for secular purposes. Conrad II, the first king of the Salian house, even assimilated the lands of the royal abbeys with the lands of the fisc. In 1002, there were eighty-five "royal" abbeys carried on the ledgers of the kings. Partial compensation was made to the monasteries for this diversion of their funds to secular purposes by generous grants of toll and market rights to them.

Some additions were made from time to time to the fisc by escheat, confiscation, or forfeiture,[3] but the latter practices were not very effectual as a means of punishment of rebellious nobles, except in Franconia and other older parts of Germany where the manorial system was well established, population denser, and cultivation somewhat intensive. Along the eastern border, where land was cheap and agriculture cruder and extensive in its application, confiscation or forfeiture did not penalize a culprit baron to any serious degree.[4] In fact, Otto III actually bought off rebellious vassals by gifts of land from the fisc.[5]

The Saxon kings had the thriftless way of not letting their left hands know what their right hands did. While they sometimes saved at the spiggot by living at the expense of their subjects and eked out the revenues of the crown lands with those of the royal abbeys, at the same time they reck-

---

[1] For the number and extent of these domains see Waitz, *Jahrb. Heinrich I*, 193. The *Reichsgüter* in the Harz originally pertained to the Liudolfinger. For the fisc in Italy see Darmstädter, *Das Reichsgut in der Lombardie und Piedmont (568–1250)*, and a review of same in *Archivio Storico Lombardo*, Vol. XXIII, fasc. 11 (1896); C. W. Previté-Orton, *History of the House of Savoy*, pp. 233, 239, 254, 368, 429–30; Gregorovius, *The City of Rome in the Middle Ages*, III, 453–55.

[2] Nitzsch, *Deutsche Gesch.*, I, 556–67.

[3] Waitz, VIII, 252–55; Inama Sternegg, *DWG*, I, 283; II, 112–16. For a remarkable instance see Wipo, *Vita Chuonradi*, chap. xxv.

[4] Lamprecht, *DG*, III, 93, 117–18; Inama Sternegg, II, 113, n. 4; Schröder, *Rechtsgesch.* (4th ed., 1902), p. 531; Eggers, p. 102.

[5] ". . . . regendo, indulgendo, largiendo et remunerando" (*Annal. Qued.* [anno 1000]).

lessly squandered the royal domains in lavish gifts to the church, especially the bishops. Otto I is said to have given one-fifth of the crown revenues in Saxony to the Archbishop of Magdeburg and other sees in Saxony; Otto II gave away seventy-one manors of the fisc in ten years. The disastrous defeat of this king in Italy in 982 and his death the next year, to be succeeded by his infant son Otto III, was a turning-point in the history of the fisc. For then began a general spoliation of it by the bishops and the feudality which the empress-mother as regent was unable to stop.[1] Henry II, most lavish of all the Saxon kings, endowed his pet bishopric in North Germany, Merseburg, with all the royal manors in Saxony and Thuringia which the Ottos had not disposed of already, and what was left of the fisc in Franconia he divided between the bishoprics of Würzburg and Bamberg.[2] The coronation of the kings always cost them dear in presents, in Rome more than at Aachen, and many of these donations were made at the expense of the fisc.[3]

Thus the fisc was unequal to the drains made upon it and steadily decreased.[4] With colossal shortsightedness the Saxon kings made no attempt to reserve for the crown certain portions in the "colonial" lands east of the Elbe River,[5] as the United States government reserved for its use enormous tracts of federal land in our Great West, but let the hungry bishops, abbots, and feudality engross the whole of it. Yet it was just there that, with a formative policy, the enlargement of the royal domain might have been provided for. The splendid expansion of the German people eastward was a wasted opportunity so far as the German crown was con-

[1] Wattenbach, *Deutschlands Geschichtsquellen* (5th ed.), II, 75.

[2] Thietmar, *Chronicon*, V, 39; VI, 43; *Vita Heinrici*, I, chap. iii, in Migne, *Pat. Lat.*, CXL, 115.

[3] Waitz, VIII, 233–35, 236, nn. 1–4.

[4] For these dissipations, in addition to Waitz, *loc. cit.*, see Eggers, pp. 97–112; Gerdes, *Gesch. d. deutschen Volkes*, I, 447–51; Gengler, *Beiträge zur bayerischen Gesch.*, IV, 81.

[5] The few crown lands in this region are discussed by Kurze, *Gesch. der sächsischen Pfalzgrafschaft* (Halle, 1886), pp. 24–31. See Lamprecht's poignant words in *DG*, IV, 14.

cerned. The kings had nothing to do with it and got nothing from it. The Saxon kings had no constructive policy in the matter of economic administration; they formulated no laws like Charlemagne's famous capitulary for management of the crown lands. A few fragmentary registers or surveys of some of the monasteries have been preserved, and that is all.[1]

The same indifference and wastefulness also character-ized the history of German forest management under the last Carolingian and all the Saxon kings. Legally, all forest lands pertained to the fisc, and only the king could make appropria-tion therefrom to private persons or corporate foundations like bishoprics and monasteries. But the coil of private pro-prietorship had tended, even from late Merovingian times, more and more to be thrown around the forests. Bishops, ab-bots, nobles, sought to add land to land and to exploit the peasantry by forced labor. The monasteries in particular, which, economically speaking, were often huge ranches, coveted thousands of acres of forest for stock-raising pur-poses. In Saxony after the Frankish conquest, in Wendish Hesse and the middle and upper Main Valley, the real or suspected persistence of pagan practices in the depth of the forests was made a pretext for extending ecclesiastical control over them, and what the clergy did with some show of church authority, the feudality did by sheer usurpation.[2]

Yet the forests of medieval Germany were so vast and the population so slight in comparison that it was centuries be-fore private engrossing of the forests became a popular grievance. The period of the Ottos was one of lavish conces-sion of forest privileges to the lay and clerical feudality.[3] Thietmar, bishop of Merseburg, gratefully records the gift by Otto II in 974 to Bishop Giseler of the great forest between the Saale and the Mulde, which covered almost the whole of

---

[1] Waitz, VIII, 223, 235–36; Eggers, p. 99; Fisher, *Medieval Empire*, I, 259.

[2] Von der Goltz, *Landwirtschaft*, I, 139; Roscher, *Ackerbau* (11th ed., Stuttgart, 1885), sec. 191, n. 1. It was Justus Moeser who first pointed out that Charlemagne inforested the forests in the bishopric of Osnabrück "cum collaudatione potentium istius regionis." So also in England, Canute's forest legislation was largely in the interest of the church (Roscher, sec. 193).

[3] Gerdes, I, 340; Lamprecht, *DWL*, I, 473.

the two counties of Siusili and Plisni, in which the conquered Sorben were held down by six *Burgwarde* garrisoned with Saxon soldiery.[1] It was a princely gift. For two hundred years the servile peasantry of the bishops of Merseburg were employed in clearing it. The place-names today in this region —Wolfeshain, Ammelshain, Lindhart, Holzhausen, Fuchshain, etc.—show where the sites of those ancient forest villages were located.

Otto III and Henry II were even more lavish than their predecessors in gifts of forest tracts to the bishops, grants which carried with them the right not only to exploit the raw materials of the forest as timber, pitch pine, charcoal, etc., but also the power to establish markets on the edges of the forests or within them, to make roads through them and impose tolls thereon, and to tithe and to tax the villagers in them.[2]

The effect of these vast proprietary grants was to deprive the free German peasantry of their last place of asylum from manorial extortion, and, since hunting privileges went hand in hand with everything else, to take cheap meat out of their mouths by forbidding them to kill the game in the forests.[3] By the end of the Saxon epoch (1024), things had gone so far that the kings practically required the consent of the proprietors of a region before declaring it under forest law.[4] Certain indications point to the fact that an important change took place about the time of Otto III in the management of the fisc. The decline in resources owing to heavy largesses of crown land to the church compelled the kings more and more to depend upon the resources of the abbeys and the episcopal fisc. Henry II seems, if not the first who introduced the practice of utilizing abbey resources, to have been the king who first developed the practice, at the expense of ecclesias-

[1] Hauck, *Kirchengesch. Deutschlands* (3d ed.), III, 97; Thietmar, *Chronicon*, III, 1. The grant has been preserved, *DO*, II, 90 (August 30, 974).

[2] Friedrichs, *Burg und territorial Grafschaften* (Bonn, 1907), pp. 15–19.

[3] Karl Roth, "Ueber die Entwicklung des Jagdrechtes in Deutschland," *Allgem. Forst und Jagd Zeitung*, Suppl. VII (1869), pp. 118–39; Begiebing, *Die königlichen Pfalzen als Jagdhufenhalte der Salischer Kaiser* (Bonn, 1904).

[4] Schröder, *Rechtsgesch.* p. 521.

tical patrimony. The tenacity with which the German kings resisted the claims of ecclesiastical investiture is explained by this economic transformation. And their fiscal interest was not less than their economic.[1]

When the first Salian king, Conrad II, was elected in 1024, the dilapidation of the fisc had gone so far that only scattered remnants of the crown lands still pertained to the crown.[2] They were reduced to less than in the time of the last Carolingians.[3] In the colonial lands along the east border there was no imperial property at all. The Saxon kings had bestowed everything upon the new sees created in this region, or else upon the Billunger and Babenberger. It was absolutely necessary for the crown to husband its slender resources.

The feudal policy of the first Salian monarch is exceedingly interesting to analyze and very valuable for understanding the nature and conditions of government in the feudal age. We are here concerned, however, with only one particular feature of that administration, namely, Conrad II's management of the fisc. The reckless waste of the crown lands by his predecessors gave the King much anxiety, and he resolved upon a drastic policy of "revindication." In 1027 at the diet of Regensburg, the Emperor ordered a survey to be made of all the crown lands in Bavaria to the end of discovering what portions of them had been unlawfully or covertly appropriated. Whether this inquisition was extended to other duchies is not certain, but it seems probable.[4] For the diplomata of his reign discover considerable acquisitions or re-

[1] There was a difference between exactions imposed on abbeys and on bishoprics. The former were chiefly assessed for material supplies. The bishops' obligations mainly consisted in the exaction of *gîte* or compulsory maintenance of the court when traveling. This exaction, which became less a private right than a public law, fell most heavily upon the bishops owing to the fact that their palaces were situated in the cities and more convenient for royal sojourn than the abbeys, which were often located in rural regions. The itineraries of the German kings furnish valuable information as to these *servitia regalia*. A comparison between the itineraries of the Saxon and those of the Salian kings proves that in the tenth century the kings lodged chiefly in their royal *villae*. But in the twelfth century they generally lodged in episcopal palaces.

[2] Gerdes, I, 446–47. [3] Eggers, p. 97.

[4] Voigt, *Klosterpolitik Conrads II*, p. 7; Waitz, VIII, 244 and n. 2; Richter and Kohl, III, 2, 285, n. C; Inama Sternegg, *DWG*, II, 112, n. 3; Bresslau, *Konrad II*,

acquisitions of the fisc in Swabia, Franconia, Saxony, Lorraine, and even in Italy.[1] Because much of it was lost later, the number and amount of these reclamations are difficult to trace. It would be interesting to know how much property Conrad II's queen, Gisela, brought him as dowry, since special mention is made of the magnitude of her landed wealth.

Conrad II's great program for the revindication of the fisc was as statesman-like as it was unpopular. For it aimed to recover for the crown the huge number of manors and great tracts of forest land which logically appertained to the crown, but which had been appropriated without royal consent, and to put the administration of them in the hands of royal *ministeriales*, i.e., men of servile origin, technically trained in administrative practices, who had everything to gain by loyal service to the government.[2] As the result of Conrad II's vigorous policy of redemption and conservation of the fisc, the material condition of the German monarchy when he died in 1039 was greater than it had ever been.[3] It is this Emperor's special claim to distinction that he perceived the economic side of the problem of government and intelligently labored for its solution. He was the first German king (and save for Henry IV and Lothar II the only one) who had a constructive fiscal program.

The distinction between the private property of the sovereign and the fisc of the crown was first made by Conrad II in Italy,[4] when he went there to punish Pavia for revolt after the death of his predecessor, in the course of which

---

I, 214; Nitzsch, II, 22–24; Hauck, III, 544; Gerdes, II, 50–57. Schröder (p. 517) contends that the Nürnberger *Salzbuch* (ed. Küstler) is a fragment of the Bavarian survey instituted by Conrad II.

[1] Bresslau, II, 359–65.

[2] Bresslau, II, 364, 507–9. In addition to Waitz and Bresslau, already cited on Conrad II's revindication of the fisc, see also Nitzsch, I, 22–24; Giesebrecht, *Kaiserzeit*, II, 709; Lamprecht, *DG*, III, 330; Gerdes, II, 50; Richter and Kohl, II, 2, 271 and notes; Fisher, I, 217–18, 260.

[3] Bresslau, I, 6 f.; Steindorff, *Heinrich III*, I, 58; Häusser, *Gesch. d. rhein. Pfalz*, I, 29 f.

[4] Inama Sternegg, II, 112; Waitz, VIII, 244, 388; Nitzsch, I, 20–23.

undertaking the imperial castle in Pavia was destroyed. The Pavians pleaded that they were not guilty. "Whom have we offended?" they said. "We served the late Emperor with fidelity and honor until his death. Now that he is dead, how shall we be accused of having destroyed his castle?" Conrad II's reply to this typically medieval technicality of law is a notable one. "I know that you have not destroyed the palace of the king" he said, "since at the time it was destroyed there was no king. But if the King dies the kingdom yet remains, just as a ship endures whose pilot has been lost. They were *public* buildings, not private."[1]

Conrad II's economic policy was not one of mere retrenchment, though he was saving in cost of administration to the point of parsimony. His was a sound and constructive policy. He partially identified the management of the lands of the royal abbeys with the fisc, and contemplated—or was said to have contemplated—the assimilation of the episcopal lands also with the fisc, a policy which became part of the great Salian administrative program, and accounts for the distrust of the bishops of Henry III and Henry IV, although not all the bishops, for example, Adalbert of Bremen, were hostile to it.[2] He also endeavored to increase the incomes from the royal domains by instituting improved methods of local administration of the crown lands. Perhaps taking a hint from the practice of the church which worked to consolidate its scattered holdings into more compact groups, Conrad II likewise tried to do the same with the estates of

[1] "Dicebant Papienses: Quem offendimus? Imperatori nostro fidem et honorem usque ad terminum vitae suae servavimus; quo defuncto cum nullum regem haberemus regis nostri domum destruxisse non jure accusabimur. E contrario rex: Scio inquit, quod domum regis vestri non destruxistis, cum eo tempore nullum haberetis; sed domum regalem scidisse, non valetis inficiari. Si rex periit, regnum remansit, sicut navis remanet cujus gubernator cadit. Aedes publicae fuerant, non privatae" (Wipo, *Vita Chuonradi*, chap. vii). The distinction was not finally made and defined in law until the time of the Hohenstaufen (Waitz, VIII, 243, n. 2, quoting Gerhoh of Reipersburg, *De Aed. Dei*, chap. x). The figure of the state as a ship and the ruler thereof as a pilot is common in classical literature (Sophocles *Oedipus Tyrannus* 104; Cicero, *Oratio in Pisonem* ix. 20; Horace *Carmina* i. 14; Quintilian viii, chap. vi, sec. 44) whence it passed into the Middle Ages (Agobard of Lyons, *Opera* [ed. Baluze], II, 52; *Forged Decretals* [ed. Hinschius], pp. 34, 67; Asser, *Life of Alfred the Great*, chaps. xxi, lxxiii, xci; cf. Stevenson's ed., p. 331).

[2] See Nitzsch, II, 60–65.

the crown by trading remote and isolated tracts for others more conveniently located, or by selling them and purchasing new domains adjacent to possessions of the crown. This Emperor, too, was far more rigorous than his Saxon predecessors in enforcing escheats and forfeitures.[1]

The exaggerated piety of Henry III wasted again what his father had recovered and conserved of the fisc. The clergy were not slow to perceive that the young Emperor's weakness could be exploited. Accordingly, when the infant Henry IV became king of Germany in 1056, "what the palmer worm had left the locust had eaten; and that which the locust had left the cankerworm had consumed; and what the cankerworm spared the caterpillar had devoured." Henry III endowed his favorite church at Goslar with one-ninth of all the revenues of the royal domains in the Harz.[2] So reduced to penury was he at one time that he had to borrow 20 pounds of gold and 200 pounds of silver from the Bishop of Worms, pledging a portion of the crown lands as security; on another occasion, he was compelled to pawn the crown itself.[3]

Like Louis the Pious before him, Henry III alternately was emotionally "pious" and recklessly lavish in gifts to the church, and again absurdly inflated when he considered the pretentious dignity and authority of his imperial position. In the latter mood, he was prone to furious acts of punishment, as when he forced Godfrey, the rebel duke of Lorraine, "to labor like a serf" in order grossly to humiliate him. In a word, Henry III's fiscal policy, his inquisitions and his forfeitures, were as ill considered as his father's course had been wise and well ordered.[4]

During the long minority of Henry IV, the crown lands

[1] Bresslau, II, 366 f.; Waitz, VIII, 246–52, cites many examples.

[2] Waitz, VIII, 224, n. 4.

[3] *Ibid.*, p. 238. This is one of the earliest instances of mortgage-broking by the bishops. In the thirteenth century the practice was general among them. In the time of Otto IV and Conrad IV, who governed Germany for his father Frederick II, from 1237 to 1253 the fisc was recklessly mortgaged and dissipated by foreclosures. The whole subject has been treated by Küster, *Reichsgut zwischen 1273 und 1313,* and Werminghoff, *Die Verpfändungen der mittel- und niederrheinischen Reichstädte;* H. Niese, *Die Verwaltung des Reichsgutes im 13. Jahrhundert (1905).*

[4] Nitzsch, II, 51.

were appallingly wasted and stolen by the bishops and nobles. Force[1] and fraud went hand in hand.[2] The clergy were adepts in forging false charters of alleged donation. The greatest number of these spoliations were in Thuringia and Saxony, where the largest block of crown lands was located. The restitution of the fisc was the most pressing necessity of the crown when Henry IV attained his majority and recovered his freedom.[3]

But the young King had larger and more constructive ideas of administration than merely salvaging his own. The Harz country, where a considerable block of the crown lands lay, and Saxony, where the forest rights of the crown were extensive, were among the most backward parts of Germany in an agricultural way.[4] Henry IV resolved to make the lands of the fisc in these regions more productive and, to accomplish that end, sent down trusted *ministeriales* from Goslar to superintend the management of the Saxon and Thuringian crown lands.[5] Simultaneously, he planned to recover those portions of the fisc which had been stolen or acquired by means of forged charters during his minority.

Henry IV had his grandfather Conrad II's passion for efficiency and economical administration. He was the sole

---

[1] ". . . heredes circumvenient vi praedia tollent," Bruno, *de bello Saxonico*, chap. xxvi; cf. chaps. xviii and xcvi; *Annal. Palad.* (SS. XVI, 70); Marianus Scotus, *Chronicon.* (1075); Vogeler, *Otto von Nordheim*, pp. 41, 44–45; Schaumann, *Gesch. des niedersächsischen Volkes*, p. 190; Sudendorff, *Reg.*, II, No. 17.

[2] Burckhardt of Halberstadt, Hezil of Hildesheim, Werner of Magdeburg, and Siegfried of Mainz were notorious for their spoliation of the fisc. Dedi, margrave of Lausitz, was the chief lay offender.

[3] Waitz, VIII, 429–31. The reader will hardly fail to see, in this history of the spoliation of the German crown lands in the Middle Ages and Henry IV's attempt to recover them, a parallel with the history of federal lands in the United States. The vested interests of those days were represented by bishops, abbots, and the great feudal nobles. Times have changed, but men have not changed with time. American timber "barons," coal "barons," "oil kings," "railroad kings," waterpower and ranching "interests" have repeated the history of Germany in the feudal age, and like the barons of old seized, appropriated, and wasted the resources of the government. Roosevelt's conservation policy has its medieval prototype in that of Henry IV.

[4] Gebhard, *Handbuch*, I, 310–12, 326.

[5] Henry IV kept a flock of sheep at Goslar (Lambert of Hersfeld, *Annales* [ed. Holder-Egger], p. 171).

medieval German king who systematically surrounded himself with a corps of royal *ministeriales* who were trained as
farmers-general or intendants.[1] The management of the royal
domains was put into the hands of this class, more intensive
methods of exploitation introduced, and a larger proportion
of produce exacted from every farm. At the same time the
King revived the almost obsolete right of the crown to unappropriated forest tracts, and began to inclose them; put
his foot down upon further private inclosures; stopped the
practice of forest donations either to corporations or to individuals; and made forest proprietors prove their titles.

Of a piece with Henry IV's forest policy is that dealing
with streams, which closely touched the traditional fishery
rights of the Saxon people. The streams, too, were included
within the new regulations, forbidden free use of, made "ban
waters," and subject to license fees with punishment for
trespass.[2]

It is in his system of bureaucratic administration, which
Henry IV planned to establish through the *ministeriales* of
the crown, and in his fiscal policy, that one sees the largest
evidences of the Salian program. Until this time in medieval
history, no administrative class of technically trained officials such as Henry's *ministeriales* were, was to be found any-

[1] Lambert of Hersfeld, pp. 145, 148, 151, 154, 257; *Annal. Altah.* (1072); Bruno,
chaps. xiv, xvi, xxxi; cf. Waitz, IV, 111; VI, 292; Meyer von Knonau, *Jahrb. Heinrich
IV*, II, 153 f.; Inama Sternegg, II, 150; Roerhig, *De secularibus consiliariis Heinrici
IV* (Halle, 1866); Lamprecht, *DG*, III, 118–20. The index to Lambert's *Annales*
under the words *familiares, auricularii, consiliarii, consulatores*, etc., may be
profitably consulted for information on this head.

[2] The *Sachsenspiegel*, II, 29, sec. 4, sharply protests against this practice; cf.
Lamprecht, *DG*, IV, 239; V, 76.

"The starting-point of the German law of fisheries was the principle that the
right to fish belonged to every member of the folk, as regarded the greater streams
and lakes, and to every mark-man as regarded the water-commons of the mark
associations. . . . . When a 'stream' regality had developed . . . . the rights of
fishery in these, as 'ban-waters,' also became a regality of the crown. The king
could either exercise them himself or convey them to the territorial princes; in later
times they were generally regarded as regalities of the territorial rulers, and in many
cases were conveyed by them to manors, cloisters, communes, mills, etc., in return
for rents or services. . . . . As regards the water-commons of mark-associations,
the right of free fishery was maintained much longer than free hunting, since the
princes and manorial lords attributed much less value to fisheries than to the chase"
(Huebner, *Germanic Private Law*, p. 286).

where in feudal Europe. Henry IV was a pioneer monarch. Suggestions of this sort of a class are to be found in the *missi dominici* of Charlemagne and the *Pfalzgrafen* of Otto I. But the method of paying these officials in landed incomes or endowments was disastrous, for it too closely identified them with the feudality. In many cases, they actually converted these stipendiary rights into hereditary benefices, as the evolution of the counts palatine into feudal nobles no whit different from dukes and margraves shows.

A money economy, a *Geldwirtschaft*, was a condition precedent to the effective creation of such a body of officials. The output of the great Rammelsberg mines near Goslar fortunately provided Henry IV with the one indispensable resource necessary for his administrative emancipation, for they supplied him with the bullion required for a government keyed upon a money economy instead of a *Naturalwirtschaft*.[1] At the same time, also, an auxiliary resource was available in the increasing development of commerce and trade in Germany, signs of the awakening of which, at this time, are very interesting.

Besides reparation and improved administration of the fisc, Henry IV may have designed to put the control of all the crown lands in the hands of a single minister, as Conrad II once contemplated putting the management of all the royal abbeys in the hands of Poppo of Stavelot. Furthermore, there is ground to believe that Henry IV planned to establish a fixed capital for the German kingdom at Goslar. At least, it is not without significance that, in the historical sources of his reign, the word *palatium* is continually used to designate the royal court at Goslar (*königlicher Hof*), and the word *curtis* employed, instead, when the court is found elsewhere.[2]

The result of Henry IV's passion for administrative efficiency—and quite apart in origin from his conflict with the pope—was a widespread conspiracy of the clergy and feudality in North Germany, whose "vested interests" were jeopardized by the King's policy. In this rebellion the Saxon

[1] Schulte, *Deutsche Staats- und Rechtsgesch.*, sec. 80, 5; Nitzsch, II, 45, 51, 55.

[2] Eggers, pp. 104–5.

and Thuringian peasantry also joined because they were deprived of their time-honored rights of cutting firewood and timber in the forests, of fishing freely in the forest streams, of hunting, of feeding their swine on the beechnuts and acorns there.[1]

In this disastrous rebellion, Henry IV's splendid designs were destroyed. He was compelled to buy partisans by grants out of the crown lands to clergy, nobles, and *ministeriales;* and his enemies, when victorious, spoiled or seized the crown lands as they could.[2] When the civil war ended in 1092, having lasted for seventeen years, his dream to establish a permanent capital at Goslar, to centralize the administration there, had gone to ruin like a broken cloud.[3] The crown lands were reduced to shreds and patches.

What was left, Henry IV tried again to salvage when peace came and to reorganize the management. Perhaps owing to the fact that he had a French mother, the King had always manifested appreciation of the administrative methods of the kings of France. Indeed, his fiscal policy bears a remarkable analogy to that of Philip I of France.[4] It is not without significance that in 1105 when the German feudality again rebelled—a rebellion in which his own sons Conrad and Henry joined the enemy—throwing Germany once more into civil war, Henry IV wrote a long letter to the French King recounting his new trials and justifying his policy, a letter in which he emphasized the new spoliation of the crown lands.[5]

[1] Lambert of Hersfeld, pp. 141, 146, 147, 148, 154, 270; Bruno, chaps. xxx, xlii, lxiii, cviii; *Carmen de bello sax.,* I, ll. 42–46.

[2] Bruno, chaps. xxv, xxxviii, xxxix; Lambert of Hersfeld, pp. 201–2.

[3] Below, *Der deutsche Staat des Mittelalters,* p. 331, rightly says that Henry IV failed because of his inability to impose taxes, as the English and French kings succeeded, because of their successful imposition of the taxing power. For this failure, however, Henry IV was not to blame. For a discussion of the largeness and constructive nature of his financial and taxation policy see Below, *op. cit.,* p. 87, n. 2; pp. 290, 339 f.; and Zeumer, *Die deutschen Städtesteuern,* pp. 161 f.

[4] "Rex [Philip] autem videns dominium suum per insoltiam praedecessorum suorum esse diminutum et fere adnihilatum, cupiensque illud reaugere" (*Chron. de Morigny,* Bouquet, XI, 157–58; cf. *ibid.,* p. 394: "pro augendo dominium suum"). For the whole subject see Luchaire, *Inst. Mon. de la France* (2d ed.), I, 88–99; II, 246.

[5] "Sic spoliatum et desolatum, nam et castella et patrimonia, et quicquid in regno conquisieram, eadem vi et arte sua extorserunt a me" (Jaffé, *Mon. Bamb.,* V, 246). The whole letter is of great importance. It covers five pages.

An inquiry into the causes of this second rebellion throws light on the difficulty a medieval ruler had in maintaining a firm administration of the crown lands. The bane of every feudal government was the tendency for its lands, its offices, and its revenues to become enfeoffed. Not the least of offenders in this particular were the King's own sons. Rebellion of sons against fathers, because the latter resisted such tendency and refused to permit royal offices and crown lands to become perquisites of their children, is a chronic phenomenon of the feudal age.

When the Saxon rebellion and the conflict with the papacy was over, Henry IV determined that the crown lands which were left should be administered by the crown alone, for the benefit of the crown. It was the French practice. When his son, Prince Henry (afterward Henry V), was crowned as junior king at Aachen in 1099 (again the French practice of co-optation), it was especially provided in the act of settlement that all and every one of the crown lands were to be excepted from his son's control during his father's lifetime. This had been the grievance of his elder brother, Prince Conrad, before, and the motive which had led to his espousal of his father's enemies in the second feudal rebellion. It was shortly to become the grievance of young Henry, too, who also soon rebelled against Henry IV.[1]

The revolt of Henry V was a repetition of the anarchy of the first civil war. The crown lands which Henry IV had labored so hard to rehabilitate were wasted, squandered, sacked, destroyed, until again nothing but scattered fragments remained.[2]

The shrinkage of the royal domains partly accounts for Henry V's desperate endeavor, in 1115, to acquire Saxony for the crown when Magnus Billung, the last of his house, died. But the Salian kings were too much hated in Saxony

---

[1] ". . . . imperator minorem filium . . . . heredem regni constituit; a quo ne et ipse abiret in viam fratris sui, jusjurandum accepit videlicet ne umquam se vel de regno vel de praediis patris, eo vivente, nisi forte ex consensu ipsius, intromitteret" (*Vita Heinrici IV*, chap. vii *ad fin.*).

[2] Ortlieb, *Chron. Zwifalt.*, chap. v (SS. X, 75); cf. *Chron. Petri Erford.* (*anno* 1105), and Gerdes, II, 381.

for him to accomplish the feat, and the chagrined King had to let Lothar of Supplinburg, who had married the daughter of the last Saxon Duke, inherit the great fief of the north. Henry V was unable to escheat the fief on the ground that the male line of dukes in Saxony was extinguished, and for the first time in German history (indeed, there is but one other earlier instance, and that in Tuscany) the principle of female succession was admitted.

Too late, Henry V realized that wise economy and intelligent management of the crown lands was the only royal road to power and prosperity. He had played with fire in siding with his father's foes and was sorely burned. Henry V had not his father's moral force but he inherited Henry IV's administrative ability, and when compelled to it, revived and applied his predecessor's fiscal policy.[1] He energetically undertook the rehabilitation of the crown lands, and so efficient was his administration of them that he was credited with the intention of instituting a Domesday Survey in Germany after the manner of William the Conqueror in England.[2]

But much of the lands of the fisc had been lost beyond recall. Even the *ministeriales*, in imitation of the nobles, began to build castles for themselves on the crown lands which they had seized, a step initial to their emergence later into the lower ranks of the nobility.[3] Yet reduced as the crown

[1] For details see Meyer von Knonau, *Jahrb.*, Vol. VII, app. 3; Waitz, VIII, 399–400; Gerdes, II, 381.

[2] "Omnibus itaque bene compositis consilio soceri sui regis Anglorum totum regnum vectigale facere volens multum in se optimatum odium contraxit"—Otto of Freising, *Chron. anno* 1124; (ed. Hofmeister, 1912, p. 332; cf. *Ann. Rod.* (1114) (SS. XVI, 698); *Ann. Pegav.* (1115), *ibid.*, p. 251; Ekkehard of Aura (1125) (SS. VI, 265); Waitz, VIII, 400 and n. 2. It is to be remembered that Henry V was the husband of Matilda, daughter of Henry I of England, the youngest son of William the Conqueror; cf. Freeman, *Norman Conquest* (3d ed.), V, 185, n. 4, on this rumor reported by Otto of Freising. The pearl of the imperial fisc then was Nuremburg (Begiebing, *op. cit.*, p. 41). Most of the royal income, however, was derived from the bishoprics and "royal" abbeys (*Mon. Welforum* [ed. Weiland], chap. xvi, p. 25).

[3] Henne am Rhyn, *Deutsche Kulturgesch.*, I, 208. In the twelfth century an imperial *ministerialis*, Werner of Bolland, owned 17 castles, a widespread complex of manors, and claimed the homage (!) of 1,100 knights. He was a typical petty prince (Gislebert, *Chron. Hanon* [SS. XXI, 540 (1184)]; Lamprecht, *DWL*, I, 2, 1307, n. 5; Köllner, *Gesch. der Herrschaft Kirchheim-Bolland*).

lands had become by 1125, Henry V's policy of rehabilitation must have been somewhat effective. At any rate, they
were sufficiently extensive to excite the cupidity of the Hohenstaufen brothers when the Emperor died, and they laid
claim to the crown lands as the nephews and heirs of their
uncle.

This famous claim of Frederick and Conrad of Swabia is
a landmark in both political and legal history.

The Swabian brothers had set up the astonishing theory that as the
heirs of Henry V they were entitled not only to his private property, but
also to those lands which during his reign had been *acquired for the empire*.
This would have given them for their own the whole of the countess
Matilda's possessions [Tuscan Italy], the city and fortress of Nuremburg
and numerous other valuable holdings.[1]

No better illustration of the essentially personal nature of
government in the Middle Ages can be imagined than this
incident, which so clearly shows how concrete men's minds
were, and how little the abstract idea of the state existed.
Moreover, it exemplifies the difference between the medieval
idea of personal law and the modern conception of territorial
law.

Just a century after Conrad II's notable legal distinction
between the private property of the Emperor and the imperial fisc, Lothar II, Henry V's successor, at the diet of
Regensburg made an even more definite and explicit pronouncement to the same effect.[2]

Nevertheless, in spite of this definition, theory of law and
actual fact failed to coincide. During the reign of Lothar II
(1125–39), the crown lands were assimilated with his own
Hausgut, and considerable portions of them seem to have
passed to the Guelfs, whose leader was the Emperor's son-in-
law, Henry the Proud.[3] Indeed, one of the many grounds of

[1] E. Emerton, *Mediaeval Europe*, p. 277. Nuremburg is first mentioned in the
Annals of Altenheim in 1050, when Henry III stopped there. By Hohenstaufen
times its importance exceeded that of Bamberg.

[2] "Rege apud Radisponam in conventu principum inquirente praedia judicio
proscriptorum a rege, si juste forifactoribus abjudicata fuerint vel pro his quae regno
attinent commutata, utrum cedant . . . . vel proprietati regis. Judicatum, potius
regiminis subjacere ditioni quam regis proprietati" (*Annal. S. Disibod.* [1125], in
MGH, SS. XVII, 23; cf. *Annal. Sax.* [1127], in *ibid.*, VI, 765).

[3] Bernhardi, *Lothar II*, p. 55.

feud between the Hohenstaufen and the Guelfs was just the attempt of the former when kings (Conrad III and Frederick I, Barbarossa) to recover these ancient remnants of the fisc which Henry the Proud, like the Swabian brothers before, now seems to have regarded as part of his own (or his wife's) family possessions.[1]

Although Conrad III failed to recover all the parts of the royal domain which the Guelfs withheld, it still would have been possible for the Hohenstaufen kings to build up a new royal domain out of their own *Hausgut* in Germany, if Frederick Barbarossa had not been more interested in realizing prodigious aspirations beyond the Alps, instead of devoting himself to the extension and consolidation of the royal power in Germany. Frederick I sold or gave away the crown lands for an elusive and superficial domination in Italy, whereas, if he had devoted himself to the upbuilding and consolidation of the royal domains in Swabia, the county of Burgundy, the Rhenish Palatinate, and the Pleisner land in the northeast,[2] a substantial German monarchy might yet have been erected. A consolidated royal domain was essential in Germany, as in France, to substantial royal authority.

Unfortunately the Hohenstaufen kings, like the Saxon and unlike the Salian, had no constructive economic policy. In war, diplomacy, politics, they were experts, but they had no sound grasp of public economy. In an age when *Naturalwirtschaft* was fast disappearing before the trade and commerce of the rising towns, the Hohenstaufen were no farther

---

[1] After the coronation of Conrad III, Henry the Proud reluctantly surrendered the regalia, "sed ad ea que ulterius inter eos tractanda erant dies ei . . . . prescribitur. . . . . Mediatores ad hanc causam prenominati . . . . nichil profecerunt. Rex enim non aliter compositionem fieri voluit, nisi dux quedam de his quae a Lothario imperatore susceperat ac possederat, resignaret" (*Mon. Welforum*, chap. xxiv, p. 32).

[2] For a particular statement as to the location and extent of the Hohenstaufen lands see Toesche, *Heinrich VI*, p. 20. There is record of a Degenhard of Hellenstein as *procurator per omnia regalia praedia Suevie* between 1173 and 1178 (Niese, *Die Verwaltung des Reichsgutes im 13. Jahrhundert* [Innsbruck, 1905], pp. 22, 268), but by that time Frederick had spent a goodly part of his resources in Germany on his wars in Italy. The fragmentary inventory in *Ann. Aquienses* (Boehmer, *Fontes*, III, 397 f.) may possibly be of Hohenstaufen time though some writers attribute it to the reign of Henry IV, and Boehmer, *Vorrede*, p. lix, thinks it of the thirteenth century. Consult Waitz, VIII, 231, n. 1.

advanced in their economic theory than the Saxon kings. They had no perception of the new economic revolution of the twelfth century.[1] Yet their economic resources were immense. They possessed whole blocks of crown land on the lower Rhine, in Saxony and Thuringia, extensive allodial and feudal holdings in Alsace and Swabia, besides a huge array of ecclesiastical *avoueries*. A system of fortresses bound all these territories together as in a net, the fortresses being garrisoned by armed *ministeriales* under the command of a local burgrave.[2]

The translation of the chief seat of Hohenstaufen residence and activity to Southern Italy and Sicily by Henry VI in 1190, and more still the double election of 1198 which created two emperors, was the culminating disaster for the fisc.[3] In the furious factional strife which followed, both Guelf and Ghibbeline bought partisans by largesses out of the crown lands, while the strong and ambitious everywhere laid their hands upon them when and where they could.

Henry VI recalled the margraviate of Meissen. It is his only distinguished effort in behalf of the wasted substance of the crown. His brother, Philip of Swabia, auctioned off blocks of the royal domain in his abortive effort to buy partisans against his rival.[4] The waste went on during the "reign" of Otto IV and the minority of Frederick II, who, half Italian in blood and wholly so in spirit, at last bartered away what was left of the crown lands of Germany to bishops, abbots, nobles, for the best price he could get for them. The regency of Conrad IV, who governed Germany for Frederick II between 1237 and 1253, saw the final pillage of the fisc.[5] In this

---

[1] See Nitzsch, II, 279 f., and Karl Weller, *Zur Organisation des Reichsgutes in der späteren Stauferzeit* ("Festschrift Dietrich Schaefer," p. 211).

[2] Frey, *op. cit.*, esp. pp. 175, 220 f., 230, 285 f., 296 f., 305 f., which are separate appendixes dealing with the fisc in each region of Germany.

[3] Waitz, VIII, 243 and n. 2.

[4] Abel, *Philipp von Schwaben*, p. 320, and with it compare Philip's wailing letter to Innocent III in *MGH, Leges*, II, 210, and *Ann. Marbac, MGH. SS*. XVII, p. 168.

[5] See the extracts from the sources cited by Huillard-Bréholles, *Introd. à l'histoire diplom. de l'empereur Fréderic II*, p. ccxii n.; also Raumer, *Gesch. der Hohenstaufen*, III, 274, 410; IV, 124, 191, 339; V, 65, 362, 377, 383, and esp. K. Weller, *Zur Organisation des Reichsgutes in der späteren Stauferzeit* ("Festschrift f. Dietrich Schaefer" [1915]).

way the fisc was almost utterly dissipated. The last remnants of it were swept away during the interregnum.[1]

Lamprecht has written this epilogue upon the fate of the crown lands in the last days of the Hohenstaufen:

In area it was about equivalent to three-quarters of the margraviate of Brandenburg. It lay scattered in the region around the confluence of the Main with the Rhine, between the Neckar and the Danube, and between the Danube and the Lech. To this we may add the landgraviate of Lower Alsace, portions of the Upper Palatinate and the Saxon Vogtland, together with the Burggrafschaft of Altenburg. Pitiable fragments were they of the old property in the motherland. In the colonial lands there was as good as no crown land. And yet it was just there that with determined effort a new territorial basis of the imperial power might have been found, as the achievements of a later time show.[2]

[1] The *Sententia de non alienandis principatibus* of 1216 (*Leges*, II, 227) was too late and too impotent to arrest the process of dissipation. For the period of the interregnum see Küster, *Reichsgut zwischen 1273 und 1313*. Toesche, *op. cit.*, p. 481, pertinently says, "Das schutzlose Reichsgut war die nächste und beste Beute aller Angriffe."

[2] *Deutsche Gesch.* (4th ed.), IV, 14.

CHAPTER XI

THE SENTIMENT OF EUROPE TOWARD THE GERMANS IN THE MIDDLE AGES[1]

MEDIEVAL EUROPE did not love the Germans. The Italians hated them, the French admitted their courage, but detested their manners, the English were jealous of them, the Slavs both feared and hated them, while the Germans despised and contemned the Slavs.[2] Rodolph Glaber, a Burgundian monk who lived in the first half of the eleventh century, described Germany as a land of confused nations of unheard-of ferocity.[3] German speech and German manners are often the butt of French ridicule in the *chansons de geste*. They are *pute gent, gent defface, laide gent.*[4] Eustace Deschamps declared that the Germans were compelled to learn the language of other nations because no one would—or could—speak theirs.[5] Even the Mohammedans paid their respects to the Germans. An Islamic traveler in Germany early in the eleventh century wrote that the language sounded like the growling of dogs.[6]

The root of this general resentment is to be found in the

[1] For literature on this subject see Steinhausen in *Deutsche Rundschau* (December, 1909; January, 1910); Körtum, "Ueber den Charakter und die Bestimmung der christlichen Hauptnationen des Mittelalters, nämlich Italiener, Deutschen und Franzosen," *Zeitschrift f. Geschichtswissenschaft*, V, 439 f.; Kern, "Der mittelalterliche Deutsch in franz. Kultur," *Historische Zeitschrift*, CVIII (1912), 237.

[2] For German contempt of the Slavs see Fredegarius, *Chronicon*, IV, 68; Monachus Sangall., II, 12; Thietmar, *Chronicon*, III, 17; Adam of Bremen, *Gesta episcop. Hammaburg.*, II, 45; Cosmas of Prague, *Chronicon*, I, 40; Helmold, *Chronica Slavorum*, I, 16.

[3] *Historia*, IV, 8.

[4] Cf. Zimmerman, *Roman. Forschung.*, XXIX (1911), 257 f., 306 f. For instances see Wace, *Roman de rou*, I, 3214; *Galeran de Bretagne*, 5613 f.; *Aymeri de Narbonne*, 2464 f.; *Parthenopeus*, 8753 f.; *Saisnes*, 441 f.

[5] *Soc. Anc. Textes Fr.*, VII, 61–62. Napoleon said the same thing of the Dutch and the Russians.

[6] Jacob, *Ein Arabischer Reisender aus dem X. oder XI. Jahrhundert*, p. 13.

important historical fact that the German kings and the German people were politically and legally the dominant state in medieval Europe. They were the recognized heirs of Charlemagne and the Roman Caesars, knew themselves to be such, and were so recognized by Europe. Yet however much the Holy Roman Empire might be recognized as "a great tradition and a present necessity,"[1] the sense of German superiority rankled in the heart of Europe. The Holy Roman Empire of the German nation possessed actual sovereignty over Germany, Italy, the Low Countries, the Two Burgundies; suzerainty over Bohemia, Poland, and Hungary; and a theoretical lordship over France, England, Spain, Denmark, and Scandinavia.[2] In the twelfth century, under the Hohenstaufen, German imperial pretensions were also extended to Byzantium and the Latin Orient during the Crusades.[3] From first to last the Holy Roman Empire was an international, not a national, monarchy.[4]

In political theory the Holy Roman Empire was fundamentally of Roman origin. But the Germanic element in it was strong, although many historians have failed to perceive the parity which existed between Roman and German tradition. It is a mistake to think that even with Frederick Barbarossa the German tradition was obliterated or effaced by the Roman tradition. The Germanic character of medieval imperial authority was no less vital than the Roman. The ancient German office of *herzog*, or "war-leader," underlay the imperial office as it underlay the kingship. Even the idea of the *comitatus*, or "war-following," persisted. Before the

[1] Fisher, *The Mediaeval Empire*, II, 255.

[2] See Waitz, *Deutsche Verfassungsgeschichte*, V, 134–35, and Gierke, *Political Theories of the Middle Ages* (Maitland's trans.), n. 56, pp. 126–27, for source citations.

[3] Leopold von Ranke, *Weltgeschichte*, VIII, 246, speculates on what might have happened to Europe in the twelfth century if Frederick Barbarossa had acquired Constantinople after the dethronement of Isaac Angelos, and regrets that he failed of getting the prize. "Es war ein Moment das nicht so leicht wieder kommen konnte."

[4] This idea is reflected in the *Sachsenspiegel*, III, 71, secs. 1, 2, and in the Golden Bull of 1356, art. 30. Heyck, *Geschichte der Hohenstaufen*, exaggerates the *national* sentiment of the Germans in the time of the Hohenstaufen. It was *international*.

rise of the towns created a new social class, the word *populus*
(people) in medieval chronicles meant the warrior class,
that is to say, the feudal nobles bound to performance of
military service. Widukind of Corvey shows that the sovereignty of Otto the Great was consecrated, not by the coronation of 962, but by the acclaim of the German army on the
battlefield of Augsburg in 955. The army made the emperor.[1]
The same conception appears in the Hohenstaufen period in
Otto of Freising and other writers of the twelfth century, for
whom the coronation of Charlemagne in 800 was nothing but
a confirmation of power already vested in the German king as
supreme military commander.[2]

Certain of the publicists of the fourteenth century, notably Lupold of Bebenburg (bishop of Bamberg, 1297–1303)
and Henry of Hervord, a Dominican of Minden (d. 1370),
declared, in opposition to the papacy, that the military power
of Charlemagne was the *ratio ultima* of his sovereignty.[3] One
finds this conception consecrated by a formula of the *Sachsenspiegel*, in a gloss of the commentator Johann von Buch,
who founded the imperial law on power.[4] The king, he argued, was elected to the kingship, but imperial authority
was fundamentally a war-power! *Dat keiserrike irwirvet hei
mit stride!* Stengel finds the origin of this formula of Buch
in the phrase, *exercitus imperatorem facit*, embodied in the
Code of Gratian, but derived from an epistle of St. Jerome.[5]

---

[1] This is what Stengel has so clearly established in his book, *Den Kaiser macht
das Heer* (Weimar, 1910).

[2] A gloss of Johannes Teutonicus upon the (unprinted) *Summa* of Huguccio,
probably composed during the pontificate of Gregory VIII (d. 1187), chap. xxiv,
dist. 93, "quomodo si exercitus imperatorem facit," reads: "Quomodo: id est sicut
in presenti; eligit quidem populus imperatorem, sed non consecratur nisi a papa; et
credo quod ex electione populi et principum sit imperator, licet non sic appelletur
antequam coronam a papa" (Mario Kramer, *Quellen zur Gesch. d. d. Königswahl*
[Leipzig, 1911], p. x).

[3] On Lupold see Lorenz, *Deutschlands Geschichtsquellen* (ed. 1870), pp. 317–19;
for Henry of Hervord see *ibid.*, pp. 123–26. Other literature in Potthast, *Bibliotheca
medii aevi*.

[4] See Schulte, *Deutsche Staats- und Rechtsgesch.*, sec. 62.

[5] The phrase in this form was a gross perversion of the original phraseology.
What Jerome said was that the bishops of the early church were elected "quomodo
si exercitus faciat imperatorem."

According to this argumentation the emperor owed this authority to his sword and the army back of him; the army was the political people.

The German state was the first state in Europe to rise out of the wreckage of the Carolingian empire with a coherent and effective government. With Henry I, law and order obtained throughout Germany.[1] Less formidable criminals than rebel dukes were sent to the east border in squads, there to do military service against the Wends.[2] Under Otto the Great, after the rebellious dukes were subdued, the interior peace of Germany was complete. "The world was fortunate while Otto held the sceptre," says a contemporary chronicler.[3] Even Lorraine was quiet.[4] Thietmar of Merseburg described the reign of Otto I as "an age of gold." His justice became almost legendary in later times.[5]

In the tenth century Germany was a land of law and order and prosperity compared with the condition of France or Italy. Leibnitz said with reason that the century which was an iron age for other countries for Germany was an age of gold.[6] Neither duke nor count nor bishop had immunity from the king's justice. Otto I's own brother Henry, his son Ludolf, Eberhard of Franconia, Frederick, archbishop of Mainz, Bishop Ruthard of Strasburg, and a Count Wichmann were all imprisoned for violating the peace. The dukes themselves were compelled to obey, and to make their own

[1] *Contin. Reg.* (920); Franklin, *Das Königl. und Reichshofgericht*, IV, 465.

[2] Widukind, II, 3.

[3] Hauck, *Kirchengesch.*, III, 394–95.

[4] *Gesta abbat. Lob.*, chap. ii; *Vita Deod. Mett.*, chap. vii; Hirzel, *Abt Heriger von Lobbes* (Greifswald diss., 1910), chap. ii.

[5] Grimm, *Deutsche Sagen*, II, 169 f.; Simrock, *Walther von der Vogelweide*, II, 159. The statement of Gobelinus, *Persona Cosmodromii Aetas*, VI, xlvii, regarding Otto I, "Bi Ottenbarde he moth barden schmecken," has the ring of veritability about it. The anecdote seems genuine.

[6] "Neque Germania sibi comparata unquam magis bello et pace, armis et moribus et si novissimas binas annorum centurias demas, quibus mutata est facies generis humani etiam literis floruit, quam seculo Ottonum, id est decimo, quod aliae gentes ab hodiernis suis moribus diversis, Galli torpore, Itali etiam probris infame fecere" (*Annales Imperii*, III [*ad annum* 1002], 802).

vassals obey.[1] Eberhard of Franconia, for having stormed a castle belonging to one of his vassals, burning it and massacring the garrison, was summoned, fined a hundred marks silver, and thrown into prison. Henry of Bavaria lost the Bavarian Nordgau for his contumacy.[2] Otto II punished the Duke of Carinthia and the bishops of Freising and Augsburg. In 979 he beheaded Count Gero at Magdeburg. Henry II either hanged, exiled, or imprisoned offenders of public order. Thietmar says that in his reign Saxony was the seat of "security and fertility."[3] Another contemporary writer says: "Under his protection everything prospered. The peasant joyfully did his necessary labor in the fields as the priest in the sanctuary. Poverty increased to riches under his aegis."[4]

Wipo, the biographer of Conrad II, says that "he powerfully surrounded his states with peace and protection."[5] No person in the kingdom was too lowly or too humble to be refused prompt justice at the hands of the King. The historiographer of Cologne was justified in boasting, in 1137, that no German king had ever let justice sleep.[6] Swift and popular justice for all, rich and poor, was the pride of a German king.[7] Conrad II stopped his coronation procession to

[1] Rosenstock, *Herzogsgewalt und Friedenschutz. Deutsche Provinzialversammlungen des 9–12. Jahrhundert* (Breslau, 1910). The sources abound with instances, both as to dukes and bishops: *Gesta Camer.*, II, 7; *Chron. S. Hubert*, chap. xxxi; cf. Waitz, *op. cit.*, VII, 126; Schröder, *Rechtsgeschichte*, 567; Roth von Schreckenstein, *Die Ritterwürde*, p. 458.

[2] Widukind, II, 6.

[3] Thietmar, *Chronicon*, VII, 5, 36, 37; cf. *Annal. Qued.* (1019); Alpertus, *De diversitate temp.*, chap. xvii (SS. IV, 717).

[4] *Epp. Bamb.* (ed. Jaffé), VI, 419.

[5] *Vita Chuonradi*, chaps. vi, xviii, xxiii, xl.

[6] "Merito a nobis nostrisque posteris pater patriae appelatur quia erat egregius defensor et fortissimus propugnator nihili pendens vitam suam contra omnia adversa propter justitiam opponere" (*Chron. Reg. Col.* [1137]).

[7] "Nam publice armis rem incipere, metus imperatoris prohibebat" (Alpertus, *De. div. temp.*, II, 7). The *Cologne Chronicle* (1107) says of Henry V: "Inde Merseburg postea Goslariam adiit omnibus super causa sua eum pulsantibus regia more judicans." Frederick Barbarossa's pledge to the Pope shows the same spirit (Weiland, I, No. 137). Frederick II declared the right of the poorest to appeal to the king (Huillard-Bréholles, VI, 158).

hear the petitions of a serf of the Archbishop of Mainz, an orphan and a poor widow.[1]

The feudal anarchy which prevailed in the half-French neighboring kingdom of Burgundy under King Rudolph was regarded as scandalous in Germany. The condition in French Lorraine shocked the Germans, who were not used to that sort of thing.[2] The German clerks who compiled the *Gesta* of the archbishops of Cambrai regarded the anarchic propensities of the French feudality—"those Carlenses!"—with scorn and contempt.[3] When Henry II, attempted to introduce the Peace of God so popular in France into Germany, the act both puzzled and irritated his subjects, who regarded it as an unjust reflection upon public law,[4] and Bishop Gerard of Cambrai protested against it.[5] Henry III rigidly enforced law and order throughout Germany.[6]

[1] Wipo, *Vita Chuonradi* chap. v. Cf. the pictures of Henry II, his predecessor, administering justice, which are preserved in *Adelboldi frag. de rebus gestis Henrici*, chaps. xxii, xxix, liv.

[2] "Tempora dissensionibus nimis, regnum hac illac quoque sibi trahente fluctuant. . . . . Transrhenena interim quietim manebant" (*Vita Johan. abbat. Gorz.*, chap. civ; *Gesta abbat. Lob.*, chap. xxv; *Gesta abbat. S. Trud.* [SS. X, 304]).

[3] "Indisciplinati mores Carlensium" (SS. VII, 466). So in Book III, chap. xl, there is a scoff at *Karlensibus custumiis*. To the same effect is the stinging comment of Gerard, author of the *Miracula S. Adalhardi abbatis Corbeiensis in Gallia*: "Talis quippe consuetudo naturaliter innata est regno Galorum ut praeter ceteras nationes semper velint exercere rabiem bellorum. Sed quidmodo? non necesse est velle mori in bello quia catervatim moriuntur famis et pestis gladio" (Bouquet, X, 378). Abbot Siegfried of Gorze laments the "ignominiosa Franciscarum ineptiarum consuetudo"—quoted by Steindorff, *op. cit.*, I, 191, n. 4. Cf. Pirenne, *Histoire de Belgique*, I, 69, n. 1. In the middle of the twelfth century Otto of Freising (*Gesta*, proem.) condemns the *Gallicana levitas* of the French. M. Ferdinand Lot, *Hugues Capet*, p. 236, n. 2, however, justly makes the observation that "cette indiscipline avait des causes sociales et non éthniques; plusque deux siècles plus tard l'anarchie avait passé en Germanie et presque abandonné la France."

[4] Thietmar, VII, 5, 36, 37; *Ann. Qued.* (1019); *Epp. Bamb.* (ed. Jaffé), VI, 419.

[5] *Gesta episc. Camer.*, II, 27 (SS. VII, 474).

[6] Waitz, VI, 428, n. i; VIII, 204, n. 2. In 1047, after Henry III had crushed the formidable rebellion of Duke Godfrey of Lorraine, he commuted the public whipping and clipping of his hair for a money payment, and so reduced his humiliation. But he still compelled him in person "to labor like a serf" in rebuilding the church at Verdun which he had destroyed: Sed post modicum facti in tantum poenituit, ut publice se verberari faceret et capillos suos, ne tonderentur, multa pecunia redimeret, sumptus ad reaedificandum ecclesiam daret et in opere caementario per se ipsum plerumque vilis mancipii ministerio functus deserviret (Lambert of Hers-

Imperial feeling and tribal sentiment were strong among the Germans, but national self-consciousness never developed among them as among the French and English. The German people was an agglomeration of tribes—Franks, Saxons, Bavarians, Swabians, Thuringians, etc.—of a common blood and similar language and institutions, but actuated more by tribal traditions and feeling than by a higher national sentiment. The persistence of the idea of the personality of law in German history long after it had become obsolete elsewhere in Europe is a proof of this condition. The sentiment of local folk-right was strong; the sense of a common and national law was weak.[1]

In medieval times the Germans almost always thought of themselves in either a tribal capacity, as Saxons, Franks, Swabians, Bavarians, etc., or as citizens of the Holy Roman Empire.[2] Widukind of Corvey and Bruno, both eminent Saxon chroniclers, are deeply imbued with sectionalism. On the other hand, Thietmar of Merseburg is vaguely imperialistic, calling the Germans *Teutonici* in distinction from non-Germans within the Empire.[3] The word *Deutsch* was applied only to the German language and not to the German people until the eleventh century, and even then was infrequent. The term *patria Teutonici* first occurs in 1079.[4]

---

feld, *Annales* [ed. Holder Egger], p. 60; cf. *Laurentii Gesta ep. Virdun*, chap. ii SS. X, 492]; Giesebrecht, *Kaiserzeit* [5th ed.], II, 444, 669).

[1] "The foreigner of old German law is the man who has a different *Hantgemal*, or legal home; who has not been domiciled to the folk-right of the region into which he has wandered" (H. Fisher, *Mediaeval Empire*, I, 275).

[2] See Thietmar, *Chronicon*, II, 28. In the middle of the ninth century when the Frank race was running to seed, the Franks manifested an inflated sense of their own importance, and contempt for not only the Saxons, but the rest of the German peoples also. For contempt of the former see Rabanus Maurus, *De oblatione puerorum;* Mabillon, *Ann. O.S.B.*, II, 732. The Monk of St. Gall, *Gesta Karoli*, I, 10, says: ". . . . By reason of the glory of Charles, Gauls, Aquitanians, Aeduans, Spaniards, Germans and Bavarians thought no small honor was paid to them, if they were thought worthy to be called the servants of the Franks." The same haughtiness is in Adrevald, *Miracula S. Ben.*, chap. xxvii (SS. XV, 491).

[3] It may be doubted if Thietmar distinguishes the *patria* and the *regnum nostrum* to which he refers from the Empire. Cf. *Chronicon*, Introd. to Book I.

[4] Waitz, V, 8, 32; Grimm, *Deutsch. Gram.*, I, 15; Gerdes, I, 354. The word "Theodiscus" (Deutsch) first occurs in 786 and is then applied to the language, not to the country or people. See Michael, *Gesch. d. d. Volkes*, I, 8, n. 2.

It is impossible to think of medieval Germany dissociated from its imperial power and claims. Viscount Bryce well described the Holy Roman Empire as "an institution or system, the wonderful offspring of a body of beliefs and traditions." These beliefs and traditions were of triple origin, partly derived from Rome, partly from the church, and partly from the Frankish kingship. "The race of the Germans," wrote Emperor Louis II in 871 to Basil of Byzantium, "has brought forth the most abundant fruits to the Lord. . . . . For as God was able of stones to raise up children like Abraham, so from the barbarism of the Germans He has been able to raise up successors to the Roman emperors."[1]

The history of Central Europe in the feudal age is the history of the efforts of the German people to expand the borders of their *Regnum Teutonicum* to East, West, North, South, not in the interest of mere conquest, but in obedience to the influence of a great idea. The German kings of the tenth, eleventh, and twelfth centuries made a supreme endeavor to realize the unitary dream of the Middle Ages by political expansion over every frontier, by permanent Germanization through colonization and conversion of the peoples in the territories beyond the Elbe and the Oder rivers and in the bend of the Danube; by the effort to keep alive in Italy (then but a geographical expression) a great tradition; by the promotion of the ancient Latin culture; by great economic development.

It is easy to criticize the Holy Roman Empire; easy to charge the rulers of the Saxon, Salian, and Staufer houses with abandoning the substance for a shadow, in being jealous to preserve a chimerical power, in being tenacious of an illusory title, the effect of which was to mutilate the natural historical development of Italy, to divert the normal history of Germany out of its natural orbit, and to waste untold blood and treasure in fruitless wars with popes and Lombard cities.

But such adverse criticism fails to understand not so much the weight of tradition and the influence of great historical facts as the profound political philosophy and deep psy-

[1] Bouquet, VII, 573. Kleinclausz, *L'Empire Carolingien*, pp. 441–57 contests the authenticity of this letter.

chology which motivated such aspiration. With justice has M. Ernest Lavisse written:

> Je recommende le Saint Empire Romain avec son cortège d'idées et de sentiments aux critiques que prétendent plier l'histoire aux règles d'une science exacte. Ils y verront qu'il existe une action de l'invisible et qu'elle ne peut être ni constatée certitude ni jugée avec équité. ... Le Saint Empire, comme l'Empire Romain, a été une tentative pour organiser l'humanité. ... Et c'est parce qu'aujourd'hui nous ne savons plus définer l'humanité que nous trouvons une charme étrange à l'histoire d'une institution fondée sur le croyance en l'unité paternelle du genre humain sous la paternité de Dieu.

A vague and traditional desire for universal rule was at the bottom of medieval German history. This was the result of the imposition of the Carolingian political ideal upon the Saxon, Salian, and Hohenstaufen kings. Henry II was saluted as "lord of lands and seas"; Henry III was called "the head of the world." These encomiums were not effusive flattery or fantastic pretension in the eleventh century, but a manifestation of "that reverence for the glories of the past whereon rested the idea of the mediaeval empire."[1]

With Germany's tremendous political preponderance and territorial sway over the center of Europe, interest in the ways and manners of the German nation bulked large in the mind of the rest of Europe.

The physical and moral characteristics of the German people received interested attention from their neighbors in the Middle Ages. As specimens of physical manhood the medieval German, like the ancient German, was tall and strong,[2] and even handsome, on the word of his enemies. In the Middle Ages, when a man was unusually tall, he was

---

[1] The *Sachsenspiegel*, III, 44, sec. 1, traces the idea of empire from Babylon to Persia to Macedon to Rome to Germany. J. G. Robertson, *History of German Literature*, p. 35, writes: "*A Spiel vom Antichrist* from the monastery of Tegernsee . . . . reflects the national spirit of the German Empire under Barbarossa, for it is a German kaiser who here rules over the earth at the end of things." See Fr. Kampers, "Kaiserprophetieen u. Kaisersagen im Mittelalter," *Beitrag z. Gesch. d. dtschn. Kaiseridee.* (1895).

[2] The Suevi mocked at the small height of Caesar's troops (*De bello Gall.* ii. 30). For Roman appreciation of the German physically see Tacitus, *Annales* ii. 14; Josephus, *Antiq.* i. 15.

taken for a German.[1] The *chansons de geste* frequently allude to the tallness of the Germans.[2] A proverb ran that the prettiest women were to be found in Flanders, the handsomest men in Germany, the tallest men in Denmark. William of Apulia speaks of the high stature of the Germans he saw in Italy.[3] Albert of Aix, who met with Germans on the First Crusade, represents them as handsome of face and figure.[4] When the Bishop of Bamberg went to Palestine in 1065 his beauty made such an impression that the people ran to see him, and even routed him out of his lodgings that they might behold him.[5] Adalbert of Bremen and his great political rival, Anno of Cologne, were both remarkably handsome men.[6] A Saxon historian, in relating the massacre of a company of warriors under command of Burckhard of Halberstadt, the fiercest fighting bishop of his century, expresses astonishment that men of such physical perfection could have been overcome.[7] Bishop Udo of Trier, and Bruno, a successor in the same see, both were men of singular physical comeliness.[8] Abbot Guntram was tall, strikingly handsome, and with a melodious voice which yet could ring like a trumpet. William, abbot of Braunweiler, was so handsome that one might think him an angel.[9]

The German warriors in the Middle Ages gloried in their physical strength and beauty. The Monk of St. Gall in the ninth century tinges with romance the army of Charlemagne which conquered the Lombards of Italy in 772.[10] The same author tells of one of Charlemagne's doughtiest warriors, a

[1] Tobler, *Mitth. aus altfranz. Handschriften*, I, 23.

[2] Zimmermann, *Roman. Forschungen*, XXIX (1911), 235 f.

[3] *Historicum poema . . . . . de rebus Normannorum*, Book II, chap. v (SS. IX, 255).

[4] *Historia Hierosolymitana*, Book I.

[5] Lambert of Hersfeld, *Annales* (*anno* 1065).

[6] Adam of Bremen, *Gesta eccles. pontif. Hammab.*, III, 2; Lambert of Hersfeld, *op. cit.* (1075).

[7] *Annal. Sax.* (1088) (SS. V, 724).

[8] *Gesta Trever.*, chap. ix.

[9] *Vita Wolfhelmi*, chap. iv (SS. XII, 183).   [10] *Monachus Sangal.*, II, 17.

man of Thurgau named Eishere, "who was so tall that you might have thought him sprung from the race of Anak, if they had not lived so long ago and so far away." Before the battle of Civitate in 1053, the German knights in the papal army derided their Norman adversaries for their small stature—and Normans passed for tall men in Europe then.[1] In 1107, when the envoys of Henry V of Germany and those of the Pope met at Châlons-sur-Marne to discuss the peace of the church, the physical beauty and hauteur of the German ambassadors, especially of Archbishop Bruno of Trier and Duke Welf of Bavaria, deeply impressed the French. The elegance of figure, the pleasantness of demeanor, the natural eloquence and good sense of the Archbishop aroused the admiration of Abbot Suger of St. Denis, the French King's chief envoy. But the big, burly figure, loud voice, and ubiquitous sword of Duke Welf nettled him.[2]

As to the bravery of the Germans in the Middle Ages opinion is unanimous.[3] At Civitate they fought to the last man. Albert of Aix, a hard critic of them in the time of the Crusades, never belies their courage. Across the annals of medieval Germany the record of their feats of arms abounds on every page. In 1044 a little troop of Germans under Henry III opposed a whole Hungarian army on the Repcze.[4] In 1050 a handful of Germans withheld the fortress of Hainburg against attack after attack of Hungarians.[5] In 1060 a combat took place which has a Homeric ring about it between two German knights and a whole host of Hungarians in the narrow defile of Theben, the famous gateway from Austria into Hungary.

The Germans had been intercepted in the pass and badly

---

[1] "Teutonici quia caesaries et forma decoros
  Fecerat egregie proceri corpore illos,
  Corpora derident Normannica quae breviora
  Esse videbantur."

  Guill. Apul., Book II, *MGH*. SS. IX (p. 255).

[2] Suger, *Vita Lud. Crassi* (ed. Molinier), chap. ix, p. 27.

[3] So far as I know the sources, Petrus Diaconus, IV, chap. xxxix, is the sole Italian historian who has accused the Germans of weakness. The extract is cited in Gregorovius, *Rome in the Middle Ages*, IV, 2, 345 n.

[4] *Annal. Altah.* (anno 1044).   [5] *Ibid.* (anno 1050).

routed. William, the margrave of Thuringia, and a German knight named Poto bravely covered the rear and put up such a resistance that if Germany at this time had been as sensitive to romantic impulses as France the memory of their feat of arms would have rung down the ages like the *Chanson de Roland*. The *Annals of Altenheim* run:

> For these two, when the others were slain, took their stand upon a knoll and laid about them with such slaughter that the deeds of the very bravest men of former ages seem small in comparison. From evening until sunrise, standing back to back and facing the foe on every side, they fought, nor could they be overcome even by the thousands against them. They refused to surrender until King Bela [of Hungary] gave his word of honor to spare them.[1]

Ever afterward Poto was known as "the Brave." Forty years later the German chronicler Ekkehard of Aura wrote of him: "Truly was he believed to have sprung from a race of ancient giants."[2] In 1115, Count Otto of Ballenstadt, with 60 German warriors, fought 2,800 Slavs, of whom 1,700 were left dead on the field![3] In the terrible battle of Monte Porzio, May 29, 1167, although the Germans were as 1 to 20 against the Romans, victory rested on their banners.[4]

The *chansons de geste* abound with gallant appreciation by the French of the bravery of the Germans.[5] Bernard of Clairvaux, when urging the Second Crusade upon the Germans, wrote to the Archbishop of Cologne and other prelates of Germany: "Your land is fruitful in brave men, and is known to be full of robust youth, your praise is in the whole world, and the fame of your valor has filled the entire earth."[6]

The Italians, like the Slavs, were not capable of militarily resisting the Germans. This is admitted by medieval Italian

---

[1] This famous day is described by many chroniclers: *Annal. Altah.* (1060); *Berth. Annal.* (1060); Lambert, *Annal.* (1060).

[2] Ekkehard, *Chronicon* (1104).

[3] *Annal. Sax.* (1115).

[4] For an account of this engagement, with citations from the sources see Gregorovius, *op. cit.*, IV, 2, 579–81.

[5] See the passages collected by Zimmermann, *Roman. Forsch.*, XXIX (1911), 236 ff.

[6] Bernh. Clarv., *Ep.* 363; cf. Otto Fris., *De gestis Friderici*, I, 41.

historians time and again.[1] The German rule of Italy was not
successfully resisted until the Lombard victory at Legnano
in 1179. In battle French and Italian chroniclers agree that
their strength, courage, and ferocity were so great that the
Germans could neither be reduced nor disarmed.[2] "In battle
they are men of iron," said an Italian annalist.[3] Falco of
Beneventum compared the shouting of the Germans in battle
to the roaring of lions.[4]

The German belief that "money talks," and in the power
of gold to influence or corrupt, was proverbial.[5] German
avarice was as notorious as German prowess. *"Terra belli-
cosa et quaestuosa"* was said of medieval Germany. The spoil
out of Italy enriched Germany.[6] Lombardy especially, because of the commercial prosperity of its towns, was heavily
taxed.[7] Rather of Verona[8] and Otto of Vercelli[9] bitterly inveighed against the brutality, violence, and spoliation practiced continually by the Germans upon the Italians. The
complaints of Italy in the Middle Ages against these practices are repeated century after century.[10] Benedict of Soracte
in 966, in crabbed medieval Latin, pronounces a threnody
over Rome in the hard grip of Otto I.

[1] *Amatus de Mont. Cass.*, VII, 12; *Annal. Sax.* (1137). Petrus Diaconus, IV,
chap. xxxix, picturesquely and untruthfully says: "Habent enim aliquid simile cum
nivibus suis; nam statim ut tacti calore fuerint, in sudorem conversi, deficiunt, et
quasi a sole solvuntur."

[2] Ekkeh., *Chron.* (1099, 1117); Odilon, *Epith. Adelh.*, chap. iv (SS. IV, 639).

[3] Bened., *Chron.*, chap. xxxvi (SS. III, 710); cf. Brunon, *Vita Adalb.*, chap. x
(SS. IV, 599).

[4] *Falc. Benev.*, II, 225.

[5] Otto Fris., *Gesta Frid.*, III, chap. xxi; Adam Brem., *op. cit.*, IV, chap. xxi;
Berthold, *Annal.* (1077); *Zwifalt. Chron.*, chap. xliv.

[6] Roswitha, *ad Oddonem*, I, vs. 6. Otto of Freising, *op. cit.*, II, 13, calls Italy
"a garden of delights"—*deliciarum hortus.*

[7] *Annal. Palid.* (955); *Annal. S. Disibodi* (SS. XVII, 29); Benzo, I, chaps. v–vi;
III, chap. i; Jaffé, *Biblioth.*, III, 691; *Annal. Qued.* (1014).

[8] Folc., *Gesta abbat. Lob.*, chap. xxvii.

[9] *Polypt.*, chap. xi.

[10] Ryccardus (SS. XIX, 334); *Annal. Ver.* (SS. XIX, 10); Otto Morena (SS.
XVIII, 619).

Woe unto thee, O Rome, who art oppressed and trodden under foot by so many nations; who hast even been taken prisoner by a Saxon king, and thy people put to the sword and thy strength reduced to naught. Thy gold and thy silver they carry away in their purses. Thou wast mother, now thou hast become daughter. Thou hast lost that which thou once possesst. Long hast thou fought against foreign foes. On all sides thou didst once conquer the world from the North unto the South. . . . . Alas, thou wast all too fair.[1]

An Italian traveling in Germany in Saxon times wrote of German music at this time:

These men on the other side of the Alps, when they let the thunder of their voices rise rumbling to the sky, never are able to attain any sweetness of modulation. . . . . The roughness of their wine-guzzling throats is barbaric, and whenever they try, by lowering and then raising their voices, to express a melodious softness, Nature shudders, for it sounds like the creaking of cart-wheels over frozen earth.[2]

The difference of language accentuated and aggravated the political resentment between the Germans and the Italians. In the *Vita S. Goaris*, chapter xi, by Wandelbert, as far back as 839, there is a remarkable tirade of a German noble against all the people using the Romance tongue.[3] The Germans despised the Italians as the Italians hated the Germans. Thietmar of Merseburg wrote:

Neither the climate nor the people of Italy suit our countrymen. Both in Rome and Lombardy treason is always at work. Strangers who visit Italy expect no hospitality; everything they need must be paid for on the

[1] The passage is quoted at length in Gregorovius, *City of Rome in the Middle Ages* (Eng. trans.), III, 365–66. He goes on to describe the Germans as the Huns were described by Roman writers in the fifth century. The original may be seen in *MGH. SS.* III, 719. Yet in contrast with this note of sorrow and resentment we have a poem upon the death of Otto III in 1002 and the accession of Henry II in exactly the opposite tone (Dummler, *Anselm der Peripatetiker*, pp. 72–82):

> "Regnorum robur periit quando Otto cecidit.
> Dum Otto noster moritur, Mars in mundo oritur.
> Mutavit caelum faciem et terra imaginem."

[2] "Alpina siquidem corpora vocum suarum tonitruis altisone perstrepentia susceptae modulationis dulcedinem proprie non resultant . . . . quia bibuli gutturis barbara feritas, dum inflexionibus et repercussionibus mitem nititur edere, cantilenam, naturali quodam fragore quasi plaustra per gradus confuse sonantia rigidas voces jactat" (quoted in Hattemer, *Denkmale*, I, 420).

[3] "Cum omnes Romanae nationis ac linguae homines ita quodam gentilitio odio execraretur, ut ne videre quidem eorum aliquem aequanimiter vellet, ac si

instant, and even then they must submit to being over-reached and cheated, and not infrequently to be poisoned in addition.[1]

"Itali sua superbia elati et velut natali odio Teutonicorum . . . . dedignati," writes the annalist of Altenheim in 1068.[2]

From the time of Conrad II, Italian hatred of the Germans was deep and concerted. Landulf of Milan, the Italian chronicler of the eleventh century, abounds in passages and epithets which disparage the Germans.[3] Gregory VII heartily hated all Germans, and distrusted even his own partisans there.[4] Pope Pascal II refused to set foot in Germany alleging "the barbarous manners of the people."[5] The violence of Conrad III (1139–52) drove many Germans into exile, and numbers of them sought refuge at the Norman court of Roger of Sicily, "who might have received more of them" records the *Historia Pontificalis*, except that the Germans were a race whose barbarism he could not endure.[6]

The Italians, while incapable of governing themselves, hated the German rule over them.[7] We catch the refrain of wounded pride in Buoncompagno's history of the siege of Ancona in 1174,[8] and in the fiery addresses of the Lombard deputies and the Pope in 1177, as recorded by Romuald of Salerno.[9] The conflict of the Lombard cities against Frederick Barbarossa between 1155 and 1183 liberated the Po Valley from German thraldom. But not until 1200 was German influence expelled from the administration of Rome, then from the Tuscan towns and the Marches, by Pope

---

quos forte ex eadem familia comprehendere potuisset crudeliter nonnumquam afficeret" (cited by Ebert, *Gesch. d. Lat. Lit. im Mittelalter*, II, 190).

[1] *Chronicon*, VII, 3.   [2] SS. XX, 89.

[3] ". . . . gulositatem et animos vino deditos . . . . saevissimi Theutonici qui nesciunt quid sit inter dexteram et sinistram" (*Mediol. Hist.*, II, 22). He describes the German speech of Lothar II, whom he heard at the diet of Roncaglia, as *verba barbara* (*ibid.*, II, 44).

[4] Meyer von Knonau, *Jahrb.*, I, 140. Old Benedictinism in Germany regarded Clunyism as "French mores" (Hauck, *Kirch. Gesch.*, III, 512).

[5] Ekkehard, *Chron.* (1107) (SS. X, 105).   [6] SS. XX, 538.

[7] "Animi Italorum semper avidi novarum rerum" (Lambert of Hersfeld, *Annales* [1052]).

[8] *De obsidione Anconae Liber*, chap. iii.   [9] SS. XIX, 445.

Innocent III. German rule over Italy was strong for centuries, but the Germans never were able to impose their civilization upon the country. Germanic *Kultur* never was anything but a gloss in medieval Italy. The remnants and the tradition of Latin culture were far too old and too strong to be dislodged or obscured.[1]

The "burden of empire" is no new thing in history. The thought may be found in Otto of Freising's *Chronicon*. When stripped of their medieval husk of language Otto's reflections have an almost startling modern ring. The kings of Germany in the twelfth century regarded the half-barbaric and semi-anarchic condition of Poland in their time much as an American regards the condition of Mexico, or the Britisher looks upon the native population in many of his colonies.[2] The frightful anarchy prevailing in Italy just before Frederick I's intervention there, even if exaggerated by Otto of Freising, baffles belief. Venice was at war with Ravenna; Verona and Vicenza with Padua and Treviso; Pisa and Florence with Lucca and Siena. "The atrociously warring factions deluged all Italy with blood, fire and pillage. . . . . Castles, villages, fields, were devastated with fire and sword."[3]

The study of law did not imbue the Italians with a respect

[1] Ficker, *Forschungen*, II, 278, has gathered together some valuable evidence on this point; cf. Fisher, *op. cit.*, II, 256 f.

[2] "Haec mala nostris diebus in vicinis regnis pullulare cognoscimus, quanta vero ex remotis et transmarinis regnis in dies audiamus, pro fastidio vitando ad presens subprimimus. Tanta enim sunt quod nisi sanctorum quorum per Dei gratiam magna nunc copia est, meritis et suffragiis staret mundus, in brevi omnino eum periturum timere cogeremur" (*Chronicon*, VII, 21 end): cf. the same thought in VII, 34, end of second paragraph. Helmold, *Chronica Slavorum*, I, 1, writing at almost the same time, expresses much the same sentiment of contempt for the Poles and Bohemians.

[3] *Chronicon*, VII, 29. Landulf of Milan admits the necessity of imperial authority in Italy whose people seemed incapable of governing themselves. *Hist. Mediolanens*, II, 22; Pertz, VIII, 58: "Cum Conradus imperator Papiae [Pavia], circumstante exercitu, consedisset, universis qui ecclesiarum beneficia invaserant, aut qui homicidia injuste commiserant, aut orphanorum aut viduarum praedia devastando contriverant, et omnibus qui injuste a perfidis hominibus per aliquam causam cruciabantur, ut sui imperii vigor exigebat secundum legem facere humanam et judicare decrevit." The internecine wars of the Lombard cities ruined the country: "Magis silva ferarum videbatur quam agricultura" (Galvaneus Flamma, *Chronicon de antiq. Mediol.*, chap. cclxv). The Lombards tortured Italian prisoners while sparing those who were German (Ottonis S. Blas., *Chron.* chap. xiv).

for it. "The Italians," said Muratori,[1] "highly prized their
new liberty, but it only operated to make them more unfortunate." Otto of Freising expressed the same sentiment
with more energy: "Barbaricae fecis retinent vestigia, quod
cum legibus se vivere glorientur, legibus non obsecuntur."[2]
Similar turmoil and incapacity in the kingdom of Jerusalem elicits similar reflections from Otto of Freising, and
from all that we know of the condition of this dependency of
Latin Christianity in the Orient between 1144 and 1187, Otto
of Freising's condemnation is amply justified.[3] It was not
chauvinism that led him to depreciate the incapacity of the
Romance races in Europe for government. Only in Norman England and in Norman Italy, outside of Germany,
did any large peace and order and protection of life and property obtain. To medieval Italy, where civil war was endemic,
Roncaglia's permanent military camp of Germans in Lombardy,[4] the sharp discipline of the German armies in Italy,[5]
and the effective administration of Christian of Mainz as
Frederick I's viceroy in Italy must have been a revelation.

Quite naturally, with the possession of these qualities for
rule the German of the time of the Ottos, the Heinrichs, and
the Friedrichs developed intellectual and moral characteristics which rasped the feelings of the non-German peoples

[1] *Annales*, VI, 478.

[2] *Gesta Frid.*, II, 13. Against these harsh verdicts, however, should be set the
gentler opinion of John of Salisbury, *Policraticus*, IV, 11: "Hospitem meum
Placentinum dixisse recolo, ... hoc in civitatibus Italiae usu frequenti celeberrimum esse quod, dum pacem diligunt et justitiam colunt et perjuriis abstinent,
tantae libertatis et pacis gaudio perfruuntur, quod nichil est omnino quod vel in
minimo quietem eorum concutiat."

Savigny, *Gesch. roem. Rechts im Mitt.*, IV, 210, n. 4, mistakenly takes this as
evidence of Italian zeal for Roman law. Not Roman law but communal liberties and
free local justice are meant.

Elsewhere (III, 8) John of Salisbury relates a conversation with Pope Hadrian IV
illustrative of the polite manners of the Lombards: "memini me audisse Romanum
pontificem solitum deridere Lumbardos, dicentem eos pilleum omnibus colloquenti-
bus facere, eo quod in exordio dictionis benevolentiam captent, et eorum cum quibus
agitur, capita quodam commendationis demulceant oleo."

[3] *Chronicon*, VII, 28, 33.   [4] *Gesta Friderici*, II, 12.

[5] *Ibid.*, III, 28. There is a remarkable description of the organization and
discipline of the army of Henry VI in Italy (1194) in Otto of St. Blasien, *Chronicon*,
chap. xl.

with whom the Germans came in contact.[1] The revived study of the Roman law inflated the imperial pretensions of the Hohenstaufen, and lent tradition and historical actuality to the former vague idea of *Weltmacht*[2] embodied in the claim to *dominium mundi*. With Frederick I the antiquity of the Holy Roman Empire was pushed back to the very founding of Rome itself. He is *Divus Augustus;* his authority, though, dates from Romulus; he ascended the throne eighteen hundred years *ab urbe condita.*[3] When he summoned the Council of Pavia in favor of his anti-pope, Victor, Frederick I reminded the bishops of "the example of Constantine, Valentinian and Justinian."[4]

Yet protest must be made against absurd exaggerations attributed to the Hohenstaufen by their enemies in Europe. Wilkins[5] long ago challenged the authenticity of the alleged

[1] The *Chronicon* of Otto of St. Blasien abounds with self-flattering moral characterizations of the Germans: "ferocitas Teutonicorum" (chap. xiv); "Teutonica animositas" (chap. xx); "audacia Teutonicorum," (chap. xxiii); "Germaniae animositas et fortitudo" (chap. xxxv). Cf. Dummler, *"Ueber den furor Teutonicus,"* *SB. d. Akad. d. Wiss. Berlin* (1897), pp. 119 f.; Schulttheiss, *Gesch. d. deutschen Nationalgefühles,* I, 221 f. (1893).

[2] For the progressive development of this idea of *Weltmacht* see Gierke, *Genossenschaftsrecht,* II, 572 f.

[3] Radevic, I, 6, 12, 20; II, 76, etc. Otto Fris., *Gesta.* II, 1; Godefr. Colon., *Chron.* (ed. Boehmer, *Fontes*), III, 427; Doeberl, *Monumenta Selecta,* IV (an admirable collection of Frederick's *diplomata*).

[4] *Conc. Pap.* (*MGH.*, IV, 121). In spite of his pompous imperialistic pretensions and fondness for quoting Sallust and the *Corpus juris*, Frederick I had slender knowledge of Latin. ("Scripturas et antiquorum gesta sedulo perquirit . . . . Latinam [linguam] vero melius intelligere quam pronunciare" [Radevic, II, 76].) At Besançon in 1157 Rainald of Dassel translated the famous letter of Hadrian IV into German, sentence by sentence, as the language flowed from the lips of Roland, the Pope's chancellor (Ficker, *Rainald von Dassel*, p. 15). We possess the text of Frederick's discourse at Roncaglia on November 14, 1158, but although it is larded with scraps of Roman law and a quotation from Sallust, it was nevertheless pronounced in German (Radevic, I, 46 [*MGH.*, *SS.* IV, 110]; *Curia Roncaliae: oratio imperialis*). During the negotiations at Venice in August, 1177, with Alexander III and the deputies of the Lombard cities, Frederick made a harangue in German which Christian of Mainz translated into Italian (*vulgariter*), Romuald, *Chron.*, *MGH. SS.* IV, 155. Otto Morena (*anno* 1158) relates that one day the Emperor was walking at Roncaglia between two legists and asked them if they believed that he was lord of the world. One said "Yes." The other said the Emperor had the title but not the proprietorship!

[5] *Gesch. d. Kreuzzüge,* IV, 52.

letter of Frederick I to Saladin preserved in Matthew Paris, in Hoveden, in Ralph Diceto, and in the *Itinerarium regis Ricardi*, in which the Emperor is made to claim Persia, Syria, Ethiopia, and Mauretania as parts of his Empire, and boasts that he will come into the East and recover those provinces conquered by Crassus and Anthony, "generals of my predecessors." I have no doubt that this epistle is a fraud and probably originated as a school exercise at St. Albans or elsewhere. It certainly excites suspicion that no mention of such a letter is made by any German or Italian writer.

Frederick Barbarossa seized upon the Third Crusade in 1190 as a means to extend German domination not only over the Holy Land and Syria, but Byzantium too, if possible. When his host entered the territory of the Byzantine Empire it was compelled to fight its way through. In Bulgaria the inhabitants fled on all sides at the German approach, obstructing the roads with fallen trees. It was necessary to take Trajan's Pass by assault. When the German army arrived at Phillipopolis it found the city deserted.[1] Frederick, in wrath, deluged the environs with fire and blood, and seriously contemplated attacking Constantinople. He wrote to his son Henry to attempt to persuade the Pope to preach a crusade against the Greeks.[2] "Over remote Eastern lands, where Frankish foot had never trod, Frederick Barbarossa asserted the indestructible rights of Rome, mistress of the world."[3]

Henry VI gave sharper definition to his father's purposes. He demanded an indemnity from Constantinople for the injury inflicted upon Frederick's army. When the Byzantine emperor, Isaac Angelos, soon afterward was dethroned by his brother Alexius III in 1195, Henry VI's attitude became more menacing. He adroitly married Irene, a daughter of the exiled Emperor, to his brother, Philip of Swabia, hoping thus to create a German pretext to claim the throne of the Byzantine Empire. At the same time that he planned to conquer Constantinople, Henry VI also dreamed of establishing his

[1] *MGH*. SS. XVII, 509–10.

[2] Prutz, *Friedrich I*, I, 131; Winkelmann, I, 447.

[3] Bryce, *Holy Roman Empire*.

sovereignty over Syria and Palestine, and began that policy which later under his son Frederick II was to transfer to the Holy Land the feud of emperor and pope. The conquests of western Christendom in the Orient hitherto had been considered to be the patrimony of the church. But Barbarossa's lawyers developed the theory that there could only be one supreme and universal authority in the world, that of the German Caesar. While one expedition, therefore, was sent to Palestine, Henry VI himself in 1197 undertook the task of conquering Byzantium. His sudden death in September of that year ruined the double plan. For the second time Constantinople and the Orient eluded the attempt of the Hohenstaufen to seize them. Henry VI's sudden death ruined the prospects of German imperial power in Constantinople and the East.

One may be tempted at first to mock at the Staufen pretensions as expressions of the madness of caesarism. But it would be an error so to do. The Holy Roman Empire was not only a German institution; it was also a universal institution —at least in theory; it represented a great tradition; it was a superstate in which all the states of Christendom were vaguely comprehended. On no other hypothesis can the ascription to its supremacy made by Henry II of England in 1157 be understood. That ascription was not extorted from the English king by force, but was the voluntary recognition of a sovereign intellectually the peer of Frederick I himself.[1]

It were impossible for language to be plainer. But there is no servility in it. It is merely moral homage which Henry II attributes to the office of Holy Roman emperor—to the office, not the man. The ascription had no practical political application, and was not supposed to have. The medieval empire was a great political constellation in which the Germano-Italian state was the central sun and the other states as stars around it. Thus interpreted, the Holy Roman

---

[1] "Regnum nostrum," wrote the Plantagenet, "et quidquid ubique nostrae subicitur dicioni vobis exponimus et vestrae committimus potestati, ut ad vestrum nutum omnia disponantur, et in omnibus vestri fiat voluntas imperii. Sit igitur inter nos et populos nostros dilectionis et pacis unitas indivisa, commertia tuta, ita tamen ut vobis, qui dignitate preminetis, imperandi cedat auctoritas, nobis non deerit voluntas obsequendi" (*Gesta Frid.*, III, chap. vii).

Empire was a utopian conception which had the virtues and the weaknesses every utopia necessarily has.

Next to Italian resentment against the Germans was that of the French. The Cluny reform, which the German kings resisted, and the Crusades were the chief factors in instigating this feeling. Pignot has related a literary conflict between a French poet and a German Benedictine which casts curious light upon the amenities of literature in the twelfth century. Pierre of Poitiers, an ardent Cluniac and admirer of the great Abbot Peter the Venerable, wrote an exceedingly laudatory panegyric of him. The critic accused the poet of fulsome adulation, saying caustically that such praise of a living man was unseemly, since even the saints themselves were so praised only after their decease. This retort stung the French writer to the quick, and he retaliated with a violent and abusive characterization, not only of his antagonist, but of German culture itself.[1]

About the same time that this was written Henry V of Germany, in order to make a diversion in the interest of his father-in-law, Henry I of England, who was warring in France against Louis VI, invaded France through Lorraine. The response of the French vassals to the King's call to arms is evidence at this time (1125) of a feeling of national antagonism against the Germans.[2]

When Norbert became archbishop of Magdeburg his enemies circulated the rumor that he and "his Frenchmen" were stealing the relics and robbing the church treasury.

Until the cult of Charlemagne arose in France in the time of the Crusades there was no national feeling between the

---

[1] Pignot, *Histoire de l'ordre de Cluny*, III, 462–63

> "Non habeo mirum, te nobis frendere dirum,
> Nam quod sic saevis, proprium solet esse Suevis.
> More tuae gentis de nostro carmine sentis.
> Quid laus, quid carmen, quid vitae dulce levamen,
> Quid pax, quid pietas, quid virtus, quid sit honestas,
> Barbare, tu nescis; ideo livore tumescis.
> Ergo tace, ... etc."

[2] Suger, *Vita Ludovici Crassi* (ed. Molinier), p. 102; cf. Ekkehard, *Chron.* (SS. VI, 262). Walter Map (*De nugis curialium* [ed. Camden Soc.], Part V, chap. v, p. 219) relates that Louis VI repudiated the terms which Henry V haughtily demanded as *tpwrut aleman* [*trop allemand*].

French and the Germans. The counterclaims to Lorraine were wholly dynastic and political. But the Crusades greatly stimulated French national sentiment. The different blood groups in France—Franks, Picards, Normans, Gascons, Poitevins, Provençaux—in contact with one another and in contact with the Germans through whose country they passed to the Holy Land developed an acute feeling toward the Germans unknown before.

Lorraine was the only German duchy which displayed enthusiasm for the First Crusade. The rest of Germany viewed the movement with either astonishment or contempt.[1] Guibert de Nogent with reason entitled his history of the First Crusade *Gesta Dei per Francos*—"an unpretending title," he writes, "but which will serve to honor our nation." In Book II, chapter i, of this work Guibert tells how, meeting an archdeacon of Mainz who mocked at the French as crusaders, he replied:

> If you think the French so weak and such cowards, and believe yourself able to wound with ridicule a name whose celebrity extends to the Indian Ocean, tell me to whom was it that pope Urban II appealed for aid against the Turks if not the French? If the French had not by their strength and courage opposed a barrier to the Turks, not all your Germans whose name is not even known, would have been of use.[2]

During the Crusades there was much friction between the French and the German troops. Godfrey de Bouillon, who was half-French and half-German, and who had imbibed a large amount of the courtesy of French chivalry, is said to have apologized to the French for the uncouth manners of the Germans in the host of the First Crusade.[3] Odo of Deuil has a long passage denunciatory of the Germans in the Second Crusade.[4]

[1] *Annal. Aug.* (1096); Ekkehard, *Chron.* (1099); Bernoldi, *Chron.* (1096).

[2] Cf. B. Monod, "L'eveil du sentiment national en France au XIe siècle," *Le moine Guibert et son temps* (Paris, 1903), pp. 235 f., and G. Bourgin, *Guibert de Nogent: Histoire de sa vie* (Paris, 1907), Introd., pp. xxii–xxiii.

[3] Wackernagel, *Altfranz. Lieder und Leiche*, pp. 194–95, but I cannot trace his reference.

[4] Book III. For collected information on this head see Steinhausen, *Gesch. der deutsch. Kultur*, p. 238; cf. F. Kern, "Der mittelalterliche Deutsche in französischer Ansicht," *Hist. Ztschft.*, CVIII, 237.

John of Würzburg who visited Jerusalem between 1160–
70 inveighs against the French claim to the leading part in
the First Crusade:

> For though Duke Godfrey is honoured for himself, yet the taking of
> the city is credited to him and his Germans [they were mostly Flemings]
> although they had no small share in that exploit; but it is attributed to
> the French alone. And some dispraisers of our nation have even scratched
> out the epitaph of the famous Wigger [of Swabia] because they could not
> deny that he was a German, and have written over it the epitaph of some
> French knight or other. . . . . No part of Jerusalem, not even the smallest
> street, was set apart for the Germans.[1]

French epic literature is cleverly satirical in allusions to
Germans. The *Ecbasis* and the *Ysengrinus*, which are interesting bestiaries, give French names to the finer kinds of
animals and German names to the wolf, the ass, etc. The
wolf in *Ysengrinus* questions the lamb in German speech.[2]
The epic literature of the Hohenstaufen period resented the
French pretensions to courage. In the *Pilatus* the people of
Rome are represented as not daring to punish a German who
had killed a Frenchman because they so feared the Germans
and contemned the French as degenerate "Carlingiens."
Elsewhere the French kings of Jerusalem are styled *welsche*,
and even a Norman knight is described as trembling at the
very name of the German Emperor.

The Second Crusade disillusioned the Germans as to the
alleged effeminacy of the French, but it did not add to the
good feeling between the two nations. The French ridiculed
the arms and armor used by the Germans as old-fashioned,
and laughed at their foot forces, for in France every man was
a mounted knight.[3] There were many complaints on both
sides and not a few pitched fights between the troops. The
Second Crusade is a turning-point in Franco-German relations in the Middle Ages, and the Third Crusade (1190) when

[1] Beazeley, *Dawn of Modern Geography*, II, 193–94. This outburst is in chap.
xiii of John of Würzburg's account.

[2] V, vss. 549–50; VI, vss. 379–82.

[3] Guillaume le Breton, *Phillippide*, X, 680. For German arms and armor at this
time and the French technical superiority see Kohler, *Die Entwicklung des Kriegswesens*, I, 152–53; Delbrück, *Kriegskunst*, III, 312.

Philip II and Henry VI bitterly quarreled accentuated still more this international resentment.[1]

The pretentious claims to imperial authority made by Frederick Barbarossa, united with his ambitious political purposes, soon aroused the apprehension and resentment of Europe. John of Salisbury, whose pet aversions were monks and Germans, voiced this sentiment in the famous interrogation: *Quis Teutonicos constituit judices nationum?* ("Who has made the Germans judges of the nations?")[2] This was said in 1160. If John of Salisbury may be believed, the great Hohenstaufen Emperor regarded all the kings of Europe as *reges provinciales* and said that Louis VII of France was a *roitelet*.[3] By 1162 there seems to have been a *haro* in Europe against Frederick I—a half-formed European coalition composed of France, England, Hungary, Byzantium, Sicily, Venice.[4] William, bishop of Pavia, in 1167 wrote that the Germans were still "barbarians."[5] John of Salisbury, about 1160, inveighed against the *furor Teutonicus*, and rejoiced exceedingly over the Emperor's defeat at Legnano in 1179.[6] If his statement is true regarding the attitude of superiority assumed by German students in Paris—*loquuntur grandia, minis tument*—there must have been many a clash between the "nations" of students in Paris.

Yet when all has been said or written, how much weight may be attached to these sentiments? Does any nation ever understand another? Are not the judgments which one

---

[1] Godfrey of Viterbo, *Pantheon* (*ca.* 1184–91) is redolent of this animosity (SS. XXII, 225–28; cf. Lot, *Hugues Capet*, pp. 329, 331).

[2] Giles, *Joannis Saresburiensis epp.*,I, No. 59, p. 164; also in Doeberl, *Monumenta Selecta*, IV, No. 40B, p. 190. Giesebrecht (*Forschungen*, XXII), has endeavored to clear up two of John's letters about Frederick I (Nos. 130 and 138).

[3] *Ep. 185:* "impudenti scurrilitate regulum appelare." Cf. Ficker, *Rainald von Dassel* (1850), p. 48.

[4] See Kap-Herr, *Abendl. Politik Kaiser Manuels*, pp. 72, 85–92, and Exkurs 4; Reuter, *Papst Alexander III*, II, 247; Giesebrecht, *Kaiserzeit*, V, 496 f., 641.

[5] Bouquet, XVI, 55.

[6] "Vidimus, vidimus hominem qui consueverat esse sicut leo in domo sua . . . . latebare quaerere. . . . . Illum, illum imperatorem qui totius orbis terror fuerat, utinam vidissetis ab Italia fugientem cum ignominia semptierna." *Policraticus*, Book IV, chap. xi, ed. Webb, I, 274.

people has of another almost always shallow and unjust? It is so today. How much more must it have been so in the Middle Ages, which were without our modern means of rapid and frequent material intercourse and thought transference?

PART II

NEW EAST FRONTIER COLONIAL GERMANY

CHAPTER XII

THE GERMAN CHURCH AND THE CONVERSION OF THE SLAVS OF THE ELBE

RELIGION was a highly developed institution among the Slavs, and—at least among the Baltic and Elbean Wends—the priest class was an influential caste.[1] The most striking fact of their belief was the dualism which pervaded it.[2] It was like ancient Manicheism, or like the belief of the Cathari in this respect.[3] They deified the forces of nature like many primitive peoples, and a black horse, sacred to the local god, was an object of great veneration among them, and was used as an instrument of divination.[4]

The Wendish temples[5] were imposing structures, usually built of wood, but that of Triglav in Brandenburg was of stone. The two most famous Slavonic fanes were those of the god Riedegost or Redigast, of which the Redarii were cus-

---

[1] Upon the religion of the Wends see *Mythology of All Races* (Gray and Moore, ed.; Boston, 1918), III, 2; Lippert, *Socialgesch. Böhmens*, II, 1–11; G. Krek, *Einleitung in die slavische Literatur* (4th ed., 1906), pp. 84 f.; *Cambridge Mediaeval History*, Vol. II, chap. xiv; Hauck, *Kirchengesch, Deutschlands*, III, 69–87; Schulze, *Kolonisierung*, pp. 19–43, 86–116; Lavisse, *La Marche de Brandenbourg*, pp. 10–15; Wendt, *op. cit.*, I, 16–18; Guttmann, *Forschungen zur Preuss. und Brandenb. Gesch.*, IX, 400–403; Bernard, *De Adamo Bremensi Geographo* (1895), pp. 63–71; Fisher, *Mediaeval Empire*, II, 3–6. Adam of Bremen, II, 18; III, 50; IV, 18; Herbordus, II, 31–33, 35; III, 6–7, 22–23, 36; Ebbo, II, 13; III, 1, 3–8; Helmold, I, 6, 52, 69, 83; II, 12; Thietmar, VI, 17–18, 23–25, are the fullest sources.

[2] "Est autem Slavorum mirabilis error; nam in conviviis et compatacionibus suis pateram circumferunt, in quam conferunt, non dicam consecracionis, sed execracionis verba sub nomine deorum, boni scilicet atque mali, omnem prosperam fortunam a bono deo, adversam a malo dirigi profitentes. Unde etiam malum deum lingua sua Diabol sive Zcerneboch, id est nigrum deum, appelant" (Helmold, *Chron. Slav.*, I, 52).

[3] Gieseler, *Ueber den Dualismus der Slaven*, pp. 357 f.; Schmidt, *Histoire des Albigeois*, I, 7–8; II, 271–72.

[4] Herbordus, *Vita Ottonis ep. Babenb.* II, 33.

[5] Hauck, *Kirchengesch.*, III, 84–85, has collected all the references to them.

todians, at Rethra;[1] and that of the god Svantowit at Arkona in the island of Rügen. Rethra was so completely destroyed in 1121 by Lothar, then duke of Saxony, that its exact location was unknown for centuries, but it was supposed to have been upon the Tollensee.[2]

One of the romances of modern archaeology is the discovery and excavation of the site of Rethra. In the year before the late war the Prussian Academy granted a subsidy to Professor C. Schuchardt to make a complete archaeological survey of the remains of the Slavs in the old Wendish territory east of the Elbe. The war interrupted the plan. But in 1918 the survey was begun anew. At this time a young German Assyriologist named Robert Koldewey, whose researches in Mesopotamia were ruined by the war, was associated with Professor Schuchardt. For four summers these two scholars labored. In 1921 their excavations were in Rügen where they discovered and excavated the ruins of the temple of Arkona, disclosing a large square measuring sixty feet each way, with four columns in the interior and traces of the pedestal upon which the figure of the god Svantovit had once stood, exactly as Saxo Grammaticus described it in 1168. Then in the next summer (1922) Rethra was unearthed. The discovery was made through the description of it by Bishop Thietmar of Merseburg. Thietmar, who was of Saxon noble lineage and count of Waldeck, was related to the Saxon imperial house and regularly accompanied Emperor Henry II on his military expeditions against the Slavs. In the course of relating one of these expeditions Thietmar entered into a minute description of Rethra in his *Chronicon*, VI, 23. It is described as a "three-horned castle with three gates." On the east side it sloped toward a lake, and on the west was bor-

---

[1] It is minutely described by Thietmar, VI, 23. Cf. Adam of Bremen, II, 18, and Helmold, I, 2. According to Schafarik, *Slav. Alterth.*, II, 580, *Rethra* meant "war temple." In Adam of Bremen, III, 21, schol. 71 (77), is an account of how two Bohemian monks penetrated into this sanctuary in 1050 while a *concilium paganorum* was in session, and were discovered and after being tortured were put to death.

[2] Lisch, *Jahrb. d. Ver. f. Mecklenb. Gesch. und Alterthumsk.*, III, 21; *Jahrb. Heinr. II*, I, 260; Schmeidler, *Hamburg-Bremen und Nord-Ost Europa* (1918), pp. 341–60.

dered by a thick belt of virgin forest. Of the three gates, two
were on the land side, but the third was a water gate.

The salient point of this description was the *urbs tricornis
ac tres in se continens portas*, or "three-horned castle having
three gates." The different conjectures of historians as to the
meaning of this term explain the long and vain search for
the location of Rethra. Both *urbs* and *tricornis* had been misunderstood. The former was erroneously taken to mean "a
town," or even "a district," and the latter was thought to
signify a three-cornered structure similar to ancient Slavonic
triangular forts built by the Slavs upon peninsulas or bends
in the rivers, remains of which have been found in the Havel
at Ziegenhorn, Schildhorn, and Bestehorn.[1] Thus Thietmar's
urbs tricornis was erroneously taken to have been an island
with three points. Accordingly, previous archaeologists had
painfully and for years (1880–1908) explored all the islands
in the lakes of Mecklenburg only to find in the end that
Rethra was upon no one of them.

Professor Schuchardt, who is both a historian and an
archaeologist, knew that in feudal times the word *urbs* meant
"a castle," "a fortified place." Accordingly, he assumed that
the "horns" of the temple of Rethra must have been vertical
not horizontal projections, or, in other words, were towers
probably with gates in them, which thus would explain the
allusion to the three gates. Hence an *urbs tricornis tres in se
continens portas* meant "a castle with three towers," which,
seen from a distance, had the appearance of a trident. With
this new interpretation in mind the two scholars began a
survey of the territory and at last near Feldberg found a
physiography which seemed to answer to the requirements.
On the east side the site sloped 36 meters toward Lake Lucin.
On the west it is to this day girdled for miles by a magnificent
forest of beech. Even without digging, remains of a former
wall revealed ruins of two gates—one on the north, the other
on the south. The third had to be found by excavation, and,
as expected, the spade unearthed it in the middle of the west

[1] In each of these cases the suffix "-horn" is a later corruption of Old German
-holm, meaning "an islet," and has nothing to do with "horn."

side, toward the land. This was not all that was uncovered, however. For later a great outer wall was revealed encircling the three-towered inner *urbs*, which was at once a temple and a castle.

As the whole original structure had been built of wood, towers, gates, and palisades, almost everything had suc-cumbed to the flames when Rethra was destroyed by the Ger-man army under Lothar in 1121. But the ends of the timbers which had been set deeply in the ground on blocks of stone and charred débris plainly told the tale. The West Gate was the largest of the three gates. When the East Gate was exca-vated, striking archaeological evidence confirmatory of Thietmar's description was revealed. For it was the *tercia [porta] quae orientem respicit et minima est, tramitem ad mare*, although nothing was found by this gate to explain Thiet-mar's *visu nimis horribile*. But it may be conjectured that some imposing figure had once stood in the gate. Unfortu-nately, not a remnant of evidence remained of the carved idols of the gods and goddesses once worshiped by the Slavs in this temple and portrayed as clad in coats-of-mail, and not a vestige of the gold-and-silver adornment or votive offerings was found which the Bishop of Merseburg describes ap-parently from the description of an eyewitness.[1] Within the inner compound were found storehouses and magazines like cellars for the storage of supplies, but nothing was in them except a few pieces of shattered pottery. The castle or *urbs* was not large, measuring 115 meters long and 45 wide. But the zone between the *urbs* and the outer ringwall was large enough to accommodate ten thousand people. The whole view of Rethra must have been a striking one—the earliest rays of the rising sun reaching it across the shining

[1] "Hujus parietes variae deorum dearumque imagines mirifice insculptae, ut cernentibus videtur, exterius ornant; interius autem dii stant manu facti, singulis nominibus insculptis, galeis atque loricis terribiliter vestiti." If the statement be a true one that the name of each god and goddess was carved upon the pedestal upon which the sacred figure stood, then the Slavs of the Elbe possessed a written lan-guage which, since they were intensely pagan and hostile to Christianity, could have had no relation with the Cyrillian writing of the southern Slavs at this time.

surface of the lake rippled by the morning breeze, while behind the temple loomed the dark beech forest.[1]

Herbordus, in his *Life of Otto of Bamberg* (II, 32),[2] describes the temple of the three-headed god Triglav, one of four temples in Stettin, with some minuteness. "It had sculptures [carved wooden figures?] within and without, and from the walls projected images of men, beasts, birds, the appearance of which was so natural that they might have been thought to be living and breathing." These figures were brightly decorated with colored paints of such quality that the colors of the images outside could not be dimmed or washed off either by snow or rain. Into this temple the people brought, in accordance with the ancient custom of their ancestors, the stores and arms of their enemies which they had captured, and whatever spoils they took by land or by sea, as they were directed to do by the law relating to the giving of a tenth.[3] They had also preserved there for the honor and adornment of their gods, horns of wild bulls [the aurochs] covered with gold and set with gems, some for use as drinking horns, and others as musical instruments; swords, too, and knives, and much rich furniture which was rare and beautiful in appearance.

The temple roofs were steep and pointed. The temples often stood in a compound of considerable extent, walled in by a palisade. The right of asylum prevailed within this area, which was also used for public and tribal conferences. As among the druids, the oak seems to have been a sacred tree, and fine specimens of it grew within the temple inclosures. Often the temples were erected within groves of oaks, especially if a spring were there too.

But all this religion, about which we know so little and of which we would know more, was devoted to utter destruction by the bigotry and intolerance of the Christian church.

[1] The first revelation of these discoveries was made by Professor Schuchardt in *Sitzungsber.* of the Berlin Academy for 1921. Since then the complete history of these excavations has been published under the title *Arkona, Rethra, Vineta* (Berlin: H. Schoetz & Co.). The second edition has recently appeared (1926). A briefer notice of the history is found in *Forschungen und Fortschritte* (Berlin: November 1, 1926), pp. 178–79.

[2] Cf. another description of the temple of Triglav (II, 13, and III, 1). In III, 6, is an account of that of Gerovit (Mars) at Hologast.

[3] Helmold, II, 12, also mentions tithes—*tributa annuatim.*

Commingled with this iconoclastic spirit was also a covetousness on the part of the German clergy which almost baffles belief.

Ever since the conversion of Saxony the temple of Rethra was an object of hatred by Christian Germany. For all opposition to missionary endeavor among the Slavs of the Elbe, every Slavonic rebellion, every lapse to paganism again, emanated from the fanatical priesthood in Rethra. It was the greatest sanctuary of all the Slavs, and like Delphi among the ancient Greeks. The oracle of Rethra was consulted from far and near, even by Christian Danish kings. Upon its walls hung the colored banners of every Slavonic tribe between the Erzgebirge and the Baltic, and the trophies of victorious wars.[1] The priests of Rethra cast omens before every campaign. With them lay final determination of war and peace.

Neither the German church nor the German nobles were willing to let time work out the problem of race contact between the German and the Slav, and permit the gradual transfusion of blood between them and the slow transforming influences of civilization to resolve the issues. There can be little doubt that this might have been possible.[2]

[1] "Vexilla quoque eorum nisi ad expeditionem necessaria et tunc per pedites, hinc nullatenus moventur" (Thietmar, VI, 23 ad fin.).

[2] The chronicles have preserved a number of examples of cross-marriages between the aristocracy of both races. About the year 1000 a certain Wendish nobleman named Pribislav eloped with Matilda, the sister of Dietrich of the Nordmark, who was a nun in a convent in Magdeburg. Pribislav was assassinated by two Saxons who were hired by the angry Margrave; whereupon his brother, who had forsaken paganism and become a priest under the German name Liudolf, abandoned his cowl and set forth to avenge his brother's murder, but was apprehended and returned to the church by Henry II. (See the account in Thietmar, IV, 64.) Matilda afterward fell into the hands of a Slav adventurer named Boliliut, an ex-companion of a Saxon outlaw named Kiza, who took her to wife. Helmold, I, 13, cites the case of an Abodrite chieftain named Billug who married the sister of Wago, bishop of Oldenburg. The border was the home of the German outlaw, who fraternized with the Wends (Helmold, I, 19). The most notorious instance of this is the case of the two nephews of Hermann Billung, Wicmann and Ecbert, who quarreled with their uncle and fled to the protection of two Abodrite chieftains, Nako and Stoinef (Widukind, III, 50–51; Annals of Quedlinburg; Annals of Hildesheim (955); Thietmar, II, 6, 12–13). In this connection the observation of the Polish historian Dlugoss as to the same process in Poland is interesting ". . . . Prefecti castrorum et munitionum civitatum cis Albim sitarum ab obedientia deditioneque Miecslai regis regnique sui Poloniae deficere ceperunt ignavia desidiaque regis et Almanorum affinitate, qua invicem dando accipiendoque uxores junxerant eis defectionis materiam" (Hist. Polon. [ed. Lips, 1711], I, Book II, 184).

The missionary zeal of the medieval German church was hardened with an alloy of worldly self-interest which gave a harsh edge to its pious professions, and the cure of souls was prevailingly subordinated to its hunger for land and its appetite for rich endowments. As early as 591 the synod of Aquileia, representing the Bavarian church, had complained of the tyranny of the Frankish church.[1] Through the efforts of Boniface, the organizer of four Bavarian bishoprics, the Bavarian law of the eighth century "encouraged" donations to the church to the point of compulsion, and punished the murder of a bishop with an impossibly huge fine, or slavery. In the same century, in Ober-Franken, again through Boniface's zeal, and that of Sturm his disciple, the see of Würzburg (741) and the monasteries of Fulda (744) and Hersfeld (769) were founded and heavily endowed with manors and tithes.[2]

The avarice of the medieval church had early been manifested. A synodical letter of the second Council of Tours (566 or 567) exhorted all faithful to imitate the example of Abraham and to pay tithes. But this exhortation failed to produce the desired effect, and in 585 the Council of Macon, after having enjoined all to offer a tithe of their substance at the altar every Sunday, "in order to effectuate the removal of their sins and to have a lot in the merits of Abel" (canon 4), ordained the payment of altar tithes under penalty of excommunication (canon 5). This Council audaciously declared that the tithe was of apostolic foundation and professed the desire to "restore." Yet the formulas of Marculf (*ca.* 650) contain no allusion to the tithe.

Toward the end of the seventh century, however, the practice of the church of exacting a tithe of the price of land transfers seems to have become general. By menace of excommunication, by intimidation, by preying upon the minds of the ignorant and superstitious through attributing natural calamities like droughts and floods to failure to pay tithes, the clergy worked upon the people. In 742 Pepin con-

---

[1] Riezler, *Geschichte Bayerns*, I, 90.

[2] For Würzburg see Kretschmer, sec. 176; for Fulda and Hersfeld, sec. 103. Tangl has studied the privilege of Fulda in *Mitth. d. Inst. f. oesterr. Gesch.*, Band XX, Heft 2 (1899).

ferred the right to collect tithes upon Fulda. Under Charlemagne in 779 a capitulary converted into positive law, civil and perpetual, what had hitherto been only pious not ecclesiastical obligation, and made permanent what had been merely occasional and voluntary practice. In 794 another capitulary imposed excommunication on those who refused to pay tithes.[1] In 813 the Council of Arles extended the tithe from agricultural produce to industry and commerce. In 909 the synod of Trosly in France imposed the tithe upon servile as well as free craftsmen. In the twelfth century we find the same thing in Germany—a tithe upon agriculture, trade, and industry.

The missionary propaganda of the German church in the Middle Ages was largely a money-making proposition.[2] Christians had to pay tithes, so the "saving of souls" became a lucrative commercial interest. The border peoples, if conquered but unconverted, were subject only to tribute, and the wealth thus acquired went into secular coffers. But evangelization offered spiritual rewards and declared substantial dividends of a material nature for the benefit of the church.[3] Alcuin, in the time of Charlemagne, rebuked Bishop Arno of Salzburg for inhuman treatment of the Slavs in Styria and Carinthia, upon whom he cruelly imposed the tithe.[4]

[1] *Cap. Wormat.* (794): "Qui decimas, post creberrimas admonitiones et praedicationes sacerdotum, dare neglexerint, excommunicentur."

[2] Adam of Bremen, II, 5; III, 22.

[3] Lavisse, *La Marche de Brandenbourg*, p. 37, caustically remarks: "Charlemagne, en assignant aux sièges épiscopaux qui auraient envoyé des missionaries en pays païen une part des revenus payés par les convertis, avait excité l'avidité en même temps que l'émulation des évêques, et les conflits qui éclataient entre les divers diocèses n'étaient point faits pour persuader aux païens que les prêtres de Jésus-Christ ne voulaient que le salut de leurs âmes."

[4] *Monum. Alcuin.* (ed. Jaffé), VI, 301, Ep. 64. So, too, in 796 Alcuin, after the conquest of the Avars, asked Charlemagne to "consider whether it is a good thing to impose on a rude people like this at the beginning of their faith the yoke of tithes, exacted in full amount and from every house." Alcuin even had the moral courage and the critical acumen to challenge the whole system of imposing tithes. For he goes on: "It is to be considered whether the apostles, who were taught by Christ himself and sent forth by him for the evangelization of the world, ever ordered the exaction of tithes, or demanded that they should be given to them" (Ep. 67). For other letters of Alcuin protesting against exploitation of *rudes populi* see *MGH. Epistolae*, IV, 154, No. 107 (796); No. 110, pp. 157–59 (796); No. 111, pp. 159–62

The sordid motives of the German church, in spite of its smooth language and professions of piety, come out strongly in the correspondence between Boniface and Pope Zacharias in 751. Boniface had propounded the question to the Pope whether the tithe should be imposed upon Slav serfs working the church lands. The reply of the pontiff is luminous for the light which it casts upon the inner motives of the church. "Yes," said Zacharias, "for if they do not pay tribute they will think the land is theirs. But if they are made to pay tithes they will know who is lord of the land."[1]

The German clergy for generations connived with Jewish merchants to promote a traffic in Slavonic slaves with the Mohammedan realms of Spain and Egypt. I subjoin two quotations:

> Those who especially enjoyed his [the caliph's] confidence were the body known as "Slavs"; it is from Abd-er-Rahman's reign that their influence dates . . . . .
>
> Originally the name of "Slavs" [Arabic, *Saqâliba*] was applied to prisoners captured by the Germanic nations in their wars against Slavonic tribes, and sold by them to the Saracens of Spain; but in course of time a multitude of men belonging to other races began to be classed as "Slavs," and the name was applied to all foreigners who served in the harem, or in the army, whatever their origin. The Cordovan chroniclers call Otto I "king of the Slavs." An Arab traveller of the tenth century explicitly states that the Slavs who were the retainers of the khalif of Spain comprised Galicians, Franks [French and German], Lombards, Calabrians and natives of the northern coasts of the Black Sea. Some of them had been captured by Andalusian pirates; others had been purchased in Italian ports —for the Jews, trading upon the distress of the people, trafficked in children of both sexes and brought them to the sea-ports whence they were

---

(796); No. 113, p. 164 (796). Cf. Hodgkin, *Italy and Her Invaders*, VIII, 149; Justus Moeser, *Osnabr. Gesch.*, I, 189; Lamprecht, *DWL*, I, 2, 872.

[1] *Epp. Bonifacii* (ed. Jaffé), III, 226, No. 80: *Boniface:* "An census a Slavis Christianorum terras incolentibus recipiendus?" *Zacharias:* ". . . . si enim tributo sederint, ipsam quandoque propriam sibi vindicabunt; si vero tributum dederint, norunt dominatorem ipsam habere terram." See also Schafarik, II, 607. Cf. a similar response in *Monum. Boica*, XXVIII, 1, 268 (996), and see Giesebrecht, *Jahrbücher des deutschen Reiches unter Otto II und Otto III*, p. 29, n. 1. It is no wonder that apologists for Boniface, like Fischer (*Bonifatius*, pp. 204 ff.), endeavor to disprove the genuineness of the letters. Sommerlad, *Die wirtschaftliche Tätigkeit der Kirche in Deutschland*, Vol. I, chap. iv, and Stutz, *Gesch. des kirchlichen Benefizialwesens* (1895), are valuable accounts of the land policy of the church in Germany in the seventh and eighth centuries.

carried in Greek or Venetian vessels to their Saracen purchasers. Another class, namely the eunuchs, destined to be attendants in the harems, were imported from France, where large establishments for the supply of these creatures existed, under the direction of Jews: that of Verdun was far-famed [Liutprand, *Antapodosis*, VI, 6; Richer, IV, 103], and there were others in the south [Reinaud, *Invasions des Sarrasins en France*, pp. 233 f.].[1]

With the fourth caliph El-Mo'izz, the conqueror of Egypt [953–75], the Fatimids entered upon a new phase. . . . . He was highly educated and not only wrote Arabic poetry and delighted in its literature, but studied Greek, mastered Berber and Sudani dialects, and is even said to have taught himself Slavonic in order to converse with his slaves from eastern Europe.[2]

The Saxon clergy, perhaps more hungry for landed possessions than even the lay feudality, was not to be deterred from the lucrative business of evangelizing the Wends across the lower Elbe River, whose "conversion" would pour tithes into their coffers and whose toil could be made to exploit the church's lands. It is charitable to indulge the thought that the missionary tradition of Anskar and the monastery of Corvey inspired the aspirations of the German church at this time. But the facts belie this rosy assumption. Charlemagne's conversion of the Saxons by force of arms had established a precedent fatal to the preservation of the liberties of the Baltic Slavs. The issue of the conversion of the Wends had first been raised by Boniface, and the prospect had haunted the mind of the cultured and gentle Alcuin. Since then a century and a half had elapsed and nothing had been done. It was high time, argued the church. For it was unthinkable that the theory of the royal prerogative could tolerate rule over a pagan people.[3]

[1] Dozy, *Spanish Islam*, p. 430.

[2] Lane Poole, *Egypt in the Middle Ages*, pp. 99–101.

[3] This idea comes out clearly in the coronation of Otto I. "Accipe hunc gladium," said the Archbishop of Mainz, "quo eicias omnes Christi adversarios, barbaros et malos Christianos, auctoritate divina tibi tradita omni potestate totius imperii Francorum, ad firmissimam pacem omnium Christianorum" (Widukind, II, 1). For comment see Waitz, VI, 163 ff. The same thought is expressed by Frederick I in the *Canonizatio Caroli Magni* in 1166: "In fide quoque Christi dilatanda, et in conversione gentis barbaricae fortis athleta fuit, sicut Saxonia et Fresonia Hispanis quoque testantur et Wandali, quos ad fidem catholicam verbo convertit gladio" (Harz., *Conc.*, III, 399–400). Adam of Bremen, II, 5, thinks the Slavs of the Elbe were ingrates and should have been grateful for the blessings of Christianity and

In the case of Otto I, his religion was politic and his piety "practical" in the most concrete sense of that term. He was indifferent to the conversion of the Wends, but he could not be indifferent to the demands of the bishops. Accordingly, his reign saw a terrible series of military expeditions and missionary forays across the lower Elbe against the Baltic Slavs, by which the land was conquered as far as the Peene River.[1] Precisely as Charlemagne had utilized the administrative system of the church to extirpate the Saxon tribal organization in Saxony,[2] so the apparatus of the German church was now imposed upon the subjugated Wends in order to crush them.[3] "Ex nomine victorum provincias quoque vocabula sortitas." Beyond the Elbe, a swarm of bishoprics arose— half houses of God, half fortresses. Oldenburg was the earliest episcopal erection at an unknown date.[4] It was an ancient Wendish town, so old that it was called Old Town (Starigard).[5] Havelberg was founded in 946, Brandenburg in 948,[6] Merseburg in 967,[7] Meissen and Zeitz (later removed to

---

tribute which the German conquest imposed upon them: "Otto Sclavos tanta virtute constrinxit ut tributum et Christianitatem pro vita simul et patria libenter offerrent victori."

[1] Sommerfeld, *Gesch. der Germanisierung des Herzogtums Pommern*, p. 10.

[2] "Capitulatio de partibus Saxoniae" (Boretius, *MGH, Leges*, I, 2, No. 26, p. 68); cf. the spurious charter for Bremen in Sickel, *Acta Karol.*, II, 393–94, and the interesting statement of Adam of Bremen, I, 13: "Huic parrochiae decem pagos subjecimus, quos etiam abjectis eorum antiquis vocabulis et divisionibus in duas redigimus provincias, his nominibus appellantes, Wigmodiam et Lorgoe."

[3] Cf. Widukind, II, 38; Adam of Bremen, II, 24; Thietmar, II, 20, 22; Helmold, I, 14, 17.

[4] Hauck, III, 105, n. 5; Dehio, *Gesch. des Erzbistums Hamburg-Bremen*, Append. XII; Curschmann, *Diözese Brandenburg*, p. 19, n. 3, think the year was 948. For further information see Kretschmar, *Historische Geographie von Mitteleuropa*, sec. 258.

[5] "Ea quae Slavica lingua Starigard, hoc est antiqua civitas," says Helmoldus the Holsteiner antiquarian of the twelfth century (I, 12). The Germans simply transliterated the name. The derivation is obvious. *Stara* means "old" and *gard* is the same as *grad*, a universal Slav suffix for "town." The Serbian today distinguishes a part of his kingdom by the term *Stara Srbiya*—"Old Serbia." On the foundation of Oldenburg see Curschmann, *Hist. Vierteljahrschrift* (1911), No. 1.

[6] Kretschmer, secs. 270–71.

[7] *Ibid.*, sec. 267.

Naumburg) in 968.[1] The Archbishop of Magdeburg was ecclesiastical ruler, "tocius ultra Albiam et Salam." Manors,
tithes, tribute, were showered upon the new bishoprics in the
Slav lands by the Ottos,[2] and the "New Plantation" for a
season enjoyed great peace and prosperity.[3] "Through the
mercy of God and the valor of Otto the Great," Helmold
piously exclaims, "complete peace prevailed everywhere; the
wastes of Wagria and of the province of Schleswig began to
be peopled, nor was there any corner left which was not conspicuous for its towns and villages, and also its many monasteries."[4]

Forcible, wholesale conversion of the Abodrites, the
Wilzi, etc., and the imposition of tithes and tribute became
the order of the day.[5] The synod of Tribur in 1036 resolved
"quod omnes Sclavi decimas dent."[6] The synod of Bamberg
in 1059 expressly declared that increase of the tithes was a
just motive for forcible conversion of the Slavs.[7] These tithes

---

[1] *Ibid.*, secs. 268-69.

[2] "Munificentia principis Ottonis cumulati essent temporalium rerum affluentia,
unde possent copiose largiri et favorem sibi populi consciscere" (Helmold, I, 12).

[3] "Novella Plantacio [Helmold, I, 12, 14] . . . . in summa prosperitate" (*ibid.*,
13).

[4] Helmold, I, 12.

[5] "Ipse [Otto I] tanta virtute deinceps constrinxit, ut tributum et christianitatem pro vita simul et patria libenter offerrent victori, baptizatusque est totus
gentilium populus" (Adam of Bremen, II, 5). "Pax continua fuit, Sclavi sub tributo
servierunt" (*ibid.*, 24). "Tribut und Christentum, so heisst es in charakteristischer
Verbindung, mussten sie bieten, damit man sie bei Land und Leben lasse" (Guttmann, *op. cit.*, p. 433).

[6] "Constitutiones et acta pub. imperatorum et regum" (*MGH, Leges*, IV, 89,
sec. 6; cf. Bresslau, *Jahrbücher Konrads* II, 529.

[7] Jaffé, V, 497-98. "Decimam tributi quae de partibus orientalium Franchorum,
vel de Sclavis ad fiscum dominicum annuatim persolvere solebant quae secundum
illorum linguam steora vel ostarstuopha vocant" (Zeuss, *op. cit.*, p. 648). The
bishopric of Bamberg was founded by Henry II in 1007, who detached eastern
Franconia ecclesiastically from the see of Würzburg, the latter being indemnified
by the gift of 153 manors (Migne, CXL, 115). It was richly endowed by the Emperor
with the possessions of the banished Babenbergers, whose lands had passed by confiscation to the fisc in the reign of Ludwig the Child (900-911). Otto II gave them to
Henry II of Bavaria, through whose accession to the German kingship in 1002 they
again became a part of the crown lands. Bamberg was Henry II's favorite place of
residence and the cathedral which he built and in which he lies buried is one of the
finest examples of early Romanesque architecture in Germany. The see was ex-

were generally collected in corn, honey, flax, hemp, and cattle,[1] data which show the primitive economy of the Slavonic peoples at this time. Helmold[2] describes with particularity the nature of the tithe and the method of collection in the bishopric of Oldenburg: "Dabatur autem pontifici annuum de omni Wagirorum sive Obotritorum terra tributum, quod scilicet pro decima imputabatur, de quolibet aratro mensura grani et XL resticuli lini et XII nummi puri argenti. Ad hoc unus nummus, precium colligentis. Slavicum vero aratrum par boum aut unus conficit equus."[3]

Aside from tithes and tribute, the Wends were not long in discovering that the saints' days and church festivals were a hardship also. What with their primitive agricultural economy and the enormous tracts of waste and water, their margin of living was a narrow one at best, and they could ill spare relaxing their labors in the fields on these occasions in compliance with the church's prohibition of secular pursuits on holy days. Herbordus, III, 22, relates how one of Otto of Bamberg's companions came in conflict with this resentment:

---

pressly founded as a missionary base among the Slavs of the upper Main region. "Ut et paganismus Sclavorum destrueretur et Christiani nominis memoria perpetualiter inibi celebris habetur. . . . . Per quam [ecclesiam] et de inimico humani generis in vicinas Sclavorum gentes Deo opitulante, triumphabit" (Jaffé, V, 27 and 31; Migne, *loc. cit.*, 118). For the founding of the see, see Gebhardt, *Handbuch d. deutschen Gesch.*, I, 277, sec. 4; Stein, *Gesch. Frankens*, p. 85; Loshorn, *Die Begründung des Bistums Bamberg*; *Jahrbücher Heinrichs II*, II, 28; Bernhardi, *Lothar von Supplinburg*, pp. 152 f. For Slav serfs on church lands see Waitz, *Deutsche Verfassungsgesch.*, V, 157, n. 3; *Jahrbücher Heinrichs II*, II, 28-31.

[1] A tithe in honey in Brandenburg is mentioned in 965: "totam decimam mellis in pagis . . . . Plonim, Nicici, Sprewa ex utraque parte Sprewae" (*MGH, Dip. I*, p. 418. So in the reign of Otto II, in 973 a honey tithe is recorded in the same place: "in Ploni . . . . et in toto Morkeni totoque Drenzile et Heveldo" (*ibid.*, II, 40). A tithe in honey or linen from the Slavs of the Main was granted by Arnulf in 889 to the Bishop of Würzburg (Boehmer, *Regesta Imperii* [751–918], p. 745; Dümmler, *Gesch. des ostfränkischen Reiches*, III, 356). On this whole subject see Nitzsch, I, 342–44.

[2] *Chron. Slav.*, I, 12.

[3] Cf. I, 14, 88. He uses the words *resticuli lini* in I, 12, and *restes lini* in I, 14. The terms are interchangeable, the latter (sing. *restis*) being more usual in medieval Latin. It is used in the sense of a bundle of sticks, of a last of fish, of a roll or bale of cloth, of a measure of grain, etc. Cf. Du Cange, *Glossarium, s.v.* The use of linen as money was common among the Slavs like the wampum of the Indians.

It happened after this on the feast of St. Lawrence that a certain priest named Bockens, as he was passing by saw some peasants reaping in their fields. He endeavored discreetly to restrain them and said: "Unhappy men, what are you doing? This is the day of the blessed martyr St. Lawrence which is observed with the utmost respect by the whole church, while you presume to profane it." They answered: "We cannot always be keeping your sabbaths. It is just that we should sometimes provide what is necessary for our households." .... In a town called Games a certain peasant and his wife had gone out to reap during the festival of Mary the mother of God and perpetual virgin. When he perceived this Bockens, moved by righteous zeal, expressed his disapproval and said: "It is altogether wrong for you to labor on this great festival day of the Blessed Virgin." (It was now the second day of festival.) They replied: "Yesterday we observed Sunday as a holy day. To-day we must needs work."

It is unnecessary to add that compulsion followed upon these admonitions.

What the actual extent of the landed possessions of these bishoprics beyond the Elbe was, or what the amount of their revenues, it is impossible to say. For they were all swept away, as will be seen shortly, in the great Wendish rising of 983. Helmold confesses his inability to tell, save in general terms, the material possessions of the church in the "New Plantation." But judging from his comment, and from what we know to have been the condition in other Wendish territory—for example, in the Sorben land and in upper Franconia, where the bishopric of Bamberg was—regions which the storm of the Slav reaction did not reach, the revenues of the trans-Elbean bishoprics must have been considerable.[1] The church was a hard taskmaster and exacted heavy service from the Wendish peasantry reduced to serfdom or even slavery upon their own once free lands.[2] The cynical aphorism of Ekkehard of St. Gall, "servi qui non timent, tument,"[3] epito-

---

[1] Helmold, I, 18.

[2] Thietmar several times alludes to this unfree Wendish peasantry: II, 24; V, 6; VI, 37; VII, 15; cf. Jaffé, V, 652, 809; Waitz, V, 157, n. 3, and esp. Schulze, *Kolonisierung*, pp. 98–116, and Koeniger, *Burchard von Worms*, pp. 208–13.

[3] *MGH*. SS. II, 403. Evidently Ekkehard has here formulated in Latin the old German legal maxim later current: "Knechte schlagen wenn sie nicht zagen." The same kind of proverb occurs in France: "Oignez vilain, il vous poindra; poignez vilain il vous oindra" (Loysel, *Inst. cout.*, Liv. I, tit. 1, reg. 31). In 1009 Henry II gave a whole batch of captive Ljutizi as slaves to the Bishop of Metz (Thietmar, VI, 51 [35]). For employment of Slav slaves in the bishopric of Worms see Koeniger, *op.*

mizes the policy of the hard and worldly feudalized clergy of medieval Germany.

As early as the first Saxon kings there are evidences of peasant unrest on church lands.[1] In the reign of Otto III their discontent had become so great that the crown legislated in suppression of any manifestation of it. The document recites that all classes of the feudality frequently complain that the serfs resist the services exacted of them, advancing various kinds of false pretexts for so doing. In the case of serfs of lay nobles certain methods of proof of status and possibility of relief are provided for. But the law is absolute in declaring that "an unfree man belonging to the church may never become free. We strictly forbid the unfree of the churches to be set free, and we order all those who have by any device been freed to be reduced to servitude again."[2] The church,[3] as the greatest landed proprietor in Germany, had little sentiment and few compunctions of conscience in regard to exploitation of its dependents. Serfdom paid, therefore it was justified.[4] The Council of Pavia in the reign of Henry II decreed that the children of serf priests were slaves of the church, incapable of manumission or of owning private property.[5]

Perhaps one must go to Spanish America in the sixteenth century for an adequate parallel to this history of the spolia-

---

cit., p. 49. Burchard of Worms, the canonist, justified slavery in his treatise on canon law. As late as the thirteenth century pagan (Slav?) slaves were still sold in Germany (Caes. Heisterb., X, 44; Lamprecht, *DWL*, I, 2, n. 4 (1195). Contrary to prevalent opinion and Roman Catholic writers, the medieval church, far from opposing slavery or ameliorating serfdom, indorsed both one and the other, and promoted both practices. See Lamprecht, *op. cit.*, I, 1, 462 and notes. Many other authorities might be cited.

[1] Lamprecht, *DG*, III, 63–64, 67.

[2] This important document is in Altmann-Bernheim, *Ausgewählte Urkunden*, No. 61.

[3] For the official attitude of the Saxon church see Burchard of Worms, *Decretum, lex familiae*, secs. 2 and 11. Cf. Schroeder, *Rechtsgesch.* (4th ed., 1902), pp. 457–61; Nitzsch, *DG*, I, 360.

[4] Lamprecht, *DWL*, I, 1, 462 cites Regino, *Caus. synod.*, 1, 366, chap. li (cf. *Concil. Agath.* [*anno* 506]): "Mancipia monachis donata ab abbate non licet manumitti; injustum est enim, ut monachis quotidianum rurale opus facientibus, servi eorum libertatis otio potiantur." Cf. *Vita Oudalr.*, chap. ix (SS. IV, 96, l. 22).

[5] Labbé, *Concilia*, IX, 829–30; Hirsch, *Jhb. Hein. II*, III, 221.

tion of a weaker people by an avaricious priest class backed
up by the sword of a powerful government.[1] The pious observations of Bernal Diaz on the benefits conferred upon the
Peru of the Incas by Spanish civilization and Christianity
have their prototype in the adamantine sanctimoniousness of
Thietmar of Merseburg when he reflects upon the "mercies"
which the German church had brought to the Sorben.[2]

In its greed for land the church was even divided against
itself. This comes out clearly in the case of the diocese of
Merseburg. The see was founded in 967 or 968.[3] From 971 to
981 Gisiler was the bishop thereof.[4] But when in 981 he was
elevated to the archbishopric of Magdeburg, he maneuvered
so as to secure the abolition of the see of Merseburg under
the pretext that Halberstadt had never given its written consent to Merseburg's erection ("sine consensu atque subscrip-
tione canonica"). The bishops of Zeitz and Meissen sustained
him in this course, the motive of which was plain. The three
coveted the lands of Merseburg and plotted the spoliation
of the diocese to the aggrandizement of their own sees. The
upshot of the scheme was that the diocese of Merseburg was
abolished and its lands partitioned among the three avaricious bishops. It was not restored until 1004, when Henry II,
whose bold policy in the face of the bishops will soon be
noticed, revived Merseburg again.[5]

The church in the Wendish lands was inspired by no
genuine religious zeal. Like the bishoprics and monasteries in

---

[1] For development of this parallel see Bourne, *Spain in America*, pp. 195–201, 259–65.

[2] Thietmar, IX, 3: ". . . . Consuetudines . . . . quamvis dirae, tamen inter-
dum laudabiles." See the whole chapter as an example of clerical moralizing and
cf. the legislation of the synod of Tribur in the year 1036 (*MGH. Const. I*, 89, No.
6). Helmold, I, 84, points to the German substitution of trial by battle or by hot
plowshares for the methods of Slavonic administration of justice as an evidence of
"progress." "Sed offerebant criminibus pulsatos sacerdoti ferro vel vomeribus
examinandos."

[3] Kretschmer, sec. 267.

[4] Thietmar, I, 37. For his colonizing on the left bank of the Saale see Hauck,
III, 431.

[5] For this scandalous affair see Thietmar, III, 16; Gebhardt, I, 273; and
Kretschmer, sec. 267, with literature cited.

England along the Scotch and Welsh Marches, the churches were strategically located to guard the frontier and to hold down the conquered country.[1] Its motives were wholly material. The bishops' seats were simply offices of exploitation. Manorial bailiffs and stewards in the service of the bishops were numerous, but there was no thought of priestly ministration.[2] The only actual churches in the land were in the cathedral places, where the bishop's authority was established and where the center of the system was. Elsewhere there were merely a few scattered chapels, with a single priest, and these were not for the conversion of the Slavs, but to minister to the isolated German communities, chiefly composed of soldiers and wandering merchants. Most of the bishops were intriguing Lorrainers and Flemings like Adalbert of Magdeburg.[3] Of all the German bishops who sat in these Wendish sees in the tenth and the early eleventh centuries, there is only one in whom any real spirituality is discernible—Boso of Merseburg, its first incumbent; and even in this case the evidence is somewhat dubious, for it rests on the flattering unction of an official document.[4] However, Thietmar has preserved for us an anecdote which is so ingenuous that it has an authentic ring, and shows that this Bavarian monk had some of the milk of human kindness in him. Thietmar records how Boso composed a little manual in the Slav tongue for the instruction of his flock, and that he taught them to chant the *Kyrie eleison*, at the same time "exponens eis hujus utilitatem." But to his bewilderment these barbarian children of the forest mistook the words *Kyrie eleison*, which they naturally did not understand the meaning of, for their own Slav word for "elderbush" (*kriolosse*), and so sang.[5]

[1] For a remarkable description of the distribution of ecclesiastical foundations in England for this purpose see Bémont, *Revue hist.*, LXX, 383–84.

[2] "Aber von Pfarren ist nicht die Rede" (Guttmann, *op. cit.*, p. 435). See the comments of Nitzsch, II, 16–17.

[3] Hauck, III, 95–97; Krabbe, *Die ostdeutschen Bistümer* (Berlin, 1906).

[4] "Multum jam in eadem Sclavorum gente convertenda sudavit" (Urk. Otto I, *MGH, Dip. I*, p. 502.

[5] Thietmar, II, 36–37; Koeniger, *op. cit.*, p. 182 n. 1.

A certain familiarity with the Slavonic tongue must have been not unusual among some classes of the Germans, as military officers, merchants trading across the frontier, and at least some of the priesthood.[1] Otto I spoke Slavonic,[2] and Thietmar, for all his Saxon scorn of the race, must have understood the language. The internal evidence of his *Chronicon* proves it.[3] A few of the Wendish chieftains embraced the Christian religion for self-advantage.[4] But the mass of the Slavs must have accepted Christianity as they accepted German domination, superficially and morosely.[5] To most of them for generations the founder of Christianity was the "Teutonicus Deus,"[6] who, they must surely have thought, had come to bring not peace but a sword. Even as late as the twelfth century the Christianity of the Sorben was very superficial and chiefly inspired by dread of the German power.[7] And yet the armies of Otto I in his Italian

[1] Hauck, III, 136, and n. 1. Some common German words are of Slav origin, as *Dolmetsch*, "interpreter"; *Grenze*, "border"; *Kummet*, "horse collar"; *Peitsche*, "whip lash"; *Petschaft*, "signet ring"; *Schöps*, "wether, mutton." For the modern Sorbisch speech see Tetzner, p. 291. H. Witte, *Wendische Bevölkerungsreste in Mecklenburg* (Stuttgart, 1905), has tried to prove that German colonization did not exterminate, but Germanized, the Slav.

[2] Widukind, II, 36.

[3] Cosmas, I, 23, speaks of "Dethmarus Saxo olim, orationis causa Pragam profectus"; and of "Theadagus Saxo, lingua perfecte imbutus Sclavonica."

[4] A Sorben knight named Zolunta was a member of Otto II's bodyguard in his ill-fated Calabrian expedition in 982 (Thietmar, III, 23; cf. Giesebrecht, *Kaiserzeit*, II, 168), and there is mention of some others like him (*Ann. Altah. mag.* [1041]; Helmold, I, 16 [Schol. 30]; *Gesta episcop. Camerac. Contin.* [*MGH*, SS. VII, p. 518]). Liutprand, *Legatio*, chap. xxiii, alludes to Wendish hostlers and stablemen.

[5] Adam of Bremen, III, 1, distinguishes the Slavs in the archiepiscopal diocese of Bremen-Hamburg into *pagani* and *pseudo-Christiani*. Cf. the comment of Wipo: "Liutici vocantur, qui olim semichristiani, nunc per apostacam nequitiam omnino sunt pagani" (*Vita Chuonradi*, chap. xxxiii).

[6] Ebo, *Vita S. Ottonis episcop. Babenb.*, III, 1.

[7] *Vita S. Winthar.* (1062–63), ep. Merseb. (*MGH*, SS. XII, 246): "Sclavorum genti, quorum copiosam multitudinem error adhuc ydolatriae detinebat"; *Mirac. Heinr.* (*MGH*, SS. IV, 816): "vix vel tenuem fidei videntur habere scintillam." The *Miracula* were written at the end of the twelfth century (Wattenbach, *DGQ*, II, 384; cf. Hauck, III, 135, n. 6). A letter written by a clerk of Liège to Udo of Naumburg (d. 1148) is to the same effect: "Ultra non christianam Salam inter agrestem et barbaram Sclavorum nationem" (cited by Hauck, III, 135, n. 7). Thietmar of Merseburg (I, 3) says that the Wends venerated their own temples more than the Christian churches: "Hunc [Glomuzi fons] omnis incola plus quam aec-

campaigns seem to have had among them considerable numbers of Slavs in the capacity of campfollowers, hostlers, etc.[1]

The blame for the inhuman treatment of the Wendish
peoples along the German border must be divided between
the Saxon clergy and the Saxon nobles, especially the ruling
house of the Billunger. The feud between the church and the
nobles was a bitter one and lasted for years.[2] The nobles resented the fondness of the Ottos for churchmen. Above all,
they resented the policy of converting the Slavs, for the
church's tithes reduced the tribute proportionally. They
were content to leave the Wends their own religion, their own
leaders, their own laws, provided the Wends regularly paid
tribute to them.[3] Saxon avarice, both of the nobles and of the
clergy, is alleged time and again by Adam of Bremen and
Helmold as the cause of German overthrow beyond the Elbe
and the arrest of the eastward expansion of German colonization for one hundred and fifty years.[4] Adam of Bremen
writes:

I have heard that the honest king of the Danes said that the Slav
peoples would long since have been converted to Christianity if it had not
been for the avarice of the Saxons.[5]

and Helmold mournfully records:

---

clesias spe quamvis dubia, veneratur et timet." The whole paragraph is interesting
for the light it throws upon the Slavonic religion. The bulk of the population around
the confluence of the Ohre and the Elbe so late as 1161 was still Slav. For Slav
paganism around Ratzeburg (1177) see Hauck, IV, 589, n. 2. ". . . . quarum in-
colae adhuc Sclavi erant" (from a deed cited by Zeuss, *op. cit.*, p. 660). See Hauck,
pp. 555–63, for the general growth of the church in the Sorben March in the twelfth
century.

[1] Otto rex veniente Italico regno, tanta bene multitudo gentis in Italia, que sic
impleverunt faciem terre, sicut situle. Habebat autem secum gentes nationes quorum lingue non agnoscebant gentis. Insuper haec habebat gens que Guinula voca-
bantur sarcinas et carros et machina portantes. Erat enim aspectus eorum orribilis
et curbis properantes, carpentes iter et ad prelium ut ferro stantes. *Benedicti S.
Andreae monachi Chronicon* (SS. III, 717); cf. Adam of Bremen, II, 42, Schol. 27(30).

[2] Cf. Giesebrecht, *Otto II*, pp. 91 ff.; *Kaiserzeit*, I, 604 ff., 850; L. Giesebrecht,
Wendische Geschichten, I, 264 ff.; Hirsch, *Jahrbücher Heinrich II*, III, 183–87;
Guttmann, *op. cit.*, p. 420.

[3] Sommerfeld, *op. cit.*, p. 6.

[4] See Hauck, III, 250–51; Hirsch, *Jahrb. Heinrich II*, III, 93 ff.; cf. Adam of
Bremen, II, 46; III, 22; Helmold, I, 14, 16, 18, 19, 21, 25, 26.

[5] Adam of Bremen, III, 22.

The princes divided the tribute among themselves. But no mention was made of Christianity. From which the insatiable avarice of the Saxons may be appreciated. They excel all other peoples in arms and the art of war; but they care more for tribute than they do for the winning of souls.[1]

As early as 983 the Abodrite prince, Mistivoi, whom the Saxons had greatly offended, aligned himself with the priests of Rethra and thus brought about a general rising of the Slavs of the Elbe against the Christians.

Under Henry II (1002-24) the German border policy initiated a new and striking course. At this time Boleslav of Poland was formidable to Germany, for he aimed to unite the whole group of separate and detached Slavonic tribes into one body, and narrowly missed so doing. The danger was a real one to Germany, for Boleslav had friends at the German court, among them Henry, margrave of the Bavarian Nordgau, Ernest of Austria, and the king's own brother Brun.[2] In this peril Henry II, adroitly taking advantage of the hostility of the Ljutizi and Redarii to the Polish policy of forcible union, promised them the unmolested enjoyment of their pagan religion in return for their support of the German cause against Boleslav.[3] Henry II was not the supine instrument of the church that tradition has represented him to have been, but a resolute, farsighted ruler without illusions.[4] His statesmanship foiled the probable unification of the western Slavs and diverted Polish ambition eastward toward Russia, while at the same time allowing liberty to the slow process of Germanization of the border peoples to work out the solution through natural contact instead of by compulsory means.[5]

[1] Helmold, I, 21; cf. Sommerlad, *Die wirtschaftliche Tätigkeit der Kirche in Deutschland*, II, 209.

[2] Thietmar, V, 32, 35, 36, 38.

[3] Thietmar, V, 21; VI, 23-25, 28 (*Anno* 1003); Pueschl, *Das Anwachsen der Deutschen*.

[4] See on this Hirsch, *Jahrbücher Heinrich II*, I, 257 ff.; III, 364 ff. (by Bresslau); Matthai, *Die Klosterpolitik Kaiser Heinrichs II* (Göttingen, 1877); Nitzsch, *Deutsche Gesch.*, I, 367; Guttmann, *op. cit.*, p. 419.

[5] For a eulogy of Henry II's border policy see Thietmar, V, 21. He was at Merseburg in November, 1014, and liberated Miesko, son of Boleslav of Poland, there (Thietmar, VII, 5-8), who showed his gratitude by burning Meissen in the next year. Thietmar, VII, 25, gives a vivid account of the heroic resistance.

The wisdom of Henry II's course was soon manifested. The bishops of Havelberg and Brandenburg returned to their devastated sees, and they and other former German towns, like Arneburg, were rebuilt. But unfortunately, some of the German bishops learned nothing and forgot nothing. Benno, bishop of Oldenburg, instituted an inquisition into the former possessions of the diocese which so exasperated the Abodrites that they declared that rather than submit again to the heavy exactions of the church they would quit the country.[1] A second Slav rebellion came in 1018, in which Mistislav, the Abodrite chieftain, and his half-Christianized adherents—for there were some Christian Slavs among them —severely suffered, and the trans-Elbean bishops were again driven out.[2]

This second Slav revolt completed what that of 983 had left unfinished. The first blow had fallen upon Brandenburg and the Havelland,[3] but Nordalbingia had escaped. Now it too was devastated with fire and sword. The priests were slaughtered, the inhabitants dragged off to glut the slave marts along the Baltic Coast, especially in the island of Rügen. Bishop Benno, the man primarily responsible for the insurrection, was absent from his post when this second wave of Slav fury swept the land. But sixty priests were captured and with hands tied behind their backs were whipped through

[1] See the detailed account in Helmold, I, 18.

[2] Thietmar, III, 17 [10]; VIII, 5 [4], distinguishes between the reaction of 983 and 1018. The first was against the German Herrschaft, the second against the Fürsten and the church. He names the Wend leaders as Mistui and Mistivoi. The names mean two separate persons, and not the same man as Adam of Bremen, II, 40–41, and Helmold, I, 16, who follows Adam, say. Cf. Hirsch, *Jahrbücher Heinrich II*, I, 478–86 (excursus of Usinger). In the middle of the reign of Henry IV, as the result of the Slav reaction of 1066, 600 Saxon families which were settled in Holstein and Ditmarsch emigrated to Thuringia (Helm., I, 26). They must have settled in their first home after the Slav insurrection of 1018 had subsided. The early Angle colony around Merseburg, often alluded to by German historians, never existed. The oldest manuscript of the text (*MGH*, SS. VII, 285) contains no mention of it. It is an interpolation in later manuscripts. Cf. Lot in *Revue hist.* (May-June, 1915), p. 31, n. 3.

[3] *Vita Henrici II*, Book I, chap. iii (Migne, *PL*, CXL, 110): ". . . . Sedes episcopales Missnam et Merseburch quae barbarica immanitate adjacentium Sclavorum vastatae fuerant, restauravit." In *ibid.*, chap. iv, it is related that the treasures, etc., of Merseburg were transferred to Magdeburg for safekeeping at this time.

the native towns and villages until they died of exhaustion.
The work of the church for seventy years past in Nordalbingia went down in a twelvemonth.[1] Gottschalk, the Abodrite chief, who at first had been tolerant of Christianity,
and whose son was educated in the cloister school in Lüneburg, became the formidable avenger of the wrongs of his
people.[2]

More than a century and a half later, when the labors of
Adolph of Holstein and Henry the Lion permanently established German domination across the great river, Helmold,
the Holsteiner priest and author of that vivid record of German eastward expansion, the *Chronica Slavorum*, picturesquely described the ruins which still could be seen of churches,
monasteries, and tiny German hamlets which were destroyed
in these two uprisings of the Slavs.[3]

But neither the violence of this second Slav rebellion nor
the imprecations of the clergy frightened Henry II into renouncing the alliance he had made with the Slavs of the Elbe.
Unexpected and ferocious as the insurrection of 1018 was,
bitter as the blow must have been to his liberal practice,
hostile as the resentment of the bishops was—especially of
those who had lost their seats—yet the Emperor's confidence
in the essential justice and wisdom of his policy was un-
shaken. He had the justice to perceive that the Wilzi, the
Wagri, the Abodrites, etc., had been "driven to the necessity
of paganism" by the cruel oppression of the clergy and Duke
Bernhard of Saxony.[4]

---

[1] "Omnes igitur Sclavi qui inter Albiam et Oddaram . . . . absiderunt a corpore Christi" (Adam of Bremen, II, 42–43; cf. Helmold, I, 19; Thietmar, IX [VIII,
4]; Hauck, III, 253).

[2] See the interesting conversation of Gottschalk, reported by Helmold, I, 19,
with a Holsatian refugee whom he met unrecognized in the way.

[3] "Adhuc restant antiquae illius habitacionis pleraque indicia, precipue in silva,
quae ab urbe Lutilinburg per longissimas tractus Sleswich usque protrahitur, cujus
vasta solitudo et vix penetrabilis inter maxima silvarum robora sulcos pretendit,
quibus jugera quondam fuerant dispertita. Urbium quoque seu civitatum formam
structura vallorum pretendit. In plerisque etiam rivis qui propter molendina stipan-
dis aquis aggeres congesti sunt ostendunt omnem saltum a Saxonibus quondam
inhabitatum" (Helmold, I, 12).

[4] Thietmar, VIII, 4; Adam of Bremen, II, 40, 41, 42, 46; Hirsch, *Jahrb. Heinrich II*, III, 93 ff.

Conrad II (1024–39), no friend of churchmen, attempted to adhere to the policy of Henry II. But the prejudice of the clergy and the continual molestation of the Abodrites and the Wilzi by the Saxons jeopardized this statesman-like course more and more.[1] For over thirty years the strong hand of these two rulers sought to restrain both the Saxon clergy and the Saxon nobles. Wipo, the biographer of Conrad, relates an incident which strikingly illustrates the conditions and the difficulties along the frontier. In 1033 the border situation became so tense that the Emperor went thither to investigate. The Wends accused the Saxons of continually breaking the peace. The Saxons blamed the Wends. The latter offered to put the determination of the question to the judgment of God in trial by battle. Conrad at first hesitated, having scruples whether a heathen could participate in a process of law in which the invisible presence of God was supposed to be, but finally consented. Each side chose a champion, and the Slav champion won, to the great elation of his compatriots and the chagrin of the Saxons, especially the clergy, whose prestige as dispensers of the will of the Almighty was somewhat injured.[2]

But the wise plan of the Salian emperors was increasingly imperiled by the ambition of the Billunger dukes of Saxony and the avarice of the Saxon clergy. Up to the death of Duke Benno in 1011 the Billungers had been loyal, though with diminishing fidelity, to the German crown. But with the accession of Bernhard to the dukedom the Billunger breach both with the crown and with the church widened. As we have seen, the Abodrites were the mildest of the Slav tribes of the lower Elbe, and when the first wild flame of rebellion subsided, Christianity began slowly to recover in Wagria under the active policy of Archbishop Unwan of Bremen (d. 1029) and Bishop Benno of Oldenburg, whose tactless inquisi-

[1] *Heiden sollen nicht erben* ("Heathen have no right to inherit") was a popular medieval proverb in North Germany.

[2] Wipo, *Vita Chuonradi*, chap. xxxiii; for a commentary on the legal technicalities see Waitz, VIII, 30; Bresslau, II, 96–97.

tion into the former possessions of the church there precipitated the rebellion of 1018.[1]

The Saxon Duke, jealous of the enrichment of the church,
did everything he could to thwart the Bishop, and at the same
time attempted to double the tribute exacted of the Abodrites.[2] Four manors, in particular, were a bone of contention
between the Duke and the Bishop.[3] The Abodrites, caught
between the hammer of the Bishop and the anvil of the
Duke, preferred the Bishop's rule as the less of two evils
and when the dispute was referred to the Emperor, testified
to the previous existence of the episcopal tithe and promised
to pay it as before.[4] This was in 1021, and was the immediate
ground of the fierce feud which widened into open war between the Billunger dukes and the bishops of Northern Germany, and which reached an acute phase in the war of Duke
Ordulf against Adalbert of Bremen in the early years of the
reign of Henry IV.

Thus the peace and prosperity of Nordalbingia and Holstein after the second Slav rebellion subsided, of which Adam
of Bremen boasts, was actually as precarious as the quarter
of a beleagured town beyond the immediate reach of the
shells. Billunger hatred of the church's ascendancy left nothing undone to embarrass it.[5] Moreover, the new King of Denmark, whose ambition for Danish expansion on the mainland
had been nourished by Canute, coveted a wider dominion.
Conrad II, Canute, and Archbishop Unwan of Bremen had
amicably arranged their somewhat conflicting interests in the
north.[6] But when Canute died in 1035 and Conrad II in 1039,

---

[1] Helmold, I, 18. Thietmar of Merseburg, when Henry II restored the bishopric
and appointed him to it, exhibited the same greed for land and started proceedings to
recover possession of the lands which had passed to others in the dismemberment of
the diocese. He did not recoil from acts of violence in so doing, and became bitterly
involved with Hermann and Eckhard, sons of Margrave Eckhard, as a result
(Thietmar, IX, 20–22).

[2] Wendt, I, 69.

[3] Helmold (ed. Schmeidler), I, 18, and nn. 4–6.

[4] *Ibid.*; cf. Giesebrecht, *Kaiserzeit*, II, 619 f.

[5] Adam of Bremen, III, 22.

[6] *Ibid.*, II, 54; Bresslau, *Jahrb. Konrad II*, I, 101–4. In 1019 Canute made a
campaign against the Slavs (*Jahrb. Heinrich II*, III, 185).

political conditions in Northern Germany were changed. Duke Bernhard's son Ordulf was married to a daughter of Magnus of Denmark. The alliance boded ill for the interests of either emperor or church in the north. Things became tenser than before. The Danish King coveted possession of the mouths of the rivers flowing into the Baltic in the interest of Danish Baltic trade,[1] while the Saxon Duke wanted to provoke the Abodrites and Wilzi into a new revolt which would destroy the churches again being established in their lands, use the rising as a pretext for Saxon intervention, and so establish his dominion and tribute over them without any competition from the church.

The Saxon-Danish alliance was formed with the object of effecting this double partition. In pursuance of the plan Ordulf and King Magnus, in 1043, fell upon the Wends at Lyrskog Heath, near Hadeby in Schleswig (September 28) a victory which clinched the Danish capture of Wollin, the most important trading town of the Baltic Slavs at the mouth of the Oder River in 960, which the Danes had renamed Jomsburg.[2] The future was to see a bitter strife between the Germans and the Danes for possession of the Pomeranian coast as a result of this intrigue. But of more immediate importance was the effect upon Nordalbingia. Against the double onslaught the Abodrites were powerless. Their capacity to resist was also hampered by their division into a pagan

---

[1] In the reign of Otto the Great the ambition of the Danes was a greater menace to Germany in the far north than the Slavonic tribes beyond the lower Elbe were (Sommerfeld, op. cit., p. 7).

That propulsive and expansive energy in the Viking spirit which had made Europe ring with the achievements of the Norsemen in the ninth century was hardly abated in the tenth. Denmark, in the time of Henry the Fowler and Otto the Great, cherished dreams of Baltic dominion which the Saxon could not look upon without anxiety. In 934 Henry I had warred with Gorm of Denmark, strengthened the ancient limes established by Charlemagne by carrying the frontier beyond the Eider to the river Schlei, and erected the tiny March of Schleswig between the rivers where a Saxon colony was established at Haddeby (Waitz, Jahrb. Heinrich I, pp. 277 f., Exkursus 24). King Sweyn Forkbeard of Denmark (985–1013) built the rampart or dike across the peninsula from Haddeby to protect the kingdom from further German expansion. See article by La Cour, Historisk Tidsskrift (8th series, 1909–10), Vol. II; cf. Biereye, Beiträge zur Gesch. Nordalbingiens im 10 Jahrhundert (Berlin diss. 1909), p. 192; Ztschft. f. Ethnologie, XXXV (1904), 688, with map.

[2] Schafarik, II, 383, 575–77.

and a Christian group, the latter under another Gottschalk. Probably nothing but the loyalty of these Christian Wends to the faith, in spite of all the abuse of them by the church, saved Nordalbingia and Holstein from a second eclipse of the church there at this time.[1] Unfortunately for Germany, the Emperor Henry III during this time was warring against the Bohemians and Hungarians, or else in Italy, and could not interfere. Helmold's comment, which echoes Adam of Bremen's doleful observation, is full of depression: "De Christianitate nulla fuit mentio."[2]

Painfully and slowly civilization began to pick up again in Nordalbingia; peasant settlers from Saxony, and not merely land-hungry nobles, began to filter once more into the region. In the middle of the eleventh century Adam of Bremen proudly says: "Per idem tempus in Sclavania res maximae gestae sunt";[3] and the picture of the prosperity which he paints, if perhaps overcolored, is nevertheless significant of the changed order of things along the lower Elbe.[4]

At this critical juncture, when the affairs of the north were full of tension, friction, and peril, Henry III died (October 5, 1056), leaving the crown to Henry IV, who was a little child, and Germany fell upon evil days. The most statesman-like man in the country was the great archbishop of Bremen, Adalbert (1043–72). But he had bitter enemies in the Saxon Duke and his son, and in his rival for the regency, Archbishop Anno of Cologne. Adalbert was of a noble Saxon family and the ambition which, if he had been a layman, would have driven him to strive for the enlargement of his feudal prerogative and the widening of his feudal lands found a broader field of ambition in his ecclesiastical office. His dream was to convert his archdiocese into an immense patriarchate, having ecclesiastical sway over Lower Germany,

---

[1] For the extensive source references and literature to the battle of Hadeby and its results see Richter, *Annalen*, II, 361–63; cf. K. Gjerset, *History of the Norwegian People*, I (1915), 275.

[2] Adam of Bremen, III, 22; Helmold, I, 21.

[3] Adam of Bremen, III, 21.

[4] *Ibid.*, III, 18–21; cf. Helm., I, 20.

Denmark, Sweden, Norway, Iceland, and even Greenland.[1]
For the realization of this dream of creating a gigantic principality covering the whole Christian north of Europe, Adalbert actually declined the papacy in 1044.[2]

The Baltic Slavs were to have formed a vassal state of the
German kingdom within this huge orbit,[3] with the Christian
Abodrite duke, Gottschalk, as prince, after the manner of the
relation of Poland and Bohemia to the German crown.[4] To be
sure, the Abodrites were yet half-pagan and the Wilzi wholly
so. But Gottschalk's loyalty and organized missionary effort on the part of the church were counted upon to remedy
this condition. Adalbert, unlike any former bishop in the
north, worked hand in hand with the Christian Abodrites.
He divided the bishopric of Oldenburg into three parts, creating two new Slavonic dioceses for them—Mecklenburg and
Ratzeburg—and founded cloisters in Oldenburg, Ratzeburg,
and Lenzen.[5] Henry III while he had lived had furthered
Adalbert's ideas, for their realization would have spread the
power of the Empire too. Moreover, the Emperor needed the
support of Adalbert in Saxony which was now dangerously
alienated and even hostile to the German crown. The absence
of Anno of Cologne at the Council of Mantua gave Adalbert
his chance to take advantage of the favor of young Henry IV,
and for two years (1064–66) he had things much his own way.

But the prospect of the speedy conversion of the Baltic
Slavs roused the fury of the Billunger, for they had no mind
to see the tribute diminished by the extension of the church's

[1] Cf. Adam of Bremen, *Descriptio Insularum Aquilonis*, 10, 36, 37. For the
medieval church in Greenland see K. Gjerset, *op. cit.*, I, 197–204; Major's ed. of
Voyages of the Venetian Brothers N. and A. Zeno (Hakluyt Soc., 1873), pp. lxxxvii f.,
Beamish, *Saga of Eric the Red*; and esp. L. M. Larsen, *Catholic Historical Review*
(July–October, 1919).

[2] Adam of Bremen, III, 7.

[3] "Sclavos ita perdomuit ut eum [Adalbertum] quasi regem timerent" (Adam
of Bremen, III, 18).

[4] "Gottschalk's Plan war die Gründung eines grossen wendischen Einheitstaates
auf christlicher Grundlage und im Bunde mit dem Reich" (Otto Bitense, *Mecklenb.
Gesch.* [1912], p. 19; cf. Guttmann, *op. cit.*, p. 419; Wendt, I, 73). Gottschalk married
a sister of the Danish King (Adam of Bremen, III, 18).

[5] Adam of Bremen, III, 20; Helmold, I, 22; Dehio, *op. cit.*, Exkurs XIX.

tithe.[1] "He shall not rest," said Duke Ordulf of Adalbert, "while I or my house last." Both parties assiduously built castles, and the north country flamed with war.[2]

The German church was divided into two camps. Anno of Cologne was supported by the Archbishop of Magdeburg and the bishops of Halberstadt, Trier, Minden, and Utrecht, as well as by the leading Saxon nobles.[3] At Tribur in January, 1066, Henry IV was forced to dismiss Adalbert, who fled to Bremen. Then followed four terrible years. The Billunger fell upon Bremen with fire and sword and wrecked the land. Adalbert found refuge in the strong imperial fortress of Goslar, whence he sent the proffer of a thousand manors of his diocese as the price of peace, to Magnus Billung, Duke Ordulf's son. In the end the bishopric was deprived of two-thirds of its possessions, half of the spoil going to the Billunger and half to their partisans. The indomitable Adalbert spent three years in his ruined city, still dreaming of the grandeur he had hoped for and laboring for the reconstruction of the dilapidated diocese.[4] At last Henry IV, who had emancipated himself in 1070 from the control of the combined clerical and feudal opposition around him, recalled Adalbert. But in March, 1072, Adalbert died, as tragically as Wolsey, save for the love of his king for him. Adam of Bremen says that in his last hours he reproached himself for having wasted his life in pursuit of earthly power. But the pious historian's moralizing does not disguise the fact that Adalbert was a big and forceful personality who wrought strenuously for the enlargement of the life and the history of Northern Germany. In the same year his great enemy, Duke Ordulf, also died.

Meanwhile, what had been the effect of these events upon the border situation?

The Saxon greed for the Wendish lands, coupled with the

[1] Adam of Bremen, III, 40, 42.

[2] Adam of Bremen, III, 43; cf. 47–48. For the earlier history of the feud see II, 69; III, 21.

[3] Adam of Bremen, III, 34, 46.

[4] See Adam of Bremen's detailed account (III, 48, 54–56).

bitter feud between the church and the Saxon nobles for control of the Wendish tribute, was a perpetual source of disaffection, and continually tended to upset peace on the frontier. The nobles by trespass and exasperation goaded the Wends into reprisal and thus created a pretext for a war of dispossession in order that they might acquire the coveted lands. The leader of this policy of forcible expropriation was Bernard Billung, duke of the Saxons. The Billunger hatred of the clergy was intense because they did not want the Wendish tribute reduced by the imposition of the tithe. The border was the prey of unceasing predatory raids by the Saxons who bled the wretched Abodrites and Ljutizi of tribute.

Moreover, the pro-Christian inclinations of Gottschalk and the Abodrites had slowly provoked the wrath of the other pagan Slavs along the Baltic Coast farther toward the east, especially the Wilzi and the wilder Rugians, the guardians of the great Slavonic fane on the island of Rügen. They perceived what was quite true, that the extension of Christianity would carry with it the subjugation of the free Slav tribes and that they were likely to pass under the onerous domination of the Saxon dukes. "They preferred to die rather than to become Christian," says Helmold, "or to pay tribute to the Saxon dukes."[1] The sight of the newly established bishoprics of Mecklenburg and Ratzeburg infuriated them, and the pagan priests of their temples seem to have fanned the flame, as the Aztec priesthood inspired their people against the Spanish conquerors in Mexico.

In 1066 a third Slavonic rebellion came, the most formidable and effective of them all. The Wilzi, maddened by Saxon abuse and border aggression, rose in fury and decisively defeated the Saxons.[2] The Christian Abodrite chief Gottschalk was killed at Lenzen, but his wife, who was a daughter of the Danish King, escaped naked to Mecklenburg. Ratzeburg was attacked, the Christian priests and many of the people stoned to death. The sack of Mecklenburg soon followed. The furious Wagri and Wilzi stormed one after an-

[1] Helmold, I, 25.   [2] *Chron. Wirzib.* (*MGH*, SS. VI, 31); Wendt, I, 75.

other the long line of Burgwärde which extended from
Mecklenburg (formerly the Wiligrad or Great Burg of the
Abodrites) through Wismar, Ilow, Bukow, Schwerin, and
Dobbin. These Burgwärde were interspersed with lesser posts
or forts, between which was an earthen and palisaded wall,
some remains of which are still visible between Schwerin and
Wismar. The key fortress along this frontier, Mikilinburg,
gave the name of Mecklenburg to the land.[1] Bishop John of
Mecklenburg was dragged off a captive to the pagan temple
at Rethra and there immolated to the high Slav god Redigast
(November 10, 1066). Squads of Christian priests were
whipped through the Slav towns until they died of exhaustion.
The Slavonic bishoprics of Mecklenburg and Ratzeburg were
obliterated; the cloisters at Oldenburg, Lenzen, and Ratzeburg
destroyed. Even the bishopric of Hamburg was overrun.[2]
Hundreds of the population were carried off into slavery, the
castle demolished, the garrison thereof being derisively cruci-
fied by the furious victors. "Omnes Sclavi," says Adam of
Bremen, "facta conspiratione generali ad paganismum denuo
relapsi sunt."[3] "Thereafter until the end of his life," writes
Helmold, "Duke Ordulf vainly fought against the Slavs, but
was never able to win a victory. Many times was he beaten
by the pagans and was an object of derision unto his own
people."

The few Christian Abodrites in the ruined land lapsed to
paganism once more. The entire achievement of German
civilization and Germanic Christianity, save around Bremen
and in Holstein, was wiped out. Both paid dearly for the
cruelty, injustice, and avarice with which they had operated.
In completeness of destruction this third great Slav rising
excelled those of 983 and 1018.[4]

[1] See Otto Vitense, *Mecklenburgische Geschichte* (1912), p. 11; Kretschmar,
Historische Geographie, p. 357. Cf. Old English *mickle*; Anglo-Saxon, *micel*=
"much," or "great."

[2] Hauck, III, 594.

[3] Adam of Bremen, III, 49–50; Helmold, I, 22–24.

[4] For the history in detail of this Wendish reaction see Adam of Bremen, III,
49–50; Helm., I, 22–25; Wendt, I, 75–79; Raumer, *Regesta*, Nos. 550, 585, 592–93;
Breska, *Untersuchungen*, pp. 31–41; Meyer von Knonau, *Jahrb. Heinrich IV*, II,
854–56; Lavisse, *La Marche de Brandenbourg*, pp. 33–34.

The Christian hero of the border was the fierce Burck-hardt, bishop of Halberstadt, who in the winter of 1067–68 made a successful raid across the frozen marshes, devastated the country of the Wilzi, burned the Wendish temple at Rethra, and triumphantly rode back to Saxony upon the sacred black horse.[1] In the next winter—winter campaigns were the only practicable method of invasion of so swampy a country[2]—young Henry IV repeated this feat.[3] But the Wends more than held their own. In 1072 they twice at-tacked Hamburg. All Nordalbingia was a solitude.[4] So great was the danger even west of the Elbe that Bishop Benno II of Osnabrück in 1070 built Aschenberg castle and walled the monastery of Iburg.[5]

The Pontiac of this successful rebellion of the Baltic Slavs to throw off the German yoke was a Rugian chief named Kruto, who fixed his capital on the island of Buku at the confluence of the Trave and the Wochnitz rivers, where later in 1143, Adolph of Holstein founded the present city of Lübeck.[6] For years Duke Ordulf or his son warred against Kruto in vain.[7]

In 1074 or 1075 Gottschalk's son Buthue, with the aid of a force of Holsteiners and men of Ditmarsch furnished him by

[1] *MGH*, SS. III, 128; *Ann. Altah. Maj.* (1069). German children in this region still sing an ancient nursery jingle reminiscent of this event:

> "Buko von Halberstadt,
> Bring doch meinen Kinde wat.
> 'Wat sall ik em denn bringen?'
> 'Goldne Schoh mit Ringen.' "

Literally:

> "Buko of Halberstadt,
> Bring something to my child.
> 'What shall I bring to him?'
> 'Golden shoes with buckles.' "

[2] "Terra etenim illa paganorum aquis et paludibus est plena" (*Annal. Altah.* [1069]).

[3] *Annal. Weissemb.* (1069); *Sigeb. Gembl.* (*MGH*, SS. VI, 362).

[4] "Pagani victores totam Nordalbingiam deinceps habuerunt in sua ditione, bellatoribusque [i.e., the vassals of the bishop] occisis aut in captivitatem ductis, pro-vincia in solitudinem redacta est" (Adam of Bremen, III, 63).

[5] *Mitth. d. Ver. f. d. Gesch. von Osnabrück*, Band XXVII (1902).

[6] Helmold, I, 25, 57.   [7] Adam of Bremen, III, 50; *ibid.*, I, 24.

Duke Magnus, who succeeded Ordulf in 1072, seized Kruto's castle of Plön, on an isthmus between the Grosse and the Kleine Plöner-See, north of Kruto's capital at Buku.[1] It had been craftily left without defenders by the wily Rugian, and Buthue was warned by a German woman against the trap. Morning showed a Slav army in boats around the castle. A parley followed at the end of which the Germans in pairs crossed a bridge of boats into Kruto's camp where, when they had surrendered their arms, they were all put to the edge of the sword. Helmold's epilogue on this catastrophe is as follows:

And Kruto prevailed and the work prospered in his hands. And the strength of the Saxons was worn down and they served Kruto under tribute . . . . All the territory of the Nordalbingians, which is divided into three peoples, the Holsteiners, the Sturmarians and those who live in Ditmarsch—these bore the heavy yoke of servitude during the whole life of Kruto, and the land was filled with robbers, who visited rapine and death upon the people of God.

From his rise to power in 1066 until his death in 1093 Kruto was lord of the north.[2] Hundreds of the German population which had settled across the Elbe forsook the country. "In those days more than 600 families of the people of Holstein emigrated across the river [Elbe], seeking a better place where they might be free from danger. And they came into the Harz Mountains and there they themselves and their sons and their grandsons have remained unto this time."[3] The memory of Kruto is still preserved in North German legend as a terrible ogre. I have heard children singing jingles

---

[1] Helmold, I, 25. The line between the Germans and the Slavs, separating Holstein from the Wendish land, was the little river Schwale, near modern Neumünster, west of the Trave River (see Wigger; *Meck. Annalen*, p. 100, n. 7; Bahr, *Studien zur nordalbingischen Gesch. im 12. Jahrh.* [Leipzig, 1895], pp. 1–9).

[2] "Invaluitque Cruto . . . . obtinuitque dominium in universa terra Slavorum. Et attritae sunt vires Saxonum, et servierunt Crutoni sub tributo, omnis terra videlicet Nordalbingorum quae disterminatur in tres populos: Holzatos, Sturmarios, Thethmarchos [Holstein, Sturmaria, Ditmarsch]. Omnes hii durissimum servitutis jugum protaverunt omni tempore Crutonis" (Helmold, I, 26; cf. Schafarik, II, 537 f., 574; Hauck, IV, 595).

[3] Helm., I, 26. Probably the settlement of Elbingerode, in the Brockengebirge, is here indicated, for it is not mentioned before the twelfth century, and the name indicates that it was founded by some people from the Elbe Valley.

about him in the streets. The border situation was as if here in America Pontiac's conspiracy in 1763 had been successful, and the Indian tribes west of the Alleghanies combined. German colonization toward the northeast was given a serious setback. "The land was almost reduced to a solitude," is the mournful record. "Travel beyond the Elbe was difficult and hazardous."[1]

In defense of their farms and hamlets the peasantry walled and towered churches, and even cemeteries. The interior chapels of the larger churches sometimes were remodeled so as to be like the courts of a medieval castle. In the open country even corncribs were transformed into local points of resistance.[2]

Under other conditions the formation of a powerful pagan Slavonic state on the north and east of the German kingdom would have been regarded with immense anxiety by the Emperor. But at this juncture (1075) Henry IV had just become involved in the dual conflict with Pope Gregory VII and the revolted Saxons. The year before the Saxons had pleaded the border danger from the Wilzi as a pretext more than an excuse to avoid military service against the Poles.[3] Henry IV must have penetrated the real reason of their evasion, and considering that Saxony was on the verge of open rebellion against him regarded the menace hovering upon the edge of Saxony with some satisfaction, if not elation. According to one account, he even offered money to the Wilzi if they would attack the Saxons, but the Saxons outbid him. Another version is to the effect that Henry offered the Wilzi all the territory which they might conquer from the Saxons.[4]

Henry IV, although he had come forth victorious out of

[1] *Sidonis Epist.* (ed. Schmeidler), p. 236.

[2] See the interesting article of Haupt on the fortified churches of the duchies of the lower Elbe, in *Ztschft. d. Gesellschaft f. Schleswig-Holsteinische Gesch.*, Band XXXII (1902). It applies to an epoch later than this, but yet is not without bearing.

[3] Lambert of Hersfeld (ed. Holder-Egger), p. 147.

[4] Raumer, *Regesta*, Nos. 611, 613, 616. For this pro-pagan policy of Henry IV and Henry V see Schmeidler's edition of Helmold, Praef., p. xvi, and references.

the conflict with the papacy and the revolted German baronage, was friendly to them. Saxony had been the storm center
of opposition to the Salian house, and the King perceived the
strategic value of a border state friendly to him and hostile
to the Saxons lying along the edge of Saxony. To the wrath
of the Saxon clergy Henry IV not only befriended the Slavs,
but even favored the continuance of paganism among them
and opposed the church's missionary activity. His son Henry
V, save for one isolated campaign against the Wilzi, adhered to the same policy.

Whatever be the real truth, it is at least certain that
Kruto was able for years to hold his own against the aggression of Magnus (duke of Saxony), Eric (the Danish king),
and the Margrave of the Nordmark. Of these three, Eric of
Denmark was the most dangerous, for the ancient bargain
which Conrad II had made with Cnut whereby he resigned
Schleswig to Denmark in return for Danish support against
the Baltic Slavs was bearing bitter fruit for Germany.
Charlemagne's policy and that of the Saxon emperors had
been to coop up the Danes within their peninsula. The failure
of the Salians to adhere to this course and the alliance between the Danish ruling house and the Billunger whetted
the appetite of Denmark so that she hungered to extend her
domination along the Baltic Coast, where she had already
acquired Jomsburg[1] at the mouth of the Oder. Henry IV for
years was too involved with the revolted Saxons and the
papacy to be able to give attention to this danger of Denmark
becoming the possessor of the mouths of the German rivers.
Under the circumstances the presence of a strong Slav state
on the north and east as a check to both a hostile Denmark
and a hostile Saxony was a great advantage to him.

But the realm created by Kruto was outwardly stronger
than it actually was within. His power rested on his own
personal achievements and prestige. A Rugian himself, the
two other pagan tribes, the Wagrians and Ljutizi, still retained chiefs of their own, though in a subordinate capacity,

[1] Schmeidler (ed. Adam of Bremen), p. 79, n. 1, in a note to "nobilissima
civitas Jumne" writes: "Nach allgemeiner Ansicht die berühmte Jomsburg mit den
Jomsvikingern, auf dem Silberberge nördlich von Wollin bei Divenow."

who were jealous of Kruto, even if not open rivals. A greater source of weakness to Kruto, though, arose from the fact that the Christian wing of the Abodrites and the Low German population under Kruto's sway—in Holstein and Ditmarsch —secretly connived with the Saxons against him, and found a leader in a son of the late Abodrite duke, Gottschalk, named Henry.[1] In 1093 the united Christian forces, aided by some Saxons, won a great victory over the pagan Wends at Schmilow near Ratzeburg, conquered fourteen Wendish towns, and reduced the Wagrians and Ljutizi to tribute once more.[2]

Holstein and Ditmarsch were free again. But the Christian Abodrite Duke was wise enough not to attempt to impose Christianity upon all the people of his tribe, deeming it better to pay tribute to the Saxons for the indulgence of paganism.[3] Of the German population once there, many had emigrated, the rest had maintained a precarious existence under the Wendish and pagan domination, living in the vicinity of a few Burgwärde which seem never to have been taken by the Wends.[4] The people gladly went back to their abandoned farms. German civilization and Germany's ecclesiastical system returned to the land, "and the houses and churches which had been destroyed were rebuilt."

[1] Helm., I, 34, is much confused in his chronology at this point, and the dates and main facts of this paragraph are established from the *Annals of Hildesheim* (*MGH*, SS. III, 106). Schirrin (*op. cit.*, pp. 114 ff.) regards the whole account in Helm., *loc. cit.*, as romance. Contra are Wigger, pp. 44 ff., and Breska, *Untersuchungen*, pp. 41 ff. According to Helmold, Henry treacherously slew Kruto with the connivance of the latter's Wendish wife, whom Henry married.

[2] On this important battle see L. Giesebrecht, *Wend. Geschichten*, II, 167; Meyer v. Knonau, *Jahrb. Heinrichs IV*, IV, 416; Wendt, I, 80.

[3] "Porro in universa Slavia necdum erat ecclesia vel sacerdos, nisi in urbe tantum quae nunc Vetus Lubika [Alt-Lübeck at the confluence of the little river Swartowe with the Trave] dicitur, eo quod Heinricus cum familia sua saepius illic moraretur" (Helm., I, 34). Breska, *Ztschft. f. Lübeckische Gesch.*, Band IV (1881), argues, against Schirren, for the accuracy of Helmold's assertion that the Christian Abodrite Duke Henry made an expedition in 1100 against the pagan Wends of Brandenburg. On the Abodrite dukes see Schmeidler, *Hamburg-Bremen und Nordost Europa*, etc., pp. 318–30; Marquart, *Osteuropäische und ostasiatische Streifzüge* (Leipzig, 1903), pp. 305–29; Biereye, *op. cit.*, pp. 169–76.

[4] Helmold does not call them Burgwärde, as Thietmar a century and a half earlier denominated the Saxon strongholds in the Sorben land. Instead he calls them *munitiones* (I, 34) or *praesidia* (I, 19, 25). He gives the name of two of these— Echeco and Bokeldeburg.

The year 1093 may be regarded as a turning-point in the history of the Baltic Slavs. The three great Slavonic revolts of 983, 1018, and 1066, in spite of their success, had depleted the energies of the tribes, and the residue of their power, after victory, was worn down by almost continuous border warfare with the Saxons. The offensive history of Wendish paganism was ended. At the close of the eleventh century the liberty and the religion of the Baltic Slavs stood upon the defensive.[1] Slowly the ring was tightening around the last devotees of the Slavonic gods, in the territory between the lower Elbe and the Oder. Poland menaced them on the east; Germany on the west. The conversion of the Poles at the end of the eleventh century was followed by a crusade of Boleslav III in 1102 against the Pomeranians. In the ensuing years the land lying between the lower Oder and the Peene and Havel rivers, with the important Wendish towns of Stettin and Wollin, was overrun by the Poles. It was the high-water mark of Polish westward expansion.[2] For the coming of Albrecht the Bear into Brandenburg in 1134 and the extension of German domination over the Uckermark were soon effectually to check the ambition of Poland to acquire the Baltic seaboard.

Perhaps a ray of hope came to the hard-pressed Wends when, in 1106, Magnus Billung,[3] the last of his line, and Udo III, the formidable margrave of the Nordmark, died. But it must have vanished at once. The fatal turning-point in the history of the Baltic Slavs is the year 1106 when Magnus Billung, the last of his house, died and was succeeded in the duchy of Saxony by Lothar of Supplinburg. The new Duke was politically as powerful as his predecessor, and by tradition and family ties represented more than the Billunger the real interests of the Saxon people. The Billunger, as we have seen, were hostile to the conversion of the Slavs because the tithes of the church reduced the tribute which they exacted from the conquered Wends. Their interest had been to pre-

---

[1] In 1100–1101 Margrave Udo III of the Nordmark recovered Brandenburg for a brief moment (Raumer, *Regesta*, No. 667; *Ann. of Hild.* [*MGH*, SS. III, 107]; *Ann. Sax.* [1101]; *Ann. Rosenv.* [SS. XVI, 102]).

[2] Sommerfeld, *op. cit.*, pp. 16–18; Wendt, II, 4–5.

[3] See B. Köster, *Sachsen unter Herzog Magnus* (1881).

vent missions among the Slavs. But Lothar was an ardent
supporter of the church. His accession was followed by a
renewal of church energy. For the first time church and state
in Saxony were united in a common purpose. The sword of
the Duke was extended in favor of the clergy, and a series of
attacks began upon the Wends which were at once military
expeditions and missionary campaigns. It has been truly said
that no such formidable person had appeared in the north
since the days of Gero.[1] In 1110 Lothar avenged the murder
of one of his vassals, Godfrey of Holstein, in the Abodrite
country, by conquering nine of their towns.[2]

The seeming strength and security of the Baltic Slavs was
illusory. In the first quarter of the twelfth century it is undeniable that Slavonic paganism was upon the defensive. Although it was true that "ultra Albiam illis temporibus rarus
inveniebatur Christianus,"[3] nevertheless Christianity was
slowly seeping into the trans-Elbean lands, especially in the
territory of Brandenburg, where the extension of the church
can be obscurely discerned. There is record of a church at
Leitzkau in 1114, and the Archbishop of Magdeburg had a
Christian Wendish *praefectus* in his service at Loburg in 1115.

It is fair to say, however, that at this time the Rugian
Slavs furnished some provocation for these feats of arms,
apart from the religious zeal which actuated the Saxons. Like
the Vikings of the ninth century, the Rugians, whose capital
was situated on the island of Rügen, were a sea-robber folk,
adventurous and fiercely pagan.[4] Their depredations along
the Baltic Coast, in Mecklenburg, Holstein, and Schleswig,
whence they carried off men, women, and children into
slavery, and immense booty, were serious. In 1110 their robber bands fell upon Holstein and penetrated nearly to Hamburg. A cry of protest went up from the land.[5] In 1111 (the

---

[1] Bernhardi, *Jahrbuch*, p. 19.

[2] Helm., I, 35; *Ann. Hild.* (*MGH, SS.* III, 112).

[3] *Annal. Pegav.* (*MGH, SS.* XVI, 252).

[4] L. Giesebrecht, *Wend. Gesch.*, I, 205 f.; Barthold, I, 324 f.

[5] *Annal. Hildesh.*; *Annal. Sax.* (1110); see the anecdote related by Helmold, I,
35, of a peasant (*rusticus*) whose wife and children had been carried off, who met
Count Godfrey of Sturm in the way and bitterly upbraided him.

date is not certain) they again invaded Nordalbingia "as if they were going to possess the land," says Helmold. But Henry, the Christian Abodrite duke, was ready for them, and so great a slaughter of the invaders was made that out of the bodies of the slain a huge mound was erected called the Rani-berg, which was long pointed out to the curious. This victory raised the prestige of the Abodrite chief to a high pitch both among the Germans of the lower Elbe and among the converted Wends. When, soon afterward, Duke Henry's son was killed by the Rugians, a united Wendish-Saxon host was gathered to the number of sixteen hundred men, it is said. No Saxon or Christian army had been beyond the Peene River since the time of Otto I.

The campaign was purposely undertaken in the winter season in the hope that it might be possible to cross from the mainland to the island of Rügen upon the ice. The plan was as successful, perhaps, as the leaders had dared to hope. After nine days' march the army reached the Baltic, where they burned all the Rugian fishing villages. When nothing but the frozen strait separated the attackers from the island, the priests of Arkona took alarm and sent a humble message through a Rugian priest (Helmold calls him a *flamen*, not the medieval Latin word for "priest," i.e., *sacerdos*)[1] with the proffer of 400 and then 800 marks. But immunity was not to be purchased so cheaply. In the end the Rugians gave hostages for the payment of the astonishing sum of 4,400 marks. The imposition of this huge indemnity stripped their temple and even private persons; messengers had to be sent to the mainland for contributions. The heart of Baltic Slavdom was shaken to the core by this expedition.[2]

In 1114 Hartbert, titular bishop of Brandenburg, then *in partibus paganorum*, invaded his see and returned, boasting

[1] *Sacerdos* and *presbyter* were used interchangeably. In towns one sometimes finds *parochianus* or *rector* or *pastor ecclesiae*, and *plebanus* in the fourteenth century (Koeniger. *op. cit.*, p. 92, n. 3).

[2] Helmold, I, 38; *Annal. Corb.* (*MGH*, SS. III, 8); *Annalista Saxo* (*MGH*, SS. VI, 75). The date of this expedition is put by Wendt, I, 84, in the winter of 1123-24. Schmeidler, the latest editor of Helmold, places it in 1113-14. Personally I incline to the date 1113-14, for such a campaign as this would naturally follow in retaliation for the great piratical raids of 1110-11.

that he had destroyed many idols of the pagan Wends.[1] On February 9, 1115, Count Otto of Ballenstadt won a crushing victory over the Wends at Köthen.[2] In the winter of 1124–25 Lothar, the Saxon duke, in company with a force of Christian Abodrites, destroyed the temple at Rethra,[3] and would probably have destroyed that of Arkona in Rügen if a thaw had not inopportunely broken up the ice and prevented the army from crossing the strait.[4] In that very spring the Christian Abodrite chief, Henry, died (March 22), and in the ensuing August, Lothar, the Saxon duke, succeeded Henry V, the last of the Salian house, as king and emperor.

It is manifest to the student who reads the history of this time that by 1125 the independence and the religion of the Baltic Slavs were clearly doomed to extinguishment. The division of the Abodrites into a Christian and a pagan group, the careers of such Wendish chieftains as Gottschalk and Henry, are evidences of it. Above all, the change of dynasty in Germany in 1125 was a bad omen for the Baltic Slavs. The old Saxon tradition of conquest and expulsion of the Wends was now identified with the power of the German kingship. Moreover, Lothar was a zealous Christian, not of the calculating Salian kind, and warmly espoused the Saxon clergy's program of forcible conversion of the Wends.

The times were propitious for such achievement. History sometimes has a singular way of clustering men and events within a brief space of years—often, too, within a limited geographical area. Such was the case in North Germany at this time, where a remarkable combination of men and events is to be found. The rise of Conrad the Great of Wettin (1124–56), of Adolph of Holstein in 1130, of Albrecht the Bear in 1134, of Henry the Lion in 1139, was destined to revolutionize the history of Lower Germany. Moreover, by the side of these great lay princes lived and labored church-

[1] "Ritum sum persecutus paganorum .... multa atque innumerabilia destruximus idola" (Riedel, *Codex Diplom. Brand.* [1114], X, 69).

[2] *Annal. Sax.* (1115).

[3] Helmold fails us of this information, but the fact is attested by Ebbo, III, 5; cf. Wendt, I, 85, n. 14.

[4] Helmold, I, 38 end; *Anselmi Cont. Sigab.* (*anno* 1124) (SS. VI, 379).

men of a new and progressive type, such as Norbert of Magdeburg (1126–34), Vicelin of Oldenburg (d. 1154), and Otto of Bamberg,[1] the apostle to the Pomeranians (d. 1139).

Born in Swabia in 1060 and early left an orphan, Otto's first recognition came in 1087 when he became chaplain to Judith, the sister of Henry IV, who married Wladislaw, duke of Poland in that year. His early career in Poland made an ineffaceable impression upon Otto. After Judith's death he returned to Germany, was for some time administrator of a monastery in Regensburg, and then entered the service of Henry IV, who, perceiving his remarkable ability, intrusted him with the superintendence of the erection of the cathedral of Speyer. A few years later Otto entered the imperial chancellery. He refused appointment to the sees of Augsburg and Halberstadt, but finally in 1102 when Ruprecht of Bamberg died, Otto became bishop of Bamberg, where he remained until his decease in 1139.

His talent for administration found ample opportunity there, for the diocese had been badly neglected by his predecessors. He busied himself in restoration of the cathedral, in building new churches and convents, and founded a school at Bamberg which shortly became the intellectual center of Germany. It was he who appointed the famous historian Ekkehard of Aura to that abbey. He was not always loyal to Henry IV. In September, 1105, he advocated the cause of Prince Henry, afterward Henry V. He labored to reconcile Pope and Emperor, and was sent on an embassy to Pascal II in 1107. His loyalty to Henry V incurred the anathema of Gelasius II in 1118, and his restoration to his see was due to Calixtus II. During the reign of Lothar II we find Otto deeply interested in the issues of that reign, especially in the papal schism between Anacletus II and Innocent II.

It is, however, as apostle to the Pomeranians that Otto of Bamberg[2] is known to history. In 1122 or 1123 Boleslav III

---

[1] Bossert, *Württemb. Vierteljahrshefte für Landesgesch.*, Band VI, Heft 4 (1884).

[2] Until the appearance of Georg Jüritsch's masterly *Geschichte des Bischofs Otto I von Bamberg, des Pommern-Apostels* (1102-39) (Gotha: Perthes, 1889) there was no other adequate biography of this greatest missionary of the Latin church among the Slavs. The literature is large: Roepell, *Gesch. Polens*, I, 267–85; Zimmermann

of Poland urged the conversion of the Pomeranians upon him.[1]

Astonishing as it seems, at this time even some of the clergy appear for a brief moment to have been actuated by a new and softer spirit. The German church, in some degree reintegrated by the Cluniac reform, and given new ideals of practical humanitarianism and spiritual enterprise by the spread of French monastic foundations like the Cistercians, began to manifest a refreshing missionary zeal and partially to abandon its brutal desire for increase of tithes merely. Vicelin of Oldenburg and especially the saintly Otto of Bamberg represent a new type of bishop practicing gentle methods, learning the Slav tongue, and considerate of the customs and prejudices of the Wends.[2]

Let us first glance at the history of the conversion of Pomerania. Henry II had founded the bishopric of Bamberg in 1007 as a missionary station among the Wends of the upper Main and the Neckar, and something of the pious spirit of Henry and his empress, the gentle Cunigunde, seems to have affected the traditions of the see. A bishop endued with sincere religious zeal, who learned the Slav language and

---

Otto, Bischof von Bamberg (Freiburg, 1875); Looshorn, *Der heilige Bischof Otto* (Munich, 1888); Maskus, *Bischof Otto von Bamberg, Reichsfürst und Missionar* (Breslau, 1889); Giesebrecht, *Kaiserzeit* (5th ed.), III, 987 ff.; Sommerfeld, *Gesch. der Germanisierung des Herzogtums Pommern*, chap. i (in Schmoller's *Forschungen*, Band XIII [Fünftes Heft, 1896]); Hauck, *Kirchengesch.*, III, 564–87; Lehmann, *Pommern zur Zeit Ottos von Bamberg* (1880); Wehrmann, *Monatsbl. von d. Gesellschaft für Pom. Gesch.* (1887) (on the relations between Bamberg and Pomerania after Otto's death. The anniversary day of the old Bishop, October 1, is still widely observed in Pomerania (Wehrmann, *op. cit.*, p. 66). The Russian scholar Kotliarevsky has supplemented these sources by use of Russian hagiographic sources, which are particularly valuable for elucidating Slavonic racial practices and characteristics. A. Kotliarevsky, *Documents Concerning Otto of Bamberg Illustrative of the History and Archaeology of the Slavs; The Antiquities and History of the Maritime Slavs in the Twelfth Century* [Prague, 1874]). See review by A. Maury, *Journal des savants* (September and October, 1877).

[1] Jüritsch, *op. cit.* p. 252.

[2] Helmold's knowledge of the tongue must have been large, for his observations upon the words and the language are too intimate for it to have been otherwise (see I, 1, 12, 20, 25, 50, 52, 84, 88. In I, 84, he lauds the labors of a priest of Oldenburg in the twelfth century, named Bruno, who "sufficienter amministravit verbum Dei, habens sermones conscriptos Slavicis verbis, quos populo pronuntiaret oportune").

mingled with the hated race with the loving-kindness of a father among his children, is a novel and refreshing type of German ecclesiastic.[1]

The conversion of Pomerania by evangelization and not by the sword is Otto of Bamberg's title to fame. He literally created a new Baltic state in the first half of the twelfth century. Pomerania was nominally under the sway of Poland, and it was the initiative of Duke Boleslav III which first interested Otto in the project of converting the Pomeranians. "Durch sein Verdienst wurde die seit einem Jahrhundert unterbrochene Mission im Osten neubelebt und deutscher Sitte und Sprache die Bahn und Ostseeküsten gebrochen."[2]

In 1107 Duke Boleslaw III, the Wrymouthed (1102–39), had overcome and subjugated the heathen Slavic Pomeranians after the death of the Pomeranian chieftain Swantibor, who had left "Slavia" to his eldest son and Pommerellia to the two younger sons, Stettinberg being the capital of the former and Danzig of the latter. This new acquisition extended far across the Oder to the Baltic coast, including the city of Demmin on the Peene River, its southern boundary touching Dobrilugk in Lusatia.

The Pomeranians were a cognate Slavic people, but they were separated from Poland by a primeval forest, of which Herbord says:

. . . . A terrible, enormous forest divides Pomerania and Poland. This wood had not been traversed before by any mortal, except that the Duke of Poland in earlier years, before he had conquered the whole of Pomerania, had cut a way for himself and his army by felling and marking the trees.[3]

The inhabitants of Pomerania for a long time were able to resist the numerous attempts at their subjugation. Ancient traditions, however, assert that Pomoří (Pomerania) at one time formed an integral part of Poland, as witnessed by the

---

[1] See the comments of Lavisse, *La Marche de Brandenbourg*, p. 52; Guttmann, in *Forschungen zur Brand. und Preuss. Gesch.*, IX, 439–40.

[2] Richter, *Annalen*, II, 634 n. The text of Boleslav's charter to the first Christian establishment in Pomerania is in Herbordus, *Dialogus*, II, 20 (Jaffé, V, 775–76).

[3] II, 10.

fact that the capitals of Poland, Gnesen and Kruszwice, were placed so far north.[1]

Though attempts at Christianization had been carried on ever since Boleslaw Chrobry ruled the land and Kolberg was set up as the seat of the Pomeranian bishopric, the inhabitants either resisted the attempts or relapsed into heathenism. Boleslaw the Wrymouthed soon after his subjugation of Pomerania set a Spanish monk, Bishop Bernhard, to convert the people, but he soon had to give up his attempt, for he was laughed to scorn for his humble attire and his bare feet. From among the Polish clergy the Duke could not find a man who could undertake the difficult task, so at last he turned to Bishop Otto of Bamberg. He, having been a chaplain at the court of Boleslaw's father, knew the language, and was generally well adapted to the task. Otto was certainly animated by religious motives when he undertook this great work, for, as Schafarik says of him: "He was one of the most noble of the apostles of the Slavs";[2] but this does not preclude the possibility that even political motives entered into his considerations.[3] Otto was no visionary. He saw a possibility of an extension of his diocese, and the consequent increase of the income of his office, and this also entered into his calculations. Although over sixty years old, he could not refuse, in spite of the hardships he knew it would be necessary to endure. Twice he made the long and arduous journey to the far Baltic coast towns of Stettin and Wollin.

Pomerania then was a land of marsh and fen, of sluggish streams and stagnant lakes, inhabited by a pure Slav people who still lived after the primitive manner of their kind and were absolutely untouched by Christo-German civilization. A fisher-folk chiefly, wealth was estimated in lasts of dried fish and in hives of bees, for honey was a staple article of production. Their food was fish and rye and a few vegetables; they drank a mead of cherry and honey. Their textile skill was considerable, but they were poor farmers. The towns at the mouth of the Oder and the Peene had considerable com-

[1] Schafarik, II, 399.   [2] *Ibid.*, p. 404.

[3] Cf. Wehrmann, *Gesch. von Pommern*, p. 61.

merce in raw productions like dried fish, furs, tar, rope, etc., but were astonishingly squalid and miry.[1] The only structures of prominence were the temples.[2] Here, too, was a sacred black horse. Amid this population, which was spared the intolerance, the bigotry, and the greed which were so heavily inflicted upon the Slavs of the Elbe, Otto lived and labored, winning the confidence of the Pomeranians by gentle means.[3] Pomerania was the only Slavonic land under the domination of the Latin church in the Middle Ages which made the transition from paganism to Christianity and from barbarism to civilization by transformation and not by force.[4] Among the many canonized but unhallowed saints of the Roman church Otto of Bamberg justly deserved the halo with which Clement III crowned his memory in 1189.

Otto started out on his journey in 1124, being accompanied by two monks of Michelsberg, Ebo and Herbord, about twenty ecclesiastics of Bamberg, and a numerous retinue of servants. They passed through Bohemia, Silesia, and Poland, and were received with a great pomp by Boleslaw at Gnesen. There they were joined by an escort of Polish soldiers, and by three chaplains from the Polish court, one of whom, however, Adalbert, was a German. It is therefore interesting to note how thoroughly German this mission was. Then the whole company set out across the border forest, following the cleared path which the Duke had made on his warlike expedition. Otto and his company were received by the Pomeranian duke, Warcislaw, or, as Herbord calls him, Wratislaw, who was already a Christian. The Duke treated them kindly, but this may have been the result of his fear of the Polish soldiery which accompanied the Bishop. How Otto

[1] Sommerfeld, *op. cit.*, pp. 62–66.

[2] In Herbordus, II, 32, is a remarkable description of the temple at Stettin. It was adorned with carved wooden figures of men and beasts and birds, brilliantly painted and so true to nature "ut spirare putares ac vivere."

[3] See the anecdote in Herbordus, III, 19, of the boys playing in the street whom Otto spoke to in their own language, and who followed him.

[4] Otto sent the three-headed head of the idol Triglav to Pope Honorius II as a proof of the conversion of the Pomeranians (Kanzow, *Pomerania, oder Ursprunck, Altheit und Geschichte der Völker und Lande Pommern, Cassuben, Wenden, Stettin, Rügen* [ed. Kosegarten], p. 107).

was received by the populace we may judge from the following extract from Herbord:

> We have nothing in common with you. The laws which we inherited from our fathers we will not give up; we are content with the religion which we have. Among the Christians there are thieves and robbers, whose feet are cut off and eyes gouged out; the Christian practices all kinds of crime and punishments upon the Christian. Far from us be such a religion. . . . . Among them were no beggars, no locks and keys; they were highly surprised at the fastened chests of the bishops. Their table was always decked with food, and every stranger could enter and satisfy himself.[1]

However, Otto, in his gorgeous vestments and with his splendid retinue, partly intimidated and partly overawed, and, most assuredly, partly won his audiences. We learn that at the very first town, that of Pierzysk (Pyritz), he won a considerable number who submitted to baptism, although the number usually stated (3,585) people is not to be taken as accurate. Unlike the humbler Bernhard, Otto merely put the question before his hearers as to whether or not they wanted to be baptized. Those who then consented to be baptized were instructed in the Christian faith after baptism, and by priests left in the city for that purpose after the Bishop had left.[2]

In Kammin the missionaries found ready listeners, and built there a small wooden church. When they passed on to Wollin,[3] for the first time they met with opposition. This was a city where the heathen party was strong and active, although it would be a mistake to suppose that it was absolutely untouched by Christianity. One of the richest of the inhabitants, Nedamir by name, was a Christian, who had learned Christianity and had been baptized in Saxony.[4] After a prolonged struggle, the people of Wollin agreed that if the people of Stettin should accept the new faith they would then follow the example. But the people of Stettin, who were

[1] II, 10, 25, 40.

[2] Hauck, *Kirchengeschichte Deutschlands*, IV, 575.

[3] Wollin was the first bishopric established in Pomerania. In 1180, however, the see was removed to Kammin (Wiesener, *Ztschft. f. Kirchengesch.*, Band X, Heft 1 [1888]). The monastery of Stolp (founded in 1153) became an important center for evangelization (Schultz, *Baltische Studien*, Band, XXXI [1881]).

[4] Hauck, IV, 568.

strongly under the domination of the priests of the local
temple of Triglav, scornfully rejected the offer of the missionaries, and refused to be intimidated by the Polish soldiery under Count Paulicius into the acceptance of Christianity. At last the threat of the vengeance of Duke Boleslaw
induced them to promise to accept the new faith, but they
exacted the condition that a part of their heavy taxes be re-
mitted them. The Duke promised to do this, but accompanied his promise with a threat that if the people should fail
to live up to the conditions he would bring them to submission by force. Therefore, the people finally yielded and allowed their celebrated temple of Triglav to be destroyed.

Otto founded two churches at Stettin, and then returned
to Wollin; the people of that city faithfully kept their promise, and thus Otto was able to establish two churches at that
city also. In fact, Otto intended to make Wollin the center of
the Pomeranian episcopal diocese, and left Adalbert there
with the intention of procuring for him the episcopal dignity.
Then Otto pursued his way to Kolberg and Belgrad, and
after visiting these cities, returned through all the places
where he had planted Christian work, and returned home,
arriving at Bamberg at Easter, 1125.

Of course, this short ministry could not do much more
than open the land to the Christian missionary work, and
predispose it to tolerance of that religion. Still even at that,
much was accomplished. Hauck states that the number of
the baptized ran up to over twenty-two thousand people, and
that in nine places there were eleven mission churches established.[1] But what had been accomplished had been done by
reason of the fact that in spite of the constant threat of force
which was exerted by the soldiers accompanying Bishop
Otto, we do not read of any actual bloodshed or great cruelty
committed by these rough champions of Christianity. The
Pomeranians were won as far as they were won, because
Christianity came to them largely in a peaceful manner, although not entirely without coercion. Thus we can at least
partially understand why some Slavic nations—like the
Moravians, the Bohemians, to some extent the Poles, later

[1] *Ibid.*, IV, p. 578.

the Russians, etc.—accepted Christianity peaceably and retained it ever after, while other Slavic tribes opposed Christianity with furious and agelong struggles. The reason for the stubborn struggle of the Baltic and the Elbe Slavs is to be sought in the circumstance that Christianity came to them with fire and sword, and that its messengers sought to enslave and exploit these nations in such a shameful manner that this chapter of the history of the expansion of Christianity is one of the blackest.[1]

And yet heathen Pomerania could not give up its struggle quite so easily. Although Christianity came into the land more or less peaceably, still it represented the hated overlordship of Poland and the threatening might of Germany. Therefore, moved by the stirring appeals of the patriotic heathen priests, Pomerania—especially Wollin and Stettin—rose in reaction against Christianity and the accompanying foreign domination. After Otto's departure the pagan priests endeavored to arouse the people against the "German God" (*Teutonicus Deus*). The Christians resisted, not without peril to themselves, and Otto, in spite of his sixty-eight years, resolved to return to Pomerania in April, 1128. He selected Usedom as his headquarters, convoked an assembly of the nobles of the country, and was successful, with the aid of Wladislaw, in baptizing a great number, so much so that he dreamed of converting the island of Rügen.

Otto's second journey was not conducted under Polish auspices, but with the aid of Emperor Lothar, who now realized the political possibilities of the missionary work of the Bishop of Bamberg. The party, which besides the clerics, consisted of German knights and soldiers, and was accompanied with ample provision packs, went from Halle down the Saale River to the Elbe, and then up the Havel River. It is interesting to note that the practical Bishop bought a load of salt which he intended to sell in the land of the Slavs.[2]

On Pentecost, 1128, the party arrived at the city of

[1] Schafarik, II, 560.

[2] "So verband er mit dem religiösen Zwecke der Fahrt auch die Absicht, dem Lande, das bisher dem deutschen Handel und Verkehr noch wenig erschlossen war, wirtschaftliche Vorteile zu bringen und aus ihm zu gewinnen" (Wehrmann, *Geschichte von Pommern*, p. 69).

Uznoimia (Usedom), where the missionaries had a considerable success, which followed them to Wolgast also. Thence
Otto went on to Stettin and to Wollin, at both of which places
the reactionary element was subjugated and the Christian
work reinstated. In November, 1128, Otto left Pomerania
and returned via Gnesen to his home at Bamberg.

From the fact that Boleslaw the Wrymouthed selected
Otto for the difficult task of Christianizing Pomerania, and
from the general influence which Otto exercised over the
Polish Prince, it is not impossible to believe that Otto tried to
induce Boleslaw to put the Polish bishoprics again under the
jurisdiction of the Magdeburger metropolitan, as they were
before the year 1000. But Boleslaw was not the man to commit such a blunder, and it seems that even the papacy did
not favor this plan, because Poland paid the "Peter's pence"
regularly, while in Germany this was not a fully established
custom.[1]

Nordalbingia, too, at this same time had its Otto of Bamberg in the person of a devoted priest named Vicelin. But in
his case his gentle labors among the Wagrians were neutralized by the fierce violence of Henry the Lion and the bigotry
of St. Bernard. The work of Vicelin of Oldenburg among the
unconverted Abodrites and Wagri is closely interwoven with
this period of German trans-Elbean expansion. Helmold
writes:

> In these days there was neither church nor priest among all the people
> of the Wilzi, Abodrites and Wagri, except only in the city of [Alt-]Lübeck,
> because there the court of Henry [the duke of the Abodrites, who person-
> ally was Christian] was established (1126). And at this time there came a
> certain priest named Vicelin who came to the "king" of the Slavs in
> [Alt-]Lübeck and asked to be given the right to preach the word of God
> in his land.[2]

Vicelin was born in a little Saxon hamlet near Minden
and was educated in the episcopal school at Paderborn under
a then-distinguished master named Hartmann; thence he

[1] Grünehagen, *op. cit.*, p. 15.

[2] I, 41. For critical study of Vicelin's life see C. Schirren, *Beitraege zur Kritik
aelterer Holsteinischer Geschichtsquellen* (Leipzig, 1876) (originally in *Ztschft. der
Gesellschaft für Schleswig-Holstein-Lauenburg Gesch.*, VII, 281 f., and in the *Forschungen zur deutschen Gesch.*, Band XVII).

passed to the instruction of his uncle, a priest of Fuhlen, in the county of Schaumburg,[1] who seems to have had more than local fame as a scholar. When his uncle died Vicelin went back to Paderborn and afterward to the episcopal school in Bremen. Here his winning personality and high moral qualities exercised a great influence over his clerical pupils, who were accustomed, like boys in a boarding-school, to get "out of bounds" and roam the streets at night, or find unlawful pleasure in frequenting taverns. His efficiency drew the praise of his superior, Bishop Frethericus, who, however, expressed misgivings of the disciplinary value of moral suasion when compared with the time-honored school-master's rod. But Vicelin could not be persuaded to use the whip upon his pupils, saying that many a good student was ruined by cruelty.[2] In the year 1122–23 Vicelin went to France, then the educational center of Europe, and pursued his studies at Laon under the famous masters, the brothers Anselm and Raoul,[3] "qui in explanacione divinae paginae fuerant eo tempore precipui."

But Vicelin had no taste for the "empty subtleties and mere battles of words"[4] which characterized scholastic education at this time. He pined for some more practical interest. In 1126 he returned to Germany and sought out Norbert, the famous Praemonstratensian archbishop of Magdeburg, who in Brandenburg had begun to imitate the enlightened policy which Otto of Bamberg was so successfully employing in the conversion of the Pomeranians. Although Vicelin did not become a Praemonstratensian,[5] he imbibed the generous missionary enthusiasm of the Norbertines. It was from Nor-

---

[1] See von Mooyer, *Die vormalige Grafschaft Schaumburg*, p. 25.

[2] This paragraph is derived from Helmold, I, 44.

[3] See G. Le Fevre, *De Anselmo Laudunensi scholastico* (Evreux, 1895).

[4] "Quaestiones supervacuas pugnasque verborum."

[5] See Hirsekorn, *Die Slavenchronik Helmolds* (Göttingen, 1873), p. 42. Helmold (I, 47) gives the form of their agreement together: "Hii ergo sacris connexi federibus statuerunt amplecti celibatum vitae, perdurare in oratione et jejunio, exerceri in opera pietatis, visitare infirmos, alere egentes, tam propriam quam proximorum salutem curare." One MS bears the marginal comment that Vicelin was probably an Augustine. But this form does not appear in the rules of that order.

bert himself that Vicelin first learned of Duke Henry, the Christian Abodrite prince, and speedily conceived the idea that the conversion of Wagria was his appointed task. "At once he took the road into the land of the Slavs" with two companions, Rodolph, a presbyter of Hildesheim, and Ludolf, a canon of Verdun.[1]

The Abodrite ruler received them graciously and they joyfully returned to Saxony in order to bring back the vessels and garments and other apparatus of church worship. The new gospel station was established at Neumünster on the boundary line between German Holstein and Slavonic Wagria.[2] It was a rough and uncouth frontier community in which Vicelin undertook to minister, predominantly Wendish, but with a considerable sprinkling of a hardy, lawless pioneer element—Helmold says it was a *gens bruta*. One is reminded of the frontier missionary labors of Peter Cartwright in America, for even in religion, as in many other aspects of the frontier, the medieval German border reminds one of our own West in pioneer times. A wave of crude revivalism stirred these rude border folk which impressed Helmold with its intensity.[3]

But Vicelin's hopes were soon dashed. Duke Henry died shortly after the mission was established; his sons quarreled until both were killed, and the land was rent with dissension, in the midst of which a band of pirates from Rügen descended upon the country. Border ruffianism prevailed. Peace and order were not restored until the rise of those two strong men of lower Saxony, Adolph of Holstein and Henry the Lion.[4]

[1] These were later joined in their labors by four others, "of whom," says Helmold (I, 47, quoting I Cor. 15:6), "the greater part are fallen asleep" (cf. I, 54). Did Helmold derive his account from actual comrades of Vicelin?

[2] Helmold, I, 47.

[3] "Denique incredibili dictu est, quanta plebium caterva in diebus illis ad penetentiae remedium confugerit, insonuitque vox predicacionis ejus in omni Nordalbingorum provincia"(I, 47). ". . . . Jactumque est misercordia Dei . . . . seminarium novellae plantacionis in Slavia" (I, 54).

[4] This account of Vicelin's early life has been drawn from Helmold, I, 42-49. For literature see A. Boehmer, *Vicelin* (Rostock, 1887); Höhlbaum, "Vicelin und seine Biographen," *Forschungen zur deutschen Gesch.*, XVII, 209-29; Schirren, "Über Vicelins Priesterweihe," *ibid.*, pp. 376-89; Bernhardi, *Lothar II*; cf. Dáhlmann-Waitz, *Quellenkunde der deutschen Gesch.* (last ed., 1912), No. 5477.

Yet in spite of these adverse conditions Vicelin's labors managed to prosper, and a half-dozen wilderness missionary stations were founded.[1] But there were few Germans living across the lower Elbe[2] at this time, except in Holstein[3] where some scattered Burgwärde gave greater security.[4] The private chapel of the Abodrite Duke in Alt-Lübeck was the only Christian edifice in the land before Vicelin's coming.[5] The best element in the country was a considerable colony of German merchants[6] settled in the Abodrite capital. But the new Abodrite Duke Pribislav[7] had apprehensions of the political effect upon his people which might arise from the establishment of a church in the capital of the Abodrites[8] and refused permission. Accordingly, the first public church in Alt-Lübeck was set up across the Trave River on a hill outside the city.[9] The precaution was wisely taken, for the irritation of the Abodrites daily increased because of the steady

[1] Helmold, I, 53, says: "sex vel eo amplius oppida." In I, 58, he describes them as "incommoda fori—forensis ecclesia." The names are recorded in some verses commemorative of Vicelin printed in the Appendix to Schmeidler's edition of Helmold, p. 229, vss. 125 ff. They also are mentioned in a diploma of Lothar II, March 17, 1137, and another of Conrad III, dated January 5, 1139 (Boehmer-Mühlbacher, *Regesta*, Nos. 3348, 3384). But there is some doubt of the trustworthiness of the documents. Cf. Bernhardi, *op. cit.*, p. 800, n. 27; Bahr, *Nordalbing. Studien*, pp. 37 ff.; Schultze, *Die Urkunden Lothars II* (Innsbruck, 1905), pp. 129 ff.

[2] This is established from the testimony of Helmold, I, 8, 48, and 56, though he contradicts himself in I, 24, where he falls into error by following Adam of Bremen. See edition of Helmold by Schmeidler, p. 96, n. 1. It is confirmed by the *Ann. Pegav.* (*anno* 1115). "Ultra Albiam illis temporibus rarus inveniebatur Christianus" (*MGH*, SS. XVI, 252).

[3] Helmold, I, 41. "Sed et Slavorum populi agebant ea quae pacis sunt, eo quod Heinricus Slavorum regulus [observe that he is not called *dux*] comitem Adolfum et contiguos Nordalbingorum populos omni benivolentia amplexatus fuerit."

[4] *Ibid.*, I, 34, 56.

[5] *Ibid.*, I, 34, 41.

[6] *Ibid.*, I, 48: "a mercatoribus quorum non parvam coloniam."

[7] Nine coins of Pribislav have been preserved, which perhaps are testimony of the commercial relations between the Germans and the Elbean Slavs. They were found in 1880 at Michendorf near Potsdam (Eckstein, *Mitth. d. Ver. f. Vaterländische Kultur* [1881–82]).

[8] "Protestatus est omnem Slavorum gentem divinae religioni subjugere" (Helmold, I, 53).

[9] *Ibid.*, I, 48; cf. Ohnesorge, *op. cit.*, p. 69.

encroachment of German settlers into their territory, and the feeling was all the more aggravated by the intolerant preaching which Vicelin could not control and the popular hatred with which the religion of the Slavs was regarded by the German incomers, which found vent in attacks upon their sacred groves and their temples.[1]

The Abodrites and Wagri were dangerously aroused and on the verge of open war to protect their liberty. The pagan population still cherished the memory of the pagan hero Kruto, and was sullenly hostile to their ruler and his and their German Christian neighbors on the edge of the country. They were intensely suspicious—and with good reason—of Adolph of Holstein and the Emperor, who seems to have been resolved upon a policy toward the Abodrites of complete subjugation and compulsory conversion. To that end Lothar II energetically began the building of castles in Wagria, in particular that of Sigberg, and summoned the Saxons dwelling along the border to help in the undertaking. The Abodrites grew furious. To make matters worse Cnut of Denmark seized the opportunity to strengthen and extend Danish sway upon the mainland and invaded Wagria, an incursion in which the Holsteiners who hated the Abodrites and Wagri, co-operated with him. In the excess of his pride Cnut even dragged Pribislav and Niklot (next to the Abodrite duke the greatest lord in Wagria) off into captivity in Schleswig, loaded with chains.[2]

On the German mainland, by 1136, the religion and the independence of the Wends—the latter not complete, for they were subject to Saxon tribute—were confined to the ancient territory of the Abodrites and the Wagri, Old Saxon Nordalbingia (modern Mecklenburg), and Brandenburg.

Unfortunately the moderation of such men as Otto of Bamberg, Norbert of Magdeburg, and Vicelin of Oldenburg was out of temper with the spirit of the twelfth century. It was the age of the Crusades—that great manifestation of medieval bigotry. In 1144 Edessa had been captured by the Moham-

---

[1] "Lucos et omnes ritus sacrilegos destruens" (Helmold, I, 47; cf. I, 52, which is a dissertation on the religion of the Slavs).

[2] Helmold, I, 49.

medans and Jerusalem was in peril. Europe was fired to a new Crusade. St. Bernard of Clairvaux was the archpreacher of the new expedition. Having prevailed upon Louis VII of France to take the cross at Vézelay, Bernard came to Germany, and on December 27, 1146, Conrad III of Germany also espoused it. But the Saxons held aloof from the movement. The fanatical saint sharply reproached the Saxons for their negligence in not having more earnestly propagated the gospel among their neighbors.[1] He upbraided them for ever having compromised with paganism and permitted the Wends to preserve their religion upon condition of paying tribute, condemning Saxon avarice in hard and heated terms.[2] To the exhortations of Bernard, Henry the Lion and other nobles of the north replied that it was senseless for them to expend blood and treasure beyond sea when the pagan Wends were on the border of Germany. The saint yielded the point and released them from service in the east on condition that they forcibly converted the Wends.

So was engendered the Wendish Crusade of 1147, the effect of which was to break the power of the Baltic Slavs and annex their territory to the German kingdom. It was a sinister mixture of bigotry and lust for land. "They agreed to this: either utterly to destroy the pagan race of the Slavs, or to compel them to become Christian," runs a chronicle of the time.[3] While Conrad III went off to the east, Henry the Lion, Conrad of Wettin, Adalbert of Salzwedel, the archbishops of Magdeburg and Bremen, organized a "home crusade" against the Abodrites and the Wagri. The Abodrite Duke was not without warning of the coming storm, and hastily began to erect a *castrum* at Dubin on the isthmus[4] between Lake Schwerin and a lesser lake, for the protection of his people. At the same time he sent messengers to Adolph of Holstein, asking his protection and reminding him of their

[1] Heinemann, *Albrecht der Bär*, pp. 162, 369–70.

[2] See the collection of references illustrating the complaint of the church on this head in Lavisse, *La marche de Brandenbourg*, p. 68, n. 1.

[3] "Conserserunt in hoc ut viciniam sibi Slavorum gentem paganam aut omnino delerent aut Christianos fieri cogerent" (*MGH*, SS. VIII, 392).

[4] Schmeidler, *Neues Archiv*, XXXIV, No. 3.

friendship. But the Count dared not make so overt a move, whatever his sympathy, for fear of offending the Saxon princes.

Adolph of Holstein had vainly hoped that he might avert the Crusade. He is the first German noble who manifested an intelligent, clear appreciation of the nature and the magnitude of the huge Slavonic problem to the expanding German nation. He could speak the Slav language fluently, and he understood the Slav character.[1] Certain of the impending crusade, Niklot resolved to anticipate the attack as far as possible, and secretly prepared a fleet at the mouth of the Trave in order to strike the province of Wagria before the Saxon forces had crossed his frontier. True to his word, he sought to apprise Adolph of his preparations, but the Count was not at Sigeberg where the messenger endeavored to find him. At dawn on June 26, 1147, the day of the passion of John and Paul, the fleet pushed up the river. Lübeck was in a panic. The merchant ships along the water front were burned. More than three hundred of the citizens were slain. Two squadrons of Niklot's horsemen ravaged the country roundabout. The Westphalian and Dutch colonies on the lower course of the Trave were fired and plundered. Adolph's own Holsteiner settlers alone were spared.[2] But the blow was a serious one to Adolph's colonization schemes, for many of the survivors returned to Flanders.[3]

Meanwhile, the news spread through all Saxony and Westphalia of the rising of the Slavs, and hastened the crusade. By August, 1147, two armies were on foot against them: one under Henry the Lion advanced upon Dubin and was accompanied by the Archbishop of Bremen and a host

[1] Helm., I, 49.

[2] *Ibid.*, I, 63. The Slavs did not molest in person or goods the settlers around Bornhöved and between the Schwale and the Plöner-See. It is not certain that the Abodrites were the ones who fired the farmsteads of the Flemish and Dutch settlers in the region. The hatred of the German settlers, particularly the Holsteiners, for these incomers (*odium advenarum* [*loc. cit.*]) was intense and honest. Helmold records that the belief was current that they, and not the Slavs, were responsible for this destruction.

[3] *Ibid.*, I, 64. The whole chapter is interesting for the evidence it affords of the hatred of the Germans for foreigners. "Nulla gens detestabilior Fresis."

of Saxon nobles; the other massed at Magdeburg under the margraves of Meissen and the Nordmark, Albrecht the Bear of Brandenburg and Conrad of Wettin. With it were the bishops of Havelberg and Brandenburg and the Archbishop of Magdeburg.

Niklot's two strongholds, Dubin and Dimin, which he erected to hold the road between Magdeburg and Hamburg,[1] were besieged, a Danish army lending aid to the attack upon the former, though the Germans looked with scant appreciation upon the unsolicited assistance.[2] They were too suspicious of Denmark's ambition to acquire a foothold on the mainland. "The Danes are warlike at home, but not fond of fighting when abroad," said the Germans scornfully.[3] The land was swampy, and the besiegers could not bring their engines of war up to the walls. Dissension broke out in the army. The lesser fighting men complained that the great nobles and the high clergy wanted to deprive them of their just share of the conquered land. "Is not the land which we have devastated our land?" they said. The Slavs fell back into the marshes and could not be captured. But their towns and villages were given to the flames and the land so reduced to desolation that in the next year a terrible famine came.[4] In the end Pribislav and Niklot succumbed. Their people accepted the Christian faith and were baptized at the edge of the sword. Niklot's despondent words to Henry the Lion need no comment: "Let the God who is in heaven be our god and it will suffice. You may worship your God. We will worship you."[5]

[1] Von Boenigk, *Baltische Studien*, Band XXXIII (1883).

[2] Not until after the Danish defeat at Bornhöved in 1227 was Denmark's claim to the Baltic strand extinguished.

[3] Helm., I, 65; cf. I, 51 and 84, for similar judgments.

[4] On this Crusade see Wendt, II, 20; Hauck, IV, 563 ff., 594–608; All the chroniclers and modern historians have noticed it. The point of view of a Christian Slav is given by Vincent, *Prag. Ann.* (*MGH*, SS. XVII, 663).

[5] Helmold, I, 84. The Abodrites agreed to recognize the Christian religion, to pay a yearly tribute to Henry of Saxony, and to release the captives which they had taken. But of the Slavs who had been taken only the old and the "useless" were released. The younger and more robust were reduced to servitude upon the manors of the church and the nobles (Helm., I, 65).

Adolph of Holstein patched up a peace with Niklot, though there must have been heartburning on each side, and began the heavy task of reconstruction of his wasted province, bravely telling his people that some adversity was unavoidable and that border folk must be strong and not afraid of bloodshed. "He did justice unto his people, suppressing turmoils and liberating the oppressed from the hand of the feudality [*potentiorum*]," says Helmold.[1] With splendid honor he ransomed many captives of his people.[2] But his hopes of establishing a *modus vivendi* between the two races were ruined by the crusade. The nascent civilization of the Wends was nearly destroyed. Border strife and predatory thieving by the Wends became a chronic evil.[3] Adolph's policy of firmness and tact, which deserved to succeed, was ruined by his rival in North Germany, Henry the Lion, whose Slavonic policy was the drastic Roman practice— *divide et impera*—and whose avarice was notorious.[4]

Henry and his Saxon vassals were greater gainers from this crusade than the church. The Saxon Duke collected tribute from the conquered Abodrites, divided the conquered lands among his vassals, and left the church in the lurch. As long as Niklot punctually paid the tribute (which he acquired by pirate raids upon the Danish islands)[5] Henry was indifferent to the church's welfare in the Slav land, and even pretended to be Niklot's friend. He used the situation to his own advantage. The "conversion" of the Abodrites had accentuated the difference between them and the other pagan Wendish tribes, and two of these, the Kycini and the Circipani (stems of the Wilzi), rebelled against Niklot, refusing either to become Christian or to contribute to the tribute exacted by the Saxon Duke. The result was that in 1151 a joint expedition was made by Henry the Lion and Niklot and Adolph of Holstein against them. The celebrated fane at Goderak was destroyed and an immense amount of booty

[1] I, 67.   [2] *Ibid.*, I, 66.

[3] "Nam latrocinia Slavorum eo tempore solito plus invaluerunt" (*ibid.*, I, 67).

[4] "In variis autem expedicionibus, quas adhuc adolescens in Slaviam profectus exercuit, nulla de Christianitate fuit mentio, sed tantum de pecunia" (*ibid.*, I, 68).

[5] *Ann. Colbaz* (*MGH*, SS. XIX, 715).

in gold and silver taken from the coffers of the Wendish priests.[1]

In the midst of these waves of war Vicelin had labored with a heavy heart. The destruction of its edifices and farms threw a great burden on the church for the care of the destitute. He was joined at this time by one of his former pupils in Bremen who also had studied in France and who now came to Neumünster.[2] Together Vicelin and his companions worked for the feeding of the hungry, for actual famine prevailed.[3] The door of opportunity was opened to the church to extend its power in Nordalbingia and Wagria as never before. For all the area which had once been Christianized and had been lost in 1066 in the great Slav rebellion under Kruto eighty-four years before[4] lay open again. The restoration of the destroyed sees of Oldenburg, Ratzeburg, and Mecklenburg was now possible. In this work Hartwig I, archbishop of Hamburg-Bremen, who strongly reminds one of Adalbert of Bremen, was a prominent figure.[5] In 1149 he consecrated Vicelin as bishop of the revived see of Oldenburg, where he continued to labor until his death in 1154. Already he had been over twenty-two years in Holstein.[6] In the same year Mecklenburg was filled and Ratzeburg was restored in 1152.[7] The establishment of rural churches was also rapidly pushed, as at Bornhöved and Högersdolf (near Sigeberg, called in the Slav tongue Cuzalina). These sanctuaries were all built of wood cut in the nearby forests by the peasantry.

The natives were quiet but sullen, especially around Oldenburg, where a local Slav cult of the god Prove obtained, whose priest (*flamen*) was a descendant of the pagan chieftain

---

[1] Helmold, I, 71. This temple could not have been the *fanum celeberrimum* at Rethra, though that is often said; for Rethra was south of the Peene in the country of the Redarii and was destroyed by Lothar II in the expedition of 1124–25. See Wendt, *Germanisierung*, etc., II, 47, and cf. Arnold of Lübeck, *Chron. Slav.*, V, 24.

[2] Helmold, I, 58.   [3] *Ibid.*, I, 66.   [4] *Ibid.*, I, 24, 69.

[5] Dehio, "Hartwich von Stade, Erzbischof von Hamburg-Bremen," *Bremisches Jahrbuch* (Göttingen, 1872), VI, 35–154, and separately.

[6] Jaffé, *Lothar*, p. 233.

[7] Dehio, p. 147; Hauck, IV, 618, n. 1, disagrees. Cf. *Neues Archiv*, XXXII, 514, n. 19.

Kruto and was "an idolator and a great pirate."[1] Timidly
civilization and Christianity crept into the land, for a new
native outbreak was always feared, for which reason castles
were again built as before.[2]

Under these strained conditions the public, voluntary
espousal of the Christian faith by Pribislav must have come
as relief. It was in the dead of winter, in January, 1156, that
the summons came to Oldenburg that a priest be sent to him
to explain the sacred mysteries. Helmold apparently was one
of the little company of priests appointed to accompany the
Bishop. After wading through snowdrifts (*inter cumulos
nivi*), they came to an abandoned castle where was a little
ruined chapel which Vicelin had once built. There they met
Pribislav. Helmold, in telling of this adventure, says:

> After having expounded the sacred mysteries, Pribislav asked that we
> would go with him to his own dwelling-place which was a castle farther off.
> He received us with much readiness and made things very pleasant for us.
> A table was set which they heaped with twenty kinds of food. There I
> learned by actual experience what I had heard before in popular talk that
> there is no people decenter in the graces of hospitality than the Wends.[3]

Having remained with Pribislav for two days and nights,
the little band of cross-bearers went on into Farther Slavonia
(*in ulteriorem Slaviam*) in response to another summons from
a lesser Wendish chief named Thessemar, who lived near Lake
Schwerin. Let Helmold again tell the tale:

> We came to a wood which is the only one in that region, for the whole
> land stretches away in a plain. There among trees hoary with age we saw
> the sacred oaks which are dedicated to the local god who is named Prove,
> enclosed in a court having two entrances, and constructed like a palisade
> of logs. Besides being sacred to the "penates" and the idols which each
> [Slavonic] town has, this place was the sanctuary of their whole country to
> the god, to which a "flamen" and sacramental and sacrificial rites are ap-
> pointed. There every fortnight the people of the land with a judge and
> a priest are accustomed to convene for justice. It is forbidden unto all to
> enter this court save only the priest and those wishing to offer sacrifice,

[1] Helmold, I, 69.

[2] "Jam enim circumjacentia oppida incolebantur paulatim a Christicolis, sed
cum grandi pavore propter insidias latronum" (*ibid.*, I, 75). Eight years after the
Wendish Crusade, the region of the Plöner-See was still a desert (*ibid.*, I, 83).

[3] Helmold, I, 83. Cf. this judgment with I, 1, and II, 12 (*ad fin.*); also with
Adam of Bremen, II, 19.

or those in peril of death, for the right of asylum is not denied. The Slavs display so much reverence for their gods that they do not allow even the blood of their enemies to pollute the approach to the temple. . . . . There is a great variety of idolatry among the Slavs, for all do not follow the same superstitions. Some of their gods are represented in the form of idols in temples, as the idol at Plönen, which is named Podaga; others dwell in groves or forests, like Prove, the god at Oldenburg, who has no idol-form. Many have two or three or even more heads. Among the great variety of divinities who preside over fields and forests they do not recognize a single ruling deity above the rest. . . . .

The bishop had strongly enjoined upon us that we should insist upon the destruction of this sacred grove. The bishop himself leaping down from his horse with his staff struck down the emblems at the gates of the temple, and then, having entered the atrium, we piled wood around the sacred trees and fired a huge pyre—not without fear, however, lest we would be stoned by the crowd. But heaven protected us. After these things we were hospitably entertained at a sumptuous banquet by Thessemar. But the liquors of the Slavs were not sweet and pleasant to us.[1]

A long colloquy followed between Pribislav and the Bishop, at the termination of which the Wend chief said:

If it please the lord duke and you that we have the same worship, let our rights be recognized in the manors and the revenues of the Saxons, and then we shall willingly be Christians. We will build churches and we will pay our share of the tithes.

Pribislav had laid his finger on the sorest and the traditional grievance of the Slavs in their long resistance to Christianity—the land-grabbing of the church and its merciless imposition of the tithe.[2] Only in their consent to use the Slavonic tongue in preaching does the Saxon clergy seem to have advanced beyond the time of Thietmar of Merseburg.[3] They were the same hard, ambitious, avaricious priests as before. In the reconquered dioceses, after the crusade of 1147, the surveyors of the church had set busily to work with

[1] Helmold, I, 84.

[2] "Principes enim vestri," said Pribislav, "tanta severitate grassantur in nos, ut propter vectigalia et servitutem durissimam melior sit nobis mors quam vita . . . . cotidie emungimur et premimur usque ad exinanicionem. Quomodo ergo vocabimus huic religioni novae, ut edificemus ecclesias et percipiamus baptisma, quibus cotidiana indicitur fuga? Si tamen locus esset, quo diffugere possemus. Transeuntibus enim Travenam, ecce similis calamitas illic est, venientibus ad Penem fluvium nichilominus adest. Quid igitur restat, quam ut obmissis terris feramur in mare et habitemus cum gurgitibus?" (Helmold, I, 84, p. 161.)

[3] "Habens sermones conscriptos Slavicis verbis" (ibid.).

their measuring ropes to retrace the lines of the former ecclesiastical manors and to mark out new ones. The labor was
long and tedious and hard, so much so that it was not completed for years. But as the church practiced surveying, the
result was lucrative to it; for swamps and even forest land
were not included within the measurement, but were "thrown
in," to be cleared and drained afterward, so that the aggregate land acquisitions of the church were very great—"fecit
maximum agrorum numerum," says honest Helmold.[1]

Fortunately for Brandenburg, the storm of the Wendish
Crusade had not driven over it. The raid of Hartbert, the
bishop of Brandenburg, in 1114 to recover his see *in partibus
paganorum*, though unsuccessful in its main purpose, seems
to have been followed by a slight restoration of Christianity,
however, in the region.[2] Henceforward, although the great
Slavonic gods Gerovit and Triglav were worshiped at Havelberg and Brandenburg, there was, nevertheless, a handful of
Christian Wends in the Brandenburg territory, notably a
Wendish chief with the German name Widukind, whose seat
was in Havelberg, and another named Pribislav (not to be
confused with the Abodrite Pribislav), who dwelt at Brandenburg, whose policies were pro-German and pro-Christian.
Since the conversion of the Poles the Wends of the Havel and
the Spree were fiercely menaced by them, and between the
two alternatives preferred German domination. It was for
this purpose that Widukind had sought the Emperor at
Merseburg in 1128. The half-French archbishop of Magdeburg at this time, Norbert, a man who expressed the new
spirit of the church, as we have seen, seized the opportunity
to extend the church into Brandenburg. A church was built
in Havelberg, and for a few years the protection of Widukind
gave it a precarious security. But the natives were sullenly
hostile to the policy of their chief, for they feared with good
reason the extension of the church's system of taxation over
them again. Accordingly, when Widukind died, in 1136,
pagan resentment broke out and destroyed the church. The

[1] Helmold, *ibid.* Cf. I, 69, 71, 77.

[2] *Annal. Pegav.* (*MGH*, SS. XVI, 252).

permanent re-establishment of Christianity in Brandenburg was not made until Albrecht the Bear got control of Brandenburg.[1]

Albrecht the Bear in an age of religious bigotry was not a bigot. In an age when German hatred of the Wends was rancorous, he was friendly to them. His policy was a rare combination of firmness and tact. He fended off the Wendish Crusade from his country and largely was content to let time work out the solution of things. He was justified of his enlightened resolution. In 1136 when Widukind died and his sons headed a pagan reaction, the new Margrave acted promptly, and by 1144 Anselm of Havelberg returned to the long-abandoned bishopric.[2]

Most of the Wendish population in Brandenburg accepted the *fait accompli*, both in its political and its religious bearing, without opposition. They acknowledged the faith and the authority of the German church and even began to live German law.[3] But vestiges of Slavonic paganism persisted for many years around Spandau in the heart of the marshes of the Havel and in the Spreewald.[4]

Albrecht kept a restraining hand upon the church in his dominions, and would not let the Wends be taxed with a heavier tithe than German subjects.[5] He was neither a bigot nor an iconoclast. While every other Slav temple had been ruthlessly destroyed, to the regret of the student of history as well as of comparative religion, in Brandenburg Albrecht spared the temple of Triglav. It was converted into a Christian church consecrated to the Virgin, and lasted until

[1] Wendt, I, 83; Ebbo, *Vita Ottonis ep. Babenb.*, III, 3; *Annal. Magdeb.* (*MGH*, SS. XVI, 186); *Annal. Hild.* (*ibid.*, SS. III, 116).

[2] Riedel, *Codex diplom. Brand.*, I, 15, p. 6; Sommerfeld, p. 132. Cf. Helmold, I, 88.

[3] Riedel, II, 2–39; Wohlbrück, *Gesch. des Bistums Lebus*, I, 323 ff. Albrecht's successors unfortunately abandoned this policy of toleration and the Wends were wantonly hunted down and out (Hauck, IV, 558 and n. 3; p. 609 and nn. 1 and 2).

[4] See the long and interesting note in Wendt, II, 21.

[5] "Si Slavi vel in foro vel quacumque commutatione sibi contraxerint aliquos mansos Teutonicorum ejusdem villae, eandem decimam sine contradictione persolvent, quam Teutonicus inde persolvit" (*Urk. des Kl. S. Marien in Erfurt*, quoted by Guttmann, p. 448; cf. Tuttle, *History of Prussia*, I, 26).

Frederick the Great, with unforgivable vandalism, pulled it down in order to use the stones for the erection of his palace at Potsdam. The marvel is that this Wendish sanctuary had been built of stone in a country so devoid of stone that even today brick is the almost universal building material. The first building of modern Berlin made of stone and not of brick was the Bourse, erected in 1859. Think of the devoted labor which must have been expended by this simple people in building a massive stone temple in such an early period, and under such adverse physical conditions; for every block of stone must have been freighted from the mountains of Bohemia, down the Elbe, and up the Havel!

By the middle of the twelfth century only a single islet of independent Slavdom west of the Oder River yet survived. This was the pirate state of Rügen, in its island fortress. Protected by its difficult location, environed by rough and stormy waters,[1] and defended by the bold and fanatical priests of the great temple of Arkona, Rügen held out until 1168.[2] In that year Waldemar of Denmark, who cherished ambitions for the expansion of Danish power along the Baltic coast which were destined to be a source of danger to future Germany,[3] and who also hated the Rugians because of their piratical forays upon the Danish coast and in the Danish islands, organized a formidable expedition against them. Even Christian Slavs participated in it, notably Kazamir and Buggeslav, two Pomeranian princes, and Pribislav

---

[1] See the description of the great storm of February, 1164, in Helmold, II, 1.

[2] "Sola Rugianorum gens durior ceteris in tenebris infidelitatis usque ad nostra tempora perduravit, omnibus inaccessibilis propter maris circumjacentia" (*ibid.*, I, 12). For a graphic account of this sanctuary, which gathered tribute from all Slavonia see Saxo Grammaticus (ed. O. Elton), pp. 393–95.

[3] Cf. Sommerfeld, chap. v. Although the island of Fehmern is said to have been chiefly settled from Ditmarsch around the middle of the fifteenth century, it is much more probable that this island (which was still purely Slav in the twelfth century) before it fell to Denmark was colonized by Holsteiners from conquered Wagria (Waitz, *Schleswig-Holst. Gesch.*, I, 345; Mannhardt, *Der Baumkultus*, pp. 190–91), and the so-called "Lowlanders," partly from Westphalia, partly from Frisia and Holland who in the twelfth and thirteenth centuries flocked into the lands formerly occupied by the Slavs in order to find new homes there (Helmold, I, 57; Waitz, I, 56). In 1242 we find mention of a *platea Flamingorum* (*Schleswig-Holst., Lauenb. Jahrb.*, IX [1866], 12).

the Abodrite—the last reluctantly, "because the duke [of the Saxons] commanded him."[1] Arkona was captured, the famous temple of the god Svantovit destroyed, the statue of the god dragged through the midst of his subjugated votaries and chopped to pieces and burned, the population scattered or else sold into slavery. Twelve churches were established in Rügen in honor of the extinguishment of the last stronghold of Slavonic paganism in Germany.[2] The last vestiges of the religion of the Baltic Slavs in Rügen were stamped out. The temples and sacred groves were destroyed. The native cult ceased to be a national expression. Where it survived at all, it was furtively practiced around some ancient oak, or by a spring or holy stone,[3] and so degenerated to folk-lore and popular superstition, snatches of which still persist among the peasantry, having lost their heathen label.[4]

There is always a certain melancholy attending the death of the gods, and one feels the pathos and romance of this *Götterdämmerung* as he feels the tragedy in the ancient cry, "Pan is dead," or the fall of Wodan. As with the Druids, as it was in Rome in the fourth century, as it was with the Aztec religion in Mexico, when the body of the votaries had become cowed by force, or grown lax and indifferent to the national religion owing to the attrition or the attraction of a new faith, so it was with the religion of the Baltic Slavs. The priests of the high temples at Rethra and Arkona made the final and futile struggle to preserve the tribal faith.

It is a pity that the Slavic side of this story has been lost. It was of the nature of medieval Christianity to be bigoted

[1] Helmold, II, 12.

[2] *Ibid.*, II, 12–13; Wendt, II, 57–60. Schafarik, II, 537–40; Beyersdorf, *Baltische Studien*, Band XXXIII (1883); Leger, "Svantovit et St. Vitus," *Revue d'histoire des religions*, XLI, No. 3 (1900); Jacob, *Baltische Studien*, Band XLIV (1894). The Slav tongue ceased to be understood in Rügen after the sixteenth century. The half-German, half-Wendish law of the island was compiled at that time by a Rugian noble (Frommhold, *Ztschft. der Savigny-Stiftung, für Rechtsgesch.*, Band XVI, Heft 1 [1895], *Germanische Abteilung*).

[3] "Et inhibiti sunt . . . . jurare in arboribus, fontibus et lapidibus."—Helmold, I, 84. Cf. Mannhardt, *Der Baumkultus*, 31 and 57.

[4] Albertus Magnus was sent into Pomerania in the thirteenth century to suppress these vestiges (Ozanam, *Les Germains*, p. 287).

and intolerant; the church in its mistaken zeal destroyed every vestige of the conquered faith. We know this sad history only from the German enemies of the Baltic Slavs. But if one reads the record between the lines and with sympathetic eyes, it is apparent that there surely was another side. One cannot refuse the meed of honor to those pagan priests of the Wends who were loyal with a desperate fidelity to their historic religion. What Sir Gilbert Murray has said of the dying paganism of the fourth century is applicable here: "Like other conquerors these conquerors were often treacherous and brutal; like other vanquished these vanquished have been tried at the bar of history without benefit of counsel. .... Only an ignorant man will pronounce a violent or bitter judgment."[1]

[1] *Four Stages of Greek Religion*, p. 180.

Spread of German Settlements to the Eastward, 800—1400.

Scale 1:10000000

Miles

Spread of German Settlement to the Eastward, 800-1400.

Germans
Slavs
Letts
Magyars (Hungarians)
Rumanians
Seat of an archbishopric
" " a bishopric
Monastery
C.-Cistercian, P.-Premonstratensian
T.O.-Teutonic Order Temp-Templars
St. John-Knights of St. John.
Boundary between Germans and Slavs about 800. Figures indicate date of founding city or monastery. Cities in which the German population in 1400 formed a minority of the inhabitants are underlined, thus: Kuttenberg.

CHAPTER XIII

THE EXPANSION AND COLONIZATION OF THE GERMAN PEOPLE BEYOND THE ELBE; THE CONFLICT OF SAXON AND SLAV[1]

GERMAN eastward expansion, from the time of the first manifestation of the eastward swing in the eighth century to the termination of the great movement when the last energy spent its force in the conquests of the Teutonic Knights in the morasses of Kurland and Esthonia, advanced in a series of waves whose lengths are measured by the distance between the rivers of Northern

[1] A reviewer of von der Goltz's *Geschichte der deutschen Landwirtschaft* in *Journal of Political Economy*, XII (1903-4), 114 said, à propos of the history of German east colonization: "It is but characteristic of the ignorance of this period prevailing in America that a work on colonization issued some years ago and pretending to treat of every phase connected with colonization at all periods contained not a word about this very important movement, to which the present German Empire so largely owes its existence." Historical study of the western Slavs dates from Christian Hennig (1649-1719). See Tetzner's biographical sketch of Hennig in *Ztschft. d. hist. Ver. f. Niedersachsen* (1903), Heft 2. The next important work was by J. C. von Jordan, *De originibus Slavicis, opus chronolog.-geograph.-historicum ab antiquitate literis nota in seculum usque ad Christianum decimum* (2 vols.; Vindob., 1745). Comparative philology opened a new line of attack for Karl Gottlieb Anton (1751-1818) who published at Leipzig in the years 1783-89 two volumes entitled *Erste Linien eines Versuches über der alten Slaven. Ursprung, Sitten, Gebräuche, Meinungen und Kenntnisse.* Anton had been a student at the University of Leipzig where he became intimately acquainted with some fellow-students from Lausitz of Sorb descent. All previous work, however, was superseded in the middle of the nineteenth century by P. J. Schafarik, *Slovanské Starožitnosti* (Prague, 1837); German translation, and the version usually consulted, by Mosig von Aehrenfeld, entitled *Slawische Alterthümer* (2 vols.; Leipzig, 1843-44; 2d ed. Jireček, 1862-63). In the same year with Schafarik's classic volumes also appeared Zeuss's *Die Deutschen und ihre Nachbarstämme*, which is very valuable for the history of the Slavs in Germany. L. Giesebrecht, *Wendische Geschichten*, although an old book, is valuable. At the present time the Czech scholar Lubor Niederlé and the Austrian scholar Peisker, of the University of Graz, are leading authorities upon the history of the Slavs. For a bibliography of their works see *Cambridge Mediaeval History*, II, 775. Leger has translated Niederlé's *Slavonic Mythology* and his *Slav Antiquities* into French, and extensively reviewed his writings in the *Journal des savants* (1907), pp. 70 and 128; *ibid.* (1908), p. 141; and those on Schaffarik, *ibid.* (1910), pp. 115-24, 155-67; *ibid.* (1911), p. 125.

451

Europe. The time element, however, in this immense expansion was not always or even nearly uniform. The current moved now slow, now fast. Three times the Germans crossed the lower Elbe and three times were thrown back by the Wends—in 983, 1018, 1066. It was over two hundred years before the Saxons utterly broke the power of the Slavonic tribes situated between the Elbe and the Oder, before they acquired a permanent foothold in Mecklenburg and Brandenburg. At the end of the *Völkerwanderung* the Slavonic western edge impinged on the lower Elbe and the Saale rivers. The Slav world between the eighth and the twelfth century was of huge extent. A line drawn from the mouth of the Elbe to the head of the Adriatic would roughly mark its western boundary.[1]

In general, until the conquest of the Saxons by Charlemagne in the last quarter of the eighth century shook Germany and the Slavonic tribes as no force had since the great migration, the relations between the Germans and the Slavs were amicable. Boniface's missionary labors were peacefully pursued among the Slavs of the Main. A Wendish peasantry cleared the lands around Fulda, and Slavonic colonies were established by Boniface in the territory of the future of Bamberg, where they worked the mines and raised cattle. Some such Slav colonists were even settled in Swabia as far over as the Rhine.[2]

The Wendish Slavs were the western edge of the great Slavonic race which, in the fifth century, extended westward to the Elbe and the Saale rivers and bordered the Baltic.

[1] Adam of Bremen (II, 21), in the eleventh century roughly indicated the area tof he western Slavs: "Sclavania igitur . . . . decies major esse fertur quam nostra Saxonia, praesertim si Boemiam et eos trans Oddaram sunt, Polanos, quia nec habitu nec lingua discrepant, in partem adjeceris Sclavaniae. . . . . Ejus latitudo est a meridie usque in boream, hoc est ab Albia fluvio usque ad mare Scythicum. Longitudo autem illa videtur, quae initium habet ab nostra Hammaburgensi parrochia et porrigitur in orientem, infinitis aucta spatiis, usque in Beguariam, Ungriam et Greciam." By "Beguariam" Adam undoubtedly means *Bulgariam*, not *Bavariam*, as Pertz, *Archiv.*, III, 658, thinks. One MS reads "Bulgariam," and the sense so requires.

[2] Lamprecht, *Deutsche Geschichte* (3d rev. ed., 1906), p. 345; Riedel, *Die Mark Brandenburg*, II, 10, nn. 10–11; Lavisse, *La marche de Brandebourg*, p. 7; Werneburg, *Mitt. d. Vereins f. d. Gesch. von Erfurt* (1882), Heft 10.

Today the Slavonic frontier is marked by a line drawn from the head of the Adriatic to Prague and to Danzig, that is to say, roughly the line of the Vistula River and its vertical projection southward. The Poles and Bohemians are the two greatest surviving blocks of the once widely extended Slavonic occupation of Central Europe.

According to the most probable conjectures, the original country of the Slavs was in the marsh land of the Pripet and the basin of the middle Dnieper. This was Polesie, a triangular area less than half as great as England, the angles of which are roughly indicated by the modern towns of Brest-Litovsk, Miholev, and Kiev.[1] The physical features of the great isthmus between the Baltic and the Black Sea, with the Oder and the Vistula flowing into the former, and the Bug, the Pruth, and the Dniester emptying into the latter, profoundly conditioned the mode and the direction of early Slav expansion. From earliest historic times one can discern those differences which later created the distinction between the northern and the southern Slavs. But early Slav history had no center. The Slavs, unlike the early Germans, had no great tradition to grasp, as the Germans adopted the idea of the Roman Empire and perpetuated it.[2]

It formerly was the prevailing belief of historians of the Slavs that the race remained confined to their original home until the fifth and sixth centuries when they began to expand down the valleys of the Dnieper and Vistula rivers. But recently Niederlé[3] has combated this theory and endeavored to demonstrate that the Slavs, not *en masse* but in small groups, little by little quitted their original country and filtered out

---

[1] For a study of the evidence leading to this conclusion see Peisker, "The Expansion of the Slavs," *Cambridge Med. Hist.*, Vol. II, chap. xiv. For modern literature in English on the Slavs see Bury, *History of the Eastern Roman Empire*, chaps. xi–xii; Beazeley, *Dawn of Modern Geography*, II, 467–574; Gibbon, *Decline and Fall of the Roman Empire* (ed. Bury), VI, 543–44, with valuable bibliography.

[2] See the suggestive memoir by Hoefler, *Sitzungsb. Akad. d. Wiss. zu Wien*, XCVII (1881), on the nature of medieval Slav history. He distinguishes five periods: (a) 375–626; (b) 626–895; (c) 895–1205; (d) 1205–1396; (e) 1396–1526.

[3] Lubor Niederlé, *Slovanské Starožilnosti* ("Slav Antiquities") (2 vols.; Prague, 1902–10). The first volume is available in French, *Manuel de l'antiquité Slav* (1923), and L. Leger, *La race Slave* (Paris, 1910), a French translation of an earlier work by Niederlé. The "Antiquities" is reviewed in *Journal des savants* (March, 1911).

and among the surrounding peoples at a remoter epoch than usually believed. This infiltration may have begun before the beginning of the Christian Era. According to archaeological evidence, the earliest expansion was into present Eastern Germany and Northern Hungary. Emigration *en masse* into the regions abandoned by the Germans of the *Völkerwanderung* took place between the second and the fourth centuries.

By the end of the fifth century the mighty westward and southward movement of the German race had almost run its course. The dark woodland east of the Rhine for centuries had poured out tribes and nations—Goths, Franks, Vandals, Burgunds—who had overwhelmed the Roman Empire. The Goths settled in Spain and Italy, the Vandals in Africa, the Franks and Burgunds in Gaul. And ever behind the German nations treading westward the Slavonic tribes crowded in, occupying the abandoned territory until the Slavonic western edge rested on the Elbe and the Saale.[1]

A little later than this northern and northwestward expansion of the Slavs, a southward drift also took place. By the sixth century the forerunners of the southern Slavs had

---

[1] C. Plattner, "Ueber Spuren deutscher Bevölkerung zur Zeit der slavischen Herrschaft in den östlich der Elbe und Saale gelegenen Ländern," *Forschungen zur deutschen Gesch.*, XVII (1877), 409-526. Cf. *ibid.*, XVIII, 629-31; XX, 165-202. O. Montelius, "Die Einwanderung der Slawen in Norddeutschland," *Mitt. d. Anthrop. Gesellschaft in Wien* (Vienna, 1900), Band XXX; Schafarik, II, 1-50. The radical pro-Slav view is represented by Boguslawski, *Dowody Autochtonizmu* (Warsaw, 1912), who contends that the Slavs were autochthonous in Northeast Germany. His strongest evidence is philological, but the book is nevertheless a pamphlet against the Berlin-Austrian School. The author has considerately given a résumé of his contentions in German in an Appendix. See, further, *Revue critique* (1915), No. 29. One may read S. Zaborowski, "L'autochtonisme des Slaves en Europe, *Revue de l'école d'anthropologie* (1905), as a corrective to such extravagant opinion. In Charlemagne's time there were certainly no great masses of Germanic peoples east of the Elbe and Saale. But Plattner has raised the question whether isolated fragments of German stock did not still remain in the east, not participating in the westward migration. His contentions are combated by Wendt, *Ueber die Nationalität der Bevölkerung der deutschen Ostmarken vor dem Beginne der Germanisierung* (Göttingen, 1878). Haag (*Gesellschaft f. pommersche Gesch. u. Alterthumskunde*, 1878) argues that long before the appearance of the Slavs there the Baltic Coast was peopled by Germans; Schwartz, *Markische Forschungen*, Band XX (1878), from a study of local folklore and popular survivals, concludes that Brandenburg and Pomerania were originally populated by German stock, and that fragments of these peoples remained and even preserved their racial institutions to some degree under the Slav superstratum imposed upon them.

reached the middle Danube through Bohemia and Moravia via the Nab and the Theiss rivers, while farther east the Pruth and the Bug had facilitated their spread around the Carpathians and into the lands along the lower Danube. Thus the huge isthmus of Europe between the Baltic and the Black Sea became a great Slavonia.

At this epoch one distinguishes the broad difference between the northern and the southern Slavs,[1] the differentiation being greater among the former than among the latter. For three distinct groups were now to be found north of the Danube: the Poles of the Vistula, the tribes of the Elbe and Baltic seaboard, and finally the Czechs in the mountainous region of Bohemia. Nothing but conjectures can be made with reference to the eastward and northeastward expansion of the Russian group before the seventh century, for the earliest texts, Byzantine and Arab, pertain to the ninth and tenth centuries. It is true that archaeology has supplemented this paucity of evidence, but the ground is nowhere firm.[2]

As with all primitive peoples the observations and criticisms of their manners and customs[3] made by observers

---

[1] This separation of the northern and southern Slavs was made permanent by the establishment of the Avars and Magyars between the two groups (600–900). "Ce peuple [the Hungarians] qui devait changer si profondement les destinées de la race slave. ... Les Hongrois implantèrent une domination étrangère au cœur des pays slaves. Ils dispersèrent les membres de la grande famille. ... Dès lors, le fait que, sur le Danube, au point de la réunion de toutes les races slaves, existait un état magyar, finno-ouralien, inattaquable au slavisme par l'énergie de son caractère national, fut la pierre d'achoppement de toute grande tentative d'agglomération slave" (Rambaud, L'empire grec au Xe siècle, pp. 335–36).

[2] The earliest allusion to the Slavs by any historian seems to be Procopius De bello Gothico, III, 14. After that come the Strategon or Ars militaris, IX, 3; XI, 5, of Emperor Maurice about 600; the Tactics of Emperor Leo in the eighth century; the De administrando imperio, chaps. xxxvii–xxxviii, of Constantine Porphyrogenitos in the tenth century. It is difficult to know whether the Arabic sources refer to the Russian Slavs or to the Scandinavians in Russia (Schafarik, I, 9–14). For modern literature see Lippert, Sozial Gesch. Böhmens, I, 121 f.; Bury, History of the Eastern Roman Empire, chaps. xi, xii; Cambridge Mediaeval History, Vol. II, chap. xiv; Meitzen, Siedelung und Agrarwesen, II, 141–64; Beazeley, Dawn of Modern Geography, II, 467–514; Gibbon, Decline and Fall of the Roman Empire (ed. J. B. Bury, 1900), VI, 543–44, with valuable bibliography; Peisker, Camb. Med. Hist., Vol. II, chap. xiv, with bibliography (pp. 770–84); Sir H. H. Howorth, in Journal Anthrop. Inst., VII, 329; VIII, 65; IX, 181.

[3] Schafarik, I, 536–43.

of a different or higher culture must be taken with reservation.

We do not know what rites accompanied the birth of a babe among the early Slavs. We know only from the *Vitae* of Otto of Bamberg that infanticide was sometimes practiced among the Baltic Slavs. The first clipping of a child's hair seems to have been a sort of rite. Whether any ceremony accompanied the advent of puberty is not known. Marriage, as nearly as we can discern from the texts and the evidence of folk-lore, was sometimes by capture,[1] sometimes by purchase. The Russian chronicle attributed to Nestor alludes to violent seizure of young girls at natural springs. According to Saxo Grammaticus, the Danish king, Fritho, after vanquishing the Russians compelled them to substitute marriage by purchase for the more barbaric marriage by capture. In the eleventh century the code of Jaroslav Vladimirovitch imposed heavy penalty for seizure of a woman. Yet many texts attest the persistence of this primitive practice, and it still survives among some of the Balkan Slavs. Other evidence indicates that daughters were purchased of their parents, so much so that a blooming family of daughters was regarded as a source of wealth.

Endeavor has been made to reconstitute the primitive Slavonic rite of marriage after observances which still obtain. Early texts throw little light. In the *Chronicle of Kiev* we learn that the newly married wife was compelled to take off her husband's shoes as a sign of obedience. Marriage usually took place in the autumn in order that the woman might have passed the time of pregnancy before the period of spring planting arrived. On the night that she was wedded the young woman was veiled, sprinkled with millet or rye as a symbol of fecundity, and conducted to the house of her husband. Three times she walked around the house, bending her knees to do homage to the tutelary household genii. On the morrow the pair were purified in running water. All these rites were accompanied with dancing and singing. That polygamy existed along with monogamy among the primitive

---

[1] Marriage by capture prevailed among the Bohemians in early times (Lippert, *Sozial Gesch. Böhmens*, I, 203).

Slavs is attested by Russian and Czech chroniclers, and by the biographers of Otto of Bamberg. Even polyandry and incest occurred. Yet female morality was high. Boniface commended the prevalence of conjugal fidelity among the Slavs in the eighth century, and is confirmed by Thietmar[1] in the early eleventh century.

The ancient Slavs practiced two modes of disposing of the bodies of their dead—cremation and interment. Their cemeteries, in which an enormous amount of archaeological material has been found, are almost innumerable between the Vistula and the Dnieper rivers, a territory essentially *urslawisch*. In 626 the Slavs who attacked Constantinople burned their dead. The same practice is recorded among the Russians by Arab texts, by Leo the Deacon, by Nestor. Place-names derived from the custom of incineration are common in Slavonic lands. Boniface in 734 tells us that Polaben wives voluntarily caused themselves to be burned with the bodies of their husbands. The Polish chronicler Martin Gallus records the use of funeral urns in 1018. In 1218 the Pomezani, the Natangi, and the Varmians, in a treaty with the Teutonic Knights, agreed to abandon the practice of cremating their dead as a heathen rite. The graves were filled with gifts of food and drink, weapons, instruments, and often the wives, men and women servants, horses and dogs, were slain that the deceased might have comfort and company in the tomb. The practice of placing articles of food in the grave lasted until the eighteenth century, according to the philologist Dobrovsky, and it is said still to obtain in remote parts of Poland, and Great and Little Russia. To Swedish influence must be attributed the occasional practice of burying the dead in a boat.[2]

With regard to food, though the Slavs knew meat and milk, their chief flesh nourishment was fish, living as they did in a world of marsh and a network of rivers. "Instead of in towns they live in marshes and forests," wrote Jordanes in the sixth century. The word for "milk" (*melko*) reminds one of the German *Milch*, and the cow may have been intro-

---

[1] *Chron. Slav.*, VIII, 2.   [2] Schafarik, I, 578.

duced from the Germans. Dlugosz, a Polish chronicler in the fifteenth century, described the Poles as living "frumento, carne, pisce, melle, lacte et olere." The names for the common cereals—rye, wheat, barley, millet, oats—are identical among all Slav peoples. Rye seems to have been originally a Slav grain. The word for "bread" (*chleb*) was borrowed from the German *Laib* (cf. Eng. "loaf"), and probably replaced an ancient word now lost. Of fruits, some were indigenous, some imported. The most familiar were plums and pears. But the harshness of the climate made fruit cultivation difficult, and Byzantine peddlers soon brought fruits and wines from the south to them. When Prince Oleg in 907 returned from a trip to Constantinople he brought back fruits and wine. In 969 Sviatoslav thought of transferring his capital from Kiev to Periaslavets on the Danube "since all manner of riches were to be found there, silver from Greece, silk, fruits and different wines." The spread of the southern Slavs must have been powerfully influenced by the lure of the orchards and vineyards of the balmier southland. The Slavs' favorite drink was hydromel or beer, of which Otto of Bamberg makes glowing eulogy.[1] This statement applies to both branches of the Slavs. Another fermented drink was *kvas*, made of fermented bread with an admixture of malt. Grape culture was unknown among the primitive Slavs, but they were heavy drinkers. Vladimir, prince of Moscow in the tenth century, told an Arabic traveler that the Mohammedan injunction against the use of alcoholic liquors was an insuperable bar to the conversion of the Slavs to Islam.

Except for the few observations to be found in the writings of Boniface[2] and casual allusions in Carolingian sources, we know little[3] of the history of the Elbean Slavs until the time of Bishop Thietmar of Merseburg, about 1000 A.D. The first

---

[1] Herbordus, II, 1.

[2] Notably the saint's uncharitable characterization of the "Winedi, quod est foedissimum et deterrimum genus hominum . . . ." (Schafarik, II, 515).

[3] The earliest mention of the Slavs of the Elbe is in Vibius Sequester, *De fluminibus*, in the sixth century, in which he says: "Albis Suevos a Cervatiis dividit," i.e., from the Sorben. Cervetii, Ciervisti, Zerbisti, Kirvisti of Saxon charters are all one and mean Zerbst (Niederlé, p. 131).

attempt of a western writer to describe the western Slavs, i.e., those of the basin of the Elbe and the south coast of the Baltic Sea, was made by Adam of Bremen in the latter half of the eleventh century.[1]

[1] *Gesta Hammaburgensis ecclesia pontificum:* Inestimably valuable as Adam of Bremen is, yet he is often vague and obscure, and his account of the Slavonic tribes between the Elbe and the Oder rivers, especially their geographical distribution, has given rise to extended controversy. According to Giesebrecht (*Nordlandskunde*, pp. 157–66; *Baltische Studien*, VI, 192) Adam was well informed. But the text of Adam of Bremen is notoriously corrupt, and Giesebrecht accuses the scholiast of many blunders and alterations. After the great revolt of the Slavs of the lower Elbe in 983, he argues, the land between the Elbe and the Oder was shut off from Christian knowledge and commercial intercourse, so that ignorance and erroneous ideas of Slavonia naturally came to prevail among the Germans. Lappenberg (*Archiv*, VI, 864), on the other hand, finds the chief source of Adam's limitations in popular German prejudice against the Slavs and contempt for their language, which prevented any intimate knowledge of them from being acquired. Slavonic tribal names and the places occupied by them might interest a diocesan historian of Hamburg, but the Saxons were too indifferent to the promotion of Christianity among the Slavs and too contemptuous of them to be interested.

Giesebrecht has endeavored to control Adam's account by Helmold's *Chronica Slavorum*, written in the last half of the twelfth century by one who dwelt long among the Slavs and knew them more intimately than any other German writer of the Middle Ages. He accepts Adam's testimony when the two agree, provided Helmold has not—as he sometimes has done, especially in the early chapters—slavishly copied his predecessor. The difficulty of clearly distinguishing the tribal names of the Slavs between the Elbe and the Oder and of accurately locating them is very great. Helmold is of better use in amplifying than in emending Adam.

However, it is to be observed that Adam's description of Slavonia falls into two parts: one dealing with the region west of the Peene River, the other with that beyond and eastward of the Peene. The former, which Adam calls Hither Slavonia (*In Sclavania citeriori*, III, 18), was comprehended within the diocese of Hamburg. He is diffuse concerning the first, but brief and obscure about things across the river. He knows a great deal about things which happen around Magdeburg, but is hazy about things *ultra Panim* (III, 21). Beyond the Oder, Adam's ideas are very nebulous, as the use of words implying indirect knowledge, like *comperimus, dicunt*, etc., indicates (e.g., IV, 11).

Adam uses the words Sclavi and Winuli interchangeably to denominate the Slavonic peoples between the Elbe and the Oder. (The latter proper name is a variant of the earlier word Winedi used by Einhard. See Pertz, I, 658, where the examples are cited.) The territory he calls Sclavania, but he is loose in application of the term, sometimes using it in a broad sense, sometimes in a narrow sense (e.g., II, 13, 19; IV, 13, for the former usage; II, 40, 46, 69, for the latter usage. In II, 24, "ecclesiae in Sclavania ubìque erectae sunt" and "Sclavaniam in duodeviginti pagos dispertitam" undoubtedly refer to Slavonia in the strict sense of the term). The hardness of heart and lack of sympathetic imagination for any culture save their own of tenth-century German historians is a striking and depressing fact. It is glaring in Widukind and Thietmar of Merseburg (e.g., IV, 31 [22]; VI, 46; VII, 4), to whom, for example, Boleslav Chrobry, who is really a heroic figure, appears

The Baltic Slavs lay in modern east Holstein and Meck-
lenburg-Schwerin.[1] The Wilzi and kindred tribes extended
over modern Mecklenburg-Strelitz, Brandenburg, Mittel-
mark and Uckermark, in the moor and marsh land of the
Spree, the Havel, and the Peene rivers; the Pomeranians were
in what is today known as Pomerania along the seaboard; the
Sorben were in the triangle included between the upper Elbe,
the Erzgebirge, and the Saale. They reached eastward to the
Bober, and westward to the Werra, Fulda, and upper Main.[2]
The blood affinity between the Wilzi and the Poles was close;
on the other hand, the Sorben were akin to the Czechs, or

---

only contemptible ("cujus nomen et conversacio .... sacius lateret" [IX, 2]).
Even Adam of Bremen, although in the eleventh century a greater objectivity of
treatment and stronger disposition to record history truthfully is discernible, is
greatly tinctured with this contempt for things other than German and Christian
(e.g., I, 63; II, 17, 20). A unique source for our knowledge of the Elbean Slavs is
the *Relation* of Ibraham Ibn Jakub, a Jew of North Africa who probably was a
member of the Mohammedan embassy sent to Otto I in 973. It is of considerable
value. The Arabic text has been established by the Dutch orientalist Goeje. For
studies upon it consult Haag, *Baltische Studien*, Band XXXI (1881); Wigger,
Jahrbücher und Jahresbericht des Vereins f. Mecklenburgische Gesch. (1880), and
Westburg's commentary in *Mem. de l'Acad. des sciences de St. Petersbourg, Hist.-
Phil.-Kl.*, VIII, 32 f. A German translation may be found in *Geschichtschreiber d.
deutschen Vorzeit*, Band XXXII. Ibrahim's important observations are given by
Lippert, *op. cit.*, 5, 64, 69, 83 f., 125, 229, 432. Peisker has an excellent article
on "The Relations of the Slavs with the Turco-Tartars and the Germans," in
the *Vierteljahrschrift f. soz.-wirt. Gesch.*, III, Nos. 2, 3, 4 (1905).

[1] Witte, "Wendische Bevölkerungsreste in Mecklenburg," *Forschungen zur
deutschen Landes- und Volkskunde*, XVI (1905), 1–124. The line is indicated by
modern Kiel, Neumünster, Alster, and Hamburg (Adam Brem., II, 15; *Visio
Godeschalci*; Helmold, II, 14; *Annal. St. Bertin* [anno 845] [Prudentius the author]).
The Alt Mark perhaps once was Slav, but from 822 one finds names of German
villages. In Thuringia between the Elbe, Ohre, Bode, and Saale was a thin sprinkling
of Slavs. East of the Saale everything was Slav. Even west of the Saale were certain
scattered Slav settlements. Thus villages are mentioned in a charter of Dagobert
III of 706 (if the act is not spurious), and some inventories of Fulda and Hersfeld
confirm this of the eighth century. In the eleventh century, the region around Saalfeld was still Slav.

[2] Cf. E. Muka, "Die Grenzen des serb. Sprachgebietes in alter Zeit," *Archiv.
f. slav. Phil.*, XXVI, 543; Guttmann, "Die Germanisierung der Slawen in der
Mark," *Forschungen zur Brand. u. Preuss. Gesch.*, IX (1897), 396–97; Wendt, I,
10–16. "Sorabi Sclavi qui campos inter Albim et Salam interjacentes incolunt"
(Einhard, *Annales Lauresh.* [anno 782]).

Bohemians.¹ Of these four grand groups of the Baltic Slavs, the confederacy of the Wilzi was most formidable.²

The Wilzi were sworn foes of the Franks and allied with the Saxons during the period of Charlemagne's Saxon wars, while, on the other hand, the Abodrites sometimes co-operated with the Franks against both Wilzi and Saxons.³ The Abodrites appear to have been late comers into the Elbean lands, and seem to have been driven from the region of the Danube, perhaps by the Hun invasion of the fifth century, or possibly by the Avars in the sixth. In the time of Pepin, before he became king, when his half-brother Grifo made trouble and fled to the Saxons, the Sorben offered their aid to Pepin. During the Saxon wars Charlemagne looked with friendly eyes upon the Sorben and the Abodrites. The former fought in the Frank armies, and the latter, in 804, when the Saxons living north of the Elbe were deported into Franconia, were colonized in their room in order to prevent the Saxons from forming an alliance with the warlike Wilzi.⁴

Unfortunately, throughout the Middle Ages the Baltic Slavs produced no historian who wrote in their idiom or in Latin. Their whole history has to be sought in German annals, notably in the chronicles of Helmold and Arnold of

---

¹ Guttmann, p. 397, n. 1. The formidability of the Sorben is attested by Charlemagne's military legislation (*Capitulare* 807, sec. 5; Baluze, I, 459).

² Adam of Bremen, III, 21.

³ "Sclavi nostri qui dicuntur Abotridi" (*Annales Lauresh.* [anno 798]). The military assistance given by the Abodrites to Charlemagne during the last stages of the war with the Saxons [797] was not forgotten by Charlemagne. They were rewarded by being permitted to move into and settle Wagria (East Holstein), which was totally bereft of its Saxon inhabitants (799) and utilized as a buffer people between the Saxons and the Danes. But the latter were too formidable, and in 805 the Emperor annexed Nordalbingia to the Empire, and established the Danemark in the valley of the little river Eyder. With the entry of the Slavs into Wagria, the German world of the Middle Ages shrank to its narrowest area. "Das Deutschtum am Ausgang des 8. Jahrhundert auf die schmalste Basis beschränkt die es je vorher und nachher gehabt hat" (Pueschl, *Das Answachsen der deutschen Städte*, p. 1).

⁴ Stein, *Gesch. Frankens*, II, 258; *Ann. Lauresh:* "Imperator . . . . omnes qui trans Albiam et in Wihmuodi habitabant Saxones, cum mulieribus et infantibus, transtulit in Franciam, et pagos transalbianos Abodritis dedit" (804); *Annales Altah.* (803); cf. Wendt, *Germanisierung d. Länder östlich d. Elbe*, I, 19; Guttmann, *op. cit.*, p. 403. The warlike character of the Wilzi is noticed by Einhard both in the *Annales* (789) and the *Vita Karoli*, chap. xii.

Lübeck, the latter being his thirteenth-century continuator. A *corpus* made of all these texts, a French historian has remarked, might take for its epigraph the words of the Saxon chronicler Widukind: "Transeunt sane dies plurimi Saxonibus, his pro gloria et pro magna latoque imperio, illis pro libertate ac ultima servitute varie certantibus."[1]

The Baltic or Wendish Slavs[2] formed a separate group, distinct from the Poles and Bohemians as well as the Litu-Slav stems extending around the bight of the Baltic from the mouth of the Oder to the mouth of the Düna in modern East Prussia and Kurland. They were loosely known as Polaben or Elbslaven,[3] and were divided into four grand divisions—the Abodrites, the Ljutizi (Ger.: Welataben or Wilzi), the Pomeranians, and the Sorben, each of these major groups in turn being subdivided into lesser stem-groups.[4]

[1] Leger, "Les Slaves Baltiques," *Journal des savants* (Jan., 1916). Widukind was more generous in appreciation of the Slavs than later German historians: "Illi vero nichilominus bellum quam pacem elegerunt, omnem miseriam carae libertati postponentes. Est namque hujuscemodi genus hominum durum et laboris patiens, victu levissimo assuetum, et quod nostris gravi oneri esse solet, Slavi pro quadam voluptate ducunt. Transeunt sane dies plurimi, his pro gloria et pro magno latoque imperio, illis pro libertate et ultima servitute varie certantibus" (II, 20).

[2] The only account in English of the Baltic Slavs is the memoir by Sir H. H. Howorth, *Journal Anthrop. Inst.*, IX, 181–232. Since it was written in 1879 some of his conclusions must now be regarded as antiquated or amended.

[3] From the word *po*, meaning "by," and *Labe*, meaning "Elbe" (Wendt, *Die Germanisierung der Länder östlich der Elbe*, II, 11). See Meitzen, *Siedelung und Agrarwesen*, II, 475–93. For a dissertation upon the Polabish language see Morfill, *Trans. Philol. Soc.* (London), XXV, 74 f.

[4] Kindred to the Abodrites were the Wagri, or Waarii of Widukind and Adam of Bremen, III, 68, in east Holstein, the Lingones on the Elbe (*ibid.*, III, 19), the Warnabi on the Warnow (*ibid.*; Helmold, I, 87), and the Dravani west of the Elbe in the Hanoverian Wendland around Lüchow, Gartow, and Wustrow (Wendt, I, 11; Brückner, *Die slavischen Ansiedelungen in der Altmark*, p. 8; *Mecklenburg. Jahrbücher*, VII, 156). The Ljutizi were bitter foes of the Abodrites (Schafarik, II, 576, 587). Akin to the Wilzi were the Redarii and the Uckri (Widukind, III, 54, "Uchri"), whence the name Ucker-Mark; the Lini or Lingones (Helmold, I, 2); the Hevelli (Thietmar, IV, 20; *Annal. Qued.*; *Annal. Magdbg.*; *Annal. Palid.*; Helmold, I, 88). Offshoots of the Sorben were the Lusizi (Thietmar, I, 9; VI, 39, 48), the Milzi, the Glomuzani or Daleminzi, the Siusli, the Plisni (Andree, *Wendische Wanderstudien*, pp. 29–38). Ljutizi was the Slav term; Wilzi the German. Adam of Bremen fantastically derives Wilzi from German *wild* and Ljutizi from German *Löwe!* His philology is at least a tribute to their warlike character. Widukind (III, 54) is the first author to indicate the territory occupied by the Wilzi. This German nomenclature first appears in the tenth century (cf. *Annal. Sangall. maj.*, 955). The earlier German

Little by little, conquered and dispossessed or else absorbed by the German race, today the Wends and their language have almost disappeared, the clearest traces of the wide empire they once ruled being afforded by the mutilated and distorted Germanic form of hundreds of place-names upon the map of Germany, especially in Mecklenburg, Pomerania, Saxony, and Brandenburg-Prussia, although Württemberg, Bavaria, and Austria also show traces of former Slav occupation in the names of places, as the Regnitz River by Bamberg and the Pegnitz by Nürnberg.[1]

---

name for the Wilzi was Welatabi (see Einhard, *Vita Caroli*, chap. xv). Adam (II, 18, schol. 17) professes to have learned the early history of the warfare between the Saxons and the Redarii from an old Nordalbingian noble. The word Wend is technically not of racial significance, though it came to be used as such by the Germans, and always to signify the Slavonic peoples of the eastern border, whatever their tribal names. Various forms of spelling of the word Wend are met with in the chronicles (Guinidini, *Chron. Moissac.* [809]; Windei, *Einhardi Annales* [798, 804]; Winuli, *Adam of Bremen*, II, 18; IV, 13; cf. II, 13 and 19, where he uses Sclavi in the sense of Winuli). The earliest western mention of the Slavs as Wends which I know is in *Vita St. Columbani*, chap. lvi. For further references see Pertz, *Mon.*, I, 658, *s.v.* "Winedi." Considerable Wendish groups are still to be found in the Spreewald between Lübben and Kottbus, in Ober and Nieder Lausitz, and around Dresden. The latter still call themselves Sorben or Soraben. Altogether they now number about 170,000, scattered in over 700 villages, mere islets of people surrounded by German waters, remnants of the Slavs of the Elbe and the Oder valleys—Polabs, Ljutizi, Abodrites, Sorben, etc., who once played a great and sometimes formidable part in medieval German history from the eighth to the end of the thirteenth century (see Tetzner, *Die Slawen in Deutschland* [Braunschweig, 1902]).

[1] The Slav origin of many German place-names is manifest to the historian under mutilated or translated current form. Zerbst recalls the Sorben, whose prowess once taxed the arms of Charlemagne. Rostock in Mecklenburg bears a name which is found in six Czech localities. It is situated at the mouth of a river whose estuary is large enough to accommodate considerable shipping, and the name is derived from *roz*, a prefix implying "width or breadth of room," and the word *tek* or *tok*, meaning "to flow." Leipzig is simply "Linden-tree Place" (*Lipazig*) (Naebe, *Schriften d. Ver. f. d. Gesch. Leipzigs*, Band VII). Chemnitz in modern Saxony at first glance does not easily show a Slav derivation. But the primitive form was Kamenica, from *Kamen* ("rock," "stone"), a word reminding one of the mineral resources of the region. The name appears in no less than twenty-two places in Bohemia and Moravia. Torgau in Silesia is derived from the Slav root *terg* or *torg*, and corresponds to the German *Markt* ("market"). Pomerania is a pure Slav word, from *po* ("along" or "by the side of") and the word *morze*, meaning "the sea."

It is to be borne in mind that the persistence of Slavonic place-names is not necessarily an evidence of survival of a Slavonic stock in the locality. The Germans adopted local native names in the course of their eastward expansion precisely as the American pioneer adopted Indian names. See the cautious pronouncement of

The monarchical institutions of the Baltic Slavs were not highly developed.[1] The tribes were not compact entities, nor did they exhibit that capacity for union manifested among the early Germans. Evidences of a closer union appear about 800, when the pressure of Charlemagne's conquests began to be felt, and a tendency is noticeable toward hereditary succession in the chieftainship.[2] But no ruling dynasty was ever established among the Baltic Slavs as in the case of the Poles and Bohemians, who early developed a strong ducal power, which with the former even grew into a kingship. Political tendencies among them were centrifugal, and there seem to have been many small chieftains.[3]

As to social structure: There was a landed nobility,[4] a

Guttmann, "Die Germanisierung der Slawen in der Mark," *Forschungen zur Brandenburgischen und Preussischen Geschichte*, IX (1897), 431–32. In general, place-names with suffixes in -*itz*, -*in*, -*zig*, etc., are Slavonic endings, and many other places which appear to have German names are actually Slavonic, for example, Stettin, Wollin, Küstrin, Kamin, Danzig, Leipzig, Chemnitz, Lausitz, etc. Brandenburg is Germanized Brunabor; Merseburg is Germanized Mesibor, i.e., "the place in the woods," from Sorab, *mes* meaning "in" (Pol. *miedzy*; Bohem. *mezy*) and *bor* meaning "forest" (Schafarik, *Slav. Altherthümer*, II, 620). Schkeitbar, between Lützen and Zwenkau, commemorates a sacred wood of the Slavs, from Pol. *Swiety* ("sacred"), *Bor* ("wood"); Belgern, a castle near Torgau, means "White Hill" from Pol. *bielo* ("white") and *gora* ("hill"); the Bober River comes from Pol. and Bohem. *bobr* meaning "beaver." In Starigard, near Stettin, which Helmold (I, 12) explains, "Hoc est antiqua civitas," and in Belgrad, the suffix is akin to the *grad* ("a walled inclosure"), which is seen in Petrograd, Belgrade, Gratz, etc. Mecklenburg in Slavonic was called Wiligrad, or "Great City." Adam of Bremen (III, 19, 50) and Helmold (I, 88, 108) repeatedly call it Magnopolis. In Mecklenburg, Brisan signifies a locality planted with birch trees; Cowale, the place of a forge; Krukowe, a crow's roost. Königgrätz is Bohem. *Hradec* (pronounced *Hradets*); Kralove is "Queen's Castle," so named because it was given in 1363 by Charles IV to his wife, Elizabeth of Pomerania. To be consistent the Germans should have called the place Königinburg. The literature pertaining to Slavonic *Ortsnamen* is enormous: see Alfred Hennig, "Zur Entstehung der ländlichen Ortsformen," *Königreich Sachsen-Deutsche Erde*, XI (1912), 74–81, with an excellent map; Kühnel, *Die slavischen Ortsnamen in Mecklenburg-Strelitz* (2 vols., 1881–83); Hay, *Die slav. Siedelungen im Kgr. Sachsen* (1893); R. Virchow, "Wie lange waren Slaven in diesem Lande?" *Korrespondenzblatt der deutschen Gesellschaft f. Anthropologie*, Band XXVIII (Munich, 1890); Bronisch, *Die slavischen Ortsnamen in Holstein und im Fürstentum Lübeck-Sonderburg* (1901); Müller, *Frankenkolonisation auf dem Eichfelde* (Halle, 1911),

[Continued on next page]

[1] Lippert, *Sozial-Gesch. Böhmens*, I, 121, 227.

[2] Einhard, *Annales*, p. 823; Guttmann, *op. cit.*, p. 398, n. 2.

[3] Guttmann, p. 399, nn. 3, 4.   [4] *Ibid.*, n. 1.

large free class composed of rude farmers,[1] cattle-raisers, and bee-keepers; fishing, perhaps, was the main source of livelihood, as was natural with a people living in so wet a country as Lower Germany was in the Middle Ages; slaves were numerous and were employed as field hands and artisans;[2] tribe enthralled tribe, and for centuries the slave marts of the Slavonic peoples supplied both Byzantium and the Germans of the West.

The westward drift of the Slavs was first acutely felt by the Thuringians, who were driven from their homes in the land between the Elbe, the Saale, and the Mulde rivers into the Thüringerwald and the Harz by the fifth century. There-

---

pp. 53–58; Stechele, *Ztschft. d. Ver. f. Thür. Gesch. und Altertumsk.* (N.F.), Band I (1879); Schulze, *Mitt. f. Anhaltische Gesch.*, Band VI (1884); Witte, "Wendische Bevölkerungsreste in Mecklenburg," *Forschungen zur d. Landes- und Volkskunde*, Band XVI, Heft 1 (1905); Witte, "Wendische-und Familienamen aus Mecklenburgisch. Urkunden," *Verein f. Meckl. Gesch.*, Band LXXI (1906); Kühnel, *Ztschft. d. histor. Verein f. Niedersachsen* (1902); Legowski, *Baltische Studien* (N.F.), Band III (1899); Vieth *et al.*, "Beiträge zur Ethnographie der hannoverischen Elbslawen," *Archiv. f. slav. Philologie*, XXII (1900), 107–43; Kühnel, *Finden sich noch Spuren der Slawen im mittleren und westlichen Hannover?* (Hannover, 1907). Bronisch, *Die slawischen Ortsnamen in Holstein und im Fürstentum Lübeck* (1901); Hilferding, "Die Ueberreste der Slawen auf der Südküste des baltischen Meeres," *Ztschft. f. slawische Literatur*, I (Bautzen, 1864), 81–97, 230–39; II, 85–111. For Slav placenames in the Moseltal see Lamprecht, *DWL*, I, 1, 152, nn. 3–4.

Several European princes still bear titles which are reminiscent of the history of German eastward expansion in the twelfth and thirteenth centuries. The late German Emperor and King of Prussia was also "duke of the Wends"; the grand duke of Mecklenburg is *Fürst zu Wenden;* even the king of Denmark yet bears the title "king of the Wends," though Danish power in Germany ceased with the battle of Bornhoeved in 1227. The question of how far the Slavs in Germany were dispossessed, and how far they were conquered and absorbed by the Germans instead, is a matter of controversy among historical scholars, unfortunately accentuated by too much race prejudice, for Russian and Polish students have entered the lists. See

[Continued on next page]

[1] Meitzen is of opinion that it is very difficult to say with certainty what the agrarian system of the primitive Slavs was. The transition from fishing and hunting with them to agriculture cannot be studied with any accuracy. The oldest sources which we have must be used with great caution since they deal with Poland, Moravia, Bohemia, Silesia, countries in which the Germans early got a foothold. But no part of Slav history indicates that they were ever nomads.

[2] Hauck, III, 86–87; Wendt, II, 9. For Wendish glass-making in Thuringia see Heim, *Correspondenzblatt der deutschen Gesellschaft für Anthropologie und Urgeschichte* (1885). The common boat was short, and made of alder wood, so light that two men could carry it. It was not rowed with oars but poled like a punt (see Herbordus, III, 17).

by the Saale River became the boundary between the two
races. The Frankish conquest of the Thuringians in 531
drew the frontier sharp and clear, and the historic conflict between the Slav and the German peoples united under the
rule of the Franks began.[1] During the reign of Dagobert
(629–39) there were incessant Slav attacks on the eastern
frontier.[2] In 630 the Slav fortress of Wogastisburg (today
Wüstenburg, between Bamberg and Bayreuth)[3] was captured by the Franks. Between 674 and 687 the Franks were
involved in bitter civil war and could not push an aggressive
border policy. Fortunately for the German world at this
perilous time, the racial unity of the Slavonic world did not

---

Pawinski, *The Slavs of the Elbe* (1871); J. A. Lebedev, *The Last Conflict of the Slavs
of the Elbe against Germanization* (2 vols.; Moscow, 1878); Majewski, *Traces of the
Wends in Franconia* (Warsaw, 1900). The earliest serious study of the subject
dates back to 1789, when L. A. Gebhardi published at Halle his *Allgemeine Geschichte
d. Wenden und Slaven und der Wenden in nördl. Teutschlande.* The controversy was
given a new impulse in 1907 by an article by Kühnel in the *Forschungen zur Geschichte Niedersachsens* to which a reply was made by W. Ohnesorge (*Ausbreitung
und Ende der Slawen zwischen Nieder-Elbe und Oder* [Leipzig, 1911]). Ohnesorge contends that the Slavs were not driven out, but were gradually absorbed. F. Tetzner,
*Die Slawen in Deutschland. Beitr. z. Volkskunde d. Preuss., Litauer u. Letten, der
Masuren u. Philipponen, der Tschechen, Mähren u. Sorben, Polacken u. Slowinzen,
Kaschuben u. Polen. M. 215 Abbildgn., Krtn. u. Plänen, Sprachproben u. 15 Melod.*
(Brschwg., 1902), contains the fullest information, with maps, for the Wends,
Masurians, Cassubians, and Prussian Lithuanians. A Russian scholar, D. N. Iergo-
rov ("Slaviano-Guermanskia Otnochenia v. Srednia Veka," *Colonisatzia Meklen-
bourga v. XIII Veke* [2 vols.; Moscow, 1915]), has learnedly endeavored to show that
the nobility of Mecklenburg was not Germanized until the sixteenth century, and
that German influence did not wholly displace that of the Slav until the Thirty
Years' War. I do no profess to know this Russian literature at first hand, but only
from German book reviews.

[1] For the Slav pressure upon Thuringia and the historical significance of the
year 531 see Schafarik, II, 607–9; Schulze, *Kolonisierung,* p. 2; Posse, *Die Markgrafen
von Meissen* (1881), p. 3; Lamprecht, III, 343; Meitzen, *Siedelung und Agrarwesen,*
II, 149–51; Leo, *Untersuchungen zur Besiedelungs-und Wirtschaftsgesch. des Thüringischen Osterlandes in der Zeit des früheren Mittelalters* (Leipzig, 1880); Schottin, *Die
Slawen in Thüringen;* Schlueter, *Die Siedelung im nordöstlichen Thüringen;* cf. *Hist.
Vierteljahrschrift,* IX, No. 2.

[2] Schafarik, II, 419, 514. In the *Jahresschrift. f. d. Vorgesch. der Sächsisch-
Thüringischen Länder,* Band III, is an archaeological article by O. Foertsch on
remains found in ancient Slav tombs in Thuringia.

[3] Ernest, Baron von Aufsess, *Archiv f. Gesch. . . . . . von Oberfranken,* Band XIX,
Heft 1 (1893). For Slav place-names in Lorraine see Lamprecht, *DWL,* I, 1, 154,
nn. 3–4.

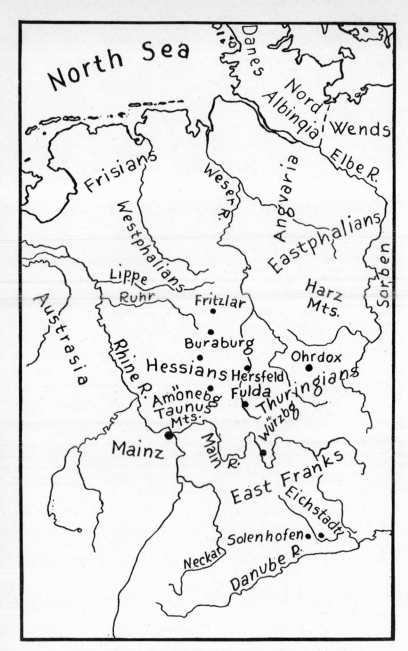

BONIFACIAN MISSION STATIONS IN HESSE

imply political unity as well, so that the Slav pressure was spasmodic and intermittent.

We can fix the time of the change in the relation of the two races with some precision. The real German anti-Slav offensive began with the founding of the mission posts of Boniface. Regensburg (739), Würzburg (741), and Eichstädt (743)[1] were half houses of God, half border fortresses designed for the conversion of the Slavs, buttressed by the genuine forts of Bremburg and Wogastisburg in the Bavarian Nordgau and Castle Salzburg (near Neustadt) in Franconia.[2]

In addition to these episcopal seats which lay echeloned along the eastern border of the Frank realm from the Danube to the mouth of the Rhine, a cluster of monasteries garrisoned Thuringia, Hesse, and the Nordgau: Disibodenburg (675), Amönaburg (722), Fritzlar (732), Buraburg (741), Fulda (744), Heidenheim (750), Hersfeld (759). With the eye of a military commander contemplating a frontal attack upon the enemy, Boniface unerringly perceived the strategical position of Thuringia as a *point d'appui*.[3]

The Thuringia of the eighth century (including Hesse) was far larger than the territory of the same name later. It was a tributary duchy of the Austrasian power which extended over the whole of Central Germany. Charles Martel had administratively included within its sphere a part of Austrasia and the Bavarian Plateau. It comprehended the valleys of the Lahn, the Main, and the Neckar. Southward and eastward the Thuringian frontier reached as far as the Raab. On the north it sloped through the valleys of the Werra and the Fulda toward the plain of Saxony. Militarily, politically, ecclesiastically, control of Thuringia carried with it the domination over Central Germany, and it was the natural base of operations for any forward movement, whether to the north, the east, or the southeast.

The social texture of Thuringia also was as firm and solid as the hills themselves. The admixture of Frankish blood, the

[1] Kretschmer, *Hist. Geog.*, p. 417.

[2] On this last place see Reiniger, *Archiv d. hist. Ver. von Unterfranken und Aschaffenburg*, Band XXV (1879).

[3] See Willibald, *Vita Bonifatii*, chap. v, sec. 15.

Saxon ingredient introduced from the north and east, acted as an alloy to gold to harden the rugged native Thuringian stock. By the side of the Thuringian nobility, among whom land monopoly had nothing like the enormous influence possessed by the same class in the Frankland, there was a numerous class of free peasant farmers. Serfdom prevailed but again not so widely or hardly as elsewhere. A few traders and artisans made up the residue of the population exclusive of the clergy.[1]

With the completion of the Frank conquest of the Saxons in 804 the *Drang nach Osten*, or, as it has been more accurately called, *Die Besiedelung von Ostdeutschland durch die zweite germanische Völkerwanderung*,[2] got in full swing. The history of the gradual dispossession and almost complete extermination of the Wends is a long and terrible one, and extends from the time of Charlemagne to the middle of the thirteenth century. Lamprecht's words have become a classic utterance: "Weit mehr als die Eroberung der Slawenländer im zwölften und dreizehnten Jahrhundert erscheint deren Germanisation als ein wahrhaft erstaunlicher Vorgang: es ist die Grosstat unseres Volkes während des Mittelalters."[3]

In 789 Charlemagne began the long and relentless war between the races which was to endure for centuries by attacking the Wilzi. In 806 he fixed the official frontier along the Elbe and Saale rivers, which was protected by a line of posts.[4]

---

[1] The evidence for this paragraph may be found in Willibald, chaps vi, vii, and viii; *Acta*, SS. XI, Octobris die xxvi, 950; but the fullest light is cast by Boniface's own sermons, which are of great value for evidence as to the social texture in Thuringia. See Migne, *Patrol. Lat.*, LXXXIX, 843 f., sermo III, 849, A, B; V, 853, A, C, D; IX, 861, A, C, D; XI, 864, B; cf. Kylie, "The Condition of the German Provinces as Illustrating the Methods of Boniface," *Cambridge Journal of Theolog. Studies*, VII, 32.

[2] Beheim-Schwarzbach, *Sammlung . . . . Vorträge* (Berlin, 1882), p. xvii.

[3] *Deutsche Gesch.* (5th ed.), III, 363; cf. Nitzsch, II, 215.

[4] Einhard, *Annales* (anno 806); *MGH, Leg.*, III, 133; Lippert, I, 137. There is an excellent map by Peisker in *Camb. Med. Hist.*, Vol. II. For traces of Charlemagne's Saxon limes see Adam of Bremen, II, 18; F. Bangert, "Spuren der Franken am nordalbingischen Limes Saxoniae," *Ztschft. d. hist. Ver. f. Niedersachsen* (1904), pp. 1–62; Schuchhardt, "Ausgrabungen am Limes Saxoniae," *Ztschft. d. Ver. f. Lübeck. Gesch.*, XV, 1–26. The posts were Bardowick, Magdeburg, Erfurt, Halstadt, Schesel, Pfreimt, Regensburg, and Lorch. Intermediate fortified points connected

But though actual Frank sovereignty was not extended farther, it was to the interest of the Frankish monarchy to keep
the border peoples in a state of intimidation.[1] The expedition
was a military demonstration. The Wilzi were beaten but not
intimidated. In 810 they stormed the Frankish border fort at
Hobucki on the Elbe near Gartow,[2] and in 812 three Frankish
armies had to be sent against them.[3] Then it was that Charlemagne was compelled to reorganize the east border on firmer
lines and the scattered Marches were all linked together in a
chain stretching from the North Sea to the head of the
Adriatic.

It was an irrepressible conflict in which race supremacy,
religion, language, trade, customs, and land to live in were
the issues.[4] On the part of the Germanic people the struggle
became a gigantic series of missionary campaigns and colonizing conquests protracted through centuries. Monk missionaries penetrated the Slavonic wilderness bent on peaceable or
compulsory conversion of the Wends, and the sword of a
semi-theocratic kingship was stretched out to protect or

these. One of these lesser fortresses has been identified, the Chat near Bamberg, so
called from the medieval Latin word *catus* (see Klieber, *Bamberger Historischer
Verein* [1882], Bericht 45). The Carolingian Limes has been thoroughly studied by
Beyer, *Der Limes Saxoniae Karls des Grossen* (1878) (cf. *Jenaer Literaturzeitung*
[Feb. 15, 1879] and *Hist. Ztschft.* [N.F.], V, 1879); and two articles by Handelman
in *Archiv d. Vereins f. deutschen Gesch. des Herzogtums Lauenburg*, Band II, Heft 3
(1879); Band III, Heft 1 (1880); Lipp, "Das fränkische Grenzsystem unter Karl dem
Grossen," *Untersuchungen z. deutsch. Staats- und Rechtsgesch.* (1892); Blochwitz,
*Die Verhältnisse an der deutschen Ostgrenze zwischen Elbe und Donau zur Zeit der
ersten Karolinger* (1872). Henigsheim, "Limes Sorabicus," *Ztschft. d. Ver. f. Thür.
Gesch.*, XVI, No. 2 (1906), thinks that the Limes was not a fortified line, but merely
a border patrol between fortified posts. The Karlschanze near Willebadessen in
Westphalia was a Saxon castle destroyed by Charlemagne (Schneider, *Festschrift
f. d. Gesch. Westdeutschlands.*, Band VIII (1888).

[1] Guttmann, *op. cit.*, p. 408, compares Charlemagne's expedition in 789 across
the Elbe to Caesar's crossing of the Rhine.

[2] Dehio, *Gesch. des Erzbistums Hamburg-Bremen*, I, 38, n. 5.

[3] Einhard, *Annales* (812); *Chron. Moissac* (812); Schafarik, II, 319 f., 423–25,
456 f., 517–21. The most recent history of the conflict between the Germans and
the Slavs before the time of Henry I is Merbach, *Slawenkriege d. deutschen Volkes*,
Part I (1914).

[4] Hauck, III, 89–91. His ferocious characterization is not exaggerated.

avenge the priests whom the Wends slew or expelled.[1] But
back of the enmity of race and religion was the fierce land-
hunger of both peoples fighting for fields to till in order to
feed millions of mouths whose hunger it was hard to satisfy
in the primitive conditions under which agriculture was then
practiced.[2]

The eastward drift of the German peoples, intimations of
which are observable in the sixth century, and which by 800
had become a definite trend,[3] was powerfully influenced by
the slow economic, especially agrarian, revolution which took
place in Frankish Gaul and the Rhinelands in the seventh
and eighth centuries. The increase of the benefice system,
the extension of the manorial régime, the adoption of more

---

[1] "Eroberung und Missionierung Hand in Hand," *ibid.*, III, 79.

[2] For detail see Joh. Müller, *Frankenkolonisation auf dem Eichfelde*, pp. 12–13;
cf. *Hist. Ztschft.*, CXIV, No. 3; Meitzen, *Siedelung und Agrarwesen*, II, 401–6;
Lamprecht, III, 311–65. Absolute statistics are, of course, impossible as to population in the Middle Ages. But modern scholars have made some relative determina-
tions. In Carolingian times, favorable regions like the valley of the Moselle, seem
to have had a fairly dense population. Indeed, along rivers which were important
highways of trade the place-names seem to have been more numerous than now,
particularly along the Meuse. In late Merovingian times and down to the invasions
of the Northmen, between the Seine and the Rhine the density of population is
estimated to have been as much as 300 per square mile. The population of the East
Frank kingdom, i.e., Germany, in late Carolingian times is estimated to have been
two and one-half to three millions. It certainly increased under the Saxon rule and
probably was between three and three and one-half millions; the Franconian period
(1024–1125), in spite of the civil war in the reign of Henry IV, was one of great
economic prosperity for Germany, and the population may have been five to six
millions by the beginning of the twelfth century. In the Moselle region the population doubled between 900 and 1100, and by 1200 was quadrupled (Lamprecht,
DWL, I, 1509; 1235–36). In Frederick Barbarossa's time it probably was between
seven and eight millions. At the accession of the Saxon house in 919 there were not
over 30 towns in Germany; at the end of the Franconian period (1125) there were
above 150. In the ninth and tenth century not over 1 to 2 per cent dwelt in towns;
in late Franconian times (1075–1125) from 3 to 5 per cent were town people. Consult R. Kötzschke, *Deutsche Wirtschaftsgesch. bis zum 17. Jahrhundert* (1908), pp.
50–52; Beloch, "Die Bevölkerung Europas im Mittelalter," *Zeitschrift f. Soz. u.
Wirtschaftsgesch.*, III, 417 f.; G. Caro, "Zur Bevölkerungsstatistik der Karolingerzeit," in his *Beiträge*, pp. 38 f.; Lamprecht, *DWL*, I, 181 f.; Inama Sternegg,
DWG, I, 514 f.; II, 29 f.; Curschmann, *Hungersnöte im Mittelalter* (1900). The
author of the *Descriptio Theutoniae*, written at the end of the thirteenth century
derived "Germania" from the Latin *generare*. "Dicitur Germania, quia multos
homines dicitur generare; nulla enim terrarum in tanto spatio dicitur tot homines
continere" (*MGH*, SS. XVII, 238 [cf. Michael, *Gesch. d. deutsch. Volkes*, I, 128, n. 2]).

[3] Kötzschke, pp. 47 and 110.

intensive agricultural methods,[1] in particular on the manors of the fisc and of the church, slowly tended to depress the small free farmer into the condition of a tenant or a serf upon his own lands, the proprietorship of which passed from him to some adjacent noble or high cleric; or else the changing order of things ejected him from his ancestral holding and made him a homeless wanderer—a *homo migrans*. The small land owner could not compete with the grand proprietor in the economic and social transformation which was in process in these years.[2]

As a result the dispossessed and evicted turned to the forests for refuge, there to carve out a clearing in the wilderness and to establish a new home.[3] The forest was the poor man's home.

But the coil of private ownership gradually wound itself around the forests, too. Traces of the intrusion of private proprietorship upon the forests appear in the Burgundian and the Visigothic codes. The forests of the Vosges began to be appropriated in the time of Gregory of Tours (*ca.* 600), those of the Ardennes by the early seventh century.[4] In Charlemagne's time the upper Mosel, the Sieg, and the lower

---

[1] There are signs of soil exhaustion in the oldest parts of Germany as early as the ninth and tenth centuries (Lamprecht, *op. cit.*, I, 1, 113).

[2] E. Dobbert, *Ueber das Wesen und den Geschäftskreis der Missi Dominici* (Heidelberg, 1861) (at end). This reference and the extracts from the capitularies are cited by Hodgkin, *Italy and Her Invaders: The Frankish Empire*, VIII, 297–99. The *Paroenesis ad judices* ("Exhortation to Judges") of Theodulph graphically shows the temptations to official corruption which beset the *missi dominici*. See the long extract in Guizot, *Civilization in France*, Lect. XXIII, pp. 60–64.

[3] "Freilich spielte daneben der Wildbruch im Walde bereits eine immer grössere Rolle; in den Vordergrund aber trat er erst nach voller Sesshaftmachung des Volkes, seit etwa dem 5. bis 6. Jahrhundert. Seitdem ziehen Generationen auf Generationen nachgeborener Söhne in den Urwald und sengen und roden. Das 7. bis 9. Jahrhundert sah einen ersten grossen Ausbau des Landes hinein in die unerschöpflichen Bestände der Bergwälder. . . . . Im 6. bis 8. Jahrhundert war vor allem der gemeinfreie Träger der Waldsiedelung gewesen; im genossenschaftlichen Verbande hatten die jungen Männer des Volkes ein neues Heim in den Tiefen der Waldtäler gesucht" (Lamprecht, *DG*, III, 53). Cf. Kotzschke, p. 47, the last paragraph. For detailed exposition of the economic transformation set forth in this paragraph see von der Goltz, *Gesch. der deutschen Landwirtschaft*, I, 93–98; Inama Sternegg, *Deutsche Wirtschaftsgesch.*, I, 246 ff.; Arnold, *Deutsche Gesch.*, II, 2, 44, 100–109.

[4] Lamprecht, *DWL*, I, 1, 469–70.

Main began to be penetrated by private claims. The early years of the reign of Louis the Pious witnessed such wholesale seizure of forest tracts by private proprietors that the Emperor canceled the titles to all forest holdings of a private nature established without express authorization.[1]

In order to escape from the pressure imposed upon him by the increase in the number and the extent of these great landed estates, both lay and clerical, west of the Rhine and in the Middle Rhinelands, the small landowner and the dispossessed freeman tended to drift eastward into the upper Main and Bavaria, where land was freer and the population less dense along the border. The conquest of Saxony does not

---

[1] *Lex Visigoth.*, VIII, 3, 8; *Lex Burg.*, Art. XIII (*MGH, Leges*, III, 538), Art. LXVII (*ibid.*, p. 561). For the Vosges see Hillman, *Deutsche Finanzgeschichte des Mittelalters*, pp. 249–50; Petit du Taillis, "De la signification du mot 'forêt' à l'époque franque," *Bib. de l'École d. Chartes* (jan.-avril, 1915), pp. 118–19; for the Ardennes, Lamprecht, *Deutsches Wirtschaftsleben*, I, 93 ff.; II, 626; Petit du Taillis, *op. cit.*, pp. 112–17. In 648 Sigbert of Austrasia granted the monastery of Stablo a tract 12 miles square *in vasta Ardenna*, which Childerich II reduced to 6 miles in 667. Inama Sternegg, *op. cit.* (2 ed., 1909), I, 283, and n. 3. Karlmann in 774 gave Fulda a tract measuring 4,000 paces each way (*ibid.*, p. 284, n. 2); in 779 Hersfeld possessed a forest 2 miles in circumference (*ibid.*); in 811 and 813 two Frank nobles owned tracts 2 miles long and 2 miles broad in the Ardennes (*ibid.*, n. 6). Louis the Pious gave Benedict of Aniane's cloister of Cornelimünster a huge tract of the forest of the Ardennes (*Acta* SS. II [Feb. 12], 10). For interpretation of the terminology of the forest in the Middle Ages see Wiener, *Commentary to the Germanic Codes*, pp. 98 ff. In general see von der Goltz, *op. cit.*, I, 139–40; Roscher, *System der Volkswirtschaft; Nationaloekonomik des Ackerbaus und der verwandten Urproduction* (11th ed., 1885), sec. 191; Schröder, "Die Ausbreitung der Salischen Franken," *Forschungen zur deutschen Geschichte*, XIX, 139 f.; Maury, *Les forêts de la France* (1856), chap. vi. For Charlemagne's liberal legislation see *Cap. de Villis*, § 36 (with the notes of Gareis, *Die Landgüterordnung Kaiser Karls d. Gr.*, pp. 44–45); *Cap. Aquisgran*, § 18; cf. Dopsch *Wirtschaftsentwicklung der Karolingerzeit*, I, 175; Arnold, *Ansiedelungen und Wanderungen*, pp. 241 f. For the legislation of Louis the Pious see *Cap. 818–819*, § 7, in Boretius, I, 288; *Cap. missorum* (819), § 22 (*ibid.*, p. 291); cf. *Mélanges Bemont*, p. 63. Petit du Taillis, *op. cit.*, p. 134, makes the point: "La signification constante du mot 'forêt' dans les capitulaires permet d'affirmer que les forêts créés par des particuliers, dont parle Louis le Pieux, étaient des réserves de chasse, ou de pêche, et l'ordre d'abolir les forêts nouvellement instituées, en prouvant qu'il y avait d'autres forêts privées, de fondation ancienne, auxquelles Louis le Pieux ne voulait pas toucher, nous reporte au moins au viiie siècle."

We have no information on private forests at this early period. The increasing curtailment of the right to use the forest was a continuous grievance of the medieval peasantry. Jonas, bishop of Orleans in the ninth century, voiced their protest in a treatise entitled *De institutione laicali*, II, 23: "Deus in commune mortalibus ad utendum concessit, pauperes a potentioribus spoliantur, flagellantur, ergastulis detruduntur et multa alia patiuntur. Hoc ut justo libramine decernant utrum lex mundi legem evacuare Christi debeat, necne" (Migne, *Patrol. Lat.*, CVI, 215).

seem to have been followed immediately by any considerable immigration into the region from points farther west.

The mission of Boniface and the conquests of Charlemagne were the first important stage in the long and bloody struggle between the German and the Slav. In 822 a castle was built on the Delvenau, an affluent of the lower Elbe near Lauenburg, in order to protect Saxony from the inroads of the Abodrites.[1] Under Louis the Pious, Würzburg and Hamburg became advance posts of Christo-German *Kultur*. In 832 the former had fourteen mission churches among the Slavs of the Main.[2] In 834 Anskar founded Hamburg, henceforth the base for the conversion of the north, both Slav and Scandinavian, until the establishment of Bremen.[3]

In the early ninth century the *populi Sclavorum*[4] were as yet floating masses, without close tribal organization and without leaders. The east border was relatively undisturbed until 862 when Ludwig the German made an expedition against Dobomysl, the Abodrite duke. In 866 the Winidi gave trouble. In 869 the Bohemians and Moraven under Swatopluk invaded Bavaria, while the Sorben and Siusli, kindred to them and dwelling along the Mulde, crossed the Saale and penetrated into Thuringia whence they were expelled by a joint Thuringian and Saxon army. Ludwig the German's two sons, Charles (the Fat) and Karlmann, drove Swatopluk back. In 872, 874, 877, 880, 889, 892, 893, 898, there was heavy fighting along the border.[5]

Dopsch justly makes the point that in all likelihood the eastern colonization movement of the German people was

---

[1] *Ann. Lauresh.* (822); Giesebrecht, *Wend. Gesch.*, I, 108.

[2] Rusam, *Beiträge zur Bayerischen Kirchengesch.*, IX, 1.

[3] Adam of Bremen, I, 24, 27, 36 (= *Vita Rimberti*, chap. xvi). See Bril, "Les premiers temps du christianisme en Suède," *Revue d'hist. ecclés.*, XII (1911), 17–37, 231–41, 652–69. In 864 Nicholas I removed the seat of the diocese to Bremen. Cf. Joachim, *Mitth. d. Inst. f. oesterr. Gesch.*, XXXIII, No. 2 (1912); Reuter, *Hist. Ztschft.* (3d ser., 1910), IX, No. 2. The alleged diploma of Charlemagne for Bremen is false (Tangl, *Mitt. d. Inst. f. oesterr. Gesch.*, XVIII, No. 1).

[4] *Annales S. Bert.* (844).

[5] *Ruod. Fuld.* (for these years); the lineaments of the future Sorben Mark may be descried in these events (Schafarik, II, 460–61, 524; Lippert, I, 148). We know the names, preserved in *Ann. Fuld.*, of two of the margraves, *Ratolf* (873–80) and Poppo (880–92); cf. Dümmler, I, 714 f.; Riezler, *Gesch. Bayerns*, I, 217 f.

relatively as strong in the ninth century as later. It differed chiefly in direction, being toward the southeast instead of the northeast, and was more exclusively aristocratic and clerical in its nature than the colonization movement of the twelfth century, which was largely a popular wave. If the sources for the reigns of Ludwig the German and Arnulf were proportionately as full as those of the Salian and Hohenstaufen periods, there is little doubt that the continuity of the history of German eastward colonization would clearly appear from the time of Charlemagne onward.[1]

What Professor Turner has called "the common sequence of frontier types—fur trader, cattle raising, pioneer, small primitive farmer"[2] is true of the frontier of medieval Germany, although for lack of the abundant evidence which American history affords the differentiations cannot be so clearly established and the impression is not so definite. Yet the distinctions are perceptible. While the Rhine cities in the tenth century were obscurely building up a trade which blossomed into rich fruitage in the Salian era and the Rhinelands were intensively cultivating the grape, Mainzer merchants imported grain and cattle into the city from the estates of the Hessian monasteries of Fulda and Hersfeld or from the Slav-tilled fields of the upper Main, freighting the grain downstream to the Rhine.[3] Beyond the monastery

---

[1] Dopsch, *op. cit.*, I, 174–75; cf. Inama Sternegg, *op. cit.*, I, 280–81; Lamprecht, *DWG*, I, 245, 290–97. Even in spite of the poverty of information in the chronicles the documentary evidence is impressive. See the long list of Carolingian grants in Eggers, *Der königliche Grundbesitz im 10. und 11. Jh.*, pp. 28–32.

[2] "The First Official Frontier of Mass.," *Col. Soc. of Mass.*, XVII (1914), 254.

[3] *Translatio SS. Marcellini et Petri* (by Einhard); "Mercatores quidam de civitate Mogontiaco, qui frumentum in superioribus Germaniae partibus emere ac per fluvium Moinum ad urbem devehere solebant." Cf. Mathai, "Einhards Translatio, SS. Marcellini et Petri in kulturgeschichtlicher Beziehung," *Progr. d. Gymn. zu Laubach* (1883–84), p. 12. Mlle Bondois, *La translation des saints Marcellin et Pierre* (Paris, 1907), curiously ignores these economic data. In the eighth century wheat cultivation and spelt appear among the peoples bordering on the Franks, and, per contra, in the ninth century the cultivation of rye, the grain of the Slavs, makes its appearance in the German sources (Kretschmer, p. 201). On the economy of the Bonifacian monasteries see Sommerlad, *Die wirtschaftliche Tätigkeit der Kirche*, I, 278, 288; II, 152. Inama Sternegg, *DWG*, I, 8; Meitzen, "Der aelteste Anbau der Deutschen," *Jahrb. f. Nationaloek. und Statistik* (N.F., 1881), II, 1–46; Roscher, *Ansichten der Volkswirtschaft aus dem geschichtlichen Standpunkte* (3d ed.), I, 205–

ranches and great farms of Hesse and lower Franconia conditions became more primitive, and in their place appeared
small farms, clearings in the forest, and patches of soil crude-
ly tilled by a German peasantry in Thuringia and Saxony,
and by Wendish folk in upper Franconia, along the higher
reaches of the Main and the Regnitz. From this "back-land"
zone things rapidly shaded off into the pure frontier marked
by the Saale and the lower Elbe rivers.

The border warfare was a profitable source of serf and
slave supply for the Bonifacian monasteries, which had great
need of raw labor for the exploitation of their vast properties.[1] The greater portion of eastern Franconia, the upper
Main around Bayreuth, Bamberg, Würzburg, and Nuremberg, was solidly Slav before the year 1000.[2] It was not until
the twelfth century that the pagan Slavs in these regions were
converted, although the districts had figured as *Gaue* on German maps since 889. When the bishopric of Bamberg was
established in 1007 the synod of Frankfort decreed "ut paganismus Sclavorum inibi destrueretur."[3] Yet in the proceedings of the synod of Bamberg in 1058 one reads: "Erat enim

---

38; Waitz, *DVG*, I, 32–52; Seeck, "Die aelteste Kultur der Deutschen," *Preuss.
Jahrb.*, LXXVI (1894), 32–58; Lamprecht, "Zur Sozialgesch. der deutschen Urzeit,"
Festgabe f. Hanssen, pp. 61–72; Riedel, *Mark Brand.*, II, 10–11 and notes. For the
subject of cattle-raising in general see Langethal, *Gesch. der teutschen Landwirtschaft*,
I (Jena, 1847), 46 f.; von der Goltz, *Landwirtschaft*, I (1902), 67–84, 98–116; Lamprecht, *DWL*, I, 532 f., 543 f.; and especially Lauffer, *Das Landschaftsbild im Zeitalter der Karolinger* (Göttingen diss., 1896), pp. 63–76. Regensburg was evidently
a center of cattle-raising in the time of Otto I (Widukind, III, 36).

[1] Schafarik, *op. cit.*, II, 607. The registers of Fulda often mention clusters of
Slavonic villages in the woody districts around the abbey (Zeuss, *op. cit.*, p. 646,
quoting Schann, *Buchonia Vetus*, pp. 46–48). Of Slavs in the Lower Harz near Mans-
feld we have mention in a deed of 973: "De possessionibus S. Bonifatii martyris
[follows the names of 12 localities] .... villis villarumque partibus quas Slavuaini-
cae familiae inhabitant" (Zeuss, *op. cit.*, p. 647, after Schann, *Tradit. Fuld.*, p. 241).

[2] Seyler, *Archiv f. Gesch. und Alterth. von Oberfranken*, Band XVII, Heft 3
(1889). The Council of Tribur in 895 (*Regino*, II, cap. 5, n. 43; Burchard Worm.,
Canon 69), and the *Poenitent. Merseburg.* imposed penance for the practice of
pagan rites (Mannhardt, *Der Baumkultus*, p. 245, n. 3; p. 331, n. 1; Friedberg,
Bussbücher, pp. 24, 61, 86). For Slav paganism in the vicinity of Bielefeld (*ca.* 940)
see Giesebrecht, *Wendische Geschichten*, I, 83. For legislation of the Eastern church
against the persistence of pagan practices among the southern Slavs see Mannhardt,
op. cit., pp. 470–71.

[3] Migne, CXL, 115.

plebs hujus episcopii utpote ex maxima parte Sclavonica."
Half a century later, in 1111, Arnold, bishop of Halberstadt,
still could write to Otto of Bamberg: "Totam illam terram
paene silvam esse, Sclavos ibi habitare." Later deeds of Bamberg for many years make mention of Slavs, and the appearance and dialect of the people yet attest a large Slavonic admixture.[1]

Along the line of the Elbe from the Erzgebirge to Hamburg, German colonization annexed immense tracts of border
territory, while in the interior dukes and margraves, bishops
and abbots, vied with one another in clearing forests, reclaiming moors and swamps. In addition to these acquisitions thousands of acres of arable land in the form of farms
were given to the church by the piety of nobles and the com-
placency of kings. These gifts were manors either of the
noble donor or taken from the royal fisc. Moreover, the
church extended its manorial machinery in the imposition of
tithes and other economic obligations upon the free peasantry
more and more so that in the end they were either compelled
to evacuate their holdings all together, which the church
promptly assimilated with its own lands, or else to accept the
condition of serfdom upon their once free acres, which ceased
longer to belong to them.

The stages in the eastward expansion of the German
people are marked, though not so clearly, as the same phenomenon in the United States. In Charlemagne's reign the
frontier of settlement (for we must distinguish between the
military boundary and the edge of civilization) was barely
beyond the Rhine. A line drawn through Frankfort and
Soest, across the sources of the Ruhr and the Lippe, would
perhaps mark it. For the chain of fortified trading posts
along the course of the lower Elbe, the Saale, and the Nab
rivers from Bardowick to Regensburg was far from the civilization of the Frankish empire.[2] Under the rule of the Saxon
house (919–1024) the frontier of settlement and the military
boundary became more nearly identical. The line of civilization was extended to the Saale in Thuringia, but in Saxony

---

[1] Schafarik, *op. cit.*, II, 609; Hauck, III, 418–19.   [2] Hauck, III, 77–78.

proper stopped at the Aller and the Ocker rivers.[1] Along the middle Main civilization had also crept up as far as Würzburg, as a charter of Otto III shows, which granted special privileges to settlers who would come and reclaim the forests and drain the marshes.[2] By the eleventh century Bamberg, which Henry II founded in 1007, had succeeded Würzburg as the frontier outpost of the Main Valley.[3] The sources of the Saxon period show the large progress made in eastward colonization.[4] Along the eastern edge of the kingdom from the mouth of the Elbe to the mountains of Styria, German colonists annexed immense tracts of territory.[5] But the Elbe was not permanently crossed until the twelfth century.[6]

These pioneers were chiefly engaged in cattle-raising. Court judgments in this region were imposed in cattle fines under Otto I, and the legislation shows the prevalence of agrarian crime, especially cattle-stealing.[7]

At the opening of the tenth century, the beginning of the Saxon epoch, the population of Germany was very unevenly

[1] Gerdes, *Geschichte des deutschen Volkes*, I, 357; Schulze, *op. cit.*, pp. 50 f.: Schwarz, *Die Anfänge des Städtewesen in den Elb- und Saale-Gegenden* (1892).

[2] Gerdes, I, 371; Matthias, *Klosterpolitik Heinrichs II*, II, 74. In the time of Arnulf, a century earlier, the bishopric of Würzburg was solidly Slav (*Ep. Arnulfi*, in Jaffé, V, 477), and still must have been heavily so in the year 1000.

[3] Hauck, III, 418–19.

[4] For cattle-raising along the frontier see Sommerlad, II, 266; Wattenbach, *Deutschlands Geschichtsquellen im Mittelalter*, II, 33 f. The *Vita Meinwerci* is rich in economic data.

[5] Gerdes, I, 337 f.; Lamprecht, *Deutsche Geschichte*, III, 52 f.

[6] An exception, of course, is here inferred for Holstein and Ditmarsch. As we have already seen, in 804 Charlemagne deported the Nordalbingian Saxons, and permitted the Abodrites to settle in their room. At what subsequent period and under what circumstances the Saxons recrossed the river and acquired a permanent foothold again in Holstein and Ditmarsch is not known. History has left no record of this movement. *Holsati* simply means "settlers in the wood" (*Holz*). But the suffix *satas* or *settas* elsewhere usually indicates a "frontier," or at least a "settlement under wilderness conditions." Thus in Anglo-Saxon England we find along the western Marches the names Dorsaetas, Somersaetas. *Thiatmarsgoi* means "dwellers in the marshes of Thiatmars," hence Ditmarsch. In fine, we do not know how and when Holstein and Ditmarsch were repeopled with Saxons. Place-names are our sole historical evidence (see Hansen, *Ztschft. d. Gesellschaft f. Schleswig-Holstein. Gesch.*, Band XXXIII).

[7] Wid., II, 6; Roscher, *Polit. Economy* (Eng. trans.), I, p. 353, note.

distributed. In the Rhinelands, from the mouth of the
Rhine to the Hochgebirge, the peopling seems to have been
quite dense and there was a high degree[1] of material culture.
In Lorraine, west Franconia, and Swabia the population must
have been numerous and the material civilization considerable. But Saxony, Bavaria, and the Ostmark were still thinly
peopled, and until the forays of the Magyars were arrested
effective southeastward movement of the Germans was impossible. The upper Neckar was not penetrated by settlers
until the verge of the eleventh century,[2] and the Frankenwald[3]
and high valley of the Murg were not colonized before the
twelfth.[4]

The Wends seem to have confronted fort with fort against
the Saxons. We know from Einhard's *Annals*[5] that they had
palisaded towns, or at least *castella*, along their western
border, and modern archaeological research has discoverd
the site and explored the ruins of a considerable number of
ancient Slav fortifications. Ibrahim ibn Jakub, the Mohammedan traveler in Germany in 973, describes their town walls
as high and made of hard-packed earth.[6]

[1] For the colonization of upper Swabia see Victor Ernst, "Zur Besiedelung
Oberschwabens," *Festschrift Dietrich Schäfer* (1915).

[2] Weller, *Wuerttemb. Vierteljahrshefte f. Landesgesch.* (N.F., 1894), Band III.

[3] Meyer, *Alterthumsforschender Verein zu Holenhauben*, Band LII.

[4] Hartmann, *Wuerttemb. Jahrb. f. Statistik und Landeskunde* (1893) (with map).

[5] *Anno* 808: ". . . . captis aliquot Sclavorum castellis."

[6] Wigger, *Jahrb. f. Mecklenburgische Gesch.* (1880). See for this subject Saal-
born, *Neues Lausitzisches Magazin*, Band LV (1879); Kasten, *Baltische Studien*,
Band XXIX (1879), a study of the foundations of the castle of Winburg on the
Pregel, which are of Wendish origin; Grupp, *Jahresbericht über den historischen
Verein zu Brandenburg an der Havel* (1881), shows that the lower strata of the
ancient walls of Potsdam and Rathenow are of Wendish construction; cf. Handel-
mann, *Ztschft. der Gesellschaft f. Schleswig-Holstein*, X, 4–24, on fortifications of the
Polaben and Wagrians; Schildt, *Jahrb. d. Vereins f. Meckl. Gesch.*, Band LII (1887),
castrum Wustrord on the Tollensee; Schumann, *Baltische Studien*, Band XXVII,
Heft 1 (1887), Randow; Welter, *Ztschft. f. Kulturgesch.* (3d ser., 1893), Heft vi,
(Lüchow in Hannover). Widukind, III, 45, 51, 62, mentions three Wendish fortresses, and apparently Merseburg before Saxon conversion of it into a *Burg* was
another Slav stronghold, for Thietmar, I, 5, writing *ca.* 1000 calls it "an ancient
city," and its name, despite its apparent German character, is Slavonic, i.e., *Mesibor*, or "Town in the Woods" (Schaferik, *Slav. Alterth.*, II, 620; Meitzen, *Siedelung und
Agrarwesen*, II, 332).

The military prestige of Duke Otto the Illustrious (d. 912) acquired in warfare with the Wends, and which passed on to his son Henry the Fowler, was an important factor in securing the latter's election to the German kingship in 919.[1]

With the accession of Henry I to the German throne, the eastward pressure of the German race was actively pushed. The Sorben land between the Saale and the upper Elbe was the first territory wrung from the Slavs by the German sword and the first to be Germanized. But it is a mistake to regard the conquest and settlement of this land as a prototype of the colonization of the territory across the Elbe, i.e., Nordalbingia, Mecklenburg, and Brandenburg. The eastward expansion of the German people was not a uniform movement, nor was the process the same in every part. In Nordalbingia and the Billunger March the expansion was, as we shall see, a natural expansion and the settlement a true colonization. But in the Sorben "triangle" it was a conquest made by government and not by the people—a military occupation made for the purpose of strengthening and straightening the frontier against the Poles and the Bohemians. Over a century was to elapse before any real colonization or much exploitation of the soil began. Even the church had no part in the process until a considerable time had elapsed. The Thuringian March was a veritable *Reichsland*.

In the tenth century the eastward pressure of the German race, which was arrested during the ninth century, partly owing to the lesion of government and society within, and partly to a brief hardening of the Slavonic offensive, was aggressively resumed. This border policy was purely Saxon in initiative and interest[2] although it was destined in the ultimate to be of profound importance to the entire German people. Henry I committed Germany to a policy of a thousand

[1] Arnulf in 897 calls Otto "fidelis marchio noster" (Dronke, *Codex Fuld.*, No. 295).

[2] Hauck, III, 76: "Die wendischen Eroberungen sind die weltgeschichtliche Tat Heinrichs I. Durch sie hat er das deutsche Volk in das Gebiet geführt, in das sich nach fast einem Jahrtausend der Schwerpunkt der deutschen Macht verlegen sollte." Cf. Guttmann, "Die Germanisierung der Slawen in der Mark," *Forsch. zur Brand. u. Preuss. Gesch.*, IX, 411.

years. Yet purely Saxon as it was, Henry's border policy was in alignment with the Carolingian tradition. His aim was to make the trans-Elbean Wendish peoples tributary again to the German power, from which they had escaped in the ninth century. In pursuance of this course, in the winter of 928–29 Henry made a campaign across the frozen marshes of the Havel River and "by hunger, sword and cold," as Widukind[1] says, took Brunabor, the chief town of the Hevelli, and converted it into a *Burg* after the fashion of the fortified places he had established in Saxony and Thuringia. Such is the particular beginning of Brandenburg. Before the force of this drive was spent the Saxon arms had advanced up the Elbe clear to Meissen, conquered the Daleminzi in this region, and gained a vantage-point of great importance for the future.[2] The Saxon menace was so great that it inspired a coalition of the threatened tribes—Abodrites, Wilzi, Hevelli, Daleminzi, and Redarii—of whom the last were the warlike custodians of the shrine of Slavonic faith at Rethra and the leaders of the war for independence. A furious battle was fought at Lenzen on the right bank of the Elbe below Wittenberg, in September, 929, the issue of which left the Wends broken and shattered.[3] A Saxon expedition in 932, up the Elster, culminating in another engagement at Lebusa, completed the reduction of the Slavs between the upper Elbe and the Saale.[4] The German "sphere of influence" extended to the Oder and the Erzgebirge. Even Bohemia, with Bavarian assistance, was reduced to tribute.[5]

Of the importance of these achievements Henry the Fowl-

[1] I, 35: *fame, ferro, frigore* (Schafarik, II, 372). For the cruelty of Henry I see Hauck, III, 74–78; for the retaliation of the Wends see *ibid.*, p. 91.

[2] "Hic montem unum juxta Albim positum et arborum densitate tunc occupatum excoluit, ibi et urbem faciens, de rivo quodam, qui in septentrionali parte ejusdem fluit, nomen eidem Misni imposuit; quam ut hodie in usu habetur, presidiis et imposicionibus caeteris munit" (Thietmar, *Chron.*, I, 9).

[3] All the chroniclers notice this battle (Wid., I, 36; Thietmar, I, 10; *Annal. Corb* [929]; *Chron. Breve Brem.*, *MGH*, SS. VII, 391).

[4] *Annal. Hildesh.*, *Annal. Weissenb.* (932); Thietmar, I, 16. For nearly a century, until repeopled by Henry II in 1012, it was desolate (*ibid.*, VI, 59). The territory between the Mulde and the Saale was called Osterland.

[5] Lippert, I, 170.

SLAVONIC TRIBES ALONG EASTERN FRONTIER IN TENTH AND ELEVENTH
CENTURIES

Barred marking in Wagria = Half Germanized

er seems to have had a slight appreciation. He was content merely with the payment of tribute.[1] He had no constructive ideas to apply to the conquered territory for its pacification and civilization, such as Charlemagne had applied in Saxony. There was no thought of a March of Meissen under him, although nearly the whole line of the Elbe was under Saxon control.[2] He established no systematic defensive organization along the eastern frontier. He made no effort to promote colonization or Christianity in the region.[3] Henry I seems to have valued the Slavonic tribute chiefly as a means of defraying the cost of his military reforms in Saxony[4] and the warfare on the border principally as a training school for his soldiery against the Hungarians. He did not even attempt to extend the Burgward system, which he had so successfully instituted in Saxony and Thuringia, beyond the Elbe and the Saale rivers. Brandenburg and Meissen were isolated frontier posts with no chain of forts to sustain them. No effort was made to colonize the country. The land lay undeveloped, peopled by a cowed but sullen and hostile population. The real Germanization of Meissen begins with Wiprecht von Groitsch.[5]

Yet for his failure to promote German settlement in these regions Henry I is hardly to be blamed. The Saxons were still dwelling in an almost primitive culture. Their social structure was simple and without the firmer distinctions of privilege and property which were attached to the more complex feudal society of France and the Rhinelands as well as Swabia and Bavaria. Saxony was a whole century and more behind them in social and economic development. Land was still cheap and abundant. Saxon feudalism was still simple and elementary in its form. The Saxon people had yet to experience the stress of social transformations and the thrust of economic pressure, such as prevailed farther west. That change came to Saxony in the late eleventh and twelfth cen-

[1] Wid., II, 20 and 30; Waitz, *Heinrich I*, p. 95; Hauck, III, 77.

[2] Richter, *Annalen*, II, 14*b*; Gebhardt, *Handbuch*, Vol. I, p. 249.

[3] Guttmann, *Forschungen zur Brand. u. Preuss. Geschichte*, IX, 417–18.

[4] Wid., II, 30; Wendt, I, 21.   [5] Tetzner, *op. cit.*, p. 293.

turies, but in the tenth century there was neither a surplus
population nor social and economic discontent in Saxony
sufficient to induce the Saxon peasantry to migrate to the
"New East" which was just being opened up by the sword.[1]

Henry I had contented himself with reducing the Sorben
to tribute. Established political forms in the Thuringian
March began with Otto I who divided the country into *pagi*
which roughly followed the older Slav lines.[2] These distinctions, however, seem to have been chiefly for topographical
convenience. Effective German occupation was insured by
division of the territory into military *cadres*, each district
having a military base (Burgward),[3] which seems usually to
have been a former Slavonic village fortified and garrisoned
by the conquerors. In the course of natural evolution, in
time these became units in the civil and ecclesiastical administration of the country. But in the Saxon epoch the administration was a purely military one.

This practice on Otto's part was actually the extension to
the Sorben land of the military measures which Henry I had
instituted in southeastern Saxony and Thuringia.

It was his father's tested-and-tried military system which
Otto I and his successors extended over the new Sorben
Reichsland. Like a huge net a meshwork of Burgwärde was
spread over the country.[4] A map of the region exhibits that
"exceedingly neat and artificial scheme of political geography" presented by the English Midlands at the same
time.[5] It is not possible to locate every Burgward that is
mentioned in the documents; but enough can be identified
to show the thoroughgoing nature of Otto I's practice. The

---

[1] See the remarks of Schulze, *Die Kolonisierung und Germanisierung der Gebiete
zwischen Saale und Elbe* (Leipzig, 1896), pp. 78–80; Wendt, I, 43, n. 3.

[2] Guttmann, p. 417, n. 6.

[3] These Burgwärde were all built of timber, as were the churches too. Thietmar,
II, 36, mentions with astonishment that Zeitz in 970 had a stone church.

[4] "Das ganze Land muss mit einem Netz von Burgen bedeckt gewesen sein"
(Gerdes, *Gesch. d. deutschen Volkes*, I, 431). It is interesting to observe that in 1830
a French writer substantially recommended this same practice to the French
government for the conquest of Algeria (*La féodalité comme moyen de conserver et de
civiliser l'Algérie* [Paris, 1840]), published anonymously.

[5] Maitland, *Domesday Studies*, p. 187.

PRINCIPAL GERMAN BURGWARDE

Notice their density in the Sorben Land

Burgward system was based upon the rivers of the region, namely, the Saale, the Weisse Elster, the Mulde, and the Elbe, all of which flow north and roughly parallel. On the Saale lay Nienburg, Bernburg, Wettin, Giebichenstein, and Merseburg; on the Elster were Schkeuditz, Leipzig, Taucha, Zwenkau, Groitzsch, Döbilzschen, Teilzig, Zeitz; on the Mulde and its affluents, the Zwickauer Mulde and the Freiberger Mulde, lay Düben, Eilenburg, Püchau, Wurzen, Döben, Rochlitz, Kohren, Allenburg, Colditz, Leisnig, Döbeln, Lobnitz, Nerschav; on the Elbe, Wörlitz near Dessau, Torgau, Mühlburg, Belgern, Strehlen, Boritz, Zehren, Zadel, Meissen, Pesterwitz, Briesnitz; Dohna commanded the Nollendorf Pass over the Erzgebirge into Bohemia. The four rivers formed a quadruple line of occupation and defense. In order to connect them, transverse lines of Burgwärde were established so that the country was not unlike a vast gridiron. For example, between the upper Saale and the Elster were Hohen and Mölsen; between the Elster and the Mulde lay Altenburg; between the Mulde and the Elbe were Oschats, Jana, Lommatzsch, and Mügeln.[1]

[1] The paragraph above describes the system in result rather than in process. Many of the Burgwärde were founded in the time of Otto II, Otto III, and Henry II —or at least not mentioned in sources of Otto I's reign. For example, Merseburg and Meissen were founded by Henry I. Kühnau and Steene, near Dessau, appear in 945; Osmünde, Trotha, and Groitzsch appear in 952; Giebichenstein, Wettin, Löbejün, Rothenburg, and Bernburg in 961; Rosenburg and Grimschleben in 965; Brachstedt, Oppin, and Gutenberg in 966; Pratau, Torgau, Belgern, and Rädewell in 973; Nerschau and Zwenkau in 974; Norits in 979; Schkeuditz (though it probably was older), Tauscha, Wurzen, Püchau, Eilenburg, Düben, Lobnitz, and Geserzisca in 981; Mügeln in 983; Treben, Kreuschberg, and Schkölen in 993; Seusslitz in 997; Strehlen in 1003; Rochlitz in 1009; Leisnig in 1040; Colditz and Zschaetz in 1046, etc. Leipzig is mentioned as a Burgward first in 1050, but it must have been such before.

Interspersed between the Burgwärde were also many *castella* or *oppida*, especially in the north and middle. Thietmar mentions sixteen of these, and others are referred to in the *diplomata*. They may be described as finer meshes of the network which covered the country. These castles seem to have been intrusted to single captains having a mere handful of men, perhaps not over a dozen. Generally a few Wendish villages were attached to them. Smaller still than these and of less number, pointing to the fact, perhaps, that the manorial régime in Saxon times was yet young in the land, we find mention of *curtes* and *villae*—communities consisting of but one hamlet. Thietmar mentions seven of the former and eleven of the latter. The distinction between them is to be observed. The *curtis* was a fortified manor-house (*villa munita*). The *villa* an open, unfortified village (*vicus*). The relatively slight number of these communities, when compared with the large number of Burg-

Within this conquered triangular area, where peace was maintained by the sword, scattered between the lines of the Burgwärde and castles lay the hamlets of the Sorben people. In the vicinity of Zwenkau in the time of Otto I a Wendish chieftain of some eminence is found. To this day the well-watered and fertile country west of Dresden is predominantly occupied by a Wendish peasantry. Judging from the numerous localities of Slavonic name which Thietmar mentions, and the many Wendish place-names which still survive, the Sorben population must have been fairly dense for the time.

A paragraph from Schulze describes the actual state of the Sorben land at the end of Saxon times:

[There was] an unfree, half-pagan Sorb population mixed with a few German serfs, ruled over by a great number of German lords and military *ministeriales*, who occupied the Burgorte and Burgsitze throughout the land, and lived upon the products of the acres which these (and the landless house-servants) cultivated for them, or from which they made various payments in kind. There was no Germanization, no penetration or permeation of the land with German customs and German life. It was a condition of affairs analogous to that in the Russian Baltic provinces, where a German sphere of domination grew up as a result of the settlement of German knightly families. The Germanization was neglected because the occupants failed to attract German peasants. The towns do not come into consideration because they were essentially but slightly connected with the land and found their centre of gravity and the focus of their interest in their relations with the west.[1]

The few Saxon settlers who came brought with them into the newly conquered country their own method of measuring

---

wärde and castles, shows how much of a conquered country the region was thought to be. For further details see Waitz, VIII, 192 f.; von Essenwein, *Kriegsbaukunst*, p. 6; Delbrück, *Kriegskunst*, III, 70 f.; Lipp, *Das Fränk. Grenzsystem*; Hellwig, *Städtewesen zur Zeit der Ottonen*; Köhler, *Kriegswesen*, III, 1, 343 f.; Schulze, *Kolonisierung*, pp. 63–69; Kaemmel, *Sächsische Geschichte*, pp. 22–25; Wendt, I, 32–43; Gerdes, I, 459–61. In the Salian period the word Burgward became obsolete, the usual term being *castellum* (Waitz, VIII, 210). It is noteworthy that only in the cases of Meissen and Merseburg had the population grown to such proportion that the walls could not include it all, and a part of it was clustered outside *in suburbio* (Thietmar, VI, 55; VIII [VII], 23 [15]; Widukind, II, 3). With the development of town life and trade in the thirteenth century the Pfahlburg (=*faubourg*) became a characteristic of almost every German city. For a description of that around Worms see *Ann. Wormat.* Fontes, II, 190.

[1] Schulze, *Kolonisierung*, p. 120; cf. Hauck, III, 97; Hanstein, *Siedelung des sächs. Vogtlandes* (1904).

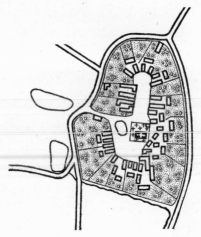

Ground-Plan of a Slavonic Runddorf or Round Village

the land and their own land unit.[1] The rudely cultivated fields of the Wends were too irregular and probably too scattered to admit of any other form of survey.[2] Consequently, the incoming Germans do not seem to have made any effort to preserve either the native method of survey or even native lines of division, but to have "dealt out" the conquered lands after the manner with which they were familiar. Such surveying was probably simple when confined as it was to the tilled acres of the Wends. Owing to their primitive rural economy,[3] the farms of the Wendish folk must have usually been of small extent, so that a considerable number of native villages with fields, pasture, and woods must often have been included in a single grant. The larger domains of the church must frequently have embraced within their complex hundreds of the small farms of the Wendish people. In these early days there was tillable land enough without the necessity of breaking new ground in forest and marsh as developed later. Resort was not made to this pioneer practice until the twelfth century when there was an enormous influx of immigrants into the trans-Elbean lands.

In the submissive Sorben land the courts of the margrave, the clergy, and the nobility were naturally German, although there are traces of a Wendish upper class, even a few of knightly rank.[4]

[1] The Germans, like the Norse, measured land by means of a rope (*funiculum*). Helmold, I, 83 (pp. 162–63), and II, 14 (p. 218), describes the method. For the same practice in Normandy see Freeman, *William Rufus*, I, 68 n.; II, 562–64. For France see Suger, *Vita Ludovici* (ed. Molinier), p. 48; *Cart. de l'abbaye de St. Bertin*, III, 344.

[2] Meitzen, *Ausbreitung der Deutschen*, p. 39; Inama Sternegg, I, 443.

[3] Oxen were scarce and horses even rarer among the Wends. Two oxen or one horse was reckoned to the "plowland," which implies that the Wendish farms were very small (Helmold, I, 12, 14, 89). Two hundred years later, in the twelfth century, the same condition of agriculture still prevailed (Helmold, I, 88; Heinrici, *Chron. Lyvoniae*, II, 7). The German plow was like that of the Romans. In the Slavonic plow the angle of beam and point was more acute. It had no share and no knife-edge. See on this subject Rau, *Gesch. des Pfluges* (Heidelberg, 1845); Anton, *Gesch. der deutschen Landwirtschaft*, I, 51, 96, 379; II, 256; Langethal, *op. cit.*, I, 551 f.; II, 344 f.; von der Goltz, *op. cit.*, pp. 29, 128 f.; Dopsch, *Wirtschaftsentwicklung der Karolingerzeit*, II, 136.

[4] Thietmar, II, 24: "Cuchovic senior Slavorum"; Lepsius, *Naumburg*, I, 203: "quidquid per beneficium Sememizl tenuit" (1040); *Codex diplom.*, A, I, 79–142:

The great mass of the population in the Sorben March was an unfree Wendish peasantry. For many years Meissen was the sole important German town.[1] Leipzig is first mentioned by Thietmar of Merseburg in 1015, but of trace of trade yet there is no evidence.[2] In 1104 the colony of Franken settled by Margrave Conrad of Wettin (1123-57) in his forest by Lausigk appears.[3]

The jealous eye with which Otto the Great regarded the Sorben land, the value of which both as a buffer and as a connecting link between Saxony and Bavaria he fully appreciated, is in sharp contrast to the relative indifference he displayed toward Brandenburg and Nordalbingia. In the north, Hermann Billung was made both duke and margrave.[4] But Gero, despite his long and loyal service in the Thuringian March, was always kept in a distinctly official capacity. No feudal dignity or rank was attached to his position. He was not even made a margrave,[5] although his deeds and daring found him a place as "marcgrâve Gêre" in that hall of fame— the *Nibelungenlied*. "Great was he and so was called," says Thietmar in eulogy of him.[6] Yet to the end of his days Gero's

---

"Liber homo Bor, natione Slavus," (1071); "Szwizla fidelis" (1031); "Moic miles" (1042); "Jarmir miles" (1045). See Winter, *Cistercienser*, I, 35-37; Wendt, II, 5 n. Meitzen, *Jahrb. f. Nationaloek. und Statistik*, XXXII, 879, gives special attention to the partition of the Wendish lands. He argues that the race mixture necessarily compelled a supreme military organization. For the church in the Sorben land see H. H. Grössler, "Die Begründung der christlichen Kirche in dem Lande zwischen Saale und Elbe," *Ztschft. d. Ver. f. Kirchengesch. in d. Prov. Sachsen*, Band IV (Eisleben, 1907).

[1] Lippert, *Geschichte Böhmens*, I, 11, 69, 70, 79, has collected the few data in regard to trade at Meissen.

[2] *Chronicon*, VIII, 25, 66; IX, 7.

[3] *Annales Pegav.*, SS. XVI, 247; cf. Posse, *Die Markgrafen von Meissen*, p. 297. For the growth of the church in the Sorben March at the end of the eleventh and in the early twelfth century see Hauck, IV, 555-63.

[4] Widukind, II, 4; Adam of Bremen, II, 7.

[5] Gero's title *marchio* was not an official one, and was not current during his lifetime. It grew up when legend began to gather around him, as it did early. "Gero .... olim licet multis gestis insigniis clarus haberetur" (Widukind, III, 54). Widukind only styles him *comes* or *praeses* (see Guttmann, p. 415, n. 2).

[6] III, 54 and 75; VI, 57. For a modern appreciation see Heinemann, *Markgraf Gero*, p. 117.

office was an inferior one, either because Otto I was determined to hold the newly conquered territory as a *Reichsland* and was jealous of even a delegation of authority,[1] or because he hesitated to promote to one of the highest of feudal dignities a man of low birth, whatever his capacities, whom the Saxon nobles hated.[2]

If now we turn to the territory bounded by the Baltic, the Oder, the marshes of the Havel and the lower Elbe—to Brandenburg and Nordalbingia, in a word—we find that here the border problem and its solution were very different. There was here no compact Slavonic mass like the Sorben, but detached and often mutually hostile Slav tribes, Abodrites, Wilzi (or Ljutizi), Redarians, Polabians, Hevellians, etc., whose division naturally weakened their power of resistance to German pressure.[3] In 936 Otto I erected this whole region from the Trave to the Peene rivers into a March and put it in the care of Hermann Billung,[4] who was given far larger liberty than Gero in the Sorben March. Otto's lack of vision was destined to throw future control of German colonization toward the northeast out of the hands of the German kings, who in their national office should have been the directors of it, and into the hands of the feudal princes.[5]

The loose and lavish nature of this grant is in sharp contrast with Otto's jealous retention of the Thuringian March

[1] "Der König als Eroberer betrachtete sich als Eigenthümer alles Bodens" (Guttmann, p. 416).

[2] Their hatred of Gero is creditable to Gero's sense of rectitude: "Cum milites ad manum Geronis presidis conscripti crebra expeditione attenuarentur et donativis vel tributariis premiis minus adjuvari possent, eo quod tributa passim negarentur, seditioso odio in Geronem exacuuntur" (Widukind, II, 30; cf. Schulze, p. 54; Nitzsch, I, 333, 342).

[3] Cf. Sommerfeld, *Geschichte d. Germanisierung des Herzogtums Pommern*, in Schmoller's *Forschungen*, XIII, No. 5 (1896), 7.

[4] *Annales Corb.* (934); Widukind, I, 40; Thietmar, I, 9; Adam of Bremen, I, 57, 59; Waitz, *Jahrbuch*, pp. 277 ff., Excursus 24. The account of the origin of the Billunger in Adam of Bremen, II, 9, is saga; cf. ed. Schmeider, p. 67, n. 2; Dümmler, *Otto I*, pp. 570–76.

[5] See the observations of Lamprecht, IV, 13–14, on the bearing of this course upon the future history of Germany and cf. Fisher, *Medieval Empire*, I, 263, 314–15. More foresighted than the crown the church made use of the tithe in the colonial lands from the very beginning (Lamprecht, *Deutsche Geschichte*, III, 116).

in his own hands. The original trans-Elbean policy of Otto I seems to have been to adhere to the Carolingian tradition of exacting tribute of the border tribes, partly as a guaranty of keeping the peace, partly as a means to defray the cost of policing the border. He never seems to have contemplated carving another crown land out in Nordalbingia, as he did between the Saale and the upper Elbe. Hermann Billung was far more independent than Gero.[1]

Hermann Billung, in his new and powerful capacity as "lord of the north," immediately set to work to make his office profitable to himself and his house. Avarice was a notorious Billunger attribute from generation unto generation.[2] The Saxons were proverbially land greedy.[3] The Slavonic tribute, by diligent manipulation, soon was made a lucrative source of revenue by the Billunger.

Unfortunately, we know nothing in detail of the degree of German colonization instituted at this time by Hermann Billung and the Saxon church across the lower Elbe. Judging from Helmold's observations made regarding it two hundred years later, there must have been a considerable pioneer movement into the Wendish lands. But the occupation was doomed to be of short duration. A generation of clerical and feudal tyranny was certain to bear bitter fruit.

Modern history both in Spanish America and in North America offers a melancholy example of the contact of a "higher" with a "lower" race.[4] The history of the long and harsh relations of the Germans with the Baltic Slavs in the

[1] "Interim Hirimannus dux Saxoniam *regebat*" (Thietmar, II, 28). Weiland, *Entwicklung des Sächsischen Herzogtums*, p. 1, has shown that officially the future Billunger duchy was not the old tribal duchy of Saxony, but a command of the Marches; cf. Sommerfeld, *op. cit.*, p. 10, n. 8. Otto I really kept Westphalia as crown land and gave the country between the Weser and the Elbe to Hermann. The test of ducal independence was exemption from the royal fisc. "So lange ein Land noch an den königlichen Fiscus steuert, ist es kein Herzogthum" (Giesebrecht, *Wendische Geschichten*, I, 186). Ekkehard, *Casus S. Galli*, IV, 83, is specific in this particular: "Nondum adhuc illo tempore Suevia in ducatum erat redacta, sed fisco regio peculiariter parebat sicut hodie et Francia."

[2] Adam of Bremen, II, 46; III, 22; Helmold, I, 16, 21.

[3] "Saxonibus vero pro gloria et pro terra adquirenda certantibus," says Widukind (I, 9).

[4] Cf. Bourne, *Spain in America*, p. 256.

Middle Ages is a medieval and relatively unfamiliar example of a "phenomenon of familiar occurrence in later history of the contact of nature peoples with a ruling race."[1] Considering the fact that the Baltic Slavs had no inheritance of civilization from Rome and the church to help them along as the Germans of the fifth century had possessed, their culture was quite as high as that of the early Germans and promised as much. The utter destruction of their material and moral culture between the tenth and the thirteenth centuries is a fact which every student of the history of civilization must deplore. Henry I, when he captured Jana, put the village to pillage and massacred the adult inhabitants.[2] After the battle of Lenzen all prisoners were put to the edge of the sword.[3] Otto I was no more humane. The victory of Racknitz was followed by a butchery which lasted until nightfall; several hundred prisoners were massacred before the eyes of the conquered Slav chief. Gero, the famous margrave, treacherously slew thirty Wendish chieftains whom he had lured to a banquet under pretense of peace.[4] Henry the Lion and the Teutonic Knights in the twelfth and thirteenth centuries were no whit less cruel.[5]

The reigns of Henry I and Otto the Great (936–73) constitute the heroic period of German eastward expansion. But only in the Thuringian March—the triangle between the Saale, the upper Elbe, and the Erzgebirge—was the result

[1] E. G. Bourne, *Spain in America*, p. 211, and n. 2. Widukind, II, 20, is interesting as the reaction of a tenth-century German's *Kultur* toward the culture of the Wends.

[2] Widukind, I, 35.   [3] *Ibid.*, 36.

[4] *Ibid.*, II, 20; III, 55. But Tetzner, p. 292, thinks this mere legend. Thietmar of Merseburg, IX, 2, approves of these cruelties. The events here alluded to completely conquered the Sorben, who henceforward were passive. Their further history does not enter into this chapter.

[5] See Hauck, III, 88–89. For German contempt of the Slav see Fredeg., *Chron.*, IV, 68; *Ann. Fuld.* (871); *Monk of St. Gall.*, II, 12; Thietmar, III, 17; VIII (VII), 59 (44); Adam of Bremen, II, 45 (schol.); Helmold, I, 16.

The comment of Cosmas of Prague (*ca.* 1045–1125), the first Slavonic historian of the western Slavs, is interesting in this particular: "Perpendit enim innatam Teutonicis superbiam, et quod semper tumido fastu habeant despectui Sclavos et eorum linguam" (*Chron.*, I, 40; *MGH*, SS. IX, 62; cf. *ibid.*, X, 84). For centuries *Wend* and "heathen" were synonymous terms to the Germans (Widukind, III, 68; *Annal. Hildesh.* [anno 1056]; *Dipl.* [anno 945], I, 146, No. 65; cf. Hauck, III, 84).

permanent. The death of Gero in 965 may be said to mark the term of this first period. Not until 1125 was the eastward movement of the German people resumed, when the great constructive work of Adolph of Holstein, Henry the Lion, and Albrecht the Bear began.

The Wends were not pliant subjects, and their tribal organization, their religion, their language, energetically resisted the assault of German militarism and ecclesiasticism. In 955 the Wends, presumably taking advantage of the great Magyar invasion of that summer, raided the Thuringian March so terribly that all Saxony trembled. Widukind,[1] who tells the story, interrupts the history of the Hungarian invasion to relate it, and reports a speech of Otto I which manifests the grave anxiety of the King.

In 983 the whirlwind came. The recoil of Otto II's crushing defeat in Calabria[2] was felt along the whole course of the middle Elbe, where a formidable Slavonic uprising and pagan reaction took place. Havelburg, Brandenburg, and Zeitz were desolated; Hamburg was plundered. The three margraves of the Nordmark, Meissen, and Lausitz, with contingents of troops furnished by the bishops of Halberstadt and Magdeburg, defeated the revolted Slav tribes at Belkesheim (near Stendhal), but the victory was without permanent effect.[3] Fortunately for Germany in this time of national reverse and peril the iron administrative system established by Otto I in the Sorben land held good, else the whole eastern border of Saxony would have been driven in. But Germany's trans-Elbean power, save in Nordalbingia and Holstein, went down like a house of cards.[4] Not until the twelfth century was the river crossed again. For more than a century and a half

---

[1] III, 45–47.

[2] Bruno, *Vita S. Adalb.*, chap. x (*MGH*, SS. IV, 598); Hauck, III, 251; Usinger, *Jahrb. Heinrichs II*, I, 478–86. For other sources and literature see Richter, *Annalen*, II, 135–38.

[3] Thietmar, III, 10–19; Bruno, *loc. cit.*; *Ann. Sangall. maj.*, 983; Giesebrecht, *Kaiserzeit*, I, 604 ff., 850, and his *Otto II*, pp. 91 ff.; L. Giesebrecht, *Wend. Gesch.*, I, 264 ff.

[4] "Die deutsche Herrschaft nach halbhundert jähriger Dauer einfach wegzublasen war" (Guttmann, *op. cit.*, p. 418).

the bishops east of the great river were in exile and only titular holders of sees which were *in partibus paganorum.*

The desolation was complete.[1] In the twelfth century, when Lower Germany, under the great leadership of Adolph of Holstein, Henry the Lion, and Albrecht the Bear, had recovered the "lost provinces," Helmold of Holstein, whose intelligent observation entitles him to no mean honor as an archaeologist, found a melancholy charm in surveying the ruins and churches and monasteries in Schleswig and Wagria and in "the land which is called Balsemerlande and Marscinerlande, where the Saxons are said once to have dwelt"[2]— crumbled memorials of German power there in the days of the Ottos. He says:

> There still remain many evidences of that former occupation, especially in the forest which extends from the city of Lütjenburg through the mighty [*longissimas*] tracts of Schleswig, in whose vast and almost impenetrable solitudes yet may be descried the furrows which once marked out the plowlands. Even the lines of former towns and villages may be traced in the ruins. Along the streams in many places mounds of earth and silt, formed by the tributary waters, yet testify that every such site was once inhabited by Saxons—when Saxon valor was formidable.

Helmold sighs over the spacious and fertile soil once radiant with the harvest, but now gone over to bramble and brier and scarce inhabited. It is the same even on the left bank of the Elbe between the great bend and the upper Aller (today the territory around Halberstadt, Stendhal, and Salzwedel), "where still may be seen the ruins of old levees which were constructed in the lowlands along the banks of the Elbe. When the Slavs overran the country the Saxons were cut off, and the land was possessed by them down to our own time."[3]

[1] When Henry II in 1017 crossed the Elbe in an expedition against Boleslav he came to a *curtis* of the Bishop of Magdeburg named Leitzkau, ruined and inhabited by wild animals. "Albim ad Liesca, curtem quondam Vigonis episcopi et tunc feris innumerabilibus inhabitatam venit" (Thietmar, VIII, 57).

[2] Helmold, I, 12 and 89.

[3] Balsamerland (Beleseim, Belesem, Belshem, Belsheim, Balsamia terra) answers to the later Altmark. The name was derived from the Slavic *Bielazemia,* or "White Land." It was a prolongation of the marshes on the eastern side of the Elbe (Schafarik, *op. cit.,* pp. 593–94). The difference in the way in which Helmold writes of the former occupations of the Saxons in Schleswig and Wagria, on the one

For years the conflict between the Germans and the Wends of the middle and lower Elbe was a series of border forays and grim reprisals.[1] Magdeburg stood like a rock in a flood, a single point of German Christendom in a welter of barbarism and paganism; half the ecclesiastical province, as it was, was lost.[2] There was danger lest even the heart of Saxony be pierced, so that Bishop Bernwald of Hildesheim built a Burgward at the confluence of the Ocker and the Aller.[3] The weakest feature of the weak reign of Otto III

hand, and of the marsh land of Balsemerlande and Marscinerlande, on the other, is to be noted. In the first case he speaks from personal observation; in the latter he is apparently writing from hearsay ("feruntur . . . . ut videri potest" [I, 89]). It is not always possible to distinguish between the direct and the indirect sources of Helmold's information. For example, in I, 18, where he relates the circumstances of the death of Benno of Hildesheim, he almost paraphrases the Bishop's epitaph in part of the account, which makes Lüntzel (*Gesch. der Diöcese u. Stadt Hildesheim*, I, 181, n. 3) and the latest editor of Helmold's *Chronica* (Schmeidler's ed., 1909), p. 39, nn. 1 and 3, believe that Helmold actually had visited Hildesheim. The history of dikes and dike-building in medieval Germany is a very interesting one. "Forces tending toward associational organization found here a fruitful field of action. The dikes along the sea-coast and in the lowlands of the greater rivers were originally constructed by voluntary colonizing associations [*Siedelungsgenossenschaften*] as a preliminary to the original settlement of marshy districts, and later by communes after the settlement of the diked land thus created, for the better security of their economic interests. From the end of the Carolingian period onward, particularly in the 1100's and 1200's, there appeared, in addition to the old communal dikes built by associations, others constructed by ecclesiastical and secular lords, churches, cloisters, and cities, usually in connection with great colonizing enterprises, and upon the basis of land grants given for enclosure. But dikes continued to be erected by individual 'dike lords,' or by free peasant communes, or by 'dike unions,' that had nothing to do with such colonial settlements" (Huebner, *History of Germanic Private Law*, p. 288, sec. 40). For literature on this subject see Anschütz, "Deichwesen," *HWB der Staatsw.* (3d ed., 1909), III, 462–81; Stengel-Fleischmann, *Wörterbuch* (2d ed., 1911), Band I, "Deichwesen"; Detlefsen, *Holsteiniche Elbmarschen*, I, 57, 89; Gierke, *Die Geschichte des deutschen Deichrechts* (cf. *Hist. Vierteljahrschrift*, Band XIV, Heft 2 [1903]); Eckermann, *Ztschft. d. Gesellschaft f. Schleswig-Holstein-Lauenb. Gesch.*, Band XXI (1891); Band XXIII (1893); Band XXV (1896); Hansen, *ibid.*, Band XXIV (1894). Koegel, "Beowulf," *Ztschft. f. deutsches Altertum*, Band, XXVII, Heft 3 (1893), thinks that Beowulf was the personification of agriculture, and the killing of Grendel, the sea monster, symbolically represents the construction of dikes along the North Sea Coast in order to protect the fields from inroads by the ocean.

[1] *Ann. Hildesh. Annal. Qued.* (985–87); Thietmar, IV, 7–10; *Ann. Hildesh.* (990).

[2] For the "appeal" of the bishops of the province of Magdeburg against the Wends see Tangl, *Neues Archiv*, Band XXX, Heft 1.

[3] *Vita Bernwardi*, chap. vii (*MGH*, SS. IV, 779). It was called Mundburg. *Origines Guelf.*, IV, 435. Bernward of Hildesheim was also compelled to erect two

was the defense of the eastern frontier. In 992 Brandenburg was won and lost again. By 994 all the Slav tribes of the middle and lower Elbe except the Sorben had thrown off the German yoke. In the year 1000 a part of Nordalbingia for the first time was devastated with fire and sword. A few years later, in 1018, the whole region was again overrun by the infuriated Ljutizi and Wagri. The churches were destroyed, the clergy slaughtered. Even Hamburg was stricken, for many of the priests and people there were carried off into captivity. Sixty priests of Oldenburg, with the sign of the cross derisively cut in bleeding characters upon their tonsured heads, with hands bound behind their backs, were dragged and beaten through the towns of the Slavs until they perished from exhaustion.[1]

For 142 years—from the great Wendish rebellion in 983 to the accession of Lothar II in 1125—the eastward expansion of the German people across the Elbe was stopped by the Slavs. After two hundred years of effort the Franconian period ended with pitiably insignificant results, so far as east German colonization was concerned. In 1125 the linguistic frontier was still where it had been in the reign of Charlemagne.[2] Yet within the term of the next generation,

---

Burgwärde in 995 against pirates of the coast who penetrated inland (*Vita, loc. cit.*; cf. Adam of Bremen, II, 33 and 69; III, 3). Bremen and Hamburg were walled by Archbishop Unwin (1013–29). Rietschel, *Markt und Stadt* (Leipzig, 1897), p. 82, contends that Adam's words, ". . . . ipsa Brema vallo muniri cepit fortissimo," do not mean the *Stadt*, but the cathedral. At any rate, Bremen seems to have had immunity from pirates henceforth (Thietmar, VII, 28 [VI, 53]). For Hamburg see Adam of Bremen, II, 60.

[1] Cf. Hirsch, *Jahrb.*, III, 93 ff.; Adam of Bremen, II, 40–46. Adam honestly recognizes the just grievances of the Wends and condemns the avaricious policy of both the Saxon dukes and the Saxon clergy as being responsible for this rebellion: "plures etiam propter odium Christianitatis. . . . . Bernardus enim dux, ... per avaritiam gentem Winulorum crudeliter opprimens, ad necessitatem paganismi coegit." He quotes Rom. 9:18; Ps. 7:12; Acts 13:19, not with the whining piety of so many medieval chroniclers, but with some of that lofty ethical sense and resignation which Lincoln manifests in his "Second Inaugural."

[2] Wendt, II, 5–7; cf. Lavisse, *La marche de Brandebourg*, p. 36. Hauck, IV, 555: "Man hat bemerkt, dass die wenigen Kirchen, die es gab, fast alle in Burgorten lagen. . . . . In den Burgorten sassen die deutschen Herren mit ihren Mannen und ihrem Gesinde. Ihnen dienten diese Kirchen. Sie waren weniger Missionposten als Gotteshäuser für eine kleine christliche Diaspora in einem heidnischen Lande"

in the middle of the twelfth century, the entire fabric of
Slavonic tribal independence collapsed. Mecklenburg, Brandenburg, and Pomerania were conquered and settled by the
German people; the native population was converted and
reduced under German domination. The speed and effectiveness of this rapid change is to be ascribed partly to the breakdown of the capacity of resistance among the Wends; more,
perhaps, to the accumulated pressure of things in Germany
which bore down all barriers of opposition.

The economic and social transformation of Germany, especially Saxon or Lower Germany, during the Franconian
epoch was enormous, and it is in these changes that the causes
of the German people's eastward expansion in the twelfth
century are to be found. The evidences of this important
revolution are manifold. They are to be seen in the manifestations of peasant unrest, which can be discerned as early
as the tenth century; in the slow depression of the Saxon
freeman to the status of a serf; in the extension of manorial
rights over mills, bake ovens, wine presses, breweries, and
other activities of the economy of the German village; in the
increase of "split" holdings, a tendency observable in France
as far back as the reign of Charles the Bald, who forbade the
practice in the Edict of Pîtres in 864;[1] in the transition from a
freehold to a rent system; in the break-up of the ancient
mark community and the dissolution of the *Allmend;* in the
evolution of the *ministerialis* class; in the extension of the

---

(cf. Schulze, pp. 294, 316). Yet he cites instances of a few churches outside of the
Burgorten (p. 141).

[1] B. Guérard, *Polypt. d'Irminon,* I, 494. Not only the fields but also the taxes in
produce in course of time became divided into two, three, four, and even more portions, giving rise to social distinctions in the codes like *Halbbauern, Halbspaenner,
Halbhufner,* etc. As early as 808 we find village plowlands divided into three parts
(there is a case of six parts in 797); and no less than sixteen parts occur in 1141. The
Polyptique d'Irminon (about 820) gives an instance of twelve peasants who shared
one carucate between them, another of sixteen households having six carucates, a
third of one hundred and eighty-one owning eighty-one carucates, etc. The tendency
toward "split" holdings became so common that the charters make particular mention of the occurrence of undivided plowlands (*hoba integra*) (Roscher, *Ackerbau,* sec.
71). Lamprecht, *DWL,* I, 2, 705, cites 50 *Morgen* in the ninth century lying in three
places: 25 in one place, 13 in another, 6 in the third, and 6 in the fourth; 17 *Hufen*
scattered in two counties; 4 *Hufen* divided in thirteen different localities.

tithe from grain and wine (*der grosse Zehnt*) to include small produce like vegetables, fowls, eggs, honey, etc. (*der kleine Zehnt*); in the engrossing of the land by the nobles and the clergy, even the forests, so that lay and ecclesiastical estates ranging from eight thousand to sixty thousand *Morgen* were not uncommon; in the agricultural revolution, largely due to the superior methods of the French Cistercians who introduced new and more scientific practices of farming; in the rise of land values, which Lamprecht estimates to have been as much as 40 per cent in older provinces like Swabia, Franconia, and the Rhinelands between the tenth and the thirteenth century; in the extension of private ownership to the forests, hitherto ever the poor man's home (the Frankenwald was appropriated in Saxon times, the Harz by the middle of the twelfth century); in the changes in social texture from a simple to a complex composition; in the movements of the lower population into new localities, frequently forest and marsh, where in "clearings" or patches of soil laboriously drained the peasantry tried still to preserve their freer form of living; in the development of commerce and industry; in the rise of the towns, a social phenomenon which strikingly characterizes the reign of Henry IV.[1] The great rebellion of Saxony during the war of investiture which Henry IV so drastically suppressed left in its train large numbers of impoverished and broken freemen, who sought to begin life over again beyond the Elbe.[2]

Under these new and changed conditions it was natural that the "New East" beyond the Elbe beckoned to the Saxons of the twelfth century much as the "New West" beckoned to the American pioneer. In both cases the sparsely populated back lands tempted men from the more settled regions. The frontier of medieval Germany lay at "the hither

[1] This long paragraph merely makes "points." The reader is referred to Lamprecht, *DG*, III, Book 8, chaps. 1–2; *DWG*, I, 149, 163–64, 368–73, 603–22; 862–70, 1235–36; Schulze, *op. cit.*, pp. 122–27; Sybel, *Hist. Zeitschft.*, IX, 409; Inama Sternegg, III, 386 f., 407 f.; Nitzsch, II, 8 ff.; Below, "Zur Entstehung der deutschen Städte," *Hist. Zeitschft.*, LVIII, 193–244; Wendt, II, 7–8.

[2] *De unit. eccles. conserv.*, chap. xxviii; *Ann. Sax.* (*MGH.* SS. VI), p. 723; Ebbo, *Vita Ottonis, ep. Bab.*, I, 32; *Vita Bennonis*, chap. xix; cf. the remarks of Fisher, *op. cit.*, I, 137–38, 141.

edge of free land" as truly as did the American frontier. The increasing economic and soil pressure in the older parts of Saxony and elsewhere pushed the hardier and the braver spirits across the line. They "trekked" eastward to establish new homes for themselves in the wilderness, leaving the great manors of church and noble—in particular the former,[1] which had supplanted the Saxon free farmer—to be farmed more intensively by Flemish and Dutch settlers used to deep plowings in the heavy soils of the Low Countries, who were imported by Adolph of Holstein, Henry the Lion, and many of the bishops. "Hard times" and feudal oppression were powerful factors in the migration of peoples in the Middle Ages.[2] The Bavarian colonization of the Ostmark, the Frankish colonization of parts of Saxony and the Thüringer March, the settlement of Westphalian, Dutch, and Flemish colonists east of the Elbe, are examples.

The relation of these internal changes in Germany to the peopling of the border needs further investigation. The history of German eastward expansion has been studied more in the results than in the formative processes which produced the movement. A remarkable proclamation (probably of the

---

[1] Kötzschke, *Quellen*, p. 48; Pueschl, p. 8.

[2] A few references, from many which might be given, must suffice: "Hanc silvam incole propter diversas pauperum necessitates adgressi sunt cedere et facere novalia [*anno* 1101]" (*Mittelrhein. Urk.-B.*, I, 401).

". . . . Qui autem pauperiores erant, faciebant sibi novalia et villas in memoribus et forestis S. Bonifacii" (*Gesta Marcuardi abbat. Fuld.*, Boehmer, *Fontes*, III, 166; also in Dronke, *Trad. Fuld.*, p. 154). The date is between 1150 and 1165.

"Exactores—ad ultimam homines nostros pauperiem redegerunt et exire de patria et de hereditate sua mendicandi coegerunt causa [1102]" (Martène, *Coll.*, I, 595). "Dum quidam pauperum de familia ecclesie nostre [S. Pantaleon in Cologne] in curtes nostras Embe et Anhe pertinentes frequenti nos proclamatione merendo pulsarent, eo quod ad jus eorum, qui plenum debitum solvunt, compulsi tanta saepe violentia comprimerentur. ut nonnulli vacuas quas tenebant possessiunculas relinquentes patriis et sedibus migrare disponerent" (Lacomblet, *Urk.-B.* [*anno* 1141], I, 344): "Avaritia et rapina potentum pauperes et ruricolae opprimuntur et ad judicia injusta trahuntur. Haec lues peccati multos vendere patrimonia et ad peregrinas migrare terras compulit." This significant reference was first pointed out by Teutsch, *Zehntrecht*, p. 7; cf. Sybel, *Hist. Zeitschrift*, IX (1863), 409, and Schulze, *Kolonisierung*, p. 125, n. 4. It relates to the Sieburger region. The date is 1183. Cf. also I (1149), 367; *Mittelrhein. Urk.-B.*, II (1197), 171; Lacomblet (1099), p. 256; *Cod. Lauresh.*, I (1148), 153; Seibert, *Urk.-B.*, I (1166), 56, cited by Inama Sternegg, II, 19, n. 2; p. 24 n. In general see Curschmann, *Hungersnöte im Mittelalter* (Leipzig, 1900).

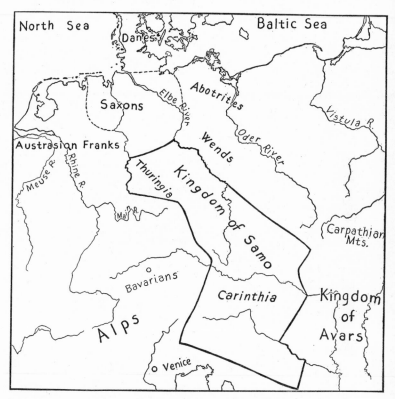

The Kingdom of Samo

year 1108) cleverly calculated to promote settlement in the
new land, and signed by the leading bishops and Fürsten of
Saxony, clearly expresses the motives of the time:

They [the Slavs] are an abominable people, but their land is very rich
in flesh, honey, grain, birds, and abounding in all products of the fertility
of the earth, when cultivated, so that none can be compared unto it. So
they say who know. Wherefore, O Saxons, Franks, Lotharingians, men of
Flanders most famous—here you can both save your souls, and if it please
you, acquire the best of land to live in.[1]

Mixed with that negative ingredient to be found in every
complex society, vaguely seeking a way out of its discontent
by change, was a large element of the best blood and bone of
the German race in this migration. A large proportion of the
emigrants in the twelfth century were men of firm fiber actuated by a determination to better their condition, and ambitious to seize the opportunities offered in a new country.
Many of these settlers came from Westphalia and eastern
Franconia,[2] regions which had themselves been frontier districts in the tenth and eleventh centuries, what might be
called the "Old East" in contrast with the "New East" just
opening up.

The rival political ambitions of the Germans and the
Danes for control of the Baltic strand in the first half of the
twelfth century complicated the border question, and drew
both the Count of Holstein and the Duke of Saxony into the
vortex. The Danes hated the Saxon incomers,[3] and naturally

[1] This remarkable document is to be found in Kötzschke, *Quellen zur Gesch. der
ostdeutschen Kolonisation im 12. bis 14. Jahrhundert* (Teubner: Leipzig, 1912), pp.
9–10. It may also be found in *Codex Diplom. Sax. Reg.*, II, i, No. 40; *Codex
Diplom. Anhalt.*, I, No. 172; *Mecklenb. Urk.*, X, 457 ff.; *Neues Archiv.*, VII, 624;
Archiv für slavische Phil., VI, 216. For commentary see Hauck, *Kirchengesch.
Deutschlands*, IV, 599, n. 4; Tangl, *Neues Archiv.*, XXX, 183; Meyer von Knonau,
Jahrb. d. deutschen Reiches unter Heinrich V, VI, 79 ff.; Lubenecker, *Regesta Hist.,
Thur.*, I, No. 1048 (pp. 1039 ff.).

[2] F. Boll, "Mecklenburgs deutsche Kolonisation im 12. und 13. Jahrhundert,"
Jahrb. f. Mecklenburg. Gesch., XIII (Schwerin, 1848), 57–112, with an Appendix by
Lisch on the places whence these settlers came (pp. 112–15); H. Ernst, *Die Kolonisa-
tion Mecklenburgs im 12. und 13. Jahrhundert* (Schirrmacher's Beiträge), pp. 98–
130; Ahlers, "Das bäuerliche Hufenwesen in Mecklenburg zur Zeit des Mittelalters,"
Jahrb. f. Mecklenb. Gesch., LI (1886), 49–97; Michael, *Gesch. des deutschen Volkes*,
I, 91–94.

[3] "Rex Danorum pluribus advenis Teutonicis terram suam incolentibus trunca-
tiones membrorum facit. Hac de causa imperator expeditionem super eum movere

the Abodrites became involved much as the Indian country
in America was the bone of contention between the English
and French.[1]

Schleswig, as a Danish duchy, was a *point d'appui* of
Danish mainland aggrandizement. This Lothar II perceived,
and he endeavored to take advantage of a conflict for the
Danish succession to attach Schleswig to Germany again. In
1103 Eric I of Denmark died leaving a minor son Knut Laward[2] under the regency of the deceased King's brother Niels
(or Nicholas). But the latter plotted to secure the succession
for his own son Magnus, and accordingly sent his nephew into
Schleswig in 1115, as duke of Schleswig. Here his pro-German affiliations became so evident that in 1125 Lothar II
invested Knut Laward with the overlordship of Wagria to

---

intendit" (*Ann. Erphesf.* [*MGH*, SS. VI, 539]; Bernhardi, *Lothar II*, p. 538, n. 34).
For the Germanization of Schleswig see Hansen, *Die Besiedelung der Marck zwischen
Elbe- und Eidermündung;* Petermann, *Mittheil.* (1893), p. 177.

[1] In 810 Charlemagne, it will be remembered, wrested Schleswig from the pagan
Danes and erected it into a German March. In 1027, after the conversion of the
Danes, Conrad II ceded the tract which the Danes had ever struggled to recover to
Denmark for Danish assistance against the Baltic Slavs. It was this dangerous
policy on the part of the first Franconian king which whetted Danish ambition to
acquire control of the Baltic strand by conquering Wagria and Pomerania, and
compromised the political relations between the two crowns. Canute had Slav
blood in him through his mother, who was a sister of Boleslav Chrobry of Poland
(Larson, *Canute the Great*, pp. 15, 33). The famous Jomsburg Vikings played a
striking part at this time in Pomerania.

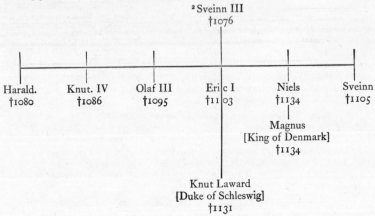

[2] Sveinn III
†1076

| Harald. | Knut. IV | Olaf III | Eric I | Niels | Sveinn |
| †1080 | †1086 | †1095 | †1103 | †1134 | †1105 |

Magnus
[King of Denmark]
†1134

Knut Laward
[Duke of Schleswig]
†1131

whom the Christian Abodrite chieftain Henry and his pagan people became vassal. Later (in 1128?) when Henry died, the Emperor judged the time to be opportune both to extinguish the quasi-independence of the Abodrite-Wagrian principality and at the same time to bind Knut Laward and Schleswig closer to Germany, and accordingly sold the *Regnum Abotritorum* to Knut Laward, who with a force of Holsteiners and Sturmarians, and in conjunction with Count Adolph of Holstein, invaded Wagria and captured Werle, but was soon recalled by a raid of the Rugian pirates upon the coast of Holstein. Niels of Denmark and his son Magnus regarded Knut Laward's course with intense animosity[1] and the Abodrites found national leaders of their cause in two new chieftains, a son of Butue, Pribislav, and his cousin, Niklot, the latter of whom was to prove the greatest leader the Baltic Slavs ever produced.

This triangular condition produced a state of things approaching anarchy along the border of Holstein and lower Saxony.[2] Knut Laward energetically set himself to establish law and order in this penumbral tract, and, after the ancient Danish fashion of punishment, nailed some of the worst offenders of the border to ships' spars in sight of all.[3] He then began to make good his claim to sway over Wagria, calling to his standard every pioneer German who hated the Wends and coveted the lands of the Abodrites, and began the erection of a castle on the site of an ancient Slavonic hill-fort which the Germans called Eilberch or Alberg. Pribislav and Niklot, the Abodrite chiefs, were dragged off in chains to Schleswig. Alt-Lübeck, the Slav capital, where the Christian Abodrite Duke had kept his court and maintained Christian worship in his private chapel, was captured. Apparently this warlike Danish Prince, by the accident of fortune become a

[1] Schafarik, II, 539.

[2] "Cepitque vir pacificus [Knut Laward] regionem compacare, auferens desertores de terra. Precipue vero Sleswicensibus beneficus erat. Contigit autem latrones forte comprehendi in mirica, quae interjacet Sliam et Egdorem, et perduci in faciem Kanuti" (Helm., I, 49).

[3] *Ibid.* On Knut's history in detail see H. Reich, "Knut Laward, Herzog von Schleswig," *Jahrbuch für Landeskunde der Herzogtümer Schleswig, Holstein und Lauenburg,* X, 203–54.

German vassal, promised to become the ruling prince in the north and the destined conqueror of the last of the independent Slavonic tribes along the Baltic. One wonders, had he lived, if he would have anticipated the career of Henry the Lion. But as it befell, Knut Laward was assassinated in 1131 at the instigation of his jealous cousin, Magnus. Intrigue and turmoil ensued in Denmark, which reminds one of Hamlet's time, and Danish enterprise upon the mainland was arrested, though for years border strife between Denmark and Holstein obtained.[1]

The death of Lothar II in 1137 precipitated a new storm against the Wends. The rebellion of Henry the Proud and the feud between Saxony and Brandenburg speedily involved the border. Pribislav destroyed the Saxon castle at Sigeberg and devastated the German settlements roundabout it. A new oratory and a new monastery there were burned. One of the monks was killed; the rest escaped to Neumünster. "In Slavia," writes Helmold, "affairs of the church lapsed."[2] A "Slavicus furor propter occupationes Saxonum"[3] swept over the border, and so many settlers quitted the country that in some places the land was reduced to a solitude. In retaliation, Henry the Proud in the winter of 1138–39 made a punitive expedition against the Abodrites and fearfully wasted the territory. Border strife became a chronic condition with no attempt on the part of the feudal nobles to restrain it.[4] In Nordalbingia the rivals were Adolph of Holstein and Henry the Lion. For a short time Albrecht the Bear fished in the troubled waters, seized the ancient commercial town of Bardowick and the castle of Sigeberg, and even extended his sway to Bremen and Hamburg, in the latter territory capturing a stone castle—a novelty in Lower Germany at this time—which the mother of Count Adolph had erected as a protection against pirates penetrating up

---

[1] For all this see Helm., I, 49–51; W. Fricke, *Untersuchungen zur älteren Holsteinischen Gesch.* (Jena, 1907), pp. 42 ff.; A. F. H. Schaumann, *Gesch. d. niedersächsischen Völker von der ersten Hervortreten auf deutsch. Boden an bis 1180* (1839); *Neues Archiv*, XXXIII, 561 ff.; Bernhardi, *Lothar II*, pp. 396 ff.

[2] I, 54.   [3] I, 56.

[4] "Nemine obsistente principum Christianorum" (*ibid.*).

the estuary of the Elbe. However, he soon found more practicable compensation farther east in Pomerania and left the field of Nordalbingia to Adolph and Henry, who in 1143 divided it between them, the former taking Wagria with the castle of Sigeberg, the latter the Abodrite land (or Polabia) with Ratzeburg as its chief seat. Roughly, the Trave River was the boundary between.[1]

The result of the reduction of the Wagri and Abodrites by Adolph of Holstein and Henry the Lion in 1143 was a large influx of German immigrants into the trans-Elbean lands, which were thrown open to settlement.[2] Settlers thronged in "cum equis et bubus, cum aratris et plaustris et personis ad opus idoneis,"[3] to the exasperation of the Wends who could do nothing but sullenly submit.[4]

Nothing so much resembles it as the American "rush" after the War of 1812 into the Western Reserve and the Ohio Valley. In the older parts of Germany the exodus was so great that manorial proprietors were compelled to ameliorate the condition of their peasantry lest they run away to the new lands beyond the Elbe.[5] It requires no stretch of imagination for the American scholar, who is familiar from his birth, through family tradition and education, with the history of the "making" of the New West, to visualize the nature and importance of this emigration across the Elbe. Helmold's paragraphs have the vividness of a panorama to his eyes. This great movement almost seems to be a chapter of the history of his own forebears. He says:

Because the land was without people Adolph sent messengers into all the regions roundabout, even into Flanders and Holland, the bishopric of Utrecht, into Westphalia and Frisia, to proclaim that all who were in want of land might come with their families and receive the best soil, a spacious

[1] Helm., I, 54, 56; Bernhardi, *Konrad III*, pp. 61, 318.

[2] For extended treatment of this subject see Detlefsen, *Geschichte des Holsteinischen Elb-Marschen* (2 vols., with map; 1891–92); Niemeyer, *Das Slavenland unter Herzog Heinrich dem Loewen.*

[3] *Sidonis Epist.* (ed. Schmeidler), p. 240.

[4] "Slavi .... terram suam a Christianis Teutonicis incoli, exarserunt" (*ibid.*, p. 241).

[5] Kovalevsky, *Die ökonomische Entwicklung Europas*, III, 321–22.

country, rich in crops, abounding with fish and flesh and exceeding good pasturage.[1]

Like a true land-promoter Adolph deftly advertised the region. He said unto the people of Holstein and Sturmaria:

Do you not see that you have subjugated the land of the Slavs—that you have bought it by the death of your brothers and your fathers? Why, therefore, do you not at once enter in and possess it? Be the first, and come into this delectable land, and cultivate it, and have a share of its products. For you should have the best of that which you have wrested from the hands of your enemies.

The response was a "rush" of settlers from the older parts of Germany, notably Westphalia, and even of immigrants from Holland and Flanders. "An innumerable multitude of various nations," we are told, "responded to the invitation." The Holsteiners took the nearest and safest stretch of land along the Trave and Schwentine as far as the Plöner-See;[2] the Westphalians settled in the Gau Dargunensis;[3] the Hollanders around Eutin; the Frisians around Süssel.[4] "And Adolph gave Oldenburg and Lütjenburg and the rest of the lands along the sea to the Slavs to cultivate, and they were made tributary to him."[5] They were driven, like the Indians of the Everglades, into the swamps and forests, where they eked out a wretched living on fish and game[5] or took to piracy among the Danish islands.[6]

[1] Helmold, I, 57.

[2] There is today a village named Holstendorf in this region between Ahrensboeck and Eutin.

[3] This location cannot be ascertained. Wendt (*Germanisierung*, etc., II, 15) thinks it near Lübeck; Schmeidler (ed. Helm.), p. 112, n. 3, fixes it near Ahrensboeck. Von Schröder and Biernatzki (*Topographie der Herzogtümer Holstein und Lauenburg* [Oldenburg, 1855], p. 6) incline to the vicinity of Rostock.

[4] All historians of medieval Germany touch upon this subject but add little to Helmold, I, 57. The most recent study is A. Gloy, *Der Gang der Germanisation in Ostholstein* (Kiel, 1884), esp. pp. 17 ff.; cf. Meitzen, *op. cit.*, II, 354 ff.; Wendt, II, 14–17.

[5] Helm., I, 69, 83; II, 13; Ebbo, *Vita Ottonis episc. Babenberg*, III, 4.

[6] Helm., I, 102. In II, 13, Helmold gives a graphic picture of their fugitive, predatory life. The island of Rügen, the last stronghold of independence of the Baltic Slavs, was the seat of these forays, which were not ended until the Danish capture of the island in 1168 and the complete destruction of the great temple of Arkona there. The Saxon princes, who hated the Danes, connived at these forays and even per-

Adolph of Holstein, if he had not been molested in his plans by his feudal neighbors, might have worked out some accommodation in the strained relations between the two races. He understood the Slavonic tongue and the Slavonic character as no other German of his time, save possibly Albrecht the Bear; without recourse to force he persuaded the Abodrite nobles to do him homage and induced them to open their lands to German settlers.[1] But Adolph's policy of peaceful colonization and benevolent intercourse between the two races was frustrated by the Wendish Crusade in 1147, by the enmity of Henry the Lion, by the land-greed of the Saxon baronage, by the eagerness of the inrushing settlers, who clamored for the expulsion of the Wends as loudly as the American settlers for the removal of the Indians. The middle of the twelfth century was no moment to advocate moderation. The Crusades, at once a fanatical religious war and a colonizing movement, were in full swing.

When the bloody strife was over, Nordalbingia was again a smoking wilderness.[2] Once more the work of colonization and settlement was resumed, and a veritable invasion of monks into the land of Wagria (East Holstein) followed as a matter of course,[3] along with a wave of new colonists who introduced the superior methods of German tillage.[4] The Germans brought both a higher form of economic life and a higher capacity for exploitation of the soil.

The end of I, 84, in Helmold's *Chronica* is an epilogue:

---

mitted captive Danes to be sold into slavery in the market places of German cities. Helmold, II, 13, says that he had heard from eyewitnesses of the exposure of 700 Danish prisoners for sale in Mecklenburg.

[1] Helm., I, 57 (end); cf. Hauck, IV, 603-4.

[2] "Omnis igitur terra Obotritorum et finitimas regiones quae pertinent ad regem Obotritorum, assiduis bellis, maxime vero hoc novissimo bello tota in solitudinem redacta est" (Helm., II, 5).

[3] *Sidonis Epist.*, p. 244; Kötzschke, *op. cit.*, p. 112. In *Meckl. U.B.*, I, No. 52, is a privilege of colonization granted by Conrad III to the Bishop of Havelberg in 1150.

[4] "[Henricus] precepit Slavorum populo, ut coleret vir agrum suum et exercerent laborem utilem et commodum" (Helm., I, 84).

"The Slavs little by little failed in the land, and the Saxons came in and dwelt there."[1]

Yet we must be cautious lest we take Helmold too literally. The German conquest of Mecklenburg and Pomerania was not completed until the thirteenth century, and until then the German settlers were quite certainly a minority of the population.[2] Indeed, the peasantry continued to speak the Slavonic idiom until the seventeenth century. It was the Thirty Years' War which exterminated the last vestiges of Slav culture in ancient Wagria and Pomerania, and completed the Germanization of the country.[3]

Says Schulze:

Up to the twelfth century conditions in Germany had not developed to a point which necessitated an overflow of the excess population into distant border territory. The homeland still furnished sufficient land even for the younger sons, and the settling and exploitation of regions within the kingdom, the clearing of the extensive forests and wild land at home yet absorbed the energy of the peasant. Only as the available area grew narrower and narrower, when the land in many cases had been subjected to cultivation beyond the limits of productivity, and recourse had to be made to division of the Hufen, did the call of the princes and the nobles from

---

[1] *Mecklenb. Urkundenbuch*, I, 56: "Slavis ejectis"; *Codex Anhalt.*, I, 347, 414. Heinemann, *op. cit.*, p. 466; Guttmann, *Forsch. z. brand. u. preuss. Gesch.*, IX, 427–28.

[2] A MS book of tithe registers of Ratzeburg for the years 1229–30, preserved in the archives at Neu-Strelitz, shows that as late as that date not all the Slavs had been converted. In the property registers of the parishes one not infrequently finds opposite the name of this or that locality: "Sclavi sunt, nullum beneficium." See Koetzschke, *Quellen*, No. 44, from *Meckl. U.B.*, I, No. 375.

[3] Besides the literature already cited on the subject of the German colonization east of the Elbe, the following monographs or articles are important; Kuehnel, *Jahrb. und Jahresbericht d. Ver. f. Meck. Gesch.* (1881) (on Slav place-names in Mecklenburg); Malchow, *Gesch. des Klosters Doberan* (1881); Prümers, *Pommersche Urkundenbuch* (1254–78), and cf. *Hist. Ztschft.* (N.F., 1882), Band XII; Kuehlmann, *Neue Mitth. aus dem Gebiete historisch.-antiquarisch. Forschungen*, Band XV, Heft 2 (1882), important for the Germanization of the district of Plonim. Eichhorn, *Schriften d. Ver. f. Sachsen-Meiningische Gesch.*, Heft 20 (1895); Curschmann, *Die deutschen Ortsnamen im nordostdeutschen Kolonialgebiet*. Pyl, *Beiträge zur Gesch. der Stadt Greifswald* (1892), shows the existence of many Westphalian and Rhenish family names in Pomerania and Rügen; Fabricius, *Hans. Geschichtsblätter* (1894), a study of the municipal law in Schwerin, shows that it was introduced by German colonists in the twelfth century. On the *Bede* in Mecklenburg, see Techen, *Mecklenburg Jahrb. d. Ver. f. Meckl. Gesch.*, Band LXVII (1902). Witte, *Wendische Bevölkerungsreste in Mecklenburg* (1905), argues for the Germanization, not the expulsion of the Wends.

the Wendish lands meet with response. Thousands then emigrated, full of fresh courage and cheerful hope, into the east, where land in plenty and freedom and independent living upon their own acres awaited them.

Nor did they come with empty hands. Just as to-day the greater portion of rural emigrants is made up of the most efficient and energetic elements, who as a whole are not utterly without means, men to whom their home has grown too narrow, and which has ceased to provide sufficient play either for their economic or for their social energies, so it was then— that enterprise, energy, and rich experience which they had gained in farming the home acres these settlers brought with them. They could not have afforded to have been wholly without some material means. The hard labor of clearing the wilderness promised success and reward to their arduous endeavors only after years of toil. At the very outset the conditions of border life demanded the application of all their strength and skill, the expenditure of a not inconsiderable capital in the form of implements and tools, equipment and supplies, and at times also of ready cash.[1]

The Saxon population along the border (*Marcomanni*, or "Marchmen," they were called)[2] had need, as Helmold says, to be of strong endurance, and to be ready to risk their blood. These medieval German frontiersmen were resolute and hardy, hard working, and given to a rough hospitality toward strangers provided they were Germans and lived Saxon law like themselves, but hated the Wend, and detested foreign incomers like the Dutch and Flemings.[3] Both their culture and their Christianity were rude and crude when compared with the more refined German life of the cities in old Franconia and the valley of the Rhine.[4] In Helmold's *Chronica*

[1] Schulze, *Kolonisierung*, p. 79.

[2] Helm., I, 66, 67, 87. A map showing a multitude of Slav *Ortsnamen* in present Saxony may be examined in *Deutsche Erde*, XI, 92.

[3] For evidence of the contempt of the Germans for the Wends see Fredegar, *Chron.*, IV, 68; Monk of St. Gall, II, 12; Thietmar, III, 17; Adam of Bremen, II, 43 (schol.); Helm., I, 13 and 16: Cosmas of Prague, I, 40 (*MGH*, SS. IX, 42); *ibid*. X, 84. For Saxon hatred of Flemish *advenae* see Helm., I, 63–64.

[4] "Tres autem sunt Nordalbingorum populi: Sturmari, Holzati, Thetmarki, nec habitu nec lingua multum discrepantes, tenentes Saxonum jura [cf. *Sachsenspiegel*, Book III, art. 64, § 3] et Christianum nomen, nisi quod propter barbarorum viciniam furtis et latrociniis operam dare consueverunt. Hospitalitatis gratiam sectantur. Nam furari et largiri apud Holzatos ostentacio est. . . . . Habitudinem loci campumque vasta et sterili mirica perorridum, preterea accolarum genus agreste et incultum, nichil de religione nisi nomen tantum Christianitatis habentes" (Helm., I, 47). Helmhold frequently uses the word "uncouth" (*agrestis*) to describe border conditions, e.g., I, 13; in I, 67, the Holsteiners are "gens libera et cervicosa, gens agrestis et indomita."

There are two paragraphs in the *Dialogus* of Herbordus (II, 2, pp. 60–61;

Slavorum we get authentic glimpses of German frontier life, of new settlers pressing into the region, chiefly Flemings and Dutch, who redeemed the fenlands around Bremen and in the Havelland.[1] As in America in the seventeenth and eighteenth centuries the blockhouse guarded the frontier settlements against Indian foray, so in the debated land between the Saxon and the Slav timbered castles (*munitiones*, *oppida*, *castra*, *castella*) protected the sparse and scattered pioneer German population. "Around them," says Helmold, "the settlers clustered, but in great fear of attacks."[2] One sees the barbarian side of the picture, too: the gradual dispossession of the Wends and the seizure of their lands by German colonists, whose hunger for land and faculty for establishing settlements roused the ire of the Slavs.[3]

In all this energy and violence upon the border the part which the Saxon people played in it, and not merely nobles and bishops, is to be observed. German eastward expansion had ceased to be only the covetous land-grabbing aspiration of the great, and had become a deep and strong national movement. "Die Grosstat unseres Volkes während des Mittelalters," as Lamprecht has styled it—the conquest of two-fifths of modern Germany was beginning its historic work.

Henry the Lion's seizure of Lübeck in 1158 from Adolph of Holstein made the position of Niklot and his people more precarious than ever.[4] By that time the very sight of any Slavs along the Baltic between him and the sea had grown intolerable to Henry. In 1160 he invaded the Abodrite territory "with fire and sword." Niklot, in desperation, after

---

30, p. 143), which interestingly depict the impression the cultivated clerical society of Michelsberg, in Bamberg, had of German wilderness life.

[1] I, 57, 88–89.

[2] "Jam enim circumjacentia oppida incolebantur paulatim a Christicolis, sed cum grandi pavore propter insidias latronum. Castrum enim Plunense necdum reedificatum fuerat" (Helm., I, 75). So it was in America: "A log hut, a little clearing edged by the primeval forest, with the palisaded fort near by—this was the type of home they made" (Turner, *American Historical Review*, I, 73).

[3] "Slavicus furor propter occupationes Saxonum" (Helm., I, 56).

[4] Hauck, IV, 620.

an unsuccessful attack upon Lübeck, burned his towns—
Mecklenburg, Schwerin, Dubin, Ilow (near Wismar)—and
fled to the marshy tract around Wurle in the valley of the
Warnow.[1] From this place he carried on a guerilla warfare.
Henry's practices were merciless, for he hanged every Wend
who fell into his hands. Niklot himself was finally killed and
his head brought into the Saxon camp. His sons burned
Wurle, too, and fled into the deep forests near the coast.
Henry offered them and the broken fragments of the Abodrites the territory around Wurle, the ancient land of the Kis-
sini and Circipani. But they refused it, and the bitter strife
went on for some years. In 1163 Wertislav, one of the brothers, was captured and carried in chains to Brunswick. The
elder, Pribislav, in retaliation, in the dead of winter, sur-
prised the garrison of the castle of Mecklenburg while the
commandant was away, and put the whole garrison together with all the refugees within it to the edge of the sword.
The capture of Ilow followed and a terrible devastation of
the province.[2]

Again the border was in a panic. It was the last flurry of
the Baltic Slavs. The call to arms went wide and far—to all
Saxony, to Waldemar of Denmark, to Adolph of Holstein,
though the Christian Slav soldiery of the last, intermingled
with his Holsteiners and Sturmari, were looked upon askance.
Pribislav's base was at Dimmin where he had massed all his
horse and foot forces. A bloody battle was fought near the
Kummerower-See in July, 1164, in which twenty-five hundred Wends were slain. On the German side the most conspicuous who fell was Adolph of Holstein. The shattered
remnant of Pribislav's forces fled to Pomerania. In 1177 the
end came, when Henry the Lion destroyed Dimmin and
Lauenburg and Niklot became a fugitive.[3]

But Pomerania offered no asylum. In the winter of 1124–
25 Lothar of Saxony, as we have seen, had made a victorious
expedition against the Rugians, destroyed their temple at

[1] Today Wyck between Schwaan and Bützow-Lisch (*Mecklenb. Jahrb.*, VI, 88).

[2] Helm., I, 93, 97, 98.

[3] Arnold of Lübeck, II, 4; III, 4.

Rethra, and broken their power.[1] The missionary labors of
Otto of Bamberg in Pomerania at the same time completed
the German conquest. The *terra Rugianorum*, too, was coveted and conquered by the Germans. For the land was boasted to be "ferax frugum, piscium atque ferarum."[2] The
Pomeranian duke, Kazimir, even if he had dared, would
have been unable to sympathize with the cause of the
Abodrites, girdled as Pomerania was by Brandenburg and
Poland. The survivors of the tribe were sold by people of
their own blood into slavery among the Poles, the Bohemians,
and the Sorben. The last independent group of the Baltic
Slavs upon the mainland was obliterated.[3]

The conquered country was secured by garrisoned castles
and thrown open to settlement, the best tracts being apportioned like military bounty lands, among Henry's vassals
and the Saxon clergy.[4] The nature of these settlers' holdings
varied.[5] Many of them were not large—a circumstance which
points to a considerable influx of peasantry. What the extent of the peasant grants was is left to conjecture. But the
minimum area must have been at least three *Hufen*, for,
according to the *Sachsenspiegel*, the possession of three *Hufen*
was a qualification of a *Schoffenbarfreimann*.[6]

[1] Helmold fails to give us this information, but the fact is recorded by Ebbo,
Vita Ottonis episc. Babenberg., III, 5; cf. Wendt, I, 85, n. 1.

[2] Helm., II, 12.

[3] *Ibid.*, II, 4–5; Arnold of Lübeck, III, 4, 7.

[4] "Porro terram Obotritorum divisit militibus suis possidendum . . . confluerent
de terris suis homines Teutonici ad incolendam terram spaciosam, fertilem frumento,
commodam pascuarum ubertate, abundantem pisce et carne et omnibus bonis"
(Helm., I, 88). "Slavi usquequaque protriti atque propulsi sunt, et venerunt . . .
populi fortes et innumerabiles et obtinuerunt terminos Slavorum et edificaverunt
civitates et ecclesias et increverunt divisiis super omnem estimacionem" (*ibid.*, I,
89; cf. I, 102).

[5] We find a variety of terms as *praedium, allodium, villa, curtis*, etc. The distinctions are more legal than economic. See Kretschmer, *op. cit.*, p. 198, and bibliography.

[6] Schulze, p. 117. The *Hufe* was not invariable in area. Its size was fixed by
regional custom and varied greatly, from 15, 20, 36, 45, 60, 120, 160 *Morgen* (Lamprecht, *DWL*, I, pp. 366–70; Kovalevsky, *Oekonomische Entwicklung Europas*, III
[1905], 217). But a *Hufenmass* of less than 30 *Morgen* was rare. An *aratrum theu-
tonicale* was equal to $2\frac{2}{3}$ *mansi* or *Hufen* (Michael, I, 116, n. 4). The same variableness is attached to the term *Morgen*. Defined as "ein Landstück für welches die

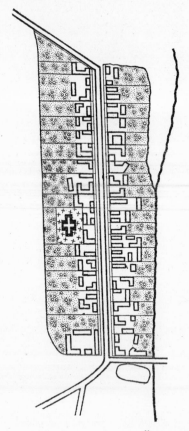

GROUND-PLAN OF A TYPICAL GERMAN "STREET" VILLAGE

In general, in the method of surveying the land there was a manifest tendency to discard the traditions and practices of the familiar manorial system, with its demesne, its strips of glebe land and dividing "balks." Instead, the land was marked out in rectangular or oblong blocks—the *mansus regalis* (720 rods long, 30 rods broad) of the Carolingian fisc.[1] Meitzen has shown that this division of allotments into rectangular or oblong blocks obtained in Frisia as early as the time of the Frank mayors, although it was originally foreign to the Frisians. The first obscure traces of the granting of *Hufen* of this form do not, in Frisian lands, antedate Karl Martel. The extension of the system along the whole Frisian Coast and to the *Waldhufen* of the royal domain is ascribed to the Carolingian administration. In Holland, Zealand, and Frisia the cultivation of the moorlands began very early. These marsh and moor *Hufen* were surveyed almost without exception in straight strips, a practice which also soon came to obtain in forest clearings, or *Waldhufen*. In the level moor-

---

Pflugarbeit eines Morgens, von Sonnenaufgang bis Mittag, erfahrungsgemäss in Anspruch genommen wurde" (Kötzschke, p. 68), the measurement was naturally conditioned by the nature of the soil, the size of the team, and the length of the working day. A *Morgen* in one place was not the same in area as a *Morgen* in another place. But it was a definite unit for the manor, or the region, concerned. Thirteen *Morgen* usually equaled *ca.* 10½ *hectares* (Lamprecht, *DWL*, I, 346; Langethal, *Landwirtschaft*, II, 362, 373; Hanssen, "Die Ackerflur der Dörfer," *Abhandl.*, II, 179 f.). See, further, Schmidt, *Zur Agrargeschichte Lübecks und Ostholsteins;* Kovalevsky, *op. cit.*, III, 193 f. The Dutch colonists in the region preserved their own ancestral law for centuries (*Hollensch. Recht*), for in 1438 the Holsteiner towns Zarneckau and Gumale went over to *Holsten Recht* (Wendt, II, 15).

[1] The earliest mention of the *mansus regalis* in legislation is in *Cap.* 801–813 (*MGH, LL*, p. 189). The rod is approximately 16 feet, varying by a few inches in different regions, except in Lorraine, where it was only 10 feet. The "royal rod" was 5 feet longer. If 16 feet be taken as the normal German rod this would make the royal rod measure 21 feet, which would nearly agree with the English "perch of the king" (20 ft.), the "lawful perch of the vill" being 16½ feet. Inama Sternegg, I, 439, n. 3; II, 25, following Meitzen, says that the customary German rod was 10 feet and the royal rod 15 feet. But Lamprecht, I, 343, has shown that the short 10-foot rod was customary only in Lorraine. If, therefore, the royal rod was 5 feet longer than the customary rod it was probably 21 feet, or even 21½ feet. Meitzen has estimated that the *mansus regalis* included from 48 to 50 *hectares* of land, (one *hectare* equals 2.47 acres) nearly 125 acres. But on the assumption that the royal rod was 21 feet the *mansus regalis* would be proportionally larger than this estimate. The Bremen tract must have been at least a mile and a half square. See next page, and also chapter xiv.

lands there was no difficulty in following this simple plan. The axis of both kinds of *Hufen* was a main road along which the homesteads were in a row, the houses being situated either at the end or in the middle of the strip.[1]

This rectangular system of survey was imported into the German borderlands by Frisian and Dutch settlers from the Low Countries. A charter of Albrecht the Bear specifically mentions these "manors of Dutch measurement."[2] The earliest recorded example of this form of settlement in Germany is that of a colony of Hollanders settled by the Archbishop of Bremen in 1106 in the marshes of the Weser near Bremen.[3]

These villages established in the German colonial lands were very different in appearance from the older, manorial type of village. They formed a long street, with dwellings on either hand, each set in the midst of a separate rectangular subdivision, with the kitchen-garden or orchard around the house near the road, then the farm acres, then the pasture, and last the wood lot. Of course, the order would be subject to natural features, but this was the preferred arrangement if possible. Holstein, Mecklenburg, and Brandenburg were largely colonized in this way. The system in time was widely extended, however, as the restless population of Germany in the twelfth and thirteenth centuries searched out for themselves new homes in the wilderness or in less-frequented localities. Parts of the Black Forest and the Odenwald, of Upper Bavaria, of the upper reaches of the Mulde and the Pleisse, of the region between the Lippe and Luneburg, were so settled. The same is true of nearly one-quarter of Silesia and

[1] Meitzen, *Siedelung und Agrarwesen*, II, 47–53, 343–44; Inama Sternegg, *DWG*, I, 439–43. Since Meitzen wrote, Blanchard (*La Flandre* [Lille, 1906]) has thrown new light upon this subject. See esp. pp. 151–57, 423–27. On p. 424 is a map of one of these "street" villages in East Flanders. A lucid, untechnical account of these villages east of the Elbe (based on Meitzen) is by Schmid-Kunz, *Nord und Süd*, No. 257 (June, 1899).

[2] *Mansos Hollandriensis dimensionis* (Riedel, *Die Marck Brand.*, II, 51; *Codex Diplom.*, I, 338; Lavisse, *op. cit.*, p. 187).

[3] See the document in Kötzschke, *Quellen zur Geschichte der ostdeutschen Kolonisation im 12. bis 14. Jahrhundert* (Leipzig, 1912), pp. 1–2; also in *Bremisches U.-B.*, I, No. 27; Altmann-Bernheim, *Urkb. z. Verf. Gesch. Deutschlands*, I, No. 80; Inama Sternegg, *DWG*, II, 13. There is an English translation of the charter in Thatcher-MacNeal, *Source-Book for Mediaeval History*, No. 298.

the marsh land in the basins of the Oder, the Wartha, and the Netze. But the whole practice goes back to the original colony of Hollanders who settled in the Weser marshes in 1106.[1]

In Brandenburg the administrative machinery for the encouragement of settlement was better organized than in other parts of Germany. The immediate instrument in the promotion of colonization was a contractor (*locator*), which may be appropriately translated "promoter" in American parlance. These agents would contract with a large landed proprietor—bishop or baron, abbot or noble—to bring settlers in and establish them upon the grants which they had acquired from the margrave. For this purpose the tract was rectangularly subdivided after the manner which has been described. One "section" in every such rural community (*Landgemeinde*) was set aside for the parish priest. But the rights of the priest were strictly defined. There was no room in Brandenburg for the intrusion of priestly authority. One-tenth went to the *locator* as his fee. The balance of the land was apportioned among the incomers by lot, who lived under German law and worked the farms on the three-field system.[2]

[1] Meitzen, *op. cit.*, III, 264–68, and cf. the map illustrating "Die Holländer-Kolonien in den Marschen um Bremen," *ibid* (Atlas), No. 86.

[2] The influence of the practice of the Carolingian fisc was a factor in promoting the extension of the *Dreifeldersystem*. It seems to me that it is a defect of Meitzen's and Hanssen's treatment of the subject of the history of medieval German agriculture that both ignore too much this influence. Meitzen (I, 33–36, 67, 169) and Hanssen (*Agrarhistorische Abhandlungen*, I, 171) have focused their attention too exclusively upon the important three-field region east and south of the Weser and overemphasized the influence of the system there upon other localities. It should be added, however, that in Brandenburg and Austria, owing to the large proportion of Wendish peasantry there, the agricultural régime shows admixture of Slavonic land survivals. Kovalevsky, *Oekonomische Entwicklung Europas*, III (1905), 191, 215. On the institution of the *locator* see Riedel, *Die Marck Brandenburg*, I, 196; Wohlbrück, *Gesch. des ehemaligen Bistums Lebus*, I, 200 ff.; Lavisse, *La marche de Brandebourg*, pp. 201-2; and esp. Schulze, *Kolonisierung*, pp. 154–66. The following excerpts illustrate the form: "Nos Henricus, Dei gratis episcopus .... volumus esse notum quod nos .... perspeximus, quod de Suscoutz villa nostra episcopali .... nobis et nostrae ecclesiae modicum utilitatis et commodi perveniret, praedictam villam .... fideli nostro .... ad locandum *iure teutonico* tradimus" (Wohlbrück, I, 201; cf. Heinemann, *Albrecht der Bär*, Nos. 39–41). On p. 204 Wohlbrück cites the sale by the prior of a women's convent situated at Czarnovans, in Upper Silesia, of 21 manors to a *locator* named Siegfried, who formed a new town in the way described, which was called Frauendorf. Riedel, *loc. cit.*, instances a large number of places terminating

The land which was to be settled was divided into equal strips of land,[1] the rent for each of which amounted on the average to a quarter of a mark.[2] Besides this rent which was paid to the margrave, they had to pay a "malter" of three kinds of grain in the form of a tithe to the parish church. The owner, lay or clerical, would call to himself a colonization agent (called *advocatus*, or more commonly *Vogt*) and would enter into a contract with him for the colonization of his unoccupied lands. These lands were surveyed and partitioned into equal strips (*Lehen, lanens, mansi,* or *Hufen*), and each colonist received one of these *Lehen*. When the colonist had made the purchase, he gave a deposit on the first payment (*arrha, anleit*), which generally ranged from one to ten pieces of silver, according to the grade of the land, and then he obligated himself to pay interest from the remaining sum. But besides these stipulated payments, the colonist generally bound himself to pay the lord certain commodities, such as a few measures of the three kinds of grain, a few head of poultry, some dozens of eggs, etc. The settler became a hereditary renter of the fields and of the house he lived in. For the uncleared ground the rent generally was not paid until the eighth year after clearing.

The reward of the *Vogt* who colonized a particular locality consisted of a free and hereditary holding, for which neither he nor his posterity paid any payment whatever. Besides, the *Vogt* held the office of the *Dorfmeister*, which office (the *justicium*) combined the administrative with the judicial functions. The proceeds of the legal suits determined before him were divided into thirds, two of which went to the lord, and one was his own. Furthermore, the occupant of the *justicium* was given the free use of the village mill, the management of the village inn, and other similar privileges. Both he and his parents had the privilege of free fishing and the permission to cut the wood in the forest for their use. An

---

in the suffix *dorf*, as Mertinstorf, Cunradstorf, Michelstorf, Gerhardstorf, Wilkendorp, etc. Schultze, *Rechtsgeschichte* (5th ed., 1881), § 148, 5, claims that the German system of title-deed and land registration goes back to this form of grant.

[1] *Hufen, sortes, mansi.*

[2] "Also etwa fünf Mark unseres Geldes" (Grünhagen, p. 39).

energetic *Vogt* often colonized more than one village, and thus attained the *justicium* with its incomes and privileges in all the places he had colonized.

The settlements thus founded received their names either after the "lay" of the land or other such local circumstances, or after the *Vogt* or the colonists themselves. The most common endings of such names are: *-berg* ("hill"), *-au* ("meadow"), *-bühel* ("hill"), *-hart* ("woods"), *-bach* ("brook"), *-dorf* ("village"), *-schlag*, *-reut*, or *-rote* ("a clearing in the woods").[1]

Helmold, though with some exaggeration, described Nordalbingia as a great Saxon colony by 1171:

> The whole land of the Slavs, beginning at the Eyder [River], which is the boundary of the Kingdom of Denmark and lies between the Baltic Sea and the Elbe, and extends through a vast tract of country clear to Schwerin —a country which was once vexed with war and almost without population—now, through the grace of God, has all been conquered and, as it were, formed into a single colony of the Saxons. Towns and castles are being builded there, and the churches and ministers of Christ are increasing.

The last paragraph of this most original narrative of German medieval frontier history tells how Pribislav, the Abodrite duke (the only one of his family left, for Henry the Lion had hanged his brother), "sate quiet and content with the portion of territory allotted him 'by the rope' [i.e., surveyed], and rebuilt the towns of Mecklenburg, Ilow, and Rostock, and collected his people therein."[2]

Thus was the German feudal system extended over the Slavonic lands. Helmold says:

> But because some of the Slavs were prone to robbery and molested the Germans who were settled in Schwerin and roundabout, Gunzel, commandant of the castle, a brave man and vassal of the duke, ordained that whoever of the Slavs thereafter was found travelling, not on the mainroads, but in the bye-ways, unless the reason was evident, should be hanged at once.[3]

---

[1] For a typical example of this nature see Kötzschke, *Quellen*, No. 8.

[2] Helm., II, 14 (end); cf. I, 84. This method of surveying with a rope also obtained in France: "... mansiones et funiculos possessionum colonis distribuit" (*Cart. de l'abbaye de St. Bertin*, III, 344; Suger, *Vie de Louis le Gros* [ed. Molinier], p. 48). It was the ancient Hebrew system of allotment (II Kings 8:2; Amos 7:17).

[3] Chap. cx. Cf. Arnold of Lübeck, III, 4.

Pribislav became an avowed if not a sincere convert to Christianity, and personally participated in the foundation of the Cistercian monastery at Doberan near Rostock, by Bishop Berno in the year 1170, providing the new foundation with lands. But in spite of this there was for the present no extensive settling of German colonists. Pribislav sought to collect the remnants of his own people and to accustom them to a peaceable manner of life. After his death, however, the suppressed hatred of his subjects toward the German incomers once more asserted itself in a wild deed of revenge. The monastery of Doberan was destroyed in 1179 by the surrounding population, every one of its inmates, seventy-eight in number, suffering violent death. But the son and nephew of Pribislav, Henry Borwin and Niklot, who succeeded him in the government of Mecklenburg, were both friendly to the Germans at the outset, and found ways and means to give new life to colonization very soon. At the court of Niklot, whose residence was at Rostock, we already, in the year 1189, meet with several German nobles. With the help of Berno he also refounded the monastery at Doberan, which a few years later already possessed four German and twelve Slavonic villages. Henry Borwin, as early as 1179, is said to have turned over to the German knight Heinrich von Bützow half of the district of Marlow in northeastern Mecklenburg, immediately contiguous to the northwestern boundary of Pomerania, for the purpose of colonization. At any rate, we find here eight places with German names as early as 1210.

Thus, at the end of two centuries and a half of effort, after three severe reverses to their arms and years of wasting war and border strife, at last the combined strength of the feudal princes of Saxon Germany and of the no less warlike feudal bishops of the German church—men like the fierce Burckhard of Halberstadt, for example—united with the material assistance of thousands of nameless colonists who occupied the conquered lands, wore down the opposition of the Baltic Slavs.[1]

[1] In 1221 Wizlaw of Rügen said: "Gott möge es verhüten dass das Land jemals wieder in seinen früheren Zustand zurückfalle, dass die Slawen die deutschen Ansiedler vertreiben und wieder anfangen, das Land zu bebauen" (*Meckl. U.B.*, I. No. 278); quoted by Pueschl, pp. 4–5 and n. 1).

Henry the Lion was undeniably one of the greatest, perhaps the greatest, and most constructive statesmen, whom Germany possessed in the Middle Ages except Henry IV. He was a true empire-builder endowed with imagination, daring, will, and like almost all such statesmen was not averse to the use of blood and iron in achieving his imperious purposes.

Arnold of Lübeck, recognizing the continuity of history as recorded by Adam of Bremen and Helmold, and aspiring to be their continuator into the thirteenth century, appropriately pays tribute to the genius of Henry the Lion in the Prologue to his *Chronica Slavorum:*

> Et quia usque ad tempora Heinrici ducis Saxoniae atque Bavarie series decurrit, ipsum in fronte ponamus; qui super omnes, qui ante ipsum fuerunt, duritiam Sclavicam perdomui et non solum ad tributa solvenda coegit, sed etiam erga veri Dei cultum, relictis superstitionibus idololatrie, humiliatis cervicibus promptissimos fecit. Pacem etiam maximam in omni terra Sclavorum firmavit, et omnes provincie aquilonares Wagirorum, Holzatorum, Polaborum, Obotritorum ocio et quieti vacabant, et prohibita sunt furta et latrocinia terra marique, et fruebantur mutuis mercationibus et negotiationibus.

And yet, how strongly the need of German colonists was felt is indicated by a contract made in 1210 between Bishop Dietrich of Lübeck, and Heinrich Borwin, a half-Slav noble. The latter, according to the contents of the document in question, had settled German colonists on the little island of Poel, near Wismar (which politically belonged to Mecklenburg, ecclesiastically to Lübeck), "because of the poverty and small number of Slavs in that neighborhood, who were insufficient for the cultivation of the land." He insisted, as the Bishop says, that these settlers should not be held to the payment of all the church tithes, which the peasants always felt to be a very oppressive burden. The Bishop finally, though seemingly not without demur, contented himself with one-half the tithe, rendering the other half to Heinrich Borwin as a fief, an arrangement which with greater or less variation is found repeated in many of the other colonized regions.[1]

[1] Hauck, IV, 589, n. 2; 620–25. For fuller comment see Sommerfeld, pp. 136 ff.; Guttmann, *Forsch. zur Preuss. und Brand. Gesch.*, IX, 429; Wendt, II, 20 n. Many of the Slav serfs were yet pagan (Michael, I, 94–97; Kötzschke, *Unternehmerthum*, pp. 24–36).

The district of Schwerin (the region west and south of the Schweriner-See) as well as the neighboring localities, Ratzeburg and east Holstein, in the course of a short time were heavily colonized with Germans. In the diocese of Ratzeburg two generations later, among 277 settlements only 8 are mentioned as having Wendish inhabitants.

There still is one region of Transalbingia—namely, Brandenburg—whose colonization remains to be briefly considered. The two German nobles of the twelfth century who exhibited a keen yet sympathetic understanding of the problem involved in the relation of the Germans and the Slavs along the Elbe frontier were Adolph of Holstein and Albrecht the Bear of Brandenburg. The moderate and statesman-like policy of Adolph, as we have seen, was ruined by the Saxon princes, especially Henry the Lion. But Albrecht was strong enough to hold his own against the pressure and to carry out his own ideas within his territories without molestation or inhibition. In Tuttle's words:

> Albert was a statesman as well as a soldier, and by a politic liberality insinuated first his religion and then his authority upon many of the most influential Wends. Arms and diplomacy thus composed a hostile and refractory people into a body of sympathetic subjects. At the same time he fixed the conditions of his social policy on such a firm yet prudent basis that even before his death the prosperity of the Mark had begun to excite the envy of his neighbors.[1]

While yet Albrecht von Ballenstedt, before Brandenburg fell to him by the favor of fortune, Albrecht had followed Otto of Bamberg's pacific labors in Pomerania with interest, if we may believe the biographers of the bishop.[2] Certainly after 1134, in which year he acquired the Nordmark, an opportunity to study the effects of Otto of Bamberg's course in Pomerania was afforded, for the lines of the Nordmark were vague and Albrecht, in denial of the claims of Poland to

---

[1] Tuttle, *History of Prussia*, I, 13–14. For a fuller discussion see Guttmann, *op. cit.*, IX, 444–50; Passew, *ibid.*, Band XIV, Heft 1 (1901); Schillmann, *Grundsteinlegung zum Brand.-Preuss. Staat um die Mitte des 12. J.* (1883); Krabbo, "Albrecht der Bär," *Forsch. zur Brand.-Preuss. Gesch.*, XIX, 253.

[2] Ebbo, III, 10; Herbordus, III, 8.

Pomerania, claimed jurisdiction clear to the Oder River.[1] This Mark, in Prussian history known as the Alt-Mark, lay along the left bank of the Elbe in the bend below Magdeburg and was roughly included in the quadrangle made by the Ohre, the Aland, and the upper Aller. The eastern part formed the *pagus* Belinesheim and ecclesiastically was attached to the bishopric of Halberstadt; the western part, the *pagus* Osterwolde, belonged to the diocese of Verden.[2] In the eastern part the ancient fortresses of Werben, Tangermünde, and Arneburg guarded the Elbe; the most important place in the western half, which less needed protection, was Salzwedel. At the time of Albrecht's acquisition of the Alt-Mark the population was thin. Most of the places mentioned in documents of the tenth century as pertaining to the churches of Havelberg or Magdeburg had disappeared in the eleventh in the various wars of Slavonic reaction, or in the struggle for supremacy, in Saxony, between Albrecht and Henry the Lion.[3]

What little population there was in Brandenburg at Albrecht's accession was mixed German and Slav, a forecast of the future social composition of the country.[4] Albrecht had

---

[1] *Codex diplom. Pom.*, I, 33; Rachfahl, *Forsch. z. Brand. Gesch.*, Band V, Heft 2 (1892); L. Giesebrecht, *Wend. Gesch.*, II, 363; Heinemann, *Albrecht der Bär*, p. 344.

[2] Kretschmer, p. 337.

[3] "Siquidem has terras Saxones olim inhabitasse feruntur, tempore scilicet Ottonum, ut videri potest in antiquis aggeribus qui congesti fuerant super ripas Albiae in terra palustri Balsamorum, sed praevalentibus postmodum Sclavis, Saxones occisi et terra a Sclavis usque ad nostra tempora possessa" (Helm., I, 88). A charter of Conrad III to the church of Havelberg in confirmation of its possessions and privileges is unusually vivid for an official document in describing the deserted state of the Alt-Mark: ". . . . Et quoniam praenominatae civitates et villae saepe irruentibus paganis vastatae sunt ac depopulatae, adeo ut vel nullo, vel raro habitore incolantur, volumus atque praecipimus ut idem episcopus liberam absque contradictione habeat facultatem ibidem ponendi et locandi colonos, de quacumque gente voluerit vel habere potuerit" (Riedel, *Die Marck Brand.*, II, 40).

[4] "Gens illa saxonica slavica" (Riedel, *Codex diplom. Brand.*, IV, 2); "gens permixta Slavonica et Saxonica" (cited by Wendt, II, 21 n.). Both allusions are from the *Pulcavae Chronica*, which is of the fourteenth century. This, of course, would normally vitiate its evidence for the twelfth century. But Riedel (*Codex diplom. Brand.*, IV, 1; Introd., pp. ix–xvi), Heinemann (*op. cit.*, pp. 421–22, and Schillman, *op. cit.* [1882]) have shown that this chronicle embodies extracts derived from an earlier and lost Brandenburger chronicle. They have attempted to restore it. Cf. Lavisse, p. 61, n. 1; p. 71, n. 2. Of course the statement in the paragraph involves the

wisely held aloof as much as he could from participation in the Wendish Crusade of 1147, so that the broken fragments of the pagan Slavs looked upon him with a not unfriendly eye, and in 1150, when the Christian Wendish chieftain in Brandenburg died without heirs and left his territory by bequest to Albrecht, a German extension over Brandenburg was made possible without friction.[1]

Albrecht the Bear's firm yet tactful policy reconciled the Wends in his domains to German domination, while a liberal land policy induced heavy immigration by settlers from regions farther west. Brandenburg and Pomerania, where the ministry of Otto of Bamberg (1124–25, 1128–29) peacefully paved the way for the extension of German rule, are the only two Wendish lands not acquired at the price of bloodshed in the twelfth century.[2] Before Albrecht died this region, so uninviting and sparsely peopled by a mixed Wendish and German population, had become so prosperous that Brandenburg excited the envy of the Margrave's neighbors.

It is worth observing that in Brandenburg there is a striking absence of those meticulous rights, services, and obligations in this new country such as were familiar to the emigrants in their former homes. The multitude of trivial and exasperating obligations imposed upon the peasantry of older Europe at this time, and from which they had fled, is

---

burning question of whether, and how far, the population of modern Brandenburg is mixed German and Slav. For literature on this subject, in addition to that already cited, see Lavisse, *La Marche de Brandebourg*, pp. 188–94, esp. p. 192, n. 2; Guttmann, *op. cit.*, IX, 395–514, and Wendt, *Die Nationalität der Bevölkerung der deutschen Ostmarken vor dem Beginne der Germanisierung* (Göttingen, 1878). Mielke, in a remarkable study of house architecture in Brandenburg, finds Slav, Saxon, Flemish, and French types surviving, interesting evidence for the mixed ingredients of colonization in Brandenburg. See *Archiv der Gesellschaft f. Heimatskunde der Provinz Brandenburg*, Band I (1894).

[1] For an analysis of the evidence concerning this remarkable measure see Lavisse, p. 61, n. 1; Wendt, II, 21. For Albrecht's policy see Hauck, IV, 608–20.

[2] Brückner, *Die slavische Ansiedelung in der Altmark* (Leipzig, 1879); Ernst, *Forschungen zur Brand. und Preuss. Gesch.*, Band XXIII (1910); von Flans, *Ztschft. d. hist. Ver. f. Marienwerder* (1897), No. 35. For the missionary work of the Norbertiner and Cistercians (Danish) in Pomerania in the twelfth century see Hauck, IV, 588–90.

not found in Brandenburg.[1] Law and government in the early centuries of Germany's New East were simpler and more wholesome than in Western and Central Germany. The social spirit and temper of the people who settled the border provinces of Germany in the twelfth and thirteenth centuries were freer and more democratic (I use this word in a relative sense only, of course), less permeated by that class feeling which accentuated social relations in older and more feudal Germany, for the reason that the social texture of German frontier society was less complex, less closely knit. Albrecht was the freest and most untrammeled prince in Europe in the twelfth century. He was like William the Conqueror in 1066. There were few "traditional" rights and no antiquated feudal interests burdening the soil of Brandenburg when he acquired it. He could build a state and establish a society almost *de novo*. His political authority was simple and complete. Every person from peasant to baron and bishop was a subject of the Margrave.[2]

[1] Conrad III (*anno* 1150) for Havelberg: "ea videlicet libertate, ut nullus dux, nullus marchio, nullus comes, seu vicecomes, nullus advocatus seu subadvocatus aliquam exactionem exinde extorquere audeat, nullus aliquod dominium sibi usurpare presumat, nullas petitiones publicas ibi faciat, nullus eos ad ligna portanda vel secanda vel faciendas fossas cogat." Riedel, *Die Marck Brandenb.*, II, 40. The same was true of the colonists around Bremen. *Henric. Wolteri Chron. Brem.* (*ca.* 1142): "Item voluit idem archiepiscopus, quod omnes villici et cultores agrorum ejusdem ecclesiae liberi esse deberent ab omni censu civitatis vel villae et quod essent liberi ab omni advocatia" (cited by Inama Sternegg, *DWG*, II, 29, nn. 1 and 2). "Just as it was earlier customary to make leases of freshly cleared woodlands in return for a heritable rent, in order to have them cleared (*Waldhufen, assart, virgate*) so a free tenancy of inheritance known as *Gründerleihe* ("colonial tenure") was the favored form in which the colonization of Eastern Germany was realized. The German colonists were granted heritable holdings as freemen by the founders of marks, or villages, and, aside from a nominal rent paid to the owner of the land (i.e., to the territorial princes or to ecclesiastical or secular magnates) in recognition of their title, were subject only to public taxes and services which left entirely unaffected their personal status. The favorable situation of these colonists in Eastern Germany reacted in turn upon the position of the peasant population in the older parts of Germany, and caused a recedence of manorial types of tenancy. To this end the decay of the manorial organization also contributed" (Huebner, *Germanic Private Law*, sec. 45, p. 325).

[2] It must be admitted that this state of things changed with the decline of the Ascanian house in the fourteenth century and that Brandenburg in time was assimilated to the condition of the other and older principalities of Germany. But this history is later than the period with which this chapter is dealing. G. F. Knapp (*Grundherrschaft und Rittergut* [Leipzig, 1897] and *Die Bauernbefreiung und der*

The colonizing genius of the Ascanian house showed un-
impaired vitality down through the thirteenth century, and
then only began to decay. The progress of the margraves
across the Oder after 1242 brought them into conflict with
Poland. The founding of towns in the Neumark began with
Frankfort on the Oder in 1253 and ended with Falkenberg in
1337. Yet great as was the importance of towns for the development of new Germany, their influence was less than that
of the towns in Western Germany. On the other hand, if the
burgher population was stronger in the west than in the east,
the condition of the peasant population in the east was better
than in the west.[1]

The peasants of Brandenburg as well as knight, baron,
and bishop were all alike indebted to the Margrave for their
titles to the land. If they paid established taxes, which were
few and simple when compared to what obtained elsewhere
in Germany, they were free.[2] No wonder, as Lavisse, writing
in 1875 well said, "the German emigrant in the Middle
Ages went beyond the Elbe in order to find free land as today
he is crossing the Atlantic."[3]

The speed and effectiveness of this transformation of

Ursprung der Landarbeiter in den aelteren Teilen Preussens) has demonstrated that
the great oppression of the peasantry does not date from the Middle Ages, and that
the manorial régime in medieval Germany was not abusive, however onerous, to the
rural classes. The real sufferings of the German peasantry date from the reception
of the Roman law in the fifteenth century, and more still from the horrors of the
Thirty Years' War. The height of oppression was in the eighteenth century, after
the Seven Years' War. Cf. S. B. Fay, "The Roman Law and the German Peasant,"
American Hist. Review, XVI, 234.

[1] Niessen, *Forschungen zur Brand. und Preuss. Gesch.*, Band IV (1891); Band
XVI (1903).

[2] Cf. Tuttle, *History of Prussia*, p. 29. A gloss of the *Sachsenspiegel*, which dates
from the early fourteenth century, emphasizes this relation between a free soil and a
freeman in Brandenburg. The peasants were free because they were the first to
clear the land. "Mit uns aber, das ist in der Marck, haben die gebawer auch Erb am
zinsgut, und mögen es lassen, wenn sie wollen, welches daher kommen ist, dass
unser landt also sindt besatzt worden. Denn do solches gesehen, hat man den bawern
die huffen erst wildt und unangebawet ausgethan, welche, nachdem sie nochmals
durch der leute arbeit sindt gebessert worden. Darumb mögen sie dieselbingen auch
ihres gefallens verkeuffen" (cited in Riedel, *Die Marck Brand.*, II, 281 n.; also
Lavisse, *op. cit.*, p. 204, n. 1).

[3] *Loc. cit.*

provinces and peoples which had so long resisted German
sway cannot be wholly ascribed to the colonizing genius of
Henry the Lion and Albrecht the Bear. Things are stronger
than men. The push of two centuries of endeavor and experience was behind the movement. It does not rob them of
the laurel to say that they were fortunate in their day and
generation, or that they were the unconscious instruments of
potential forces in the Saxon nation operating for expression
and solution.

Saxon Germany had been partially transformed in economic conditions and in social texture under the rule of the
Ottos. But the Salian period was a melting-pot, a vast
crucible, out of which North Germany emerged with tremendous and unguessed forces pent up within her and struggling for expression. Within the two centuries represented by
the rule of the Saxon and Salian houses, Germany—especially
North Germany—was radically transformed, in economic
and social condition. Population had become denser; competition keener; life more complex.[1] In a word, old Germany
had become feudalized.

Colonization and reclaiming of land entirely changed the condition of
the rural population between the tenth and thirteenth centuries. In the
time of the Carolingians wood and land had still been regarded as inexhaustible goods of the nation, like the sun, air and water. But now the
limitations of the geographical basis of national life appeared more and
more clearly. There had been an immense range of land to grow food upon;
but now the supply became limited, chiefly and first on the Rhine, in
Swabia and Franconia, afterwards in Saxony, and finally in Bavaria, the
Tyrol and Styria. The people had to shift on a limited area. The soil became more than before an object of economic value. Its price kept continually increasing. In the twelfth century in some prosperous districts,
land seems to have attained twelve times the value it had in the ninth
and afterwards even down to the second half of the thirteenth century an
increase of about 50 per cent is to be observed. Taking into consideration
that land was still regarded, especially by the ruling classes as the only
basis of social and political influence (though already other sources of large

[1] In 1222 Caesar of Prüm wrote of the advancement of agriculture and the
agrarian civilization of Germany since 893 as follows: "In tempore tam diuturno
constat multas silvas esse extirpatas, villas edificatas, decimas auctas, multa
molendina sunt in praefato tempore edificata ac multe vinee plantate, terre infinite culte" (*Mittelrheinisches Urkundenbuch*, I, 201; cf. Lamprecht, *DWL*, II, 50).

incomes were gradually arising), we may understand how intense the struggle for the possession of the soil must have been at this period.[1]

On the other hand, we also find that increase of population induced emigration from the older parts of Germany into the New East.[2]

A knowledge of American history is not without value for an understanding of this movement. A young nation discovers the marks and *indicia* of its growth which are undiscernible in the early history of an old nation, whose tree trunk is covered with the lichen and moss of centuries. The newer, fresher, nearer history of America embodies principles of social development and the play of economic forces which have been foreign to Europe for six hundred years. It still holds in solution, as it were, institutions which have been crystallized for generations across the sea. Friedrich List, the German economist, when he visited America early in the nineteenth century, clearly perceived the sequence of frontiers in our history. Indeed, he is the first who formulated the fact historically. In his *National System* he wrote:

> There one may see wildernesses grow into rich and mighty states; and progress which requires centuries in Europe goes on there before one's eyes, viz.: that from the condition of the mere hunter to the rearing of cattle, from that to agriculture, and from the latter to manufactures and commerce.

More than thirty years ago the Italian economist Loria said that "America has the key to the historical enigma which Europe has sought for centuries."

Every student of American history knows the effect of the westward movement upon New England in the depletion of the population, the increase of the number of abandoned farms, the gradual degeneration of the "stay-at-homes" owing to the fact that the strongest and sturdiest blood had

---

[1] Lamprecht, *DG*, III, 56–57. See also G. von Buchwald, *Zur deutschen Wirtschaftsgesch. in endenden Mittelalter* (1885) and an article by Schaeffler and Brandl in *Archivalische Ztschrift*. (1880).

[2] "Multa milia puerorum a sex annis et supra usque ad virilem aetatem . . . . quidam aratra vel currus quos minabant, alii pecora, que pascebant, vel si qua alia habebant pre manibus relinquunt" (Lamprecht, *DWL*, I, 1, 463 and n. 1, from *Chron. Reg.* [1213], p. 191). The exodus was so great that there is complaint of abandoned farms and even whole villages in Hohenstaufen times.

emigrated, empty houses and grass-grown streets in the towns, etc. But it comes with something like a shock to discover these same phenomena and identical complaints with reference to the older parts of Germany in the late Middle Ages.[1]

The frontier between the German and the Slav in the twelfth century interestingly exhibits characteristics which are familiar to every student of the history of American westward expansion. That "return to primitive conditions in a continually advancing frontier line, and a new development of that area," which Professor Turner has pointed out as so significant in the history of the formation of the West is true of the east border of Germany in the twelfth century. Border ruffians and robbers infested the Marches.[2] One is reminded of Morris Birkbeck's observation touching the condition of southern Indiana in 1817:

> The inhabitants of Indiana . . . . are lawless, semibarbarous vagabonds, dangerous to live among. . . . . An unsettled country, lying contiguous to one that is settled, is always a place of retreat for rude and even abandoned characters, who find the regulations of society intolerable.

By the beginning of the twelfth century Germany had become historically conscious of the worth of its frontier and as eager to occupy it as our forefathers here in America were. What the trans-Allegheny country was to the United States in 1800 that the trans-Elbean country was to Germany in 1200. The hardy rustics who tilled their little farms redeemed from marsh and swamp and forest in Ditmarsch and Holstein, in Mecklenburg and Brandenburg, were men like unto our own ancestors in conditions of livelihood, in courage, in hope, in perseverance. Life on the East German border then was rude and crude and impinged as sharply upon the feelings of the cultured and refined society of older Germany as the Kentucky of Boone grated upon the sensibilities of staid tidewater communities like Baltimore or Philadelphia. The frontier as it advanced geographically reflected the reactions

[1] See Lamprecht, *DWL*, I, 2, 871, for citations.
[2] Helm., I, 49, 66, 67, 87.

between the physiography and the society settling it by modifying inherited institutions to meet new conditions.[1]

An analogy between the two frontiers, though so far removed in time and place from each other, is not a fanciful one. The greed of the Americans for the lands of the Indians, and the intolerance of the rifleman toward the Red Man, has a parallel in the conduct of the Saxons toward the Wends. The history of the Cherokees has its prototype in medieval Germany. The protest of the nameless Abodrite chief in Helmold, I, 53, against the erection of the *castellum* of Sigeberg reminds one of the harangue of that Delaware chief recorded by Heckewelder. Niklot's reply to Adolph of Holstein

[1] By far the most important difference between East-Elbean and West-Elbean Germany was in the character of the agrarian system prevailing. The researches of G. von Below, *Territorium und Stadt;* of T. Knapp, *Gesammelte Beiträge zur Rechts- und Wirtschaftsgeschichte;* of Fuchs (translated in Carver's *Readings in Rural Economics,* pp. 223–53, under the title "The Epochs of German Agrarian History and Policy"), have done much to modify or supplement the earlier work of Meitzen and Hanssen. The country east of the Elbe was, and still is, pre-eminently the region of great patrimonial landed estates (*Gutsherrschaften*). In the words of Fuchs: "It was a threefold landed proprietorship, that of the reigning prince, of the German cloisters, which received as gifts vast tracts of land for colonization with German peasants, and of the great vassals constituting the high German and native nobility. .... The large manorial estates in the East were from the very beginning geographically closed domains." For excellent general accounts of the contrast between these great produce-yielding estates of the cultivating lords to the east of the Elbe (*Gutsherrschaften*) and the rent-yielding estates of landlords in the south and west of Germany (*Grundherrschaften*) see G. v. Below, *op. cit.* (Leipzig, 1900), pp. 1–96, and T. Knapp, *Gesammelte Beiträge zur Rechts- und Wirtschaftsgeschichte* (Tübingen, 1902), pp. 348–88 (reprinted from *Zeitschrift d. Savigny-Stiftung,* XIX [1898], 16–51). Monographs on special regions are noted in Dahlmann-Waitz, *Quellenkunde der deutschen Geschichte* (8th ed.; Leipzig, 1912), Nos. 2173–2275. The ground plans of these new towns in the East, the structure of villages, and the history which may be read in different forms of house- and barn-building types which moved with the German colonists across the whole of North Germany from the Low Countries to the Vistula, may be mentioned here as subjects which have yielded rich results to German scholarship. See Fritz, *Deutsche Stadtanlagen* (Strassburg, 1894), with ground plans of German "colonial" towns; Heil, *Die deutschen Städte und Bürger im Mittelalter* (Leipzig, 1912); Meilke, *Das deutsche Dorf* (Leipzig, 1913), and especially Püschel, *Das Anwachsen der deutschen Städte in der Zeit der mittelalterlichen Kolonialbewegung* (Berlin, 1910), which shows the relation between German eastward expansion and agricultural prosperity and urban growth. He has studied the topography of fifteen towns. There is an admirable map in *Deutsche Erde,* VIII, 256, illustrating East German colonization by the spread of types of German house architecture. It interestingly confirms the historical facts set forth in this chapter. In the same volume, p. 80, may be seen ground plans of these various house types.

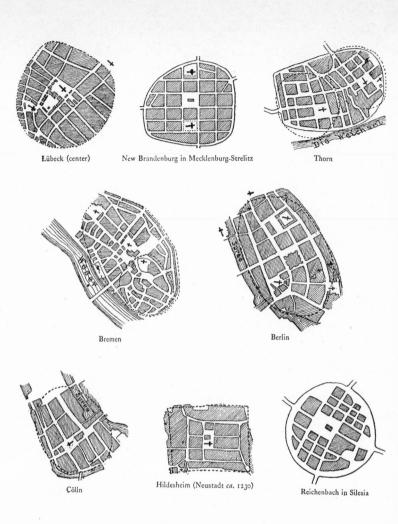

Łübeck (center) New Brandenburg in Mecklenburg-Strelitz Thorn

Bremen Berlin

Cölln Hildesheim (Neustadt *ca.* 1230) Reichenbach in Silesia

UNTER WARNOW

Rostock Demmin in Pomerania

GROUND PLANS OF "NEW TOWNS" IN EAST GERMANY

is like that of a friendly Indian chief whose friendship has been betrayed.[1]

Every great nation, however old, has gone through a long, formative stage of development. If we could clear away the mold of ages of history around the roots of the nations, we not only would know more of their history but we probably would also perceive that there are certain primary characteristics which are roughly common to the formative period of every people. There is a parallel, not absolute, of course, but relative between the border history of medieval Germany and that of America. The German pioneer faced the wolf and the Wend; he endured the isolation and sometimes the desolation of his settlements; he felled the forests; he drained the swamps; he built up a civilization—often, it is true, with crude instruments and with unskilled hands. But for his own time, for his own country, for his own people, he accomplished a work as large and as lasting as the formation of our own Ohio and Mississippi commonwealths has been for the United States.

The endeavor has been made in this chapter to trace the history of German eastward expansion from its inception down to the time when the Elbe became a German river. Perhaps one might take as culminating dates of the movement the year 1134, when Albrecht the Bear acquired Brandenburg, and 1158, the year in which Henry the Lion became possessed of Lübeck. Effective, permanent German life across the great river practically began with these two events. It is to be noticed, however, that these dates terminate only the first period of the history of German colonization.

While the rulers of Brandenburg, Mecklenburg, and Pomerania were slowly building the superstructure of a great Germanic civilization in North Germany, which was to reach brilliant culmination in the cities of the Hanseatic League, the forward movement still drove on eastward over Pomerellia and Livland, and clear around the bight of the Baltic into Kurland and Esthonia.[2] When once the Baltic Slavs were crushed, the tribes east of them, long since de-

[1] Helm., I, 62.   [2] Cf. Hauck, IV, 627-57.

serted by Christianized Poland and Bohemia, fell an easy conquest to the German sword. Once the Elbe was permanently crossed, the other rivers were slight barriers to German advance. One after the other, in rapid succession, the Slav towns at the mouths of the Baltic rivers—Danzig, Riga, Reval—fell into German hands.

It is with a sensation akin to astonishment that the historian reads the record of this continued eastward expansion. For over three hundred years the fecund *Mutterland* sent her children forth from the Old West into the New East, to build roads, to bridge rivers, to clear forests, to drain swamps, to establish towns, to found a civilization in the wilderness. As a story of a great people, as the history of empire-building, the making of the German Northeast in the Middle Ages is matched only by the formation of our own great Northwest. What Burke said of the American colonists when he made the rafters of St. Stephens ring with his oratory in that masterful speech on conciliation with the colonies, "We cannot, we cannot falsify the pedigree of this fierce people," may be as well applied to the German settlers of Mecklenburg, Brandenburg, Pomerania, Livonia, as to the New England colonists.

In the year of the incarnation of the Word, 1186, the episcopal see in Livonia was founded in the place called Riga. And because that region abounded in many good things owing to the beneficence of the soil, Christian settlers never failed there, and planters of the new church. For the land was one of fertile fields, of abundant pasture, well watered by rivers full of fish, and well covered with trees. . . . . Moved by the impassioned preaching of the lord abbot Berthold of Loccum not a few well to do and gentry, for to break the strength of the heathen and to establish the religion of Christ took the road of migration. . . . . A vast number of them came from all Saxony, from Westphalia, from Frisia, prelates and priests, soldiers, merchants, rich and poor, unto Lübeck where were vessels laden with arms and foodstuffs, whence they went to Livonia.[1]

These words were written by Arnold of Lübeck concerning the colonization of Livland between 1186 and 1196. The spirit of these settlers in the Slavonic wilderness beyond the Vistula is not far from that which actuated those who came to America in the seventeenth century.

[1] Arnold of Lübeck, *Chron. Slav.*, V, 30.

It is a long tale, this history of German eastward expansion and colonization, to which I now bring a term. It is a history of blood and iron, of strong men and women, of lusty strife, of daring adventure, of hard work. As the dust cloud of the arena sometimes obscures the figures of the racing horses, so in the thick turmoil of this strenuous expansion of a great people we may sometimes lose sight of the greater process which worked itself out.

For there was a great process in the movement and an increasing purpose striving for realization. The colonization of the New Northeast was the product of a great faith and great works. It had in it that elemental energy which all discovery and new conquest possess.

It was the great deed of the common people of medieval Germany,[1] just as the making of the American West has been the achievement of the common people of America, from whose loins, "new birth of a new soil," sprang the first American. What the "Old Northwest" has been to the United States, that, in much the same degree and similar way, was the Northeast—the trans-Elbean-Oder country—to medieval Germany.

Nor were the conditions which these German colonists encountered in the new land so different from those endured by the settlers of New England. With change of time and place, this extract from Peter von Dusburg's *Chronicon terrae Prussiae*[2] would fit into Winthrop's *Journal*, or Bradford's *Plymouth Plantation*:

For they had left the sweet soil of their native country and entered into an alien land, in which their future was to be, where for many years they were destined to endure hardships without hope of return homeward even unto the fourth or sixth generation of them. They came from a fertile homeland, peaceful and quiet, and penetrated a country of horror and

[1] "In den Landen deutscher Zunge, in denen die traditionelle Macht des Adels heute noch am besten erhalten ist, ist er fast völlig frei von allem Blute der altfreien Edelgeschlechter. An der Kolonisation des deutschen Ostens hat der altdeutsche Adel keinen anderen Anteil gehabt, als ihn die wenigen Dynastenhäuser dieser Gebiete und einige wenige Prälaten und Ordensritter nahmen. Schon Hermann von Salza war ein Dienstmann" (Aloys Schulte, *Der Adel und die deutsche Kirche*, p. 300).

[2] *SS. rerum Prussicarum*, quoted in Kötzschke, *Quellen*, No. 39; cf. Hauck, IV, 642–52.

vast solitude and filled with baneful war. In a word, putting behind their backs an abundance of everything in this world, liberty, home, honor, they accepted hunger and thirst, endured infinite poverty, endless discomfort, failures and perils.

For about seventy-five years the Vistula River remained the boundary between the expanding German and the shrinking Slavonic world. Then, early in the thirteenth century, the Teutonic Knights, having no longer a field in the Holy Land, and driven out of Hungary, found a new field of conquest, in 1231, in Prussia.

By 1346 their rule extended clear to the Gulf of Finland. Prussia, Courland, Livonia, and Esthonia were conquered in succession. As each region was conquered a fortress was built to enforce obedience and to serve as a base for further operations; that of Marienburg is a conspicuous example of such a castle. German settlers were introduced to colonize and redeem the devastated lands. The energy of the Knights in building towns was remarkable. By 1400 they had ninety-three cities, the most important of which were Riga and Reval.

CHAPTER XIV

EARLY TRADE RELATIONS BETWEEN THE GERMANS AND THE ELBEAN AND BALTIC SLAVS

THE HISTORY of German eastward expansion in the Middle Ages is the *Vorgeschichte* of the Hanseatic League. Unfortunately few Hanseatic historical writers go back to the founding of Lübeck in 1143, and none farther than Lothar II's diploma of 1134. It is true that effective commercial life did not begin in North Germany until the rise of Lübeck. But the founding of Lübeck was as much the term of one epoch as it was the point of departure for a new period. Bächtold in his excellent *Der norddeutsche Handel im 12. und beginnenden 13. Jahrhundert*[1] perceived that the history of the genesis of the Hansa had not received its due proportion of treatment; but the limitations of his subject prevented him from going farther back than the twelfth century. It is this neglected aspect of the history of medieval German commerce which I have tried to relate in this chapter.

In spite of the immemorial antagonism between the two races, from early times a certain amount of border trade seems always to have existed between the Germans and the Slavs. Desire for commercial aggrandizement was a not unimportant motive of German eastward expansion and subjugation of the Slavs.[2] As far back as the first half of the

[1] Rothschild (Berlin and Leipzig, 1910).

[2] "Kaufleute, Krieger und Priester," Wendt, *Die Germanisierung der Länder östlich der Elbe*, I, 10. (Liegnitz, 1884). Bugge, "Die nordeuropäischen Verkehrswege im frühen Mittelalter," *Vierteljahrschrift f. Soz. und Wirtschaftsgesch.*, IV, 237, has written: "Die grösste Bedeutung der nördlichen Völker für die Handelsgeschichte liegt doch darin, dass sie überall im Auslande, wo sie im 9., 10. und 11. Jahrhundert als Eroberer hinkamen, Städte und Handelsniederlassungen gründeten. Dadurch wurde dem ganzen Verkehrsleben des nördlichen Europas neues Leben eingehaucht und der Welthandel in neue Bahnen gelenkt."

seventh century there is mention of adventurous Frankish traders penetrating into the Slavonic wilderness, bartering for slaves, amber, and beaver and marten skins.

In the reign of Dagobert I (629-39) an alleged renegade Frankish trader named Samo established commercial relations with the pagan Bohemians, Moraven, and Carinthians, and is said finally to have abjured Christianity and to have established a short-lived barbarian state which extended from the Drave and Silesia[1] to the frontier of Thuringia, and which was powerful enough to defeat the Frankish arms and important enough to have its alliance sought by the Byzantine emperor Heraclius.[2]

That a brisk commercial intercourse between the Frankish state and Samo's kingdom existed in the seventh century is

[1] Grünhagen, *Gesch. Schlesiens*, p. 4.

[2] Fredegar, *Chronicon*, IV, 48, "ex pago Senonago" (cf. 68 and 75). Usually this reading has been accepted as meaning Sens or Soignies. If so this would make Samo a Frank. But there is room for doubt. Apart from the dubious geographical reading and translation thereof, the name Samo does not sound like a German name, but a Slav. Certain it is that Czech tradition has connected Samo with the Bohemian national house of Przemysel-Schreuer, *Vierteljahrschrift f. Soz. und Wirtschaftsgesch.*, V, No. 2 (1907), 197-213; Goldmann, *Mitteil. d. Inst. für oesterr. Gesch.*, XXX, No. 2 (1909); Schafarik, *Slawische Alterthümer*, II, 416-20. For the extension of Samo's rule to Thuringia see Peisker, *Cambridge Med. Hist.*, II, 451 and note; for Samo and the Slavs in Carinthia, J. Goll, "Samo und die Karantischen Slawen," *Mitteil. d. Inst. für oesterr. Gesch.*, XI (1890), 443-46. Inama Sternegg, *DWG*, I, 234; Schulze, *Die Kolonisierung und Germanisierung der Gebiete zwischen Saale und Elbe*, pp. 5-7; Meitzen, *Siedelung und Agrarwesen*, II, 150, 405-6; Lippert, *Sozial-Gesch. Böhmens*, I, 219, all notice the trade importance of this item.

Peisker, in his article on the expansion of the Slavs in the *Cambridge Mediaeval History*, II, 451, argues that the chronology of Samo's reign must be corrected, for his overthrow of the Avars must have taken place some time between 602 and 605, most probably in 603. He points out that the revolt of the Croats and the Serbs, and finally the Bulgar Khan's revolt, followed in the years between 635 and 641. However, other dates also in Peisker's article differ from those commonly accepted, and no explanation is offered for this change of chronology. It is interesting to note in this connection, however, that another circumstance seems to favor Peisker's contention. According to his chronology, Samo died about the year 637-40. Duke Radulf (Fredegarius, *Chronicon*, IV, 75, 77) was put in command of Thuringia, to protect that territory from the inroads of the Slavs. He, however, became involved in some difficulties with Sigibert, the son of Dagobert, and finally rebelled against him. In order to strengthen his position, he sought alliance with the neighboring peoples, and most probably with the Bohemian Slavs also. This was in 641 (*ibid.*, IV, 77, 87), and it is noteworthy that the name of Samo—who certainly was an outstanding character and was well known to the chronicler—is not mentioned. This would indicate that he may have been dead by that time.

evident from the incident that some Frankish merchants were killed in Bohemia in 631, and when King Dagobert sent an ambassador to Samo, this untactful messenger insulted him and Samo had him literally thrown out of the country.[1] After that Dagobert invaded the country with an army composed of Allemanni, Bavarians, and even of Longobards from Italy, but was decisively defeated at Wogastiburc. As a positive result of this victory of Samo's, the Sorben chieftain Drevan fell away from his allegiance to the Frankish state and joined Samo's kingdom. Samo became thoroughly domesticated in the country of his adoption, and is said to have married at least twelve wives; if we may believe Fredegar, he had twenty-two sons and fifteen daughters. He ruled thirty-five years; when he died, the great territory which he had consolidated seems to have fallen back into its component parts again.

In the next century the *Life of Sturmi*, Boniface's disciple, and abbot of Fulda, who died in 779, shows that a regular trade route ran from the Saale River to Mainz through the Thuringian Forest.[2] In 805 (probably, the date is not certain) Charlemagne for the first time legislated in regulation of this border traffic, and established a chain of fortified trading posts along the Slavonic frontier from the mouth of the Elbe to the middle Danube. These posts were Bardowick and Schesel (near later Hamburg), Erfurt[3] in Saxony, Magdeburg on the great bend of the Elbe, Halstat (near later Bamberg), Pfreimt (in the later Ober Pfalz), at the confluence of the Wald Nab and the Pfreimt to form the Nab, Forchheim, Lorch, and Regensburg on the Danube at the mouth of the Nab.[4]

[1] *Ibid.*, "aejectus est Sicharius de conspectu Samonis."

[2] "Tunc quadam die . . . . pervenit ad viam a Turingorum regione mercandi causa ad Mogontiam pergentes ducit . . . . ibi magnam Sclavorum multitudinem reperit" (*MGH*, SS. II, 369, chap. vii). Cf. Rettberg, *Kirchengesch. Deutschlands*, I, 372; Dopsch, *Wirtschaftsentwicklung der Karolingerzeit*, II, 191.

[3] A letter of Pope Zacharias in 742 mentions Erfurt as "jam olim urbs paganorum rusticorum."

[4] Cap. Miss. in Theodonis Villa, chap. vii (*MGH*, SS. XI, 1, p. 133); ed. Boretius, 123, No. 44. For discussion of this legislation see Schulze, *op. cit.*, pp. 13–14; Dopsch, *Wirtschaftsentwicklung der Karolingerzeit*, II, 190; Waitz, *Deutsche Verfassungsgesch.*

Although the Frankish sources are silent as to the nature
of this border trade, except the mention of arms, the exporta-
tion of which Charlemagne forbade, we know from other evidence what its character must have been. This evidence has
to do with the economy of the Baltic Slavs.

They were a lowland people by nature, and the western or
Baltic Slavs in the course of their expansion found a natural
habitat in the vast marsh and lake region of modern Mecklenburg, Brandenburg, and Pomerania. Even at the present
time these regions abound with lakes. There are 329 in
Mecklenburg, the largest of which is the Schweriner-See; and
more than 450 in East Prussia. Geologists estimate that in
the twelfth century there were over 2,000 lakes in East
Prussia alone. Medieval chroniclers show, and modern
geology confirms their statements, that the whole territory
in the valleys of the Elbe, the Oder, and the Vistula in the
Middle Ages was dotted with lakes and ponds and covered
with swamps.

The alluvial soil was fertile. Fish and game abounded.
Communication was much by means of boats made of alder
wood, so light as to be easily carried. They were poled or
punted instead of rowed. Horses were used for war, but not
for farming. The nobles estimated their wealth in terms of
possession of horses. In the Wendish towns a market was
held twice a week.[1]

In such a country only the dry islets were capable of
cultivation, so that the agriculture of the Baltic Slavs was
never as highly developed as that of the Germans. Cattle
were scarce and horses even rarer. Two oxen were reckoned
to the "plowland," which shows that the farms of the Slavs
were small. Their plow was a tree, the trunk being the beam
and the lopped-off projection of a strong limb the plowshare.
It had no share and no edge.[2]

(2d ed.), IV, 51; Mühlbacher, *Deutsche Gesch.*, p. 285; Wendt, I, 21–22; Püschl, pp.
107–8. For the location of these posts see Maps 26A, 26B, in *Cambridge Mediaeval
History*, Vol. II.

[1] Herbordus, *Dialogus*, II, 1, 21, 23, 26, 41; III, 17.

[2] For contemporary comment see Helmold, *Chronica Slavorum*, I, 12, 14, 88;
Heinrici, *Chron. Lyvoniae*, II, 7; *Monumenta Lubensia* (ed. Wattenbach), p. 15.

FRONTIER TRADING POSTS WITH SLAVS IN TIME OF CHARLEMAGNE (UNDERLINED)

Bee-keeping with all Slavonic peoples almost amounts to a passion, and the Baltic Slavs plied a brisk trade with the Germans in honey and wax for church candles and the sealing of documents.[1] Flax was much grown in the lowlands, and linen cloth or canvas an article of export.[2] Herbordus, the biographer of Otto of Bamberg, the apostle to the Pomeranians in the first quarter of the twelfth century, says that the Pomeranians wore shirts and trousers made of linen in summer.[3] Before this time, when German coin began to circulate among them,[4] strips of linen passed as currency like wampum among the American Indians in early colonial times. Weaving, pottery-making, and wood-carving were the principal industrial occupations.[5] Fishing, both fresh- and salt-water fishing, was a universal means of livelihood. Like the Norse, the Slavs of the Baltic coast were pirates and slave traders.[6]

We know nothing about the trade intercourse between the Germans and the Slavs in the ninth century, and it may be doubted if, in those tumultuous days of the break-up of the Frankish Empire, there was much. On the other hand,

---

For modern commentary see Langethal, *Gesch. der deutschen Landwirtschaft*, I, 51, 96, 379; II, 246; von der Goltz, *Gesch. der deutschen Landwirtschaft*, I, 128–29; Dopsch, II, 136; Michael, *Gesch. des deutschen Volkes*, p. 100.

[1] The church in Otto I's reign collected the Slav tithe in honey (*MGH*, Dip. I, 418, 603; II, 40). Payments in wax, furs, hemp, and flax are also recorded. Silver is first heard of along the Wendish border in 965 (Guttmann, *Forschungen zur brand. und preuss. Gesch.*, IX, 416).

[2] Adam of Bremen, II, 19; IV, 18; Helmold, I, 12, 14, 88. The merchants in Wagria in the time of Vicelin (1127) must have been buyers of Slav linen and furs.

[3] Herbordus, *ibid.*, II, 28. These linens were sometimes embroidered (*picturata*).

[4] Helmold, I, 38 (ed. Schmeidler, pp. 76–77). "Porro apud Ranos [Rugians] non habetur moneta, nec est in comparandis rebus nummorum consuetudo, sed quicquid in foro mercari volueris, panno lineo comparabis. Aurum et argentum quod forte per rapinas et captiones hominum vel undecumque adepti sunt, aut uxorum suarum cultibus impendunt, aut in erarium dei conferunt." Saxo Grammaticus describes at length the great Slav temple at Arcona sacred to the god Svantovit, with the tributes brought thither from all Slavonia. See English translation by O. Elton, pp. 393–95.

[5] Herbordus, II, 32.

[6] L. Giesebrecht, *Wendische Geschichten*, I, 205 f.

the Danes, with whom piracy and trade went hand in hand,[1] established commercial relations with the Slavs of the Baltic early in the period of their expansion. The little port of Reric (near later Wismar[2] which was not founded until 1237), where the Danes had got a foothold on the mainland, is mentioned in the *Annals* of Einhard (*anno* 808) as being frequented by Danish merchants.[3] These traders were chiefly men of Schleswig, from the port of Hadeby.[4] Fish and fur were the principal articles of trade, the importance of the former appearing as early as the ninth century;[5] as for fur, a yearly gift of marten skins was exacted by the Danish king of the Schleswiger merchants as late as the middle of the twelfth century.[6]

At the end of the tenth century, the piracy of the Danes, while not yet wholly abandoned,[7] had passed through the stage of foray. Their expeditions in the time of Harold Bluetooth (935–85), Sweyn (985–1014), and Knut (1014–35) took the form of territorial conquest and commercial expansion beyond sea. The Baltic policy of Denmark was to get a foothold at the mouths of the rivers, and so control the Wendish trade. The most important of such possessions was Jomsburg, on the island of Wollin at the mouth of the Oder, the seat of the famous brotherhood of pirates known as the Jomsvikings, which seems to have been established in the time of Harold Bluetooth.[8]

---

[1] See my article, "The Commerce of France in Ninth Century," *Journal of Political Economy* (November, 1915), pp. 865–67; Bugge, *loc. cit.;* Dopsch, II, 183–86.

[2] "In portu qui Wissemer dicitur" (*Codex Pomer. Diplom.*, No. 31).

[3] Bugge, *op. cit.*, p. 237, n. 243; Biereye, *Beiträge zur Gesch. Nordalbingiens im 10. Jahrhundert* (Berlin diss., 1909), p. 15. In Herbordus, III, 2, is an account of a Pomeranian of Stettin who traded with Denmark, and had six vessels.

[4] Biereye, *op. cit.*, p. 9 and n. 2; Bugge, *op. cit.*, pp. 232–33. Schwerin is first mentioned in 1018 by Thietmar, *Chronicon*, IX, 5.

[5] Herbordus, II, 1, p. 51; Vogel, *Hansische Geschichtsblätter* (1907), Heft 1, p. 56. Marten skins were much imported from Birka in Sweden (Adam of Bremen, II, 62).

[6] Biereye, *op. cit.*, p. 9, n. 3.

[7] For a mass of evidence see Richter, *Annalen der deutschen Gesch.*, III, 154–55; Haskins, *Normans in Europe*, p. 43.

[8] Wollin—or at least the Slav tribe Vuloini, whence the name came—is first mentioned by Widukind, *Rerum gestarum Saxonicarum*, III (*anno* 967), 69. Cf.

Wollin, at the mouth of the Oder, which must have been the chief point of connection between the Danish-Baltic trade and that of Eastern and Southeastern Europe,[1] reached its height in the first half of the eleventh century.[2] While Rurik and the Swedes in the ninth century had opened the famous Varangian Route from the Baltic to the Black Sea and Constantinople via Lake Ladoga, Novgorod, and the Dnieper, yet the shortest route between the two seas was across the isthmus via the Oder or the Vistula to Cracow and thence down the Pruth or Dniester.[3]

Adam of Bremen, *Gesta Hammaburg, eccl. pontif.*, II, 19; Herbordus, *Dialogus*, II, 24 and 34. Ebbo, *Vita Ottonis*, II, 7, severally describes it under the name of Jumna or Jumneta in the eleventh and twelfth centuries. It was the seat of the famous Jomsburg vikings, on which see Ersch and Gruber, *Encyclopädie*, XXII, 370–78; Bugge, *op. cit.*, pp. 242–43; Larsen, *The King's Household in England before the Norman Conquest*, pp. 154–57. Giesebrecht, *op. cit.*, I, 205, thinks Wollin was the present Swinemünde. But all other historians and philologists like Schafarik, *Slawische Alterthümer*, II, 576; Kemplin, *Baltische Studien*, XIII, 1, are agreed that Jomsburg, Wollin, Jumna, Jumneta, Vineta, were one and the same place. For latest information on this obscure question see C. Niebuhr, "Die Nachrichten von der Stadt Jumne," *Hans. Geschichtsbl.*, XXIII (1917); J. F. Leutz-Spitta, "Neues Material zur Vinetafrage," *Ztschft. Mannus*, VIII (1917). Another port, Truso, now Drausen, near the mouth of the Vistula, is mentioned in the travels of Wulfston by Alfred the Great (see Sweet's ed. of *A-. S. Orosius*, p. 19). Whether the Danes were trading there as early as the tenth century is not known (Bugge, *op. cit.*, p. 238).

[1] ". . . . apud Sliaswig, quae et Heidaba dicitur. . . . . Ex eo portu naves emitti solent in Sclavaniam vel Suediam vel ad Semlant usque in Graciam" (Adam of Bremen, *Descriptio insularum Aquilonis*, 1).

[2] See the long description of it in Adam of Bremen, *Gesta*, etc., II, 19. For the magnitude and extent of Danish trade at this time, in addition to the article by Bugge already cited, see *Baltische Studien von der Gesellschaft für Pommersche Geschichte und Alterthumskunde* (Stettin, 1885–92), Nos. 7, 13, 25.

[3] There is a very extensive literature upon the subject of early Balto-Slavonic-Byzantine commerce. See Peisker, *Vierteljahrschrift f. Soz- und Wirtschaftsgesch.*, III, Nos. 2, 3, 4 (1905); Heyd, *Histoire du commerce du Levant*, I, 68–86; Wilken, "Die Verhältnisse der Russen zum byzant. Reich im 9.–12. Jahrh.," *Abhandl. der Berl. Akad.* (1829), pp. 75 ff.; Lelewel, "Tableau historique du commerce des Slavons," *Numismatique du moyen-âge*, Part III, pp. 98 ff.; Jacob, *Der nordisch-baltische Handel der Araber im Mittelalter* (Leipzig, 1887) (with bib., pp. 126–27); Bugge, "Der Untergang der norwegischen Schiffahrt," *Vierteljahrschrift für Soz. und Wirtschaftsgesch.*, XII, 1, 245–50; Bury, *History of the Eastern Roman Empire* (802–67), pp. 402 f.; Guttmann, *Forschungen zur brand. und preuss. Gesch.*, IX, 399–400; Lamprecht, *Deutsche Geschichte*, III, 346–51; Fisher, *Mediaeval Empire*, II, 4–5; Wendt, *Germanisierung der Länder östlich d. Elbe*, I, 14–15; Schumann, *Baltische Studien* (N.F., 1902), VI; Fiddichow, *Monatsbl. v. d. Gesellschaft für pom. Gesch.* (1896);

But independently of this Wendish-Byzantine commerce, the nearer commerce of the Baltic Slavs was worth striving for by Denmark. Stettin, at the mouth of the Peene, Danzig at the mouth of the Vistula, Colberg, were rivals of Wollin, while inland the Slav towns of Wiligrad (Mecklenburg), Stargard (Oldenburg), Demmin, Cammin, and Schwerin, which have preserved their original Wendish name, were important places long before Bremen and Hamburg and Lübeck, the last of which was not founded until 1143.[1]

The long and bloody warfare waged against the Baltic Slavs by the Saxon Germans was partly motivated by religious bigotry, partly by land-hunger, and partly by a wish to acquire possession of the mouths of the rivers flowing into the Baltic, in order to control the Wendish[2] trade. The conquest was not completed until the Wendish Crusade (1147) finally subdued Mecklenburg and Brandenburg beyond all

---

Beltz, *Jahrb. f. Mecklenb. Gesch.*, LVIII (1893); Fischer, *Ztschft. f. Harz Ver. f. Gesch.*, XXIX, Heft 2 (1896); Bender, *Ztschft. f. d. Gesch. und Alterthumskunde Ermlands*, VI (1878).

[1] Herbordus, II, 25, in the middle of the twelfth century calls Stettin "civitatem antiquissimam et nobilissimam in terra Pomeranorum matremque civitatum." For other mention of it commercially see II, 40. Stettin is first mentioned under the name Schinesge in 995 (*Codex Pomer. Diplom.*, No. 503, p. 1026). Danzig appears as Gyddanizc in 997 (*Vita S. Adalberti-SS. rerum Pruss.*, I, 228.) Colberg, on the coast between Wollin and Danzig, traded especially with the "outer islands" (Herbordus, II, 39; cf. Martin Polonus, II, 28). It is interesting to observe that though the center of trade shifted from the island of Wollin, whose period of greatest prosperity was during the Danish occupation of the Baltic seaboard, to the mainland at Stettin and Danzig after the German conquest of Mecklenburg and Pomerania in the twelfth century, yet the configuration of the coast has not changed since the Middle Ages. For Adam of Bremen, II, 19, describes the three mouths of the Oder in terms which would hold today. Adam of Bremen, III, 19, describes the Abodrite city of Wiligrad (Mecklenburg) as "Magnopolis . . . civitas inclita Obodritorum," and mentions Ratzeburg and Stargard (Alt-Lübeck or Oldenburg), the latter of which Helmold I, 12, characterizes as "antiqua civitas." There is an excellent history of Danzig by Hirsch, and one of Stettin by Wehrmann. Stargard has found a historian in F. Boll.

[2] The word "Wend" was used (and still is) by North Germans to describe the Slavs of the Elbe and the Baltic coast, without distinction of tribe. The name was derived from the Wenidi or Winidi, a formidable Slavonic tribe in the time of Charlemagne, and came to be used to indicate the Slavs much as the word *waelsch* (English Welsh) was employed to indicate foreigners in general, e.g., French and Italians. A modern parallel is the Boer word *Uitlander* ("Outlander") in South Africa, to describe the English and Portuguese there.

hope of Slav recovery, and German domination was firmly fixed in the country by the vigorous rule of Henry the Lion and Albrecht the Bear.

But the Germans fought for the mouths of the Baltic rivers not only in order to capture the Wendish trade in the Baltic, but also to find an exit for their own inland commerce. The natural exits for products of the German Hinterland were the Elbe, the Trave, the Peene, and the Oder rivers. The Germans always controlled the mouth of the Elbe, but its middle course was not permanently secure until after 1147, when it became a German river from Meissen to the sea. Nor was full control of the other rivers acquired until after the Wendish Crusade. Leipzig appears by the year 1000 but was insignificant until the twelfth century.[1]

Heinemann thinks[2] that even as early as the Saxon period (919–1024) the border traffic between the Germans and the Wends was of sufficient importance to be taxed; but Gutt-mann believes this to be *ganz unwahrscheinlich*.[3] However, the growth of German trans-Elbean trade can be obscurely traced even in Saxon times. In 975 Otto II, at the prayer of Adalbert, archbishop of Magdeburg, granted protection "to merchants dwelling in Magdeburg" and freedom "every-where in our realm, in Christian and in barbarous lands, to go and come unmolested."[4] In 1025 Conrad II reaffirmed this decree, and specific mention is made of the trade of Magdeburger merchants on the Havel and the Spree, i.e., in Brandenburg.[5] Intermediate between these two dates we have the statement of Bishop Thietmar of Merseburg (d. 1018), whose youth was spent in Magdeburg, that he had seen guards in the churches watching the goods of merchants

---

[1] Thietmar, VIII, 25, 66. Even in Martin Polonus, II, 39; III, 1, it is not yet important. In his *Proem* he writes: "Sed quia regio Polonorum ab itineribus peregrinorum est remota, et nisi transeuntibus in Rusiam pro mercimonio paucis nota . . . ." Cf. L. Giesebrecht, *op. cit.*, I, 23.

[2] *Markgraf Gero*, p. 42.

[3] *Forschungen zur brand. und preuss. Gesch.*, IX, 417, n. 5.

[4] *Hansisches Urkundenbuch*, I, No. 1.

[5] Boehmer, *Regesta*, No. 1272; Stumpf, *Regesta*, No. 1871.

deposited there for safekeeping.¹ These merchants were both Germans and Jews, chiefly engaged in the slave trade.²

The Slavonic reaction of 1018 must have given this frontier trade a setback. Yet by the middle of the century it is evident from Adam of Bremen that adventurous German merchants were again penetrating into the Wendish lands, going as far as Wollin, which was eight days' journey from Hamburg. They seem to have been unmolested provided they did not parade their faith. Apparently these merchants, or others like them, also went on to the Swedish coast and to Ostrogard-Novgorod, which was eighteen days' journey farther.³

When we reach the twelfth century evidence accumulates in regard to this trans-Elbean and Baltic trade. In the Abodrite country (it did not become the Duchy of Mecklenburg until after the conquest in 1147), at Stargard, later Germanized into Oldenburg, which was the capital of the Abodrite

¹ Thietmar, *Chronicon*, I, 12.

² *Ibid.*, III, 1; IV, 12; VI, 16. *MGH*, Dip. I, p. 416, associates German and Jew merchants together. These slaves were recruited from the border warfare between the German and the Slav peoples, and also from the internecine strife between the Slav tribes (Adam of Bremen, *Descriptio*, 18). The strife also between the Danes and the Germans furnished slaves. Helmold, II, 13, relates that 700 Danish captives were exposed for sale in the market at Mecklenburg in 1168. Thietmar of Merseburg deplored the barbarity of the Saxons in dividing up the families of prisoners when sold as slaves (Giesebrecht, *op. cit.*, I, 35). The Jews controlled the border slave trade upon which they paid a tax (Thietmar, VI, 12; Gerdes, *Gesch. d. d. Volkes*, I, 357, and n. 3, 359). Würzburg was an important base of slave supply in 1006. The better public opinion reprobated the practice, yet it flourished for centuries. Margrave Gunzelin was criticized for selling Wendish captives to Jew merchants (Thietmar, VI, 36); the Bohemians were reckoned "bad Christians" because they disposed of captives in war to the Jews (*Vita S. Adalberti*, chap. xii; cf. *Vita Johan. Gorz.*, chap. cxxi); Henry II in 1012 endeavored to restrain the traffic (*Ann. Qued., MGH*, SS. III, 81). Slaves are mentioned as articles of commerce in a Bavarian tariff list on the Danube in 904 (Dümmler, *Ostfränk. Reich*, III, 533). Slaves are often mentioned with transfers of land (see Gerdes, I, 418–20, and Waitz, V, 207–8, for references). In 914, 23 slaves and 27 *Hufen* of land were exchanged for 30 slaves and 19 *Hufen*, which shows that a slave was valued about at the price of a *Hufe*.

³ Adam of Bremen, *Gesta*, II, 19; *Descriptio*, 18, 21; Helmold, I, 6. The Gothland merchants had reached Novgorod long before the twelfth century (Bächtold, *op. cit.*, p. 256; Bugge, *op. cit.*, p. 251). A charter of 1023 mentions an "international" bridge where the German merchants changed wares with the Russians. A Russian chronicle mentions St. Peter's Church in 1184. First mention of the factory at Novgorod is made in 1199 (Bächtold, *op. cit.*, p. 256).

duke Pribislav, there was a considerable colony of German merchants settled in 1129.[1] German trading operations extended clear to the island of Rügen, whose inhabitants were still fiercely pagan, and where the famous Slavonic fane of Arcona was located,[2] and before the storming and capture of this sanctuary by a joint German and Danish expedition in 1168, it was necessary for the merchants not only to avoid parading their Christianity, but also to offer substantial presents to the god in order to be permitted to buy and to sell.[3]

Among the Rani, or Rugians, conditions of trade were so primitive that strips of linen cloth served for currency, like wampum among the Indians of America.[4]

Every year, in November, at the time of the "big wind" a fleet of western craft came for dried fish and furs.[5]

This Alt-Lübecker merchant group even penetrated into the Baltic and sought to capture the ancient Swedish-Russian trade of Novgorod and the Varangian route and had a "factory" or trading post on the island of Gothland. For in 1124 the emperor Lothar II took them under imperial protection.[6]

[1] Helmold, I, 48: "a mercatoribus quorum non parvam coloniam."

[2] *Ibid.*, 38.

[3] *Ibid.*, 6 (p. 17); cf. Breska, *Forschungen zur deutschen Gesch.*, XXII, 585–87.

[4] "Porro apud Ranos non habetur moneta, nec est in comparandis rebus nummorum consuetudo, sed quicquid in foro mercari volueris, panno lineo comparabis. Aurum et argentum, quod forte per rapinos et captiones hominum vel undecumque adepti sunt, aut uxorum suarum cultibus impendunt, aut in erarium dei sui conferunt" (Helmold, I, 38; cf. 36). This cloth currency was also once current among the Bohemians. In Czech the word for "linen" and the word "to number" come from the same root (Lippert, *Sozial Gesch. Böhmens*, I, 84).

[5] Helmold, I, 48, and II, 12; *Ann. Erphesf.*, 1135 (*MGH*, SS. VI, 540), supply other details as to the nature of this commerce. There is still a little village, now a watering-place, near Stettin named Heringsdorf. For the importance of the Baltic herring trade see Bächtold, *Der norddeutsche Handel im 12. und beginnenden 13. Jahrhundert* (Berlin, 1910), p. 261, and especially K. Jagow, "Die Heringsfischerei an den deutschen Ostseeküsten im M. A.," *Archiv f. Fischereigesch.*, Band V (1915). In Herbordus, *Dialogus*, III, 30, and Ebonis, *Vita Ottonis*, III, 23, is a curious account of how the conversion of the peoples of the mainland of Pomerania interrupted for some time the trade with the Rugians, who would have nothing to do with the converted Slavs.

[6] The original charter of Lothar is lost. But it is referred to by Henry the Lion in a privilege dated October 18, 1163, granted to the merchants of Lübeck (*Lübecker Urkb.*, I, 4, n. 3. Cf. Richter, *op. cit.*, III, 690 nn.; Jaffé, I, 155).

We know little more about this farther commerce until the formation of the Hanseatic League and the incorporation of the Wisby group with it in 1298.

Of the trade of the Pomeranian mainland in the first half of the twelfth century we have interesting information in Ebbo's *Life of Otto of Bamberg*, who twice visited Pomerania (in 1124 and again in 1128), and also in the *Dialogus* of Herbordus.[1] With the fall of the Jomsburg vikings[2] Wollin had begun to decline, though when Adam of Bremen wrote in the middle of the eleventh century it was still the most important port on the Pomeranian coast.[3]

By the next century, however, Stettin appears as the *totius Pomeraniae metropolis*, although it could not possibly have had a population of from six to seven thousand, as said.[4] Its chief rival was Camin. The spongy, marshy soil, upon which both towns were built was a serious drawback. Stettin was girded with swamps,[5] and the streets in Camin were so miry that bridges, which seem to have been nothing but planks, were everywhere. Otto himself fell off one of these planks and was pitched into the mud.[6] The people were hospitable, though rude and crude in manners.[7] Each town had a *forum* where business was done, and a certain degree of money economy obtained.[8] There were warehouses, chiefly, one imagines, for the curing and storing of fish. Fishing was the main activity of the inhabitants, though furs[9] and slaves were also articles of commerce.[10] The herring ran in

---

[1] *Vita*, II, 41; *Dialogus*, I, 36; II, 7, 12, 28; III, 1.

[2] Ersch and Grüber, *Encyc.*, XXII, 370–78; L. Giesebrecht, *Wendische Geschichten*, I, 205 f.; *Baltische Studien*, No. 13; Bugge, "Die nordeuropäischen Verkehrswege, etc.," *Vierteljahrschrift f. Soz. und Wirtschaftsgesch.*, XII, 92 f.; Sommerfeld, *Gesch. d. Germanisierung Pommern* [Schmoller's *Forschungen*, Band XIII, Heft 5, p. 15]; Lamprecht, *Deutsche Gesch.*, II, 267–69; III, 345; Barthold, *Gesch. von Pommern*, I, 360 f.; S. A. Krijn, *De Jomsvikingsaga* (Leiden, 1914).

[3] *Gesta*, II, 19.

[4] Herbordus, II, 5, 25, 34; Sommerfeld, *Gesch. d. Germanisierung des Herzogtums Pommern*, p. 54 n.

[5] Herbordus, II, 5.   [8] *Ibid.*, 9 and 26.

[6] *Ibid.*, 24.   [9] *Ibid.*, 28.

[7] *Ibid.*, 41.   [10] *Ibid.*, III, 2.

shoals in the Baltic; but there was a brisk trade in fresh-water fish, too.[1] The coastwise trade must have been considerable, for Otto easily traveled by water from port to port of the river mouths.[2]

By 1125 it is evident that there was a through route from the eastern parts of "New" Germany to the farther Baltic coast. Halle, on the Saale River, was the clearing house and emporium of all this eastern German commerce. Both times when Otto of Bamberg made his trips to Pomerania he "stocked up" at the fair (*nundinae*) in Halle, and thence traveled by boat down the Saale to the Elbe, down the Elbe to Werben at the mouth of the Havel, and up the Havel and down the Peene to Uzedom.[3]

If one were not already convinced of the activity of Lower Germany in the Baltic trade, the founding of Lübeck in 1143 by Adolph of Holstein ought to resolve his doubt, for its establishment was a turning-point in the history of North Germany. The site was not unknown before. In days gone by Kruto, the powerful Wendish chieftain who broke the German domination east of the Elbe by the great rebellion in 1066, had erected a castle surrounded by a wooden palisade on the large island where the Trave and the Wochnitz flowed together. Adolph's clear eye saw the advantage of the location in spite of its swampy nature. The new place, which was called New Lübeck, to distinguish it from

[1] *Ibid.*, II, 41; III, 21.

[2] *Ibid.*, II, 37; III, 14, 15.

[3] *Ibid.*, I, 36; III, 1. For further information on this trade see Giesebrecht, *Wend. Gesch.*, I, 16–35; Herzberg, *Gesch. d. Stadt Halle im Mittelalter* (1889); Sommerfeld, *op. cit.*, pp. 62–66; K. F. Klöden, *Beiträge zur Geschichte des Oderhandels* (Berlin, 1847–52), in eight parts. It seems to me that Wendt, *op. cit.*, II, 6, underestimates this commerce. For routes by road and water in Germany in this time see Kretschmer, *Historische Geographie von Mitteleuropa*, pp. 212–13; Gasner, *Zum deutschen Strassenwesen von der ältesten Zeit bis zur Mitte des XVII. Jahrhundert* (Leipzig, 1889), pp. 31–58; Lauffer, *op. cit.*, pp. 53 f.; Knull, *Historische Geographie Deutschlands im Mittelalter* (Breslau, 1903). The Baltic trade to South Germany was mainly up the Mulde and down the Nab to Regensburg, the former taking the place of the Saale when that stream was made the eastern edge of the German world in Charlemagne's time. In Bohemia a trade route ran from Prague up the Moldau and over the divide to Linz on the Danube. Another road was up the Eger—or through the Nollendorf Pass—and down the Nab to Regensburg.

Alt-Lübeck (the Wendish Stargard, now Oldenburg), and later merely Lübeck, soon became an important port.[1]

The rapid growth of Lübeck[2] aroused the resentment of Henry the Lion, for it cut into the trade of Bardowick, Charlemagne's ancient trading post, which belonged to the Saxon duke, and in order to get a share of the Baltic trade Henry founded Löwenstadt, named after himself, on the Wochnitz between Lübeck and Ratzeburg.[3] But his new city did not prosper. Lübeck, as Helmold says, "was more prosperous and better located."[4] Henry the Lion was not the man to brook a successful rival. In 1158 he seized Lübeck by force, removed the markets of Bardowick and Löwenstadt there, and established a mint. It soon became the emporium of the whole Baltic trade. Merchant vessels from England, Denmark, Sweden, Norway, and even Russia crowded the port.[5] Stettin was Lübeck's closest rival.[6] The Low German speech became the language of trade throughout the whole north, and the *Elbslavische* speech, which hitherto had been necessary for the conduct of Baltic trade,[7] gradually died out. More than a hundred years later the records of the Hanseatic League began to be written in it. The destruction of Bardowick in 1189 by Henry the Lion, after his return from exile, further contributed to Lübeck's growth.[8]

[1] Helmold, I, 57 and 63; *Ep. Sidonis* (in Schmeidler's ed. Helmold, p. 245); Hoffman, *Gesch. der Stadt Lübeck* (1889).

[2] Helmold, I, 48, 57, 63, 71, 76, 85.

[3] *Ibid.*, I, 86; cf. Simonsfeld, *Jahrbuch*, I, 555–56.   [4] Helmold, I, 90.

[5] *Ibid.*, I, 86; Arnold of Lübeck, II, 5. Henry the Lion founded the monastery of St. Mary and St. John in Lübeck (1177) and because of slenderness of episcopal revenues there endowed it with half of the villa Renseveld (*Urkundenbuch der Stadt Lübeck*, I, n. 5), a second "villula" across the river called Cleve, but in the same parish, and a third of the tithes in Greater and Lesser Gladenbrugge (parish of Sigeberg) and in Stubbendorf. Certain property within the city of Lübeck (*curtes*) bringing eight marks rent annually and fields around Lübeck were also donated. The Duke's liberality, we are assured, stirred the envy of others.

[6] Wehrmann, *Gesch. von Pommern*, I (1904), 95, 112; Bächtold, p. 246: record of a citizen of Bamberg who had lived for years in Stettin as a merchant, and at his death left his property to the church in Stettin.

[7] Guttmann, *op. cit.*, IX, 408; Bugge, *op. cit.*, p. 240, n. 3; Iken, *Bremisches Jahrbuch*, XVII (1895).

[8] Helmold, I, 73; Arnold of Lübeck, V, 2. Cf. Hüllmann, *Ztschft. f. Geschichtswiss.*, IV, 1–9. Rostock is first mentioned in 1160 by Saxo Gram., SS. XXIX, 108.

A similar progress of German commerce, although not in the same degree, is observable at this time also farther inland.

In Brandenburg, when Albrecht the Bear fixed his capital upon the Spree, where Berlin now is situated, there were already there two Slavonic villages, Kollin (Ger., Kölln) on the island and Berlin on the right bank. Both names are of Slavonic origin. The German incomers settled on the river edge, while Kölln was chiefly inhabited by Wendish fisher folk. It is not without significance that the first Christian church erected on the island was dedicated to St. Peter, the fisherman, and that the German settlers in Berlin built their first church to St. Nicholas, the patron saint of merchants. The fact is typical of the difference between the two communities. In Berlin today the island part of the city is known as Alt-Kölln, where the fish market even yet is hard by the ancient church of St. Peter's. The two communities each received a separate charter and were not united into a single city until the fourteenth century, when Berlin became a member of the Hanseatic League.[1]

Ably seconded by the energetic archbishop of Magdeburg, Wichmann, the Margrave furthered the immigration of settlers, among them many Dutch and Flemish colonists, planted towns and granted town charters and commercial privileges which were models of their kind; on the rivers of the Mark plied the barges of merchants, whose goods were protected from brigands and predatory attacks of the hostile Wends by armed guards.[2] Warehouse privileges and toll stations were established at convenient points, such as Werben and Wittenberg on the Elbe, Potsdam and Heiligensee on the Havel.[3] The number of mints shows that a money economy prevailed by this time.[4] The traffic must have been

---

In 1189 a market was established there for the benefit of the monks at Dobberan. In 1218 Duke Heinrich Borwin of Mecklenburg granted the inhabitants *Zollfreiheit* and Lübecker law (Pueschl, *op. cit.*, p. 22). But Soesten law still continued inland away from the coast, and east of the Elbe Magdeburger law (*ibid.*, p. 7).

[1] Lavisse, *La marche de Brandenbourg*, pp. 134–35 and notes.

[2] Riedel, *Die Marck Brandenburg*, II, 99.

[3] *Ibid.*, II, p. 103; Lavisse, p. 128.

[4] Riedel, II, 97, n. 1.

almost exclusively in raw products, especially furs,[1] though the German colonists must have drawn some supplies, particularly domestic utensils and farm tools, from farther west, and the church and the Margrave's court created some demand for the luxuries of older Germany. There is no doubt that the towns of the margraviate commercially prospered under the enlightened régime and efficient protection given them by Albrecht the Bear.[2]

But one must not exaggerate the size or prosperity of these towns. In the twelfth century they were much behind the older cities of Central and Western Germany both in wealth and population, and, indeed, not until well down in modern times did Berlin and Frankfort-on-the-Oder come to rival Cologne or Nürnberg, or Frankfort or Lübeck. Brandenburg was located on the outer edge of the great commercial zone created in Northern Germany by the later formation of the Hanseatic League.

The conquest of Mecklenburg and Pomerania from the Slavs in the twelfth century had given the Germans control of the mouths of the German rivers, and Lübeck at the mouth of the Trave, Stettin at the mouth of the Peene, Wollin at the mouth of the Oder, and Danzig at the mouth of the Vistula, became not only outlets for the interior trade of Germany, but *points d'appui* whence German trade dominion was extended.

Beyond Danzig and the Oder mouth German commercial enterprise had expanded into Livonia before the end of the twelfth century (1186).[3] In Prague, in the reign of Wratislav (1061–92), there is mention of a group of Bavarian merchants, but of none from the north.[4] In Poland there is scarcely a trace of German commerce before 1175.[5]

---

[1] Lavisse, *op. cit.*, pp. 231–32.

[2] Tuttle, *History of Prussia*, Vol. I, chap. i.

[3] Heinrici, *Chron.*, I, 2, 11.

[4] Wendt, II, 6.

[5] *Ibid.* A papal privilege of 1155 for Breslau contains only one German name in a long list. In the thirteenth century a market was established before the church of St. Adalbert (Pueschl, 47).

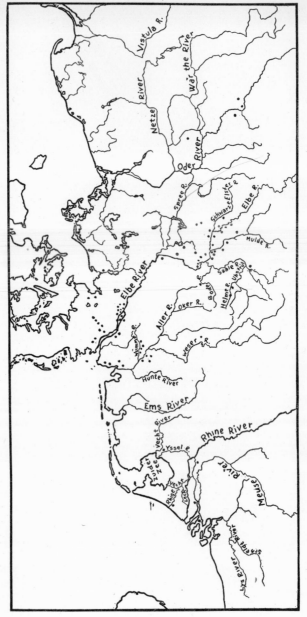

DISTRIBUTION OF MARSHLAND SETTLEMENTS MADE BY DUTCH AND FLEMISH COLONISTS

CHAPTER XV

DUTCH AND FLEMISH COLONIZATION IN MEDIEVAL GERMANY[1]

THE progress made in recent years in economic and social history has changed both the axis and the orbit of historical interpretation. Political, dynastic, and military history, the history of governments, laws, and institutions, has ceased to interest many students of history in these days. The Aristotelian mind of Western Europe and America has discovered new sources of information and new subjects of investigation. No one of these questions is more important to the medievalist than that of demography.

Among the discoveries which the modern study of medieval history has made is the profoundly organic and heterogeneous nature of medieval society—the complexity of its composition, the variety of its texture. The sharp cleavage once supposed to have existed between the three classes of medieval society, we now know, was not a hard-and-narrow line of separation, but a series of social gradations, some of them so slight that their parallax, so to speak, has not yet been accurately determined.

[1] The literature upon this subject is very large. It is cited fully in Kretschmer, *Historische Geographie von Mitteleuropa* (Berlin, 1904), pp. 371–72; in Schulze, *Die Kolonisierung und Germanisierung der Gebiete zwischen Saale und Elbe* (Leipzig, 1896), p. 129; in Kötzschke, *Deutsche Wirtschaftsgeschichte*, p. 109. The earliest important study of the subject was done by E. Borchgrave, in "Mém. de l'Acad. roy. de Belgique," Vols. XXVII, XXXII, XXXVI. Grünhagen has an article on the Walloon colonies in Silesia in the same series, Vol. XXXIII. Lamprecht, *Deutsche Geschichte* (3d ed., 1906), III, 309–42, has a great amount of suggestive material packed into a small compass. R. Kötzschke's *Quellen zur Geschichte der ostdeutschen Kolonisation im 12. bis 14. Jahrhundert* (Leipzig: Teubner, 1912), Nos. 9–20, is an indispensable collection of the charters. Helmold's *Chronica Slavorum* (ed. Schmeidler; Leipzig: Hahn, 1909), is the best narrative source. There are isolated examples of Flemish settlements in Germany before the twelfth century, but they have no continuity with the history of Flemish colonization in the high feudal age. Thus, for example, as far back as the sixth century a colony of Flemings seem to have settled at *Belgesheim* near Altmark. Some Flemings followed St. Adalhard and settled around New Corvey between 822 and 827, and others followed Anskar into the diocese of Hamburg.

The light cast upon the condition of the medieval peasantry in the course of these social and economic researches has been enormous. One of the most interesting of these findings is the startling discovery that the rural population of Europe in the Middle Ages was probably more nomadic and less sedentary than the lower classes of society today.[1] These displacements of population were not upon the gigantic scale of the German migrations in the fifth century or the Norse and Hungarian invasions of the ninth and tenth centuries. Nevertheless they were mass movements of large dimension —waves of popular migration sometimes succeeding one another through a series of years, which were primarily motivated by desire for improvement of material condition and powerfully affected by economic distress and the pressure of social forces. The Frankish colonization of the Spanish March in the time of Charlemagne and Louis the Pious is an example of such a movement.[2] More important and more typical is the history of the eastward expansion of the German people under the Saxon, Salian, and Hohenstaufen rulers, and their colonization of Mecklenburg, Brandenburg, Pomerania, and Silesia.

In this pioneer labor Dutch and Flemish immigrants from the Low Countries played no unimportant part. The emigration of the peasantry of modern Holland and Belgium in the twelfth and thirteenth centuries and their settlement in numerous scattered colonies in Lower Germany was due to the simultaneous operation of expulsive forces at home and the attraction which a new land presented. In the Middle Ages Belgium shared with Lombardy the honor of being the most densely populated region of Western Europe. The heart of the Frankish monarchy had been there, and the inti-

---

[1] This the late Achille Luchaire, *Social France at the Time of Philip Augustus* (Eng. trans.), pp. 404–6, clearly demonstrated. Cf. Powicke's review of the French original in *English Historical Review*, XXV, 565. The conclusion amply confirmed the previous researches of Lamprecht, *Études sur l'état économique de la France* (Fr. trans., Marignan), pp. 138–39, 222–23; Flach, *Les origines de l'ancienne France*, II, livre iii, prem. partie. For Germany the last half of Lamprecht, *Deutsche Gesch.*, Vol. III, to mention no other work, shows the same thing.

[2] See Imbart de la Tour, "Les Colonies agricoles et l'occupation des terres désertes à l'époque carolingienne," *Questions d'Histoire*, pp. 31–68.

mate association between the Merovingian and the Carolingian sovereigns and the church had resulted in the founding of many monasteries in the land. Nowhere else in Europe perhaps were they more thickly clustered, with their ample lands and their thousands of serfs exploiting the rich glebe farms. Here were the great historic abbeys of St. Vaast in Arras, St. Bavon in Ghent, St. Martin in Utrecht, St. Géry and St. Sepulchre in Cambrai, St. Laurence and St. Lambert in Liège, St. Omer, St. Quentin, St. Bertin, and St. Riquier, with their clustered communities of artisans, craftsmen, and petty tradesmen dwelling in separate "quarters" around the monastery walls, with the scattered villages of servile husbandmen on the abbey lands stretching roundabout,[1] and in the eleventh and twelfth centuries grown into more or less independent towns. Besides these great abbeys there were many others, Corvey, Lobbes, St. Trond, Nivelles, Andennes, Calmont, St. Hubert, Stavelot, Fosses, Alden-Eyck, Brogne, etc.

What these great monasteries did on a large scale in clearing forests and draining moor and swamp lands[2] those among the peasantry who were free did in less degree. For, as lay and ecclesiastical feudalism expanded, throwing its coils over the persons and lands of the free peasantry, rather than submit to servile conditions and bondage to the glebe they found refuge in remoter parts of the wide waste of moor and fen,[3] exactly as the population of the uplands fled to the forest, and there established their tiny villages, and by ditching and diking and draining redeemed a few acres of soil from the reluctant grasp of the sluggish waters. Cubes of turf served for building blocks for their cottages, and peat was their fuel.[4]

But in the course of time, as in the uplands the feudality appropriated the forests and reduced the free forest villages to serfdom, so in the Low Countries the feudal nobles gradually penetrated into the remote fen regions and extended

---

[1] See Flach, *op. cit.*, chap. vii; Blanchard, *La Flandre*, pp. 153–69; and my article in *Journal of Political Economy* (November, 1915), pp. 872–73.

[2] Blanchard, pp. 170–201.

[3] *Ann. Fuld.* (885): "Frisones .... pravissimis [parvissimis?], ut eis consuetudo, naviculis vecti. ...."

[4] Lamprecht, *Deutsche Geschichte* (4th ed.), III, 336.

their seigniorial sway over the free marsh villages.[1] With the spread of the feudal and manorial régime came the evils of private war, which neither the Truce of God nor the civil power (for the civil power was that of the lords themselves) was able to suppress, in addition to which the burden of heavy and vexatious manorial exactions was imposed upon the peasantry. From this condition of things emigration was the readiest form of relief.

Furthermore, the lot of the peasantry was made worse by the vicious commercial policy of some of the nobles, whose heavy taxation upon production, distribution, and consumption in the form of numberless *tonlieux*, *péages*, and *maltôtes* impoverished the peasants and discouraged or even ruined enterprise. The Bishop of Münster, for example, closed to the Frisians their market of the Ems, whither they had been accustomed to bring their cattle for barter. No other market was open to them because the Danes and the merchants of Bremen and Hamburg demanded money, a commodity which was very scarce in Friesland. As a consequence the Frisian cattle, practically the sole resource of the country, became diseased from inbreeding, and starvation ensued.[2]

Industrial coercion, again, was a factor in provoking emigration, for nowhere in North Europe in the eleventh and twelfth centuries was the development of industry and town population greater than in Belgium. If the burghers secured freedom of work and measurable political rights they stayed; if coercion succeeded they sought to migrate. What development had industry attained and in how far was it emancipated from the influence of agriculture and a rural environment and become urban? Levasseur has shown that a change had supervened in the relations between agriculture and industry by the beginning of the twelfth century.[3] It

---

[1] The history of this swamp reclamation and forest clearing in medieval Belgium has been the subject of various studies: Blanchard, chaps. xi–xiii; Duvivier, "Hospites: défrichements en Europe et spécialement dans nos contrées aux XIᵉ, XIIᵉ, et XIIIᵉ siècles," *Révue d'histoire et d'archéologie*, Vol. I; Van de Putte, "Esquisse sur la mise en culture de la Flandre occidentale," *Ann. de la soc. d'émulation de Bruges*, Vol. III.

[2] Curschmann, *Hungersnöte im Mittelalter* (Leipzig, 1900), p. 23.

[3] *Histoire des classes ouvrières* (1st ed.), I, 173 f.; cf. pp. 320–21, and Lamprecht, *L'état économique de France*, pp. 241–47.

goes without saying that this change was intimately connected with the emancipation of the servile classes and the birth of the burgher class in the towns. There is no need to enter here into consideration of this complex and thorny question. But the tendency to freedom of industry and the formation of industrial combinations like the gilds, as everyone knows, were bitterly resented by the nobility, who tried to maintain the serfdom of industry quite as much as the serfdom of agriculture.[1]

An additional factor which induced migration in the Middle Ages, perhaps the most general of all influences, was famine. The occurrence of famine was not always due to adverse weather conditions. It is true that a hard winter which killed the peasant's seed corn in the pits, or a drought, or a prolonged wet season was often terribly destructive of the crops. But aside from these physical phenomena famine was often engendered, at least locally, by other causes, such as feudal war, exhaustive taxation both of production and distribution, in addition to which the rudimentary system of agriculture prevailing, with crude farming implements and ignorance of the use of fertilizers, must be taken into account.

Since Lamprecht deplored the absence of any monograph upon the history of medieval famine, the gap has been filled, at least for Germany and the Low Countries, by Curschmann's admirable book.[2] He has shown that in Belgium famine occurred four times in the eleventh century, nine times in the twelfth, and twice in the thirteenth. There is most certainly a connection between these hunger conditions—there was a three years' famine in 1144–47—and the huge emigration which took place from Belgium in the twelfth century.[3]

[1] Levasseur, I, 167; Guérard, *Polyptique d'Irminon*, I, 471 f., 717 f., 729 f.

[2] See n. 2, on previous page.

[3] Curschmann, pp. 40 and 140–41. He compares it (p. 8) with the great drought in Europe in 1847 and its effect upon emigration, particularly from Germany and Ireland. In the latter country the potato crop had also failed the year before. The effect of these "hard times" in provoking popular discontent and so promoting the revolution of 1848 has not yet been studied. Overpopulation and underproduction are sometimes the positive and the negative way of saying the same thing, and overpopulation in the Middle Ages was a very prevalent cause of migration. See for Belgium: Blanchard, pp. 485–88; Curschmann, p. 199; Pirenne, *Histoire de Belgique*, I, 135–40; for Germany: Püschel, *Anwachsen der deutschen Städte in der Zeit der*

Under stress of such privation no feudal lord could have been able to retain his tenantry. "Propter caristiam colono fugiente, plurimi vici deserti remansere," reads a chronicle. The cattle were slaughtered for lack of fodder and to furnish food. When they were consumed nothing but flight remained as a recourse. It is impossible to avoid this conclusion, even if one is not always able to establish a direct nexus between any given famine and any given migration. The simultaneousness of the two events was not accidental.

When the Frisian and Flemish peasant betook himself to the refuge of the marshes in order to escape from feudal oppression he found only a precarious freedom even there. For he lived ever in peril of the sea. The low coast, the many deep tidal estuaries, the flat plains across which the Rhine, the Vaal, the Meuse, the Scheldt, and their affluents meandered, and which often overflowed their low banks in time of freshet, the salt marshes, the swamps—all these conditions exposed the population to floods which were sometimes terrible in their devastation.[1] Inundation was a powerful incen-

---

mittelalterlichen Kolonialbewegung, pp. 13–15; Wendt, *Die Germanisierung der Länder ostlich der Elbe*, II, 17–18.

[1] In the middle of the first century A.D. Pliny the Elder, who had seen service in the Roman province of Lower Germany, described the condition of the Frisians in terms which are applicable to them a thousand years later. He says: "In this region the wretched natives, occupying either the tops of hills or artificial mounds of turf raised out of the reach of the highest tides, build their small huts, which look like sailing vessels when the water covers the land, and like wrecks when it has retired. For fuel they use a kind of turf [i.e., peat] dug by hand and dried rather in the wind than in the sun, and with this earth they cook their food and warm their bodies. Their only drink is rain-water collected in ditches under the eaves." Cf. Elton, *Origins of English History*, p. 49. Nearly a thousand years later, the *Anonymous* of Utrecht early in the ninth century described the Frisians as "living almost like fishes amid the waters which hemmed them in on all sides, so that they rarely had access to outside countries unless in ships." There is an ancient study of inundations in Flanders in the *Séances de l'Académie ... de Belgique*, I (1777), 63 f. Blanchard, chaps. ix-xi, is very interesting, as is also Curschmann, who gives extracts from the sources. See also Klopp, *Ostfriesland* (Hanover, 1854), pp. 98–100, 139–44; Wiarda, *Die geschichtliche Entwicklung des wirtschaftlichen Ostfriesland* (Jena, 1880), pp. 13–14; Spruner-Menke, *Handatlas*, No. 39, carton 5. Montagu Burrows, *Cinque Ports*, chap. xi, deals with tidal and storm effects of the English Channel on the south coast of England. The year 1405–6 wrought terrible havoc along all the North Sea Coast. It was perhaps the greatest storm in history, for it practically raged, with brief intermissions, over the whole of Europe from November, 1405, to April, 1406. Bruges, the greatest commercial emporium of the north,

tive to emigration.[1] The peasant who saw his little farm-
stead destroyed in a day, the labor of years of tilling, draining, ditching, diking, go for worse than naught, his crops
ruined, his cattle drowned or lost in the awful confusion of a
great flood, had no heart left to begin the struggle all over
again in such a land.[2]

---

was ruined by it, for the sea overwhelmed the great tide gates at the mouth of the
Zwin, regarded even in Dante's time as an engineering wonder, and so filled the
harbor of Bruges with sand that nothing but the lightest draft vessels could enter.
At the same time this great storm cleared a huge island of sand out of the mouth
of the Scheldt and opened Antwerp, which hitherto had been a mere fishing village,
to trade, and so it succeeded Bruges in commercial history. Popular opinion associated this mighty storm with the death of Tamerlane, who died February 19, 1405,
but the news was not known in Western Europe until March, 1406. Wylie, *History
of the Reign of Henry IV*, II, 470–75, has gathered a mass of data regarding its
effects in England. The winter of 1407–8 was the "Great Winter"—one of the most
famous known.

[1] Püschel, *Das Anwaschen der deutschen Städte in der Zeit der mittelalterlichen
Kolonialbewegung* (1910), p. 15.

[2] It is curious to note that the regions of Flanders most subject to inundation
were least likely to suffer from famine. Curschmann (p. 21) suggests that the reason
may be found perhaps in the fact that the peasants were often able to drive their
cattle out of reach of the floods and so preserve them. When this chapter was first
published in the *American Journal of Sociology* (September, 1918), Mr. Maurice B.
Hexter, secretary of the United Jewish Charities of Cincinnati, wrote me: "I have
a suggestion to make as to the reason that in the regions of Flanders most subject to
inundation the individual was least likely to suffer famine. For some years I have
been getting data from American life on the adaptation of people in geographical
sections of American cities to sudden changes. In a certain portion of Newport,
Kentucky, inundations occur with a specific periodicity. I have noticed that other
portions of Newport, Kentucky, less likely to be inundated have fewer inhabitants
than the portion most likely to be inundated. This led me to study the people most
likely to be flooded. I find that amongst these people there is a series of social gradations, the parallax for which can be accurately determined. There is, first, the
group of newcomers attracted to this locality by low rents. There is, second, a class
of inhabitants who have lived in this section for years. The third class falls in between these two just delineated. The class which has lived in this section for years,
as I have witnessed during five or six floods, have a certain calm and a definite
precision and methodology in rescuing their stuff from the ravages of the flood.
They have lived there for years, and have learned to forecast the height of the water
to be expected with an uncanny precision, and even go so far as to look upon the
labors of the newcomers with a certain naiveté and supercilious contempt. The newcomers, on the other hand, after going through one or two floods usually move out.
I think that a similar explanation can be made with reference to your note about the
apparent paradox concerning the fact that the regions most subject to inundation
were least likely to suffer famine. I do not think that Curschmann's suggestion can
be demonstrated. Curschmann's suggestion is based upon ability; whereas the suggestion I offer is based upon practice. I think there is a difference."

Constant warfare against the sea was required despite the partial protection of a strip of sand dunes on the coast.[1] In Holland and Friesland, to the east of the Scheldt, this barrier had been broken down by inundations early in the Christian Era, and as the land progressively sank, relative to the sea, district after district was turned from arable land to swamp or perhaps completely submerged. So the islands along the coast were reduced in size, cut to pieces, or washed away; so the inland Zuider Zee was made an arm of the ocean in the years following 1200; and so shortly afterward were the Dollart and the Jadebusen scooped out by the voracious sea, which took, along with the land, the villages that happened to stand upon it. A flood of November 18, 1421, at the mouth of the Vaal River, destroyed no less than seventy-two hamlets.[2]

To the Frisian and Flemish peasantry, which in the eleventh and twelfth centuries suffered under the combination of adverse conditions which I have endeavored to summarize, Lower Germany beckoned invitingly, and thousands of them trekked eastward filled with new energy and fresh hope, seeking to found new homes for themselves and to find new economic and political freedom in a land where the population was sparse, land cheap, and little or no capital necessary to begin with.

We catch the echo of this hope of the lowland emigrants of this time in the text of an old Flemish ballad which has been preserved:

> Naer Oostland willen wy ryden,
> Naer Oostland willen wy mêe,
> Al over die groene heiden,
> Frisch over die heiden.
> Daer isser een betere stêe
> Als wy binnen Oostland komen
> Al onder dat hooge huis,
> Daer worden wy binnen gelaten,
> Frisch over die heiden;
> Zy heeten ons willekom zyn.[3]

[1] Blanchard, chaps. ix and xi. An early mention of these dunes is in *Ann. St. Bert.* (839).

[2] Knüll, *Historische Geographie Deutschlands im Mittelalter*, pp. 5–7.

[3] Quoted in Schulze, *Die Kolonisierung und Germanisierung der Gebiete zwischen Saale und Elbe*, p. 79; Lamprecht, *op. cit.*, III, 342. Willems, *Oude Vlaemsche*

The *Drang nach Osten* of the German peoples had long since been under way when the first "rush" of settlers out of Friesland and Flanders into North Germany began early in the twelfth century. From the time of Henry the Fowler, under the lee of the battle line, the frontier of colonial settlement had advanced, conquering the stubborn soil and the no less stubborn resistance of the Wends, until by the term of the Salian epoch Mecklenburg, Brandenburg, Pomerania, and the Thuringian Reichsland were studded with German settlements; the initial stages of a permanent political and ecclesiastical system were firmly grounded; Magdeburg, Bardowick, and Lübeck had become important trade centers; and colonies of German settlers from farther west, tempted by cheap land and the easy terms under which titles might be acquired, were established.

But the Flemish and the Frisian pioneers did not come into these regions until the subjugation or expulsion of the former Wendish peoples there had been accomplished by the sword of the Saxons through two centuries of almost unremitting warfare against them, and the preliminary work of settlement made by German colonists. They were not men of the battle edge, but of the rear-guard.

For the land into which they came the Fleming and the Frisian were singularly adapted. In the high feudal age Lower Germany along the coast of the North Sea was an almost uninterrupted series of marshes and fens, which, owing to the sluggish flow of the rivers across the flat plain and the deep indentation of estuaries like the mouths of the Weser and the Elbe, sometimes extended a considerable distance inland. Mecklenburg and Pomerania were dotted with lakes. Even in the interior there was much bog land and some areas which were huge morasses.

The first German incomers into these regions had naturally avoided these places and appropriated for themselves the tilled soil of the conquered Wends. When almost all of this had been occupied, chiefly by the clergy and high feudality, the settlers, where possible, still clung to high ground and cleared the forests.

Liederen (Ghent, 1848), p. 53, has claimed that this ballad is not of the twelfth century, but later. He prints the complete text on p. 25.

Before the coming of the Dutch and Flemings into Germany in the twelfth century the swamps and marshes, if used at all, were used only for pasturage[1] and occasionally, if not too wet, for hay meadows. But the German peasantry before their immigration knew little or nothing of the process of making such bottom lands arable.[2] The German feudal princes and prelates who imported these lowlanders by hundreds knew their value for swamp reclamation.[3] They had an ancestral affinity for swamps and flats. Since Roman times dike-building and artificial drainage had been practiced in Flanders and Holland.[4]

It was the slow increase of population in Germany,[5] and especially the enormous land-hunger of the great proprietors, both lay and clerical, which gave a new value to these neglected spots and was the primary factor in inducing the bishops, abbots, and princes of Germany to bring in colonies of Dutch and Flemings. They were used to deep plowings in heavy soils. Moreover, the labor was without peril. It was a new country, but it was not exactly the frontier.

Intelligent nobles like Adolf of Holstein, Henry the Lion, and Albrecht the Bear vied with churchmen like the four great archbishops of Hamburg-Bremen, Adalbert, Adalbero, Frederick, and Hardwich, with Bernhard of Hildesheim and Wichmann of Magdeburg, in promoting the immigration of these Frisian and Flemish settlers. The Cistercian monasteries, however, were the most active promoters of lowland colonization. Having been but recently established, this order found little place for itself in older Germany, where

---

[1] Heinemann, *Albrecht der Bär*, p. 227; Meitzen, *Siedelung und Agarwesen*, II, 451.

[2] Vogel, *Ländliche Ansiedelungen der Niederländer*, p. x.

[3] Alpertus, *De div. temp.*, II, 20–21, has a remarkable tribute to the capacity of the Frisians to redeem swamp lands for cultivation. "[Frisi] . . . . praedones vero, eis postea subjugatis, singulis ad modum uniuscujusque culturae ad extirpanda novalia terram diviserunt eamque colere jusserunt et sibi vectigales fecerunt." For the skill of the Flemings in gardening see Michelin, *Der Mainzer Hof zu Erfurt* (Jena, 1853), pp. 3–6.

[4] Heinemann, p. 143.

[5] For information on this head see Kötzschke, *Deutsche Wirtschaftsgesch.*, pp. 50–52, where much literature is cited.

enormous areas of land had been for centuries in the hands of the Benedictines and Cluniacs. In consequence the Cistercians were compelled to found their houses in the unsettled parts of Germany, where land was still cheap, and, in the case of monks, could be acquired for nothing.

Within the space of a hundred years the lower Weser, the whole valley of the Elbe from Meissen to Hamburg, the marshes of the Havel, the bottom lands of the Mulde, the Black and the White Elster, the banks of the Oder below Breslau, together with its affluents like the Netze, were peopled with these Dutch and Flemish settlers. Place-names like Hollern, Hollen, Hollernweg, Hollernklink, Hollernstück, Hollanderhof, Hollerndick, Hollerwisch, Hollerwettern, Hollerbrock, and other names of localities of Flemish origin like Flemsdorf, Flemingsthal, Vlammingen, tell the tale, which is legible even today upon the map of Germany.[1]

Broadly speaking, these groups of Flemish settlers in Germany may be divided into two categories: Those founded by the church, by bishops and abbots, and those founded by German nobles upon their lands or within their provinces. Among the first group we find the colonies established around Bremen, in Holstein, at Wilster, Stoer, and Elmshorn in Thuringia, in the Goldene Aue, at Erfurt, Naumburg, near Meissen, in Anhalt, in the archbishopric of Magdeburg, in lower Lausitz and in Silesia. In the second group are included the Flemish settlements at Bitterfeld, Jüterbock, in Wagria, Brandenburg, Uckermark, Mecklenburg, Pomerania, the circle of Leubus, and in Austria and Hungary.

The methods of colonization varied between the extremes of the individual pioneer settler and the migration and settlement of groups of colonists, great or small in number. In the main, however, the latter was the practice. The day of the *homo migrans* of the Salic Code, and of the *hospes* of the annals and cartularies of the ninth, tenth, and even eleventh centuries,[2] had passed. While doubtless much forest land still

---

[1] Meitzen, III, 352–54; Kretschmer, *Historische Geographie*, sec. 227, where much local literature is referred to.

[2] See Du Cange, *Glossarium*, and cf. Lamprecht, *L'état économique de France*, pp. 230–41; Henri See, *Les Classes rurales et le régime domanial en France au moyen-âge*, pp. 212–38.

continued to be cleared by the lone pioneer, or bog land drained, or waste redeemed, the group idea was dominant. It was real colonization—the simultaneous co-operative migration of blocks of people, who took their cattle and household effects with them from the ancient homeland, and their settlement in a new country. This was the fashion in which the first important settlement of lowlanders was made in Germany, that of 1106 in the marshes of the Weser near Bremen.

The organized nature of these displacements of population in the twelfth and thirteenth centuries is one of the first things to strike the student. In another chapter I have endeavored to show this in the case of the history of the colonization of the trans-Elbean Hinterland by peoples of German stock who moved eastward from the older and more densely populated parts of Germany like Westphalia and Franconia. In the history of the influx of the lowland Fleming and Frisian, although the localities where they settled were different, we see the same purpose, the same motives, the same organization, and similar conditions of settlement.

One of the most interesting and most difficult questions in the history of these Flemish and Dutch colonies in Germany is that of ascertaining from what localities in Flanders or Holland these settlers emigrated. The sources in this particular are either silent or vexatiously indefinite, merely saying Flanders, Holland, the region of Utrecht, or more rarely Brabant. But the evidence of place-names enables us to make partial amend for this deficiency. Among localities in the Low Countries from which we may be sure some of these Flemish pioneers came may be mentioned Antwerp, Arras, Ghent, Lembeke, Bruges, Lille, Stockem, Daelhem, Velthem, Durstadt, Molhuysen, Herstal, and Liège.

But a word of caution is necessary. While some of them were initially formed of original settlers from Flanders and Frisia, which in course of time grew both from natural increase of the population and from agglomeration owing to the occasional arrival of new immigrants, on the other hand numbers of these Flemish and Frisian colonies in Germany evidently were not composed of *original* lowlanders,[1] but were offshoots of the mother-group. Confusion arises from the loose terminology of the sources, which do not always distinguish between Flemish and Dutch settlers, nor between original lowlander settlements and colonies derived from these. The lowland strain inclined to thin with each succeeding generation as the newcomers intermarried with their German neighbors, or with the local Wendish population which remained in its ancestral habitat. Finally, to confuse the investigator still more, the institutions of these lowlander colonies were sometimes copied by real German colonies, so that there are examples of the latter which bear the earmarks of Holland or Flanders, though they actually contained no inhabitant of that stock.[2]

The chief source of information for the history of these lowlander colonies is of a documentary nature.[3] Of the chronicles Helmold's *Chronica Slavorum* is far the most valuable. Philology has been an important auxiliary science in tracing the genesis of surnames and the names of places; and archaeology has thrown some light upon the subject.[4]

These Dutch and Flemish colonies in medieval Germany, as might be expected, were more numerous near the country whence the settlers came. The marsh lands of the lower Weser were the earliest place of settlement, then the lower and middle Elbe and its tributaries, then the Oder region. Traces of Netherlanders are to be found in Galicia, in Austria, and in the Carpathians. But little positive information is to be had concerning them.[5] The farther Baltic Coast

[1] For example, Lüntzel, *Gesch. der Diöcese und Stadt Hildesheim*, in mentioning the settlement established by Bishop Udo of Hildesheim calls it a "Flemish colony," whereas the names of the four men with whom the Bishop made the contract are obviously Frisian, i.e., Dutch, as Vogel, *op. cit.*, p. xi, has pointed out. Again, the fact that the Flemish form of landholding is found to obtain around Uebigau, Schweinitz, and Domnitzsch in the later Middle Ages does not prove that these places were settled by original Flemish colonists (Schulze, p. 127).

[2] Schulze, p. 126.

[3] Kötzschke, *Quellen zur Gesch. der ostdeutschen Kolonisation im 12. bis 14. Jahrhundert* (Leipzig, 1912).

[4] Meitzen, II, 358; Kretschmer, p. 374.

[5] Kaindl, *Gesch. der Deutschen in den Karpathenländern* (2 vols.; Gotha, 1907), II, 208; Knüll, pp. 94–95.

seems to have been settled chiefly by immigrants from Westphalia, although the dune and marsh topography might be
presumed to have attracted the people from the Low Countries.[1] The high uplands of Germany and the mountainous
region of the Erzgebirge and the Carpathians were usually
avoided by them. They preferred cutting reed grass and
digging turf to clearing timber and mining. The Flemish settlements near Waldheim and Altenburg (where even now
there is a locality named Flemmingen) and the Dutch and
Flemish (*qui et Flamingi*) colony near Koesen, which were
certainly established there before 1140, that is, before the
foundation of the Cistercian abbey of Pforta, are exceptional,
for the reason that they found lodgment in a mountainous
and forest country instead of a river plain.[2]

The earliest record of Netherlandish settlement in Germany is found in the *Bremisches Urkundenbuch* for the year
1062, when a small group of these immigrants was settled in
the moors along the left bank of the Weser by the great archbishop Adalbert.[3] The fall of Adalbert and the plundering
of the bishopric by the Billunger, coupled with the anarchy
of Germany for so many years during the reign of Henry IV,
probably deterred further immigration for a long time.

Things rapidly changed, however, soon after the century
mark was turned. In 1106 Archbishop Frederick of Hamburg-Bremen energetically revived his predecessor's policy,
and granted "certain lands which are uncultivated, swampy,
and useless" to his own people to persons "who are called
Hollanders," and who were apparently refugees, for the
charter recites that they came to the Archbishop and "earnestly begged" for leave to settle on the moors.[4] The prelate,
"considering that their settlement would be profitable,"
granted their request. The lands were divided into rectangular blocks measuring 720 "royal" rods in length and 30 in
width. The settlers were to pay one penny (*denarius*) annu-

---

[1] Kretschmer, pp. 367–68; Lamprecht, III, 305.

[2] Schulze, p. 129 n.   [3] Lamprecht, III, 372.

[4] Kötzschke, *Quellen*, No. 1. There is an English translation in Thatcher-
MacNeal, *Source Book for Mediaeval History*, No. 298. For commentary, see
Meitzen, III, 264–68. Map 86 is a luminous exposition of the text.

ally for each hide or holding, to give every eleventh sheaf of grain, every tenth lamb, every tenth goat, every tenth goose, and a tenth of the honey and flax for tithes, besides a penny for each colt and a farthing (*obolus*) for each calf on St. Martin's Day. A tithe of these tithes was set aside by the Archbishop for the support of the parish churches, and each priest was to have one hide of land. They agreed to pay every year two marks for every one hundred hides for the privilege of retaining their own law and holding their own courts for the settlement of all their differences in secular matters. This they asked "because they feared they would suffer from the injustice of foreign judges." But the bishop's court was to be a court of appeal.

The success of the enterprise must have been soon manifest. For almost immediately afterward Bishop Udo of Hildesheim established a colony of Flemings at Eschershausen, west of the Harz,[1] and Dietrich of Halberstadt undertook the settlement of the lowlands between the Bode and the Ocker rivers.[2] Within two years after 1106 the promotion of Dutch and Flemish immigration for the redemption of swamp land became an organized effort of the clergy and lay nobles of Lower Germany. In 1108 the Archbishop of Magdeburg, the bishops of Merseburg, Naumburg, Meissen, Brandenburg, and three counts, Otto of . . . . , Wicbert of . . . . , Ludwig of . . . . , whose territories are not mentioned, "and all the greater and lesser lords of eastern Saxony" (*universi orientalis Saxonie majores et minores*) united in a joint circular petition to the Archbishop of Cologne, the bishops of Aachen and Liège, the Duke of Lower Lorraine, Robert, count of Flanders, and others, urging them to encourage the emigration of their surplus and hungry population into Lower Germany, which was represented, not unlike land-promotion schemes today, as a land flowing with milk and honey.[3]

[1] Kötzschke, *op. cit.*, No. 2. The original charter is lost. We know the fact from the confirmation of it by Udo's successor, Bernhard. For another such colony see Schulze, p. 158, n. 3.

[2] Vogel, *op. cit.*, p. vii.

[3] The text of this remarkable document is in Kötzschke, *op. cit.*, No. 3, where references are also given to a large amount of literature dealing with it.

We do not know what the immediate effect of this endeavor was. But by the middle of the century Flemish and Frisian immigration into North Germany was in full swing. Of the German nobles at this time Adolph of Holstein was the most active in this effort. Helmold says:

> In 1143, because the land was sparsely peopled, Count Adolph sent messengers into all the regions roundabout, even into Flanders and Holland, [the bishopric of] Utrecht, Westphalia, and Frisia, to proclaim that all who were in want of land might come with their families and receive the best of soil, a spacious country rich in crops, abounding in fish and flesh, and of exceeding good pasturage.[1]

The marsh lands of the lowest course of the Elbe at this time were the special region of colonization, where Eutin and Süssel were settled by Dutch and Frisian pioneers.[2]

The furious racial and religious war which broke out in 1147, known as the Wendish Crusade, devastated the whole eastern frontier of Saxon Germany from Magdeburg to Holstein. The new Flemish and Frisian settlements were imperiled at the moment when many of the men had returned to their old homes in the Low Countries to bring back the residue of their possessions which they had left there. When the infuriated Wagri burst into the region with fire and sword they found less than a hundred fighting men in the blockhouses which had been erected to protect the villages, instead of four hundred. Fortunately the Wends, while they hated the Saxons for their oppression of them, did not confound the Flemish and Dutch incomers with their German enemies. The frightened villagers, who could not have resisted if they had so dared, were spared, they and their herds and crops.[3] Alone the garrison in the blockhouse at Süssel, under the leadership of a priest named Gerlach, braved the foe.[4] What destruction did befall the colony, not without

[1] Helmold, *Chronica Slavorum*, Book I, chap. lvii.

[2] *Ibid.* Helmold confuses "Frisians" and "Flemings." For full information regarding these settlements see Gloy, *Der Gang der Germanisation in Ost-Holstein* (Kiel, 1894), pp. 17 f.; J. von Schröder and H. Biernatzki, *Topographie der Herzogtümer Holstein und Lauenburg*, I (Oldenburg, 1855), 6. The settlement of the Elbe marshes must, however, have been begun before 1144. For evidence see Wendt, *op. cit.*, II, 31.

[3] Helmold, Book I, chap. lxiii *ad fin.*   [4] *Ibid.*, Book I, chap. lxiv.

reason, was attributed to the violence of their Holsteiner neighbors, who were jealous of the industry of the settlers and hated them as "foreigners."[1]

The effect of the Wendish Crusade in 1147 was to open large tracts of border land to occupation which hitherto had been still precariously held by the Slavs, and a wave of Dutch and Flemish settlers followed hard upon a great influx of Westphalian colonists into the territory east of the Elbe, along both the lower and the middle course of the river.[2]

The promotion of this movement was participated in by all classes of landed proprietors—dukes, margraves, counts, bishops, abbots. The amount of lowlander blood infused with German in the middle of the twelfth century in the basin of the Havel River must have been considerable.[3] These tenacious lowlanders eagerly attacked the sodden soil. Thousands of acres of swamp land in course of time were redeemed by them. For example, documents of the year 1148 describe the region around Brettenburg on the river Stör as a huge morass. In the year 1340 the Dutch communities of Cronenmoor and Lütteringe are described as prosperous farming localities.[4] That the main body of settlers in Holstein was of Dutch origin Meitzen has shown from the fact that Christian I of Denmark in 1470 issued a decree canceling the jurisdiction of Dutch law in the Kremper and Wilster marshlands and substituting Danish law instead.[5]

No lord of North Germany was more active in promoting the colonization and settlement of these Dutch and Flemish

---

[1] The Holsteiners called these lowlander incomers "Rustri" (*ibid.*, p. 158 and n. 1). The term first appears in Schol. 3 in Adam of Bremen's *Gesta Hammaburgensis ecclesiae pontificum*, from whom Helmold, Book I, chap. lxxxiii, borrows it. See Pertz's edition of Adam of Bremen, the note to the scholium.

[2] This appears from a survey made by Bishop Anselm of Havelberg in 1150, after the Wendish Crusade was over, and is contained in the new *Fundationsprivileg* of Conrad III: ". . . . et cum praenominatae civitates et villae saepe irruentibus paganis vastatae sunt ac depopulatae adeo, ut vel nullo vel raro habitatore incolantur, volumus atque praecipimus, ut idem episcopus liberam absque contradictione habeat facultatem ibidem ponendi et locandi colonos de quacunque gente voluerit vel habere potuerit" (Riedel, *Codex Diplom. Brand.*, II, 438).

[3] Kötzschke, *Staat und Kultur im Zeitalter der ostdeutschen Kolonisation* (Leipzig, 1910), pp. 30–34.

[4] Meitzen, III, 354.   [5] Heinemann, *Albrecht der Bäer*, p. 222.

immigrants than Albrecht the Bear of Brandenburg. In this policy he was ably assisted by the bishops, especially Wichmann of Magdeburg. Except possibly Rainald of Dassel, Frederick Barbarossa's heroic archbishop of Cologne, and the versatile Christian of Mainz, who was for so long his viceroy in Italy, twelfth-century Germany had no abler prelate than Wichmann. On the paternal side he was descended from the Billunger dukes of Saxony, on his mother's from the margraves of Lausitz and Meissen.[1] After having completed his theological studies at Paris, Wichmann was successively prior of the chapter of Halberstadt, bishop of Naumburg (1148), and in the first year of Frederick I's reign was made archbishop of Magdeburg by him. He was a faithful adherent of the Emperor through all the long conflict with Alexander III and one of the chief negotiators of the Peace of Constance in 1183. He was an implacable adversary of Henry the Lion and a principal in the catastrophe which overcame the mighty Saxon Duke in 1181. In that year, with the aid of the Bishop of Halberstadt, he laid siege to Haldensleben. But the Count of Lippe, who defended the place, diverted the course of the Ohre River. Nothing daunted, Wichmann threw up dikes around the town so that the water overflowed the walls and drove the inhabitants to seek refuge in church towers and granaries. Wichmann then built a fleet of boats and with this little navy triumphantly sailed over the walls of Haldensleben and so captured it.[2]

Although Albrecht had received titular investiture of the margraviate of Brandenburg in 1134(?), the Slav element in the Mark was not wholly subdued until 1157,[3] an achievement materially aided by Wichmann. Already in the last year of his episcopacy at Naumburg, Wichmann had imported a colony of Flemings and settled them at Schul-

[1] Kechner, "Leben des Erzbischofs Wichmann von Magdeburg," *Forschungen zur deutschen Gesch.*, V, 417-562.

[2] *Chron. Montis Sereni* (*anno* 1181), in *MGH*, SS. XXIII, 158; Raumer, *Reg. historiae Brandenb.*, No. 1558.

[3] This information is contained in the fragments of the *Old Chronicle* of Brandenburg, to be found in Heinemann, p. 422; cf. Lavisse, *La Marche de Brandenbourg sous la dynastie Ascanienne*, pp. 71-72.

Pforta, where they long retained their own laws and gave their name—Flemmingen or Flaminghe—to the locality.[1] Six years after his transference to Magdeburg, when Albrecht's domination had been made complete in Brandenburg, Wichmann began the active importation of Flemish and Dutch settlers into the unoccupied marsh lands of the Havel. Wichmann, however, was not the original pioneer in thus settling these colonies along the upper Elbe, for already in 1154 Bishop Gerung of Meissen had established a group of them at Kühren near Wurzen.[2] But Wichmann was the greatest promoter of these enterprises, more so even than Albrecht the Bear himself.[3]

Of all the regions in North Germany in which these Flemish immigrants settled, perhaps the two most interesting colonies are those of Jüterbog and Bitterfeld. This is certainly true from the cultural point of view, for in these two places, as nowhere else, the descendants of the original settlers preserved for centuries the idiom of their ancestors. Jüterbog, a former Wendish village and the place where free and pagan Slavdom made its last stand in Brandenburg, fell into the hands of Albrecht the Bear in 1147. Perhaps this first margrave took the initiative in colonizing it. But the actual promoter was Wichmann, and the time of settlement between 1163 and 1167. The prosperity of the colony is evidenced by a charter of April 29, 1174, in which the Law of Magdeburg is granted to it,[4] and in the grant of which, to use the Archbishop's own words, he sought to "mitigate and to ameliorate" the condition of the inhabitants by exempting them from tolls and ordaining certain market privileges. Furthermore,

[1] Kötzschke, *Quellen*, No. 9; Wendt, II, 35. For a complete study see Rudolph, *Die niederländlichen Kolonien der Altmark im 12. Jahrhundert* (Berlin, 1889).

[2] Kötzschke, *Quellen*, No. 10; Vogel, p. vii; Schulze, p. 159.

[3] Kötzschke, *op. cit.*, Nos. 14, 15, 16, 18; Wendt, II, 30 f.; Heinemann, *Urkunden*, Nos. 38–41; Rudolph, *op. cit.* Hollanders were established at Krakau near Magdeburg, and at Kleutsch near Dessau; Flemings around Naundorf and Pechau near Magdeburg; Westphalians at Poppendorf, across the Elbe, opposite Magdeburg, *in pratis et paludibus*.

[4] Kötzschke, *op. cit.*, No. 31.

since the grace of God has followed our labor so that in Jüterbog where once pagan rites were carried on and frequent persecution of Christians practiced, now the Christian religion and the firm and guardian protection of Christianity obtains, on account of the devotion to the faith of all those who have migrated into this region or who may yet wish to come,

Wichmann grants the right of free pasturage to the people for their cattle "from Jüterbog to the farther hill of Zinna, and across the Bridge of the Flemings."

We know also from another source that these hard-working diggers and ditchers from the heavy soil of Flanders constructed a dike which first extended from Jüterbog to Nutritz and Dennewitz and later was prolonged to Schweinitz and Wittenberg. Around the point of intersection of the dike with the town grew up a *faubourg* called Damme. Was it so named from Damme in their homeland? In 1182 Wichmann, still liberal, established a mint at Jüterbog, the coins of which bore the superscription: *Moneta Nova Flamingorum Jutreboc.*

The details of the history of the settlement of these Dutch and Flemish colonies by Albrecht and Wichmann may be traced in the *Urkunden*. But Helmold's *Chronica Slavorum* has one chapter[1] descriptive of Albrecht's colonizing policy which is so excellent that it is here translated:

> In that time [*ca.* 1157] the margrave Adalbert, surnamed the Bear, had possession of eastern Slavia, who by God's care over him very greatly prospered in his lot.[2] For he conquered [*misit sub jugum*] all the territory of the Brizani,[3] Stoderani,[4] and many other tribes dwelling along the Havel and the Elbe, and overcame those of them in rebellion.[5] Finally, as the Slavs gradually disappeared [*deficientibus sensim Slavis*], he sent to Utrecht and the regions of the [lower] Rhine, as well as to those peoples who live near the ocean and suffer the violence of the sea [*patiebantur vim maris*], namely, Hollanders, Zealanders, Flemings, and brought a great multitude of them and caused them to dwell in the towns and villages of

---

[1] Book I, chap. lxxxix.

[2] Helmold's phrase is *in funiculo sortis*. The figure is derived from the method of surveying land by measuring it off with a rope. Helmold several times mentions this form of mensuration, e.g., chaps. lxix, lxxi, lxxvii, lxxxiv.

[3] The Brizani were one of the small tribes belonging to the Baltic branch of the Slavs; they dwelt near Havelberg (Riedel, *Der Mark Brandenburg*, pp. 271 f.).

[4] A similar tribe in the same region (Riedel, pp. 306 f.).

[5] Albrecht the Bear recovered Brandenburg (the city) in 1157.

the Slavs. He greatly furthered the immigration of settlers [*advenae*] into the bishoprics of Brandenburg and Havelberg, wherefore the churches multiplied there and the value of the tithes greatly increased.

In this time Dutch settlers began to occupy the east bank of the Elbe. From the city of Salzwedel these Hollanders settled all the marsh and meadow land [*terram palustrem atque campestrem*] which is called Balsemerlande and Marscinerlande,[1] being very many towns and villages as far as the Bohemian frontier.[2] The Saxons are said formerly [*olim*] to have inhabited these lands in the time of the Ottos,[3] as can still be seen in the remains of old levees which had buttressed the banks of the Elbe in the swampy land of the Balsami. But afterward, when the Slavs prevailed[4] the Saxons were killed and the territory has been possessed by the Slavs until our time. But now, because God has generously given health and victory to our duke and the other princes, the Slavs everywhere have been worn down [*protriti*] and driven out, and peoples "strong and without number"[5] have been brought in from the borders of the sea, and have taken possession of the fields [*terminos*], and have built towns and churches and increased in wealth beyond all expectation.

Bitterfeld, between Wittenberg-on-the-Elbe and Leipzig, according to tradition, owes its foundation to a colony of Flemish refugees who were driven out of Flanders in 1153 by flood, and who were welcomed by Albrecht the Bear. Legend says that the original name was Beterveld (Besser Feld). Its history is a close repetition of that of Jüterbog.[6]

[1] Balsemerlande, Pagus Belxa, was the territory around Stendal in the diocese of Halberstadt. Marscinerlande is supposed to have been between Arnesburg and Werben, but Rudolph (*op. cit.*, p. 37) has questioned it.

[2] Helmold's words are *usque ad saltum Boemicum*. In chap. lxxx, p. 150, he uses the same phrase. Whether Helmold, who lived in Holstein, knew the difference between the Boehmerwald and the Erzgebirge may be doubted. Dehio (*Brem. Jahrb.*, VI, 85 f.) thinks the phrase refers to the Erzgebirge; Rudolph (*loc. cit.*), to the Boehmerwald. Schmeidler, the last editor of Helmold, is sure that the latter is not meant, and not certain that it applies to the former. I have translated the word *saltum* as "frontier," which, while not an exact rendering of the word, is sufficiently indefinite to express the hazy state of Helmold's mind.

[3] Cf. Helmold, Book I, chaps. xii and xviii.

[4] This refers to the great Slav rebellion in 1066.

[5] The words are quoted from Joel 1:6.

[6] There are several neighboring villages, as Puch and Muldestein, which are also of Flemish origin, and daughter-hamlets of Bitterfeld. In the latter are still the ruins of the castle and the chapel, today a church, which once belonged to the Bora family, to which Luther's wife, Catherine von Bora, pertained. An ancient lime tree near by long was called "Heinrich Flemming."

But the place in North Germany where either the Flemish colonization was densest, or the Flemish tradition longest preserved, is the region just east of Magdeburg, which is still known as the Fläming. It is the plateau which separates the Elbe from the Havel. All this district was peopled by the Flemings and became divided into Hohe Fläming and Nieder Fläming. Singularly enough, it was not the marshy nature of this locality, but its aridity that destined it for Flemish settlement. By reason of physical feature it was a waterless region and one never occupied by the Wends. But the Lowlanders were as expert in ditching as in diking, as skilled in making irrigation canals as in making fosses for drainage. Not all of the settlers here, however, were from Flanders; some were Hollanders. Upper Fläming was chiefly settled by Flemings; Lower Fläming by colonists from Holland. The place-names show it. We find Rohrbek, strikingly akin to Roosebeek in Flanders, Heinsdorf (from Henriksdorp), Markendorf (Marggravendorp), Woltersdorf (Wolterdorp), Gräfendorf (Grevendorp), Niemek, Genthin (from Ghent?), Kameryk (Cambrai), Brugge (Bruges), Aaken, Leeuweeden (Leuwarde), Eyper (Ypres) Lichtervelde. Significant, too, is the pronunciation of Mügeln, which is pronounced "Mecheln" in local idiom and reminds one of the medieval Flemish Mechelin (modern Malines). Among names of Dutch origin we find Stolzenhain (Stoltenhagen), Kaltenhausen, and Seehausen, all three in Nieder Fläming, Nimwegen, Gravenhage. It might be added also that family names in the Fläming even today bear out the double Flemish and Dutch lineage of the inhabitants.

Albrecht the Bear seems to have preferred the agency of others in promoting lowlander colonization of his territories to direct enterprise by himself. His favorite agencies were the Cistercians and the Praemonstratensians. In 1159 Abbot Arnold of Ballenstadt purchased two localities "formerly possessed by the Slavs" from the margrave, and sold holdings in them to "certain Flemings who had petitioned permission to occupy them and to preserve their own law."[1] In 1170 Otto of Brandenburg gave two villages, Dalchau and Druse-

[1] Kötzschke, op. cit., No. 13A.

dow, to the Johannite Order, which had been settled by Hollanders during his father's lifetime.[1]

In the Weser region the initiative begun by Frederick of Bremen was continued by later archbishops. In 1158 Archbishop Hartwig I established a colony of Hollanders on the Ochtum, a small affluent of the Weser.[2] In 1170 Friedrich von Machenstedt, founder of the monastery of Heiligenrode, southwest of Bremen, received permission from his successor, Archbishop Baldwin, to settle the swamp lands between Brinkum and Machenstedt, west of the Ochtum, with Hollanders.[3] This example is interesting because Baldwin himself was a Hollander by birth, and in 1178 returned to his native land as bishop of Utrecht, over which he ruled until his death in 1196.

In Saxony the precedent of Dutch and Flemish colonization, which Adolph of Holstein was the earliest of the lay nobles of Germany to introduce, was followed by Henry the Lion, whose intelligent rule owes more to Adolph's example than his biographers have admitted. After all but the last remnants of the wretched Abodrite population were driven out of Mecklenburg in 1160, by a joint expedition of Henry and King Waldemar of Denmark, hundreds of lowlanders were imported into the bottom lands around Mecklenburg and Ratzeburg.[4]

As the end of the twelfth century approaches there is a noticeable falling off in Dutch and Flemish immigration into Lower Germany. How far this decline was due to the great revolution made in North Germany by the fall of Henry the Lion in 1181, or to the growing prosperity of the Low Countries, which, as every scholar knows, reached a high degree of economic development at this time, it does not seem possible to determine. One factor in "slowing down" this immigration perhaps may be found in this, that as the Weser and Elbe marshes increasingly became settled, the next available tracts, in the basin of the Oder, were so far away from the source of immigrant supply that it required unusual ac-

---

[1] *Ibid.*, No. 19.   [2] Vogel, p. iv.   [3] *Ibid.*

[4] Heinemann, p. 227; Henry the Lion founded a colony of Hollanders in 1164 around Erteneburg (Meitzen, III, 358).

tivity and unusually favorable terms to induce new settlers
to go so far. Probably also the fact that the best marsh lands
by 1200 had been taken up had its influence. What remained
unoccupied was so huge and so hopelessly miry that simple
peasants had neither the capital nor the engineering means to
undertake its reclamation. Such enormous tracts of swamp
as the Goldene Aue could be successfully drained only by
corporate enterprise like that of the Cistercians.[1]

Almost without exception the Cistercian cloisters in
medieval Germany were located in swamp or marsh regions,
so that a system of drainage had to be worked out. The ruins
of many of their foundations in North Germany still retain
traces of these improvements. In the Harz and the hill country of Thuringia the tourist will come upon these remains.
The swamps were drained, and the redeemed land (known
as "polders" in Holland) was made fit for tillage and grazing.
The water was impounded in reservoirs by dams and walls
and used for both irrigation and milling purposes. The
ditches were used as fishponds.[2]

As interesting as their use of engineering was the German
Cistercians' effort to utilize the forests. Much of the face of
the country was covered with dense forests. But instead of
the former haphazard way of making clearings without
reference to the value of the soil underneath, the Cistercians
studied both the timber and the soil. They knew, or discovered, that where hardwoods grew there good land was to

[1] The standard work upon the German Cistercians is that of Franz Winter, *Die
Cistercienser des nordöstlichen Deutschlands* (Gotha), Vol. I, 1868; Vol. II, 1871;
Vol. III, 1871. For more recent literature see Werminghoff, *Verfassungsgesch. der
deutschen Kirche im Mittelalter* (2d ed.; Leipzig: Teubner, 1913); Krüger, *Handbuch
der Kirchengesch.* (Tübingen, 1911–12), Vol. I, Part 2, sec. 19, 5.
The economy of the German Cistercians has been made the object of a special
study by E. Hoffmann, "Die Entwicklung der Wirtschaftsprinzipien im Zister-
zienserorden während des 12. und 13. Jahrhunderts," *Historisches Jahrbuch der
Görres-Gesellschaft*, Band XXXI (1910); Dolberg, "Zisterzienser-Mönche und Kon-
versen als Landwirte und Arbeiter," *Studien und Mitteilungen aus dem Benediktiner-
und Zisterzienser-Orden*, XIII (1892), 216–28, 360–67, 503–12. In general, for this
colonization, see Winter, I, 137 f.; Hauck, *op. cit.*, IV, 326 f.; Lamprecht, *Deutsche
Gesch.*, III, 386 f.; Michael, *Gesch. des deutschen Volkes*, pp. 91–120.

[2] Winter, II, 169. At Luttenbach, near Münster, water from the hills was conducted in underground conduits to freshen the orchard, to drive a mill, and to fill
the fishpond.

be found. They never wholly denuded the forest but left patches of standing timber.[1] Moreover, they studied plant life for food purposes: seed germination, grafting of fruit trees, and mayhap even cross-fertilization. We know that in 1237 Doberan had a glass-roofed house for purposes of plant experimentation.[2]

When a brother went on his wanderings he always took with him plants and seeds and slips of trees and brought home whatever herbs and seeds he thought might flourish in the locality of his monastery. In this wise the culture of the grape was extended from the Rhinelands into Central Germany. The monks of Altencampen imported the prized vine slips of the vineyards of Basigny around Morimond to Cologne, whence other shoots were taken to Walkenried in Thuringia, and thence to Pforta and Leubus.[3]

The particular history of a few of the more notable Cistercian enterprises in medieval Germany may be of value as illustrative of the nature and extent of their labors. One of the most famous of their achievements was the creation of the Goldene Aue, or Golden Meadows.

The traveler who today traverses by railroad the fertile region from Naumburg to Artern, which passes through Memleben, with the ruins of the old Benedictine monastery there, where Otto the Great died, would not know that the broad tract, waving with corn in the summer wind, lying between Rosaleben and Artern, was once one of the most terrible swamp lands in all Northern Germany. For these Golden Meadows are in the very bottom of the Thuringian Basin.[4] Until the coming of the Cistercian monks hither in the middle of the twelfth century, this region was a wilderness of bog, morasses, and tree stumps.[5] In prehistoric times

---

[1] *Ibid.*, p. 171.

[2] *Ibid.*, p. 175. It was on the Baltic between Rostock and Wismar.

[3] *Ibid.*, pp. 173–74.

[4] For the geographical formation of the Thüringisches Becken see Kretschmer. *Historische Geographie von Mitteleuropa*, sec. 24.

[5] There is a valuable study on this subject, namely, R. Sebicht, *Die Cistercienser .... in der Goldenen Aue* (Halle, 1887); printed in *Ztschft. d. Harzvereins f. Gesch.*, Vol. XXI.

a lake had been here. The lake had now degenerated to a huge marsh whose sluggish waters found a partial exit through the little river Helme into the Unstrut and thence into the Saale. It was in the shape of a three-pointed star, one extension reaching from Sachsenburg to Meuthen, another, Untere Helmerieth, from Brücken to the Unstrut, and the third, Obere Helmerieth, from Brücken to Sundhausen.[1]

In 1144 Count Christian of Rothenburg a-d. Saale gave a portion of this boggy area near the village of Görsbach to the Cistercians of Walkenried, and later much enlarged the tract by subsequent grants. At the same time the Archbishop of Magdeburg exempted from payment of the tithe all the land which they might redeem. Within four years there was meadow where once there had been morass only. The monks then turned their attention to the lower Rieth. In the last years of his reign Frederick Barbarossa, who had learned to esteem those whom he had once persecuted, gave permission to Jordan, a monk of Walkenried, to drain the whole region of the lower Rieth. The Emperor gave Walkenried a *Hofstätte* (a manor court and farm buildings), with two hides of land, together with area sufficient for the erection of a mill, to which the water was carried by a canal. Not many years afterward the monks of the Goldene Aue[2] had mills in operation at Riethof, Bernigen, Görbsach, Windelhausen, and Kaldenhausen.[3]

Whatever the reasons, it is certain that there are proportionally fewer examples of the establishment of colonies of Dutch or Flemish in Lower Germany after 1180 than before that date. Hartwig II of Bremen in 1201 established a colony of Hollanders near Bremen, but it is noteworthy that exceedingly attractive terms were required to prevail upon them to come.[4]

[1] Winter, II, 190–93. For other literature on the Goldene Aue see Knüll, *Hist. Geogr. Deutschlands im Mittelalter* (Breslau, 1903), p. 93; Lamprecht, *Deutsche Gesch.*, III, 371–72; Schulze, *Koloniesierung*, p. 130.

[2] The term "Aue" first appears in the *Walkenried Urkundenbuch*, I, 10, 14 (Winter, II, 191).

[3] Winter, I, 193.

[4] Meitzen, II, 350–51; Kretschmer, p. 368; Knüll, pp. 7–8; Lamprecht, III, 326; Kötzschke, *Das Unternehmertum in der ostdeutschen Kolonisation des Mittelalters*

By the beginning of the thirteenth century the Hinterland of medieval Germany was not the valley of the Elbe,
but the valley of the Oder. The "Far" East of earlier Germany had now become the "Middle" East,[1] and Breslau had
taken the place of Magdeburg and Brandenburg as a frontier
city. In the thirteenth century Silesia and the territory of
Lebus in farther Brandenburg, where the March touched the
Oder, not the bottom lands of the Weser and the Elbe, not
lower Saxony and Mecklenburg, were the parts of Germany
whither the tide of overflow population from the Low Countries directed itself. In Lebus, where the population still was
heavily Slavonic (it was the ancient land of the Leubuzzi),
the local house was very active in attracting colonists from
Flanders and Eastphalia, from Hesse and Thuringia. In the
thirty-five years between 1204–39 it is said that over 160,000
acres of waste or bottom land was redeemed by them.[2] In
lower Silesia, where the people were Polish in blood, there
was a great influx of German colonists in the time of Boleslav
the Tall and his son Conrad, who seem chiefly to have come
from Westphalia, and it may be surmised that most of the
Flemish immigrants who entered Silesia came into the country in the wake of these. Zedlitz, west of the Oder near
Steinau, seems to have been one of these settlements, and
Pogel near Wohlau certainly was a Flemish colony.[3]

(Bautzen, 1894), pp. 5–8. It is unfortunate that Kötzschke has not included this
record in his *Quellen*.

[1] Professor F. J. Turner has made this distinction classic for the history of the
American frontier between the "Old West," the "New West," and the "Far West,"
and I have applied it here.

[2] Fisher, *Mediaeval Empire*, II, 16. I do not know upon what authority he de-
pends for this statement.

[3] In the middle of the twelfth century the Augustinians of Breslau brought a
colony of Walloons into the Altmark (Grünhagen, *Les colonies wallones de Silesie*
[Brussels, 1867]), and later some serfs from Namur are found in Silesia. The Walloon
immigration into Silesia preceded that of the Flemings, but they were never numerous. Their coming was rather an infiltration than a migration. Since Grünhagen's
study, Levison ("Zur Gesch. des Bischofs Walter von Breslau, 1149–1169," *Zeitschrift des Vereins für Gesch. und Altertum Schlesiens*, XXV [1901], 353–57) has
thrown new light upon this obscure Walloon population. Cf. Pirenne, *Histoire de
Belgique*, I, 138, n. 3. Among these Flemings in Silesia it is of special interest to
follow the career of two brothers, Everard and Simon, whose names appear in the
charters for a space of thirty years. In 1261 they are merely mentioned as "Everard

In general, it may be said that east of the Elbe River the
Cistercian monks and the Praemonstratensian canons were
more active in furthering lowlander immigration than either
the bishops or the feudal nobles, while as to Prussia, the
whole exploitation of the land was in the hands of the Teutonic Order. But the activities of the great military order of
the north territorially fall outside of Germany proper.

As to Dutch and Flemish immigration into Southwestern
Germany, there is little to be written. Leopold VI of Austria
in 1106 issued a charter bestowing certain rights and liberties
upon "burgenses nostros qui apud nos Flandrenses nuncu-
patur in civitate nostra Wiena."[1] But the intensely mountainous nature of much of the Austrian and Hungarian lands
repelled settlers who were used to a fen country. The Erzgebirge and the Carpathians had more attraction for Saxon
miners from the Harz than for them. There is no evidence
of organized or group colonization by Flemings or Dutch in
Southeastern Europe. The few lowlanders found in Vienna
or Hermannstadt probably percolated into the country indi-
vidually or at the most in family groups.[2]

It was natural that the changes and new conditions here
outlined should develop new institutions. Almost from the
very inception of the movement it acquired an organized
character. The joint proclamation issued in 1108 by Adolph
of Holstein and other Saxon nobles is an indication of this.
The mechanism of both feudal and ecclesiastical government
was early used to promote and govern the movement of
Dutch and Flemish colonization in medieval Germany. In
the rivalry between the two forms that of the church was

---

et Symon fratres, Gallici [Walloon?]." In 1268 the latter is Burgrave of Steinau,
two years later *castellanus* of Welun [from Walloon?], then *prepositus*; in 1274 the
two brothers have become *comites*, and three years later Simon blossoms forth as a
palatinus.

[1] This valuable charter is reprinted from Herrgott, *Monumenta domus Austri-
acae, etc.* (1750–72), in Reich, *Select Documents Illustrating Med. and Mod. History*,
pp. 264–65. Kaindl, *op. cit.*, II, 206–10, has summarized the information to be
found. For other special literature see Schwind-Dopsch, *Urkunden zur Verfassungsgesch. d. deutschoesterr. Erblande* (Innsbruck, 1895), p. 38.

[2] Kötzschke, No 53A; *Archiv f. Kunde d. Oesterr. Geschichtsq.*, X. 92; Huber,
Gesch. Oesterrich, I, 488.

superior to that of the secular nobles; and of the two branches of the clergy the system of the Cistercian Order was superior to all.

One of the earliest and most influential institutions that developed was the office and profession of "promoter," or *locator*. Usually he was a bailiff or steward of the feudal domains of some prince or prelate, who as agent of the lord surveyed the tract intended for colonization, and then, armed with the terms of settlement, betook himself into the Low Countries and there organized a company of "homeseekers" whom he conducted into the new territory. His fee was commonly a preferred share in the enterprise in the form of an allotment of land. Naturally he often also became an important official in the new community and a medium between the settlers and the reigning noble. The first mention of a *locator* occurs in the year 1149.[1] But it is evident from the allusion that the office was already an established one. In fact, this sort of real estate agency became a profession.[2] Even cities were established in the same manner.[3]

There is much variation in detail in these settlements, but a striking general uniformity both in method of distribution of the allotments and in institutions. The model for almost all agreements seems to have been the charter of Archbishop Frederick of Bremen to the men of Utrecht whom he settled in the Weser marshes in 1106. Instead of the nucleated manorial village, with its peasant strips or plowlands in the spring and autumn "plantings" separated by dividing "balks" of turf, its demesne land, its group of huddled cottages in one corner of the manor, its array of irksome farm tasks and "boons," these colonial villages were laid out in rectangular blocks—an American would call them "sections" and "quarter-sections"—of 40, 60, 80, or more acres, so that each homesteader had a farm composed of contiguous land,

---

[1] Meitzen, II, 348.

[2] On the institution of the *locator* see Kötzschke's *Unternehmertum, etc.*, which is the most recent study of it.

[3] Poeschl, *op. cit.*, is full of evidence on this point. More briefly described in Heil, *Deutsche Städte und Bürger im Mittelalter* (Teubner's "Sammlung," Band XLIII).

and not, as under the manorial régime, an assembly of widely scattered holdings. We find these "manors of Dutch measurement" among both the Dutch and the Flemings and among new settlements of German colonists, who recognized the enormous advantage of the practice over the old system.[1]

The village, instead of being a huddled group of cottages, was a long street, every house situated at the near end of the holding facing the road. Behind it lay the farm acres, the meadow, the wood lot, in this order if the "lay" of the land so permitted. Somewhere, usually near the center of the village, were the church and the priest's house, the priest, besides the local tithe, having a holding of his own (called "Goddes peece" in England) which was worked either by parish serfs or by the peasantry of the village. If there were several villages close together, a number of them collectively were formed into a parish.[2] The priest's house and that of the *locator* were generally the most substantial and commodious structures in the community.[3]

These Flemish and Dutch settlers brought their own house architecture with them in many cases. While doubtless the original "shack" might have been rudely built of logs, the permanent edifice was often of homemade brick made out of the local clay, with timber travesses and, of course, timbered superstructure. The floors too were brick; peat, with which the lowlander was familiar, but which the German peasant had no knowledge of, was burned in the fireplace. Sometimes the front of the house was decorated with rude and curious carvings, or painted pictures of horse heads,

[1] These *mansus Hollandriensis dimensionis* are frequently mentioned in the charters, e g., Kötzschke, *Quellen*, No. 19; Riedel, *Der Mark Brandenburg*, p. 51; *Codex Diplom.*, I, 338. Elsewhere they are called "Flemish"—*mansos ad mensuram Flandrensium* (Kötzschke, *Quellen*, Nos. 13C and 50C). They were also known as *mansus regales* or *Königshufen* (Sommerfeld, "Gesch. der Germanisierung des Herzogtums Pommern" in Schmoller's *Forschungen*," XIII, Heft V, 140, 149). Meitzen has an exhaustive monograph, *Volkshufe und Königshufe* (Festgabe f. G. Hanssen, 1889), pp. 1-60, republished in Conrad's *Handwörterbuch*, IV, 496.

[2] On these Flemish "street" villages see Blanchard, *op. cit.*, pp. 423-27, who gives some interesting maps. Cf. Meitzen, II, 47-53, 343-44; Inama-Sternegg, *Deutsche Wirtschaftsgesch.*, I, 439-43.

[3] Lamprecht, III, 364-65.

swans, windmills, etc.[1] Of course these luxurious appointments obtained only among the more well-to-do settlers who possessed considerable land which was well diked and drained. Poorer settlers on small holdings frequently exposed to flood and freshet had no means to indulge in the blandishments of art.

One of the primary inducements always offered to these settlers was exemption from the exasperating and multiple manorial obligations which burdened them in the homeland to such a degree that these grievances were a real cause of emigration. The sources abound with evidence on this point. The charter clearly defined what should be the rights, duties, and obligations of both parties to the transaction, which, so to speak, became a written constitution for the government of the community. Sometimes, however, in order to make the colonists doubly assured, after reciting the duties and obligations the charter went on specifically to narrate from what the settlers should be exempt, so that their freedom was doubly defined.[2]

But in common with much that was new these settlers commingled some things that were old. They tenaciously clung to the preservation of their own native legal customs in the new land. The persistence of this characteristic trait of feudal particularism, which itself is traceable to the old Germanic legal theory of the personality of law,[3] in spite of the fluxing of the old order of things and the development of so many new institutions, is a striking example of the conservatism of things of the law.[4]

[1] See Hübbe, *Jahrb. und Jahresberichte d. Ver. f. Meck. Gesch.*, Band LXI (1896); Vigenes, *Bezeichnungen zum Volk und Land der Deutschen vom 10. bis zum 13. Jahrh.* (Heidelberg, 1901); Alfred Ronse and Theo. Raison, *Fermes-Types et constructions rurales en West-Flandre* (2 vols.; Bruges, 1919), I, 29 f. Meitzen, II, 359–60, has a detailed account.

[2] Item voluit idem archiepiscopus, quod omnes villici et cultores agrorum ejusdem ecclesiae liberi esse deberent *ab* omni censu civitatis vel villae et quod essent liberi *ab* omni advocatia, etc." (Henric. Wolteri, *Chron. Brem.* [*ca.* 1142], cited by Inama-Sternegg, II, 29 n.). For other examples see Schulze, p. 157, n. 1.

[3] Meitzen, II, 349.

[4] Even the *Stadtrecht* of Goslar (1256), although it was a mining-town where few lowlanders settled, shows traces of Flemish law, e.g., the *institutio que vulgar. Kura*

The charters abound with records of this privilege. It appears in the charter of Archbishop Frederick of Bremen (1106), in the earliest instance of Dutch colonization, where their traditional *judicia et placita* are guaranteed;[1] in that of Bishop Wichmann of Naumburg (1152) to the Hollander colony in Schul-Pforta;[2] in that of Bishop Gerung of Meissen (1154), where the provision is curiously worded: *in placitis que cum ipsis et apud ipsos;*[3] in 1159 in that of Abbot Arnold of Ballenstedt (*jure suo*); in that of Wichmann of Magdeburg in 1166 (*jure Hollandensium*); in the swamp colony established by Archbishop Baldwin in 1170 between Brinkum and Mackenstedt;[4] in the Kremper and Wilster marsh settlements.[5]

In the nature of things these imported judicial institutions were assimilated in course of time with those of the German population among whom these Dutch and Flemish incomers settled. But in some cases these special laws endured a long time. The Dutch colonies of Zarnekau and Gumale in Holstein preserved their "Hollensch Recht" and did not go over to "Holsten Recht" until 1438;[6] Christian I of Denmark in 1470 canceled the Dutch law of the Hollander settlement around Breitenburg in the marshes of the Stör;[7] the statutes of the Flemminger *Societät* in Bitterfeld were in vogue as late as the eighteenth century, and remains of them are still traceable in this locality.[8]

It is a noteworthy fact that these Dutch and Flemish

---

points to the Keuren of Flanders. The town coinage of Jüterbog and Bitterfeld for many years showed the Flemish origin of the places (Schulze, pp. 126–27, n. 2). The Belgian scholar Van Houtte has made a special study of the survival of Flemish law among these Flemish colonies in medieval Germany (*Le Droit flamand et hollandais dans les chartes de colonisation en Allemagne au XIIe et au XIIIe siecle* [Bruges, 1899]).

[1] Kötzschke, *Quellen*, No. 1.

[2] *Ibid.*, No. 9.

[3] *Ibid.*, No. 10.

[4] *Ibid*, Nos 13A, 14; Vogel, p. v.

[5] Kötzschke, *Quellen*, No. 6.

[6] Wendt, II, 16. The word *Strantorosen* in Hanseatic charters means "Frisians."

[7] Meitzen, II, 354.

[8] Schulze, p. 130.

immigrants, especially the latter, were almost wholly a rural peasantry and not a townspeople, although the Flemish towns by the twelfth century were already well developed. The attractions of commerce and industry dissuaded this latter class from emigrating. In consequence the history of German town life in the Middle Ages shows little evidence of Flemish influence.[1] Nor do Dutch or Flemings appear in the records as servile *ministeriales* and household servants. In the war of 1166 waged by Henry the Lion's rebellious vassals, Count Christian of Amerland seized Bremen with a body of "Frisian" troops,[2] but this is the only instance of the kind which I have met.

On the other hand, Flemish effect upon the material development of the open country, especially bottom lands, was very great. While the Wends were traditionally a marsh folk, their crude agriculture was incapable of the engineering necessary to drain the swamps. As for the German, he was a woodlander by ancestral association and by preference; even the Low German of the North German plain usually avoided the river bottoms, until the process of feudal inclosure of the Almend and the forests drove him to them.[3]

But the incoming Flemish and Dutch settlers had a natural aptitude for this kind of labor. They were used to bog and fen, to peat marshes and swamps, and by inclination preferred lowlands to uplands. The great landed proprietors of Germany who promoted their settlement had a clear perception of their economic worth; hence the large privileges accorded them. The charter of Bishop Gerung lauds the "strong men of Flanders" (*strenuos viros ex Flandrensi*) who will redeem the waste of swamps around Meissen. Besides ditching, diking, and draining these lowlander immigrants

---

[1] *Ibid.*, n. 3. Gilds of Flemish weavers are traceable in Nordhausen, Langensalza, and Görlitz.

[2] Helmold, Book I, chap. ciii: *Fresonum manu.*

[3] On this process of "inclosures" see Lamprecht, *op. cit.*, III, 53–58; von der Goltz, *Landwirtschaft*, pp. 93–98; Roscher, *Ackerbau, etc.* (11th ed., 1885), secs. 79–80.

materially helped the country by building roads.[1] Another service to which we find several allusions is the extermination of snakes by them.[2]

One might think that these humble laborers who settled where others would not go and hardly competed at all with the German would have been welcomed by him. But this was not the case. Helmold relates that the Holsteiners, not without reason, were suspected of firing the villages of Flemish and Dutch settlers during the Wendish Crusade "on account of hatred of these immigrants" (advenae).[3]

The resentment of the Wends toward them was more reasonable, for the Wends were a fen people who often were actually dispossessed by these settlers from the Low Countries. This was particularly the case in Brandenburg around Dressau, Wörlitz, and Pratau, where a ruthless expulsion of the Wends took place under Albrecht the Bear and Wichmann of Magdeburg.[4] In the really eloquent complaint of Pribislav, the Abodrite chieftain, relating the sufferings of his people, which is given at length by Helmold,[5] Flemings and Hollanders are mentioned along with Saxons and Westphalians as those by whom his people have been expelled from their homelands. "Worn down by the coming of these settlers," as honest Helmold says, "the Slavs forsook the country." It was the fate of the Red Man in America.

Lamprecht has said that the greatest deed of the German people in the Middle Ages was their eastward expansion over, and colonization of, the Slavonic lands between the Elbe and the Oder. Most of this long and important labor was done by

[1] Kötzschke, Quellen, p. 11 n.

[2] Ibid., Nos. 2 (p. 7), 4 (p. 11).

[3] Helmold, Book I, chaps. lxiii–lxiv. Ibid., chap. lxiv, quotes at length the harangue of a German priest named Gerlach against the Flemings, in which he said: "Nulla gens detestabilior Fresis. Sane fetet eis odor noster." Every anthropologist and ethnologist knows the importance of this phenomenon among primitive peoples. So the children of Israel in Egypt complained to Moses and Aaron: "Ye have made our savor to be abhorred in the eyes of Pharaoh" (Exod. 5:21). Even to this day in Germany, from the Weser to the Oder, the terms Vlämsch, Vlämischer Kerl, Vlämisches Gesicht, etc., signify "uncouth," "heavy," "rough," "having bad taste" (Schulze, p. 130, n. 3 at end).

[4] Schulze, p. 130.   [5] Chron. Slav., Book I, chap xcviii.

the Germans themselves. But a not inconsiderable portion of this achievement was due to these nameless pioneers dwelling by the ocean and suffering the violence of the sea, who came to redeem the marshes of the Weser, the Elbe, and Havel, the Oder, and even the Vistula.[1]

[1] "Dieser Pionierdienst in der Kolonisation des deutschen Ostens ist unter den vielen Grosstaten unserer westlichen Brüder eine der grössten; er soll ihnen unvergessen bleiben in jeder deutschen Geschichte" (Lamprecht, *Deutsche Gesch.*, III, 342).

CHAPTER XVI

GERMAN SOUTHEASTWARD EXPANSION AND THE FORMATION OF AUSTRIA

NO ONE needs to be told that South Germany differs from North Germany in physical formation, in racial ingredients, in history. North Germany, save for the massif of the Harz, is a great plain. South Germany is a rugged, broken, mountainous country, the great trough of the Danube being the only physical feature giving unity to the region.

As are the physical differences, so are the racial differences. North Germany had but two peoples in contact or composition, Saxon and Slav. The history of South Germany was the achievement of two Teutonic peoples of equal importance, the Swabian and the Bavarian, each of whom occupied a different part of the country, each of whom made his own distinct history.

The history of South Germany, moreover, is more complex than that of North Germany for the reason that the South was included for centuries, first within the great Celtic empire of Central Europe, and then within the orbit of the Roman Empire (the Danube provinces of Rhaetia, Noricum, and the two Pannonias, which extended from the source to the great bend), so that, in spite of the Germanic dominant in this region, the history of South Germany is a palimpsest, for deep below, in the very fibers of the parchment, may be read the record of earlier Celtic and Roman occupation of the country. Finally, later, a considerable infusion of Slav blood entered into the composition of Southeastern Germany.[1]

---

[1] For a general ethnographic survey of the populations of the Danube see Van den Ghyn, *Polybiblion* (1888); for the Celts in Germany, A. Bachmann, "Die Kelten im Norden der Donau," *Ztschft. f. d. österr. Gymn.*, XXX (1879), 81–93. Kämmel, *Die Anfänge deutschen Lebens in Oesterreich* (Leipzig, 1879), pp. 313–14, gives interesting examples of the survival of old Celtic names in Pannonia. For

The making of Southeastern Germany was the work of the Bavarians, as the making of Northeastern Germany was the work of the Saxons. These are the two great pioneer Germanic peoples. An offshoot or a remnant of the formerly great Marcomanni, whose prowess had taxed the arms of Marcus Aurelius in the second century, the Bavarians seem originally to have been settled between the Saale and the Erzgebirge, whence they expanded up the Elster and down the Nab, across the Vogtland and Nordgau of later times, to and beyond the Danube. Once having reached the right bank of the Danube further expansion was easy, via the valleys of the Lech, the Isar, the Inn, the Enns, those Alpine affluents of the great river.

The time of this migration was for the Bavarians that epoch when their tribal sentiment and tribal institutions

Celtic survivals in Swabia see Buck, *Württemb. Jahrb. f. Statistik und Landeskunde* (1879); for Austria, R. Müller, *Blätter d. Ver. f. Landesk. v. Niederöst.* (N.F., 1888), XXII, Nos. 1–2, a study based on place-names. Buck has also a study of 45 charters of St. Gall pertaining to the ninth and tenth centuries demonstrated the persistence of Romanized Celtic blood in Rhenish Switzerland and the valley of the upper Inn (*Ztschft. f. roman. Philologie*, Band XI, Heft 1). Schulte, from an examination of the oldest lists of monks in the monasteries of Gengenbach, Ettenheim, Schuttern, and Schwarzbach in Baden, concludes that the ancient Roman population there preserved some traces until the ninth century. Krones, *Mitteil. d. hist. Ver. f. Steiermark*, Band XXVII (1879), thinks the Romanized Celtic population in Noricum did not disappear until the sixth century, when it was effaced by Slav immigration. The Bavarian penetration, which took place later, was accomplished without violence and not only absorbed the greater part of the Slavs there, but also assimilated Celto-Roman fragments which had escaped fusion with the Slavs. For Slav traces in Bavaria see Zapf, *Beiträge z. Anthrop. und Urgesch. Baierns*, Band IV (1881), and for Slav survivals in the Alps, Dopsch, *Die ältere Soziale und Wirtschaftsverfassung der Alpenslaven* (1912), a review of which may be read in the *Hist. Ztschft.*, CVIII, No. 2 (1912). In this long article Dopsch seeks to refute Peisker upon the economic and social institutions of the Slavs in Styria and Carinthia. Peisker has claimed that there existed among the Alpine Slavs two sharply differentiated classes: (1) the *zupani*, former nobles reduced by the conquering Germans, but living like their forefathers by cattle-raising; and (2) the peasants, who were serfs. Dopsch holds that these contentions are untenable; that the *zupani* were nothing more than manorial agents like the German *ministeriales*, and were not to be distinguished from the peasantry except by their function. Automatically the other contentions of Peisker fall to the ground. The original meaning of the word *zupan* seems to have been that of "clan chieftain," then official of the lord enjoying a servile benefice, later possibly, like the *ministerialis*, developing into a petty *dominus*. Usage of the word with a territorial application like *pagus* is modern (Lippert, *Soz. Gesch. Böhmens*, I, 120, n. 2, and his article in *Mitteil. d. Ver. f. d. Gesch. der Deutschen in Böhmen*, XXXI, No. 3).

seem to have acquired fixity of form and to have crystallized. The dissolution of the Ostrogothic kingdom in the sixth century indubitably facilitated the spread of the Bavarians in the middle Danube region. But, at the same time, that very decline of Ostrogothic power north of the Alps tempted the Frank to expand his power farther eastward down the Danube. Nominal subjugation of the Bavarians to Frankish sway was accomplished between 552 and 555. But it was not a conquest of violence. For the Bavarian needed the strong protection of the Frank in his new land owing to the formidable pressure of the Avars below him in the bend of the Danube.[1]

But if the Bavarian had need of Frank protection against the Avar, the need of the Danubian Slavs for protection against him was greater. Soon after 611 all the Slavs between the Alps and the middle Danube seem to have fallen under Avar sway, from which Samo (628–38?) had for a time released them. But with Samo's death the Avar peril returned, and in 745 Borut of Carinthia in return for Bavarian help recognized some sort of Bavarian control over Carinthia. The early history of Bavaria before the rise of the Agilofinger ducal house is very obscure, and our information is wholly of an ecclesiastical nature. From the time of St. Severinus (d. 481?), whose *Vita* throws some light on conditions in Pannonia in the last half of the fifth century, until the seventh century, there is hardly a shred of information with reference to the history of Bavaria. Although remnants of Christianity from Roman times survived in the middle Danube lands, the Bavarians were and remained pagan until the coming of St. Eustasius (d. 625) among them from the Irish monastery of Luxeuil in the Vosges. Progress was slow, however, until the end of the seventh century, when the effect of St. Rupert's missionary work began to become evident. The first bishopric established was Salzburg in 696. Rupert, we are told, traveled by boat up and down the valley of the Danube as far as the border of lower Pannonia,

---

[1] Bachmann, "Die Einwanderung der Bayern," *Sitzungsb. der K.K. Akad. d. Wiss. in Wien*, Band XCI; Mehlis, "Beiträge z. Anthrop. und Urgesch.," *Münchner Gesellschft. f. Anthrop., Ethnol. und Urgesch.* (1877–78).

scattering the seed of life. He came to Walarius (Seekirchen am Wallersee), where he built a church in honor of St. Peter, and another at the place anciently called Civitas Juvavensis (Salzburg), where in former times there had been churches which were then fallen utterly to ruin and covered by forest.

This early Irish missionary endeavor soon began to experience the superior competition of a similar movement which emanated from Frankish Benedictinism. It was through the latter influence that the cult of St. Martin penetrated into Württemberg, where before the eighth century places named Kirchheim are to be found, and where there were five churches founded in Merovingian times dedicated to St. Martin. From Swabia these Frankish black-frocked missionaries passed over into Bavaria, where we find the first churches of the Latin faith under the protection of St. Michael and St. Stephen, to the prejudice of favorite Irish saints.

But effective organization of the church in Bavaria did not begin until the coming of Boniface, who founded the sees of Regensburg, Freising, and Passau, and refounded that of Salzburg on a Roman basis. At the same time a swarm of Benedictine cloisters began to be established in Bavaria. Neither the Bavarian Duke nor his people seem to have taken kindly to this monastic invasion. It savored too much of Frankish and Roman domination, and local sentiment in favor of the Irish form of Christianity was vivid. Nevertheless, the progress of Benedictinism was not slow in Bavaria. The Agilofinger dukes had to promote it for expediency's sake.[1] But their veiled conciliatory policy did not save the Bavarian dukes from complete Frankish conquest. The deposition of Tassilo, the last Agilofinger duke, in 788 by Charlemagne was the sequel of the alliance between the Frankish crown and the papacy, made in 751.

The progress of Frankish monastic colonization in Bavaria was given new impulse by this event, and ere long we find direct contact of Frankish secular and ecclesiastical power with the southeastern Slavs. These mission posts cleared the

[1] See Fastlinger, *Die wirtschaftliche Bedeutung der Bayerischen Klöster in der Zeit der Agilofinger* (Freiburg im B., 1903), for details.

forest and worked the salt springs found in the region and mark the beginnings of German colonization among the Danubian Slavs.[1]

The fall of Bavarian independence in 788 opened Southeastern Germany as never before to an influx of Frankish colonists and settlers, chiefly monks and nobles, who vied with each other in hunger for land and desire to exploit the native border population in the development thereof. The *monastic* and *aristocratic* nature of the colonization of the middle Danube lands is marked. It is evident that this mixed missionary and colonizing movement was directly inspired by the Frankish court, and far less a natural and spontaneous expansion of the people than was the case with the eastward spread of the Saxons. As early as Charlemagne's reign swarms of settlers from the more densely populated regions of the Moselle and the Rhine seem to have poured up the valley of the Main and so over into Bavaria and Carinthia. The bishopric of Würzburg, founded by Boniface in 741, was the Carolingian base for the evangelization and subjugation of the southeastern Slavs, and not Salzburg, as one might expect. For the Slavs of the Main, among whom Charles the Great established fourteen churches, were the connecting link between the Slavs of the Danube and the Frankland.

The heavy labor on these plantations of the church in the Bavarian Hinterland was done by the "converted" Slavs. Already as early as this the word "Slav" had become equivalent to "slave,"[2] and the systematic exploitation of them by the church through the imposition of the tithe an established and onerous practice.[3]

---

[1] In 770 the little stream of the Mühlbach seems to have formed the dividing line between Bavarian and Slav territory. We know that in the eighth century the village of Bischofshofen on the Pongau was neighbored "a vicinis Sclavis" (*Salz. Urkundenb. des Landes ob der Enns*, II, 2, 6, 13), and another document of 834 describes the territory around Kronsdorf on the Enns as "pars Sclavorum"; a third of 906 of St. Florian mentions "Bavari vel Slavi istius patriae" (*ibid.*, 55). Today this region on the right bank of the Danube is pure Bavarian, the trace of Slovenism once there having been absorbed (cf. Niederlé, *La Race Slav*, pp. 80–81).

[2] *Mon. boica*, XXVIII, 1, 45; XXXI, 1, 55. Schober, *Die Deutschen in Nieder- und Ober-Österreich, Steiermark, Kärnthen und Krain*, I (1881), 17–18.

[3] Already in the cartularies *labores* is the equivalent of *decimae*. For the brutality of the tithes imposed upon the "converted" Slavs see Zeissberg, "Arno, erster

In the still unappropriated lands the villages of the Slavs maintained a precarious existence, beset on every side both by newly established monasteries and settlements of German immigrants from farther west, who hewed out clearings for themselves in the forests. But most of these German in-comers, as said, were not free, but serfs belonging to great Frankish proprietors and to the abbeys, who moved them *en masse* from their crowded domains in the Frankland into these new and sparsely peopled regions along the frontier. Commingled with these dependents, however, doubtless was a sprinkling of the lower grades of Carolingian society, the *hospites, peregrini et pauperes* of the great capitulary of 789 (art. 75), whom economic distress and social strain had de-tached from their old homesteads. Such people, without family or village ties, or deprived of them by misfortune and poverty, were only too glad to find refuge, even at the ex-pense of privation, in the new lands of the southeast. The great famine of 791 must have increased this class of homeless and destitute, and so have promoted a drift of population into the region of the middle Danube. For Saxony was not yet subdued, and any strong northeastward drift of the Frankish population is not yet perceptible.[1]

But all this southeastward progress, which had extended the sphere of German occupation as far as the Enns before the end of the eighth century, was arrested, and much of it even destroyed, by the Avars. In 791, 793, 796, Charles the Great made campaigns against these formidable marauders. Two subsequent campaigns, in 803 and 811, completed their conquest. At the diet of Regensburg in 803 the Emperor formally organized the Ostmark, destined so many years later to grow into the duchy of Austria, and linked it up with the chain of Marches which guarded the eastern frontier of

---

Erzbischof von Salzburg," *Sitz. d. kaiserl. Akad.*, XLIII, 24; Dümmler, "Ueber die südöstlichen Marken des fränk. Reiches unter den Karolingern (795–907)," *Archiv f. Kunde österr. Geschichtsquellen*, X (1854), 21, and Schröder, "Arno v. Salzburg," *Neue Heidelb. Jahrb.*, II, No. 2.

[1] Of 119 place-names in the charters of Freising before 800, 24 per cent end in *inge*, which indicates settlements of Swabian origin (Sommerlad, *Die wirtschaftliche Tätigkeit der Kirche in Deutschland*, II, 214).

the Empire from the mouth of the Elbe to the head of the Adriatic. At the same time, as in Saxony, whose conquest was just completed, forcible conversion and the heavy weight of the tithe were imposed upon the Avars in order to complete their subjugation.

The destruction of the Avar power opened the door wide to colonization of the Danube lands both for German and southern Slav. For, while there is reason to believe the statement is exaggerated to the effect that the Avar land was left utterly uninhabited[1] after the conclusion of the conquest, yet there can be no doubt that the land within the new Ostmark was very much reduced in population.[2] The repopulation of this vast devastated territory, together with that of the similarly decimated Spanish March, was one of the keenest interests of Charlemagne during his last years. In both countries settlers began to flow in from the more densely peopled central provinces of the Frank Empire. But the border condition in the Ostmark (and the same is true of the Spanish March) was such that haphazard settlement was unthinkable. Both territories were regarded as *Reichsländer*, primarily occupied by the military, who strictly regulated the colonization. Allotments of land seem to have been systematically made to bishops, abbots, and great nobles, who imported settlers, many of whom were serfs, from Bavaria, the lower Main and middle Rhine regions into old Pannonia and the Riedmark.[3]

The German colonization, then, of the Ostmark was made by collective groups, chiefly of servile condition, under the direction of a feudal and ecclesiastical aristocracy, and not by individual free settlers.[4] In this particular, as well as in the

[1] Einhard, *Vita Karoli*, chap. vi.

[2] "Quos [Avaros] invictissimus Karolus ita in annis viii perdomuit ut de eis minimas quidem reliquias remanere permiserit" (*Monachus Sangall.* [written about 885], II, 1); Regino, *Chron.* (889), refers to the "Pannoniarum et Avarum solitudines."

[3] See the long list of Carolingian grants from the crown lands in what is now Austria, Steiermark, Carinthia, Carniola, and the Isar Valley, as given in Eggers, *Der königl. Grundbesitz im 10. und 11. Jh.*, pp. 26–28, in proof of this statement.

[4] Inama-Sternegg, II (1891), 7, fails to make the essential distinction between German northeast expansion and southeast expansion. "Die Rodung des kleinen

government supervision of the movement, the settlement of Southeast Germany differs greatly from the nature of the expansion toward the northeast, where a large proportion of the settlers were freemen and the expansion natural and un-controlled (except in the Thuringian March between the Saale and upper Elbe) by government. Dopsch has made the point that the tide of German immigrants was probably as strong in the one direction as in the other, though, owing to the poverty of the sources, we cannot measure the depth and swiftness of the current setting toward the Danubian lands as we can that setting toward the trans-Elbean lands. But the new territory of the Ostmark was not to be undisputedly of Germanic settlement. For there is faint trace of the influx of Czech settlers also into this old Pannonian land, especially from Moravia.[1]

Now, for the first time, in the ninth century, the Adriatic Slavs became a factor in German history. The Frankish de-struction of the Avar power had removed the bulwark which for years had hindered the expansion of the Bulgars. They now began to penetrate into the eastern part of the former Avar territory. By the middle of the ninth century their in-fluence extended as far as the Theiss and the Timok rivers and brought the Bulgars and Serbs into conflict.[2] The effect of this pressure by the Bulgars was to drive some of the Slavonic peoples, notably the Slovenes, into Carinthia and later Styria.

---

freien Mannes" is largely true of the former provinces (except the land between Saale, Elbe, and Erzgebirge); it is not true of the Danubian lands. At p. 8, n. 2, he cites an exchange of a manor (*praedium*) in Bavaria with two serf families upon it for one in Carinthia with eight such families as an instance of voluntary settlement of simple freemen.

[1] *Conversio Bag. et. Car.*, chaps. vi, x, xi; cf. Niederlé, *op. cit.*, pp. 82–86.

[2] "Tunc vero Sclavi post Hunos inde expulsos coeperunt istis partibus Danubii diversas regiones habitare" (*Conversio Car.*, chap. vi); "In Slavoniam, in partes videlicet Quarantanas atque inferioris Pannoniae," etc. . . . . Coeperunt populi sive Sclavi vel Bagoarii inhabitare terram unde illi expulsi sunt Huni, et multiplicari" (*ibid.*, chap. vii). For this westward drift of the Slovenes see Dümmler, *op. cit.*, pp. 25–29, 33. Down to 828 the Drave formed not only the diocesan limit, but also a frontier between the counts of lower Pannonia and Friuli. The Count Odalric, men-tioned in 860 and 869, administered upper not lower Pannonia (Pirchegger, *Mitteil. d. Inst. f. österr. Gesch.*, XXXIII [1912], No. 2).

What the relative proportions were of the mixed peoples which were gathered together here in the middle Danube lands it is, of course, impossible to say. But it will escape no one that the intricate and varied racial composition of old Austria dates back at least as far as the ninth century. The process of assimilation or fusion of these various ingredients was a slow and unsuccessful one, in spite of the influence of the church and the military organization which obtained. For that influence was political and administrative in its nature, not social, except in the matter of depressing the population to a condition of serfdom. It requires more than a mortar and a pestle to effect the fusion of peoples. It takes time to change a mechanical mixture into a chemical compound by transfusion of blood. From its inception down to its latest history, Austria always has been a state which grew *par agglomération*, instead of organically *par assimilation*.

Historians have endeavored, on the evidence of place-names, to determine which localities were German and which were Slav in the old Ostmark. But apart from the fact that much of the Carolingian régime was destroyed at the end of the ninth century by the inroads of the Magyars and the work of recolonization had to be begun anew after 955, the findings cannot be conclusive. For in any case the distinctions would hold good only of the free villages (and these were few), and not of the manors of the *Grundherrschaften*, on which German, Slav, and even Avar serfs toiled side by side.

The physical area of this colonization, however, is not a matter of dispute. By the end of the ninth century the German sphere of influence extended beyond the Enns, which had been the farthest east of German expansion in pre-Avar times, and had reached the Raab. The civilization in this land was lustily, even brutally, materialistic in its character. "Wer mit der einen Hand den Pflug fasst und die andere am Schwertgriff halten muss, der hat für die Feder keine frei." The social texture was that of a warlike feudal and ecclesiastical aristocracy imposed upon a servile peasantry. The three-field system of farming was practiced, at least upon the manors of the church, along with some grape-growing on the sunny slopes. Other activities were lumbering, beer-making, salt-making, and bee-keeping.

But, once more, as in the eighth century, again at the extreme end of the ninth and beginning of the tenth, most of this hard labor of colonization in the lands of the middle Danube was doomed to go for naught. The history of German southeastward expansion exhibits the same alternation of advance and retreat that characterizes the history of northeastward expansion. Just as the Slav reactions of 983, 1018, and 1066 undid the work of trans-Elbean colonization, and threw the Saxon pioneers back across the Elbe three several times, so in the Ostmark the labor of settlement was twice undone, first by the Avars and then by the Magyars.[1]

By 896 the Magyars were settled upon both banks of the Theiss, and thenceforward for years both Germany and Northern Italy were harried almost annually by their depredations. In 900, the margrave Liutpold built the Ennsburg out of the stones of Passau's old Roman wall. The military reforms of Henry the Fowler of Saxony, and his victory on the Unstrut in 933, partially abated the Magyar danger. But effective check to their inroads was not made until Otto I's smashing defeat of them near Augsburg in 955. After that date a steady stream of German colonists seems to have flowed into the twice-wasted land of the Ostmark. The body of these pioneers probably came from Bavaria. But there is reason to believe that with them was a considerable proportion of Franconian and Swabian immigrants from farther west.[2]

---

[1] The eastward drift of the Carolingian Pfalzen is marked in the middle of the ninth century (Schröder, pp. 20–21). Ludwig of Bavaria is found at Tuln in 864 in the Ostmark (Jaffé, 2758). Pertz, *Mon. Ger. Hist.*, SS. I, 378, n. 52, thinks that Tuln was Theben, in the defile at the confluence of the March with the Danube, which Dümmler, *Ostfränk. Gesch.*, I, 528, n. 37, holds to be impossible. In 884 Charles the Fat was at Tuln (*Annal. Fuld.*). Until the coming of the Magyars the Raab was the eastern boundary of the Ostmark (Pritz, *Gesch. des Landes ob d. Enns*, I, 317; *Mon. Boica*, XXVIII, 1, No. 72, a charter of Charles the Fat). The first Carolingian castle at Regensburg was built by Charlemagne.

[2] When Adalbert of Babenberg and his house were exiled from Franconia in 906, their lands there were confiscated to the fisc. From this circumstance it was long believed that the Babenbergers were natives of Franconia. But evidence has been found to indicate that they came originally from Swabia (Stein, *Forschungen z.*

The history of Austria in the first decade of the tenth century begins obscurely to revolve around the great house of Babenberg, as the vaporous rings of superheated gas in the cosmic world slowly congeal around some stellar sun to form a new world. But, unfortunately, no contemporary writer has left us an account of the early history of the Babenbergers in Austria, such as Widukind and Adam of Bremen wrote of the Billunger dukes in Saxony. But it admits of no doubt that effective and permanent political formation of the Ostmark really began with the Babenbergers.

But that the progress of German southeastward colonization, however, was slow and not without arrest and interruption may be inferred from the fact that the Magyar peril, while much allayed, was not wholly removed by the German victory on the Lechfeld. For as late as 1020 Vienna was taken by the Magyars, and in 1043 Henry III was compelled to make a complete reorganization of the Marks which buttressed the southeastern flank of the German kingdom.[1]

Nevertheless, after 955, in spite of obstacles and setbacks, the advance of German southeast colonization, if slow, was sure. The stages by which the great Böhmerwald region and the Riedmark were settled by German colonists are very obscure.[2] But it is certain that there was a rather steady in-

---

d. Gesch., XII, 113–36; Hüber, Mitteil., II, 374–82), whence it has been inferred more than demonstrated that there was a considerable commingling of Swabians among the German settlers who flowed into the Ostmark after 955 (Budinger, Österr. Gesch., p. 161; Kötzschke, Deutsche Wirtschaftsgesch., p. 110). The truth is that the place of origin of these pioneers and the stages by which the territory beyond the Enns and between the Danube and the upper Drave was resettled in the last half of the tenth century are not clear. The most complete examination of the subject has been made by Hasenörhl, "Deutschlands südöstliche Marken im X., XI. und XII. Jahrhundert," Archiv f. österr. Gesch., LXXXII, 419 f. The maps are valuable.

[1] The term "Terra Ostarrichi in regione vocabulo Ostarrichi . . . . dicto" first appears in 996 (Meiller, Regesten, I, p. 2, No. 2); the form "Austria" in 1074 (Hasenörhl, p. 452, nn. 1–2). For Henry III's reorganization of the Ostmark in 1043, when the Neumark is first mentioned, see Thausing, "Die Neumark Österreich und das Privileg. Heinrici," Forschungen, IV, 361 f. The earliest mention of the Riedmark is in 1155 (Hasenörhl, p. 450, n. 33).

[2] Since Hasenörhl's monograph and maps were published Julius Strandt has studied the history of the Riedmark anew ("Die freien Leute der alten Riedmark: Wenden und Bajuwarensiedelung" [with 2 maps], Archiv f. österr. Gesch. [1915]).

GERMAN SOUTHEASTWARD EXPANSION   591

flux of settlers through the whole Saxon and Salian period,
and that the process was pursued with little conflict. For the
Bohemian forest was too dense for habitation hitherto, and
clearings had to be painfully and laboriously made with the
ax, which was far more useful than the sword as a weapon of
expansion. As before, so now again, the work was done by
big "operators," namely, the high clergy and great feudal
nobles. Unfortunately there is no chronicle of the Babenbergers to tell us the tale of this recovery and renewed expansion like Helmold's *Chronica Slavorum* for the German
northeast. The history has to be traced through detached
and often widely separated pieces of evidence in Meiller's
Regesten der Babenberger and the charters in the *Monumenta
Boica*. Historical imagination, from later facts which have
come to light, and from the analogous history of the northeastward expansion of the German people, often must visualize the nature of the movement by a process of inverse
reasoning.

Important, positive facts are few and far between. By
994 we know that Leopold of Babenberg had carried the
frontier of the Ostmark down to the Wienerwald. For in that
year, in which he lost his life by an accident, he organized the
Traungau on the right bank of the Danube,[1] and the Riedmark and the Machland upon the left bank.[2] These three
military erections must have been made to cover the thin line
of German pioneers pushing eastward. This forward movement seems to have been quite sudden and of considerable
pressure. For as late as 985 much of the bishopric of Passau
is described as a wilderness, so bereft of serfs that freemen had
to do villein service on the church patrimonies.[3] Yet when
Pilgrim of Passau died in 991, the land between the Wienerwald and the Enns seems to have been fairly well settled.[4]

[1] For the Traungau see Strandt, "Das Gebiet zwischen der Traun und der
Enns," *ibid.*, XCIV, 466 and 662.

[2] For Machland see Strandt, "Das Land im Norden der Donau," *ibid.*, p. 282.

[3] Meiller, *Regesten*, Vol. I, No. 3: "Ut liberi cujuscunque conditionis sint qui
destinantur coloni in locis pertinentibus ad sanctae patauiensis aecclesiae, etc."

[4] Huber, I, 177. For examples of settlements of free peasants and serfs here see
Mon. Boica, XXVIII, A 216, 243; B 88; XXXI, A 223.

North of the Danube at the same time a similar colonization in the Böhmerwald was effected by Wolfgang of Regensburg (d. 994).[1] The explanation of this sudden bulge of the frontier toward the southeast is probably to be found in the successful rebellion of the Slavs of the Elbe in 982, which destroyed all the German settlements across that great river, and set back the eastward expansion of the Saxon people for nearly a generation.

Leopold's son and successor, Henry I of Babenberg, continued to promote his father's work of colonization, and at this time we find Franconian settlers among the Bavarian and Swabian incomers. The record is to be read in ecclesiastical grants, not all of which, however, are genuine. For the church, taking advantage of the obliteration of the earlier boundary lines in these localities, which had been run in times preceding the Magyar invasions, forged new deeds in the effort to enlarge its already enormous possessions. In particular, the forgeries made by Pilgrim of Passau were notorious. The devastated monasteries of St. Polten, Kremsmünster, and St. Florian made paper claims of vast extent.

The magnitude of the tracts which the church claimed was only exceeded by the brazen effrontery with which these forgeries were fabricated. According to the *Passauer Saalbuch*, some time between 985 and 994 Duke Henry of Bavaria held an inquest, at which the bishops and abbots and nobles of the March were present, in order to determine the nature and extent of the "rights and liberties" of the Bishop of Passau, and it found that Passau's claims stretched clear up to the Wienerwald! It is evident that the Bavarian Duke who was overlord of the Margrave himself, as well as others in the region, was becoming jealous and alarmed over the land-hunger of the Bishop of Passau.

The Wienerwald seems for several years to have retarded settlement. But more important than the resistance of the

---

[1] *Mon. Boica*, XXVIII, A 227. For the date see Ficker, *Urkundenlehre*, I, 197. In 1010 the Böhmerwald, sometimes known as the Nordwald, is described as "silva quae vocatur in comitatu Adalberonis in longitudine a fonte flumenis quod dicitur Ilzisa sursum usque ad terminum praedictae silvae qui separat duas terras Baioriam videlicet et Boemiam et ita usque ad fontem fluvii qui dicitur Rotala" (cited by Hasenörhl, p. 444).

forest was the hostility of the sparse but resolute population (principally Magyars, but with some settlers of Slavonic blood) living east of the forest. This territory was a sort of "No Man's Land" between the two competitive groups, where every man's hand was likely to be against another, and certainly against any encroaching pioneers out of Germany. Thietmar of Merseburg tells the story of an Irish pilgrim named Colomannus, who was captured and killed as a spy by these borderers. A tinge of legend already when he wrote (1017) had gathered around this incident. But there is no reason to doubt the essential accuracy of the tale, which so clearly illustrates the suspicious nature of the population in this *terra nullius*. The first positive evidence of German settlement east of the Wienerwald is found in 1002, when King Henry II granted to a certain noble of Bamberg named Pilgrim a tract of territory eighteen miles square, from which in after-days the endowments of the abbeys of Zell and Heiligenkreuz were to be derived.

At some unknown date in the career of Margrave Adalbert of Austria (1018–55) the site of Vienna had been occupied by him, probably as an advance post to cover the German settlements which by that time had succeeded in penetrating the Wienerwald.[1] The establishment of these soon led to border strife between Germans and Magyars, in which apparently the former were the aggressors, so that King Stephen of Hungary interfered to protect his subjects. The danger to the Ostmark arising from this intervention was great enough to call Conrad II into the Danube lands. But in spite of the strong forces with him (the panegyrist of King Stephen says that the imperial host was drawn from "all Germany") the difficult nature of the country, which abounded with forest and swamp, made successful military operation impossible.

[1] If the author of the *Gesta Friderici I*, chap. xxxiii, in his account of Henry of Bavaria's Danube campaign in 1146 meant Vienna by "vicinum oppidum Hyenis," then the place must have been very insignificant at that time. Much discussion has revolved around the question of the origin of the word Vienna. Grienberger, *Sitzungsb. k. Akad. d. Wiss. in Wien*, Band CXXXI (1894), concedes that Roman Vindobona is of Celtic origin, but thinks Vienna of Slav origin. Müller, *Blätter d. Ver. f. Landesk. v. Niederösterreich*, Band XXX (1896), denies that the word is either Roman or Slav, but admits that its origin is unexplained.

While not actually defeated, perhaps, in a pitched battle, Conrad II lost a large number of men and was compelled to retreat, leaving the honors of the campaign with the Hungarian King, who captured Vienna.

German recovery from this reverse was slow. The narrow strip of territory between the Fischa and the Leitha rivers had to be ceded to Hungary. This frontier area, like the Scottish Border, was the scene of a strife which left a picturesque and indelible mark upon medieval German literature in the greatest of German epics; but in spite of the fact that the region was perilous ground, German settlers, and even some adventurous traders, persisted in creeping in.

The chance for German retaliation and recovery came in the reign of Henry III. In 1038 a war of succession disrupted Hungary, and Henry III was not slow to profit by it. In 1042 the country east of the March was invaded, the Maygar army terribly slaughtered, and all captives, men and women alike, massacred in cold blood. With considerable strategy the Emperor had avoided the marshy region of the Raab, which had so discomfited his father, and invaded Hungary through the Bavarian Nordgau, falling upon that part of the kingdom which lay north of the Danube. The whole valley of the Waag as far as the Gran River was fearfully devastated by the Germans. Nine Hungarian towns were taken, and two in addition destroyed by the Magyars themselves when evacuation of them was made necessary. A submissive Magyar embassy came to Regensburg in 1043 to sue for peace. Henry III demanded the cession of the debated territory between the Fischa and the Leitha, the return of all German captives, and the payment of 400 talents of gold as reparation for damage done to the German border settlements.

The Austrian Mark thus extended (the new annexation was called Neumark) entered upon a new history. More compact, though larger than before, it lay on both sides of the Danube, the rivers Thaya and March protecting its front north of the Danube, the Leitha doing the same south of the Danube, while the flank of the Mark was covered by the Mark of Carinthia. During the war just closed the Emperor had destroyed the two Hungarian advance posts, Hainburg and Pressburg, now mentioned for the first time in 1042, which lay almost opposite to each other on either side of the Danube. By the terms of peace the Germans retained Hainburg, but Pressburg had to be returned to Hungary and was at once rebuilt. Commanding the famous defile known as Theben, which forms a natural gateway, Pressburg was of incalculable importance to Hungary.

The conversion of Hungary early in the eleventh century introduced a new factor in the racial and border rivalry of the Germans and the Magyars. As early as the second half of the tenth century Christian missionary monks from Bavaria had begun to penetrate into Hungary, while at the same time the trade with Byzantium brought in missionaries of the Greek church. These rival groups in turn competed with Italian and Slovene missionaries from the dioceses of Friuli and Aquileia.

The inclination of King Géza was toward the German form of Christianity, for he feared Byzantine menace more than German pressure. Political interest, not religious "conversion," was the primary motive which inspired the marriage of the King's son Stephen to Gisela, a daughter of Duke Henry of Bavaria, with the result that many German notables swarmed into Hungary and soon came to form an influential party at the Magyar court, to the resentment of the Magyar nobles who looked with distrust upon this alien racial and religious intrusion.

But in spite of this opposition Stephen, who became king in 995, was favorable to German immigration into his kingdom, as his father had been before him. His attitude is seen in the advice he gave his son: "Hold the 'guests' [hospites] in honor, for they bring foreign learning and arms into the country. They are an ornament and a protection to the throne. For a kingdom of one language and manner of life is weak and easily destroyed." The first Christian King of Hungary modeled his administrative system after that of feudal Germany, and, in spite of hostility between the two governments and the two races, promoted the settlement of German colonists not only on the crown lands, but also on the lands of the nobles and clergy.[1]

[1] K. Schünemann, *Die Deutschen in Ungarn bis zum 12. Jahrhundert* (1923).

Abstractly considered, one may applaud the intelligence and liberality of this policy of the Magyar King in thus endeavoring to elevate the condition of his country and people by borrowing from the higher German civilization. But the policy carried with it the possibility of political reduction of Hungary to German vassalage, and evidence of strong anti-German feeling soon became manifest in the kingdom.

After the death of King Stephen, Hungary became torn by a strife between two factions: the one a pagan, national party; the other a Christian and pro-German party—a struggle in which control of the crown was the objective of each. The former was led by a pretender named Aba; the latter was represented by King Peter. In the issue, while Christianity triumphed, fortunately the Magyar nation was too vigorous to succumb to German pressure, and was able to preserve its independence and the genius of its people.

The illusions which once were cherished as to the antiquity of the early chronicles of Hungary have been dissipated by modern criticism[1] so that one is compelled to rely for information upon the sources of peoples neighbor to them, Germans, Poles, and Byzantine Greeks. One of the oldest accounts of Hungary and the Hungarians is to be found in the *Vita major* and the *Vita minor* of King Stephen (d. 1038), which were written after the canonization of that King by Benedict IX (d. 1044). Of these two sources the *Vita major* is the older. An additional source is the *Monita*[2] or book of instructions which this first Christian king drew up for his son and intended successor, Emerich, who, however, died before his father.

All three of these works were written by German monks dwelling in German monasteries established in Hungary in the years following the official recognition of Christianity by King Stephen in the year 1000.[3] They reflect German his-

---

[1] For example, the "Anonymi Belae regis notarii Gesta Hungarorum" (ed. Endlicher), *Rerum Hungar. mon. Arpad.*, I, 15–54, is now known to be of twelfth-century authorship at least, and not improbably of thirteenth.

[2] Migne, *Pat. Lat.*, CLI, 1234 f. Stephen's laws are in the same volume, cols. 1243 f., or *MGH. SS.* XI, 229–38.

[3] See the long critical dissertations upon these sources by Kaindl, *Archiv f. österr. Gesch.* (1894–1902); Heinemann, *Neues Archiv*, XIII, 63 f.; Steinacker, *Mitteilungen*, XXIV, 135 f.

torical tradition, e.g., *Regino* and the *Annals of Altaich*, and German sentiment toward the Magyars.[1]

Nevertheless, if we penetrate below the gloss of German prejudice and contempt, we discover the lineaments of a constructive administrative system of both state and church in Hungary. The episcopal system contributed much to the firm administration of the country, while the new monasteries, largely of Cluniac foundation, aided greatly the material and moral culture of the land and people. Administratively the kingdom was divided into counties. The court was organized after the German model. A landed aristocracy soon began to be formed, serfdom was introduced, though there were still many free Magyars. The penal laws were severe, especially upon pagans and heretics, although quite curiously Jews enjoyed greater liberty in Hungary than in Western Europe.

The pro-German, Christian party naturally looked to Germany for support, and Henry III was not slow in giving it. German politics and the interest of the German church were so combined together that German intervention in Hungary or war with the Magyars became chronic, on one pretext or another. In 1042 the Emperor made a formidable expedition into Hungary. He crossed the river Raab with Bavarian and even Bohemian troops, gained a great victory on July 4, captured the golden lance of the pretender Aba, and recovered many German priests and other Germans who had fallen into Aba's hands. At Stuhlweissenburg, King Peter was formally invested with the crown and scepter of Hungary as a German vassal. His first act was to ordain Bavarian law in the country for those of German lineage— a fact which shows that most of the incomers into the kingdom must have been of Bavarian stock.[2]

---

[1] "Barbarica gens Hungarorum" (*Vita minor*, 1); "filii perdicionis et ignorancie, populus rudis et vagus, culturam Dei nesciens, Ungari videlicet et Pannonie patriam inhabitantes" (*Vita major*, 1).

[2] "Illis etiam petentibus concessit rex scita teutonica" (i.e., German law and institutions); cf. Steindorff, *Jahrb.*, I, 211, n. 2. Herim. Aug. (1044), says, "Ungarios petentes lege baioarica donavit," a statement denied by Magyar historians as contradictory to Hungarian sources. For discussion of this moot point see Steindorff, I, 211; II, 452 f.; Waitz, V, 143; Giesebrecht, II, 661; Riezler, *Gesch. Bayerns*, I, 458, n. 3; Fränkel, *Forschungen*, XXIII, 125. Possibly only Christianized Hungarians are meant.

A new native and pagan reaction followed soon upon the withdrawal of the German troops, and again, in 1045, a second German intervention in Hungary took place. This time German suzerainty over Hungary was more formally declared, a process facilitated by lavish distribution of German gold among Peter's following. Pressburg, too, was garrisoned by Bavarian soldiery. The effect of the changed political condition at once was manifested in a great influx of German settlers into the Neumark. Grants of land were also made to German nobles and clergy in Transleithania, notably the gift of a hundred manors around Neusiedler See (significant name!), a big salt lake belonging to the Bishop of Freising.

But the turbulence in Hungary continued for some years yet. In 1047 German relief had again to be sent to the Christian-German party in Hungary, where, owing to the death of King Peter, a new pagan and nationalistic reaction was begun. His successor, Andreas (1047–61), attempted to reconcile the two hostile factions, and to avoid the religious issue by uniting them together in a common opposition to the growth of German ascendancy in the country. In 1051 Pressburg was captured by the Magyars, after a heroic resistance by the Bavarian garrison. Accordingly, in that same summer, for the third time Henry III invaded Hungary with a larger army than ever before, in which were Bavarians, Swabians, Franconians, Saxons, Burgundians, and even Lombards from Italy, and Slavonic troops from beyond the Elbe. Bishop Gebhard of Regensburg and Duke Welf of Bavaria were conspicuous leaders of the expedition. Immense supplies were floated down the Danube for the maintenance of the army.

In spite of the difficult nature of the country and the fact that his supplies threatened to fail, the Emperor pressed on. Relief for Hungary, which seemed likely to be crushed by this formidable host, came from a new and unexpected quarter. At this juncture the papacy was just beginning to unveil its programme of ecclesiastical reform and church ascendancy over imperial authority, although the clerically minded Emperor failed to read the signs thereof. The identification of the papacy with the radical wing of the Cluniac party had lately been effected, and Rome, anticipating the coming struggle, in order to weaken the imperial power began that policy of relaxing the German grip upon the subjugated border nations. It was an adroit stroke. For it simultaneously curtailed the imperial power and bound the newly converted border peoples closely to Rome, which posed as the protector of Bohemian, Polish, and Magyar liberty against German domination. The enormous historical significance of this course is apparent, and in the case of the Poles and the Hungarians explains their intense Catholicism even to this day. Hungary was saved from terrible punishment, perhaps even from destruction by Germany, through the intervention of Leo IX.

The clement policy of Henry III at this time undoubtedly weakened the imperial prestige. The anger of the German feudality at being thus balked of what they regarded as theirs by right of might was great. For their hearts had been set upon the spoliation of Hungary. Duke Conrad of Bavaria and Welf III, duke of Carinthia, were furious. Indeed, Bavarian disaffection at this time is the root, perhaps, of Guelf hostility toward the Salian house from this time forth.[1]

One of the things which a modern historian must guard against in studying medieval history is the error—for it would be an error—of translating later national antagonisms back into the feudal age. It is doubtful whether the hostility of the Germans as a race was greater toward the un-German peoples along the border than was the internal animosity of Frank, Saxon, Swabian, Bavarian, toward one another. Race and national feeling played a much less important part in the high Middle Ages than is usually supposed. The German border abounded with renegades from their own country and kindred, whose desertion is treated with astonishing condonation by the chroniclers. The Saxon clerk, Widukind, has no

---

[1] *Annales Altahenses maj.* (1053); Herim. Aug. (1053). Nitzsch makes much of the importance of this event. The famine at this time prevailing in Bavaria led to the flight of whole villages of peasantry, many of whom must have flowed over the frontier, "Vini frugum maxima penuria in tota pene grassabatur Baioria. Quapropter colono fugiente plurimi vici deserti remansere." *MGH.*, SS. V, 133; Curschmann, *Hungersnöte im Mittelalter*, p. 119.

word of reproach for Wichmann, who, because Otto the Great
preferred his brother, deserted to the Slavs and waged
guerilla strife with his own countrymen.

In harmony with the good old German precedent of
deserting to the enemy for revenge, Conrad, with a large
number of fellow-malcontents, now joined Andreas of Hungary, who gave the renegades a warm welcome. United, a
force of Magyars and Bavarians invaded the March of
Carinthia (it had been detached from the duchy of that name
in 1035 and became the later Steiermark or Styria, which by
this time had become fairly well populated by German settlers, although we know little about the process of this
colonization), devastated the new settlements and captured
Hengstburg on the river Mur, a northern affluent of the
Drave, which the Hungarian King at once fortified.

The folly of the enterprise became apparent within a year.
The Hungarian garrison in Hengstburg, worn out by the incessant attacks of the German population, evacuated the
stronghold and fled to Hungary. The Emperor, seizing upon
the incident as a pretext, while he nominally placed his infant son in the duchy of Bavaria as duke, practically incorporated Bavaria with the royal domain. As for Carinthia,
a new history began for it with the accession of the house of
Eppenstein. Andreas of Hungary compounded in the end for
the ravaging of Styria. But for several years the Austro-
Hungarian border was infested with border ruffians, the leaders being the outlaw Conrad and Chuon, the luckless Hungarian commander in Hengstburg, whom King Andreas
proscribed.

In 1058 an attempt to establish a firm peace between Germany and Hungary was made by the betrothal of the Magyar
prince Salomon and Judith, daughter of Henry III. But the
time was not yet ripe for so intimate a relation. The national
party rose in opposition under the leadership of Andreas'
brother Béla. A German commission composed of Eppo of
Naumburg, Margrave William of Meissen, and Duke Ernest
of Bavaria was sent into Hungary. The appearance of this
embassy, instead of ameliorating the situation, poured oil
upon the flames.

The events which immediately followed (1060) have an almost Homeric quality of action and of courage. Andreas, as the chronicler says, "feeling that he would be safer in foreign territory than in his own country," endeavored to escape into the Austrian March with his wife Anastasia, who was a daughter of the Russian Duke of Kiev, but was intercepted by forces of Béla in the narrow defile of Theben, the famous gateway into Hungary where the river March falls into the Danube, a river for centuries the boundary between Austria and Hungary. Andreas was taken alive, but was almost instantly killed in a charge of the Magyar horse. The Queen, with her son and the royal treasure, escaped, and found refuge in the monastery of Melk. But all three of the German ambassadors were captured.

Nevertheless, in spite of the rout, the honors of the day were with the Germans. For Margrave William of Meissen and a Bavarian count palatine named Poto put up such a fierce resistance that if feudal Germany at this time had been as sensitive to romance as was France, the memory of their feat of arms would have rung down the ages in a medieval German *chanson*. "For these two," run the *Annals of Altenheim*, "when the others were slain took their stand upon a knoll and laid about them with such slaughter that the deeds of the very bravest men of former times seem small in comparison. From evening until sunrise they fought, nor could they be overcome even by the thousands (?) against them. They would not surrender until king Béla's word of honour to spare them was given." Ever afterward Poto was known as "the Brave." The chronicler Ekkehard, forty years later, wrote of him: "Truly was he believed to be sprung from the race of the giants of old."[1] So impressed was King Béla with

---

[1] Ekkehard Uraugiensis, *Chron.* (1104), SS. VI, 225. The memory of this famous day lived long in German song. In *Vita Bennonis II, episcopi Osnabrugensis* (written between 1090 and 1100), there is a most interesting allusion to it: ". . . . adhuc notae fabulae attestari solent et cantilenae vulgares." Cf. Hauck, *Kirchengesch. Deutschlands*, IV, 486, and n. 1. That Germany in the twelfth century was feeling the lilt of song within her breast is evidenced by a collection of songs composed in the Rhinelands, and recently edited by Karl Breul under the misleading title: *The Cambridge Songs. A Goliard's Song Book of the XIth century* (University Press, 1915). For the collection is manifestly of German origin, and nothing but the circumstance that it reposes in the Cambridge University Library justifies the

the prowess of Margrave William that he offered him his daughter Sophia in marriage. But fate intervened. The Margrave returned to Thuringia and prepared to remove permanently to Hungary *cum magna opum suarum ostentatione*, when he was taken suddenly ill and died. The Princess married Udalric, margrave of Carinthia, instead.

The expulsion of all Germans in Hungary, including Princess Judith and her young husband, followed this reverse. The new Magyar king, Béla, tried to avert a German retaliatory expedition by alleging that they had fled voluntarily, and disavowing responsibility for the exile of German subjects in Hungary, who were represented as quitting the country of their own accord. War ensued in the summer of 1063. A large German army invaded Hungary. Béla suddenly died and his son Géza became a fugitive in Poland. The pro-German and pro-Christian party in Hungary triumphed. Young Salomon, now practically a protégé of the German crown, was carried to Stuhlweissenburg and crowned king.

For eleven years the Christian-German party ruled in Hungary. But in 1074 the exiled Géza returned, and the national party triumphed. Emperor Henry IV had just taken the government into his own hands after the disastrous regency of his early youth; the Saxons were on the point of rebellion, and already the papal policy, though masked, was apparent. Henry IV's expedition against Hungary accomplished nothing except to rescue his sister and her husband.

But if German ascendancy beyond the Leitha was checked by these events, nevertheless the Hungarian wars had strengthened the Babenberger house in Austria. Margrave

---

title. No. 12 is a song in honor of the three Ottos, and especially a laudation of the great Hunnenschlacht in 955; Nos. 13, 14, and 17 are complaints upon the death of Henry II and Conrad II; two are songs in honor of Henry III (Nos. 15 and 16); and, finally, Nos. 19 and 20 are songs in honor of Heribert, archbishop of Cologne (999–1021), and Poppo of Trier (1016–47). With these evidences we may associate the interesting statement in Widukind, I, 23, of how, in his day, the memory of a great fight around the Ehresburg between the Saxons and the Franks two hundred years before was still commemorated in song and story: "Adhuc sermo in ore ejus erat, et ecce Saxones ei occurrerunt miliario uno ab urbe, et inito certamine, tanta caede Francis multati sunt, ut a mimis declamaretur, etc." Indeed, "mimi, joculatores, histriones," are often mentioned in the sources of the ninth and tenth centuries (cf. *Epistola Ermenrici Augiensis*, SS. II, 101, n. 39).

Adalbert (d. 1055) and his son Ernest (1067–74) were lavish-
ly rewarded by Henry III and Henry IV, who saw the means
not only to guard the frontier but also to check the hostility
of Bavaria in the formation of a powerful Austria. Adalbert
had received enormous grants of land from Henry III;
Henry IV described Ernest of Austria as "our true knight,"
and rewarded his fidelity by the gift of forty manors in the
forest of the Raab.

The progress of German culture in the southeast during
this period is no less important than the political development. By the time of Henry IV, under the able administration of Bishop Altmann of Passau (1065–91), this portion of
the Danubian lands had begun to lose the shaggy frontier
aspect of a border diocese, and to acquire some of the material
amenities at least of that civilization which might be enjoyed in older Germany.

The *Vita* of the Bishop casts interesting light upon this
change. A native of Westphalia and educated at Paderborn,
in his time the most distinguished school in Saxony, Altmann
had become chaplain of Henry III at the court in Goslar, *ad
radicem montis Ramisberc de quo argentum tollitur*. In 1065,
when the wave of pilgrimages to the Holy Land was at its
height, Altmann joined the huge pilgrim host led by Gunther
of Bamberg. In Syria he, with the whole body of travelers,
narrowly escaped capture by the Turks. Shortly after his return from the East, the see of Passau became vacant and,
through Bamberg influence (for it was the favorite bishopric
of the Salian emperors), Altmann was made bishop of
Passau.

He was an enthusiastic supporter of the Cluny reform,
and thoroughly purged the monasteries in his diocese, notably
St. Hippolytus and Kremsmünster, of licentious and simoniacal monks. His labors for the material improvement of the
church in the Passauer bishopric were no less active. He
found the churches made of wood, he left them stone; he
found them devoid of decoration and without books, he left
them embellished with pictures and ornaments and equipped
with libraries. Apparently, judging from the relation of his
enthusiastic biographer, Altmann must have imported

marble columns, and possibly even expert Italian workmen, into Bavaria, for it is hardly conceivable that the elaborate decorative work he accomplished could have been done by native German artisans.

In the field of politics Altmann seems to have been no less efficient. His influence won over the Margrave Leopold (1075–96) from the imperial to the papal side during the war of investiture, and, although Henry IV made a foray into the March, ejected Altmann, and "made the see of Passau the see of Satan," the King was unable to extend his power over the Austrian March.

Of the influence of these vicissitudes, both the German-Hungarian wars and the war of investiture, upon the extension of German colonization farther down the Danube, it is difficult to say much that is particular. It would seem that the anarchy in Germany during the reign of Henry IV must have led to an exodus from the older provinces of the kingdom, where the conflict was most fiercely waged, into the newer lands of Austria. We know that this was the case in the northeast. Why not also in the southeast? It is not mere inference that colonization of the Austrian lands was stimulated by the events of Henry IV's reign. For in the next century one finds a surprising number of new German communities established there. In the narrow border strip between the Fischa and the Leitha, the territory of which had been so bitter a ground of feud between Germans and Magyars earlier in the century, we find German domination rooted and firm. The exiled Salomon here ruled like a king of Yvetot over a toy "kingdom," and was lavish in making grants to the Bavarian bishops, especially to Freising, out of his domains.

Further tangible evidence of German extension in the Mark is found in the charters of the monasteries. The colonizing activities of the bishops and abbots in Austria, in Styria, in Carinthia, in the late eleventh and through the twelfth century, were very great. The multiplication of German place-names shows it. This progress of German colonization was no less energetic north of the Danube. German and Bohemian backwoodsmen clashed in the great Böhmerwald, where their spheres of settlement met. This is the time when Melk, Klosterneuburg, Heiligenkreuz, Lilienfeld, St. Maria Zell, Zwettl, Seitenstetten, Geras, and other abbeys began to grow rich and fat on gifts of land. At the same time families of the high feudality like the Ebersberg, the Falkstein, the Schala-Burghausen, the Bogner, the Plaien-Peilstein, the Sulzbach, who naturally brought with them a crowd of colonists, free and serf, began to rise. Some of these families probably drifted into the middle Danube lands from old Germany as the result of German participation in the Second and Third Crusades.

Naturally, the Bavarian sees, Salzburg, Passau, and Regensburg, which formed the frontal line of the church in the southeast, played the largest part in this process of colonization. But the work of Bamberg in this field is a notable one. Bamberg was the favorite bishopric of the Salian dynasty, and had been originally founded by Henry II in 1007 as a mission station among the Slavs of the upper Main. The tradition thus attached to its origin soon made Bamberg a radiant point for the extension of German influence in all the border lands, both northeast and southeast. The bishops of Bamberg long regarded the promotion of missionary work among the Slavs as the peculiar duty of their see.

The history of the splendid labors of Otto of Bamberg in the conversion of Pomerania early in the twelfth century is one of the brightest pages of medieval ecclesiastical history. But in the eleventh century Bamberg's missionary zeal was especially directed toward the southeast.

Bamberg, however, did not attempt to compete with the Bavarian bishoprics in the Danube lands proper. She left these regions free to Salzburg, Passau, and Regensburg. Her special mission was to the Slavs, not to German settlers in the Austrian Mark and its dependencies. Bamberg missionaries lived and labored particularly among the Slavs of Carinthia. The effect was to bring numbers of German colonists from Franconia, and even the middle Rhinelands, down into this remote corner of Central Europe, like the Eppenstein, the Sponheim-Ortenburg, the Herren von Hennburg, the Karlsberg, the Anstein, etc.—almost all Frankish names. In a word, while the German basis of the population of Austria was Bavarian, that of Carinthia was of Frankish origin.

In like manner Freising, too, marked out a sphere of missionary activity among the Slavs of the southeast. For Freising, finding herself blocked of direct eastern extension by Salzburg and Passau, executed a flank movement, so to speak, around them and found an exit for her colonizing impulses down the Save River, in a field which she made peculiarly her own in Carniola (Krain). The detachment of Krain from Carinthia in 1040, and its erection into a separate Mark, was partly influenced by military consideration, and partly by the historical difference between the German colonization of the two regions.[1] Here, as elsewhere, the colonization was predominantly aristocratic, and made by noble Bavarian families like the Herren von Hoflein, Stein, Hertenberg, Reydeck, Rabensberg, etc., though the presence of a few families of Swabian origin is discernible, like the Auersperg, Osterberg, and Gallenberg.

A unique and puzzling German settlement in this province is the little German *enclave* of Gottschee in Carniola, southeast of Laibach. The place of origin of the original settlers of this community is unknown. It is first mentioned in 1347, when Bavarian colonists from the Ortenburgen pushed into the region, then described as a wilderness, and found there already an islet of German population in a lake of Slav blood. Some scholars have thought that possibly this strange, isolated German group in Gottschee may have been descended from original Germans of the *Völkerwanderung*, who by accident got caught in a "backwash" of the current of the German nations then drifting westward and south and down into the Roman Empire.

The Slav population found by these German incomers in Carinthia, Carniola, and Styria (Steiermark) was less driven out than depressed, as was the case also in the northeast, in

---

[1] See, on this, Krones, "Die Markgrafen von Steiermark: Ihre Anfänge, ihr Verwandtschaftskreis und ihre Kärntner Markgrafschaft vor 1122," *Archiv f. österr. Gesch.*, LXXXIV, 137 f.; Dopsch, "Die Kärnten-Krainer Frage und die Territorialpolitik der ersten Habsburger," *ibid.*, LXXXVII, 1 f.

the Thuringian Mark, in Brandenburg, Mecklenburg, and Pomerania. Unfortunately, such full and vivid chronicles as those of Thietmar of Merseburg, Adam of Bremen, and Helmold, which cast so much light upon the history of German colonization in the northeast, are wanting for the history of southeastward German expansion. In partial compensation, however, a considerable body of charters has been preserved, and in the codices and cartularies of the monasteries founded in these lands peopled by the southern Slavs, place-names and family names, both German and Slav, are of frequent occurrence, which often give us clues to larger information. The beginnings of the German colonization of Neumark in 1045, in especial, are clearly revealed in the charters of Henry III.[1]

To sum up: Everywhere in the Danube, Drave, and Save lands the political and social overstratum was German and aristocratic; but the understratum differed. In Austria it was chiefly a German servile peasantry of Bavarian blood. In Carinthia, Carniola, and Styria a German peasant stock of servile condition was settled down side by side with the native Slav peasantry, also of servile condition. The provenience of these settlers differed. Carinthia and Styria (which was separated from Carinthia in 1035) were mainly colonized by Franconians and Rhinelanders; Carniola mainly by Bavarians, but with some Swabians.

The colonial nature of the history of all these provinces of the southeast, in what may be termed the "Austrian complex," was stamped upon their physical appearance and upon their institutional organization. That organization was simple and hard. For generations the people in these regions had wrought their way through enormous forests; they had faced savage beasts and hostile foes; they had had to build blockhouses, to fortify islands, to clear the woods. The wilderness put its seal upon the people. Life was rude and crude.

The administrative development was in harmony with this stern environment. It was intensely military and more centralized than in the older parts of Germany. The land was

[1] See Steindorff, *Heinrich III*, I, 235 f.; Giesebrecht, *Kaiserzeit* (5th ed.), II, 653.

not divided into *Gaue*, that immemorial local administrative unit of the German folk. Nothing so civil as that obtained. It is true that the word *Gau* appears as an alternative to *pagus*, but the *pagi* in the Danubian provinces were primarily military *cadres*. The word had a military not a civil meaning; and all the other similar terms, as *regio* and *provincia*, have the same connotation. Again, the political authority of the high clergy, which played so large a part in the history of old, feudal Germany, was not nearly so powerful in these new lands. No bishop, no abbot, exercised a sway comparable to that possessed by the Rhenish bishops or the abbots of ancient monasteries like St. Gall, Fulda, and Hersfeld.

Technically, the tenure of the margraves was wholly at the will of the German kings. They were removable like counts. In this position their status differed from that of the dukes whom feudal traditions and tribal consciousness of Bavarians, Swabians, Franks, Saxons, girded around. But practically, at least in Austria, for two hundred years the Ostmark had descended from father to son in the Babenberger house, and what was lost of moral influence owing to the absence of any tribal self-consciousness was compensated for by the centripetal pressure arising from Austria's frontier location and formation.

In theory, all territory won from the Hungarians was held to be imperial land. In fact, it became the Margrave of Austria's own. He consolidated his power within and extended his sway without. The first mention of Vienna as a *civitas* is in 1130; but from the time when Henry Jasomirgott made it the capital of the ancient Ostmark in 1156,[1] Austria was actually a feudal state different in formation from the older feudal duchies of Germany, but quite as independent. But instead of being a political entity in itself like them, Austria was really the center of a system of which, so to speak, it was the sun. Styria, Carinthia, Carniola, and lesser territories like Riedmark, Mark Pettau, and Mark Saunien were a loose complex of which Austria was the core, vaguely

[1] Out of the recorded acts of Henry in Meiller between the years 1156 and his death in 1177, 37 are made in Vienna and 29 elsewhere, chiefly when Henry was in attendance at the diets, or in Italy with Frederick I.

adhering together more by agglomeration than by organic unity. It was adherence, not coherence, which gave the Austrian lands whatever loose unity they possessed. The most active force was external, not internal, and this emanated from Hungary.

The strip of territory between the Fischa and the Leitha, so long in dispute between the margraves and the kings of Hungary, by the end of the eleventh century had become definitely German, and formed a buffer region between the two states. But it was a weak bastion. As long as Pressburg and the Theben Pass were in Hungarian hands, the Ostmark and the Nordgau were insecure. In 1108, when the storm of the war of investiture had nearly spent its fury, Henry V beleaguered Pressburg, but retired discomfited by the prowess of the Magyars and the difficulty of the *terrain*. In 1119 the border warfare was especially fierce. In 1131 the Steiermark was invaded by Hungarian forces, a raid in which the settlements established by the bishops of Salzburg suffered severely. In 1138 an allusion of Otto of Freising shows that Hungarian expansion north of the Danube had spread so far that Poles and Magyars clashed *in silva quae Polonios et Ungarios sejungit*, as already we have seen Bohemians were in border strife with Bavarian pioneers in the Böhmerwald.[1]

A century before the Marchfeld, history had determined that the Leitha was to be and remain the "farthest east" of German expansion. At the time when Frederick I erected Austria into a duchy in 1156 Hungary had recovered from her internecine wars and developed into a strong national kingdom.

Early in the twelfth century a new impulse to German colonization was imparted by the Cistercians whom Leopold of Babenberg, father of the historian Otto of Freising, first introduced into the Austrian lands. It was he who founded the famous cloister of Heiligenkreuz, whose house yet exhibits a statue of the last Babenberger prince.

---

[1] Hasenörhl, *op. cit.*, LXXXII, 444. A *Zollverordnung* of Conrad III shows that by his time a trade route had been cut through the Böhmerwald between Bavaria and Bohemia: ".... licentiam .... mercandi habeant usque ad silvam Boemicam" (*Urkundenbuch des Landes ob der Enns*, II [1852], 54).

The middle of the twelfth century is the high-tide period of German eastward expansion. It is the time of the huge colonizing activities of Adolf of Schauenburg, Albrecht the Bear, and Henry the Lion, when Mecklenburg, Brandenburg, and Pomerania were won to German blood and German culture. The provinces of the middle Danube felt the same force, and part of the current of colonization must have flowed toward the southeast, although we know relatively little about the movement when compared with the information we have concerning the lands across the Elbe. The principal event of this time is the famous settlement of 1156 when Frederick Barbarossa erected the Austrian Mark, which Conrad III had separated from Bavarian dependency in 1142, into the duchy of Austria. This act is both the term of a long process of formation and the point of departure of a new epoch.

The history of the Babenberger house during the century after this date, until its extinction in 1254, is merely an epilogue. The formative period of Austrian history terminated in 1156; the rest was but accretion.

The chief labor of Leopold V (1177–94) was to extinguish the overlordship of the German King in Styria. Fortunately Ottokar IV of Styria was childless and related to the Babenberger house, and whatever chagrin Frederick Barbarossa may have felt had to be concealed. For at this time the Emperor was too deeply involved in Guelf and papal politics to risk arousing a new and formidable opposition north of the Alps. Even though Frederick I had won in the struggle in Saxony with Henry the Lion, he did not want that struggle to be repeated in Austria. Leopold V had the Emperor at the point of his sword, and he knew it. Nothing in feudal law could prevent the Styrian Margrave from willing his allodial lands, his ministerial rights, his advocacies, etc., to his relative; and with these in his possession the Austrian Duke was so intrenched in the Steiermark that he could have defied the imperial ban, if it had been issued. Like his father, Henry VI, too, deemed discretion the better part of valor, and in 1192 formally invested Leopold with the possession of Styria.

This acquisition carried with it an implied claim of the

AUSTRIA UP TO THE HAPSBURG CONQUEST

|||| = Probable limits of the Bavarian   \\\\ = Lands annexed to Austria by
     Ostmark, about 976   Ottocar II of Bohemia
≡ = Conquests of the Babenburg mar-
     graves and dukes

    * = Cities serving as capitals of the Austrian state at various times
    ‡ = Seats of bishoprics

Babenbergers upon Carinthia. For in 1122, when the Eppenstein house in Carinthia died out, their rich possessions had fallen to the margraves of Styria, which now in turn passed to the Duke of Austria. The new ducal house installed in Carinthia by Henry V, the Sponheimer, held the duchy as vassals of the Emperor, it is true; but the Babenbergers had a strong foothold in the territory. Yet they were never able wholly to realize their ambition there. The extinction of the Babenberger house in 1254, and of the Sponheimer family in 1269, left Carinthia open to appropriation by the first comer, and Ottokar of Bohemia temporarily acquired possession, by a bold policy, of Austria, Carinthia, and Carniola during the interregnum.

The accession of Rudolf of Habsburg, however, to the imperial throne in 1273 soon changed the political situation in Southeastern Germany. For when Ottokar fell in the battle of the Marchfeld in 1278, Austria, Styria, Carinthia, and Carniola became Habsburg possessions. Rudolf gave the last two to Meinhard, count of Görz and Tyrol in 1286, thus letting the Slav principalities of the southeastern complex go. It is a pity that the last Habsburgs did not adhere to his wise policy. The history of this angle of Europe would have been different and could not have been worse than it has been in recent years.

CHAPTER XVII

MEDIEVAL GERMAN EXPANSION IN BOHEMIA AND POLAND

THE BOHEMIANS, or Czecho-Slovaks, and the Poles were the only nations of the northern Slavs during the Middle Ages who successfully maintained their national integrity and their national self-consciousness in the face of the enormous German pressure imposed upon them. All the other northern Slavonic tribes of Central Europe, sometimes known as the Elbean or Baltic Slavs, went to ruin like a broken cloud, leaving merely the débris of themselves in the conquered country between the Elbe and the Oder.

But it was not in the nature of things that even the Bohemians and the Poles could retain their ancient racial institutions uninfluenced by contact with Germany. So it came about in the fateful centuries between 800 and 1200 that their religion, their political institutions, their culture, their very blood (that of the Czechs more than that of the Poles), were potently influenced by German attrition and penetration. This permeation of things German, however, was not everywhere either quantitatively or qualitatively in the same proportion. In Silesia, German influence was overwhelming after the twelfth century. In Bohemia, where the process was slower and sometimes not without check or arrest, the spread of German influence continued until the Hussite wars. In Poland the degree of Germanization was never nearly so great as in Silesia and Bohemia. In them all, German colonization was of varying density in different parts of the country. Before the advent of Christianity—that is to say, before the tenth century—the most active German influence was that of commerce and trade.[1]

---

[1] Cf. Waitz, *Deutsche Verfassungsgesch.*, IV, 70–73 and notes, which are very valuable.

In the feudal age, as today, wedged in between the northern and the southern Slavs, lay the Moravians, the Bohemians, and the Poles, whom we may collectively describe as the "central Slavs." Of these three peoples, the Bohemians and the Moravians became of historical importance in the ninth century. The Poles are not mentioned until the tenth. The Moravians were the first to attract the attention of Frankish historians, when their representatives are mentioned as appearing at the diet of Frankfurt in 822.[1]

The process of consolidation of their separate tribal groups seems to have preceded that of the Bohemians; for, when the Moravians first appear in history, they seem to have been a homogeneous people. Perhaps it was the first Moravian duke of whom we have record, Mojmír (830–46), who effected this union, or at least completed the process of fusion. In 831, we learn of *multae legationes Sclavorum* coming to the court of Louis the Pious at Diedenhofen, among whom Moravian chieftains must certainly have been the most prominent personages.[2]

In 855, Emperor Lothar I made a futile expedition against Rastislav, the Moravian duke.[3] Apparently at this season the whole eastern "Middle Border" was in a state of unrest. For two years later a Frankish punitive expedition was sent into Bohemia against Duke Slavitah, son of the former Duke Viztrach, and drove him to find refuge among the Moravians. But Rastislav evidently had no mind to become compromised with the Frank Emperor through giving asylum to the fugitive. In the issue, a brother of Slavitah, whom he had exiled among the Sorbs, was put up as duke in Bohemia by Frankish power.[4] That Rastislav had learned precaution is further evident by his support of Ludwig the German in 866, when the latter's son (Ludwig the Young) unsuccessfully rebelled against his father.

[1] "In quo conventu omnium orientalium Sclavorum [i.e., *Abodritorum*], Soraborum, Wiltzorum, Beheimorum, Moravanorum, etc." (*Annal. Lauriss* [822]).

[2] *Annal. S. Bertin.* (831); Thegan, *Vita Hlud.*, chap. xlvi.

[3] ". . . . . sine victoria rediit. . . . . Magnam tamen provinciae partem praedis et incendiis vastavit exercitus" (*Annal. Ruod. Fuld.* [855]).

[4] *Ibid.* (857). Cf. Dümmler, *Gesch. d. ostfränk. Reiches*, I, 397; Riezler, *Geschichte Bayerns*, I, 209.

In 869, the whole middle border of Germany seems to have been in insurrection. While the Sorbs and Siusli invaded Thuringia, the Bohemians and Moravians, under the first great Moravian leader, Svatopluk, raided the frontier of Bavaria. Three armies were at once put in the field against them: a Thuringian-Saxon army under Ludwig the Young against the Sorbs, a Bavarian army under Karlmann against Svatopluk, and a Frankish-Swabian army under Charles (the Fat) against Rastislav. The collapse of the whole rebellion followed. Rastislav was captured and immured in a monastery, and the territory of Moravia united with the East Frank kingdom by extension of German county (*Gau*) government over it.[1]

But German hold upon the annexed country was precarious. In 871 a new rising of the Moravians occurred, which spread to the Sorbs and other Slavs of the Elbe. A bloody battle was fought on the Waldaha (Vltava or Moldau), where the German army under command of Archbishop Liutbert of Mainz (by the ninth century the art of war had become an important episcopal accomplishment) won a signal victory. Submission and peace were finally made in 874, when legates of Svatopluk appeared at Forchheim. It is of interest to observe that the head of this mission sent by the Moravian Duke was a Venetian priest named John.

The vassalage of Moravia to the German kingdom was established by this settlement, the payment of annual tribute being required. At the same time the Bohemian duke Bořivoj recognized the overlordship of Svatopluk, whose domination now extended over Lusatia, the Sorb land between the upper Elbe and the Saale, Silesia, western Galicia, and lower Pannonia. This whole vast area was put under the ecclesiastical jurisdiction of the Archbishop of Velehrad (Moravia), with two suffragan bishops. "Greater Moravia" under Svatopluk extended along the eastern frontier of Germany, from the middle of the Elbe to the great plain between the Danube

---

[1] Dümmler, *Gesch. d. ostfränk. Reiches*, I, 734; "Ueber die südöstl. Marken unter den Karolingern," *Archiv. f. österr. Geschichtsquellen*, X (1854), 40. The first counts were two brothers, Wilhelm and Engelschalk, from the Ostmark (*Annal. Fuld.* [871]).

and the Theiss. But it was too brittle to endure, and fate was adverse to it. The death of the great Duke in 892, the partition of his territories between three rival sons, and the dread menace of the Magyars wrought its downfall in the last decade of the tenth century.

Yet the greatest factor in the fall of Moravia was not political, but religious, namely, the hostility of the Bavarian clergy. Legend ascribes the introduction of Christianity among the central Slavs—first among the Moravians, later among the Czechs—to the two brothers, Cyril and Methodius, but it is of slender foundation.[1] We have no precise information as to when Christian missionaries first began to labor among the Moravians, though it is almost certain that they came from Regensburg and Passau. But they were not alone and without rivals. For Italian and even Greek missionaries were also there.[2]

As late as 852, Christianity had but slight and insecure hold upon the people of Moravia. Duke Mojmír himself was not a Christian,[3] but did not oppose the missionary work being done in his territory. Privina, Mojmir's vassal duke, who held the territory of present Slovakia, although himself a pagan, aided Archbishop Adalram (821–36) of Salzburg in the erection of a Christian church in his capital city of Nitra, which was completed about 830. It may be believed, however, that this was done more for political than religious reasons.

Between the years 833 and 836, Privina was driven out of his territory by his overlord Mojmír, and took refuge with his neighbor Ratbod, who introduced him to Ludwig the German. Under the influence of the German court, Privina received baptism, and was rewarded later by the gift of a fief in lower Pannonia. Here he built a very strong castle, Moosburg, on the Platten See; and as settlers came in, this place became the oldest town in the region. Evidently, Privina's espousal of the Christian faith paid him well, for in 847, as a

[1] Lippert, *Socialgesch. Böhmens*, I, 131.

[2] Hauck, *Kirchengesch.*, II, 639.

[3] Novotný, *Česke Dějiny*, I, 291, n. 2; Lippert, I, 130 f.

reward for his zeal, Ludwig the German gave him the territory as his hereditary property. Privina's chaplain, Dominic, became famous for his missionary work. In 850, Archbishop Liutpram, in the presence of many Slav nobles, consecrated the first church built at Moosburg, and dedicated it to the honor of the Virgin.[1] Within fifteen years, we are told, lower Pannonia boasted of thirty-two churches, besides several monasteries, like that of Niederaltaich (later acquired by Bavaria), and the bishops of Freising and Salzburg received extensive lands in the region.[2]

Rastislav, who succeeded Mojmír in Moravia in 846, was already a Christian. He was a clear-headed and able man, who saw that if he was to neutralize the continual German penetration, his people must become Christian. He perceived that the German missionaries were tools for the extension of German domination. For these reasons—mainly political, be it observed—he sent (*ca.* 860–61) to Emperor Michael of Byzantium, asking him to dispatch into Moravia some missionaries who knew the Slavonic language.

In response to this invitation, the famous missionary brothers Cyril (his original name was Constantine) and Methodius were sent. Thus the labors of these two blood and spiritual brothers did not begin, but continued, the progress of Christianity, which had already a few years earlier been introduced among the central Slavs. Whether they were actual Greeks or Hellenized Slavs is not certain. They eagerly began the work of evangelization, preaching in the tongue of the people. Cyril, who is said to have invented the Slavonic alphabet, conceived the design of using the vernacular not only in liturgical parts of the service, but even in celebration of the mass.

The enterprise of Cyril and Methodius soon aroused deep resentment among the German clergy, especially that of the bishops of Regensburg and Passau, whose sees were the chief base of German propaganda among the central Slavs. Possibly because of the complaints of these, who regarded the brothers as intruders, if not worse, Cyril and Methodius were

---

[1] Hauck, II, 635. [2] Novotný, I, 314.

summoned to Rome by Pope Nicholas I. But before they reached Rome the Pope was dead (867). His successor, Hadrian II, approved the Slavonic liturgy, and Cyril was elevated to episcopal dignity. He, however, preferred to remain in Rome, and there he died in a monastery in 869. Methodius was then consecrated in his brother's stead. On his way back, he stopped at the court of the Pannonian duke, Kocel, the son of Privina, to whom the Duke seems to have suggested the restoration of the ancient metropolitan see of Sirmium,[1] with himself as archbishop. Accordingly, Methodius returned to Rome with this request, which the Pope readily granted.

But the project aroused bitter opposition among the Bavarian bishops. The Archbishop of Salzburg might have consented to the erection of a Moravian bishopric in a suffragan capacity to his own authority. But an archbishopric in a region formerly under his ecclesiastical jurisdiction, and in which Salzburg possessed many lands, was certain to incur his enmity.[2] Upon his return, Methodius seems to have fallen into the hands of these opponents, who treated him shamefully, and one of whom went so far as to slap him in the face. Hermanrich of Passau would have flogged him with a horse-whip, had he not been restrained by his cooler colleagues.[3] Finally, Methodius was dragged away to Freising, where he spent two and a half years in prison. It was not until the pontificate of John VIII (872) that his case came before the *curia* and was decided in his favor. Adalwin of Salzburg was commanded to reinstate him in his diocese, while Hermanerich of Passau and Anno of Freising were suspended from their offices.

[1] *Ibid.*, I, p. 345.

[2] Hauck, II, 646: "Die Deutschen [Bischöfe] machten Method zum Vorwurf, dass er in ein fremdes Gebiet eingedrungen sei; sie gingen davon aus, dass Pannonien zweifellos einen Theil der Salzburger Diozöse bildete. Method leugnete nicht, dass das Eindringen in einen fremden Sprengel verwerflich sei, aber er leugnete, dass dieser Vorwurf ihn treffe; Pannonien gehöre nicht zur Diözese Salzburg: es hänge von Rom ab; nur aus Ehrgeiz hätten die Salzburger die alten Grenzen ihrer Diozöse überschritten."

[3] For the history of this rivalry between the Slavonic and the Latin liturgy see Lippert, I, 154–57.

The Pope again approved the usage of the Slavonic liturgy and declared Methodius' teaching to be orthodox. Apparently, Methodius had won his long and bitter struggle with the German bishops. But the death of John VIII in 882 ruined everything and secured the triumph of the German church in Moravia. A letter purporting to be from the new pope, Stephen V, but actually a forgery made by Wicking of Passau, and a declared foe of the Moravians, was circulated. This alleged bull forbade the use of the Slav liturgy.

Methodius died in 885, having lived long enough to see the German ruination of his work. The German ecclesiastical "steam-roller" was rapidly rolled over Moravia. Some two hundred priests and deacons were driven out of Moravia, Duke Svatopluk apparently complying or conniving with the suppression because the German clergy condoned his notorious marital irregularities. Most of the exiled priests found refuge among the Bulgarians. But some were sold as slaves to Venetian slave-dealers, and probably ended their career in Mohammedan Egypt.[1]

In 890, Stephen V invited Svatopluk to Rome, but the perilous condition of his country forbade.[2] John IX recreated the archbishopric of Moravia (901), in spite of the opposition of the Bavarian bishops. But the hostility of the German clergy and the act of the Pope were alike useless. For a greater power than either had arisen in the bend of the Danube and the lands of the Theiss. By 896 the Magyars were across the latter river. In 900 Moravia was attacked and compelled to implore German assistance. By 906 the Magyars had overrun the country and the Moravian state disappeared. Down to the end of the tenth century it remained a dependency of Hungary. In 1003 it was conquered by the Poles, and in 1030 acquired by Boleslav I of Bohemia.[3]

The passing of the first and earliest Slavonic state in Central Europe, however, was not without compensation; for, as Moravia declined, Bohemia rose.

The earliest mention of the Bohemians occurs in the seventh century, and has to do with the episodic career of

[1] Novotný, I, 392.   [2] *Annal. Fuld.* (890).
[3] Bretholz, *Archiv f. öster. Gesch.*, Band LXXXI (1895).

Samo. But permanent contact with the Bohemians was not made by the Franks until 788, when Charles the Great erected the Nordgau or Bohemian Mark, with the old fortress of Wogastisburg, which Karl Martel had earlier constructed at the instance of Boniface, as the chief post. The Eger Valley, which nature indicated as the natural avenue of German penetration into Bohemia, was thereby assured to German control.

Frankish annals, however, make no allusion to border warfare at this time. In fact, Bohemia is not again mentioned until 791,[1] when Charles the Great's army touched the edge of the country while returning from the first expedition against the Avars.[2] It was not until 805 that a Frankish army of invasion entered Bohemia in order to "convert" the heathen Czechs. The Bohemian stronghold of Canburg (we do not know its Czech name) was then besieged, but there is no evidence of its capture. For fourteen days the Frankish army plundered and devastated in the thick and almost pathless Bohemian forest.[3] Then it was that Charles the Great founded the famous frontier post of Bremberg on the Nab back of Wogastisburg, which was too exposed, and linked it with the long line of border posts which extended from the mouth of the Elbe to the Danube. Two years afterward, in 807, a capitulary made provision for military service *in partibus Beheim*, and there can be little doubt that Frank domination at this time was extended over Bohemia as far as the Mittelgebirge,[4] whose basaltic peaks rise above the serpentine course of the upper Elbe halfway between Dresden and Prague, where the Pfraumberger Pass afforded ingress into the heart of the country. It seems probable that the Bohemians were at this time reduced to tribute by Charles the Great,[5] and included in the famous partition of the Empire made in 817 by Louis the Pious.[6]

[1] Lippert, I, 129.

[2] Czech pressure upon the Avars at this time is noticed by Einhard, *Annales* (805); cf. Zeuss, p. 740.

[3] Invia et saltus penetrantes (*Ann. Einhardi* [805]).   [4] Lippert, I, 137–38.

[5] Einhard, *Vita Caroli*, 15. According to tradition this was 120 oxen and 500 pounds of silver, the same amount that Břetislav paid in 1040, Lippert, I, 138.

[6] *M. G. H. Leges*, III, 198, sec. 2.

The significant features of Czech history in the ninth century are, first, the establishment of the Bavarian Nordgau in 849, as a bulwark both to guard the German frontier and to confront the Czechs; and, second, the internal hardening of the political structure of Bohemia by the consolidation of the "hrady" into counties, and the development of a national Czech chieftain or duke by the elevation of a single ruler above the various clan leaders. In a word, Bohemia began to cease to be a loose agglomeration of various Czechs stems,[1] and slowly to form a more compact national entity.

The legendary first duke of Bohemia was Přemysl, who is actually no more of a historical personage than the legendary Duke Piast, who is alleged to have founded the earliest ruling dynasty of Poland.[2] We can discern the lineaments of this process of political consolidation long before the result was achieved. In the nature of things, as long as the Bohemians were vassal to the Moravian Duke, independent political formation was slow. "Duke" Bořivoj (ca. 880–85), because he is alleged to have been baptized and thus to have become an instrument of providence for the conversion of the Czechs, is almost as much a figment of pious edification as Přemysl is of later Czech patriotism.[3]

The earliest mention of the introduction of Christianity into Bohemia is that of fourteen Czech nobles, who, on January 13, 845, appeared at Regensburg before King Ludwig the German and requested baptism.[4] No great importance, however, can be attached to this incident, for Christianity hardly began to get a foothold among the Czechs before 895.

We get on firmer ground in this year, when the two sons of Bořivoj, Spytihněv and Vratislav, recognized the German

[1] The *Annal. Fuld.*, 872, give the names of five of these clan chieftains, *cf. Lippert*, I, 143–47.

[2] Lippert, I, 112–19, has critically analyzed this "Premsylsage."

[3] Lippert, I, 145–47. It is pure legend that Cyril and Methodius ever visited Bohemia; Bretholz, *Mitteil d. Inst. f. österr. Gesch.*, XVI, Heft 1, cf. *Revue Hist.* C. 39 (review of Brückner, *Legendy o Cyrylu Metodym*).

[4] *Annal. Ruod. Fuld.*, 845. It is not said that Regensburg was the place. But this may be inferred, for Bohemia was included within the diocese of Regensburg. It is certain that the earliest missionaries in Bohemia came from Regensburg. See Pandler's *Mitteil. d. nordböhmischen Excursions-Clubs*, XVIII, No. 2 (1895).

overlordship of Arnulf at Regensburg, and fell away from the already shattered and doomed Moravian state. When Bohemia thus became a vassal state of Germany, it also entered into the German ecclesiastical system and was incorporated with the diocese of Regensburg.[1] In this double way the door was opened for the entrance of German institutions, German culture, the German church into Bohemia. Spytihněv introduced German priests who used the Latin liturgy, although the older Slavonic liturgy did not become obsolete for nearly two hundred years. It was he who founded the church of St. Peter and St. Paul at Budeč, near Prague. His brother and successor, Vratislav, established the church of St. George at the castle of Prague.

Nevertheless, although professing Christianity and ecclesiastically subject to a German bishop, the Czechs were far from supinely accepting German ascendancy over their country. Arnulf's precaution was well taken in 895 when he reorganized the Bohemian Mark, incorporating the Bavarian Nordgau with it, and intrusting the office of margrave to his nephew Liutpold.[2]

For the next thirty-four years (895–929) the history of Bohemia is very obscure. In the time of Conrad I (911–19) there is evidence of a colonization wave which threw into the Eger region a great number of Germans from the valleys of the Lahn, the Wetter, and the lower Rhine.[3] At the same time a more aggressive German penetration was taking place from the Bavarian angle of approach. Even before the end of the tenth century Bishop Wolfgang of Regensburg had claimed ecclesiastical jurisdiction over this wilderness country as far as the Chub River, where the Bayerischer Wald shaded off into the greater Böhmer Wald. In this huge forest zone Bavarian pioneers, hardy woodsmen, and border farmers clashed with the advance line of Bohemian settlers where

[1] Lippert, I, p. 167; II, 8–9. This arrangement gave great offense to the Bishop of Würzburg, who laid claim to ecclesiastical jurisdiction over the Slavs of the Main, the Sorben, and the Bohemians on the ground of the foundation of his see in 741 as a missionary station among the Slavs (Schafarik, II, 432).

[2] *Annal. Fuld.* (895); Dümmler, II, 392; Riezler, I, 245.

[3] Gradl, *Mitth. d. Ver. f. Gesch. d. Deutschen in Böhmen*, Band XVIII (1880).

the two expanding movements fused their edges in frontier strife.

Church tradition relates that Vratislav's son Václav succeeded his father in 921, but owing to his minority the administration was in the hands of his pious grandmother, "Saint" Ludmila, during whose rule there was a great influx of monks and nuns, who brought in relics and relic worship, psalters, manuscripts, and the moral and material apparatus of the German church. Modern criticism, however, reduces this alleged large growth of Christianity in Bohemia at this time to low proportions.

Yet there is some evidence of development of German influence during these years, although it was not of that pious nature alleged. It was just at this time that Henry the Fowler's (919–36) military reforms in Saxony were being instituted, and his newfangled warriors whetted their teeth in conflict with the Slavs of the middle and upper Elbe as preliminary training for the King's telling campaign against the Magyars in 933. In 929 Henry and his Saxon forces crossed the Elbe and captured Brandenburg. Before the drive had spent its strength, the Saxons had carried their victorious arms up the river as far as Prague and compelled the Bohemians to pay them tribute.[1]

The victorious drive of the Saxons brought to a head in Bohemia the latent opposition which Václav's weak and pietistic policy had created. Feeling ran high against the "foreign" priests in the land. The national party found a leader in the Duke's able brother Boleslav, the first important Czech in history who, in collusion with his mother Drahomiř, it is said, compassed the assassination of Václav. In German annals this act is represented as a bloodthirsty pagan reaction. But it was really anti-German, not anti-Christian.

A German retaliatory expedition soon afterward invaded Bohemia under command of Count Asic of Merseburg. The army was composed of Saxons, Thuringians, Hessians, and some Slav Massubians compelled to military service, and divided into two columns. Boleslav routed the Thuringians,

---

[1] Widukind, I, 35; Lippert, I, 170. Palacký, *Gesch. Böhmens*, I, 232, thinks this the earliest case of tribute.

but was defeated by the Saxons. He rallied his forces, though, and, while the victors were plundering the dead, fell upon them and put them to flight.

Fourteen years of intermittent war followed between the Germans and the Bohemians, under the pressure of which the union of the Czech stems took place and the dukedom became a solid authority.[1] Finally, in 950 Otto the Great came in person into the land and captured Nimburg at the junction of the Elbe and the Medlina, in which Boleslav's son of the same name had taken refuge. Again Bohemia recognized German overlordship and paid tribute.[2]

The long rule of Boleslav I (929–67) is the true period of the formation of Bohemia, but there is no evidence that any German colonization then took place. The most positive German activity in the country at this time seems to have been commercial. These traders, however, really were not Germans, but Jews, who dealt in furs, salt, and especially slaves.

In 971 the Pope authorized the first Bohemian bishopric, that of Prague, which Otto I two years later caused to be erected, not, however, under the jurisdiction of the Bishop of Regensburg, as that prelate had fondly hoped, but under the Archbishop of Mainz.[3] The Emperor was too cautious to permit any political power to pass from Northern to Southern Germany, especially into such a feudal storm center as Bavaria notoriously was.[4] The first bishop of Prague was a Saxon monk from the Benedictine monastery of St. John in Magdeburg, who had lived in Bohemia for a long time and spoke the Czech language. He was not installed until 975 and then the coronation took place at Brumpt in Alsace. At his installation later at Prague in the church of St. Vitus, we are

[1] Lippert, I, 169, 177. The process is evident in Widukind's terminology. He calls Boleslav *rex* and the other Bohemian chiefs *duces*.

[2] Thietmar, *Chronicon*, II, 1; Lippert, I, 173, n. 2.

[3] Spangenberg, "Die Gründung des Bistums Prag," *Hist. Jahrb.*, XXI (1900), 758–73; Schulte, *ibid.*, XXII (1901), 285–97.

[4] Kretschmar, *Hist. Georg.*, p. 433; Lippert, I, 178. This arrangement offended the Archbishop of Magdeburg, who held all the newly established sees in Brandenburg and the Thuringian *Reichsland* under his authority. Perhaps Otto I was afraid of making Magdeburg too powerful.

told that the nobles and the priests chanted in German: "Christe keinado . . . . und die hailigen alle helfuent unse . . . . ," while the common people merely shouted "Krleš."[1]

Twenty years after this event the first monastery was founded in Bohemia, that of Břevnov (993) near Prague. It was richly endowed by Boleslav II. The first monks, twelve in number, are said to have been brought from the mother-monastery of Benedictinism, Monte Cassino, by Bishop Adalbert of Prague, who himself had once been an inmate of it. In 999, just before his death, Boleslav II founded the second Benedictine house in Bohemia, that of St. John on the Ostrov, named from the circumstance that it was situated on an island (*ostrov*) in the Moldau near Davle, south of Prague. This one was filled with monks from Kloster Altaich in Bavaria. The earliest nunnery in Bohemia was that of St. George, established hard by the old chapel of St. George in Prague, the first abbess of which was Boleslav II's youngest daughter, Mlada-Marie.

German influence, with a little Italian admixture, now flowed deeply and rapidly into Bohemia. In addition to things ecclesiastical like relics, missals, manuscripts, etc., a great impulse seems to have been given to trade.[2] The household of the Duke was largely German; Emma, the wife of Boleslav II, was of German birth. The higher and court clergy were German born and German educated. The Duke's own brother, Strachkvas (Christian), was educated in the monastery of St. Emmeran in Regensburg. When Boleslav II was stricken with paralysis he was cared for by Thiddag, a medical monk from Corvey in Westphalia.[3]

It must not be assumed, however, that the political relations between Germany and Bohemia were amicable during these years. German civilization and Christianity were one

[1] See A. Sedláček's article on Bohemia in Otto's *Encyclopaedia*. Novotný explains it by saying that the German chant was used because there was as yet no hymn in the Czech tongue. The later consecration chant "Hospodine pomiluj ny" had not yet been written.

[2] See the documents cited by Lippert, I, 227, which list a long series of articles.

[3] In accordance with Boleslav's wish Thiddag was made the third bishop of Prague, but was so drunken that Boleslav III expelled him, and he sought refuge with Ekkehard of Meissen.

thing, German domination quite another. In 976–77 Otto II made campaigns against Bohemia,[1] and from 985 to 987 there was war between the two states, the rebellion of Bohemia perhaps having been encouraged by the death of Dietrich of the Nordmark and Margrave Rikdag of Thuringia in 985, which relaxed German control of the middle border.[2] The effect was to clamp German overlordship and imposition of the tribute upon Bohemia more heavily than before.[3]

Boleslav II died in 999, and was succeeded by Boleslav III. An insurrection, led by his brother Spytihněv, soon drove him out, together with his mother Judith. It is evident that this rising was motivated by both anti-Christian and anti-German sentiment,[4] combined with the resentment of some of the great families in Bohemia against the ducal house because of its rapidly growing political authority, and who leaned toward German ecclesiasticism as a counterbalance to its increase. One of the most influential of these clans was that of the Slavnik, which Boleslav disposed of by massacre in 995, save a single scion.

This sole survivor was Vojtěch, more famous in history as St. Adalbert (b. 956), the martyred saint of both the Bohemians and the Poles. Adalbert, as we may call him, had been intrusted by his family, who early embraced the Christian faith, to the care of Archbishop Adalbert of Magdeburg, whose name he adopted as his own. In 983 he received orders from Dithmar, bishop of Prague; and in the same year, when Dithmar died, the popular Christian voice in Prague chose Adalbert as the new bishop, in spite of his youth, and he was consecrated by the Archbishop of Mainz on June 29, 983. His asceticism, his intense religious emotionalism, his vigils, so early as this gave him a reputation for sanctity.

---

[1] K. Uhrlirz, *Die Kriegszüge Kaisers Otto II nach Böhmen* (Prague, 1902).

[2] *Annal. Hild.* (985–87); Thietmar, IV, 7–8; *Ann. Necrol. Fuld.* (985), SS. XIII, 205.

[3] Stumpf, No. 942, grant by Otto III, May 1, 990, to the Moritzkirche in Magdeburg of a third of all the tribute "de tota Boemia in qualicunque re sit, sive in auro, sive in argento, vel pecoribus."

[4] Thietmar, V, 23 (15); Loserth, *Mitteil. d. Inst. f. österr. Gesch.*, Band IV, Heft 2 (1883).

For six years, secretly opposed by the Bohemian Duke, Adalbert labored in a diocese still largely pagan. In 989 he went to Rome and asked for papal permission to resign his see and to enter the monastery of St. Boniface in Rome. John XV granted his request and he became a monk, together with his brother Gaudentius. But the German primate demanded Adalbert's return to Prague. Again, however, he quitted it for Rome, where he became the most intimate friend of Otto III. For the second time the Archbishop of Mainz demanded Adalbert's return to his abandoned diocese. Obedient to the command of Gregory V, he was preparing to go when news of the murder of his family by Boleslav arrested him. Instead he went to Poland, resolved to become a missionary among the wild pagan peoples bordering upon Poland. The Pope gave him an itinerant episcopal title (*episcopus regionarius*). No Christian priest had yet penetrated among the heathen Prussians, whose ferocity was notorious, and thither he and his brother went.[1]

Duke Boleslav the Brave of Poland gave him a boat and a guard of thirty soldiers, and Adalbert floated down the Vistula River to Danzig, whence he went by sea to Samland. At Romowe, now Fischhausen, near Königsberg, he was murdered (April 23, 997). His two companions, having been spared for the moment, made their escape to Poland. Boleslav the Brave recovered Adalbert's remains and removed them to the church of Our Lady in Posen. Thither in the year 1000 came Otto III to do reverence to the memory of his friend.[2]

In Bohemia the insurrection of Spytihněv and the expulsion of Boleslav III and his mother Judith coincided with this event, and an imputation of paganism, or at least of pagan sympathies, rested upon the Bohemian Duke. Moreover, the

[1] Thietmar, VII (VI), 58 (35). Thietmar had a relative and intimate friend named Bruno, son of Count Bruno of Querfurt, who perished as a missionary among the Prussians in 1009, together with eighteen companions.

[2] *Ann. Qued.* (1000); Thietmar, IV, 44 (28), 45; Gregorovius, *Rome in the Middle Ages*, III, 415–16; Zharski, *Die Slavenkriege zur Zeit Ottos III und dessen Pilgerfahrt nach Gnesen;* Zeissberg, "Über die Zusammenkunft Ottos III mit Herzog Boleslav von Polen zu Gnesen," *Ztschft. f. d. österr. Gymn.*, XVIII (1867), 313–48.

anti-German nature of the movement was unmistakable. The Emperor took prompt action. Upon his return from Italy in 1004 a great flotilla of boats was collected at Merseburg to carry munitions and supplies, and a mixed army of Saxons, East Franks, Bavarians, invaded Bohemia via the upper Elbe River, which gave entrance into the heart of the country. Saaz, Vyšehrad, and finally Prague were taken. The rebel Bohemian Duke fled into the wilds of the Erzgebirge and disappeared from history. On its return the German army, in spite of fatigue and hunger, reconquered upper Lusatia from Poland.

The next two dukes of Bohemia, Jaromír and Oldřich (1004–37), were mere puppets of the German crown. The Czech people still lacked sufficient coherence and compactness to resist German influence. In 1032 the Duke refused to come to Merseburg to do homage to Conrad II, but an expedition soon brought him to reason. Balked of expansion westward (for although Czechs and Bavarians clashed in the Boehmer Wald the German eastern frontier was too hard to be pierced), the Bohemian Duke turned instead upon Poland. Moravia, which Poland had seized from the Magyars, was his first conquest.[1]

The anarchy of Poland after the expulsion of Kasimir was taken advantage of by Břetislav I (1037–55) to seize Silesia and Chrobatia from Poland and to conquer Cracow. But in addition to territory the Bohemian Duke was endeavoring to rehabilitate the stain of having persecuted Adalbert of Prague and indirectly of having superinduced his death among the heathen Prussians. Accordingly, in 1039, the body of Adalbert was forcibly removed by the Bohemians from Gnesen to Prague, where it was interred with magnificent honors. On the strength of his new evidence of zeal, Břetislav asked the Pope to elevate the see of Prague to an archbishopric. But Benedict IX, who was incensed at this bold piece of body-snatching, not only refused to do so, but imposed a penance upon the Bohemian Duke.[2]

[1] Bretholz, *Archiv f. österr. Gesch.*, Band LXXX (1895).

[2] For years historians have had doubts in regard to the reality of this translation of Adalbert's remains, and upon the authenticity of his remains at Prague. The

Břetislav I is the first distinguished ruler of Bohemia. His conquest of Silesia and seizure of Chrobatia from Poland was the realization of that Greater Bohemia of which he and his people dreamed.[1] War always increases one-man power; and Břetislav I saw in successful war not only the means of gratifying Czech ambition, but also of suppressing the authority of those local leaders who inhibited his own power. On the other hand, the German kings looked with resentment and suspicion upon this enlargement of Bohemia, and it was their interest to prevent either the enlargement or the consolidation of the ducal power.

Probably it was this fear of Germany that led Břetislav I, in 1039, to make an alliance with King Peter of Hungary, for both states were apprehensive of the extension of German domination over them. But the experiment was a disastrous one. Emperor Henry III, who had just come to the German throne, was the last man to brook such an arrangement. The result was a formidable campaign against Bohemia and the humiliation of Břetislav I at the diet of Regensburg, where he was compelled to pay the huge sum of 8,000 marks as tribute,[2] to restore Chrobatia to Poland, to permit German garrisons in the military posts which he had built in the Böhmer Wald and the Erzgebirge, to repatriate the captive Poles whom he had taken, and to give hostages for future good behavior.

From this time forth the Bohemian court was thronged

---

life of the saint early became the object of pious legend, and moreover the national patriotism of the Bohemians and Poles has mutilated actual history. But all doubt as to the genuineness of the remains interred at Prague was removed in 1880 when Adalbert's tomb was discovered. See a long article in *Theologisch-praktische Quartal-Schrift*, XXXIII, Heft 3 (1880), 437–69. A copious abstract of this may be read in *RQH*, XXIX (1881), 533–52. The literature on Adalbert is enormous, e.g., H. G. Voigt, *Adalbert von Prag: ein Beitrag zur Gesch. der Kirche und des Mönchtums* (1898); and his "Der Missionversuch Adalberts von Prag," *Altpreuss. Monatsschrift*, XXXVIII (1901), 317–97; Lohmeyer, "St. Adalbert, Bischof von Prag," *Zur altpreuss. Gesch.* (Gotha, 1907), 134–79.

[1] "Die Boleslavischen Ideen, die auf die Gründung eines unabhängigen grossslavischen Reiches hinausliefen, hatten in ihm einen fruchtbaren Boden gefunden" (J. Kröger, *Gesch. Böhmens* [from 1041 to 1086]; Leipzig diss. [1880], p. 1).

[2] This tribute was commuted in 1041 to military service of 300 Bohemian knights.

with Germans.[1] The two margraves, Otto of Schweinfurt, of the Nordgau, and Ekkard of Meissen were the Duke's close friends. The former, indeed, was Břetislav's brother-in-law, for the Duke had spectacularly abducted Otto's sister, Judith, from the convent of Schweinfurt, where the lady was being educated. She belonged to one of the oldest and noblest families of Germany, the Babenbergers.

Henceforth, through all the wavering allegiance or hostility of Poland and Hungary in the middle of the eleventh century, Bohemia held fast to Germany. This loyalty must not, however, be wholly attributed to spontaneous wish or to fear of Germany's heavy hand coming down again. The territorial ambition of Poland on his north, and the aggressive policy of the Hungarian kings on his south, made it expedient for the Duke of Bohemia to court German favor. Břetislav's donations to the first Bohemian cloister, Břevnov, and also to St. John-on-the-Island, and the erection of a stone wall around Prague are examples of the influence which German ecclesiastical and secular culture had upon him.[2] When he came to die Břetislav manifested that political judgment which so characterized him. Instead of dividing Bohemia up among his sons and thus perpetuating her weakness, he willed old Bohemia to his eldest son, Spytihněv II (1055–61), the three younger sons holding lands only in appanage.

This settlement soon gave ground for a family feud, and Spytihněv II has been represented by Cosmas as a hater of the Germans, who alleges that he expelled all Germans within three days from Bohemia.[3] It is true that his mother, Judith,

---

[1] "Fidelibus regis ad se vocatis" (Herim. Aug., *Chronicon* [1041]).

[2] Cosmas, I, 12.

[3] *Ibid.*, II, 14. "Prima die, qua intronizatus est, hic magnum et mirabile ac omnibus seculis memorabile fecit hoc sibi memoriale; nam quotquot inventi sunt de gente Teutonica, sive dives sive pauper sive peregrinus, omnes simul in tribus diebus iussit de terra Boemia. . . . ." But this particular passage of Cosmas has for a long time been held in suspicion. Giesebrecht, II, 525, 679, accepts it conditionally, i.e., doubts only that it happened on the day of the coronation; Steindorff, *Heinrich III*, II, 347, accepts it with the reservation: ". . . . ja, wenn man dem Geschichtschreiber Cosmas unbedingt Glauben schenken dürfe. . . . ." Loserth and Bretholz contend that Cosmas cannot be credited here. Novotný, II, 84, also expresses strong doubt as to the accuracy of the passage, and thinks that in this instance Cosmas' strong wish was the father of the statement.

left the country; but the reason for her expulsion is to be found in political complications, not in any anti-German sentiment as such. Cosmas expressly mentions the German abbess of St. Gregory's nunnery as another who was exiled because she had violently protested when Spytihněv demolished a portion of the convent to make room for the palisade he began to erect around Prague. This reputed antagonist of the Germans in Bohemia also drove out Slav monks of Sázava into Hungary and settled the monastery (where the Slavonic liturgy had survived until then) with monks using the Latin liturgy, and under a German abbot. Furthermore, it is certain that numbers of Germans remained in Bohemia; for we find them among the clergy, the traders, and around the court. Spytihněv's wife, Hidda, was related to the powerful German family of Wettin.

The epoch of the war of investiture in Germany decisively fixed the friendly relations between Bohemia and the German kingdom. Henry IV adroitly played off the enmity of Bohemia against the Poles, whose Duke was a strong adherent of the papal cause. In 1080 Duke Břetislav, fighting under the banner of the Emperor, captured the golden lance of the papal counter-king, Rudolf of Swabia, at the battle of Flarchheim. Bohemia's reward for this loyalty came six years later, in 1086, when Henry IV elevated the Duke to the rank of king,[1] but the pope refused to recognize the change. When the Concordat of Worms (1122) concluded the struggle of emperor and pope, the King of Bohemia still retained the old-fashioned sort of control over clerical offices within his kingdom.

The profoundest change in Bohemian life since the introduction of Christianity began just at this time, in the middle of the eleventh century, namely, the influx of German colonists and traders in large numbers. The order and the stages of this movement may be distinguished: first, the trader; second, the monk; third, the farmer in search of cheap land;

---

[1] Cosmas, II, 37; Kröger, *Gesch. Böhmens*, p. 66. The popes refused to recognize this elevation, and Lothar II, partly owing to his conciliatory ecclesiastical policy, partly owing, one may think, to the notorious hatred of the Bohemians by the Saxons (Otto of Freising, *Gesta Frid.*, I, 22), adhered to the same policy. Full royal recognition of Bohemia came in 1158 (*ibid.*, III, 14).

fourth, the miner. This period coincides with the reign of
Břetislav II (1061–92). Commerce was active and of increasing volume. Below the castle of Prague on the Hradčany and
in the Vyšehrad Street, besides the rich Jew slave traders,
there was gathered a medley of various merchants. This also
was the place where the fairs were held. The Prague Fair
shortly became famous and attracted merchants from Germany, France, Italy, Poland, Russia. Many of these remained and settled permanently in Prague, especially Italian
and French traders. But the German group always predomi-
nated, and they formed a compact community near the
church of St. Paul, on the Poříči. Břetislav II granted them
important privileges, notably the right of self-government
under magistrates of their own election, and the right of living
under German law. In course of time this German community filled an entire quarter of Prague.

Vladislav I, who drove out his brother Bořivoj II in 1120,
was a great promoter of monastic colonization in Bohemia.
His most important foundation was the Benedictine abbey of
Kladruby (Ger., *Kladrau*) west of Pilsen, in 1115. This monastery was richly endowed; for the original grant comprised
no less than 25 manors and the lordship of Zbraslav, in addition to small parcels of land scattered far and wide. The abbey was at first organized with Bohemian monks and a Bohemian abbot. But in 1117, perhaps because of pressure from
his German wife, Richenza of Berg, Vladislav I enlarged the
house by the introduction of six monks and six lay brothers
from the Swabian monastery of Zwifalten. These newcomers, who were deeply imbued with the ideas of monastic reform which the abbey of Hirsau espoused (it was the center
for the dissemination of Cluniac ideas in Germany), were
scandalized at the looser life which prevailed at Kladruby,
and also objected against serving under a Bohemian abbot.
Within a year, they left the cloister, telling the King that they
would not return unless these objectionable conditions were
removed.

The main cause of disaffection was soon made manifest.
In 1120 a new colony, which now amounted to twenty members, appeared at Kladruby, and this time the monks brought

along their own abbot, whose name was Wizmannus.[1] The Bohemian abbot had to give way, while the German monks contemptuously tolerated the native brothers. The feud between the factions endured for years. After Wizmann's death, in 1124, and that of King Vladislav in 1125, the German monks chose to leave rather than submit to the rule of a Bohemian abbot. In 1130, however, they returned, bringing with them another German abbot, Berthold, who had gained the favor of the new king. After Berthold's death there was no acute struggle over the election of his successor, for by this time the German members seem to have become more contented.

Although the establishment of the Benedictine monasteries in Bohemia was mostly of foreign (German) origin, yet in course of time the incomers seem to have become adapted to the new and strange environment, and gradually the native Czech element became predominant. The history of Kladruby probably illustrates what happened elsewhere— the antagonism between the two races[2] slowly lost the sharpness of its edge, and the native representation finally rose to be the controlling influence in the monastery.

The Premonstratensian canons and the Cistercian monks followed hard upon the Benedictines. The first Premonstratensian house was established in 1140 at Strahov, near the castle of Prague, and was called Mount Zion. In that year, Prior Eberwin of Steinfeld-am-Rhein arrived, and the next year Abbot Geza came with a colony of German brothers to occupy the new foundation. Within ten years four other houses were established.

The Cistercians founded richly endowed monasteries at Plass, north of Pilsen, Sedlec, Mnichovo Hradiště, and Svaté Pole. That of Plass was colonized by monks from Langheim near Bamberg; Sedlec was settled by Bavarian monks.

There is an episode related as to the way in which the monastery of Želivo was refounded by the Premonstratensians which illustrates the competition of the various

---

[1] Novotný, II, 694.

[2] Ortlieb, *Zwif. Chron.*, chap. i; "quod isdem locus et abbatem et monachos habere de eadem nacione dicebatur"; cf. Novotný, II, 741.

orders for political preferment and for generous donations of land. When Daniel of Prague was elected bishop in 1148 he promised the Premonstratensians of Steinfeld the foundation of Želivo, which was a Benedictine house, and by a trick succeeded in dispossessing the lawful occupants.[1]

Generally speaking, until the end of the twelfth century, German colonization did not penetrate into the mountainous parts of Bohemia.[2] When German occupation of the territory of the Elbean Slavs was at its height, after the Sorben land, Mecklenburg and Pomerania, had been Germanized, the overflow of German settlers from points farther west began to pour over in some volume into Bohemia. The valley of the Eger was the great gateway of ingress for these pioneers. This movement was much aided by the fact that the Sedlec region came into the possession of the margraves of Wohlburg and of Frederick I in the twelfth century; furthermore, the important monastery of Waldsassen, which owned lands in Bohemia, lay right in the heart of the Eger Valley. The first German villages known in Bohemia are those of Penerit and Neudorf (although it is possible that these are two different names for the same locality) and were settled in 1196.

The group identity and provenience of these German settlers in Bohemia may be discerned and their geographical distribution perceived by a careful examination of the map. Broadly speaking, it may be said that Bavarians and Austrians settled in the south, East Franks from the middle Rhine and Main lands in the west, Saxons—almost all of them miners—in the Erzgebirge. But one finds numbers of examples of scattered *enclaves* of Germanic population, like islets surrounded by a pure Czech people.[3]

[1] Novotný, II, p. 836.

[2] Loserth, *Mitth. d. Ver. f. die Deutschen in Böhmen*, Band XXI, Heft III (1883).

[3] See articles by Schmidt, *ibid.*, Band XXXVI, Heft 3; Klimesch, *ibid.*, Band XXVIII (1890); and especially Hauffen, *ibid.*, Band XXXIV (1895). Schmidt has studied the German islet of Stritschitz (*ibid.*), and Simboeck that of Iglau in *Ztschft. d. Ver. f. d. Gesch. Mährens und Schlesiens*, Band VII (1903). Other places lured the German settlers because of the newly discovered silver mines; thus Jihlava (Iglau) on the Moravian border, first named in the contemporary documents in 1227, grew with unexampled rapidity. Later on Kutná Hora (Kuttenberg) became the most

It is necessary, however, to notice that while German colonists penetrated the Bohemian Grenzwald[1] in their restless search for free land, fully as important an inner Slavonic colonization went on also at the same time, by which the Czechs themselves founded new villages, cleared forests, and drained swamps and moors.[2]

Unlike the cases of Brandenburg, Mecklenburg, Pomerania, and Silesia, the Germanization of Bohemia was not so heavy nor were the settlers so evenly distributed throughout the country. The native Czech population never so lost its identity nor was reduced to such subordination as was the case with the Slav population in the Thuringian Mark, in Brandenburg, Mecklenburg, and Pomerania. On the other hand, it is an exaggeration of the self-sufficiency of medieval Bohemia to say that all the usual trades were practiced in Bohemia before the colonial era began, and that the Germans only brought the German miner's skill and German craft guilds,[3] or to argue that medieval Bohemia owed little to German enterprise outside the great towns.

By the end of the twelfth century the economic development of Bohemia had reached such proportions and the population in the more favorable localities had become so dense that now, on account of the steady pressure from the interior of the country toward the frontiers, settlements of colonists who cleared the forest and wrested for themselves enough tillable land to suffice for their needs grew in numbers. Hitherto the great forests encircling the country on all sides and which screened the frontier had been untouched. This was especially true of such border forests as those separating regions inhabited by populations of the same nationality, as was the case with the southwestern frontiers. The region of the ancient Vitorazsko (Weitra), south of Gratzen, lay in Austria at a later date. This territory, at the time with which we are dealing, politically pertained to Bohemia and was

famous of the mining cities. Likewise the origin of the cities of Německý Brod (Deutsch Brod), Krucemburg, Humpolec, and Příbram is connected with the mining industry.

[1] Kötzschke, *Quellen*, etc., Nos. 22, 23, 24, 25, 26, 27, 37, D.
[2] Lippert, I, 107 f.; 273 f.   [3] Novotný, II, 836.

peopled by a Czech population. But because of its remoteness and isolation it was gradually colonized and Germanized by the Austrian house of Künring.

It fell to Soběslav II's lot to be the defender of the rights of this Czech population, which, penetrating from the Bohemian side, came into collision with the German settlers drifting in from Austria. Soběslav was not minded to allow himself to be robbed of a portion of his territory by these squatters and therefore in 1175 asked the Austrian Margrave to surrender the title to the lands thus alienated. The demand met with a refusal, and a protracted conflict ensued, so bitter and so bloody that both the Emperor and the Pope protested. In the end Soběslav lost his throne in Bohemia, and Emperor Frederick Barbarossa seized the opportunity at the diet of Eger to settle the controversy to the advantage of Austria.[1]

In such manner the Germans settled during the thirteenth century the southern, the western, and the eastern frontiers of Bohemia. As an example of a systematic colonization may be cited the case of the monastery of Břevnov, whose Abbot gave the forests of Politz (near the Silesian border) to two German *Vögte*, Pertold and Wickmann, to be cleared and settled.[2] The vicinity of Litoměřice (Leitmeritz) was the first to be settled; the next settlements were those of Ellbogen (near Karlsbad) and at Saaz (on the Eger).[3]

Sometimes a Bohemian village received so many German colonists that it was practically changed into a German settlement, and then even its ancient name was changed. Thus the counts of Bogen, who held much land in the vicinity of the Bohemian forest, colonized the Czech village of Sušice with so many Germans that its name was changed to Schuttenhofen. When the Teutonic Knights received in 1252 the village of Chomútov (near the Erzgebirge; Ger., *Komotau*) they soon Germanized it so completely that a proverb arose: "You

[1] *Ibid.*, II, p. 1054.

[2] For the history of Břevnov *in extenso* see Winter, *Studien und Mitth. aus dem Bened. und Cisterc. Ord.*, Band XVI, Heft 1 (1895), and Schramm's study of the registers of Břevnov, *ibid.*, Band III, Heft 1 (1882).

[3] Palacký, II, 93.

can find people everywhere except at Chomútov, where there
are Germans." Many of these villages were known by two
names: thus Teplice was also known as Weckelsdorf, Skalice
as Langenau, etc. Some Czech village names were frightfully
distorted by this process of Germanization—for instance,
Modlibohov was distorted into the impossible appellation of
Nudelbaum.

Sometimes a Czech village was compelled to change its
ancient character and conform to German practices. The
nobles began to re-survey and to partition anew the lands
appertaining to these villages, and the Czech peasants were
forced to pay rent and to assume all other obligations in the
same fashion as the newer settlers. They were compelled to
do this for fear of being ejected from their ancient holdings in
favor of the German colonists. This process of readjustment
went on throughout the fourteenth century, and was not completed until the beginning of the Hussite wars.

King Václav (Wenceslas) was a great friend of the German colonists, and during his reign Bohemia was started on a
road which would have led to a complete Germanization of
the land. He even went so far as to drive the Czech peasants
—his own distant relatives—out of Stadice, from which the
founder of the Přemyslid dynasty came, and to settle it
with Germans. It is no wonder that with such an example
before their eyes the nobles assiduously followed in his steps.
Both the King and the nobility, when building or rebuilding
a castle (and the land soon bristled with castles,[1] especially
after the Tartar invasion of 1241), would give them such
names as were in vogue in Bavaria and Swabia. Thus Přimda
was changed to Pfrimberg, Zvikov to Klingenberg, Hrádek
to Burglin, Hluboká to Froburg, and Loket to Ellbogen. As
for the new castles, we find Plankenberg (1220), and soon
after that appear Lewenberg, Sternberg, Rysenburg, Rosen-
berg, Winterberg, and Rosenthal (now Rožmitál), so that a
castle with a Czech name soon became a great rarity. This
custom of giving the castles German names continued down
to the fifteenth century.

[1] Building in stone first appears in the twelfth century in Bohemia (Lippert, I,
229–30; 432–33).

The monasteries, those very active centers of Germanizing influence, also did their share in the work of colonization in the thirteenth century, both in Czecho-Slovak and Polish lands. The Premonstratensians had a monastery at Chotěšov (Choteschau, southwest of Pilsen), and the Benedictines a priory at Politz (near the Silesian Glatz), both of which were founded in 1213. A commandery of the Teutonic Knights was instituted at the church of St. Benedict at Prague, and the first Dominican preaching friars were housed at St. Clement's in Prague in 1226. In Moravia, Vladislav Heinrich founded the Cistercian monastery at Velehrad in 1201. That the first monks were Germans is evident from those of their names attached to the charter: the abbot's name was Ticelin, and the names of the monks are Walkun, Eberhard, Gerung, Hartmut, and Pertold—all Germans.[1] They came from the Plass monastery in Bohemia. To these monks the ancient Slavic liturgy and customs savored too much of heathenism, and therefore we find a studied neglect as far as concerns any mention of the ancient glory of Velehrad, where the body of Archbishop Methodius lay. In 1211 a nunnery of the Cistercian Order was founded at Doubravník, and in 1225 the pious Hedwig of Znojmo founded and richly endowed the nunnery at Oslavany (or Marienthal) near Brno. In 1232 the widowed Queen Constance established another cloister at Tišňov, which was called "The Door of Heaven"; in 1251 Boček, the lord of Kunštát and Poděbrady, founded the monastery at Žďár (Saar) on the Bohemian frontier. The Premonstratensians built a monastery at Zabřdovice (Obrowitz) and a nunnery at Nová Říše (Neu-Reisch).

As for the military orders, the Knights of St. John were permitted by Markgrave Vladislav to settle the German colonists anywhere on their lands, and these settlers were exempted from the local (župan) laws and permitted to be governed by their own written law. The main feature of this German right was the fact that the Germans were thus freed from the various local (župan) duties and obligations, such as the upkeep of the fortifications, bridges, and roads, and the

---

[1] Dudik, Dějiny Moravy, VI, 23.

transportation, accommodation, and the boarding of the traveling district or crown officials. Other military orders were introduced into the country in the reign of King Václav I (1230–53). The Templars came in 1232, and twenty years later built the church of St. Lawrence in the old part of Prague; the Hospitalers came to Prague in 1238, and occupied two churches, that of St. Francis on the bridge, and the old German church of St. Peter.

The Dominicans came to Moravia shortly after 1227, as is evident from two bulls of Pope Gregory IX sent to Bishop Robert of Olmütz, who—it is interesting to note in passing—was an Englishman. As early as 1230 there is record of a convent of the Dominicans in Olmütz, and in 1239 in Znojmo, and in 1241 in Brno. The Franciscans, who arrived within the lifetime of the founder of their order, established their first house at Doubravník. Among these begging friars were not only Germans, but also Italians, and we find that they held services in their own language. Both these orders soon became involved in commercial enterprises, and thus interfered with the native interests.

Town-planting also went on apace with colonization during these eventful years of the twelfth and thirteenth centuries. The German colony in Prague, as we have seen, was the oldest, the greatest, and the richest foreign group within the country. Prior to 1203 it was the only important German urban element. All other German settlements in the land were either in rural localities or in the mountainous mining regions. Soběslav II (1173–79) demands special attention because of his very favorable attitude toward the German merchant colony in Prague. It was in his time that this group overflowed its original street and spread over a whole quarter. He not only confirmed the old privileges granted by Břetislav II, but materially extended them.[1] It would be an error, however, to think that Soběslav II so favored the Germans in Prague because of sentiment or attachment. His motives were those of practical advantage, of commercial and econ-

[1] Kötzschke, *Quellen*, No. 32; Lippert, I, 98–99; Werunsky, *Mitth. d. Ver. f. d. Deutschen in Böhmen* (1881).

omic expediency. Thus the Prague colony continued to grow apace. By the time of Otakar I (1198–1230) it occupied almost the whole area of the Old Town, was surrounded by its own wall and moat, and formed a veritable town apart.

The first town in Bohemia to receive Magdeburg law (the basis of most of the municipal law in the country) was Litoměřice, but it is not certain whether this took place in the time of Otakar I or not until the time of Václav I. Then follow Kadaň on the Eger, Hroznětín (1213), Hradec on the Elbe (1225), Kynšperk (1232), Roudnice (1237), etc. Many of these originally were German foundations, but in the course of time a Czech population settled in them and gradually changed the social texture of these towns into that of its own nationality.[1]

The Poles were the latest of the Slav race to emerge into the light of recorded history, their prehistoric history extending almost to the year 1000. Roman and Byzantine historians and geographers knew nothing of the so-called Lekhites. Our knowledge of them is of an archaeological character. The Poles claim a legendary dynast in Piast.[2] But historical Poland only begins dimly to emerge out of the age of myth-making late in the tenth century under the rule of Mieszko of Poznan or Posen (963–92), when German subjugation of the Ljutizi and Milzini, with whom the Poles had affiliation if not affinity, began to fill the Poles with apprehension.[3] This conquest was the achievement of the heroic Margrave Gero, after whom the whole territory between the upper Elbe and the Bober rivers was first called Marca Geronis. Here, too, as in the Sorben Mark, the native Slavonic population was reduced to serfdom.[4] Already as early as 963 we find Mark Lausitz distinguished from the Ostmark, and even a vague

[1] Palacky, II, 93.

[2] Gajsler, *Przegl. Hist.*, Vol. VI (1900), detected an analogy between the legend of St. Germain d'Auxerre and that of Piast, and has shown that each is derived from the same source, which is still unknown. Cf. *Revue hist.*, C, 398.

[3] Widukind, *Rerum gest. Sax.*, III, 68; Thietmar, *Chronicon*, II, 14; Schafarik II, 392.

[4] Ermisch, *Archiv f. sächs. Gesch.*, V, 73 f.

cleavage between upper and lower Lausitz.[1] When the great[2] Margrave died in 865 the middle border was divided by Otto I into several marks, which remained separate or were combined in the years which followed according to the influence of events. But in the fluctuation the Mark Lausitz stands out more and more clearly as the German bulwark against the Poles.

The future German conquest of Silesia is also foreshadowed as early as the reign of Otto I. For German political ambition, German expansive energy, the German colonizing spirit already in the tenth century dreamed of possessing the big tract of Slav land inclosed between the Katzbach, the Glatzer Neisse, and the upper Oder, the most striking feature of whose physiography was Mount Zlenz or Mount Zobten, a rugged mountain twenty-three miles southwest of a still undreamed-of Breslau. At some unknown date in the reign of Otto I a German Burgward was built at Nimptsch on the little river Lohe. Probably the site was originally an important palisaded Slavonic runddorf, like so many other German places in this land.[3] We are ignorant of the German name of this remote Burgward, indeed it may never have had one, but may have been called Nemzi, as it was named by the Slavs.[4]

With a rashness bordering upon foolhardiness German imperialism even coveted possession of the land beyond the Oder. In 979 Margrave Hodo, with the design of compelling the Polish Duke to pay tribute to Germany for the territory between the Oder and the Warthe rivers, made a foolhardy expedition into this region and was badly defeated near

---

[1] Thietmar, *Chronicon*, II, 9.

[2] He is called *magnus* by Widukind, III, 54 and 75; Thietmar, VI, 57; *Annal. Qued.* (1013).

[3] Soehnel, *Schlesiens Vorzeit in Bild und Schrift*, Band VI, Heft I (1894).

[4] It must have been lost by the Germans in 979 though no chronicler records the fact. Thietmar, VIII, 59, is the only historian who records the foundation of Nimptsch, and he is indefinite: ". . . . ad urbem Nemzi eo quod a nostris olim sit condita." The Polish word *niemiec*, Bohemian *nĕmec*, Sorab *nimz*, Russian *niemetz*, all signify one who does not understand the Slav language and hence a foreigner, primarily a German. The usage is exactly similar to German use of the terms *Wend* and *Wälsch*.

Zehden, a Polish village on the right bank of the Oder.[1] But while the Poles were able to resist German military pressure by force of arms, they nevertheless began to succumb to the penetrating influence of the German church. For in 966 Mieszko married Dobravka—*quod Teutonico sermone Bona interpretatur*—a sister of Duke Boleslav II of Bohemia, in whose train the first Christian priests entered Poland.[2] Two years later the bishopric of Poznan was established, whose first incumbent was Jordan, a German.[3]

The great uprising of the Slavs of the Elbe in 983 might have been more compromising than it was to Germany if it had not been for the fortunate fact that the dukes of Bohemia and Poland fell out in 990 in spite of the marriage alliance between them. The former sought the alliance of the recently subjugated Liutizi, whereupon Mieszko appealed to the Germans for assistance. The empress-mother, Theophano, played her hand adroitly. In the upshot Poland recognized German overlordship over the territory between the Oder and the Warthe, and Bohemia was subjected to greater tribute.[4] For the first time in history a Polish duke visited Germany. Mieszko was present at the Easter celebration at Quedlinburg on April 5, 991. Both the clever woman who had brought him to terms and he died soon afterward—the Empress on June 15, 991; Mieszko in the following year.

His successor was his son, Boleslav Chrobry, or "the Brave,"[5] who at first dissembled his conquering ambition, and when the Slavs of the Elbe rebelled in 994, all except the Sorben, he came to the support of Otto III with a joint Polish-Bohemian army,[6] and kept the Ljutizi overawed while

[1] Bruno, *Vita S Adalb.*, chap. x (SS. IV, 598); Thietmar, II, 29; Giesebrecht, *Otto II*, p. 147.

[2] Thietmar, IV, 55.   [3] Schafarik, II, 393.

[4] *Annal. Hildesh.* (990); Thietmar, IV, 9–10; Diploma of Otto III (May 1, 991), in Stumpf, *Regesta*, No. 942, endowing the church of St. Moritz in Magdeburg with a tithe "de tota Boemia in qualicunque re sit, sive in auro, sive in argento vel pecoribus."

[5] Thietmar, V, 23, explains the word literally to mean "potestas exercitus."

[6] "Cum magno exercitu necnon Boemani cum filio alterius Bolizlau" (*Annal. Qued.* [995]).

the Saxon army campaigned in Mecklenburg and the Havel land.[1] But while the young Emperor was away in Italy in the next year (996) the Slavs of the Havel and the irrepressible Ljutizi raided the German frontier settlements and again had to be drubbed into submission by the Westphalian heerban.[2] The Polish Duke shrewdly took advantage of these circumstances and seems coolly to have paid himself for his recent aid by extending his sway across the Oder as far as the Bober River, an extension to which Otto III seems to have acquiesced.[3] Perhaps the young Emperor was influenced by his projected sentimental journey to the tomb of his friend, Adalbert of Prague, who had been murdered while laboring as a missionary among the heathen Prussians, and whose remains had been recovered by Boleslav and were now interred in the cathedral church of Gnesen.

Boleslav Chrobry resolved to utilize the imperial pilgrimage for his own advantage, and persuaded the Emperor to permit the erection of Gnesen to an archbishopric, the Pope's sanction having been previously secured by a promise that Poland would pay Peter's pence to Rome.[4] Breslau, Cracow, and Kolberg (Polish, Kolobrzeg) were put under Gnesen's ecclesiastical jurisdiction.[5] Only the bishopric of Poznan remained still subject to the Archbishop of Magdeburg, to his vast indignation.

The sequel soon showed the cunning of Boleslav Chrobry. Emperor Otto III died in 1002, and in the same year Margrave Ekkehard of Meissen, whose prowess had made him the bulwark of the eastern border of Germany, also died.[6] While the new emperor, Henry II, was engaged in subduing the rebellious margrave Henry of the Bavarian Nordgau, he fell upon the Lausitzer and Milziener Marks—"omnem Gero-

---

[1] Otto III was at Wismar on Sept. 10, at Neustrelitz on Oct. 3, at Havelberg on Oct. 6.

[2] *Annal. Qued.* (997).   [3] Thietmar, IV, 45.

[4] Grünhagen, p. 7.

[5] Stumpf, No. 1213. The date is March 15, 1000.

[6] Thietmar, V, 7 (5), eulogizes him as "decus regni, solatium patriae, comes suis, terror inimicis et per omnia perfectissimus."

nis marcham comitis citra Albim jacentem," wails Thietmar of Merseburg,[1] including Bautzen, Strehla, and Meissen. The whole Thuringian Mark east of the Elbe was lost.[2] The booty was immense. The rugged Bishop of Merseburg whose father had been a soldier in these border lands vents his indignation in no measured words: "God forgive the Emperor," he exclaims, "for ever having elevated Boleslav of Poland after he had once been reduced to tribute."[3] Flushed with this victory the Duke then turned his arms on Moravia, in dispute between Poland and Bohemia, and conquered it.

The Poland of Boleslav Chrobry was a country of formidable but fragile power. It was a country without natural frontiers, whose borders were easy to expand but difficult to retain. The Poles were warlike and brave, but incapable of making solid conquests. Poland's expansion at this time was more due to the weakness or divided state of her neighbors than to Polish prowess and Polish discipline.

But for the time being the militant ambition of Boleslav Chrobry now became a formidable bar to German eastward expansion and a menace to the whole middle border. Moreover, the critical condition of German politics in Italy handicapped Henry II and prevented effective measures against him for years. Fortunately for Germany the Redarii and the Ljutizi remained quiet, although the Milzini joined the Poles. An expedition made in the midst of winter for the purpose of punishing the Milzini and destroying the strongholds which Boleslav Chrobry had erected failed on account of the severity of the weather.[4] But in the next year (1005) Henry II invaded Poland in a devastating raid almost as far as Posen. Yet it was a futile military gesture. For the Poles fell back into their forests and swamps, to emerge in 1007 when the Emperor was in Flanders and deluge the whole part of the Mark beyond the Elbe again with fire and sword.[5] The entire province east of the river was devastated *juxta Magadaburch*, the settlements destroyed, the settlers either slain or taken

---

[1] V, 9.   [2] *Ibid.*, V, 18.   [3] V, 10.

[4] *Annal. Qued.* (1003); Adalboldi, *Vita Heinr.*, chap. xxx (SS. IV, 691).

[5] Thietmar, VI, 33, 34; *Annal. Qued.* (1007).

captive. Only the brave Margrave Hermann of Bautzen held out until succor proved impossible. There was a rude sense of honor in the surrender. The Polish Duke permitted the Margrave, his garrison, and all others within the fortress to return with their possessions, sad but free, to Germany.[1]

For three years the Poles remained unmolested in the conquered territory. A new German campaign in the summer of 1010 was frustrated by heavy rains which inundated the rivers and drowned the land.[2] But Henry II was determined to bring the Poles to terms. In 1012 Lebusa near the confluence of the Warthe with the Oder was converted into a gigantic military base. The stockade was large enough to hold ten thousand men within it, had twelve gates, and was built in two weeks. The Bishop of Merseburg grows so enthusiastic about this camp that he compares it with the camp of Caesar near Dyrrhacium, which shows that the Bishop had read Lucan's *Pharsalia*.[3] How far the Emperor relied upon church contingents is shown by the interesting fact that the Archbishop of Magdeburg and the bishops of Meissen, Halberstadt, Paderborn, Havelberg, Hildesheim, and Zeitz were all called upon for military service. But misfortune befell. Tagino of Magdeburg died on June 9 and his successor Walthard on August 12. Thietmar of Merseburg, the historian, after starting for Lebusa, was forced to return owing to illness. Henry II had not yet joined the army and the host had not entirely gathered, when on August 20 Boleslav Chrobry suddenly stormed Lebusa, slew a thousand of the garrison, and captured more. The Poles gorged themselves with the food and wine found there, divided the plunder, fired the fortress, and retired victoriously.[4] It was the darkest day the middle border had ever seen.

Not content with this success, the ambitious and energetic Boleslav also hatched a design for extension of Polish power

---

[1] "Licentiam hinc exeundi cum omnibus quae habebant . . . . urbem ei reddiderunt tristesque patriam repedebant" (Thietmar, VI, 34).

[2] ". . . . Crebra imbrium inundatione nostri tardarentur" (*ibid.*, VI, 56).

[3] Thietmar, VI, 59.

[4] Thietmar, VII, 20; *Annal. Magdeb.* (SS. XVI, 164).

in Russia. Diplomacy and war were his two agents. By means of the first he had succeeded in betrothing his daughter to the son of Vladimir, grand duke of Kiev, and force of arms was soon to follow. At this moment (1013) the Russian Duke was involved in trouble with the Tartar Petchenegs in the south, with whom Boleslav connived.[1] Accordingly he feigned to desire peace with the Germans, and in February, 1013, sent his son Mieszko II to Magdeburg, *cum magnis muneribus*, with an overture of peace, and later in May himself came to Magdeburg for a conference with the Emperor. Henry II was on the eve of his second Italian campaign, and was only too ready to make terms with Poland,[2] and resigned upper and lower Lausitz to Poland on condition of Polish recognition of German overlordship over the territories. So eager was the Emperor for this diversion of Polish interest away from Germany that he even furnished a contingent of German troops to the Polish Duke.[3]

But the event was soon to prove that "the Poles lied according to their custom."[4] For in 1015 while Henry II, having returned from Italy, was occupied in the western part of his kingdom,[5] Boleslav overran the Thuringian Mark and stormed Meissen. For the time being the Emperor's hands were tied and he could merely send an embassy to protest against the act and demand the restoration of the territory, to which Boleslav haughtily replied that Lausitz pertained to Poland and that he would keep it.[6] A war of two years' duration followed in which Saxon and Bavarian troops, assisted by Bohemian forces, were poured into the east border.[7] Nothing was spared from fire or sword in all the territory between the Elbe and the Bober. The outstanding

---

[1] Thietmar, VII, 31. See also Röpell, *Gesch. Polens*, I, 145; Hirsch, *Jahrb.*, II, 392.

[2] ". . . .Cum benefitio diu desiderato" (Thietmar, *loc. cit.*).

[3] "Nostris ad hoc auxiliantibus" (*ibid.*; cf. Hirsch, *op. cit.*, II, 396).

[4] *Annal. Hild.* (*anno* 1013).   [5] Thietmar, VIII, 9.

[6] *Annal. Qued.* (1015): "Addidit etiam imperator hoc anno legationem mittere ad Boleslavum pro restituendis regionibus quas abstulerat. Ille, ut solebat, superbe respondit se non solum propria retinere velle, quin potius non sua diripere malle."

[7] It is related at length by Thietmar, VIII, 16–24.

event was the siege of Nimptsch by the German forces, which
was unsuccessful owing to an outbreak of pestilence in the
army. At Bautzen in January, 1018, peace between Germany
and Poland was made by the terms of which Poland was to
retain possession of Lausitz, as before, under German suzerainty. The impelling motive of this peace, however, was not
the failure before Nimptsch, but the great Slav and pagan
reaction at this time in Wagria and the Billunger Mark.[1] The
bellicose Boleslav Chrobry now turned his arms against
Russia and sacked Kiev, to the vast enrichment of Cracow.[2]
But in 1025 Boleslav repudiated the terms of Bautzen,
flouted German overlordship over Lausitz, and renewed the
war, even having the hardihood of appeal to the Abodrites
and Wilzi again to rebel.[3] Yet Polish enmity toward Germany was political, not religious.

For in Poland Boleslav Chrobry's policy was favorable to
the church. He tried hard to rid the country of the last vestiges of paganism, and for this reason called foreign monks
into the land. In 997 he brought in a few monks of the rule of
St. Romuald (Camaldulians), whom he settled near Posen.
But they were soon murdered by robbers. The Benedictines
were brought into the country about the year 1006, and were
settled at Sieciechowie in Radomsko, at Miedzyrzeczi, on the
Lysa-Gora at Sandomierz, and at Tyniec upon the Vistula
near Cracow.[4] He transferred the bishopric of Kolobrzeg in
Pomerania to Kruszwice in Poland, erected another bishopric
at Lubush (=Lebus), and finally incorporated the bishopric
of Posen with the archbishopric of Gnesen, and thus consolidated all Polish dioceses under one Polish archbishopric.[5]

Boleslav Chrobry is the true founder of Poland. He en-

---

[1] See Thietmar, IX, 5; Adam of Bremen, II, 40–46; Hirsch, *Heinrich II*, III, 93 f.

[2] According to Thietmar, IX, 32, Kiev had eight markets, which if true attests its commercial importance as a mart between the Baltic and the Black seas and an intermediate between Europe and Constantinople and Baghdad. Cf. Röpell, *Gesch. Polens*, pp. 145 f.; Strahl, *Gesch. d. russischen Staates*, I, 155; Hirsch, *op. cit.*, III, 89.

[3] *Annal. Qued.* (1025); *Annal. Corb.* (1025); Wipo, *Vita Chuonradi*, chap. viii.

[4] Baczynski, *Dzieje Polski*, p. 51.   [5] Tatomir, *Polish History*, p. 16.

larged Poland's frontiers to the edge of the Baltic by overcoming the Pomeranians; he conquered Silesia, Chrobatia,
and Moravia from the Czechs; he wrested Lausitz from the
Germans; he was the first Polish ruler to war against the
Russians. He established bishoprics and monasteries. He
had no fixed capital, dwelling turn by turn at Posen, Cracow,
Plock, and Breslau.

Boleslav Chrobry died in the year 1025 and was succeeded
by his son Mieszko II (1025–34), whose wife Richenza was
German.[1] The new Polish Prince, inspired by his father's
achievements, was ambitious to do no less than conquer the
March of Thuringia for Poland, and in 1028 fell upon the middle border.[2] At this critical juncture Conrad II was in central
Saxony,[3] and lost no time in reaching the imperiled tract.[4]
While a son of Bretislav of Bohemia invaded Moravia (which,
as we have seen, Boleslav Chrobry had wrested from Bohemia
in 1003), and successfully recovered it, a German army advanced through "pathless forests, swamps and deserted
tracts of territory"[5] upon Bautzen, only to beleaguer it in
vain. The German campaign was a dismal failure. The protection of the Saxon Ostmark that winter of 1029–30 was left
to Margrave Thietmar and Count Dietrich of Wettin, while
the Emperor was in the Rhinelands.[6] But unfortunately the
Margarve died early in January, and, taking quick advantage of the event, Mieszko II in the depth of winter fell upon

[1] She was a daughter of the count palatine, Erenfrid (Grünhagen, p. 8), and a
sister of Hermann, archbishop of Cologne (*Ann. Magdeb.* [1034]).

[2] *Annal. Hildesh.* (1028): ". . . . Orientales partes Saxoniae cum valido suorum
exercitu violenter invasit et incendiis ac depraedationibus peractis . . . . etc."

[3] He was at Dortmund on May 24–26 (Stumpf, Nos. 1972–73); at Paderborn
probably in June (*ibid.*, No. 1974); and in Magdeburg on July 1 (*ibid.*, No. 1975).

[4] The charters indicate his continued stay in the east Saxon *pfalzen:* Allstedt,
Aug. 1; Wallhausen, Aug. 20, 23; Imbshausen, in Leinegau, Sept. 11; Pöhlde, Oct.
10 (Stumpf, Nos. 1976–80, 1982–83: Bresslau, *Jahrb.*, I, 254, n. 5). Early in 1029
we find him still there (*Vita Godeh.*, chap. xxxv; *Annal. Hildesh.* [1029]).

[5] . . . . silvis deviis, palustribus desertisque locis (*Annal. Hildesh.* [1029]).

[6] "Imp. nat. dom. Paderbrunnen celebravit [he was there on Dec. 31 (Stumpf,
No. 1998)], peractisque diebus festis ultra Rhenum ire proposuit." He was in Basel,
March 18, in Ingelheim the first week of April where he celebrated Easter (Wipo,
Vita Chuonradi, chap. xxv; Bresslau, I, 286, n. 1).

the Middle Border with appalling devastation. A hundred towns and villages were fired and destroyed and ten thousand captives carried away.[1] The work of years of German expansion and colonization was undone by one fell stroke. It was not until the next century that the damage was fully repaired.[2]

But Conrad II was made of sterner stuff than his predecessor. Realizing that the situation on the Polish border was an acute one, and not comparable in importance to that in Austria, he made peace (1031) with the Hungarians by yielding the territory between the Fischa and the Leitha to King Stephen of Hungary in order to have a free hand against Poland.[3] In the autumn of the year he drove the Poles out of Nieder Lausitz, and followed up this stroke by a crushing campaign in the next summer. The cards were in the Emperor's hands, for Mieszko II and his brother Otto— the German name is interesting—were at odds, the latter apparently being opposed to the Polish Duke's hostility toward Germany. Driven from Poland into Russia, the fugitive Otto made his way into Germany, where the Emperor welcomed him. The Thuringian Mark and Lausitz were cleared of the invading Poles, and in his turn Mieszko II became a fugitive.

Then followed the first partition of Poland. Lower Lausitz was given to Conrad of Wettin, with whom the particular history of the future great Wettiner house begins; Upper Lausitz was attached to the Mark of Meissen, and the residue of the territory given to Otto as duke under German overlordship. Otto was soon murdered by an unknown assassin, and Mieszko II, whose spirit adversity had now broken, returned to Poland whence he despatched emissaries to Conrad II saying that he would abide by the condition of Polish vassalage to Germany.[4]

[1] *Annal. Magdeb.* (1030); Bresslau, I, 291.

[2] Hauck, IV, 558.

[3] Wipo, *Vita Chuonradi*, chap. xxvi; *Annal. Hildesh.* (1031); *Annal. Altah.* (1033); in error for 1031.

[4] Wipo, *op. cit.*, chap. xxix; *Herim. Aug.* (1032); *Annal. Ratisb.* (1032); Bresslau, II, 481 f.

In 1034 the Polish Duke died, and his son Casimir succeeded him. The event was followed by a simultaneous Polish national, anti-German, and pagan reaction against German ascendancy and influence.[1] The three motives were combined, or rather confused. If it had not been that Christianity in Poland was represented by the German element, the reaction might possibly have been avoided. Poland's policy was anti-German and anti-imperial, not anti-Christian and pagan. It was opposed to German political and ecclesiastical imperialism, but not hostile to Latin Christianity.[2] Richenza was driven out of the country by this faction, and either at the same time with her, or soon afterward, Casimir, who was too much under the influence of his German mother, was also forced to leave the country and sought protection in Saxony. Chaos prevailed in Poland for the next six years (1034–40).

At this time the hostility of all three of the states on the east border, Hungary, Bohemia, and Poland, was pronounced against the Germans. But fortunately for Germany they could not make common cause together, and both Hungary and Poland were torn with internal dissension. Henry III's policy was to let Hungary exhaust herself in internal distraction, crush Bohemia by force of arms, and watch his opportunity in Poland. Accordingly, in 1040, when the Emperor was waging victorious war against the Bohemians, Casimir, whose cause was sustained by the Polish bishops, slipped back again into his own country with German consent, apparently on the understanding that Germany would assist Poland to recover Crobatia from Bohemia in return for Polish recognition of Germany's claim upon Silesia.[3] For eighteen years Casimir managed to hold his own in Poland. But when

[1] *Annal. Magd.* (1034); *Annal. Hild.* (1034); *Chron. Polon.*, I, 19 (SS. IX, 437); Bresslau, II, 491 f.; Roepell, *Gesch. Polens*, I, 174 f.

[2] Zeissberg, "Die öffentliche Meinung im XI. Jahrhundert über Deutschlands Politik gegen Polen," *Ztschft. f. oesterr. Gymn.* XIX, 83–90.

[3] "Primates ergo nostri ejus miseriae compassi . . . . regi decenter dant consilium ut supplicem clementer susciperet et priorem dominatum illi redderet. Quem ubi recepit, jusjurandum regi fecit ut tam fidelis illi maneret, quam miles seniori esse deberet, omnibus amicis ejus fore se amicum, inimicis inimicum, et nihil plus Bolaniae vel ullius regalis provinciae sibimet submittere, nisi duas regiones quas ibi meruit suscipere" (Cosmas, II, 12; Steindorff, I, 112, n. 5).

Boleslav II succeeded in 1058 a situation in Poland adverse to German interest developed.

The precarious internal politics of the middle border in the reign of Henry IV emboldened the Polish policy. The middle border at this time was divided into four segments: the Saxon Ostmark, Mark Lausitz, Mark Meissen, and Mark Zeitz. In the tenth century the crown's control over the margraves in these four areas had been whole and complete. But with the development of feudalism the margraves evinced a disposition to make themselves as independent as possible, and, further, endeavored to establish the hereditability of the margraviates in their houses, as the German duchies were hereditary. Conrad II and Henry III were able to check this inclination, but during the minority of Henry IV it became strongly manifest. When William, Margrave of Meissen, the hero of the engagement in the Theben Pass in 1060, died in the following year, his brother Otto succeeded for a brief season. But when Otto died, the widow of Margrave, William married the ambitious and turbulent Dedi, Margrave of the Saxon Ostmark, who laid claim to Mark Meissen in right of his wife (!), in which he was sustained by that far-from-gentle dame—Lambert of Hersfeld describes her as *saevissima uxor*. The energy of Archbishop Adalbert of Bremen, regent for the young King and loyal to the interests of the crown, however, frustrated this design and the Mark Meissen was intrusted to Count William of Weimar,[1] who in turn was followed by his brother, Otto of Orlamünde. When he died in 1067, the last scion of the Weimar house, Mark Meissen passed to Ekbert of Brunswick (1067), and a year later to his son Ekbert II.

At this juncture Henry IV had reached his majority and assumed personal rule. He was far from being content with seeing the territories of the middle border slip from crown control and become hereditary fiefs, half-independent of the royal authority. The result was that when the great rebellion of Saxony broke out in 1075 and was speedily followed both by revolt on the part of the high feudality and conflict with Gregory VII, Margrave Ekbert II joined with the King's

[1] Lambert of Hersfeld (1062); *Annal. Sax.* (1062).

enemies. The Poles were dangerously near taking advantage
of this situation but were foiled by the adroitness of Henry
IV, who, as we have seen, played Bohemia against Poland, detached Upper Lausitz and gave it to Wratislav of Bohemia,
and thereby accomplished the double result of foiling Poland's designs to attack the middle border once more and acquired Bohemian support as well.

The Pope retaliated by sending the first papal legate to
Poland who crowned Boleslav II as king in 1076.[1] Such bold
action on the part of the Polish Duke could not go without
punishment. A joint German-Bohemian army, in spite of the
fact that civil war raged within Germany, soon invaded
Poland, and Boleslav II, like the "Winter King" of Bohemia
centuries later in 1618, was compelled to fly ignominiously
from his realm. He sought refuge in Hungary. His fate is unknown.

Yet contrary to what we might expect, in spite of Polish
sympathy with the papal cause the Gregorian reforms had
slight effect upon the development of the church in Poland.
The Polish episcopate developed without any great dependence upon either Germany or the papacy. In fact, we
find that the reforms of Gregory VII hardly penetrated into
Poland. The Piast dynasty considered the church to be a political institution, and the bishops were used as the first
officials of the crown. The limits of the dioceses were not well
defined. Celibacy was unknown. The Polish secular clergy,
up to the end of the eleventh century, was composed mostly
of foreigners, and therefore could not exert much influence
over the people.[2]

On the other hand, monasticism of French Cluniac or Ital-

[1] The strong adherence of Poland to Rome at this time is in contrast with the
attitude of Bohemia, which advocated the imperial cause in the struggle of pope
and emperor. This attitude of Poland may be attributed to the large influence which
Italian monks had in the land (Grünhagen, p. 20). The "Galli" of the chronicles of
this time were not all French and Walloons, as is frequently asserted. Some were
Italians whose influx and influence have been studied by A. Ptásnik, *Italian Culture
in Med. Poland* (in Polish), Warsaw, 1923. Cf. *Revue historique du Sud Est Européen*,
I, 296.

[2] Tatomir, *Polish History*, p. 36. Even polygamy obtained among the Poles as
late as the time of Cosmas (Lippert, *op. cit.*, I, 205).

ian nature exercised more than slight influence. The monks introduced improved methods of agriculture and brought with them the elements of higher culture. The first chronicler of Poland arrived in 1109 in the person of Martin Gallus, probably a monk from St. Gilles in Provence who entered the country via Italy and Hungary, having been invited by the Bishop of Posen who was a former inmate of the monastery at St. Gilles. The comminglement of foreign cultures—Italian, French, and Flemish—in Poland from now on is interesting. At the beginning of the twelfth century a daughter of a French count, Godfrey of Lyons, was married to a Polish nobleman; another Polish nobleman was the husband of a Flemish wife who in 1109 founded at Gorka a house of Flemish Augustinians who came from Artois. A colony of Walloons was settled in Silesia who introduced flax-raising and linen-making into the land. Russo-Byzantine influence also is observable in the Polish coinage and in the architecture of the church of St. Michael which was built in the first half of the twelfth century by Count Jaxo, a nephew of Count Peter Vlast, the same who founded a house of Flemish Augustinians.

The fall of Boleslav II in 1079 marks a significant development in Polish history. It was less due to German intervention by force of arms than to an uprising of the Polish nobility, the *szlachta*, against him. The fact that this word is not a Polish but a German word (*die Schlacht*) indicates the historical origin of the Polish nobility and points to the fact that there must have been an obscure but influential penetration of German nobles into the land. This class was less pro-German in its sympathies than pro-feudal in its interests. Its aim was similar to that of the great German dukes—to localize and intensify their own power and to make the King their creature. In Germany feudalism did not triumph over the crown until 1250. In Poland it was an ever present factor from now on. In 1093 the magnates, conniving with the discontent of the two sons of the weak Vladislav Hermann, compelled him to divide the kingdom—a second partition, but one due to domestic disaffection and not imposed by foreign force. Great Poland was given to Zbiegniev, Little Poland to

Boleslav, and the king retained Mazovia under his personal domination. The pretext or occasion for this manifestation of power by the nobles was the ineffectual resistance made by the King to Bretislav of Bohemia, who in 1093 invaded Silesia and plundered the whole left bank of the Oder from Castle Ritschen to Glogau, with the exception of Nimptsch, which resisted all attack.

But if selfish and unpatriotic at home, the Polish nobles were warlike and ambitious for conquest abroad. They warred with the Bohemians and Hungarians, conquered Pomerania, even checked Henry V in 1109 before Glogau,[1] and during the troubled reign of Borivoj III (1100–20) of Bohemia overran Silesia, which Poland retained until 1163. The pacific mission of Otto of Bamberg redeemed Pomerania from Polish possession, while the ambition of the Polish magnates continued to rend the kingdom within. Again Poland was partitioned, this time into five parts: Mazovia was retained by the King, but the provinces of Great Poland, Silesia, Sandomir, and Cracow were allotted to his four sons, the eldest of whom, Vladislav II (1138–46), received the territory around Cracow which was now raised to the rank of a grand duchy. His attempt in 1146 to oust his brothers was prevented by the nobles who drove him into exile. His successor was Boleslav IV (1146–73), who was to all intents and purposes a puppet of Frederick Barbarossa and the half-German magnates. His wife was a daughter of Albrecht the Bear of Brandenburg. The discomfiture of the Pope at this ascendancy of German political influence in Poland was so great that anathema was decreed against the Emperor, the Polish magnates, and the Polish bishops for their part in the change. But by this time many of the Polish high clergy were Germans who were more interested in advancing their own ecclesiastical sway in Poland than in promoting papal prerogative there.

Vladislav never regained his throne, but after his death

---

[1] The *Chron. Polon.*, III, chaps. iv–xiv, gives a long and detailed account of this campaign, not without flattery of the Poles. For it is alleged that the masterly tactics of Boleslav III elicited German praise of him—"cantilena Allemannorum in laudem Boleslavi" (chap. xi).

in 1163 Silesia was divided between his two sons, Boleslav the Tall and Mieszko. Boleslav received Glogau, Liegnitz, Breslau, and Oppeln, while Mieszko received only Ratibor and Teschen.[1] Both princes had spent seventeen years in Germany, and were Germans by education and spirit. Thus the year 1163 is an epoch-making one in the history of the relations between Germany and Poland.

Boleslav the Tall resolved to redeem the land by calling in German settlers. The colonization was conducted systematically by dividing the tracts to be settled into great blocks of a thousand *Hufen*, or about three German square miles in area, partitioning these blocks into farms and intrusting the whole matter of settlement to a contractor, lay or clerical. The rent for these equal areas averaged five German marks.[2] German Cistercians and Premonstratensians were very active in this kind of enterprise. The founding of the Cistercian house of Leubus in 1175 may be regarded as a turning-point in the history of Silesia.[3] Scattered bits of evidence show, however, that the land had been traversed occasionally by German missionaries, merchants, and warriors from as early as the tenth century, and it is logical to conjecture that some of these people took up residence, but no proof is forthcoming in documents that there was any permanent colonization of German stock in Silesia before 1175. An early written record dating back to 990 mentions the presence of German knights at Nimptsch in Upper Silesia, in the pay of Polish landowners of the region.[4] In the early part of the twelfth century we learn of Augustinian monks from the county of Artois, in France, penetrating into the country and establishing in 1109 a monastery on the summit of the Zobten Mountains.[5] These French monks, following the usual practice of the time, introduced Flemings and Walloons into the land, partly as mer-

[1] Grünhagen, p. 23.

[2] Grünhagen, p. 39. The Polish mark was worth less than one-fifth of the German mark.

[3] Charter in Kötzschke, *Quellen zur Geschichte der ostdeutschen Kolonisation*, No. 35; for the history of Leubus see Schulte, *Die Anfänge deutscher Kolonisation in Schlesien* (Festschrift f. Grünhagen, p. 35).

[4] Lamprecht, III, 400.   [5] Michael, I, 89–90, n. 3.

chants and artisans, partly as farmers.[1] Proof of this is found, according to Weinhold, in certain place names, such as *Walgasse* (i.e., *Walhengasse*) to the southeast of Breslau, which name survived as late as the fifteenth century. Jankau and Kreidel also exhibit positive evidence of Walloon habitation introduced by the Augustinians. But, on the whole, French influence as introduced by the Augustinians was never large, and was extinguished by the Germans toward the beginning of the thirteenth century, when they began coming into the country in great numbers.

Even before the establishment of Leubus, there seem to have been two other sources of German penetration and influence into Silesia. One of these had its origin in the war of Frederick I, Barbarossa, against Poland as a consequence of his adopting the cause of the dispossessed claimant to the Polish throne, Vladislav II. His march into Poland as far as Posen in 1157[2] undoubtedly brought in German ways and innovations into the country. This was followed by the importation of German knights by the first Duke of Silesia to help him against the Poles, and also by the invitation to Germans to come into the land and trade and settle there. The other possible source of German penetration anterior to the founding of Leubus is much more dubious. It is the theory of Weinhold that the route of the Rhinelanders who, in the middle of the twelfth century, came into Siebenbürgen upon the invitation of King Geisa II of Hungary, passed through Silesia and that many of them chose to remain there without proceeding farther.[3]

Thus one may distinguish two distinct waves of German immigration into Silesia: an earlier one made up of Low Germans mainly from the Lower Rhine and by people from Holland and Flanders, and a later and more important penetration of Middle Germans. This earlier, or Low German penetration, was part of the general eastern movement of these peoples, the majority of whom came by invitation of

[1] Weinhold, *Die Verbreitung und die Herkunft der Deutschen in Schlesien* (1887), p. 164.

[2] Lamprecht, III, 402; Roepell, pp. 358–60.   [3] Weinhold, p. 206.

monasteries, the secular clergy, and the feudal lords. Along with these lowlanders came some colonists from Hesse, the Lower Rhine, Westphalia, and other western and Rhine regions.[1] It is difficult to determine just what share the Low Germans had in the founding of German villages and cities in Silesia, but probably it was considerable. From linguistic evidence it would seem that the penetration by the Low Germans extended throughout the land. Weinhold cites lists of words and family names that are of Low German origin, pointing out that while the language of Silesia is undoubtedly of a Middle German dialect, the vocabulary reveals words of Low German origin which are clearly not of recent importation.

But, on the whole, this Netherlandish–Low German colonization was small and was followed almost immediately afterward by people of Middle German stock, which soon became the chief source of German settlers into the country and whose dialect became that spoken by the German Silesians today. In the early days these incomers came chiefly from Thuringia and the neighboring regions where Germans had already settled. In fact, there is little difference in the type and culture of the inhabitants who took up residence in Silesia from those that colonized the German regions of Bohemia, Moravia, or Upper Lausitz, Meissen, and the Pleisner country. To these can be added the Germans who came into Zips, and the Burzenland. The proof of this is found in the language, in the place and proper names, in the plan of house and farm, and in the national traditions, says Weinhold. Under Bishop Siroslav, between 1170 and 1189, Germans were settled in the district of Treibnitz; by 1202–3 they were found between Jauer, Schonau, and Bolkenhain; by 1206, around Goldberg; in 1207, around Striegau and Frankenstein; in 1210, in Kittlau near Nimptsch; in 1211 Goldberg adopted German law, as did Breslau in 1214, and all contained German inhabitants. The pattern for the German law and city constitutions seems to have been furnished by Magdeburg.[2]

All the German immigrants into Silesia were freemen and

[1] Michael, p. 102.   [2] Weinhold, p. 167; Michael, p. 102.

were protected by the dukes of Silesia in this status, whenever the Polish nobility or others sought to interfere with them. The Poles living in the German cities, or cities under the German law, enjoyed all the rights and freedom possessed by the German inhabitants. The lot of the German newcomer was vastly better than that of his Polish neighbor. For the first few years after his arrival in Silesia, the colonist that had been invited by the Cistercians was exempt from all dues. Later he had only to pay a moderate yearly rental and to work certain days of the year, especially during harvest time, for the monastery. This improved standard of living and greater liberty of the Germans from the feudal lord had the effect indirectly of improving the lot of the Polish peasant, which heretofore was an exceedingly miserable one.

The coming of the Germans into Silesia immediately benefited the land in the most material way. Heretofore, Silesia had been largely a waste land of sand and swamp and rock, sparsely populated, with no cities and only a few villages of a very rude order, such as Breslau; agriculture was exceedingly elementary, cultivation being performed by a rude wooden plow; the industries of a very primitive order. All this the German *Einwanderung* transformed. Cities and villages were made to flourish, the swamps were drained, the land forced to yield rich harvests, and German civilization brought in.

The contrast along the middle border between the lands peopled by thrifty German colonists and the territory inhabited solely by a Polish population was a striking one. A Cistercian poet, even as late as the fourteenth century, pictures the country of the Poles as a land of forest and fen inhabited by wretchedly poor and lazy Poles who used the forked trunk of a tree for a plow, drawn by a pair of scrawny oxen or cows. The people lived without salt or metal or shoes, and were pitiably clothed. Nowhere was a town to be found. Markets were held in the open air, where barter took the place of coin.[1]

[1]   "Nam sine cultore tellus jacuit nemorosa,
        Et genus Polonie pauper fuit, haut operosa,
        Sulcans in sabulo lignis uncis sine ferro
        Et vaccis bobus nisi scivit arare duobus.

The wonder of it is that all this settlement was accomplished peaceably, without bloodshed, and in this fact German colonization of Silesia is quite distinctive from its history in other Wendish lands.

They conquered the land not in war with the sword, but instead as peaceful incomers they occupied it, coming with plow and harrow as peasants, with the spindle, the loom and other hand-labor devices as Burgers, and occupied it entirely through agreements and arrangements. They did not oppress the natives or drive them out. In many parts of the country these two unlike peoples fused together through intermarriage. But the children of such marriages did not follow the servitude of the Poles; instead they followed freedom; they became German.[1]

Under Henry the Bearded (1202–38), whose capital was Breslau, Silesia became an independent and progressive duchy, by a curious reversal of history exercising sway over all the Piast princes. Monastic and lay colonization, commerce and trade and town life, rapidly increased. Neumarkt (formerly Szroda), Löwenburg, Goldberg, Naumburg, Steinau, Guhrau, Ohlau, and Ratibor received Magdeburg law. German colonization progressed so rapidly that along the left bank of the Oder from the river to the mountains, and in the territory between the Bober and the Neisse rivers, the population is estimated to have been between 150,000 and 180,000.[2] Even the old Polish towns of Cracow, Lwow (Lemberg), Poznan (Posen), and Plock received a great influx of German settlers and became German outposts of commerce and political influence. Magdeburg or Halle town law was widely spread; German silver money became the predominating currency; even the municipal records of these Polish towns in the fourteenth century were kept in the German language.

Civitas aut oppidum per terram non fuit ullum,
Sed prope castra fora campestria, broca, capella,
Non sal, non ferrum. numismata nonque metallum,
Non indumenta bona, sed neque calciamenta.
Plebs habuit ulla, pascebat sola jumenta."
—*Monumenta Lubensia* (ed. Wattenbach), p. 15.

[1] Michael, I, p. 104.

[2] Grünhagen, 62; Schmoller, *Forschungen*, XIII, 41, who cites Meitzen.

APPENDIX

TABLE OF POPES AND EMPERORS, 800–1273*

Popes		Emperors	
795	Leo III	Deposition of Constantine **VI** by Irene	797
		Charles I (the Great)	800
		(*Following henceforth the new Western line*)	
		Louis I (the Pious)	814
816	Stephen **IV**		
817	Paschal I		
824	Eugenius **II**		
827	Valentinus		
827	Gregory **IV**		
		Lothar I	840
844	Sergius **II**		
847	Leo IV		
855	Benedict III	Louis II (in Italy)	855
855	(Anastasius, anti-pope)		
858	Nicholas I		
867	Hadrian II		
872	John VIII		
		Charles II, the Bald (W. Frankish)	875
		Charles III, the Fat (E. Frankish)	881
882	Martin **II**		
884	Hadrian III	*Interval from* 888	
885	Stephen **V**		
891	Formosus	Guido (in Italy)	891
		Lambert (in Italy)	894
896	Boniface **VI**	Arnulf (E. Frankish**)**	896
896	Stephen **VI**		
897	Romanus		
897	Theodore **II**		
898	John IX		
900	Benedict **IV**	Ludwig (*the Child*)[1]	899
		Louis III, king of Provence (in Italy)	901
903	Leo V		
903	Christopher		
904	Sergius III		

* The names in italics are those of German Kings who never made any claim to the imperial title.

659

Popes		Emperors	
		Conrad I	911
911	Anastasius III		
913	Lando		
914	John X		
		Bérenger (in Italy)	915
		SAXON HOUSE.	
		Henry I the Fowler of Saxony	919
928	Leo VI		
929	Stephen VII		
931	John XI		
936	Leo VII	Otto I (the Great), crowned E.	
939	Stephen VIII	Frankish king at Aachen	936
941	Martin III		
946	Agapetus II		
955	John XII		
		Otto I, crowned emperor at	
963	Leo VIII	Rome	962
964	(Benedict V, anti-pope?)		
965	John XIII		
972	Benedict VI		
		Otto II	973
974	(Boniface VII, anti-pope?)		
974	Domnus II (?)		
974	Benedict VII		
983	John XIV	Otto III	983
985	John XV		
996	Gregory V		
996	(John XVI, anti-pope?)		
999	Sylvester II		
		Henry II (the Saint)	1002
1003	John XVII		
1003	John XVIII		
1009	Sergius IV		
1012	Benedict VIII		
		SALIAN HOUSE	
1024	John XIX	Conrad II (the Salic)	1024
1033	Benedict IX		
		Henry III (the Black)	1039
1044	(Sylvester, anti-pope)		
1045	Gregory VI		
1046	Clement II		
1048	Damasus II		
1048	Leo IX		
1054	Victor II		
		Henry IV	1056
1057	Stephen IX		
1058	Benedict X		

Popes		Emperors	
1059	Nicholas II		
1061	Alexander II		
1073	Gregory VII (Hildebrand)		
		(Rudolf of Swabia, rival)	1077
1080	(Clement, anti-pope)		
1086	Victor III	(Hermann of Luxemburg, rival)	
1087	Urban II	(1081)	
1099	Paschal II	(Conrad of Franconia, rival)	
1102	(Albert, anti-pope)	(1093)	
1105	(Sylvester, anti-pope)		
		Henry V	1106
1118	Gelasius II		
1118	(Gregory, anti-pope)		
1119	Calixtus II		
1121	(Celestine, anti-pope)		
1124	Honorius II		
		Lothar II (of Saxony)	1125
1130	Innocent II		
		HOUSE OF SWABIA OR HOHENSTAUFEN	
	(Anacletus, anti-pope)	Conrad III†	1138
1138	(Victor, anti-pope)		
1143	Celestine II		
1144	Lucius II		
1145	Eugenius III		
		Frederick I (Barbarossa)	1152
1153	Anastasius IV		
1154	Hadrian IV		
1159	Alexander III		
1159	(Victor, anti-pope)		
1164	(Paschal, anti-pope)		
1168	(Calixtus, anti-pope)		
1181	Lucius III		
1185	Urban III		
1187	Gregory VIII		
1187	Clement III		
		Henry VI	1190
1191	Celestine III		
		Philip (of Swabia),	
1198	Innocent III	Otto IV† (Guelf)	
		(rivals 1197–1208)	
		Frederick II	1212
1216	Honorius III		
1227	Gregory IX		
1241	Celestine IV		
1241	Vacancy		

† Never actually crowned at Rome.

Popes		Emperors	
		Emperors	
1243	Innocent IV	(Henry Raspe, rival)	1246
		(William of Holland, rival)	1246–7
		Conrad IV†	1250
1254	Alexander IV	*Interregnum*	
		Richard† (earl of Cornwall), Alfonso† (king of Castile) (rivals)	1257
1261	Urban IV		
1265	Clement IV		
1269	Vacancy		
1271	Gregory X		
		Rudolf I† (of Hapsburg)	1273

† Never actually crowned at Rome.

THE WELF AND BILLUNGER FAMILIES
DESCENT OF LOTHAR II AND OTTO OF NORDHEIM*

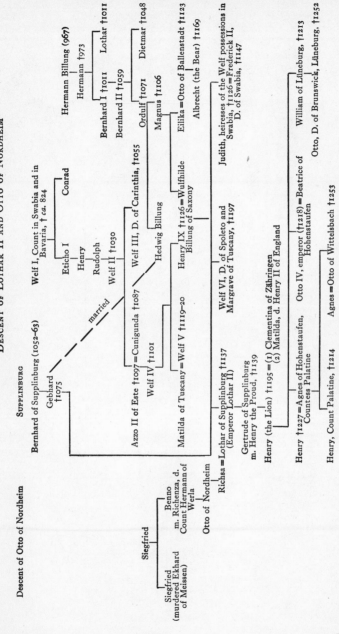

*This table shows the marriages between these families.

THE WELF AND HOHENSTAUFEN FAMILIES

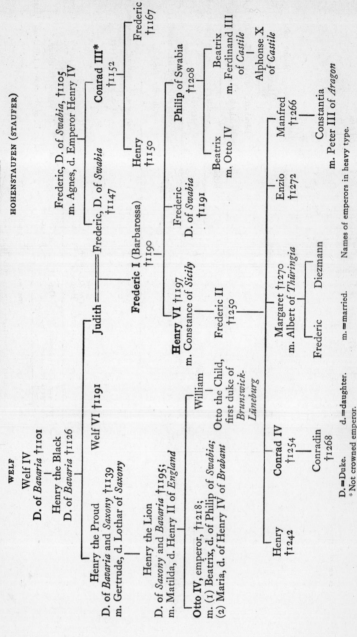

D. = Duke.   d. = daughter.   m. = married.   Names of emperors in heavy type.
* Not crowned emperor.

THE ABODRITE AND WAGRIAN DUKES

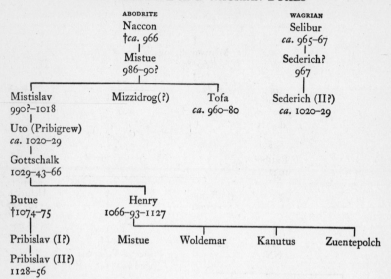

ABODRITE

Naccon
†ca. 966

Mistue
986–90?

WAGRIAN

Selibur
ca. 965–67

Sederich?
967

Mistislav
990?–1018

Uto (Pribigrew)
ca. 1020–29

Gottschalk
1029–43–66

Mizzidrog(?)

Tofa
ca. 960–80

Sederich (II?)
ca. 1020–29

Butue
†1074–75

Pribislav (I?)

Pribislav (II?)
1128–56

Henry
1066–93–1127

Mistue   Woldemar   Kanutus   Zuentepolch

THE SLAVONIC DUKES OF WAGRIA [LATER MECKLENBURG]

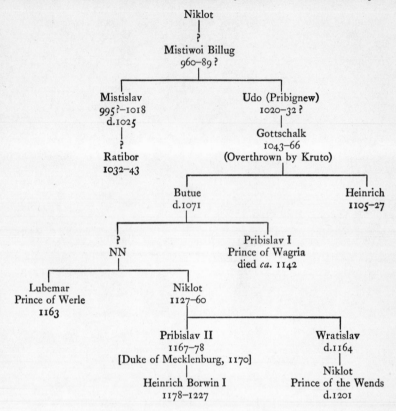

Niklot
|
?
|
Mistiwoi Billug
960–89 ?

Mistislav
995 ?–1018
d.1025
|
?
|
Ratibor
1032–43

Udo (Pribignew)
1020–32 ?
|
Gottschalk
1043–66
(Overthrown by Kruto)

Butue
d.1071

Heinrich
1105–27

?
NN

Pribislav I
Prince of Wagria
died *ca.* 1142

Lubemar
Prince of Werle
1163

Niklot
1127–60

Pribislav II
1167–78
[Duke of Mecklenburg, 1170]
|
Heinrich Borwin I
1178–1227

Wratislav
d.1164
|
Niklot
Prince of the Wends
d.1201

PRINCES OF MORAVIA, BOHEMIA, AND POLAND

Moravia	Bohemia	Poland
Mojmír, 830–46	Bořivoj I, —894	Mieszko I, 960–92
Rastislav, 846–70	Spytihněv, 894–905	Boleslav I (Chrobry),
Svatopluk, 870–94	Vratislav I, 905–21	992–1025
Mojmír II, 894–906	Václav I, 921–29	Mieszko II, 1025–34
	Boleslav I, 929–67	Kazimir, 1034–58
	Boleslav II, 967–99	Boleslav II (Szczodry),
	Boleslav III, 999–1003	1058–79
	Jaromír, 1003–12	Vladislav Herman,
	Oldřich, 1012–34	1079–1102
	Břetislav I, 1034–55	Boleslav II (Krzywou-
	Spytihněv II, 1055–61	sty), 1102–38
	Vratislav II (king),	Vladislav II, 1138–46
	1061–92	Boleslav IV (Kedzie-
	Conrad (duke), 1092	rzawy), 1146–73
	Břetislav II, 1092–1100	Mieszko III the Old,
	Bořivoj II, 1100–1120	1173–77
	Vladislav, 1120–25	Cazimir the Just,
	Soběslav I, 1125–40	1177–94
	Vladislav II, as king,	Leszek I the White and
	I, 1140–73	Mieszko III, 1194–
	Soběslav II, 1173–78	1202
	Bedřich, 1178–89	
	Conrad Otto, 1189–91	
	Václav II, 1191–92	
		Vladislav III (Lasko-
		nogi), 1202–06
		Leszek I the White,
	Přemysl Ottokar I,	1206–27
	1192–93	Henry I the Bearded,
	Jindřich Bedřich, 1193–	1231–38
	97	Henry II the Pious,
	Vladislav II, 1197	1238–41
	Přemysl Ottokar I,	Boleslav V the Bash-
	(again), 1197–1230	ful, 1243–79
	Václav I, 1230–53	

INDEX